CIMA
STUDY TEXT

Stage 3 Paper 9

Financial Reporting

New in this July 1999 edition

- FRS 11 *Impairment of fixed assets and goodwill*

- FRS 12 *Provisions, contingent liabilities and contingent assets*

- FRS 13 *Derivatives and other financial instruments: disclosures*

- FRS 14 *Earnings per share*

- FRS 15 *Tangible fixed assets*

- FRED 18 *Current taxation*

- The revised *Statement of Principles*

- Current international issues

FOR EXAMS IN NOVEMBER 1999 AND THE YEAR 2000 .

BPP Publishing
July 1999

First edition 1994
Sixth edition July 1999

ISBN 0 7517 3123 4 (previous edition 0 7517 3108 0)

British Library Cataloguing-in-Publication Data
A catalogue record for this book
is available from the British Library

Published by

BPP Publishing Limited
Aldine House, Aldine Place
London W12 8AW

http://www.bpp.co.uk

Printed in Great Britain by Ashford Colour Press

We are grateful to the Chartered Institute of Management Accountants for permission to reproduce past examination questions in our Exam Question Bank. The Exam Answer Bank has been prepared by BPP Publishing Limited.

Contents

		Page

Contents

BPP PUBLISHING

HOW TO USE THIS STUDY TEXT

Aims of this Study Text

To provide you with the knowledge and understanding, skills and application techniques that you need if you are to be successful in your exams

This Study Text has been written around the **Financial Reporting** syllabus (reproduced on pages (xi) and (xii), and cross-referenced to where in the text each topic is covered) and the 1999-2000 syllabus guidance notes (which we set out on pages (xiv) to (xvi)).

- It is **comprehensive**. We do not omit sections of the syllabus as the examiner is liable to examine any angle of any part of the syllabus - and you do not want to be left high and dry.

- It keeps you **up-to-date** in developments in financial reporting, the way in which the examiner is examining the subject and relevant legislation etc.

- And it is **on-target**. We do not include any material which is not examinable. You can therefore rely on the BPP Study Text as the stand-alone source of all your information for the exam, without worrying that any of the material is irrelevant.

To allow you to study in the way that best suits your learning style and the time you have available, by following your personal Study Plan (see page (ix))

You may be studying at home on your own until the date of the exam, or you may be attending a full-time course. You may like to (and have time to) read every word, or you may prefer to (or only have time to) skim-read and devote the remainder of your time to question practice. Wherever you fall in the spectrum, you will find the BPP Study Text meets your needs in designing and following your personal Study Plan.

To tie in with the other components of the BPP Effective Study Package to ensure you have the best possible chance of passing the exam (see page (vi))

BPP PUBLISHING

Recommended period of use	Elements of the BPP Effective Study Package
Three to twelve months before the exam	**Study Text** Use the Study Text to acquire knowledge, understanding, skills and the ability to use application techniques.
One to six months before the exam	**Practice & Revision Kit** Attempt the tutorial questions and complete the interactive checklists which are provided for each topic area in the Kit. Then try the numerous examination questions, for which there are realistic suggested solutions prepared by BPP's own authors. May 2000 examinees will find the 2000 edition of the Kit invaluable for bringing them up-to-date as at 1 December 1999, the cut-off date for May 2000 examinable material.
From three 3 months before the exam until the last minute	**Passcards** Work through these short, memorable notes which are focused on what is most likely to come up in the exam you will be sitting.
One to six months before the exam	**Success Tapes** Cover the vital elements of your syllabus in less than 90 minutes per subject with these audio cassettes. Each tape also contains exam hints to help you fine tune your strategy.
Three to twelve months before the exam	**Breakthrough Videos** Use a Breakthrough Video to supplement your Study Text. They give you clear tuition on key exam subjects and allow you the luxury of being able to pause or repeat sections until you have fully grasped the topic.
Three to twelve months before the exam	**Master CD** Take advantage of an Interactive CD-ROM containing questions on all aspects of the syllabus, cross referenced to help topics.

Settling down to study

By this stage in your career you are probably very experienced at learning and taking exams. But have you ever thought about *how* you learn? Let's have a quick look at the key elements required for effective learning. You can then identify your learning style and go on to design your own approach to how you are going to study with this text - your personal Study Plan.

Key element of learning	Using the BPP Study Text
Motivation	You can rely on the comprehensiveness and technical quality of BPP material. You've chosen the right Study Text - so you're in pole position to pass your exam!
Clear objectives and standards	Do you want to be a prizewinner or simply achieve a moderate pass? Decide.
Feedback	Work through the examples in this text and do the Questions and the Quick quizzes. Evaluate your efforts critically - how are you doing?
Study Plan	You need to be honest with yourself about your progress - don't be over-confident, but don't be negative either. Make your Study Plan (see below) and try to stick to it. Focus on the short-term objectives - completing two chapters a night, say - but beware of losing sight of your study objectives.
Practice	Use the Quick quizzes and Chapter roundups to refresh your memory after you have completed your initial study of each chapter.

These introductory pages let you see exactly what you are up against. But however you study, you should:

- **read through the syllabus and syllabus guidance notes** - these will help you to identify areas you have already covered, perhaps at a lower level of detail, and areas that are totally new to you;

- **study the examination paper section,** where we show you the format of the exam (how many and what kind of questions) and analyse all the papers set so far under the syllabus, **including the one set in May 1999.**

BPP PUBLISHING

Key study steps

The following steps are, in our experience, the ideal approach to studying for professional exams but you can of course adapt it for your particular learning style (see page (ix)). Tackle the chapters in the order you find them in the Study Text. Taking into account your individual learning style, follow these key study steps for each chapter.

Key study steps	Activity
Step 1 *Chapter topic list*	Study the list. Each numbered topic is a numbered section in the chapter.
Step 2 *Introduction*	Read through it. It is designed to show you *why* the topics in the chapter need to be studied - how they lead on from previous topics, and how they lead into subsequent ones.
Step 3 *Knowledge brought forward boxes*	In these we highlight information and techniques that it is assumed you have 'brought forward' with you from your earlier studies. If there are topics which have changed recently due to legislation for example, these topics are explained in full. Do not panic if you do not feel instantly comfortable with the content of the box - it should come back to you as we develop the subject for this paper. If you are really unsure, we advise you to go back to your previous notes.
Step 4 *Explanations*	Proceed methodically through the chapter, reading each section thoroughly and making sure you understand. Where a topic has been examined, we state the month and year of examination against the appropriate heading. You should pay particular attention to these topics.
Step 5 *Key terms* and *Exam focus points*	• **Key terms** can often earn you *easy marks* if you state them clearly and correctly in an appropriate exam answer (and they are indexed at the back of the text so you can check easily that you are on top of all of them when you come to revise). • **Exam focus points** give you a good idea of how the examiner tends to examine certain topics - and they also pinpoint *easy marks*.
Step 6 *Note taking*	Take brief notes if you wish, avoiding the temptation to copy out too much.
Step 7 *Examples*	Follow each through to its solution very carefully.
Step 8 *Case examples*	Study each one, and try to add flesh to them from your own experience - they are designed to show how the topics you are studying come alive (and often come unstuck) in the real world.
Step 9 *Questions*	Make a very good attempt at each one.
Step 10 *Answers*	Check yours against ours, and make sure you understand any discrepancies.
Step 11 *Chapter roundup*	Work through it very carefully, to make sure you have grasped the major points it is highlighting.

Key study steps	Activity
Step 12 *Quick quiz*	When you are happy that you have covered the chapter, use the **Quick quiz** to check how much you have remembered of the topics covered. The answers are in the paragraphs in the chapter that we refer you to.
Step 13 *Question(s) in the Question bank*	Either at this point, or later when you are thinking about revising, make a full attempt at the **Question(s)** suggested at the very end of the chapter. You can find these at the end of the Study Text, along with the **Answers** so you can see how you did. We highlight those that are introductory, and those which are of the standard you would expect to find in an exam.

Developing your personal Study Plan

Preparing a Study Plan (and sticking closely to it) is one of the key elements in learning success.

First you need to be aware of your style of learning. There are four typical learning styles. Consider yourself in the light of the following descriptions and work out which you fit most closely. You can then plan to follow the key study steps in the sequence suggested.

Learning styles	Characteristics	Sequence of key study steps in the BPP Study Text
Theorist	Seeks to understand principles before applying them in practice	1, 2, 3, 4, 7, 8, 5, 9/10, 11, 12, 13 (6 continuous)
Reflector	Seeks to observe phenomena, thinks about them and then chooses to act	
Activist	Prefers to deal with practical, active problems; does not have much patience with theory	1, 2, 9/10 (read through), 7, 8, 5, 11, 3, 4, 9/10 (full attempt), 12, 13 (6 continuous)
Pragmatist	Prefers to study only if a direct link to practical problems can be seen; not interested in theory for its own sake	9/10 (read through), 2, 5, 7, 8, 11, 1, 3, 4, 9/10 (full attempt), 12, 13 (6 continuous)

BPP PUBLISHING

Next

Work out the time you have available per week, given the following.

- The standard you have set yourself
- The time you need to set aside later for work on the Practice & Revision Kit and Passcards
- The other exam(s) you are sitting
- Very importantly, practical matters such as work, travel, exercise, sleep and social life

Note your time available in box A.   A ▭

Now

- Take the time you have available per week for this Study Text show in box A, multiply it by the number of weeks available and insert the result in box B.   B ▭
- Divide the figure in Box B by the number of chapters in this text and insert the result in box C.   C ▭

Then

Set about studying each chapter in the time shown in box C, following the key study steps in the order suggested by your particular learning style.

This is your personal **Study Plan**.

Short of time?

Whatever your objectives, standards or style, you may find you simply do not have the time available to follow all the key study steps for each chapter, however you adapt them for your particular learning style. If this is the case, follow the Skim Study technique below (the icons in the Study Text will help you to do this).

Skim Study technique

Study the chapters in the order you find them in the Study Text. For each chapter, follow the key study steps 1-3, and then skim-read through step 4. Jump to step 11, and then go back to step 5. Follow through steps 7 and 8, and prepare outline answers to questions (steps 9/10). Try the Quick quiz (step 12), following up any items you can't answer, then do a plan for the Question (step 13), comparing it against our answers. You should probably still follow step 6 (note-taking), although you may decide simply to rely on the BPP Passcards for this.

Moving on...

However you study, when you are ready to embark on the practice and revision phase of the BPP Effective Study Package, you should still refer back to this Study Text, both as a source of **reference** (you should find the list of key terms and the index particularly helpful for this) and as a **refresher** (the Chapter roundups and Quick quizzes help you here).

And remember to keep careful hold of this Study Text - you will find it invaluable in your work.

SYLLABUS

The syllabus contains a weighting for each syllabus area, and a ranking of the level of ability required in each topic. The Institute has published the following explanatory notes on these points.

'Study weightings

A percentage weighting is shown against each topic in the syllabus; this is intended as a guide to the amount of study time each topic requires.

All topics in a syllabus must be studied, as a question may examine more than one topic, or carry a higher proportion of marks than the percentage study time suggested.

The weightings do not specify the number of marks which will be allocated to topics in the examination.

Abilities required in the examination

Each examination paper contains a number of topics. Each topic has been given a number to indicate the level of ability required of the candidate.

The numbers range from 1 to 4 and represent the following ability levels:

Appreciation (1)
To understand a knowledge area at an early stage of learning, or outside the core of management accounting, at a level which enables the accountant to communicate and work with other members of the management team.

Knowledge (2)
To have detailed knowledge of such matters as laws, standards, facts and techniques so as to advise at a level appropriate to a management accounting specialist.

Skill (3)
To apply theoretical knowledge, concepts and techniques to the solutions of problems where it is clear what technique has to be used and the information needed is clearly indicated.

Application (4)
To apply knowledge and skills where candidates have to determine from a number of techniques which is the most appropriate and select the information required from a fairly wide range of data, some of which might not be relevant; to exercise professional judgement and to communicate and work with members of the management team and other recipients of financial reports.'

Syllabus overview

This syllabus is an advanced study of financial accounting. It links with Strategic Financial Management in Stage 4 and has as a prerequisite Financial Accounting in Stage 2. It deals with the most advanced and complex areas of the subject, in particular, accounting for groups of companies, performance evaluation and the international aspects of accounting.

Aims

To test the candidates' ability to

- prepare financial statements for organisations, including groups of companies, for publication in accordance with regulations governing preparation of accounts

- analyse and interpret financial accounting statements and recognise their limitations

- critically appraise accounting practice with particular reference to capital maintenance theory and asset valuation
- explain the international dimension to financial accounting and compare different practices.

Content and ability required

	Ability required	Covered in Chapter(s)
9(a) Company and group accounts *(study weighting 55%)*		
Preparation of consolidated accounts involving one or more subsidiaries and associated companies: inter-company transactions, problems of transfer pricing; acquisition and merger methods	4	12-19
Preparation of accounts in accordance with the requirements of the Companies Acts, Statements of Standard Accounting Practice (SSAPs) and Financial Reporting Standards (FRSs)	4	1-11
Treatment of taxation in company accounts; accounting for deferred taxation	3	6
Accounting treatment of acquisitions, mergers, capital reconstruction schemes, reduction of share capital, purchase of company's own shares	3	21
Pension costs accounting	3	7
Foreign currency translation	3	20
Implications of current Exposure Draft issues	2	All
9(b) Income and value measurement *(study weighting 15%)*		
Problems of profit measurement and alternative approaches; extraordinary and exceptional items.	4	22
Principles of current cost and current purchasing power methods	2	23
Valuation of assets: alternative bases; stocks and work in progress; investment properties; accounting for leases and hire purchase	3	3,5,10, 22,23
Intangible assets: capitalisation of research and development and interest; treatment of goodwill including brands; minority interests	3	4,12
Environmental accounting issues	2	22
9(c) Interpretation of accounts *(study weighting 20%)*		
Advanced aspects of the preparation and interpretation of accounts, cash flow statements and related reports	4	24
Calculation of stock market ratios including earnings per share and price/earnings ratios	4	25,26
Business and share valuation alternatives	3	27
Segmental reporting and trend analysis	4	28
9(d) International regulation *(study weighting 10%)*		
The international regulatory framework including international standards of accounting and auditing	2	29
Comparative accounting systems	1	29

UK legislation

The examination will be set in accordance with the provisions of relevant UK legislation passed and case law established up to and including 1 December preceding the examination. Specially relevant to the following papers: Business Environment and Information Technology; Business and Company Law; Financial Accounting; Financial Reporting; Business Taxation.

Statements of Standard Accounting Practice and Financial Reporting Standards

The examination will be set in accordance with relevant Statements of Standard Accounting Practice and Financial Reporting Standards issued up to and including 1 December preceding the examination. Specially relevant to the following papers: Financial Accounting; Financial Reporting.

This criterion also applies to material contained in Exposure Drafts which are especially relevant to the following papers: Financial Accounting; Financial Reporting.

Where examinations are not based on UK legislation and practice, overseas candidates may take appropriate opportunities to cite examples of local practice in their answers. Such examples should be supported with references which will validate the answers.

BPP PUBLISHING

CIMA SYLLABUS GUIDANCE NOTES 1999-2000

The following Guidance Notes are published by the CIMA in the August 1999 CIMA Student as an aid to students and lecturers.

'The following guidance notes have been drafted by the Chief Examiner for each of the subjects. They are intended to inform candidates and lecturers about the scope of the syllabus, the emphasis that should be placed on various topics and the approach which the examination papers will adopt.

These guidance notes are applicable immediately, insofar as they provide a general guidance on each subject. Where any major changes are indicated, these will not be applicable until the May 2000 examination (and will be highlighted, where relevant, in the notes).

Introduction

This paper not only tests the candidate's ability to prepare and interpret financial statements and reports, but also tests understanding of current accounting practice and ability to critically appraise current practice and developments. Therefore, questions will normally require candidates to *reflect* upon a particular issue and to demonstrate an understanding of the principles involved and then to *apply* those principles to a numerical scenario of some sort. It is not the Examiner's intention to set questions which simply require the mechanical application of a technique.

Candidates will be expected to be familiar with any of the following which are issued up to and including 1 December preceding the examination.

- Relevant UK legislation and case law

- All existing Statements of Standard Accounting Practice (SSAPs) and Financial Reporting Standards (FRSs)

- Pronouncements of the Urgent Issues Task Force (UITF) to the extent that the issue is not dealt with in a subsequent FRS

- The *main issues* which are being considered by the Accounting Standards Board (ASB) in their work on the preparation of a *Statement of Principles*. Details of the drafts of the statements will *not* be examined.

- The principles behind any extant Financial Reporting Exposure Drafts (FREDs) and Discussion Drafts (DDs). The detail of FREDs and DDs will *not* be examined.

Candidates will be expected to be familiar with the workings of the Financial Reporting Council and the Financial Reporting Review Panel as well as the ASB and the UITF.

Whilst the main thrust of the paper will be directed towards financial reporting in the private sector, candidates should have some knowledge of financial reporting developments in the public sector, in particular noting the convergence of practice in recent years.

The examination paper

The examination paper will consist of two sections.

Section A will contain three compulsory questions.

Section B will offer candidates a choice of answering one question from two.

In section A, questions may typically have a mark allocation of 40:20:20. The 40 mark question will usually ask candidates to consider a financial reporting issue that affects a group and prepare consolidated financial statements. Such a question will typically require understanding and application of a range of financial reporting issues. No particular form of consolidation working schedule will be required as the Examiner recognises that a variety of good practice exists in this area.

The 20 mark questions will tend to be more focused on a single financial reporting issue. Questions which have as a main theme the preparation of financial statements in compliance with the accounting requirements of the 1985 Companies Act, will *not* be set since, in the opinion of the Examiner, such a question is more appropriate to the FNA paper at Stage 2.

However, candidates will still need to be able to appreciate the extent to which the 1985 Companies Act contributes to the overall regulatory framework in the UK and will, therefore, need to retain their knowledge of its requirements.

The Section B questions will often be of a more 'reflective' nature, but will not usually be totally devoid of computational elements.

Company and group accounts	*Syllabus reference 9(a)*
	Study weighting 55%
& Income and value measurement	*Syllabus reference 9(b)*
	Study weighting 15%

These two sections of the syllabus have been grouped together deliberately in line with the philosophy of requiring reflection and application side by side in the examination. The two sections together (with a 70% weighting) could be said to encompass the theoretical and practical issues surrounding the preparation of financial reports for UK undertakings.

In particular, candidates may be required to demonstrate an ability to:

* prepare consolidated financial statements for a UK parent undertaking and discuss the underlying theoretical issues involved. One or more of the four primary statements could be involved. The group could typically contain associated undertakings in addition to subsidiary undertakings and one or more of the investee undertakings could be an overseas undertaking. Questions may involve a change in the group structure during the year.

* discuss and account for complex financial reporting issues which may have only been considered in outline in the Stage 2 FNA paper. Such issues could include, *inter-alia*:
  deferred taxation;
  pension costs in the accounts of the employer;
  capital instruments.

* be aware of financial reporting issues which have been the subject of an FRS only very recently or which are still being considered by the ASB. Such issues are clearly changing constantly but would include (at the time of writing):
  accounting for provisions;
  discussion of derivatives and other financial instruments;

* accounting for intangible fixed assets.

* account for and discuss changes in the capital structure of an undertaking, including the purchase of its own shares.

* discuss the extent to which the financial reporting regulatory framework has relevance and application in the public sector and in other 'not-for-profit' undertakings.

* discuss the extent to which financial reports prepared under the historical cost convention are distorted in conditions of changing prices and evaluate the various attempts which have been made to adapt the regulatory framework to make allowances for price changes.

The following items are not examinable:

- designing a scheme of reducing, or otherwise reconstructing, the capital structure of an undertaking;

- preparing detailed statements which are adjusted to take account of price changes, whether these be general or specific.

Interpretation of accounts

Syllabus reference 9 (c)

Study weighting 20%

As well as preparing financial statements, the Chartered Management Accountant needs to be able to interpret them and draw sensible conclusions which he or she can express in the form of a report to non-financial mangers. Such a task often involves, as a first step, the calculation of relevant accounting ratios.

However, at Stage 3 the emphasis will be shifted to the conclusions which candidates draw from the ratios and the way those conclusions are expressed in the form of a report. In questions of this nature a pass mark will *not* be gained by candidates who produce a large number of ratios unaccompanied by analysis. In addition to asking candidates to evaluate the financial performance of an undertaking (which could be a not-for-profit undertaking), a typical question might also ask candidates to reflect on the non-financial criteria which should be borne in mind to make a more rounded evaluation of the undertaking's performance.

The Examiner does not intend to set questions on the use of published financial data to suggest a valuation of a business or of shares in a business.

International regulation

Syllabus reference 9 (d)

Study weighting 10%

Chartered Management Accountants need to be aware of international accounting regulation and how it affects their own organisations. In particular, they should be aware of the fact that the nature and extent of the regulatory framework differs from country to country. Candidates should be aware of the major financial reporting issues on which opinion differs from country to country.

For example, they should be aware that deferred taxation or goodwill is one of the financial reporting issues where there exists a diversity of treatment from one country to another. However, knowledge will *not* be required of the standard accounting treatment for deferred taxation or goodwill in any other country apart from the UK. Candidates should also be aware of the existence of International Accounting Standards (IASs) and of their place within the regulatory framework for UK companies.

The following items are *not* examinable:

- Detailed knowledge of individual regulatory frameworks, other than the UK frameworks

- Details of any IASs.

THE EXAM PAPER

Format of the paper

Number of marks

Section A:	Three compulsory questions	80
Section B:	One out of two questions	20
		100

Time allowed : 3 hours

You should note that what the examiner says about the examination paper in the Syllabus Guidance Notes as the paper is analysed there in some depth.

Analysis of past papers 1995 - 1999

The analysis below shows the topics which have been examined in the nine sittings so far of the *Financial Reporting* paper and the CIMA Specimen paper. Throughout the text we highlight topics which have been examined by cross-referencing the date.

May 1999

Section A
1   Status of investment; consolidated profit and loss account
2   Analysis of financial statements
3   Deferred tax – calculation and discussion

Section B
4   Leasing – calculation and discussion
5   Related party disclosures

November 1998

Section A
1   Consolidation of foreign subsidiary
2   Earnings per share
3   FRS 5 *Reporting the substance of transactions*

Section B
4   FRS 4 *Capital instruments*
5   Sundry accounting standards

May 1998

Section A
1   Complex consolidation with subsidiary and sub-subsidiary
2   Analysis of liquidity
3   Accounting treatment for various scenarios

Section B
4   Valuation of fixed assets; FRS 3
5   Harmonisation of financial reporting practices

November 1997

Section A

1 Consolidated profit and loss account
2 Ratio analysis; contribution of published accounts
3 Treatment of transactions under FRS 3

Section B

4 Revision of FRS 1 *Cash flow statements*
5 FRS 4 and SSAP 19

May 1997

Section A

1 Consolidated cash flow statement: finance leases; acquisition of a subsidiary
2 Scheme of capital reorganisation: calculations and analysis
3 Segmental reporting: analyse results; comment on use of segmental data

Section B

4 Deferred taxation: partial and full provision
5 International accounting: harmonisation and UK to US GAAP reconciliation

November 1996

Section A

1 Consolidated balance sheet with mid-year acquisition; goodwill; fair values
2 Performance comparison of two NHS trusts
3 FRS 5: recognition and derecognition; consignment stock

Section B

4 FRS 3 statements and the *Statement of Principles*: discussion and preparation
5 Accounting treatment of various transactions, including related parties, brands and revaluation

May 1996

Section A

1 Foreign subsidiary: memo on treatment; consolidated P&L a/c and balance sheet; consolidated reserves
2 Discontinued operation per FRS 3; treatment of closures and rationalisations in balance sheet, P&L a/c and notes
3 UK subsidiary of US parent: note supporting tax charge in P&L a/c; total corporation tax and deferred tax balances; explain treatment of stocks and tax to US parent

Section B

4 Ratios for historical cost and real terms current cost accounts; explanation of differences; explain parts of CC accounts
5 Pension costs for defined benefit scheme: explanations of SSAP 24; calculations for a deficit

November 1995

Section A

1 Consolidated P&L a/c and reserves with a subsidiary, a sub-subsidiary (piecemeal) and an associate
2 Analysis of a loss-making company for a bank; effect of withdrawal of overdraft; limitations of information produced
3 Leasing: the effect on gearing; calculations for extracts from the financial statements

Section B

4 Capitalisation of borrowing costs: arguments for and against; calculations
5 Long-term contracts: explanations of SSAP 9; calculations of P&L a/c and balance sheet figures

May 1995

Section A

1 Consolidation adjustments, consolidated balance sheet, with subsidiary and associate
2 Report on French company's financial statements, and vs UK accounts
3 Long-term contract WIP, treatment of five contracts

Section B

4 Explain capital instruments per FRS 4
5 Discussion on goodwill and the forerunner of FRS 10

BPP PUBLISHING

THE MEANING OF EXAMINERS' INSTRUCTIONS

The examinations department of the CIMA has asked the Institute's examiners to be precise when drafting questions. In particular, examiners have been asked to use precise instruction words. It will probably help you to know what instruction words may be used, and what they mean. With the Institute's permission, their list of recommended requirement words, and their meaning, is shown below.

Recommended requirement words are:

Advise/recommend	Present information, opinions or recommendations to someone to enable that recipient to take action
Amplify	Expand or enlarge upon the meaning of (a statement or quotation)
Analyse	Determine and explain the constituent parts of
Appraise/assess/evaluate	Judge the importance or value of
Assess	See 'appraise'
Clarify	Explain more clearly the meaning of
Comment (critically)	Explain
Compare (with)	Explain similarities and differences between
Contrast	Place in opposition to bring out difference(s)
Criticise	Present the faults in a theory or policy or opinion
Demonstrate	Show by reasoning the truth of
Describe	Present the details and characteristics of
Discuss	Explain the opposing arguments
Distinguish	Specify the differences between
Evaluate	See 'appraise'
Explain/interpret	Set out in detail the meaning of
Illustrate	Use an example - chart, diagram, graph or figure as appropriate - to explain something
Interpret	See 'explain'
Justify	State adequate grounds for
List (and explain)	Itemise (and detail meaning of)
Prove	Show by testing the accuracy of
Recommend	See 'advise'
Reconcile	Make compatible apparently conflicting statements or theories
Relate	Show connections between separate matters
State	Express
Summarise	State briefly the essential points (dispensing with examples and details)
Tabulate	Set out facts or figures in a table

Requirement words which will be avoided

Examiners have been asked to avoid instructions which are imprecise or which may not specifically elicit an answer. The following words will not be used.

Consider	As candidates could do this without writing a word
Define	In the sense of stating exactly what a thing is, as CIMA wishes to avoid requiring evidence of rote learning
Examine	As this is what the examiner is doing, not the examinee
Enumerate	'List' is preferred
Identify	
Justify	When the requirement is not 'to state adequate grounds for' but 'to state the advantage of'
List	On its own, without an additional requirement such as 'list and explain'
Outline	As its meaning is imprecise. The addition of the word 'briefly' to any of the suggested action words is more satisfactory
Review	
Specify	
Trace	

Part A
Company and group accounts

Chapter 1

FINANCIAL REPORTING

Chapter topic		Syllabus reference	Ability required
1	The regulatory framework	9(a)	Application
2	GAAP and the conceptual framework of accounting	9(a)	Application
3	The Accounting Standards Board and FRSs	9(a)	Application
4	FRS for Smaller Entities	9(a)	Application

Introduction

Up to this point in your studies of financial accounting you have been concerned predominantly with legalities, techniques, numbers and calculations. While this text is still concerned with more advanced aspects of these functions, we are shifting our perspective towards a more conceptual approach. We now move into the realm of the theories behind financial accounting practice, the motivations behind corporate reporting, and the controversies and issues which make news in the financial press.

It is most important that you note what the examiner says about Paper 9, right at the beginning of the Syllabus Guidance Notes.

> 'This paper not only tests the candidate's ability to prepare and interpret financial statements and reports, but also tests understanding of current accounting practice and ability to critically appraise current practice and developments. Therefore, questions will normally require candidates to reflect upon a particular issue and to demonstrate an understanding of the principles involved and then to apply those principles to a numerical scenario of some sort. It is not the Examiner's intention to set questions which simply require the mechanical application of a technique.'

The debate on financial reporting has been widened and deepened by unexpected corporate failures over the last few years, particularly Maxwell, Polly Peck and BCCI. As well as focusing on the role of the auditors in these situations, the spotlight has also fallen on financial reporting as a whole, its reliability and relevance and what improvements are possible and desirable. This text will demonstrate the complexities, the difficulties and the controversies surrounding financial reporting.

1   THE REGULATORY FRAMEWORK

1.1   Unincorporated businesses in the UK can usually prepare their financial statements in any form they choose (subject to the constraints of specific legislation, eg the Financial Services Act 1986 for investment businesses). However, companies (limited or unlimited) must comply with the Companies Act 1985 in preparing their financial statements, and Statements of Standard Accounting Practice (SSAPs) and Financial Reporting Standards (FRSs). The *Foreword to Accounting Standards* states that accounting standards are applicable to all financial statements whose purpose is to give a **true and fair view**. This necessarily includes the financial statements of every company incorporated in the UK.

BPP PUBLISHING

1.2   The regulatory framework therefore derives from several sources.

    (a)   Company law

    (b)   Accounting standards and other related pronouncements

    (c)   International accounting standards (and other national standard setters)

    (d)   The requirements of the Stock Exchange

Company law

1.3   In 1985, all existing companies legislation was brought together in a number of consolidating Acts, of which by far the most important is the **Companies Act 1985 (CA 1985)**. This was substantially amended on the enactment of the Companies Act 1989 (CA 1989). You will have studied these requirements in detail in your previous studies.

The European Union

1.4   The United Kingdom is a member of the European Union (EU), formerly the European Community and it must comply with legal requirements decided by the EU. It does this by enacting UK laws to implement **European Commission (EC) directives**. For example, CA 1989 was enacted in part to implement the provisions of the 7th and 8th EC directives, which deal with consolidated accounts and auditors. You should be aware that the form and content of company accounts can be influenced by international developments, as we will see in Chapter 29.

Accounting standards

1.5   Some accounting principles (such as valuation of assets) are embodied in legislation, while others (eg cash flow statements, accounting for contingencies) are regulated by **accounting standards**.

KEY TERM

An **accounting standard** is a rule or set of rules which prescribes the method by which accounts should be prepared and presented.

1.6   In the UK, such standards were called **Statements of Standard Accounting Practice (SSAPs)** and were until 31 July 1990 formulated by the Accounting Standards Committee (ASC). SSAPs are gradually being replaced by **Financial Reporting Standards (FRSs)** produced by the successor to the ASC, the Accounting Standards Board (ASB). The ASB and FRSs are discussed in Section 3. The structure of the standard setting process, which includes the ASB, is discussed below.

1.7   Accounting standards interact with **company law** in several ways.

    (a)   'Realised' profits and losses are determined by reference to generally accepted accounting practice, ie SSAPs and FRSs: s 262 (3).

    (b)   The accounts must state whether the provisions of accounting standards have been followed or give reasons for, and disclosure of any material departure: para 36A Sch 4.

The Stock Exchange requires listed companies to comply with accounting standards; failure to do so will also usually lead to an undesirable audit qualification.

The standard-setting process in the UK

1.8   SSAPs were produced by the ASC. In 1987 the Consultative Committee of Accountancy Bodies (CCAB) established a review committee the **Dearing committee** and its report was published in September 1988. It concluded that the arrangements then in operation, where 21 unpaid ASC members met for a half-day once a month to discuss new standards, were no longer adequate to produce timely and authoritative pronouncements. The ASC was disbanded in August 1990.

1.9   The Dearing committee proposals were put into effect on 1 August 1990.

(a)   A **Financial Reporting Council (FRC)** was created to cover a wide constituency of interests at a high level. It guides the standard setting body on policy and sees that its work is properly financed. It also funds and oversees the Review Panel. It has about 25 members drawn from users, preparers and auditors of accounts.

(b)   The task of devising accounting standards is now carried out by the **Accounting Standards Board (ASB)**, with a full-time chairman and technical director. A majority of two thirds of the Board is required to approve a new standard. Previously, each new standard had to be approved by the Councils of each of the six CCAB bodies separately before it could be published. The ASB now issues standards itself on its own authority. The ASB produces standards more quickly than the ASC and it has the great advantage of legal backing (see below).

(c)   An offshoot of the ASB is the **Urgent Issues Task Force (UITF)**, whose function is:

'to tackle urgent matters not covered by existing standards, and for which, given the urgency, the normal standard-setting process would not be practicable.'

(d)   The **Review Panel,** chaired by a barrister, is:

'concerned with the examination and questioning of departures from accounting standards by large companies.'

It has about 15 members from which smaller panels are formed to tackle cases as they arise.

1.10   The activities of each of these bodies to date is considered below, but the important area is that of the ASB and its standard setting process. Important or topical points will be mentioned again in relevant parts of this text. The following diagram summarises the standard setting structure.

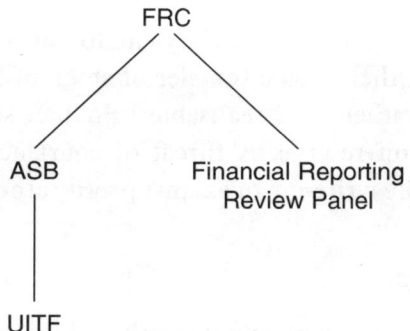

The Financial Reporting Council (FRC)

1.11   The FRC acts as an umbrella organisation to all the bodies involved in standard setting. It is responsible for **funding** and it ensures the smooth running of the standard setting process.

1.12 The FRC is also responsible for the **enforcement** of standards, particularly in relation to the Review Panel. The FRC which can take companies to court to enforce changes to accounts where a company has refused to make changes recommended by the Review Panel. The FRC makes appointments to the ASB and the Review Panel.

1.13 The most important task of the FRC is to set a **general work programme** for the ASB, along with a guide to broad policy issues. This role means that it is the FRC which determines what matters should come to the attention of the ASB.

The Financial Reporting Review Panel

1.14 The Review Panel is alerted to most cases for investigation by the results of the new CA 1989 requirement that companies must include in the notes to the accounts a **statement** that they have been prepared in accordance with applicable accounting standards or, failing that, give details of material departures from those standards, with reasons. Although it is expected that most such referrals would be resolved by discussion, the Panel (and the Secretary of State for Trade and Industry) have the power to apply the court for revision of the accounts, with all costs potentially payable (if the court action is successful) by the company's directors.

1.15 The **auditors** may also be disciplined if the audit report on the defective accounts was not qualified with respect to the departure from standards. Revised accounts, whether prepared voluntarily or under duress, must be circulated to all persons likely to rely on the previous accounts.

1.16 One of the Panel's first acts was to write to over 100 large companies informing them that they were not following a key provision in the 1989 Companies Act. This requires companies specifically to state in their accounts whether they have been prepared in accordance with accounting standards, and to detail and justify any significant **departures from the standards**.

1.17 The Review Panel has also commented on **individual companies' accounts**. The result of these comments tends to be that change is promised by the offending company in the financial accounts of the following year. Occasionally, however, the Panel sees fit to insist on an immediate change in the accounts, but so far only the *threat* of court action has been required.

1.18 The most publicised case which nearly went to court was Trafalgar House. In Trafalgar House's 1991 accounts there was a transfer of stock of land developments to tangible fixed assets at book value (rather than realisable value). A subsequent write-down (£102m) was taken to the revaluation reserve. A threat of court action was required before Trafalgar House agreed to take the write-down against profit rather than reserves.

The effect of the Review Panel

1.19 The Review Panel has not just shown its teeth since it was formed: it has bitten hard. Listed companies and their auditors are doubtless becoming far more cautious in their attempts to break or bend the rules laid out by both the Companies Act and accounting standards. To date, the actions of the Review Panel against individual companies have caused no difficulties as the companies obeyed the Review Panel dictates without any real argument. What will happen if a company argues **through the Courts**?

1.20 The Review Panel may have enough power but can it maintain a **wide enough scrutiny** of published accounts? Unlike its counterpart in the USA, where a significant number of accountants are employed to scrutinise annual reports, very few are employed by the Review Panel. Instead, the Panel relies on the Stock Exchange's Primary Markets Division to supply accounts which are believed to be defective. Other sources include the general public, MPs and the ICAEW's Professional Standards Committee.

1.21 The Review Panel may also make an effective contribution to the debate about **auditors' independence** from large clients, such as the big plcs. The Review Panel can criticise the auditors as well as the company in question. For this reason, auditors may be able to withstand pressure from client companies to accept 'suspect' accounting practices, as public exposure for both the auditor and the company by the Review Panel would be seen as a greater evil.

1.22 There has been some **criticism** of the Review Panel's 'heavy handedness'. It is generally felt, however, that the Panel must be aggressive in order to succeed. Another criticism has been that the Panel gives **insufficient information** about the reasons for its decisions.

Question 1

Look for Review Panel rulings in the financial press between now and your exam.

The Urgent Issues Task Force (UITF)

1.23 The UITF pronouncements, which are called 'abstracts', are intended to come into effect quickly. They therefore tend to become effective within approximately one month of publication date. The UITF has so far issued 22 **abstracts**. Abstracts 1, 2, 3 and 8 have all been superseded by new FRSs and Financial Reporting Exposure Drafts (FREDs). The rest are discussed in the relevant parts of this text when necessary. Three of them are discussed here.

UITF Abstract 7 True and fair override disclosures

1.24 Where the directors depart from provisions of CA 1985 to the extent necessary to give a true and fair view, the Act required that 'particulars of any such departure, the reasons for it and its effect shall be given in a note to the accounts'. Abstract 7 seeks to clarify the meaning of that sentence as follows.

   (a) **Particulars of any such departure**: a statement of the treatment which the Act would normally require in the circumstances and a description of the treatment actually adopted.

   (b) **The reasons for it**: a statement as to why the treatment prescribed would not give a true and fair view.

   (c) **Its effect**: a description of how the position shown in the accounts is different as a result of the departure, with quantification if possible, or an explanation of the circumstances.

The disclosures required should either be included in or cross referenced to the note required about compliance with accounting standards, particulars of any material departure from those standards and the reasons for it (Paragraph 36A Sch 4).

BPP PUBLISHING

UITF Abstract 14 Disclosure of changes in accounting policy

1.25 This Abstract clarifies an aspect of the statutory disclosure requirements that has caused some uncertainty as to its meaning. When there is a **change of accounting policy**, companies legislation requires disclosure of particulars, reasons and effect. The issue concerns the extent of the disclosure necessary to give the 'effect' of the change. The UITF has received legal advice that an indication of the effect on the *current* year's figures is required. This is in addition to the effect on the results for the *preceding* period, which is a disclosure requirement of FRS 3 *Reporting financial performance*. As this is a clarification of the law this consensus should be adopted as soon as practicable.

1.26 There has also been some debate about the **extent of the disclosure** necessary to cover the 'reasons' for the change. In this connection FRS 3 states that 'a change in accounting may ... be made only if it can be justified on the grounds that the new policy is preferable to the one it replaces because it will give a fairer presentation of the result and of the financial position of a reporting entity'. This, together with the requirements in companies legislation for 'special reasons', is a stringent test and directors of companies contemplating a possible change of policy should ensure that the reasons for any change are compelling.

1.27 The issue of a **new accounting standard** requiring a change would constitute sufficient reason, since accounts prepared adopting a policy no longer permitted by a new standard would normally not give a true and fair view. On the other hand, where the existing policy continues to be acceptable, either because the relevant standard permits a choice or because, in the absence of a relevant standard, both policies are generally accepted, it would not be in accordance with the legislation or FRS 3 if a change was made from one such alternative policy to another unless the reasons for the change were compelling, in that the new policy provided better information for users of the accounts.

1.28 **UITF 7** elaborates on the requirement to state 'reasons' and in the context of a change of accounting policy this would imply a statement as to why the continuation of the previous accounting policy would not be appropriate. Where the change of accounting policy was imposed on the company, for example by a new accounting standard, a simple statement to this effect will normally suffice. However, where a change has been made from one generally accepted policy to another, in the absence of a new accounting standard or other similar requirement, the reasons justifying the change need to be clearly and fully disclosed.

UITF Abstract 17 Employee share schemes

1.29 This abstract deals with the measurement and timing of the charge to be recognised in the profit and loss account in respect of employee share schemes. It requires the charge to be based on the fair value of the shares at the date an award has been made to participants in the scheme (the grant date). In the case of **long-term incentive plans (LTIPs)**, which have become common following the Greenbury Committee's report in 1995 on executive pay, the charge should be spread over the period to which the employee's performance relates.

1.30 The use of the **grant date**, rather than alternatives such as the exercise date, is consistent with the principle underlying UITF Abstract 10 *Disclosure of directors' share options* and equivalent requirements in the USA, reflecting the fact that the grant date is when the commitment is entered into by the company.

UITF Abstract 18 - Pension costs following the 1997 tax changes in respect of dividend income

1.31   This abstract is concerned with the recognition in the financial statements of employers of the loss arising as a result of the Finance (No 2) Act 1997, whereby pension schemes are no longer able to reclaim a tax credit on dividend income.

1.32   It states that this change to tax legislation does not, of itself, fall outside the normal scope of the actuarial assumptions as set out in paragraph 82 of SSAP 24 *Accounting for pension costs*. Hence, the loss should be spread forward over the remaining service lives of current employees in the scheme whatever the financial position of the scheme and regardless of any additional contributions that are made.

UITF Abstract 19 Tax on gains and losses on foreign currency borrowings that hedge an investment in a foreign enterprise

1.33   This abstract formalises the view expressed two years ago, following changes to the tax treatment of certain exchange differences, that where exchange differences are reported in the statement of total recognised gains and losses, the related tax should also be reported in that statement.

1.34   The abstract also specifies how tax should be taken into account in applying the restrictions contained in SSAP 20 *Foreign currency translation* on the treatment of gains and losses on borrowings that finance or hedge a foreign net investment and clarifies the necessary disclosures.

Foreword to UITF Abstracts

1.35   This foreword was issued in February 1994. It is closely associated with the *Forward to Accounting Standards* (see Paragraph 4.4) in its scope and application and users are asked to 'be guided by the **spirit and reasoning**' behind the abstracts.

1.36   Most importantly, the document sets out the following **criteria for compliance** with the UITF abstracts.

> 'The Councils of the CCAB bodies expect their members who assume responsibilities in respect of financial statements to observe UITF Abstracts until they are replaced by accounting standards or otherwise withdrawn by the ASB.'

1.37   The **scope** of and **compliance** with the abstracts are similar to those associated with accounting standards (accounts which show a true and fair view, non-compliance must be justified and disclosed etc).

The effect of the UITF

1.38   The prompt action of the UITF has **closed many loopholes** as soon as they have become apparent. Some of the abstracts have been triggered by the accounts of individual companies, whereas others reflect concern which has grown over time. Another aspect of the success of the UITF is the relative speed with which the abstracts have been included in new standards or exposure drafts.

1.39   In combination with the Review Panel, the UITF can **halt abuses** in financial reporting as soon as they occur. This also acts as a preventative measure, causing many companies and their auditors to hesitate before breaking (or even bending) the rules.

Question 2

Discuss the function of these bodies.

(a)   Accounting Standards Board
(b)   Review Panel
(c)   Financial Reporting Council
(d)   Urgent Issues Task Force

Answer

See Paragraph 1.9.

International Accounting Standards

1.40   International Accounting Standards (IASs) are produced by the **International Accounting Standards Committee (IASC)** which was set up in 1973 to work for the improvement and harmonisation of financial reporting. The IASC develops IASs through an international process that involves the world-wide accountancy profession, the preparers and users of financial statements, and national standard setting bodies.

1.41   The **objectives** of the IASC are:

(a)   to formulate and publish in the public interest accounting standards to be observed in the presentation of financial statements and to promote their world-wide acceptance and observance; and

(b)   to work generally for the improvement and harmonisation of regulations, accounting standards and procedures relating to the presentation of financial statements.

The use and application of IASs

1.42   IASs have helped to both **improve** and **harmonise** financial reporting around the world. The standards are used:

(a)   as national requirements, often after a national process;

(b)   as the basis for all or some national requirements;

(c)   as an international benchmark for those countries which develop their own requirements;

(d)   by regulatory authorities for domestic and foreign companies; and

(e)   by companies themselves.

1.43   As well as the *Framework* document already mentioned, the IASC has published 39 IASs, as well as revised standards. There are also various exposure drafts of IASs in existence. We will look at the procedures and practices of the IASC in Chapter 29.

Effects of IASs on UK regulation

1.44   **Before the ASB** came into existence, the effect of IASs and other IASC publications on UK standard setting was limited and haphazard. Many SSAPs and IASs were in agreement, but some were not, and some covered completely different topics.

1.45   Once the ASB was established, this situation began to change. The main impact of the IASC on the work of the ASB involved the IASC's *Framework for the Preparation and Presentation of*

Financial Statements. The *Framework* was introduced to 'set out the concepts that underlie the preparation and presentation of financial statements for external users'. The ASB has based its own *Statement of Principles* on the IASC's *Framework* and we will discuss this ASB document in Section 3. The ASB has adopted the same **conceptual approach** to financial reporting as the IASC, although some aspects of the *Statement of Principles* conflict with the international approach.

1.46 In its FRSs, the ASB states the **compliance** of the standards with IASs or IAS exposure drafts. The ASB sees itself as closely aligned with the IASC. However, it seems that the ASB will only follow the relevant IAS if it fits in with the desired UK practice. The IASC is revising and improving its current IASs and one of the reasons is the elimination or reduction of alternative accounting treatments.

The Stock Exchange

1.47 In the UK there are currently **two different markets** on which it is possible for a company to have its securities quoted:

(a) the Stock Exchange; and
(b) the Alternative Investment Market (AIM).

1.48 Shares quoted on the **main market,** the Stock Exchange, are said to be 'listed' or to have obtained a 'listing'. When a share is granted a quotation on the Stock Exchange, it appears on the *Official List* which is published in London for each business day. The Official List shows the 'official quotation' or price for the share for that particular day; it is drawn up by the Primary Markets Division of the Stock Exchange, which derives its prices from those actually ruling in the market. In practice, the buying and selling prices used by member firms will be within the prices quoted on the official list.

1.49 In order to receive a listing for its securities, a company must conform with Stock Exchange regulations contained in the **Listing Rules or 'Yellow Book'** issued by the Council of The Stock Exchange. The company commits itself to certain procedures and standards, including the disclosure of accounting information, which is more extensive than the disclosure requirements of the Companies Acts.

1.50 The requirements of the **AIM** are less stringent than the main Stock Exchange. It is for new, higher risk and smaller companies.

Effects of Stock Exchange requirements

1.51 Many requirements of the Yellow Book do not have the backing of law, but the ultimate sanction which can be imposed on a listed company which fails to abide by them is the **withdrawal of its securities** from the Stock Exchange List: the company's shares would no longer be traded on the market.

1.52 As part of the listing agreement, companies are now obliged to state whether they have complied with the **Combined Code** (the *Code* deals with matters such as the composition of the board of directors, non-executive directors, directors' contracts and reporting and controls).

BPP PUBLISHING

1.53 Section summary

This section gives you an overview of the regulatory framework surrounding financial reporting, but the best students will keep up to date by reading some or all of the following. Try a good library.

- *CIMA Student*
- *Management Accounting*
- Other accountancy journals
- *Financial Times*
- *The Economist*

2 GAAP AND THE CONCEPTUAL FRAMEWORK OF ACCOUNTING

2.1 It has been said that in the past the standard setting body took a 'fire fighting' approach to developing accounting standards. The **old SSAPs** were not based on a consistent philosophy and this led to the need for a conceptual framework of accounting.

KEY TERM

A **conceptual framework** is a constitution, a coherent system of interrelated objectives and fundamentals that can lead to consistent standards and that prescribes the nature, function and limits of financial accounting and financial statements.

Financial Accounting Standards Board (FASB)

2.2 The basic idea is to avoid the 'fire fighting' approach which characterised the development of SSAPs under the old ASC, and instead to develop an **underlying philosophy** as a basis for consistent accounting principles so that the rationale of each standard is structured into the whole framework. The process towards a conceptual framework is described briefly here.

ASC/FASB

2.3 The ASC stated in a consultative document *Setting Accounting Standards* that, whilst an agreed framework of accounting would provide a good basis on which to build accounting standards, it believed that no such framework was currently available and that conclusive results would probably not be rapidly achieved. FASB, however, began a large-scale project in 1973 to develop such a framework, with immense resources committed to the research and large volumes of material produced.

Macve Report

2.4 In the UK, a similar search for a conceptual framework was under way; a report was commissioned by the ASC from Professor Richard Macve. His report was published in 1981 and he wrote:

'the value of the current attempts to explore the conceptual framework lies, in my opinion, mainly in the discipline the process imposes of identifying the important areas where judgement is needed on questions of accounting policy, and of stimulating enquiry, with regard to users' needs and how to satisfy them.'

IASC's Framework

2.5 The IASC *Framework for the Preparation and Presentation of Financial Statements* is non-mandatory and it deals with:

(a) the objective of financial statements;

(b) the qualitative characteristics that determine the usefulness of information in financial statements;

(c) the definition, recognition and measurement of the elements from which financial statements are constructed;

(d) concepts of capital and capital maintenance.

2.6 The IASC believes that further international harmonisation of accounting methods can best be promoted by focusing on these four topics since they will then lead to published financial statements that meet the common needs of most users.

Solomons Report

2.7 The Solomons Report, published in 1989 and entitled *Guidelines for Financial Reporting Standards*, proceeds in a similar way. Chapters deal with:

(a) the purpose of financial reporting;
(b) financial statements and their elements;
(c) the qualitative characteristics of accounting information;
(d) recognition and measurement;
(e) the choice of a general purpose accounting model.

Advantages of a conceptual framework

2.8 The advantages arising from using a conceptual framework may be summarised by looking at some of the **problems** the old ASC had when developing SSAPs.

(a) SSAPs were developed on a **patchwork quilt** basis where a particular accounting problem was recognised by the ASC as having emerged, and resources were then channelled into standardising accounting practice in that area, without regard to whether that particular issue was necessarily the most important issue remaining at that time without standardisation.

(b) The development of certain SSAPs (eg SSAP 13) were subject to considerable **political interference** from interested parties. Where there is a conflict of interest between user groups on which policies to choose, policies deriving from a conceptual framework will be less open to criticism that the standard setters buckled under external pressure.

(c) Some SSAPs **concentrate** on the income statement (P&L account), some on the valuation of net assets (balance sheet).

(i) FRS 15 ensures that depreciation is charged on a systematic basis through the P&L account to comply with the accruals concept, but the net book value figure in the balance sheet has little meaning.

(ii) Conversely, SSAP 15 requires the balance sheet provision for deferred tax to be the liability currently envisaged, but the P&L charge or credit for deferred tax has no meaning other than representing the balancing figure between a provision brought forward and carried forward in the balance sheet.

An unambiguous definition of **income** and **value** would ensure all financial statements have equal usefulness to each user group.

Disadvantages of a conceptual framework

2.9 Arguments against the introduction of a conceptual framework might include the following.

(a) Financial statements are intended for a **variety of users**, and it is not certain that a single conceptual framework can be devised which will suit all users.

(b) Given the diversity of user requirements, there may be a need for a variety of accounting standards, each produced for a **different purpose** (and with different concepts as a basis).

(c) It is not clear that a conceptual framework will make the task of **preparing** and then **implementing** standards any easier than it is now.

2.10 The ASB has now focused its attention on developing a conceptual framework, based on both the IASC *Framework* and on the recommendations of the Solomons Report. The ASB conceptual framework is encompassed in a *Statement of Principles* published in **exposure draft** form. This is discussed in detail in Chapter 22.

Generally Accepted Accounting Practice (GAAP)

2.11 This term has sprung up in recent years.

> **KEY TERM**
>
> **GAAP** signifies all the rules, from whatever source, which govern accounting. In the UK this is seen primarily as a combination of:
>
> - Company law (mainly CA 1985)
> - Accounting standards
> - Stock exchange requirements

2.12 Although those sources are the basis for UK GAAP, the concept also includes the effects of **non-mandatory sources** such as:

(a) international accounting standards;
(b) statutory requirements in other countries, particularly the US.

2.13 In other words, GAAP encompasses these regulatory influences discussed in Section 1 above. In the UK, GAAP has **no statutory or regulatory authority** or definition (unlike other countries, such as the US). The term is mentioned rarely in legislation, and only then in fairly limited terms.

2.14 GAAP is in fact a **dynamic concept**: it changes constantly as circumstances alter through new legislation, standards *and* practice. This idea that GAAP is constantly changing is recognised by the ASB in its *Statement of Aims* where it states that it expects to issue new standards and amend old ones in response to:

> 'evolving business practices, new economic developments and deficiencies identified in current practice.'

The emphasis has shifted from 'principles' to 'practice' in UK GAAP.

2.15 The problem of what is **generally accepted** is not easy to settle, because new practices will obviously not be generally adopted yet. The criteria for a practice being 'generally accepted' will depend on factors such as whether the practice is addressed by UK accounting standards or legislation, their international equivalents, and whether other companies have adopted the practice. Most importantly, perhaps: is the practice consistent with the needs of users and the objectives of financial reporting and is it is consistent with the 'true and fair' concept?

3 THE ACCOUNTING STANDARDS BOARD AND FRSs

3.1 The ASB's consultative process leads to the setting of Financial Reporting Standards (FRSs). To produce an FRS, first a working **Draft for Discussion (DD)** is published to get feedback from people closely involved with or with a direct interest in the standard setting process. The DD, as a result of this process, is converted into a **Financial Reporting Exposure Draft (FRED)**. You should be aware of the contents of all the FRSs, FREDs and DDs published by the ASB. The ASB publishes other documents as Exposure Drafts, eg, chapters of the *Statement of Principles*.

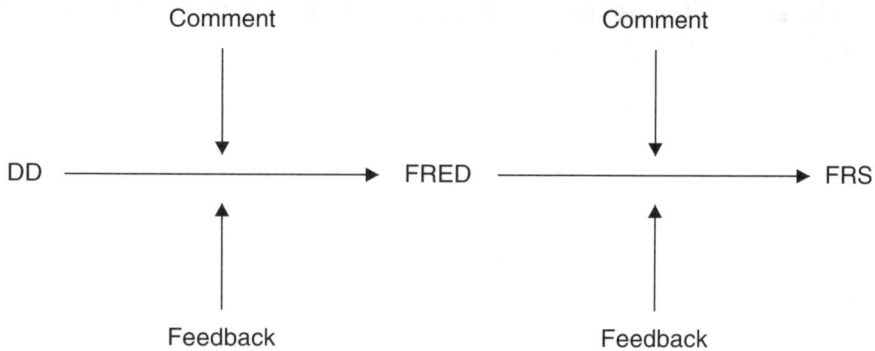

Statement of Aims

3.2 The **definitive** *Statement of Aims* was published by the ASB in 1991 and it is produced here in full as it is very brief.

> *'Aims*
>
> The aims of the Accounting Standards Board (the Board) are to establish and improve standards of financial accounting and reporting, for the benefit of users, preparers and auditors of financial information.
>
> *Achieving the aims*
>
> The Board intends to achieve its aims by:
>
> 1 Developing principles to guide it in establishing standards and to provide a framework within which others can exercise judgement in resolving accounting issues.
>
> 2 Issuing new accounting standards, or amending existing ones, in response to evolving business practices, new economic developments and deficiencies being identified in current practice.
>
> 3 Addressing urgent issues promptly.
>
> *Fundamental guidelines*
>
> 1 To be objective and to ensure that the information resulting from the application of accounting standards faithfully represents the underlying commercial activity. Such information should be neutral in the sense that it is free from any form of bias intended to influence users in a particular direction and should not be designed to favour any group of users or preparers.
>
> 2 To ensure that accounting standards are clearly expressed and supported by a reasoned analysis of the issues.

3   To determine what should be incorporated in accounting standards based on research, public consultation and careful deliberation about the usefulness of the resulting information.

4   To ensure that through a process of regular communication, accounting standards are produced with due regard to international developments.

5   To ensure that there is consistency both from one accounting standard to another and between accounting standards and company law.

6   To issue accounting standards only when the expected benefits exceed the perceived costs. The Board recognises that reliable cost/benefit calculations are seldom possible. However, it will always assess the need for standards in terms of the significance and extent of the problem being addressed and will choose the standard which appears to be most effective in cost/benefit terms.

7   To take account of the desire of the financial community for evolutionary rather than revolutionary change in the reporting process where this is consistent with the objectives outlined above.'

Foreword to Accounting Standards

3.3   This document was issued in June 1993 and the contents are listed briefly here.

(a)   **Introduction.** This is merely background information about the ASB and the documents it will produce.

(b)   **Accounting Standards Board.** Reference is made to the *Statement of Aims.*

(c)   **Authority.** This section mentions:

(i)   the legal authority of FRSs in relation to the Act;

(ii)   directors' responsibilities to prepare accounts showing a true and fair view;

(iii)   the responsibility of members of CCAB bodies in industry and practice in relation to financial statements (as preparers or auditors);

(iv)   CCAB bodies may investigate non-compliance.

(d)   **Scope and application.** The standards apply to:

(i)   financial statements of a reporting entity that are intended to give a true and fair view;

(ii)   group accounts in the UK (and Ireland) including any overseas entities.

(e)   **Compliance with accounting standards.** The following rules and comments are laid down.

(i)   It will normally be necessary to comply with the standards to show a true and fair view.

(ii)   In applying the standards, the user should be guided by their spirit and reasoning.

(iii)   In *rare* cases it may be necessary to depart from a standard to show a true and fair view.

(iv)   Departures should be dealt with objectively according to the 'economic and commercial characteristics of the circumstances'; the departure and its financial effect should be disclosed.

(v)   The Review Panel and the DTI have powers and procedures to investigate departures and to require a restatement through the court.

(f)   **The public sector.** 'The prescription of accounting requirements for the public sector in the United Kingdom is a matter for the Government.'

(g) **The issue of an FRS**. This section covers the procedures for discussion, consultation and drafting.

(h) **Accounting standards and the legal framework**. Consistency with UK and EC law is aimed for.

(i) **International accounting standards**. An FRS will contain a section explaining how it relates to the IAS dealing with the same topic. 'The Board supports the IASC in its aims to harmonise international financial reporting.'

(j) **Early adoption of FREDs**. The contents of FREDs may change before the FRS stage is reached and therefore early adoption is discouraged unless the information is shown as a supplement.

(k) **Appendix**. A new **legal opinion** by Mary Arden QC has been obtained on the true and fair requirement. This opinion endorses the legal force of standards.

> 'Just as a custom which is upheld by the courts may properly be regarded as a source of law, so too, in my view, does an accounting standard which the court holds must be complied with to meet the true and fair requirement become in cases where it is applicable, a source of law in itself in the widest sense of that term.'

3.4 As you can see, the foreword gives the FRSs a **context** in relation to other standard setting bodies, company law and users and preparers of accounts.

Current accounting standards

3.5 The following standards are extant at the date of writing. The SSAPs which were in force at the date the ASB was formed have been adopted by the Board. They are gradually being superseded by the new FRSs.

Accounting standards

No	Title	Issue date
	Foreword to accounting standards	Jun 93
FRS 1	Cash flow statements (revised) (see below)	Oct 96
FRS 2	Accounting for subsidiary undertakings	Jul 92
FRS 3	Reporting financial performance	Oct 92
FRS 4	Capital instruments	Dec 93
FRS 5	Reporting the substance of transactions	Apr 94
FRS 6	Acquisitions and mergers	Sep 94
FRS 7	Fair values in acquisition accounting	Sep 94
FRS 8	Related party disclosures	Oct 95
FRS 9	Associates and joint ventures	Nov 97
	Financial Reporting Standard for Smaller Entities	Dec 98
FRS 10	Goodwill and intangible assets	Dec 97
FRS 11	Impairment of fixed assets and goodwill	Jul 98
FRS 12	Provisions, contingent liabilities and contingent assets	Sep 98
FRS 13	Derivatives and other financial instruments: disclosure	Sep 98
FRS 14	Earnings per share	Oct 98
FRS 15	Tangible fixed assets	Feb 99
SSAP 2	Disclosure of accounting policies	Nov 71
SSAP 4	Accounting for government grants	Jul 90
SSAP 5	Accounting for value added tax	Apr 74
SSAP 8	The treatment of taxation under the imputation system in the accounts of companies	Dec 77
SSAP 9	Stocks and long-term contracts	Sep 88
SSAP 13	Accounting for research and development	Jan 89
SSAP 15	Accounting for deferred tax	May 85
SSAP 17	Accounting for post balance sheet events	Aug 80
SSAP 19	Accounting for investment properties (amended)	Nov 81

No	Title	Issue date
SSAP 20	Foreign currency translation	Apr 83
SSAP 21	Accounting for leases and hire purchase contracts	Aug 84
SSAP 24	Accounting for pension costs	May 88
SSAP 25	Segmental reporting	Jun 90

Financial reporting exposure drafts

FRED 18	*Current taxation*	June 99
Amendment to FRSSE		July 99

UITF Abstracts

Students sitting Paper 13 are expected to be aware of the issues/reasons which have led to the publication of a UITF abstract indicated as examinable in the list below, and their principal requirements.

No	Title	Issue date
	Foreword to UITF Abstracts	Feb 94
UITF Abstract 3	Treatment of goodwill on disposal of a business	Dec 91
UITF Abstract 4	Presentation of long-term debtors in current assets	Jul 92
UITF Abstract 5	Transfers from current assets to fixed assets	Jul 92
UITF Abstract 6	Accounting for post-retirement benefits other than pensions	Nov 92
UITF Abstract 7	True and fair override disclosures	Dec 92
UITF Abstract 9	Accounting for operations in hyper-inflationary economics	Jun 93
No	Title	Issue date
UITF Abstract 10	Disclosure of directors' share options	Sep 94
UITF Abstract 11	Capital instruments: issuer call options	Sep 94
UITF Abstract 12	Lessee accounting for reverse premiums and similar incentives	Dec 94
UITF Abstract 13	Accounting for ESOP Trusts	Jun 95
UITF Abstract 14	Disclosure of changes in accounting policy	Nov 95
UITF Abstract 15	Disclosure of substantial acquisitions	Jan 96
UITF Abstract 16	Income and expenses subject to non-standard rates of tax	Feb 97
UITF Abstract 17	Employee share schemes	May 97
UITF Abstract 18	Pension costs following the 1997 tax changes in respect of dividend income	Dec 97
UITF Abstract 19	Tax on gains and losses that hedge an investment in a foreign enterprise	Feb 98
UITF Abstract 20	Year 2000 issues: accounting and disclosures	
UITF Abstract 21	Accounting issues arising from the proposed introduction of the Euro	Mar 98
UITF Abstract 22	The acquisition of Lloyds business	Jun 98

Other documents

Accounting for the effects of changing prices: a handbook - ASC (Summary and Overview)

The Cadbury Report (Dec 1992), *The Hampel Report* (Jan 1998)

Operating and Financial Review - ASB (July 1993)

The old Accounting Standards Committee: Exposure Drafts

Most of the old ASC EDs have been superseded by FRSs or FREDs.

Title		Issue date
ED 55	Accounting for investments	Aug 90

Accounting Standards Board (ASB): Exposure Drafts

Title	Issue date
Statement of Principles for Financial Reporting (revised)	Mar 99

ASB Drafts for Discussion (DDs)

Title	Issue date
Accounting for tax	Mar 95
Segmental reporting	May 96
Discounting (working paper)	Apr 97
Derivatives and other financial instruments (discussion paper)	Jul 96
Aspects of accounting for pension costs (discussion paper)	Jul 98
Business combinations (discussion paper)	Dec 98
Reporting financial performance: proposals for change	June 98

Statements of Recommended Practice (SORPs)

3.6 When the ASB took over from the old ASC, it adopted all the existing accounting standards. It did not, however, adopt the ASC's SORPs 1 and 2. As far as your syllabus is concerned, you need only be aware of the relevance of SORPs to financial reporting and the principal requirements of SORPs 1 and 2. SORPs are developed as an **aid to reporting** in specific industries or for specific bodies, eg pensions (SORP 1) and charities (SORP 2).

ASB policy for the development of SORPs

3.7 The ASB produced a document laying out its policy on Statements of Recommended Practice (SORPs). That policy can be summarised as follows.

(a) The ASB will not issue its own SORPs, but will **recognise bodies** for the purpose of issuing SORPs. Guidelines are given for whether a particular body is suitable.

(b) ASB-recognised bodies must, as a condition of recognition, agree to abide by the **ASB's code of practice** on producing SORPs (included in this document).

(c) SORPs issued by such bodies will include a **negative assurance statement**, outlining the limited nature of the ASB's review and stating whether the SORP contains any unacceptable fundamental points of principle.

(d) The ASB has appointed **committees** to deal with recognised bodies and the SORPs they produce.

(e) **No other mention** should be made of the ASB within a SORP, except in the negative assurance statement.

3.8 You can see from this that the ASB is merely acting as a **quality control monitor** on SORPs. Although there will be some work involved, the ASB will not commit any major resources to aid the development of SORPs.

SORP 1 *Pension scheme accounts*

3.9 This SORP governs the form and content of **pension scheme accounts**. It does *not* cover how companies account for pension costs in their own accounts, as this is the subject of SSAP 24 (See Chapter 7).

3.10 The published pension scheme report should contain these **documents**.

- Trustees' report (growth of the scheme, scheme management)
- Audited accounts
- Actuary's statement (security of the scheme)
- Investment report (investment policies, performance of the scheme)

3.11 The **accounts** are historical statements concerning the **stewardship** of the scheme. The accounts are designed to give a true and fair view of the financial transactions of the scheme during the accounting period and of the disposition of its net assets at the end of the period. Note that the ASC could not lay down rules governing reports from other professionals (eg actuaries), so the SORP only governs the contents of the audited accounts.

3.12 The **accounts** should comprise the following.

- Revenue account
- Net assets statement
- Reconciliation of movement in net assets of the scheme to the revenue account
- Notes to the accounts

4 FRS FOR SMALLER ENTITIES

Big GAAP/little GAAP

4.1 This is a current debate in the financial accounting world. Most UK companies are **small companies**, generally owned and managed by one person or a family. The owners have invested their own money in the business and there are no outside shareholders to protect. Large companies, by contrast, particularly plcs, may have shareholders who have invested their money, possibly through a pension fund, with no knowledge whatever of the company. These shareholders need protection and the regulations for such companies need to be more stringent.

4.2 It could therefore be argued that company accounts should be of **two types**: 'simple' ones for small companies with fewer regulations and disclosure requirements and 'complicated' ones for larger companies with extensive and detailed requirements. This is the 'big GAAP/little GAAP' divide.

FRS for Smaller Entities

4.3 In November 1997 the ASB published the *Financial Reporting Standard for Smaller Entities*. This was revised in December 1998. It brings together in one brief document all the **accounting guidance** which UK small businesses will require to draw up their financial statements.

4.4 The FRSSE is applicable to all companies that satisfy the definition of a small company in companies legislation and is available to other entities that would meet that definition if they were companies. A company that chooses to comply with the FRSSE is exempt from all other accounting standards and UITF Abstracts.

4.5 The FRSSE contains in a simplified form the requirements from existing accounting standards that are relevant to the majority of smaller entities.

4.6 In order to keep the FRSSE as user-friendly as possible some of the requirements in accounting standards relating to more complex transactions, eg the treatment of convertible debt in FRS 4 *Capital instruments*, have not been included in the FRSSE, as they do not affect most smaller entities. Where guidance is needed on a matter not contained in the FRSSE, regard should be paid to existing practice as set out in the relevant accounting standards.

Measurement

4.7 The measurement bases in the FRSSE are the same as, or a simplification of, those in existing accounting standards. For example, under the FRSSE a lessee that is a small company could account for the finance charges on a finance lease on a straight-line basis over the life of the lease, rather than, as in SSAP 21, using a constant periodic rate of return.

Disclosure requirements

4.8 One of the many ways in which the FRSSE should reduce the burden for preparers of smaller entities' financial statements is likely to be its *reduced* disclosure requirements. For example, the FRSSE does not require an analysis of turnover and profits into continuing operations, acquisitions and discontinued operations, nor a reconciliation of movements in shareholders' funds.

Related parties

4.9 The disclosure requirements for related party transactions in the FRSSE represent a useful dispensation for smaller entities compared with those in FRS 8 *Related party disclosures*. Under FRS 8, related party transactions that are material to the related party, where that related party is an individual, are required to be disclosed in the accounts of the reporting entity even if the transaction is not material to the entity. This is not so for smaller entities adopting the FRSSE, as they need disclose only those related party transactions that are material in relation to the reporting entity.

Cash flow statement

4.10 Since small entities are already exempt from the requirements of FRS 1 *Cash flow statements* the FRSSE does not include a requirement for a cash flow statement. The ASB nevertheless believes that a cash flow statement is an important aid to the understanding of an entity's financial position and performance and the FRSSE therefore includes a 'voluntary disclosures' section, recommending that smaller entities present a simplified cash flow statement using the indirect method (ie starting with operating profit and reconciling it to the total cash generated (or utilised) in the period).

Small groups

4.11 Small groups are not required by law to prepare consolidated accounts, and therefore in practice not many do so, at least on a statutory basis. The Working Party and the Board, however, agreed with respondents that it would be unfair to those small groups that voluntarily prepare group accounts, if they were not able to take advantage of the provisions in the FRSSE. To import all the necessary requirements from accounting standards and UITF Abstracts into the FRSSE to deal with consolidated accounts would have added substantially to its length and complexity, even though it would have been of interest to only a small percentage of entities. Accordingly, the Working Party and the Board preferred to extend the FRSSE in certain areas and then require small groups adopting the FRSSE to follow those accounting standards and UITF Abstracts that deal with consolidated financial statements. This approach was supported by the majority of respondents to the Exposure Draft commenting on the matter.

Criticisms of the FRS

4.12 **Criticisms** of the FRSSE have been as follows.

(a) The FRSSE is unlikely to make it **easier or cheaper** to prepare financial statements.

(b) The case in favour of relaxing **measurement** GAAP for smaller companies has not yet been made convincingly. If it is ultimately decided that the only exemptions are to be from disclosure, rather than from measurement, this could be achieved more easily by simply stating in the individual FRSs and SSAPs what disclosure requirements apply to all companies and what applies only to large ones.

(c) There is concern that the FRSSE could allow smaller companies to use **different accounting measurements,** eg the straight line method rather than the current actuarial method for finance charges.

(d) It is questionable whether accounts prepared under the FRSSE would give a **true and fair view** under company law. The true and fair view requirement applies to all companies, whatever their size.

(e) The present document is not a **'stand-alone' document**. Users would still need to refer to 'mainstream' standards if they are to prepare financial statements which show a true and fair view.

4.13 However, some commentators back the concept of a financial reporting standard for smaller entities; they feel that the FRSSE provides a satisfactory and workable solution to the problems of smaller entities caused by the **increasing complexity** of accounting standards.

Future developments

4.14 With the assistance of its advisory committee, the Committee on Accounting for Smaller Entities, the ASB will update and revise the FRSSE periodically to reflect future developments in financial reporting. Any changes to the FRSSE, for example as a result of new accounting standards and UITF Abstracts, will be the subject of public consultation.

4.15 The FRSSE attempts to balance the conflicting views of those who commented on the proposals, ranging from those who believe small companies should be exempt from all accounting standards to those who favour retaining virtually the status quo. Given this divergence of views, the ASB believes that it is particularly important that, going forward, the FRSSE is carefully monitored. It is therefore proposed to review how the FRSSE, as a whole, is working in practice after two full years of effective operation and propose amendments as necessary, in addition to the routine periodic revisions of the FRSSE resulting from new accounting standards and UITF Abstracts.

Exam focus point

As with all topical issues, you should aim to read around the subject. Not all comments on the FRSSE have been favourable.

Chapter roundup

- This is a very long but also a very important chapter. You must understand all aspects of the **regulatory environment** and the arguments behind current thinking. We have put a lot in here and you may wish to refer back to this chapter as you go through the text.

- You should be able to discuss the **role and impact** of the following bodies.
  - Accounting Standards Board
  - Financial Reporting Council
  - Review Panel
  - Urgent Issues Task Force
  - European Union/European Commission
  - Company Law
  - International Accounting Standards Committee

- While this text gives you a thorough explanation of the function of each of these bodies, you will find the material much easier to remember if you **keep up to date** with developments in the accountancy or financial press. These bodies and their actions are discussed constantly.

- Whereas in the past accounting standards were produced on an *ad hoc* basis, in recent years attempts have been made to develop a **conceptual framework** of accounting, on which future accounting standards should be based.

- There have been **initiatives** in this direction by:
  - FASB;
  - IASC;
  - more recently the ASB with its *Statement of Principles*.

- **GAAP** standards for 'Generally Accepted Accounting Practice'. It signifies all rules from whatever source, which govern accounting.

- You should be familiar with the ASB's approach to **standard setting**.

- There are some important debates raging in the financial reporting world at the moment on the *Statement of Principles* and on **corporate governance**.

- The *FRS for Smaller Entities* aims to close the big GAAP/little GAAP debate by giving small entities basic accounting and disclosure rules to follow.

Quick quiz

1   From which sources does the UK regulatory framework derive? (see para 1.2)

2   What are the responsibilities of the UK statutory authorities to EC directives? (1.4)

3   What is the role of the Review Panel? (1.9(d))

4   Why is a conceptual framework necessary? (2.1, 2.2)

5   What are the disadvantages of a conceptual framework? (2.9)

6   Summarise the content of the ASB's *Statement of Aims.* (3.2)

7   Summarise the ASB's policy on the development of SORPs (3.7)

8   How does the FRSSE affect the accounts of smaller entities? (4.6)

9   How does the FRSSE modify SSAP 21? (4.8)

10 What have been the criticisms of the proposed FRSSE? (4.13)

Question to try	Level	Marks	Time
1	Introductory	n/a	n/a

BPP
PUBLISHING

Chapter 2

THE ACCOUNTS OF LIMITED COMPANIES

Chapter topic	Syllabus reference	Ability required
1 SSAP 2 *Disclosure of accounting policies*	9(a)	Application
2 Format and notes	9(a)	Application
3 FRS 3 *Reporting financial performance*	9(a)	Application
4 Filing exemptions for small and medium-sized companies	9(a)	Application
5 Summary financial statements	9(a)	Application
6 Directors' report	9(a)	Application
7 Auditors' report and chairman's report	9(a)	Application
8 Interim reports and preliminary announcements	9(a)	Knowledge

Introduction

Although you are unlikely to be asked to produce a full set of published accounts in the Paper 9 examination, you must be able to describe the **disclosure requirements** of all the component parts of the accounts, in the primary statements (the balance sheet, profit and loss account, cash flow statement and statement of recognised gains and losses), in the notes to the accounts and in supplementary reports (directors', chairman's and auditors'). We will leave cash flow statements until Part C of the text, by when you will have covered consolidations and foreign currency. New regulations over disclosure of directors' emoluments have been included in Section 4.

The requirements of **FRS 3 Reporting financial performance** are introduced here as it has a substantial impact on disclosure, particularly in the case of larger group companies. Aspects of FRS 3 will be introduced in the later chapters on consolidation and in Part B where we examine profit measurement (and in particular extraordinary and exceptional items). You may wish to refer back to this chapter when you reach these later references to FRS 3.

The material in this chapter may seem dry, you may find it rather 'heavy going', but you must realise that this chapter (along with Chapter 1) contains information which is fundamental to your financial accounting studies - so learn it properly before you go on.

1   SSAP 2 DISCLOSURE OF ACCOUNTING POLICIES

1.1   You should be very familiar with SSAP 2 *Disclosure of accounting policies* from your earlier studies, so a brief summary is given here.

Knowledge brought forward from Papers 1 and 5

SSAP 2 Disclosure of accounting policies

SSAP 2 defines three important terms.

- **Fundamental accounting concepts** are the broad basic assumptions which underlie the periodic financial accounts of business enterprises.

- **Accounting bases** are the methods developed for applying fundamental accounting concepts to financial transactions and items, for the purpose of financial accounts; and in particular:

  - for determining the accounting periods in which revenue and costs should be recognised in the P & L a/c; and

  - for determining the amounts at which material items should be stated in the B/S.

- **Accounting policies**: a business entity's accounting policies are simply the accounting bases which they have chosen to follow in a situation where there is a choice of accounting bases: eg depreciation of fixed assets.

Fundamental concepts

SSAP deals with the four fundamental concepts.

- The **'going concern' concept**: the enterprise will continue in operational existence for the foreseeable future.

- The **'accruals' concept**: revenue and costs are accrued (that is, recognised as they are earned or incurred, not as money is received or paid).

- The **'consistency' concept**: there is consistency of accounting treatment of like items within each accounting period and from one period to the next.

- The **concept of 'prudence'**: revenue and profits are not anticipated, but are recognised by inclusion in the P&L a/c only when realised in the form either of cash or of assets, the ultimate cash realisation of which can be assessed with reasonable certainty

There is always a presumption that these concepts have been observed. If this is not the case, the facts should be explained.

1.2 The CA 1985 and SSAP 2 require the following.

(a) **Accounting policies** should be applied **consistently** from one financial year to the next.

(b) If accounts are prepared on the basis of assumptions which differ in material respects from any of the generally accepted fundamental accounting concepts (principles) the **details, reasons for and the effect of, the departure** from the fundamental concepts must be given in a note to the accounts.

(c) The **accounting policies** adopted by a company in determining the (material) amounts to be included in the balance sheet and in determining the profit or loss for the year must be stated by a **note to the accounts**. For examination purposes, it is useful to give the accounting policy note as the first note to the accounts, making sure that the explanations are clear, fair and as brief as possible.

Other conventions/assumptions

1.3 There are some other conventions which, while not mentioned in SSAP 2, are usually followed by preparers of accounts.

(a) CA 1985 adds the **separate valuation principle**: 'In determining the aggregate amount of any item, the amount of each individual asset or liability that falls to be taken into account shall be determined separately'.

(b) **Business entity convention**: the business is a separate entity distinct from its directors, shareholders etc; only those transactions relevant to the business are shown.

(c) **Money measurement convention**: only those items measurable in money terms are shown in the accounts.

(d) **Cost convention**: values normally shown are at historical cost, because HC is objective and auditable, but can be modified by alternative rules allowing revaluation.

2 FORMAT AND NOTES

2.1 Part III of the Fourth Schedule deals with notes to the balance sheet and profit and loss account. These are sub-divided into:

(a) disclosure of accounting policies;
(b) notes to the balance sheet;
(c) notes to the profit and loss account.

2.2 The following example shows a pro forma profit and loss account and balance sheet with the required notes. These notes are expanded in the subsequent chapters on different accounting standards and disclosures.

STANDARD PLC
PROFIT AND LOSS ACCOUNT FOR THE YEAR ENDED
31 DECEMBER 19X5

	Notes	£'000	£'000
Turnover	2		X
Cost of sales			X
Gross profit			X
Distribution costs			X
Administrative expenses			X
Operating profit	3		X
Income from other fixed asset investments	6		X
			X
Interest payable and similar charges	7		X
Profit on ordinary activities before taxation			X
Tax on profit on ordinary activities	8		X
Profit on ordinary activities after taxation			X
Dividend paid and proposed	9	X	
Transfer to general reserve	20	X	
			X
Retained profit for the financial year			X

STANDARD PLC
BALANCE SHEET AS AT 31 DECEMBER 19X5

	Notes	£'000	£'000
Fixed assets			
Intangible assets	10		X
Tangible assets	11		X
Fixed asset investments	12		X
			X
Current assets			
Stocks	13	X	
Debtors	14	X	
Cash at bank and in hand		X	
		X	
Creditors: amounts falling due within one year	15	X	
Net current assets			X
Total assets less current liabilities			X
Creditors: amounts falling due after more than one year	17		X
Accruals and deferred income	18		X
			X
Capital and reserves			
Called up share capital	19		X
Share premium account	20		X
Revaluation reserve	20		X
General reserve	20		X
Profit and loss account	20		X
			X

Approved by the board on ....

.... Director

The notes on pages 43 to 49 form part of these accounts.

NOTES TO THE ACCOUNTS

1 **Accounting policies**

(a) These accounts have been prepared under the historical cost convention of accounting and in accordance with applicable accounting standards.

(b) Depreciation has been provided on a straight line basis in order to write off the cost of depreciable fixed assets over their estimated useful lives. The rates used are:

Buildings	X%
Plant and machinery	X%
Fixtures and fittings	X%

(c) Stocks have been valued at the lower of cost and net realisable value.

(d) Development expenditure relating to specific projects intended for commercial exploitation is carried forward and amortised over the period expected to benefit commencing with the period in which related sales are first made. Expenditure on pure and applied research is written off as incurred.

Notes

(a) Accounting policies are those followed by the company and used in arriving at the figures shown in the profit and loss accounts and balance sheet.

(b) The Companies Act 1985 requires policies in respect of depreciation and foreign currency translation to be included. Others are required by accounting standards insofar as they apply to the company.

2   Turnover

Turnover represents amounts derived from the provision of goods and services falling within the company's ordinary activities, after deduction of trade discounts, value added tax and any other tax based on the amounts so derived.

	Turnover	*Profit before tax*
Principal activities	£'000	£'000
Electrical components	X	X
Domestic appliances	X	X
	X	X

Geographical analysis	
UK	X
America	X
Europe	X
	X

Notes

(a)   Directors are to decide on classification and then apply them consistently.

(b)   Geographical analysis must be by destination of sale.

(c)   If the directors believe this disclosure to be seriously prejudicial to the business the information need not be disclosed.

(d)   The profit before tax disclosures are only required by SSAP 25 for larger companies.

3   Operating profit

Operating profit is stated after charging:

	£'000
Depreciation	X
Amortisation	X
Hire of plant and machinery (per SSAP 21)	X
Auditors' remuneration	X
Exceptional items	X
Directors' emoluments (see note 4)	X
Staff costs (see note 5)	X
Research and development	X

Notes

Separate totals are required to be disclosed for:

(a)   audit fees and expenses; and
(b)   fees paid to auditors for non-audit work.

This disclosure is not required for small or medium-sized companies.

4   Directors' emoluments

New requirements for the disclosure of directors' remuneration were introduced recently by *The Company Accounts (Disclosure of Directors' Emoluments) Regulations* 1997. A distinction is made between listed/AIM companies and unlisted companies.

	£
Directors	
Aggregate emoluments	X
Gains made on exercise of share options (listed/AIM company only)	X
Accounts receivable (unlisted company: excludes shares) under long-term incentive schemes	X
Company pension contributions to money purchase schemes	X
Compensation for loss of office	X
Sums paid to third parties for directors' services	X

BPP PUBLISHING

x directors exercised share options in the year and x directors became entitled to receive share under the long-term incentive scheme (unlisted only).

Retirement benefits are accruing to x directors under a money purchase pension scheme and to x directors under a defined benefit scheme.

	£
Highest paid director	
Aggregate emoluments, gains on share options exercised (listed/AIM company only) and benefits under long-term incentive schemes	X
Company pension contributions to money purchase schemes	X
Defined benefits pension scheme:	
Accrued pension at end of year	X
Accrued lump sum at end of year	X
	X

Notes

(a)   All companies must disclose aggregate emoluments paid to/receivable by a director in respect of qualifying services.

(b)   Unlisted companies do not need to disclose:

   (i)   the amount of gains made when directors exercise options, only the number of directors who exercised options; and

   (ii)   the net value of any assets that comprise shares, which would otherwise be disclosed in respect of assets received under long-term incentive schemes, only the number of directors in respect of whose qualifying service shares were receivable under long-term incentive schemes.

(c)   For listed companies, the disclosure requirements for share options do not refer to qualifying services, so gains made on the exercise of shares *before appointment* must therefore be included.

(d)   Information about the highest paid director only need to be paid if the aggregate of emoluments, gains on exercise of share options, and amounts receivable by the directors under long-term incentive schemes is > £200,000. For unlisted companies, state whether the highest paid director exercised any share option and/or received any shares in respect of qualifying services under a long-term incentive scheme.

(e)   The details relating to pensions are discussed further in Chapter 7.

(f)   *Definitions*

   (i)   **Emoluments**. Salary, fees, bonuses, expense allowances, money value of other benefits, except share options granted, pension amounts and amounts paid under a long-term incentive scheme. Includes 'golden hellos'.

   (ii)   **Qualifying services**. Services as a director of a company and services in connection with the management of the company's affairs.

   (iii)   **Listed company**. A company whose securities have been admitted to the Official List of the Stock Exchange (or AIM).

   (iv)   **Long-term incentive scheme**. Any agreement or arrangement under which money or other assets become receivable by a director land where one or more of the qualifying conditions relating to service cannot be fulfilled within a single financial year. Bonuses relating to an individual year, termination payments and retirement benefits are excluded.

Also, see UITF Abstract 10 *Disclosure of directors' share options* in Chapter 1.

5   **Employee information**

(a)   The *average number of persons* employed during the year was:

By product

Electrical components	X
Domestic appliances	X
	X

By activity

Production	X
Selling	X
Administration	X
	X

(b)   *Employment costs*

	£'000
Aggregate wages and salaries	X
Social security costs	X
Other pension costs	X
	X

Notes

(a)   Classification to be decided by the directors and applied consistently year on year. Must state whether executive directors are included or excluded.

(b)   Social security costs are employer's NI.

(c)   Other pension costs are contributions by the company to a pension scheme.

(d)   *Definitions*

(i)   *Staff costs*. Costs incurred in respect of persons employed under contract of service. They include part time employees under contract.

(ii)   *Average number*

(1)   Ascertain number employed under contracts each week.
(2)   Aggregate these numbers.
(3)   Divide by the number of months in the period.

Include those persons working wholly or mainly overseas.

6   **Income from fixed asset investments**

	£'000
Income receivable from:	
Group undertakings	X
Participating interests	X
Other fixed asset investments	X
	X

7   **Interest payable and similar charges**

	£'000
On loans from group undertakings	X
Other interest payable on:	
Bank overdrafts and loans	X
All other loans	X
	X

Note

Similar charges might include arrangement fees for loans.

8   Tax on profits on ordinary activities

	£'000
UK corporation tax (at x% on taxable profit for the year)	X
Tax credit on dividends received	X
Transfer to/from deferred taxation	X
Under/over provision in prior years	X
Unrelieved overseas taxation	X
	X

Note

The rate of tax must be disclosed, according to SSAP 8 (see later).

9   Dividends

			£'000
Preference:	8% paid		X
Ordinary:	interim	3.5p paid	X
	final	7.0p proposed	X
			X

Note

Show for each class of share distinguishing between amounts paid and proposed. Only advisable (and not required) to show amount per share. If the aggregate proposed dividend is not shown in the notes to the accounts, it must be shown on the face of the P&L a/c.

10   Intangible fixed assets

	Development expenditure £'000
Cost	
At 1 January 19X5	X
Expenditure	X
At 31 December 19X5	X
Amortisation	
At 1 January 19X5	X
Charge for year	X
At 31 December 19X5	X
Net book value at 31 December 19X5	X
Net book value 31 December 19X4	X

Note

The above disclosure should be given for each intangible asset. There are additional disclosure requirements for goodwill: see Chapter 4.

11   Tangible fixed assets

	Freehold land and buildings £'000	Leasehold land and buildings — Long leases £'000	Leasehold land and buildings — Short leases £'000	Plant and machinery £'000	Fixtures and fittings £'000	Assets in the course of construction £'000	Total £'000
Cost (or valuation)							
At 1 Jan 19X5	X	X	X	X	X	X	X
Additions	X	-	X	-	X	X	X
Revaluation	X	-	-	-	-	-	X
Disposals	(X)	-	-	(X)	(X)	-	(X)
At 31 Dec 19X5	X	X	X	X	X	X	X
Depreciation							
At 1 Jan 19X5	X	X	X	X	X	-	X
Charge for year	X	X	X	X	X	-	X
Revaluation	(X)	-	-	-	-	-	(X)
Disposals	(X)	-	-	(X)	(X)	-	(X)
At 31 Dec 19X5	X	X	X	X	X	-	X
Net book value							
At 31 Dec 19X5	X	X	X	X	X	X	X
At 31 Dec 19X4	X	X	X	X	X	X	X

Notes

(a)   Long leases are ≥ 50 years unexpired at balance sheet date.

(b)   Classification by asset type represents arabic numbers from formats.

(c)   Motor vehicles (unless material) are usually included within plant and machinery.

(d)   Revaluations in the year: state for each asset revalued:

(i)   method of valuation;

(ii)   date of valuation; and

(iii)   the historical cost equivalent of the above information as if the asset had not been revalued.

12   Fixed asset investments

	Group undertakings — Shares £'000	Group undertakings — Loans £'000	Participating interests — Shares £'000	Participating interests — Loans £'000	Other investments other than loans £'000	Other loans £'000	Total £'000
At 1 Jan 19X5	X	X	X	X	X	X	X
Additions	X	-	X	-	X	X	X
Disposals	-	(X)	(X)	-	(X)	-	(X)
Transfers	X	-	(X)	-	-	X	X
At 31 Dec 19X5	X	X	X	X	X	X	X
Listed	X	X	X	X			
Unlisted	X	X	X	X	X	X	X
	X	X	X	X	X	X	X

The market value (in aggregate) of the listed investments is £X.

Note

An AIM investment is *not* a listed investment. All stock exchanges of repute allowed. Aggregate market value (ie profits less losses) to be disclosed if material.

13 **Stocks**

	£'000
Raw materials and consumables	X
Work in progress	X
Finished goods	X
	X

The replacement cost of stock is £X higher than its book value.

14 **Debtors**

	£'000
Trade debtors	X
Other debtors	X
Prepayments and accrued income	X
	X

Of this amount £X of recoverable ACT is recoverable after more than one year.

15 **Creditors: amounts falling due within one year**

	£'000
Debenture loans: 8% stock 19X9	X
Bank loans and overdrafts	X
Trade creditors	X
Other creditors including taxation and social security (see note 16)	X
Accruals and deferred income	X
	X

The bank loans and overdraft are secured by a floating charge over the company's assets.

Notes

(a)   Details of security given for all secured creditors.

(b)   Include current portion of instalment creditors here.

16 **Other creditors including taxation and social security**

	£'000
UK corporation tax	X
Social security	X
Proposed dividend	X
	X

Notes

(a)   Liabilities for taxation and social security must be shown separately from other creditors.

(b)   Dividend liabilities to be disclosed separately.

17 **Creditors: amounts falling due after more than one year**

	£'000
8½% unsecured loan stock 19Y9	X

Notes

(a)   Very long-term creditors:

      (i)   disclose the aggregate amount of debentures and other loans:

           (1)   payable after more than five years;

(2) payable by instalments, any of which fall due after more than five years;

(ii) for (1) and (2) disclose the terms of repayment and rates of interest.

(b) Debentures during the year, disclose:

(i) class issued;

(ii) for each class:

(1) amount issued;

(2) consideration received.

18 Accruals and deferred income

	£'000
Government grants received	X
Credited to profit and loss account	(X)
	X

Note

Alternative presentation if not included as part of creditors, which saves dividing the accruals or deferred income amount between within and greater than one year.

19 Called up share capital

	£1 ordinary shares £'000	*6.2% preference shares* £'000
Authorised		
Number	X	X
Value	X	X
Allotted		
Number	X	X
Value	X	X

Notes

(a) Disclose number and nominal value for each class, both authorised and allotted.

(b) *Shares issued during the year*, disclose:

(i) classes allotted;

(ii) for each class:

(1) number and aggregate nominal value allotted; and

(2) consideration received.

20 Reserves

	Share premium £'000	*Revaluation* £'000	*General* £'000	*Profit and loss* £'000
At 1 January 19X5	X	X	X	X
Retained profit for the year	-	-	-	X
Revaluation	-	X	-	-
Transfers	-	-	X	X
At 31 December 1995	X	X	X	X

21 Contingent liabilities

Note: governed by FRS 12 (see later).

22 Post balance sheet events

Note: governed by SSAP 17 (see later).

23 **Capital commitments**

	£'000
Amounts contracted but not provided for	X

Note

This figure is not included in the balance sheet as it is simply a note of future obligations to warn users of likely future capital expenditure.

24 **Significant holdings in other undertakings**

(a) A holding is significant if it represents:

(i)   ≥ 20% nominal value of any class of shares in issue;

(ii) ≥ 20% of the investing company's total assets.

(b) Disclosure requirements:

(i)   name of investee company;

(ii)   country of incorporation;

(iii) description of each class of share and the nominal value held;

(iv)   aggregate capital and reserves at investee company's most recent accounting year end;

(v)   profit or loss for the period ending on that date.

This information is often attached to note 12.

3 FRS 3 REPORTING FINANCIAL PERFORMANCE   5/96, 11/96, 11/97

3.1 We will look at the basic requirements and provisions of FRS 3 here. Do not worry too much about extraordinary and exceptional items as they are discussed in more detail in Chapter 22 on profit measurement. We will also look at FRS 3 again in the chapters on consolidation, from a 'group' perspective.

3.2 FRS 3 applies to all financial statements intended to give a true and fair view, unless the entity is obliged to prepare accounts under a statutory framework which does not permit such treatment.

3.3 The objective of FRS 3 is:

> 'to require reporting entities falling within its scope to highlight a range of important components of financial performance to aid users in understanding the performance achieved by a reporting entity in a period and to assist them in forming a basis for their assessment of future results and cash flows.'

Profit and loss account

3.4 A **layered format** is to be used for the profit and loss account to highlight a number of important components of financial performance.

- Results of **continuing operations** (including the results of acquisitions);

- Results of **discontinued operations**;

- **Profits or losses on the sale or termination** of an operation, costs of a fundamental reorganisation or restructuring and profit or losses on the disposal of fixed assets; and

- **Extraordinary items.**

3.5 The following points must be noted.

(a) The analysis of results between continued (and acquired) and discontinued operations should be disclosed to the level of operating profit.

(b) All exceptional items (except those in (c) below) should be included under the statutory format heading to which they relate and disclosed by way of a note. They should only be disclosed on the face of the profit and loss account if required to do so to show a true and fair view.

(c) The following items must be shown separately on the face of the profit and loss account **after** operating profit and **before** interest:

    (i)   profits or losses on the sale or termination of an operation;
    (ii)   costs of a fundamental reorganisation or restructuring; and
    (iii) profits or losses on the disposal of fixed assets.

Statement of total recognised gains and losses

3.6 This is a **primary financial statement** (like the balance sheet and profit and loss account). It shows the profit or loss for the period along with all other movements on reserves which reflect recognised gains and losses attributable to shareholders. It does not deal with the realisation of gains in previous periods, nor with transfers between reserves. This means that the excess of the revalued amount over historical cost will *never* be recognised in the profit and loss account. Profit or loss on disposal will be calculated as the difference between the net proceeds and the net carrying amount.

Earnings per share (EPS)

3.7 (a) EPS is now calculated on the profit attributable to equity shareholders **after minority interest, extraordinary items, preference dividends and other appropriations in respect of preference shares**.

(b) If an EPS figure is given **based on any other level of earnings**, then it **cannot** be **given greater prominence** than the proper EPS figure in (a) above, and a reconciliation between the two figures must be disclosed. The alternative figure must be calculated and disclosed in a consistent manner (see Chapter 25 on EPS).

Note of historical cost profits and losses

3.8 This is a **memorandum item** which helps comparison between the results of companies which have revalued their assets with the results of those which have not. It shows the results for the period as if no revaluation had ever been made (where the results are materially different). The note should be shown immediately after the profit and loss account, or after the statement of total recognised gains and losses (see below). An example is shown in the illustrative example at the end of this section.

Reconciliation of movements in shareholders' funds

3.9 This brings together the **results of the period**, shown in the statement of total recognised gains and losses, with all other changes in shareholders' funds in the period, including capital contributed by or repaid to shareholders.

Prior year adjustments

3.10 Prior period adjustments should be accounted for by **restating the comparative figures for the preceding period in the primary statements** and notes and **adjusting the opening balance of reserves for the cumulative effect**. The cumulative effect of the adjustments should also be noted at the foot of the statement of total recognised gains and losses of the current period. The effect of prior period adjustments on the results for the preceding period should be disclosed where practicable.

Definitions

3.11 These are the more important definitions in FRS 3.

> **KEY TERMS**
>
> - **Ordinary activities** are any activities undertaken by a reporting entity as part of its business and such related activities in which the reporting entity engages in furtherance of, incidental to, or arising from, these activities. Ordinary activities include the effects on the reporting entity of any event in the various environments in which it operates, including the political, regulatory, economic and geographical environments, irrespective of the frequency or unusual nature of the events.
>
> - **Acquisitions** are operations of the reporting entity that are acquired in the period.
>
> - **Discontinued operations** are operations of the reporting entity that are sold or terminated and that satisfy **all** of the following conditions.
>
>   (i) The sale or termination is completed either in the period or before the earlier of three months after the commencement of the subsequent period and the date on which the financial statements are approved.
>
>   (ii) If a termination, the former activities have ceased permanently.
>
>   (iii) The sale or termination has a material effect on the nature and focus of the reporting entity's operations and represents a material reduction in its operating facilities resulting either from its withdrawal from a particular market (whether class of business or geographical) or from a material reduction in turnover in the reporting entity's continuing markets.
>
>   (iv) The assets, liabilities, results of operations and activities are clearly distinguishable, physically, operationally and for financial reporting purposes.
>
> Operations not satisfying all these conditions are classified as continuing.
>
> - **Exceptional items** are material items which derive from events or transactions that fall within the ordinary activities of the reporting entity and which individually or, if of a similar type, in aggregate, need to be disclosed by virtue of their size or incidence if the financial statements are to give a true and fair view.
>
> - **Extraordinary items** are material items possessing a high degree of abnormality which arise from events or transactions that fall outside the ordinary activities of the reporting entity and which are not expected to recur. They do not include exceptional items nor do they include prior period items merely because they relate to a prior period.

BPP PUBLISHING

KEY TERMS (cont)

- **Prior year adjustments** are material adjustments applicable to prior periods arising from changes in accounting policies or from the correction of fundamental errors. They do not include normal recurring adjustments or corrections of accounting estimates made in prior periods.

- **Total recognised gains and losses** are the total of all gains and losses of the reporting entity that are recognised in a period and are attributable to shareholders.

Provisions relating to operations to be sold or terminated

3.12 **FRS 3 severely limits the items which can be included** in such provisions, because companies have been known to manipulate such provisions over time to smooth the impact of disposals. Provision may only be made to the 'extent to which obligations have been incurred that are not expected to be covered by the future profits of the operation or the disposal of its assets'. The entity should be *committed* to the sale or termination, by binding contract or by a detailed formal termination plan from which it would not be practical to withdraw.

Provisions should cover only the direct costs of termination and any operating losses of the operation up to the date of sale or termination, after taking future profits or disposal profits into account.

Exam focus point

Provisions are the subject of a new accounting standard, FRS 12, covered later in this text.

3.13 **Comparatives must be shown** for all figures in the primary statements and all figures required by the FRS in the notes. The comparative figures for the profit and loss account should include in the continuing category only the results of those operations included in the current period's continuing operations.

3.14 EXAMPLE: FRS 3

The FRS contains the following example of the effect of FRS 3 on a set of group accounts using CA 1985 format 1. The following matters should also be noted.

(a) The group has made acquisitions and disposal of operations during the year under review.

(b) In this example there is no extraordinary item. However, the positioning of such an item on the face of the profit and loss account is shown, although in practice the caption would not appear if no extraordinary items existed.

(c) The profit and loss account examples include the disclosure of earnings per share numbers and a pro forma reconciliation statement for adjusted earnings per share numbers is also shown.

PROFIT AND LOSS EXAMPLE 1

	1993 £m	1993 £m	1992 as restated £m
Turnover			
Continuing operations	550		500
Acquisitions	50		
	600		
Discontinued operations	175		190
		775	690
Cost of sales		(620)	(555)
Gross profit		155	135
Net operating expenses		(104)	(83)
Operating profit			
Continuing operations	50		40
Acquisitions	6		
	56		
Discontinued operations	(15)		12
Less 1992 provision	10		
		51	52
Profit on sale of properties in continuing operations		9	6
Provision for loss on operations to be discontinued			(30)
Loss on disposal of discontinued operations	(17)		
Less 1992 provision	20		
		3	
Profit on ordinary activities before interest		63	28
Interest payable		(18)	(15)
Profit on ordinary activities before taxation		45	13
Tax on profit on ordinary activities		(14)	(4)
Profit on ordinary activities after taxation		31	9
Minority interests		(2)	(2)
(Profit before extraordinary items)		29	7
(Extraordinary items - included only to show positioning)		-	-
Profit for the financial year		29	7
Dividends		(8)	(1)
Retained profit for the financial year		21	6
Earnings per share		39p	10p
Adjustments (to be itemised and an adequate description to be given)		Xp	Xp
Adjusted earnings per share		Yp	Yp

PROFIT AND LOSS ACCOUNT EXAMPLE 2 (to operating profit line)

	Continuing operations 1993 £m	Acquisitions 1993 £m	Discontinued of operations 1993 £m	Total 1993 £m	Total 1992 as restated £m
Turnover	550	50	175	775	690
Cost of sales	(415)	(40)	(165)	(620)	(555)
Gross profit	135	10	10	155	135
Net operating expenses	(85)	(4)	(25)	(114)	(83)
Less 1992 provision			10	10	
Operating profit	50	6	(5)	51	52
Profit on sale of properties	9			9	6
Provision for loss on operations to be discontinued					(30)
Loss on disposal of the discontinued operations			(17)	(17)	
Less 1992 provision			20	20	
Profit on ordinary activities before interest	59	6	(2)	63	28

BPP PUBLISHING

Thereafter example 2 is the same as example 1.

STATEMENT OF TOTAL RECOGNISED GAINS AND LOSSES

	1993 £m	1992 as restated £m
Profit for the financial year	29	7
Unrealised surplus on revaluation of properties	4	6
Unrealised (loss)/gain on trade investment	(3)	7
	30	20
Currency translation differences on foreign currency net investments	(2)	5
Total recognised gains and losses relating to the year	28	25
Prior year adjustment (as explained in note x)	(10)	
Total gains and losses recognised since last annual report	18	

NOTE OF HISTORICAL COST PROFITS AND LOSSES

	1993 £m	1992 as restated £m
Reported profit on ordinary activities before taxation	45	13
Realisation of property revaluation gains of previous year	9	10
Difference between a historical cost depreciation charge and the actual depreciation charge of the year calculated on the revalued amount	5	4
Historical cost profit on ordinary activities before taxation	59	27
Historical cost profit for the year retained after taxation, minority interest, extraordinary items and dividends	35	20

NOTES TO THE FINANCIAL STATEMENTS

Note required in respect of profit and loss account example 1

	1993			1992 (as restated)		
	Continuing £m	Discontinued £m	Total £m	Continuing £m	Discontinued £m	Total £m
Cost of sales	455	165	620	385	170	555
Net operating expenses						
Distribution costs	56	13	69	46	5	51
Administrative expenses	41	12	53	34	3	37
Other operating income	(8)	0	(8)	(5)	0	(5)
	89	25	114	75	8	83
Less 1992 provision	0	(10)	(10)			
	89	15	104			

The total figures for continuing operations in 1993 include the following amounts relating to acquisitions: cost of sales £40 million and net operating expenses £4 million (namely distribution costs £3 million, administrative expenses £3 million and other operating income £2 million).

Note required in respect of profit and loss account example 2

	1993 Continuing £m	Discontinued £m	Total £m	1992 (as restated) Continuing £m	Discontinued £m	Total £m
Turnover				500	190	690
Cost of sales				385	170	555
Net operating expenses						
Distribution costs	56	13	69	46	5	51
Administrative expenses	41	12	53	34	3	37
Other operating income	(8)	0	(8)	(5)	0	(5)
	89	25	114	75	8	83
Operating profit				40	12	52

The total figure of net operating expenses for continuing operations in 1993 includes £4 million in respect of acquisitions (namely distribution costs £3 million, administrative expenses £3 million and other operating income £2 million).

Reconciliation of movements in shareholders' funds

	1993 £m	1992 (as restated) £m
Profit for the financial year	29	7
Dividends	(8)	(1)
	21	6
Other recognised gains and losses relating to the year (net)	(1)	18
New share capital subscribed	20	1
Net addition to shareholders' funds	40	25
Opening shareholders' funds (originally £375 million before deducting prior year adjustment of £10 million)	365	340
Closing shareholders' funds	405	365

Reserves

	Share premium account £m	Revaluation reserve £m	Profit and loss account £m	Total £m
At beginning of year as previously stated	44	200	120	364
Prior year adjustment			(10)	(10)
At beginning of year as restated	44	200	110	354
Premium on issue of shares (nominal value £7 million)	13			13
Transfer from profit and loss account of the year			21	21
Transfer of realised profits		(14)	14	0
Decrease in value of trade investment		(3)		(3)
Currency translation differences on foreign currency net investments			(2)	(2)
Surplus on property revaluations		4		4
At end of year	57	187	143	387

Note. Nominal share capital at end of year £18 million (1992 £11 million).

The following exercises should be useful revision.

Question 1

B&C plc's profit and loss account for the year ended 31 December 19X2, with comparatives, is as follows.

	19X2	19X1
	£'000	£'000
Turnover	200,000	180,000
Cost of sales	(60,000)	(80,000)
Gross profit	140,000	100,000
Distribution costs	(25,000)	(20,000)
Administration expenses	(50,000)	(45,000)
Operating profit	65,000	35,000

During the year the company sold a material business operation with all activities ceasing on 14 February 19X3. The loss on the sale of the operation amounted to £2.2m. The results of the operation for 19X1 and 19X2 were as follows.

	19X2	19X1
	£'000	£'000
Turnover	22,000	26,000
Operating loss	(7,000)	(6,000)

In addition, the company acquired a business which contributed £7m to turnover and an operating profit of £1.5m.

Required

Prepare the profit and loss account and related notes for the year ended 31 December 19X2 complying with the requirements of FRS 3 as far as possible.

Answer

B&C PROFIT AND LOSS ACCOUNT FOR THE YEAR ENDED 31 DECEMBER

	19X2		19X1	
	£'000	£'000	£'000	£'000
Turnover				
Continuing operations				
(200 - 22 - 7)/(180 - 26)		171.0		154
Acquisitions		7.0		-
		178.0		154
Discontinued		22.0		26
		200.0		180
Cost of sales		(60.0)		(80)
Gross profit		140.0		100
Distribution costs		(25.0)		(20)
Administration expenses (50 - 2.2)		(47.8)		(45)
Operating profit				
Continuous operations	72.7		41	
Acquisitions	1.5		-	
	74.2		41	
Discontinued	(7.0)		(6)	
		67.2		35
Exceptional item		(2.2)		-
		65.0		35

Note to the profit and loss account

| | 19X2 | | | 19X1(as restated) | | |
| | Continuing | Discontinued | Total | Continuing | Discontinued | Total |
	£'000	£'000	£'000	£'000	£'000	£'000
Cost of sales	X	X	60.0	X	X	80
Net operating expenses						
Distribution costs	X	X	25.0	X	X	20
Admin expenses	X	X	47.8	X	X	45
	X	X	72.8	X	X	65

Question 2

Extracts from Z Ltd's profit and loss account for the year ended 31 December 19X1 were as follows.

	£'000
Profit after tax	512
Dividend	(120)
Retained profit	392

During the year the following important events took place.

(a)   Assets were revalued upward by £120,000.

(b)   £300,000 share capital was issued during the year.

(c)   Certain stock items were written down by £45,000.

(d)   The company's investment properties previously revalued by £81,000 were written down by £110,000. The deficit is expected to be temporary.

(e)   Opening shareholders' funds = £4m.

Show how the events for the year would be shown in the statement of recognised gains and losses and the reconciliation of movements in shareholders' funds.

Answer

	£'000
Profit after tax	512
Asset revaluation	120
Devaluation of investment properties *	(110)
	522

An amendment to SSAP 19 allows a temporary debit balance on the investment revaluation reserve (IRR).

RECONCILIATION OF MOVEMENTS IN SHAREHOLDERS' FUNDS

	£'000
Profit after tax	512
Dividend	(120)
	392
Other recognised gains and losses (522 – 512)	10
New share capital	300
Net addition to shareholders' funds	702
Opening shareholders' funds	4,000
Closing shareholders' funds	4,702

Question 3

A Ltd reported a profit before tax of £162,000 for the year ended 31 December 19X1. During the year the following transactions in fixed assets took place.

(a)   An asset with a book value of £40,000 was revalued to £75,000. The remaining useful life is estimated to be five years.

BPP PUBLISHING

(b) An asset (with a five year useful life at the date of revaluation) had been revalued upwards by £20,000 (book value £30,000). It was sold during the current year (one year after revaluation) for £48,000.

Show the reconciliation or profit to historical cost profit for the year ended 31 December 19X1.

Answer

RECONCILIATION OF PROFIT TO HISTORICAL COST PROFIT
FOR THE YEAR ENDED 31 DECEMBER 19X1

	£'000
Reported profit on ordinary activities before taxation	162
Realisation of property revaluation gains	20
Difference between historical cost depreciation charge and the actual depreciation charge of the year calculated on the revalued amount (75,000 – 40,000)/5	7
	189

Exam focus point

In November 1997 you had to account for a discontinued operation, namely the disposal of a subsidiary.

4 FILING EXEMPTIONS FOR SMALL AND MEDIUM-SIZED COMPANIES

4.1 Small and medium-sized companies are allowed certain '**filing exemptions**': **the accounts** they lodge with the **registrar of companies**, and which are available for public inspection, **need not contain all the information** which must be published by large companies. This concession allows small and medium-sized companies to reduce the amount of information about themselves available to, say, trading rivals. It does *not* relieve them of their obligation to prepare full statutory accounts, because all companies, regardless of their size, must prepare full accounts for approval by the shareholders.

4.2 Small and medium-sized companies must therefore balance the expense of preparing two different sets of accounts against the advantage of publishing as little information about themselves as possible. Many such companies may decide that the risk of assisting their competitors is preferable to the expense of preparing accounts twice over, and will therefore not take advantage of the filing exemptions.

KEY TERMS

A company qualifies as a **small company** in a particular financial year if, for that year, two or more of the following conditions are satisfied.

(a) The amount of its turnover for the year should not exceed £2.8m. This amount must be adjusted proportionately in the case of an accounting period greater or less than twelve months.

(b) Its balance sheet total should not exceed £1.4m. Balance sheet total means the total of assets disclosed under headings A to D in the statutory balance sheet format (total assets before deduction of any liabilities).

(c) Its average number of employees should not exceed 50, calculated on a monthly basis.

KEY TERMS (cont)

For a **medium-sized company**, the corresponding conditions are:

(a) turnover not more than £11.2m;
(b) balance sheet total not more than £5.6m;
(c) average number of employees not more than 250.

Again, a minimum of two of these conditions must be satisfied.

4.3 Public companies can never be entitled to the filing exemptions whatever their size; nor can banking and insurance companies; nor can companies which are authorised persons under the Financial Services Act 1986; nor can members of groups containing any of these exceptions.

4.4 **Small companies** may file an **abbreviated balance sheet** showing only the items which, in the statutory format, are denoted by a letter or Roman number.

4.5 Small companies are not required to file either a profit and loss account or a directors' report. No details need be filed of the emoluments of directors.

Question 4

The chairman of Goodstart Ltd, a private company, has asked for information concerning the definition of small and medium-sized companies as set out in the Companies Act 1985.

Goodstart Ltd was incorporated and commenced to trade on 1 February 19X3. The first accounts are to be prepared to 29 February 19X4. The unaudited balance sheet prepared by Goodstart Ltd, as on 29 February 19X4, sets out the figures as follows.

	£	£
Fixed assets		
Gross amount	698,722	
Less hire purchase outstanding	55,636	
Investment at cost		643,086
		15,000
Current assets		
Stock	386,518	
Debtors and prepayments	407,419	
Cash	1,731	
	795,668	
Current liabilities		
Creditors and accruals	229,813	
Bank overdraft	85,537	
	315,350	
Net current assets		480,318
		1,138,404
Long-term liability		
Bank loan		200,000
		938,404
Capital and reserves		
Share capital		900,000
Profit and loss account		38,404
		938,404

In addition, Goodstart Ltd has provided the following information about the numbers employed during the period covered by the first accounts.

Months		
	1-3 inclusive:	4 part-time and 28 full-time
	4-7 inclusive:	6 part-time and 43 full-time

8-12 inclusive: 6 part-time and 56 full-time

All employees, whether part-time or full-time, were employed under a contract of service. Three of the full-time employees who were employed by the company throughout the period worked wholly overseas.

Turnover, including exports of £315,812, totalled £3,000,000.

You are required to write a memorandum for the chairman of Goodstart Ltd:

(a) setting out the criteria for deciding whether a company qualifies as a small or medium sized company; and

(b) indicating, on the basis of the information provided, into which category Goodstart Ltd falls. Give your reasons with appropriate calculations.

Answer

MEMORANDUM

To:	Chairman of Goodstart Ltd	Date: 9 May 19X4
From:	Accountant	
Subject:	*Small and medium sized companies under the Companies Act 1985*	

(a) Criteria for deciding small or medium size

The criteria for deciding whether a company qualifies as a small or medium-sized company are given in s 248 CA 1985.

The criteria are that a company must satisfy two or more of the following conditions.

		Small	*Medium*
(i)	Turnover not exceeding	£2.8m	£11.2m
(ii)	Balance sheet total not exceeding	£1.4m	£5.6m
(iii)	Average number of employees not exceeding	50	250

(b) Size category applicable to Goodstart Ltd

(i) Turnover

The turnover of Goodstart Ltd is £3,000,000 for its first period. Since this covers a 13 month period, it should be compared with the limit of £2.8m turnover for a 12 month period proportionately adjusted. Thus, the adjusted small company limit would be £3,033,333 (13/12 × £2,800,000) which would place Goodstart Ltd within the small company limit.

(ii) Balance sheet total

'Balance sheet total' is defined as including all items under headings A to D in the format 1 balance sheet laid down by the Companies Act 1985. This would include all assets before deducting any liabilities. Thus, for Goodstart Ltd, it would include:

	£
Fixed assets	698,722
Investment	15,000
Current assets	795,668
	1,509,390

This exceeds the small company limit but is within the medium-sized company limit for the balance sheet total.

(iii) Average number of employees

The average number of employees is defined as the relevant annual number divided by the number of months in the financial year. The relevant annual number is determined by ascertaining each week in the financial year the number of persons employed under contracts of service by the company in that week and adding together all the weekly numbers.

The calculation for Goodstart Ltd is as follows.

		Number
32 employees for	3 months	96
49 employees for	4 months	196
62 employees for	5 months	310
	12	602

Average number of employees = 615/12 = 50.17

This exceeds the small company limit, but is within the medium-sized company limit. Employees working overseas have been included since they are employed under contracts of service.

(iv) Conclusion

Since Goodstart Ltd has exceeded two out of the three limits for a small company, but is within all three limits for a medium-sized company, it would be classified as a medium-sized company.

4.6   The only **notes to the accounts** required are those dealing with:

- Accounting policies
- Share capital (including any allotments of shares)
- Long-term creditors including any security given by the company
- Basis of foreign currency translation
- The aggregate amount of debtors falling due after more than one year
- Fixed assets, but only certain details

4.7   The only exemptions allowed to **medium-sized companies** are in the **profit and loss account**.

- Turnover need not be analysed between a company's different classes of businesses, or its different geographical markets.

- The profit and loss account may begin with the figure of gross profit (or loss).

4.8   If a small or medium-sized company files 'abbreviated accounts' a **statement by the directors** must appear above the director's signature on the balance sheet. The statement must be to the effect that the directors have relied on the filing exemptions granted by the CA 1985 and have done so because the company is a small or (as the case may be) medium-sized company.

4.9   Abbreviated accounts must be accompanied by a **special report of the company's auditors** stating that, in their opinion, the directors are entitled to deliver abbreviated accounts and those accounts are properly prepared. The text of the auditors' report on the full statutory accounts must be included as a part of this special report.

Small company accounts sent to shareholders

4.10   The regulations which raised the existing limits to those given above also introduced some **new disclosure rules for small companies**. The new disclosure requirements for small companies represent, at long last, a reduction in the regulation costs borne by small businesses. This is because they apply to the full accounts sent to shareholders and not to the abbreviated financial statements filed with the Registrar of Companies. Small companies can choose not to take advantage of some or all of the new exemptions, but the statutory instrument disclosure requirements should be regarded as the minimum. Note that small companies may only need to comply with certain accounting standards in future (see Chapter 1, Section 4).

BPP PUBLISHING

4.11 Where a company takes advantage of the new exemptions, the **main headings** appearing on the balance sheet are **unchanged**, but many **sub-headings may be combined**. In addition, small companies need no longer disclose certain information, required by Sch 4, 5 and 6, CA 1985, in the notes to their financial statements.

4.12 A further set of exemptions relate to the **contents of the directors' report** (see Section 8 of this chapter), which can now be very brief indeed for a small company. It need no longer give information on matters such as fair review of the development of the businesses and so on.

4.13 Where a small company takes advantage of the exemptions, then the balance sheet must make a **statement to that effect**.

4.14 The disclosure requirements on the face of the balance sheet has hardly been reduced, and it has not changed at all for the profit and loss account. The reduction in disclosure has been in the notes to the accounts. Small companies need not disclose details of the following.

    (a) Split of freehold, long leasehold and short leasehold in land and buildings
    (b) Debentures
    (c) Long-term debt (repayment terms, etc)
    (d) Taxation (provision, other particulars)
    (e) Dividends proposed and paid
    (f) Interest payable, rental income, hire of plant and machinery, auditors' remuneration
    (g) Staff (numbers, emoluments)
    (h) Directors' emoluments
    (i) Turnover and geographical analysis.

4.15 You should note that, in a move to free more businesses from onerous reporting requirements, the DTI has suggested an increase in the ceilings in Paragraphs 4.2 and 4.3 by up to 50%, but no action has yet been taken.

5 SUMMARY FINANCIAL STATEMENTS

5.1 The CA 1989 has amended the CA 1985 so that **listed companies** need not send all their members their full financial statements but can instead send them **summary financial statements (SFSs)**. All members who want to receive full financial statements are still entitled to them, however.

5.2 An SFS must:

    (a) **state** that it is **only a summary of information** in the company's annual accounts and the directors' report;

    (b) **contain a statement** by the company's **auditors** of their opinion as to whether the summary financial statement is **consistent** with those accounts and that report and complies with the relevant statutory requirements;

    (c) state whether the **auditors' report** on the annual accounts was **unqualified** or qualified, and if it was qualified set out the report in full together with any further material needed to understand the qualification.

5.3 SFSs must be derived from the company's annual accounts and the directors' report and the form and content are specified by regulations made by the Secretary of State.

The key figures from the full statements must be included along with the review of the business and future developments shown in the directors' report. Comparative figures must be shown.

6 DIRECTORS' REPORT

6.1 Attached to every balance sheet there must be a directors' report (s 234 CA 1985). (The Companies Act 1985 allows small companies exemption from delivering a copy of the directors' report to the registrar of companies.)

6.2 The directors' report is **largely a narrative report**, but certain figures must be included in it. The purpose of the report is to give the users of accounts a more complete picture of the state of affairs of the company. Narrative descriptions should help to 'put flesh on' the skeleton of details provided by the figures of the accounts themselves. However, in practice the directors' report is often a rather dry and uninformative document, perhaps because it must be verified by the company's external auditors, whereas the chairman's report need not be.

6.3 The directors' report is expected to contain:

'a fair **review of the development of the business** of the company and its subsidiary undertakings during that year and of their position at the end of it...'

No guidance is given on the form of the review, nor the amount of detail it should go into.

6.4 S 234 CA 1985 also requires the report to show the amount, if any, recommended for **dividend**.

6.5 Other disclosure requirements are as follows.

(a) The **principal activities of the company** and its subsidiaries in the course of the financial year, and any significant changes in those activities during the year.

(b) Where significant, an estimate should be provided of the **difference** between the **book value of land held as fixed assets and its realistic market value**.

(c) Information about the company's **policy for the employment for disabled persons**:

(i) the policy for giving fair consideration to applications for jobs from disabled persons;

(ii) the policy for continuing to employ (and train) people who have become disabled whilst employed by the company;

(iii) the policy for the training, career development and promotion of disabled employees.

(Companies with fewer than 250 employees are exempt from (c).)

(d) The names of persons who were **directors** at any time during the financial year.

(e) For those persons who were directors at the year end, the **interests** of each (or of their spouse or infant children) in shares or debentures of the company or subsidiaries:

(i) at the beginning of the year, or at the date of appointment as director, if this occurred during the year; and

(ii) at the end of the year.

If a director has no such interests at either date, this fact must be disclosed. (This information in (e) may be shown as a note to the accounts instead of in the directors' report.)

(f) **Political and charitable contributions** made, if these together exceeded more than £200 in the year, giving:

    (i)   separate totals for political contributions and charitable contributions; and

    (ii)   the amount of each separate political contribution exceeding £200, and the name of the recipient.

Wholly owned British subsidiaries are exempt from requirement (f) because the information will be disclosed in the directors' report of the holding company.

(g) Particulars of **any important events** affecting the company or any of its subsidiaries which have occurred since the end of the financial year (significant 'post-balance sheet events').

(h) An indication of **likely future developments** in the business of the company and of its subsidiaries.

(i) An indication of the **activities** (if any) of the company and its subsidiaries in the field of **research and development**.

(j) Particulars of **purchases** (if any) **of its own shares** by the company during the year, including reasons for the purchase.

(k) Particulars of **other acquisitions of its own shares** during the year (perhaps because shares were forfeited or surrendered, or because its shares were acquired by the company's nominee or with its financial assistance).

(l) Public and large companies must disclose their '**creditor payment policy**', ie whether the company had one and what it was.

(m) A note on **employee involvement** etc should be given if the company employs more than 250 people.

6.6   Note that the 1985 Act requires details of important post balance sheet events to be explained in the directors' report. The requirements of SSAP 17, which should be considered in conjunction with the 1985 Act, are either for the accounts themselves to be altered, or for the amount of the adjustment to results to be disclosed in a **note** to the accounts.

7   AUDITORS' REPORT AND CHAIRMAN'S REPORT

The auditors' report

7.1   The **auditors' report** is included as a part of the company's published accounts. It is addressed to the members of the company (not to the directors). It will be **either unqualified or qualified to various degrees**. An unqualified report indicate that there are no problems with the accounts, but a qualified report shows that there has been disagreement between the auditors and the directors, or various other problems.

7.2   Most companies wish to avoid qualification of their audit report, but it is worth noting that some companies will accept a qualification, often repeated year after year, for the sake of implementing a policy or transaction with which the company agrees but the auditors do not. Analysts tend to avoid a knee-jerk reaction to qualifications; they are more interested

in whether the matter causing the qualification really matters to the value of the company or not.

The chairman's report

7.3 Most large companies include a chairman's report in their published financial statements. This is purely voluntary as there is no statutory requirement to do so and it often provides information now to be found in the **Operating and Financial Review** (OFR): see Chapter 26. It can be unduly **optimistic and subjective**.

8 INTERIM REPORTS AND PRELIMINARY ANNOUNCEMENTS

Interim reports

8.1 In September 1997 the ASB published a 'best practice' statement on **interim reports. This takes forward a recommendation made by the Cadbury Committee (see below).** The Statement is non-mandatory but is designed to be a guide to best practice. The ASB strongly encourages listed companies to adopt the recommendations when preparing interim reports and its use is recommended by the Financial Reporting Council, the Hundred Group of Finance Directors, the London Stock Exchange and the Irish Stock Exchange.

8.2 Interim reports are produced by **large listed companies** when they release half-yearly figures to the markets. Recent surveys have disclosed that current practices in interim reporting vary and have evolved considerably from the reporting requirements of the London Stock Exchange. The Statement sets out the recommended contents and measurement basis of interim reports and is designed to improve the consistency, comparability and quality of interim reporting.

8.3 The **IASC** also has interim reporting on its agenda and plans to issue an IAS in 1998. IASC proposals made so far are on similar lines to, though more detailed than, the ASB's *Statement*.

Basis of presentation

8.4 Interim reports should be drawn up using the same measurement and recognition bases and accounting policies as used in the preparation of annual financial statements, with the specific exception of taxation: the **'discrete' approach**. Under the discrete approach, the interim period is treated as a **distinct accounting period,** not as part of the annual reporting cycle. Therefore incomplete transactions are treated using the same accounting principles as are applied at the year-end.

8.5 The Statement does not favour the alternative **'integral' approach**, which views the interim period as part of the **larger annual reporting period,** predominantly to predict and explain the full year's financial information. Under the integral approach, revenues and expenses are therefore recognised in interim periods as a proportion of estimated annual amounts.

8.6 As taxation can be determined only at the end of the financial year the Statement requires that an interim period's tax charge should be based on an estimate of the annual effective tax rate, applied to the interim period's results.

Content

8.7   Interim reports should contain the following.

- Management commentary
- Summarised profit and loss account
- Statement of total recognised gains and losses, where relevant
- Summarised balance sheet
- Summarised cash flow statement

8.8   The **management commentary should highlight and explain significant events and trends** since the previous annual financial statements. Attention should be drawn to events and changes within the period that are likely to have a significant effect on the succeeding period despite having had relatively little impact in the current period. The commentary should describe and explain any seasonal activity and draw attention to a summarised balance sheet and cash flow statement.

8.9   The **management commentary** should also **analyse turnover and profit** by segment in a similar manner to that disclosed in the annual financial statements. In addition, discontinued operations and, where possible, acquisitions should be separately disclosed for turnover and operating profit.

8.10   Basic **earnings per share** should also be disclosed, as well as earnings per share using other bases, if they are also disclosed in the annual financial statements.

8.11   A **statement of total recognised gains and losses** should be included to provide a link between the P&L account and the balance sheet. It is not required, however, if there are no other material gains and losses to report in the interim period, other than operating profit.

8.12   The **summarised balance sheet** should, for consistency, be based on similar classifications to those used in the annual financial statements. Current assets should be separated into their key component parts, mentioning stock, debtors and cash, to assist users' analyses.

8.13   The **cash flow statement** should be summarised using the headings required by FRS 1 (revised 1996). Reconciliations of operating profit to operating cash flow and of cash in the period to the movement in net debt should also be disclosed.

Preliminary announcements

8.14   In 1998 the ASB published its Statement *Preliminary Announcements*. Like the Statement on interim reports, the proposed Statement will be a non-mandatory guide to best practice. Its aim is to improve the timeliness, quality, relevance and consistency of preliminary announcements within the constraints of reliability. Its main features are:

Content

8.15   The content should be **similar** to that recommended for **interim reports**.

- A narrative commentary, similar to the OFR, but not as lengthy, and focused on areas of change
- A summarised profit and loss account
- A statement of total recognised gains and losses
- A summarised balance sheet

- A summarised cash flow statement

8.16 **Segmental information** should be given for turnover and operating profit and an analysis of discontinued and continuing activities presented on the face of the summarised profit and loss account. The announcement should also provide earnings per share figures.

8.17 Traditionally, preliminary announcements focus on the **results for the full year**. However, the market tends to react more particularly to new, previously unreported, **information about the second half-year** (or fourth quarter, if quarterly interim reporting has been adopted). Consequently, the proposed Statement recommends that data for the **final interim period** should be **separately presented** and commented upon in the preliminary announcement. An alternative view given is that information on the final interim period is needed only when particularly relevant, eg where the business is highly seasonal. Comment is invited on this point.

Timeliness

8.18 Companies should be encouraged to issue their preliminary announcement within **60 days** of the year-end, as is already achieved by many listed companies.

Reliability

8.19 Information given should be **reliable and consistent** with the yet to be published audited financial statements. It should therefore be based on material upon which the audit is substantially complete. The proposals encourage companies to issue their preliminary announcement as soon as reliable figures are available, and not wait until the full accounts have been signed off.

Distribution

8.20 Although preliminary announcements are primarily designed for institutional shareholders and financial analysts, companies should **explore the use of electronic means (eg the Internet)**, as a way of disseminating the preliminary announcement to a wider audience without delay. They should also consider other means of providing all shareholders with the opportunity of receiving the announcement, on as timely basis as is practical, if they so wish.

Question 5

In between now and your examination you should obtain and examine as many sets of published accounts as possible. You can obtain these through the *Financial Times* Free Annual Reports Service - look at the Share Service page of the FT. Also look out for any interim reports.

BPP PUBLISHING

Chapter roundup

- This has been a long and detailed chapter but not a conceptually demanding one. You must have a firm grasp of its contents before proceeding to the remainder of this second section of the Study Text, in which the statutory and professional requirements on each area of the accounts are discussed in turn.

- Learn the **formats** for published accounts and the **notes** required.

- You should be aware of the substantial impact on the profit and loss account brought about by **FRS 3** and you must learn the content and layout of the new statement and notes.

- You should be aware of the definitions of **small and medium-sized companies** and the appropriate filing **exemptions**.

- There is no better way of familiarising yourself with the contents of **annual reports** than by obtaining a few and reading through them.

Quick quiz

1   What other common accounting conventions are there, apart from those in SSAP 2? (see para 1.3)

2   List the notes generally required to accompany a profit and loss account and balance sheet. (2.1)

3   What is the prescribed format for the P & L account under FRS 3? (3.4)

4   What is a statement of total recognised gains and losses? (3.6)

5   What is the definition of EPS as revised by FRS 3? (3.7)

6   Define a small company and a medium-sized company in the context of abbreviated accounts. (4.2)

7   What three items concerning disabled persons must be disclosed in a directors' report? (6.5)

8   What is the difference between the 'discrete' and 'integral' approaches to interim reports? (8.4 – 8.5)

Question to try	Level	Marks	Time
2	Exam	20	36 mins

Chapter 3

FIXED ASSETS: TANGIBLE ASSETS

Chapter topic	Syllabus reference	Ability required
1 Definitions and statutory requirements	9(a), (b)	Application
2 FRS 15 *Tangible fixed assets*	9(a), (b)	Application
3 Revaluation	9(a), (b)	Application
4 SSAP 19 *Accounting for investment properties*	9(a), (b)	Application
5 SSAP 4 *Accounting for government grants*	9(a), (b)	Application

Introduction

The **definition of an asset** is an important question and we will consider further the way the ASB defines assets (and liabilities) in Chapter 8 (on off balance sheet finance). Here, the major definitions are given, including that adopted by FASB in the USA. The **definition** and **valuation** problems described in this chapter also apply to intangible assets, at least to a certain extent and we will move on to look at these in the next chapter.

FRS 15 is a recent standard and the result of a lot of debate. SSAPs 19 and 4 will be familiar to you from your earlier studies.

1   DEFINITIONS AND STATUTORY REQUIREMENTS

1.1   Assets have been defined in many different ways and for many purposes. The definition of an asset is important because it directly affects the **treatment** of such items. A good definition will prevent abuse or error in the accounting treatment: otherwise some assets might be treated as expenses, and some expenses might be treated as assets.

1.2   Let us begin with a simple definition from the CIMA *Official Terminology*.

> **KEY TERM**
>
> An **asset** is any tangible or intangible possession which has value.

This admirably succinct definition seems to cover the main points: **ownership** and **value**. An asset is so called because it is owned by someone who values it. However, this definition leaves several questions unanswered.

(a)   What determines ownership?
(b)   What determines value?

Such a simple definition is not adequate in the current accounting climate, where complex transactions are carried out daily.

Accounting Standards Board (ASB)

1.3 In the ASB's *Statement of Principles,* Chapter 4 *The Elements of Financial Statements,* currently in exposure draft, assets are defined as follows.

> ### KEY TERM
>
> **Assets** are rights or other access to future economic benefits controlled by an entity as a result of past transactions or events.

1.4 The *Statement* goes on to discuss various aspects of this definition, and it is broadly consistent with the **IASC's** *Framework.* The *Statement* then goes further in discussing the complimentary nature of assets and liabilities.

Financial Accounting Standards Board (FASB)

1.5 The definition given by the FASB in the USA in its *Statement of Concepts* is very similar.

> ### KEY TERM
>
> **Assets** are probable future economic benefits obtained or controlled by a particular entity as a result of past transactions or events.

'Probable' is given in its general meaning merely to reflect the fact that no future outcome can be predicted with total certainty.

Comparison of definitions

1.6 It is clear from what we have seen so far that a general consensus seems to exist in the standard setting bodies as to the definition of an asset. That definition encompasses **three important characteristics**.

    (a) Future economic benefit
    (b) Control (ownership)
    (c) The transaction to acquire control has already taken place

Definition of a fixed asset

1.7 Fixed assets are defined by CA 1985.

> ### KEY TERM
>
> A **fixed asset** as one intended for use on a continuing basis in the company's activities, ie it is not intended for resale.

Statutory requirements relating to fixed assets

1.8 You have already come across these in you earlier studies, besides which FRS 15 now deals much more comprehensively with the important issues from CA 85. For completeness, a summary is given here.

Summary: statutory requirements relating to fixed assets

Initial cost

- Purchase price plus any expenses incidental to its acquisition.

- Where an asset is produced by a company for its own use, its 'production cost' must include the cost of raw materials, consumables and other attributable direct costs (such as labour). Production cost may additionally include a reasonable proportion of indirect costs, together with the interest on any capital borrowed to finance production of the asset.

Valuation: alternative accounting rules

- Historical cost is the norm, but revalued amount/current cost may be used.

- Depreciation may be provided on the basis of the new valuation.

- Where an asset is revalued, the gain or loss goes to a revaluation reserve.

- There are three alternative bases for valuation: current cost, market value and directors' valuation (for investments)

FRS 3 and revaluations

1.9 Note the effect here of FRS 3 (see Chapter 2). The **statement of recognised gains and losses** (STRGL) shows the profit or loss for the period along with all other movements on reserves which reflect recognised gains and losses attributable to shareholders. It does *not* deal with the **realisation** of gains in previous periods, nor with transfers between reserves.

1.10 This means that the excess of the revalued amount over historical cost will *never* be recognised in the P&L account; profit or loss on disposal will be calculated as the difference between the net proceeds and the net carrying amount (see Question 1 below). This is a very important FRS 3 rule; previously, on disposal of a revalued asset, companies could transfer the surplus in the revaluation reserve which related to the asset to the P&L account. The difference between historical cost depreciation and depreciation on a revaluation will appear in the **note of historical cost profits and losses**.

UITF Abstract 5 *Transfer from current assets to fixed assets*

1.11 This abstract requires transfers from current assets to fixed assets to be made at the **lower of cost and net realisable value,** in order to prevent the practice of transfers being made at a value higher than NRV. This practice avoided charging the P&L account with any diminution in value of what were, in effect, unsold trading assets. Once transferred to fixed assets, the CA 1985 alternative accounting rules could be used to take the debit reflecting the diminution in value to a revaluation reserve. This abstract follows the *Statement of Principles*. This was triggered by a Review Panel judgement on Trafalgar House's 1991 accounts (see Chapter 1).

2 FRS 15 TANGIBLE FIXED ASSETS

2.1 FRS 15 *Tangible fixed assets* was published in February 1999. It goes into a lot more detail than the Companies Act and is examinable from December 1999.

BPP PUBLISHING

2.2 FRS 15 replaces SSAP 12 but not SSAP 19. Investment properties are still accounted for in accordance with SSAP 19 (see Section 4).

Objective

2.3 FRS 15 deals with accounting for the initial measurement, valuation and depreciation of tangible fixed assets. It also sets out the information that should be disclosed to enable readers to understand the impact of the accounting policies adopted in relation to these issues.

Initial measurement

2.4 A tangible fixed asset should **initially be measured at cost**.

KEY TERM

Cost is purchase price and any costs directly attributable to bringing the asset into working condition for its intended use.

2.5 Examples of directly attributable costs are:

- **Acquisition costs**, eg stamp duty, import duties

- Cost of **site preparation** and clearance

- Initial **delivery and handling** costs

- **Installation** costs

- **Professional fees** eg legal fees

- The estimated cost of **dismantling and removing** the asset and restoring the site, to the extent that it is recognised as a provision under FRS 12 *Provisions, contingent liabilities and contingent assets* (discussed in Chapter 11).

2.6 Any abnormal costs, such as those arising from design error, industrial disputes or idle capacity are not directly attributable costs and therefore should not be capitalised as part of the cost of the asset.

Question 1

Seafood 'n' Eatitt, a trendy restaurant, opens on 1 January 19X9 with a skeleton staff. The first month is not expected to bring in many customers as it will take time to build up a reputation. Could the costs incurred in January be capitalised as start-up costs?

Answer

No. The restaurant *could* operate at normal levels immediately so the start up costs are not essential.

2.7 The above costs should only be capitalised for the period in which the activities that are necessary to get the asset ready for use are in progress.

Finance costs   **11/95, 11/97**

2.8   The **capitalisation of finance costs**, including interest, is **optional**. However, if an entity does capitalise finance costs they must do so **consistently**.

2.9   All finance costs that are **directly attributable** to the construction of a tangible fixed asset should be capitalised as part of the cost of the asset.

> **KEY TERM**
>
> **Directly attributable finance costs** are those that would have been avoided if there had been no expenditure on the asset.

2.10   If finance costs are capitalised, capitalisation should start when:

- Finance costs are being incurred
- Expenditure on the asset is being incurred
- Activities necessary to get the asset ready for use are in progress

2.11   Capitalisation of finance costs should cease when the asset is ready for use.

2.12   Sometimes construction of an asset may be completed in parts and each part is capable of being used while construction continues on other parts. An example of such an asset is a business park consisting of several units. In such cases **capitalisation of borrowing costs relating to a part should cease when substantially all the activities that are necessary to get that part ready for use are completed.**

Question 2

Why would this not apply in the case of a steel mill?

Answer

A steel mill is an industrial plant involving several processes that are carried out **in sequence** at different parts of the plant within the same site.

2.13   The following disclosures are required in respect of capitalisation of borrowing costs.

(a)   The accounting policy adopted

(b)   The amount of borrowing costs capitalised during the period

(c)   The amount of borrowing costs recognised in the profit and loss account during the period

(d)   The capitalisation rate used to determine the amount of capitalised borrowing costs

Recoverable amount

2.14   The amount recognised when a tangible fixed asset is acquired or constructed should **not exceed its recoverable amount**.

2.15   It is not necessary to review tangible fixed assets for impairment when they are acquired or constructed. They need to be reviewed for impairment only if there is some indication that

impairment has occurred. Such indications are specified in FRS 11 *Impairment of fixed assets and goodwill*.

Subsequent expenditure

2.16 **Subsequent expenditure** is repairs and maintenance expenditure which ensures that an asset maintains it originally assessed standard of performance. An example of such expenditure is the cost of servicing or overhauling plant and equipment. Without this expenditure, the depreciation expense would be increased because the useful life and perhaps the residual value of the asset would be reduced.

> ### RULE TO LEARN
>
> **Subsequent expenditure** (repairs and maintenance expenditure) should be recognised in the profit and loss account as it is incurred.

2.17 There are three exceptions to this.

(a) It enhances the economic benefits over and above those previously estimated. An example might be modifications made to a piece of machinery that increases its capacity or useful life.

(b) A component of an asset that has been treated separately for depreciation purposes (because it has a substantially different useful economic life from the rest of the asset) has been restored or replaced.

(c) It relates to a major inspection or overhaul that restores economic benefits that have been consumed and reflected in the depreciation charge.

Question 3

A building is repainted. How should this expenditure be treated?

Answer

It should be written off to the profit and loss account. This expenditure is too regular an occurrence to be seen as a separate 'component'.

Question 4

Baldwin Ltd installs a new production process in its factory at a cost of £20,000. This enables a reduction in operating costs (as assessed when the original plant was installed) of £8,000 per year for at least the next ten years.

How should the expenditure be treated?

Answer

It should be capitalised and added to the original cost of the plant as it results in enhancement of economic benefits.

2.18 An entity often has to spend material amounts on a major refit or refurbishment every few years, in order to stay in business. For example, a furnace may require relining every few years.

2.19   The same approach is applied to major inspections and overhauls of tangible fixed assets.

2.20   EXAMPLE: MAJOR OVERHAUL

An aircraft is required by law to be overhauled once every three years. Unless the overhaul is undertaken the aircraft cannot continue to be flown. The cost of the overhaul is capitalised when incurred because it restores the economic benefits of the tangible fixed asset. The carrying amount representing the cost of the benefits consumed is removed from the balance sheet.

Valuation

2.21   FRS 15 supplements and clarifies the rules on revaluation of fixed assets which the Companies Act allows. Revaluation is discussed in the next section.

Depreciation

2.22   As noted earlier, the Companies Act 1985 requires that all fixed assets having a limited economic life should be depreciated. FRS 15 gives a useful discussion of the purpose of depreciation and supplements the statutory requirements in important ways.

KEY TERM

Depreciation is defined in FRS 15 as the measure of the cost or revalued amount of the economic benefits of the tangible fixed asset that have been consumed during the period. Consumption includes the wearing out, using up or other reduction in the useful economic life of a tangible fixed asset, whether arising from use, effluxion of time or obsolescence through either changes in technology or demand for the goods and services produced by the asset.

2.23   This definition covers the amortisation of assets with a pre-determined life, such as a leasehold, and the depletion of wasting assets such as mines.

2.24   FRS 15 contains **no detailed guidance** on the calculation of depreciation or the suitability of the various depreciation methods, merely stating the following two **general principles**.

'The depreciable amount of a tangible fixed asset should be allocated on a **systematic** basis over its useful economic life. The depreciation method used should reflect as fairly as possible the pattern in which the asset's economic benefits are consumed by the entity. The depreciation charge for each period should be recognised as an expense in the profit and loss account unless it is permitted to be included in the carrying amount of another asset.'

'A variety of methods can be used to allocate the depreciable amount of a tangible fixed asset on a systematic basis over its useful economic life. The method chosen should result in a **depreciation charge throughout the asset's useful** economic life and not just towards the end of its useful economic life or when the asset is falling in value.'

Two of the most common methods – the straight line and the reducing balance method are mentioned, the former to be used where the pattern of consumption of an asset's economic benefits is uncertain.

Factors affecting depreciation

2.25 FRS 15 states that the following factors need to be considered in determining the useful economic life, residual value and depreciation method of an asset.

(a) The **expected usage** of the asset by the entity, assessed by reference to the asset's expected capacity or physical output

(b) The **expected physical deterioration** of the asset through use or effluxion of time; this will depend upon the repair and maintenance programme of the entity both when the asset is in use and when it is idle

(c) **Economic or technological obsolescence**, for example arising from changes or improvements in production, or a change in the market demand for the product or service output of that asset

(d) **Legal or similar limits** on the use of the asset, such as the expiry dates of related leases

2.26 If it becomes clear that the **original estimate** of an asset's useful life was **incorrect**, it should be **revised**. Normally, no adjustment should be made in respect of the depreciation charged in previous years; instead the remaining net book value of the asset should be depreciated over the new estimate of its remaining useful life. But if future results could be materially distorted, the adjustment to accumulated depreciation should be recognised in the accounts in accordance with FRS 3 (usually as an exceptional item).

2.27 FRS 15 also states that a **change from one method** of providing depreciation **to another** is permissible only on the grounds that the new method will give a **fairer presentation** of the results and of the financial position. Such a change does **not**, however, constitute a **change of accounting policy**; the carrying amount of the tangible fixed asset is depreciated using the revised method over the remaining useful economic life, beginning in the period in which the change is made.

Two or more components of a fixed asset

2.28 A fixed asset may comprise two or more major components with substantially different useful economic lives. In such cases each component should be accounted for separately for depreciation purposes and depreciated over its individual useful economic life. Examples include:

- Land and buildings
- The structure of a building and items within the structure, such as general fittings

Question 5

What about the trading potential associated with a property valued as an operational entity, such as a hotel or pub? Should this be treated as a separate component?

Answer

No. The value and life of any trading potential is inherently inseparable from that of the property.

2.29 In calculating the useful economic life of an asset it is assumed that **subsequent expenditure** will be undertaken to maintain the originally assessed standard of performance of the asset (for example the cost of servicing or overhauling plant and equipment). Without such expenditure the depreciation expense would be increased because the useful life and/or residual value of the asset would be reduced. This type of expenditure is **recognised as an expense when incurred**. In addition, subsequent expenditure may be undertaken that results in a restoration or replacement of a component of the asset that has been depreciated or an enhancement of economic benefits of the asset in excess of the originally assessed standard of performance. This type of expenditure may result in an extension of the useful economic life of the asset.

> **IMPORTANT!**
>
> **Subsequent expenditure does not obviate the need to charge depreciation.** The subsequent expenditure is **capitalised as it is incurred and depreciated** over the asset's (or, where the expenditure relates to a component, the component's) useful economic life.

2.30 Tangible fixed assets other than non depreciable land, should be **reviewed for impairment** at the end of the reporting period where:

- no depreciation is charged on the grounds that it would be immaterial; or
- the estimated remaining useful economic life exceeds 50 years.

The review should be in accordance with FRS 11 *Impairment of fixed assets and goodwill,* discussed in the next chapter

2.31 Many companies carry fixed assets in their balance sheets at revalued amounts, particularly in the case of freehold buildings. When this is done, the **depreciation charge** should be calculated **on the basis of the revalued amount** (not the original cost), in spite of the alternative accounting rules in CA 1985.

2.32 Where the residual value is material, it should be reviewed at the end of each reporting period to take account of reasonably expected technological changes. A change in the estimated residual value should be accounted for prospectively over the asset's remaining useful economic life, except to the extent that the asset has been impaired at the balance sheet date.

Renewals accounting

> **KEY TERM**
>
> Where **renewals accounting** is adopted, the level of annual expenditure required to maintain the operating capacity of the infrastructure asset is treated as the depreciation charged for the period and is deducted from the carrying amount of the asset (as part of accumulated depreciation). Actual expenditure is capitalised (as part of the cost of the asset) as incurred.

2.33 Definable major assets or components within an infrastructure system or network with determinable finite lives should be treated separately and depreciated over their useful

economic lives. For the remaining tangible fixed assets within the system or network, renewals accounting may be used if:

(a) the infrastructure asset is a system that as a whole is intended to be maintained at a specified level of service by the continuing replacement and refurbishment of its components; and

(b) the level of annual expenditure required to maintain the operating capacity or service capability of the infrastructure asset is calculated from an asset management plan certified by a qualified, independent person; and

(c) the system or network is in a mature or steady state.

Disclosure requirements of FRS 15

2.34 The following information should be disclosed separately in the financial statements for each class of tangible fixed assets.

(a) The depreciation methods used

(b) The useful economic lives or the depreciation rates used

(c) Total depreciation charged for the period

(d) Where material, the financial effect of a change during the period in either the estimate of useful economic lives or the estimate of residual values

(e) The cost or revalued amount at the beginning of the financial period and at the balance sheet date

(f) The cumulative amount of provisions for depreciation or impairment at the beginning of the financial period and at the balance sheet date

(g) A reconciliation of the movements, separately disclosing additions, disposals, revaluations, transfers, depreciation, impairment losses, and reversals of past impairment losses written back in the financial period

(h) The net carrying amount at the beginning of the financial period and at the balance sheet date

Criticisms of FRS 15

2.35 FRS 15 has been largely welcomed, particularly the rules on revaluations (see below). However, some commentators have found problematic the treatment of subsequent expenditure where there is a major overhaul. The treatment has been described as 'contrived'.

3 REVALUATION 5/98

3.1 Before FRS 15, companies could pick and choose which of their assets they wished to revalue and when. This allowed companies to flatter their balance sheet figures through the inclusion of meaningless out of date valuations, thereby hindering comparability between companies from year to year. FRS 15 puts a stop to this 'cherry picking'.

3.2 An entity may adopt a policy of **revaluing tangible fixed assets**. Where this policy is adopted **it must be applied consistently** to all assets of the same class.

KEY TERM

A **class of fixed assets** is 'a category of tangible fixed assets having a similar nature, function or use in the business of an entity'. (FRS 15)

3.3 Where an asset is revalued its carrying amount should be its **current value** as at the balance sheet date, current value being the **lower of replacement cost and recoverable amount**.

3.4 To achieve the above, the standard states that a **full valuation** should be carried out **at least every five years** with an **interim valuation in year 3**. If it is likely that there has been a material change in value, interim valuations in years 1, 2 and 4 should also be carried out.

3.5 A full valuation should be conducted by either a **qualified external valuer** or a **qualified internal valuer,** provided that the valuation has been subject to review by a qualified external valuer. An interim valuation may be carried out by either an external or internal valuer.

3.6 For certain types of assets (other than properties) eg company cars, there may be an active second hand market for the asset or appropriate indices may exist, so that the directors can establish the asset's value with reasonable reliability and therefore avoid the need to use the services of a qualified valuer.

Valuation basis

3.7 The following valuation bases should be used for properties that are not impaired.

(a) **Specialised properties** should be valued on the basis of **depreciated replacement cost**.

Specialised properties are those which, due to their specialised nature, are rarely, if ever, sold on the open market for single occupation for a continuation of their existing use, except as part of a sale of the business in occupation. Eg oil refineries, chemical works, power stations, or schools, colleges and universities where there is no competing market demand from other organisations using these types of property in the locality.

(b) **Non-specialised properties** should be valued on the basis of **existing use value** (EUV).

(c) **Properties surplus** to an entity's requirements should be valued on the basis of **open market value** (OMV).

3.8 Where there is an indication of impairment, an impairment review should be carried out in accordance with FRS 11. The asset should be recorded at the lower of revalued amount (as above) and recoverable amount.

3.9 Tangible fixed assets other than properties should be valued using market value or, if not obtainable, depreciated replacement cost.

Reporting gains and losses on revaluation

3.10 Revaluation **gains** are recognised in the **statement of total recognised gains and losses (STRGL)** except to the extent that they reverse revaluation losses on the same assets, in which case they should be recognised in the profit and loss account.

3.11 All revaluation **losses** that are caused by a clear consumption of economic benefit (eg physical damage or a deterioration in the quality of the service provided by the asset) are recognised in the **profit and loss account**, ie the asset is clearly impaired.

3.12 **Other losses** are recognised in the **STRGL until the carrying amount reaches depreciated historical cost** and **thereafter in the profit and loss account**. However, if it can be demonstrated that the recoverable amount of the asset is more than its revalued amount, the loss will be recognised in the STRGL to the extent that the recoverable amount exceeds the revalued amount. This is because the difference between recoverable amount and revalued amount is not an impairment and should therefore be recognised in the STRGL as a valuation adjustment, rather than the profit and loss account.

3.13 EXAMPLE: ACCOUNTING FOR REVALUATION LOSSES

The following details are available in relation to a non specialised property.

Carrying value	£960,000
Depreciated historic cost	£800,000
Recoverable amount	£760,000
Existing use value	£700,000

How should the revaluation loss be treated?

3.14 SOLUTION

(a) The revaluation loss on the property is £260,000 (ie carrying value of £960,000 compared with EUV of £700,000).

(b) The fall in value from carrying value (£960,000) to depreciated historic cost (£800,000) of £160,000 is recognised in the STRGL.

(c) The fall in value from depreciated historic cost (£800,000) to recoverable amount (£760,000) of £40,000 is recognised in the profit and loss account.

(d) The difference between recoverable amount (£760,000) and EUV (£700,000) is recognised in the STRGL.

4 SSAP 19 ACCOUNTING FOR INVESTMENT PROPERTIES

4.1 The requirement that all fixed assets should be depreciated including freehold buildings (though excluding freehold land) caused a stir amongst **property investment companies** who feared that their reported profits would be severely reduced. The lobby was sufficiently strong to gain a respite from the standard-setters and investment properties were temporarily excluded from the scope of SSAP 12, the forerunner of FRS 15. Eventually, the ASC's deliberations resulted in the publication of a separate standard for such properties.

4.2 A summary of the main provisions of SSAP 19 *Accounting for investment properties* will be given shortly, and these should be familiar to you from Paper 5. First it is worth noting the **conceptual difference** which the ASC identified between investment properties and other fixed assets. Such properties are held 'not for consumption in the business operations but as investments, the disposal of which would not materially affect any manufacturing or trading operations of the enterprise.' Contrast this with the concept underlying the FRS 15 definition of depreciation which is given above.

Knowledge brought forward from Paper 5

SSAP 19 Accounting for investment properties

Definition

- **Investment property:** an interest in land and/or buildings in respect of which construction work and development have been completed, and which is held for its investment potential, rental income being negotiated at arm's length.

- **Exceptions**: property owned and occupied by a company for its own purposes; and property let to and occupied by another group company (in company and group accounts). An associated company is not a group company.

Accounting treatment

- Such properties are **not depreciated**, except where a leasehold has an unexpired term of less than 20 years.

- **Revalue** each year to open market value.

- The increase in value is taken to the **IRR** (Investment Revaluation Reserve).

- For **diminutions** in value the treatment varies (this required an amendment to SSAP 19).

  - If **permanent**, it is charged to the P&L a/c.
  - If **temporary**, a temporary IRR deficit is allowed.

- **Disposals**: per FRS 3,

  - Profit/loss represents the sales proceeds less the carrying amount
  - Revaluation surplus transferred to the P&L a/c (as realised profits)

Disclosures

- Investment properties and the IRR should be **displayed prominently**.

- **Disclose**:

  - the name of the valuer;
  - whether the valuer is an employee or officer of the company; and
  - the basis of valuation used.

- **Non-compliance with CA 1985** for a true and fair view should be noted as required by UITF Abstract 7 (see below).

4.3   A suitable note to comply with the Companies Act as mentioned above was suggested in the APC's bulletin *True and Fair* (and reviewed by the DTI) as follows.

> 'In accordance with SSAP 19, (i) investment properties are revalued annually and the aggregate surplus or deficit is transferred to a revaluation reserve, and (ii) no depreciation or amortisation is provided in respect of freehold investment properties and leasehold investment properties with over 20 years to run. The Directors consider that this accounting policy results in the accounts giving a true and fair view. Depreciation or amortisation is only one of many factors reflected in the annual valuation and the amount which might otherwise have been shown cannot be separately identified or quantified.'

4.4   This chart will help to determine the application of SSAP 19.

BPP PUBLISHING

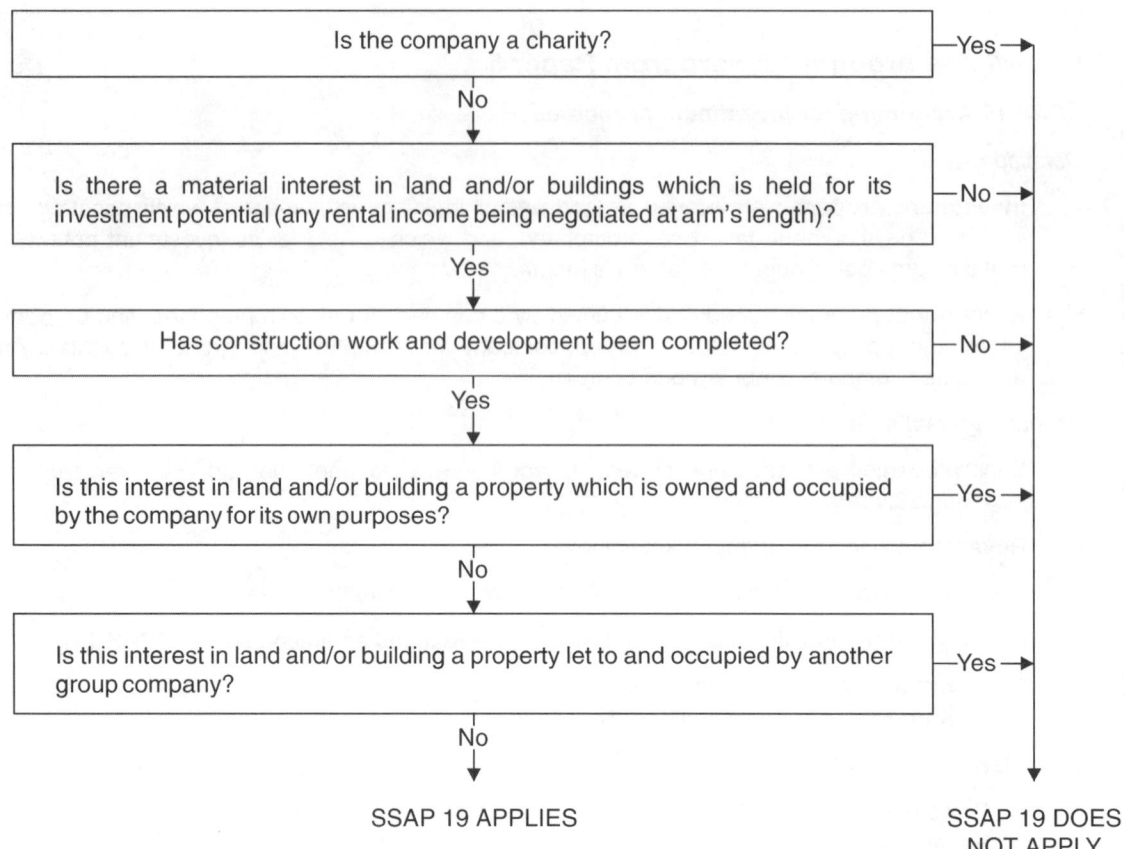

Question 6

The managing director of your company has always been unhappy at depreciating the company's properties because he argues that these properties are in fact appreciating in value. Recently he heard of another company which has investment properties and does not depreciate those properties.

You are required to write a report to your managing director explaining:

(a)   the consequences of not depreciating the company's existing properties;
(b)   the meaning of investment properties; and
(c)   the accounting treatment of investment properties in published financial statements.

Answer

REPORT

From:	Finance Director	
To:	Managing Director	Date: 31 October 19X2
Subject:	*Depreciation of property*	

(a)   All fixed assets that have a finite economic life should be depreciated in a systematic manner over that period. While it is recognised that, generally, freehold land has an indefinite economic life, the same is not true of buildings. Even if they are properly maintained, most industrial and commercial buildings will become economically obsolete in time, even if they remain structurally sound.

The failure to provide depreciation on industrial and commercial buildings over their period of use overstates the profits of the company and this could lead to over-distribution of profit.

(b)   An investment property is defined in the relevant accounting standard (SSAP 19) as one which is held for its investment potential and for which a rental is negotiated at arms length (and where construction is complete). It cannot be one which is owned and occupied by a company or its affiliated companies for its own purposes.

This means that our properties, which are used for the purposes of the company's own manufacturing, distribution and administrative activities, do not qualify for treatment as investment properties.

It also means that they could not be made to qualify as investment properties by transferring them to another group company and renting them back.

(c) Under SSAP 19 investment properties are not depreciated but are shown in the accounts at open market value. Increases in market value are credited to an investment revaluation reserve and decreases are charged to it. Falls in market value below the revaluation reserve are taken directly to the P&L account. The open market valuation, which is related to rentals, is likely to vary considerably over time and large charges against profits could occur during periods of weakness in the property market. This could lead to greater volatility of earnings than if the properties had been depreciated, but it reflects more accurately the realities of the property market.

Problems with SSAP 19

4.5 It is likely that SSAP 19 will be amended to fit in with the new FRS 15 from which it is excluded. There are criticisms of the standard, mainly because it does give a clear definition of 'market value'. The Royal Institution of Chartered Surveyors defines **market value** as the best price at which the sale of an interest in property might reasonably be expected to have been completed unconditionally for cash consideration on the date of valuation, assuming a 'willing seller'. There is no mention of a 'willing buyer'.

4.6 There are perceived to be various difficulties with this definition.

(a) **A market transaction** cannot take place without both a seller and a buyer.

(b) The concept of 'willing seller' (but not a willing buyer) is largely theoretical in depressed market conditions where no willing seller really exists, only unwilling and even forced sellers.

(c) This 'willing seller' concept inevitably leads to an over-emphasis on comparable evidence, forcing the valuer to look **backwards** rather than forwards.

(d) Following on from (c), such an approach cannot cope with **specialised assets**, such as large regional shopping centres, for which no ready market exits.

4.7 The deficiencies in the current definition of open market value do not become apparent **in normal market conditions** where there is a liquid market in actively traded properties. However, at the extremes of the cycle, the current definition is quite inadequate, producing over-valuation in times of boom and under-valuation in times of slump, exacerbating market cycles in an extremely damaging way.

5   SSAP 4 ACCOUNTING FOR GOVERNMENT GRANTS

5.1 In the UK, the government provides grants to companies which invest in assisted areas (such as development areas or special development areas). These grants may be:

(a) **revenue grants** to cover some of the costs of certain categories of revenue expenditure;

(b) **capital grants**, which are cash grants to cover a proportion of the costs of certain items of capital expenditure (such as buildings, plant and machinery).

5.2 Companies receiving such grants must account for them. No particular problem arises in respect of revenue grants as they can be credited to revenue in the same period in which the revenue expenditure to which they relate is charged. However, **capital grants** may be treated in a number of ways. SSAP 4 is summarised here as it is very straightforward and you have already studied it, look back to your previous studies if necessary.

Knowledge brought forward from Paper 5

SSAP 4 Accounting for government grants

Problems

- There is a **conflict** of the accruals concept vs the prudence concept.
- **Matching** is difficult if the expenditure is not specified to which the grant should be applied.
- It is necessary to distinguish between **revenue** and **capital grants**.

Accounting treatment

- **Government grants** should be matched in the P&L a/c with the expenditure for which they are contributed.
- For **fixed assets**, the grant is recognised over the useful economic life of the asset.
- The method of reducing the acquisition cost of the fixed asset by the amount of the grant and depreciating the net amount is **in conflict with CA 1985**.
- Grants are not recognised in the P&L a/c until **conditions of receipt** are complied with.
- If part or all recognition is **deferred**, treat this as deferred income.
- Any **potential liabilities** to repay should be provided for to the extent that repayment is probable.

Disclosure

- **Accounting policy note**
- Effect of **government grants** on the results for the period and/or the position at the B/S date.
- Any **potential liability** to repay grants according to FRS 12.

Chapter roundup

- **Assets** have been defined in various ways. The most recent definition is contained in the ASB's *Statement of Principles*, Chapter 4 *Elements of financial statements*.

- CA 1985 maintains **historical cost** principles, modified by the revaluations of certain assets.

- **FRS 15** sets out **uniform principles** relating to tangible fixed assets with regard to:

    o Initial measurement
    o Valuation
    o Depreciation

- **SSAP 19** conflicts with the statutory requirement to depreciate all fixed assets with a limited economic life, by stating that investment properties need not ordinarily be depreciated. Companies taking advantage of this provision need to justify their departure from statute as being necessary to provide a true and fair view.

Quick quiz

1 How does the ASB's *Statement of Principles* define an asset? (see key term)

2 What elements of expenditure are included in the production cost of a fixed asset? (2.5)

3 Can finance costs be capitalised? (2.8)

4 Can subsequent expenditure on a fixed asset be capitalised? (2.16)

5 Define depreciation. (2.22)

6 What accounting treatment is required if the estimated useful life of a fixed asset is revised? (2.25)

7 What is the main problem with SSAP 19? (4.5, 4.6)

8 Name the two types of grant which a company may receive from the government. (5.1)

Question to try	Level	Marks	Time
3	Exam	25	45 mins

BPP PUBLISHING

Chapter 4

FIXED ASSETS: INTANGIBLE ASSETS

Chapter topic	Syllabus reference	Ability required
1 The requirements of the Companies Act 1985	9(a)	Application
2 FRS 10 *Goodwill and intangible assets*	9(a), (b)	Application
3 FRS 11 *Impairment of fixed assets and goodwill*	9(a), (b)	Application
4 SSAP 13 *Accounting for research and development*	9(a), (b)	Application
5 Investments	9(a)	Application

Introduction

Probably the most important, and certainly the most contentious intangible fixed asset is **goodwill**. This is the subject of **FRS 10** *Goodwill and intangible assets* which was covered in your earlier studies.

The section on **SSAP 13** should be revision of a fairly straightforward topic, but you should make sure that you know SSAP 13's provisions.

FRS 11 *Impairment of fixed assets and goodwill* is a recent standard that you need to know about.

1 THE REQUIREMENTS OF THE COMPANIES ACT 1985

1.1 The statutory balance sheet format lists the following intangible fixed assets.

1 Development costs
2 Concessions, patents, licences, trade marks and similar rights and assets
3 Goodwill
4 Payments on account

1.2 With regard to concessions, patents, licences, trade marks and so on, the Companies Act states that such items should only be treated, and disclosed, as **assets** if they were either:

(a) acquired for valuable consideration; or
(b) created by the company itself.

1.3 With regard to **development costs,** the Act states that such costs may only be treated as an asset in the balance sheet (rather than being written off immediately) in 'special circumstances'. The Act does not define these circumstances and this is a case where a SSAP goes further than statute. SSAP 13 (see below) lays down strict criteria for determining when such expenditure may be treated as an asset. The Act merely states that, if it is so treated, the following disclosures must be made by way of note:

(a) the period over which the amount of the costs originally capitalised is being or is to be written off; and

(b) the reasons for capitalising the development costs.

1.4 With regard to goodwill, the Act's requirements are more than covered in FRS 10 (see Section 2).

2 FRS 10 GOODWILL AND INTANGIBLE ASSETS

2.1 You should be familiar with FRS 10 *Goodwill and intangible assets* from your earlier studies. Below is a summary of the requirements, together with one or two exercises. Look back to your earlier study material if you are unsure.

Knowledge brought forward from Paper 5

FRS 10 Goodwill and intangible assets

Accounting treatment

- Under FRS 10 both purchased goodwill and intangible assets should be capitalised as assets in the B/S. Thereafter treatment depends on the nature of investment.
  - There is a rebuttable presumption that the useful economic lives (UEL) of purchased goodwill and intangible assets are limited and do not exceed 20 years from acquisition.
  - The UEL may be regarded as greater than 20 years or even indefinite, but only if the goodwill is capable of continued measurement so that annual impairment reviews can be performed

- **Positive purchased goodwill and intangible assets**
  - Where goodwill and intangible assets are regarded as having limited UEL they should be amortised
  - Where they are regarded as having indefinite UEL they should not be amortised
  - Where they are not amortised or are amortised over more than 20 years, impairment reviews should be performed each year under FRS 11

- **Negative goodwill**

  Negative goodwill should be recognised and separately disclosed on the face of the balance sheet immediately below the goodwill heading. It should be recognised in the profit and loss account in the periods in which the non monetary assets acquired are depreciated or sold

- **Internally generated goodwill**

  Internally generated goodwill should not be capitalised and internally developed intangible assets should be capitalised only where they have a readily ascertainable market value

---

Question 1

The circumstances where an indefinite useful economic life longer than 20 years may be legitimately presumed are limited. What factors determine the durability of goodwill?

Answer

FRS 10 mentions the following.

(a) The nature of the business
(b) The stability of the industry in which the acquired business operates
(c) Typical lifespans of the products to which the goodwill attaches
(d) The extent to which the acquisition overcomes market entry barriers that will continue to exist
(e) The expected future impact of competition on the business

---

PUBLISHING

Question 2

Ashley Ltd has an income-generating unit which has a carrying value of £4,000,000 at 31 December 19X7. This carrying value comprises £1,000,000 relating to goodwill and £3,000,000 relating to net assets. The goodwill is not being amortised as its useful life is believed to be indefinite. In 19X8, changes in the regulatory framework surrounding its business mean that the income-generating unit has a value in use of £3,200,000. As a result of losses, net assets have decreased to £2,800,000 reducing the total carrying value of the unit to £3,800,000 which has thus suffered an impairment loss of £600,000. This is charged to the profit and loss account. The carrying value of goodwill is reduced to £400,000. In 19X9 the company develops a new product with the result that the value in use of the income-generating unit is now £3,400,000. Net tangible assets have remained at £2,800,000.

Can all or any of the impairment loss be reversed?

Answer

No. Despite the value in use of the business unit now being £3,400,000 compared to its carrying value of £3,200,000, it is not possible to reverse £200,000 of the prior year's impairment loss of £600,000 since the reason for the increase in value of the business unit (the launch of the new product) is not the same as the reason for the original impairment loss (the change in the regulatory environment in which the business operates).

Question 3

Brookie plc acquired its investment in Stenders Ltd in the year ended 31 December 19X8. The goodwill on acquisition was calculated as follows.

	£'000	£'000
Cost of investment		200
Fair value of net assets acquired (remaining useful life - 7 years)		
Fixed assets	350	
Stock	50	
Net monetary assets	100	
		(500)
Negative goodwill		(300)

Required

Calculate the amount relating to negative goodwill as reflected in the profit and loss account and balance sheet for the year ended 31 December 19X8.

Answer

Amortisation in the profit and loss account for 19X8

Non-monetary assets recognised through the profit and loss account for the year ended 31 December 19X8:

	£'000
Stock	50
Depreciation (£350,000 ÷ 7)	50
	100
Total non-monetary assets at acquisition	400
Proportion recognised this year	¼

This means that a credit of £75,000 (£300,000 × ¼) of the negative goodwill will be charged to the profit and loss account for the year ended 31.12.X8. The remaining £225,000 will be carried in the balance sheet as a deduction from positive goodwill as part of intangible fixed assets.

Over the next six years (the remaining useful life of the non-monetary assets originally purchased), it will be released into the profit and loss account (£37,500 a year).

Criticisms of FRS 10

2.2 The new rules will mean significant changes to the accounts of many companies. Over 95% of companies in the UK adopted the 'immediate write off' treatment permitted under SSAP 22. Some commentators have suggested that some deals will not be done because of the new, tougher rules. This is probably an exaggeration, but it is certainly possible that the new standard will not be popular.

2.3 More seriously, criticisms have been made of the thinking behind the standard by the firm Ernst & Young. The main criticisms are as follows.

(a) FRS 10 still allows a choice of accounting treatments. Companies can follow a regime that permits the goodwill to be carried as a permanent asset. This may allow some spurious assets to remain indefinitely in the balance sheet, potentially providing fuel for criticism of the profession in the next wave of accounting scandal.

(b) The impairment review, if it is to be based on FRED 15, applies 'labyrinthine methodologies to very soft members'. In other words, it is subjective, not least in determining how the business is to be segmented. Forecasting cashflows is also problematic.

(c) The importance of negative goodwill has been underestimated. It is more likely to arise now that FRS 7 bans reorganisation provisions, thus raising the value of the net assets acquired.

(d) The treatment of negative goodwill is 'strange'. It is a 'dangling credit' in the balance sheet and the profit and loss account treatment simply mirrors that required for depreciation without regard to the fact that this is a **credit** to the profit and loss account.

3 FRS 11 IMPAIRMENT OF FIXED ASSETS AND GOODWILL

3.1 It is accepted practice that a **fixed asset** should **not be carried in the financial statements at more than its recoverable amount,** ie the higher of the amount for which it could be sold and the amount recoverable from its future use. A new FRS has been produced on impairment of fixed assets and goodwill but first we will summarise the Companies Act requirements.

3.2 Under CA 85 the treatment of diminutions in value is as follows.

(a) **Assets held at cost**

(i) **Temporary diminutions** are **not recognised.**

(ii) **Permanent diminutions** are **recognised** and **charged to the profit and loss account.**

(b) **Assets held at valuation**

(i) **Temporary diminutions** are **recognised** and **debited to reserves.**

(ii) **Permanent diminutions** are **recognised** and charged to the **asset's previous surplus in reserves** and **then to the profit and loss account** for the year.

3.3 Further points to note are as follows.

(a) Where the increase in value relates to the **reversal of a permanent diminution** in value previously charged to the profit and loss account, the increase will be credited to the profit and loss account for the year.

(b) Any changes in value taken **directly to reserves** must be disclosed in the STRGL.

FRS 11 *Impairment of fixed assets and goodwill*

3.4   While statute provides some guidance, it provides none on how the recoverable amount should be measured and when impairment losses should be recognised. As a result, practice is inconsistent and perhaps some impairments may not be recognised on a timely basis.

3.5   The need for a standard on impairment is increased by the requirement in FRS 10 *Goodwill and intangible assets* (see Section 2) that, where goodwill and intangible assets have a useful life in excess of twenty years or one that is indefinite, the recoverable amount of the goodwill and intangible assets should be reviewed every year.

3.6   FRS 11 was released in July 1998. It applies to financial statements relating to accounting periods ending on or after 23 December 1998.

3.7   The objective of the FRS is to ensure that:

(a) fixed assets and goodwill are recorded in the financial statements at no more than their **recoverable amount**;

(b) any resulting **impairment loss** is measured and recognised on a consistent basis; and

(c) sufficient information is **disclosed** in the financial statements to enable users to understand the impact of the impairment on the financial position and performance of the reporting entity.

Scope

3.8   The FRS **excludes:**

(a) fixed assets which are governed by the ASB's Standard on *Derivatives and financial instruments* (see Chapter 9);

(b) investment properties as defined in SSAP 19;

(c) shares held by an ESOP;

(d) cost capitalised pending determination under the Oil Industry Accounting Committee's SORP;

The FRS applies to subsidiary undertakings, associates and joint ventures.

Indications of impairment

3.9   A **review for impairment** of a fixed asset or goodwill should be carried out if events or changes in circumstances indicate that the carrying amount of the fixed asset or goodwill may not be recoverable.

> **KEY TERM**
>
> **Impairment**: a reduction in the recoverable amount of a fixed asset or goodwill below its carrying amount.   *(FRS 11)*

3.10 Impairment occurs due to *either*:

(a) something happening to the **fixed asset** itself; *or*

(b) something occurring in the **environment** within which the asset operates.

3.11 This means that it is possible to use **indicators of impairment** to decide when an impairment review is required. Examples of such events and changes in circumstances include the following.

(a) There is a **current period operating loss** or **net cash outflow** from operating activities, combined with *either*:

(i) **past** operating losses or net cash outflows from operating activities; *or*

(ii) an expectation of **continuing** operating losses or net cash outflows from operating activities.

(b) A **fixed asset's market value has declined** significantly during the period.

(c) Evidence is available of **obsolescence or physical damage** to the fixed asset.

(d) There is a **significant adverse change** in any of the following.

(i) Either the **business or the market** in which the fixed asset or goodwill is involved, such as the entrance of a major competitor.

(ii) The **statutory or other regulatory environment** in which the business operates.

(iii) Any **indicator of value** (eg multiples of turnover) used to measure the fair value of a fixed asset on acquisition.

(e) A commitment by management to undertake a **significant reorganisation**.

(f) A major loss of **key employees**.

(g) **Market interest rates** or other market rates of return have increased significantly, and these increases are likely to affect materially the fixed asset's recoverable amount.

3.12 Where any of the above (or similar) occur, then an impairment review should be carried out. In the case of tangible fixed assets, if there is no cause to suspect any impairment, then **no impairment review** is necessary. Intangible assets and goodwill may, however, still require review.

KEY TERMS

Intangible assets: non-financial fixed assets that do not have physical substance but are identifiable and controlled by the entity through custody or legal rights.

Purchased goodwill: the difference between the cost of an acquired entity and the aggregate of the fair values of that entity's identifiable assets and liabilities.

Tangible fixed assets: assets that have physical substance and are held for use in the production or supply of goods or services, for rental to others, or for administrative purposes on a continuing basis in the reporting entity's activities.

(FRS 11)

The impairment review

3.13 The impairment review will consist of a comparison of the carrying amount of the fixed asset or goodwill with its **recoverable amount** (the higher of net realisable value, if known, and value in use). To the extent that the carrying amount exceeds the recoverable amount, the fixed asset or goodwill is impaired and should be written down. **The impairment loss**

should be recognised in the profit and loss account unless it arises on a previously revalued fixed asset.

KEY TERMS

*   **Net realisable value**: the amount at which an asset could be disposed of, less any direct selling costs.

*   **Recoverable amount**: the higher of net realisable value and value in use.

*   **Value in use**: the present value of the future cash flows obtainable as a result of an asset's continued use, including those resulting from its ultimate disposal.

3.14 Note the following **rules** here.

(a) If NRV *or* value in use is higher than the carrying amount, there is no impairment.

(b) If a reliable estimate of NRV cannot be made, the recoverable amount is its value in use.

(c) If NRV is less than the carrying amount, then value in use must be found to see if it is higher still. If it is higher, recoverable amount is based on value in use, not NRV.

3.15 When an impairment loss on a fixed asset or goodwill is recognised, the **remaining useful economic life** should be reviewed and revised if necessary. The revised carrying amount should be depreciated over the revised estimate of the useful economic life.

Calculation of net realisable value

3.16 The net realisable value of an asset that is **traded on an active market** will be based on **market value**. Disposal costs should include only the essential selling costs of the fixed asset and *not* any costs of reducing or reorganising the business.

Calculation of value in use

3.17 Value in use is **not always easy** to estimate.

(a) The value in use of a fixed asset should be estimated **individually** where reasonably practicable.

(b) Where it is not reasonably practicable to identify cash flows arising from an individual fixed asset, value in use should be calculated at the level of **income-generating units**.

(c) The **carrying amount of each income-generating unit** containing the fixed asset or goodwill under review should be compared with the **higher of the value in use and the net realisable value** (if it can be measured reliably) of the unit.

KEY TERM

An **income generating unit** is defined as a group of assets, liabilities and associated goodwill that generates income that is largely independent of the reporting entity's other income streams. The assets and liabilities include those already involved in generating the income and an appropriate portion of those used to generate more than one income stream.

3.18 Because it is necessary to identify only material impairments, in some cases it may be acceptable to consider a **group of income generating units together** rather than on an individual basis.

3.19 In some cases a detailed calculation of value in use will not be necessary. A **simple estimate** may be sufficient to demonstrate that either value in use is higher than carrying value, in which case there is no impairment, or value in use is lower than net realisable value, in which case impairment is measured by reference to net realisable value.

Identification of income generating units

3.20 Income generating units should be identified by **dividing the total income of the entity into as many largely independent income streams as is reasonably practicable.** Each of the entity's identifiable assets and liabilities should be attributed to, or apportioned between, one or more income generating unit(s). However, the following are **excluded**.

- Deferred tax balances
- Interest bearing debt
- Dividends payable
- Other financing items

3.21 In general terms, the income streams identified are likely to **follow** the way in which **management** monitors and makes decisions about continuing or closing the different lines of business of the entity. **Unique intangible assets,** such as brands and mastheads, are generally seen to generate income independently of each other and are usually **monitored separately.** Hence they can often be used to identify income-generating units. **Other income streams** may be identified by **reference to major products or services**.

3.22 EXAMPLE: IDENTIFICATION OF INCOME GENERATING UNITS

A transport company runs a network comprising trunk routes fed by a number of supporting routes. Decisions about continuing or closing the supporting routes are not based on the returns generated by the routes in isolation but on the contribution made to the returns generated by the trunk routes.

3.23 SOLUTION

An income-generating unit comprises a trunk route plus the supporting routes associated with it because the cash inflows generated by the trunk routes are not independent of the supporting routes.

Question 4

Identify the income generating unit in the following cases.

(a) A manufacturer can produce a product at a number of different sites. Not all the sites are used to full capacity and the manufacturer can choose how much to make at each site. However, there is not enough surplus capacity to enable any one site to be closed. The cash inflows generated by any one site therefore depend on the allocation of production across all sites.

(b) A restaurant chain has a large number of restaurants across the country. The cash inflows of each restaurant can be individually monitored and sensible allocations of costs to each restaurant can be made.

BPP PUBLISHING

Answer

(a) The income-generating unit comprises all the sites at which the product can be made.

(b) Each restaurant is an income-generating unit by itself. However, any impairment of individual restaurants is unlikely to be material. A material impairment is likely to occur only when a number of restaurants are affected together by the same economic factors. It may therefore be acceptable to consider groupings of restaurants affected by the same economic factors rather than each individual restaurant.

Central assets

3.24 Assets and liabilities that are directly involved in the production and distribution of individual products may be attributed directly to one unit. Central assets, such as group or regional head offices and working capital may have to be apportioned across the units as on a logical and systematic basis. The **sum of the carrying amounts of the units must equal the carrying amount of the net assets (excluding tax on finance) of the equity as a whole**.

3.25 It **may not be possible** to **apportion certain central assets** meaningfully **across the income generating units** to which they contribute. Such assets **may be excluded from** the **individual income generating units**.

- An additional impairment review should be performed on the excluded central assets.

- The income generating units to which the central assets contribute should be combined and their combined carrying amount (including that of the central assets) should be compared with their combined value in use.

Capitalised goodwill

3.26 This **should be attributed to income generating** units or groups of similar units.

Cash flows

3.27 The expected future cash flows of the income-generating unit, including any allocation of central overheads but excluding cash flows relating to financing and tax, should be based on **reasonable and supportable assumptions**. The cash flows should be **consistent with the most up-to-date budgets** and plans that have been formally approved by management. Cash flows for the period beyond that covered by formal budgets and plans should assume a steady or declining growth rate. Only in exceptional circumstances should:

(a) the period before the steady or declining growth rate is assumed extend to more than five years; or

(b) the steady or declining growth rate exceed the long-term average growth rate for the country or countries in which the business operates.

3.28 **Future cash flows** must be estimated for income generating units in their **current condition**, ie exclude:

(a) benefits expected to arise from a **future reorganisation** for which provision has not been made;

(b) **future capital expenditure** that will improve or enhance the income generating units more than originally assessed.

3.29 For the **five years** following each impairment review where the recoverable amount has been based on value in use, the **cash flows achieved should be compared with those forecast**. If the actual cash flows are so much less than those forecast that use of the actual cash flows could have required recognition of an impairment in previous periods, the original **impairment calculations should be re-performed** using the actual cash flows. Any impairment identified should be recognised in the current period unless the impairment has reversed.

Discount rate

3.30 The present value of the income-generating unit under review should be calculated by discounting the expected future cash flows of the unit.

- The discount rate used should be an **estimate of the rate that the market would expect** on an **equally risky investment**.

- It should **exclude the effects of any risk for which the cash flows have been adjusted** and should be calculated on a pre-tax basis.

Allocation of impairment loss

3.31 Allocation of any impairment loss calculated (ie where carrying amount exceeds value in use) should be allocated:

- First, to any **goodwill** in the unit;
- Thereafter to any **capitalised intangible asset**
- Finally, to the **tangible assets** (pro-rata or other method)

No asset with a readily ascertainable market value should be written down to below NRV.

Acquired business merged with existing business

3.32 If an acquisition that gives rise to goodwill is merged with an existing business, the requirements of the FRS necessitate the calculation of the amount of any internally generated goodwill in the existing business at the date of the merger because that amount will need to be used in the calculation of any subsequent impairment loss in the merged business.

(a) The value of the internally generated goodwill of the existing business at the date of merging the businesses should be estimated and added to the carrying amount of the income-generating unit for the purposes of performing impairment reviews.

(b) Any impairment arising on merging the businesses should be allocated solely to the purchased goodwill within the newly acquired business.

(c) Subsequent impairments should be allocated pro rata between the goodwill of the acquired business and that of the existing business.

(d) The impairment allocated to the existing business should be allocated first to the (notional) internally generated goodwill.

(e) Only the impairments allocated to purchased goodwill (and, if necessary, to any recognised intangible or tangible assets) should be recognised in the financial statements.

3.33 EXAMPLE: ALLOCATION OF IMPAIRMENT LOSSES WHEN AN ACQUIRED BUSINESS IS MERGED WITH EXISTING OPERATIONS

Assumptions

An entity acquires for £60 million a business having net assets with a total fair value of £40 million, resulting in purchased goodwill of £20 million. The acquired business is merged with an existing operation that has net assets with a fair value of £100 million and a carrying amount of £70 million. The value in use of the existing operation at the time of the acquisition is £150 million, implying that the existing operation had internally generated goodwill of £50 million.

Five years later, the carrying amount of the net assets of the combined income-generating unit is £105 million and the carrying amount of the purchased goodwill is £10 million (goodwill is being amortised over 10 years). Value in use is £119 million and there is no reliable estimate of net realisable value.

Calculation of impairment loss

	£m
Carrying amount of net assets	105
Carrying amount of goodwill	10
Notional carrying amount of the internally generated goodwill at the date of acquisition (assuming notional amortisation on same basis as for purchased goodwill)	25
Total	140
Value in use	119
Impairment	21

The impairment is allocated on a pro rata basis (2:5) to the purchased goodwill and internally generated goodwill, resulting in the recognition of an impairment loss of £6 million and purchased goodwill being written down to £4 million.

If value in use were £98 million, the resulting total impairment loss of £42 million would be allocated first to the goodwill (purchased and notional amount of internally generated) of £35 million, then to any intangible assets, then to the tangible fixed assets in the income-generating unit, resulting in the recognition of an impairment loss of £17 million (write-down of purchased goodwill £10 million, write-down of intangible and tangible assets £7 million).

Reversal of past impairments

3.34 Tangible fixed assets and investments are treated differently from goodwill and intangible assets.

Tangible fixed assets and investments

3.35 **If**, after an impairment loss has been recognised, the **recoverable amount** of a tangible fixed asset or investment (in subsidiaries, associates and joint ventures) **increases because of a change in economic conditions,** the resulting **reversal** of the impairment loss should be **recognised in the current period.** However, recognition is *only* **to the extent that it increases the carrying amount of the fixed asset up to the amount that it would have been had the original impairment not occurred.** The reversal of the impairment loss should be recognised in the **profit and loss account unless** it arises on a **previously revalued fixed asset** (see below).

3.36 Such events would be the reverse of those given above (Paragraph 3.11) to trigger an impairment review. Increases in value from the passage of time or through the passing of cash outflows do *not* give rise to the reversal of an impairment loss.

3.37 An increase in value above the original carrying value is a **revaluation,** and this is the case with goodwill and intangibles too.

Goodwill and intangible assets

3.38 The reversal of an impairment loss on intangible assets and goodwill should be **recognised in the current period if, and only if:**

(a) an **external event** caused the recognition of the impairment loss in previous periods, and subsequent external events clearly and demonstrably reverse the effects of that event in a way that was not foreseen in the original impairment calculations; or

(b) the impairment loss related to an intangible asset with a readily ascertainable market value and the **net realisable value based on that market value** has increased **to above the intangible asset's impaired carrying amount.**

3.39 The reversal of the impairment loss should be **recognised to the extent that it increases the carrying amount of the goodwill or intangible asset up to the amount that it would have been had the original impairment not occurred.** However, the reversal of an impairment loss recognised under (b) above should *not* be recognised **beyond the extent that it increases the carrying amount of the intangible asset to its net realisable value.**

KEY TERM

Readily ascertainable market value, in relation to an intangible asset, is the value that is established by reference to a market where:

(a) the asset belongs to a homogeneous population of assets that are equivalent in all material respects; and

(b) an active market, evidenced by frequent transactions, exists for that population of assets. *(FRS 11)*

Question 5

An income-generating unit comprising a factory, plant and equipment etc and associated purchased goodwill becomes impaired because the product it makes is overtaken by a technologically more advanced model produced by a competitor. The recoverable amount of the income-generating unit falls to £60m, resulting in an impairment loss of £80m, allocated as follows.

	Carrying amounts before impairment £m	Carrying amounts after impairment £m
Goodwill	40	-
Patent (with no market value)	20	-
Tangible fixed assets	80	60
Total	140	60

After three years, the entity makes a technological breakthrough of its own, and the recoverable amount of the income-generating unit increases to £90m. The carrying amount of the tangible fixed assets had the impairment not occurred would have been £70m.

Required

Calculate the reversal of the impairment loss.

Answer

The reversal of the impairment loss is recognised to the extent that it increases the carrying amount of the tangible fixed assets to what it would have been had the impairment not taken place, ie a reversal of the impairment loss of £10m is recognised and the tangible fixed assets written back to £70m. Reversal of the impairment is not recognised in relation to the goodwill and patent because the effect of the external event that caused the original impairment has not reversed - the original product is still overtaken by a more advanced model.

3.40 The **reversal of past impairment losses** is **recognised** when the **recoverable amount** of a tangible fixed asset or investment in a subsidiary, an associate or a joint venture has **increased because of a change in economic conditions or in the expected use of the asset**. Increases in the recoverable amount of goodwill and intangible assets are recognised only when:

(a) an external event caused the recognition of the impairment loss in previous periods; and

(b) subsequent external events clearly and demonstrably reverse the effects of that event in a way that was not foreseen in the original impairment calculations.

RULES TO LEARN

(a) **Impairment losses** are recognised in the **profit and loss account, unless** they arise on a **previously revalued fixed asset.**

(b) Impairment losses on **revalued fixed assets** are recognised in the **statement of total recognised gains and losses** until the carrying value of the asset falls **below depreciated historical** cost unless the impairment is clearly caused by a **consumption of economic benefits**, in which case the loss is recognised in the **profit and loss account.**

(c) Impairments **below depreciated historical** cost are recognised in the **profit and loss account.**

Presentation and disclosure

3.41 **Impairment losses recognised in the profit and loss account** should be included within **operating profit** under the **appropriate statutory heading**, and disclosed as an exceptional item if appropriate. Impairment losses recognised in the STRGL should be **disclosed separately** on the face of that statement.

3.42 In **the notes** to the financial statements in **accounting periods after the impairment**, the impairment loss should be treated as follows.

(a) For assets held on a **historical cost basis**, the impairment loss should be included **within cumulative depreciation**: the cost of the asset should not be reduced.

(b) For **revalued assets held at a market value** (eg existing use value or open market value), the impairment loss should be included **within the revalued carrying amount**.

(c) For **revalued assets held at depreciated replacement** cost, an impairment loss **charged to the profit and loss account** should be included **within cumulative**

depreciation: the carrying amount of the asset should not be reduced; an **impairment loss charged to the STRGL** should be **deducted from the carrying amount** of the asset.

3.43 If the impairment loss is measured by reference to **value in use** of a fixed asset or income-generating unit, the **discount rate applied to the cash flows should be disclosed**. If a risk-free discount rate is used, some indication of the risk adjustments made to the cash flows should be given.

3.44 Where an impairment loss recognised in a previous period is **reversed** in the current period, the financial statements should **disclose the reason for the reversal**, including any changes in the assumptions upon which the calculation of recoverable amount is based.

3.45 Where an impairment loss would have been recognised in a previous period had the forecasts of future cash flows been more accurate but the impairment has reversed and the reversal of the loss is permitted to be recognised, the impairment now identified and its subsequent reversal should be disclosed.

3.46 Where, in the measurement of value in use, the period before a steady or declining long-term growth rate has been assumed extends to more than five years, the financial statements should **disclose the length of the longer period** and the circumstances justifying it.

3.47 Where, in the measurement of value in use, the long-term growth rate used has exceeded the long-term average growth rate for the country or countries in which the business operates, the financial statements should **disclose the growth rate assumed** and the circumstances justifying it.

> **Exam focus point**
> As FRS 11 is relatively recent, you are more likely to get a 'written' question or a simple calculation than a complicated one.

3.48 Section summary

The main aspects of FRS 11 to remember are:

- **Indications** of impairment
- Identification of **income-generating** unit
- How an **impairment review** is carried out
- **Restoration of past losses** (tangibles vs intangibles)
- Impairment and restoration of **revalued fixed assets**

4 SSAP 13 ACCOUNTING FOR RESEARCH AND DEVELOPMENT

4.1 In many companies, especially those which produce food, or 'scientific' products such as medicines, or 'high-technology' products, the expenditure on research and development is considerable. When R & D is a large item of cost, its accounting treatment may have a significant influence on the profits of a business and its balance sheet valuation. SSAP 13 is relatively straightforward, and you have met it in your previous studies. A summary is given below, along with a revision question.

R & D in practice

4.2 In a recent survey of company accounts, it was found that 25% did not show the amount spent on R & D, even when it had been disclosed in the chairman's report that money had been spent during the period. This contradicts SSAP 13. It is obviously misleading for companies to state that they spend money on R & D unless the amount was **material**. If it was material the amount should be disclosed.

4.3 The importance of R & D disclosure was emphasised in another survey of what users really needed in financial statements. UK institutional investors said the top requirement was **future prospects and plans** (84%). R & D is seen to form a crucial quantitative element of prospects and plans. When specifically asked about R & D, 64% of UK investors said the data was very, or extremely, important to them. Unfortunately, the top companies analysed failed dismally to provide the information required. There is a wide variety of treatment and information given on R & D and improvements are required in the reporting of R & D.

4.4 The emergence of new and quickly growing **computer software companies** has brought SSAP 13, a previously uncontroversial standard, back into the spotlight. These companies have complained about the high level of write-offs of R & D costs, which has a significant impact on profits. Such costs have to be written off because they are often incurred on speculative software which is high risk and may never be produced commercially. It is unlikely, however, that the ASB will look at this topic in the near future.

Knowledge brought forward from Paper 5

SSAP 13 Accounting research and development

Definitions

- **Pure/basic research** is experimental/theoretical work with no commercial end in view and no practical application.
- **Applied research** is original investigation directed towards a specific practical aim/objective.
- **Development** is the use of scientific/technical knowledge in order to produce new/substantially improved materials, devices, processes etc.

Accounting treatment

- **Pure and applied research** should be written off as incurred.
- **Development expenditure** should be written off in year of expenditure, *except* in certain circumstances when it *may* be deferred to future periods.
  - **S** Separately defined project
  - **E** Expenditure separately identifiable
  - **C** Commercially viable
  - **T** Technically feasible
  - **O** Overall profit expected
  - **R** Resources exist to complete the project
- Show **deferred development costs** as an intangible asset amortised from the beginning of commercial production, systematically by reference to sales, etc.
- Deferred costs should be **reviewed annually**; where the above criteria no longer apply, write off the cost immediately.
- Development expenditure previously written off can be **reinstated** if the uncertainties which led to it being written off no longer apply.
- **R & D fixed assets** should be capitalised and written off over their estimated economic lives.

Knowledge brought forward from Paper 5 (cont)

- Deferral of costs should be **applied consistently** to all projects.
- SSAP 13 **does not apply to**:
  - Fixed assets used for R&D (except amortisation)
  - The cost of locating mineral deposits in extractive industries
  - Expenditure where there is a firm contract for reimbursement

Disclosure

- R&D activities should be disclosed in the **directors' report**.
- Private companies outside groups which include a plc are **exempt** from disclosing R & D expenditures (except amortisation) if they meet the criteria for a medium-sized company × 10.
- **Disclose**:
  - Movements on deferred development expenditure
  - R&D charged to the P&L a/c analysed between current year expenditure and amortisation
  - An accounting policy note

Question 6

Forkbender Ltd develops and manufactures exotic cutlery and has the following projects in hand.

	Project				
	1 £'000	2 £'000	3 £'000	4 £'000	5 £'000
Deferred development expenditure b/f 1.1.X2	280	-	450	-	-
Development expenditure incurred during the year					
Salaries, wages and so on	35	29	-	60	20
Overhead costs	2	5	-	-	3
Materials and services	3	13	-	11	4
Patents and licences	1	2	-	-	-
Market research	-	10	-	2	-

Project 1 was originally expected to be highly profitable but this is now in doubt, since the scientist in charge of the project is now behind schedule, with the result that competitors are gaining ground.

Project 2: £370,000 development expenditure on this project has been written off in previous years. Directors now believe, on the best advice, that the project will in future earn revenue considerably in excess of all development costs and they therefore wish to reinstate the expenditure of previous years.

Project 3: commercial production started during the year. Sales were 20,000 units in 19X2 and future sales are expected to be: 19X3 30,000 units; 19X4 60,000 units; 19X5 40,000 units; 19X6 30,000 units. There are no sales expected after 19X6.

Project 4: these costs relate to a new project, which meets the criteria for deferral of expenditure and which is expected to last for three years.

Project 5 is another new project, involving the development of a 'loss leader', expected to raise the level of future sales.

The company's policy is to defer development costs, where permitted by SSAP 13. Expenditure carried forward is written off evenly over the expected sales life of projects, starting in the first year of sale.

Required

Show how the above projects should be treated in the accounting statements of Forkbender Ltd for the year ended 31 December 19X2 in accordance with best accounting practice. Justify your treatment of each project.

Answer

Project 1 expenditure, including that relating to previous years, should all be written off in 19X2, as there is now considerable doubt as to the profitability of the project.

Project 2 expenditure for 19X2 can be deferred and the expenditure relating to previous years can be reinstated.

Since commercial production has started under project 3 the expenditure previously deferred should now be amortised. This will be done over the estimated life of the product, as stated in the question.

Project 4: the development costs may be deferred.

Since project 5 is not expected to be profitable its development costs should not be deferred.

BALANCE SHEET AS AT 31 DECEMBER 19X2 (extract)

	£'000
FIXED ASSETS	
Intangible assets	
Development costs (Note 2)	850

NOTES TO THE ACCOUNTS

1 *Accounting policies*

Research and development

Research and development expenditure is written off as incurred, except that development expenditure incurred on an individual project is carried forward when its future recoverability can be foreseen with reasonable assurance. Any expenditure carried forward is amortised over the period of sales from the related project.

2 *Development costs*

	£'000	£'000
Balance brought forward 1 January 19X2		730
Development expenditure reinstated		370
Development expenditure incurred during 19X2	188	
Development expenditure amortised during 19X2	438	
		(250)
Balance carried forward 31 December 19X2		850

Note. SSAP 13 does not permit the inclusion of market research in deferred development expenditure. The costs might, however, be carried forward separately under the accruals principle.

Workings

	1 £'000	2 £'000	3 £'000	4 £'000	5 £'000	Total £'000
B/F	280	-	450	-	-	730
Expenditure previously written off, reinstated	-	370	-	-	-	370
Salaries etc.	35	29	-	60	20	144
Overheads	2	5	-	-	3	10
Materials etc.	3	13	-	11	4	31
Patents etc.	1	2	-	-	-	3
C/F	-	(419)	(360)	(71)	-	(850)
Written off	321		90		27	438

* *Note.* An alternative basis for amortisation would be:

$$\frac{20}{180} \times 450 = 50$$

The above basis is more prudent, however, in this case.

---

5 INVESTMENTS

5.1 The last category of fixed assets we need to consider is investments. Not all investments are held by a company for the long term and it will be convenient to deal with **fixed asset**

investments and **current asset investments** together. Investments intended to be retained by a company on a continuing basis (for use in the company's activities) should be treated as fixed assets, while any other investments should be taken to be current assets.

5.2   All the terms relating to investments in **group companies** are explained in Part C of this Study Text.

Fixed asset investments

5.3   The provisions relating to fixed assets in general, which were given in the previous chapter, embrace investments which are held as fixed assets. But investments will not normally have a limited economic life, so that the requirement of **systematic depreciation does not apply**.

5.4   The **alternative accounting rules** allow the following bases of valuation, other than cost, for fixed asset investments.

(a)   **Market value**: if this is higher than the stock exchange value, the latter should also be disclosed

(b)   **Directors' valuation**

(c)   **Equity method**: this method will be explained during your studies of accounting for associated companies

5.5   As always when advantage is taken of the alternative accounting rules, **disclosure** must be made of:

(a)   the items affected;
(b)   the basis of valuation adopted; and
(c)   the comparable amounts determined according to the historical cost convention.

Current asset investments

5.6   Current asset investments should be shown, in accordance with the **prudence concept**, at the lower of purchase price and net realisable value.

Listed vs unlisted

5.7   Investments, whether fixed assets or current assets, must be split between any listed investments and those which are unlisted. **Income** from listed investments need not be disclosed. Shares dealt with on the Alternative Investment Market (AIM) are not 'listed' (but they are 'quoted').

5.8   If the aggregate market value of listed investments differs from their carrying value in the balance sheet, the **market value** should be disclosed.

5.9   Where an investment comprises a **substantial shareholding** in another company there is further information which must be disclosed. This is to enable the company's members to obtain a proper appreciation of the nature of the investment.

(a)   If a company owns **over 20% of the equity shares** in another company or the investment exceeds **20% of the investing company's assets**, then the name and nationality of the company should be disclosed. For each class of shares held, the identity of the class and the proportion of the nominal value held must be given. These are called 'significant investments'.

BPP PUBLISHING

(b) If **20% or more** of a company's shares are held, then the investing company must disclose its aggregate capital and reserves and profit or loss for the year.

(c) These requirements do not apply if the investment is to be treated as a **subsidiary, associate** or **joint venture,** nor if a 20% or greater investment is accounted for under the **equity method**.

We will look at these treatments and the effect of changes in holdings in the later chapters on group accounts.

Chapter roundup

- The treatment of **goodwill and intangibles** is a controversial and complex area. You must ensure that you can discuss the current thinking on the nature of fixed assets, intangible assets and goodwill and that you can discuss all the possible treatments of positive and negative goodwill in accounts and the arguments on brand accounting. You should be familiar with, and be able to explain, the ASB's requirements as set out in FRS 10 *Goodwill and intangible asset.*

- FRS 11 *Impairment of fixed assets and goodwill* was introduced to ensure that

  o Fixed assets and goodwill are recorded at no more than their **recoverable amount**

  o Any **impairment loss** is **correctly measured**

  o **Sufficient information** is disclosed

- **SSAP 13** on the other hand is a standard which is generally accepted and well understood. You should already be very familiar with its provisions, but make sure that you learn the disclosure requirements.

- **Investments** are treated according to the percentage holding of votes and shares.

Quick quiz

1 In what circumstances may concessions, patents and so on be treated as assets in a company's accounts? (see para 1.2)

2 What are the statutory disclosure requirements in relation to deferred development costs? (1.3)

3 What is the normal treatment prescribed by FRS 10 for positive purchased goodwill? (KBF box)

4 The useful economic life of goodwill or intangible assets is always 20 years or less. True or false? (KBF box)

5 How should negative goodwill be shown in the balance sheet? (KBF box)

6 What are the main indications of impairment? (3.11)

7 What is meant by 'value in use'? (Key term)

8 What is the correct treatment for central assets under FRS 11? (3.24)

9 Why do producers of computer software have a problem with SSAP 13? (4.4)

10 What methods of valuing investments are permitted under the alternative accounting rules? (5.4)

Question to try	Level	Marks	Time
4	Introductory	n/a	n/a

Chapter 5

STOCKS AND LONG-TERM CONTRACTS

Chapter topic	Syllabus reference	Ability required
1 Stocks and short-term work in progress	9(a), (b)	Application
2 Long-term contract work in progress	9(a), (b)	Application

Introduction

In spite of its importance as a component of company accounts, and its direct impact on profitability, the treatment of **stock** has become a fairly **uncontroversial area** in the financial accounting debate. This should not blind you to its importance; any auditor will tell you that one of his or her primary concerns is with stock as it provides infinite potential for problems and possible errors.

You have examined the valuation and disclosure of stock earlier in your studies. We will briefly revise stocks and short-term WIP as this is a very straightforward accounting subject which you should have studied in depth for Papers 1 and 5.

Long-term contracts only tend to arise in certain companies, for example those in the construction business. The treatment of long-term contracts is covered in Section 2. The accounting for long-term contracts is not difficult, but many students seem to have problems with it, so we have covered the subject in depth. Make sure that you work through the comprehensive exercise given here as carefully as possible.

1 STOCKS AND SHORT-TERM WORK IN PROGRESS 5/96

1.1 In most businesses the value put on stock is an important factor in the determination of profit. **Stock valuation** is, however, a **highly subjective** exercise and consequently there is a wide variety of different methods used in practice. The statutory regulations embodied in the CA 1985 and SSAP 9 *Stocks and long-term contracts* requirements have been developed to achieve greater uniformity in the valuation methods used and in the disclosure in financial statements prepared under the historical cost convention.

1.2 **SSAP 9** defines stocks and work in progress as:

(a) goods or other assets purchased for resale;
(b) consumable stores;
(c) raw materials and components purchased for incorporation into products for sale;
(d) products and services in intermediate stages of completion;
(e) finished goods.

1.3 In published accounts, the **CA 1985** requires that these stock categories should be grouped and disclosed under the following headings:

(a) raw materials and consumables ((c) and (b) above);

(b)   work in progress ((d) above);

(c)   finished goods and goods for resale ((e) and (a) above);

(d)   payments on account. This is presumably intended to cover the case of a company which has paid for stock items but not yet received them into stock.

1.4   A **distinction** is also made in SSAP 9 between:

(a)   stocks and work in progress other than long-term contract work in progress; and

(b)   long-term contract work in progress.

1.5   Stocks and short-term work in progress are revised briefly here.

Knowledge brought forward from Papers 1 and 5

SSAP 9 Stock and long-term contracts (stock and short-term WIP)

Under the **matching concept** costs must be allocated between the cost of goods sold (matched against current revenues) and closing stock (matched against future revenues).

- Stock should be valued at the **lower of cost and net realisable value (NRV)**.

- Costs should include those incurred in the **normal course of business** in bringing a product or service to its **present location and condition**.

- **Costs** include direct costs (labour, materials), production overheads and other attributable overheads. Exclude all 'abnormal' overheads, eg exceptional spoilage.

- CA 1985 also allows the inclusion of **interest payable** on capital borrowed to finance the production of the asset (allowed by SSAP 9 under 'other attributable overheads').

- **NRV** is the actual or estimated selling price less further costs to be incurred in marketing, selling and distribution.

- The method used in allocating costs to stock should produce the **fairest approximation** to the expenditure incurred.

- Methods include (per CA 1985): average cost, base stock, current cost, FIFO, LIFO, replacement cost, standard cost, unit cost; however, base stock and LIFO are not allowed under SSAP 9.

- The principle situation where **NRV will be less than cost** will be where:

  ° there have been increases in the costs or falls in selling price;
  ° physical deterioration of stock has occurred;
  ° products have become obsolescent;
  ° the company has decided to make and sell a product at a loss;
  ° there are errors in production or purchasing.

1.6   The following question is a very simple reminder of how FIFO and LIFO operate.

Question 1

A retailer commenced business on 1 January 19X5, with a capital of £500. He decided to specialise in a single product line and by the end of June 19X5, his purchases and sales of this product were as follows.

	Purchases		Sales	
	Units	Unit price	Units	Unit price
		£		£
January	30	5.00	20	7.00
February	-	-	5	7.20
April	40	6.00	25	8.00
May	25	6.50	30	8.50
June	20	7.00	20	9.00
	115		100	

Required

(a) Ascertain the retailer's gross profit for the period assuming that:

   (i) stock is valued using FIFO;
   (ii) stock is valued using LIFO.

(b) Assuming that all purchases and sales are made for cash and that there are no other transactions for the period, draw up balance sheets as at 30 June 19X5, showing:

   (i) stock valued on a FIFO basis;
   (ii) stock valued on a LIFO basis.

Comment briefly on the significance of these balance sheets.

Answer

(a) (i) *LIFO basis*

	Sales			Cost of sales		
	Unit	Unit price	Total	Unit	Unit price	Total
		£	£		£	£
January	20	7.00	140.00	20	5.00	100.00
February	5	7.20	36.00	5	5.00	25.00
April	25	8.00	200.00	25	6.00	150.00
May	30	8.50	255.00	25	6.50	162.50
				5	6.00	30.00
June	20	9.00	180.00	20	7.00	140.00
	100		811.00	100		607.50
Closing stock				10	6.00	60
				5	5.00	25
				15		85

	£
Sales	811.00
Less cost of sales	607.50
Gross profit	203.50

   (ii) *FIFO basis*

	£	£
Sales		811.00
Purchases	692.50	
Less closing stock (15 @ £7.00)	105.00	
		587.50
		223.50

(b)   BALANCE SHEETS AS AT 30 JUNE 19X5

	(i) LIFO basis £	(ii) FIFO basis £
Original capital	500.00	500.00
Profit	203.50	223.50
	703.50	723.50
Stock	85.00	105.00
Cash	618.50	618.50
	703.50	723.50

In a time of rising prices LIFO (which uses the most current costs) will tend to give a more realistic measure of profit, but results in an outdated stock valuation being disclosed in the balance sheet.

Exam focus point

It is unlikely that you will be asked a basic stock question, as the subject is covered in Paper 5. You are more likely to be asked about long-term contracts. However, in May 1996 a question required the treatment of stocks to be compared with the US treatment.

2   LONG-TERM CONTRACT WORK IN PROGRESS   5/95, 11/95

2.1   This section should also serve as revision as you will have covered long-term contracts in your earlier studies. However, we have covered the subject in some depth here because, as well as causing problems for students, the more complex forms of long-term contracts do appear in Paper 9 questions.

KEY TERM

Long-term contract: a contract entered into for the design, manufacture or construction of a single substantial asset or the provision of a service (or a combination of assets or services which together constitute a single project) where the time taken substantially to complete the contract is such that the contract activity falls into different accounting periods.   *(SSAP 9)*

2.2   SSAP 9 points out that, while such a contract will **usually extend for over one year**, a duration exceeding one year is not as important as the **materiality** of the contract. Provided that a consistent policy is used to identify 'long-term' contracts, any contract so material to the activity of the period that the profit and loss account would not give a true and fair view if it were not accounted for as 'long-term' is long-term for the purpose of implementing SSAP 9.

2.3   The SSAP argues that, owing to the length of time taken to complete such contracts, to defer recognition of turnover and profit until completion may result in the profit and loss account reflecting, not so much a fair view of the activities of the company during the year but rather the results relating to contracts which have been completed during the year. It is therefore appropriate, subject to certain limitations, to **take credit for turnover and ascertainable profit while contracts are in progress.**

2.4   This is contrary to SSAP 2, which states that 'where the accruals concept is inconsistent with the prudence concept the later prevails', but if no profit was taken until each contract was complete, the company results would be erratic from year to year.

2.5   The standard accounting practice required by SSAP 9 is as follows.

> 'Long-term contracts should be **assessed on a contract by contract basis** and reflected in the profit and loss account by **recording turnover and related costs as contract activity progresses**. Turnover is ascertained in a manner appropriate to the stage of completion of the contract, the business and the industry in which it operates.

> 'Where it is considered that the outcome of a long-term contract can be assessed with reasonable certainty before its conclusion, the **prudently calculated attributable profit** should be recognised in the profit and loss account as the difference between the reported turnover and related costs for that contract.'

KEY TERM

Attributable profit: that part of the total profit currently estimated to arise over the duration of the contract, after allowing for estimated remedial and maintenance costs and increases in costs so far as not recoverable under the terms of the contract, that fairly reflects the profit attributable to that part of the work performed at the accounting date. (There can be no attributable profit until the profitable outcome of the contract can be assessed with reasonable certainty.)   *(SSAP 9)*

2.6   Attributable profit is taken to debtors in the balance sheet, not stocks. It is apparent from the definition of attributable profit quoted above that estimates based on formulae such as:

$$\frac{\text{Costs attributable to work performed to date}}{\text{Estimated total contract cost}} \times \text{total estimated profit; or}$$

$$\frac{\text{Work certified to date}}{\text{Total contract price}} \times \text{total estimated profit}$$

are to be preferred to ones based on the difference between work certified to date and costs incurred to the date of the certificate.

2.7   An obvious advantage of the first two methods is that they will tend to ensure that a proper estimate of total profit is made, thus preventing any profits being taken on projects where outcomes are not reasonably certain. (There are, of course, occasional cases when a company knows beyond any reasonable doubt that a contract will be profitable but nevertheless finds it impossible to make a reasonable estimate of total profits in the early stages of the contract. The third method mentioned above, based on the difference between work certified to date and costs incurred to the date of the certificate, may then be adopted.)

Determination of turnover

2.8   No specific method is laid down in the standard: **turnover** is required to be ascertained 'in a **manner appropriate to the industry, the nature of the contracts concerned** and the **contractual relationship with the customer**'. This may be 'by reference to valuation of the work carried out to date' or 'there may be specific points during a contract at which individual elements of work done with separately ascertainable sales values and costs can be identified and appropriately recorded as turnover (for example because delivery or customer acceptance has taken place)'.

BPP PUBLISHING

Foreseeable losses

2.9   If it is expected that there will be a loss on a contract as a whole, provision must be made (in accordance with the prudence concept) for the whole of the loss as soon as it is recognised. The standard defines foreseeable losses as:

> 'losses which are currently estimated to arise over the duration of the contract (after allowing for estimated remedial and maintenance costs, and increases in costs so far as not recoverable under the terms of the contract). This estimate is required irrespective of:
>
> (a)   whether or not work has yet commenced on such contracts;
> (b)   the proportion of work carried out at the accounting date;
> (c)   the amount of profits expected to arise on other contracts.'

2.10   In addition, the explanatory note states that:

> 'where unprofitable contracts are of such magnitude that they can be expected to utilise a considerable part of the company's capacity for a substantial period, related administration overheads to be incurred during the period to the completion of those contracts should also be included in the calculation of the provision for losses.'

2.11   SSAP 9 seeks to produce an integrated financial statement approach. This is achieved by treating a long-term contract as if it were a series of completed short-term contracts, recognising turnover and cost of sales as the contract progresses. The steps in this process are described below.

Step 1.   Calculate **total estimated contract costs** and, if necessary, percentage completed to date.

Step 2.   Using the **percentage completed** to date or work certified to date, calculate turnover attributable to the contract for the period (for example, percentage complete × total contract value less turnover taken in previous periods).

Step 3.   Calculate the cost of sales on the contract for the period.

	£
Total contract costs × percentage complete	X
Less any costs charged in previous periods	(X)
	X
Add foreseeable losses in full (not previously charged)	X
Cost of sales on contract for the period	X

Step 4.   **Deduct** the full amount of **cost of sales** as calculated above (including any foreseeable loss) from work in progress at cost up to the total balance on the account. If the cost of sales transfer exceeds this balance, then show the excess as a provision for liabilities and charges or accrual.

Step 5.   Calculate **cumulative turnover** on the contract (the total turnover recorded in respect of the contract in the profit and loss accounts of all accounting periods since the inception of the contract). Compare this with total progress payments (payments on account) to date.

(a)   If turnover exceeds payments on account, an 'amount recoverable on contracts' is established and separately disclosed within debtors.

(b)   If payments on account exceed cumulative turnover then the excess is:

(i)   first deducted from any remaining balance on work in progress;
(ii)   then any remaining balance is disclosed within creditors.

2.12   SSAP 9 also states that, although 'amount recoverable on contracts' will not have the contractual status of a debtor in strict legal form, such a debtor may still be recorded under the normal accruals method. The main point is that such amounts should be realisable as an asset, whether classed as a debtor or an element of work in progress.

Problems with SSAP 9 and long-term contracts

2.13 Many commentators believe that the classification of a portion of long-term contract balances as debtors is **misleading and incorrect**. However, this treatment was required by CA 1985, to avoid the inclusion of attributable profit in work in progress.

2.14 SSAP 9 has also been criticised for '**scattering**' long-term contract balances around the balance sheet thus making it difficult for users of the financial statements to appreciate the full exposure of an entity to long-term contract activity. However, SSAP 9 is also seen by many as providing a comprehensive and consistent treatment.

2.15 In addition, SSAP 9 does not:

(a) specify exactly the amount to be recorded under turnover, or for attributable profit;
(b) define turnover and related costs;
(c) address capitalisation of interest on long-term capital borrowings.

Summary of accounting treatment

2.16 The accounting double entry for a long-term contract can therefore be described as follows.

(a) *During year*

(i) DEBIT   Contract account (WIP)
CREDIT   Cash/creditors
Being costs incurred

(ii) DEBIT   Trade debtors
CREDIT   Debtors: amounts recoverable on contracts
Being progress payments invoiced

(iii) DEBIT   Bank
CREDIT   Trade debtors
Being cash received

(b) *At year end*

(i) DEBIT   Debtors: amounts recoverable on contracts
CREDIT   Turnover (P&L a/c)
Being turnover recognised

(ii) DEBIT   Cost of sales (P&L a/c)
CREDIT   Contract account
Being costs matched against turnover

(iii) DEBIT   Provisions on long-term contracts (P&L a/c)
CREDIT   Provision for future losses (B/S)
Being a provision for future losses

2.17 The following summarises the accounting treatment for long-term contracts - **make sure that you understand it.**

Profit and loss account

(a) **Turnover and cost**

    (i)   Turnover and associated costs should be recorded in the profit and loss account 'as contract activity progresses'.

    (ii)   Include an 'appropriate proportion of total contract value as turnover' in the profit and loss account.

    (iii)   The costs incurred in reaching that stage of completion are matched with this turnover, resulting in the reporting of results which can be attributed to the proportion of work completed.

    (iv)   Turnover is the 'value of work carried out to date'.

(b) **Attributable profit**

    (i)   It must reflect the proportion of work carried out.

    (ii)   It should take into account any known inequalities in profitability in the various stages of a contract.

Balance sheet

(a) **Stocks**

	£
Costs to date	X
Less transfer to P & L a/c	(X)
	X
Less foreseeable losses	(X)
	X
Less payments on account in excess of turnover	(X)
WIP	X

(b) **Debtors**

	£
Cumulative turnover recognised	X
Less payments on account	X
Amount recoverable on contracts	X

(c) **Creditors.** If payments on account exceed both cumulative turnover and net WIP then the excess is taken to 'payments on account' in creditors.

(d) **Provisions.** To the extent foreseeable future losses exceed WIP, these losses must be provided for.

2.18   The question below is comprehensive and you should work through it *carefully*. Make sure that you are happy with the accounting treatment for each contract.

Question 2

	Contract 1 £'000	Contract 2 £'000	Contract 3 £'000	Contract 4 £'000	Contract 5 £'000
Total contract price	500	1,000	1,000	357	1,000
Cost incurred to date	110	510	450	250	50
Prudent estimate of costs to completion	269	355	471	197	980
Progress payments received and receivable	100	600	400	270	40
Percentage complete	29%	52%	38%	56%	5%

Required

Show the balance sheet and profit and loss account entries for each contract in turn.

Answer

CONTRACT 1

		£'000	£'000
DEBIT	Debtors: amounts recoverable on contracts	145	
CREDIT	Turnover (29% × 500)		145

Being proportion of total contract value recognised as turnover

DEBIT	Debtors: trade debtors	100	
CREDIT	Debtors: amounts recoverable on contracts		100

Being progress payments invoiced

DEBIT	Contract work-in-progress	110	
CREDIT	Cash/creditors		110

Being costs incurred to date

DEBIT	Cost of sales (29% × 379)	110	
CREDIT	Contract work-in-progress		110

*Being proportion of total costs matched against turnover resulting
in attributable profit of £35,000*

Amounts disclosed under the appropriate headings would be as follows.

Profit and loss account	£'000
Turnover	145
Cost of sales	110
Gross profit	35

Debtors: amount recoverable on contracts	
Included as turnover	145
Less payments on account	100
Debtors	45

Work-in-progress	£'000
Costs incurred to date	110
Less transfer to profit and loss account	110
Work in progress	nil

CONTRACT 2

		£'000	£'000
DEBIT	Debtors: amounts recoverable on contracts	520	
CREDIT	Turnover (52% × 1,000)		520

Being proportion of total contract value recognised as turnover

DEBIT	Debtors: trade debtors	600	
CREDIT	Debtors: amounts recoverable on contracts		600

Being payments invoiced

DEBIT	Contract work-in-progress	510	
CREDIT	Cash/creditors		510

Being costs incurred to date

DEBIT	Cost of sales (52% × 865)	450	
CREDIT	Contract work-in-progress		450

*Being proportion of total costs matched against turnover
resulting in attributable profit of £70,000*

As a result of the above entries, there is a credit balance on 'amounts recoverable on contracts' of £80,000, which represents the amount by which progress payments invoiced exceed the amount of turnover recognised.

Conversely, there is a remaining debit balance on contract work-in-progress of £60,000. SSAP 9 requires that the excess progress payments are first set off against the balance of work-in-progress and only to the extent they exceed this balance will they be included under creditors.

Thus, amounts disclosed under the appropriate headings would be as follows.

	£'000
Profit and loss account	
Turnover	520
Cost of sales	450
Gross profit	70
Debtors: amounts recoverable on contracts	
Included as turnover	520
Less payments on account	600
Excess payments on account: deduct from WIP first	(80)
Therefore, debtors	nil
Work in progress	
Costs incurred to date	510
Less transfer to profit and loss account	450
	60
Less excess payments on account (as above)	80
Include under creditors	(20)
Therefore, WIP	nil
Creditors: payments on account	20

CONTRACT 3

		£'000	£'000
DEBIT	Debtors: amounts recoverable on contracts	380	
CREDIT	Turnover (38% × 1,000)		380

Being proportion of total contract value recognised as turnover

		£'000	£'000
DEBIT	Debtors: trade debtors	400	
CREDIT	Debtors: amounts recoverable on contracts		400

Being payments invoiced

		£'000	£'000
DEBIT	Contract work-in-progress	450	
CREDIT	Cash/creditors		450

Being costs incurred to date

		£'000	£'000
DEBIT	Cost of sales (38% × 921)	350	
CREDIT	Contract work-in-progress		350

Being proportion of total costs matched against turnover
resulting in attributable profit of £30,000

In this case, there is a credit balance on 'amounts recoverable on contracts' and a debit balance of £100,000 on 'contract work-in-progress'. The excess payments on account should be set off against work-in-progress. Amounts disclosed under the appropriate headings would be as follows.

	£'000
Profit and loss account	
Turnover	380
Cost of sales	350
	30
Debtors: amounts recoverable on contracts	
Included as turnover	380
Less payments on account	400
Excess payments on account, deduct from WIP first	(20)
Therefore, debtors	nil
Work in progress	
Costs incurred to date	450
Less transfer to profit and loss account	350
	100
Less excess payments on account	20
WIP	80

CONTRACT 4

		£'000	£'000
DEBIT	Debtors: amounts recoverable on contracts	200	
CREDIT	Turnover (56% × 357)		200

Being proportion of total contract value recognised as turnover

DEBIT	Debtors: trade debtors	270	
CREDIT	Debtors: amounts recoverable on contract		270

Being progress payments invoiced

DEBIT	Contract work-in-progress	250	
CREDIT	Cash/creditors		250

Being costs incurred to date

DEBIT	Cost of sales (56% × 447)	250	
CREDIT	Contract work-in-progress		250

At this stage, a loss of £50,000 has been recognised in the profit
and loss account being turnover £200,000 less cost of sales £250,000.
Since the total foreseeable loss is £90,000, an *additional* provision of
£40,000 is required in accordance with the prudence concept.

DEBIT	Provision for losses (P/L)	40	
CREDIT	Provision for losses (B/S)		40

	£'000
Profit and loss account	
Turnover	200
Cost of sales	250
Gross loss	(50)
Additional provision for loss on contract	(40)
Operating loss	(90)
Debtors: amounts recoverable on contracts	
Included as turnover	200
Less payments on account	270
Excess payments on account, deduct from WIP	(70)
Therefore, debtors	nil
Work in progress	
Costs incurred to date	250
Less transfer to profit and loss account	250
	-
Less provision for foreseeable losses	40
	(40)
Less excess payments on account (as above)	(70)
	(110)
Therefore, WIP	nil

The remaining credit balance of £110,000 arises from two causes and will be classified as follows.

	£'000
Creditors: payments on account	70
Provision/accrual for losses	40

Note that under SSAP 9 the provision for losses is deducted from work in progress in priority to excess payments on account. This is a questionable approach and in this example makes no difference to the classification of the resultant credit balance. However, in the next example, Contract No 5, this 'order of set-off' does affect the classification.

CONTRACT 5

		£'000	£'000
DEBIT	Debtors: trade debtors	40	
CREDIT	Debtors: amounts recoverable on contracts		40

Being progress payments invoiced

BPP PUBLISHING

		£'000	£'000
DEBIT	Contract work-in-progress	50	
CREDIT	Cash/creditors		50

Note that due to the early stage of the contract no turnover and no cost of sales figures have been recognised. Since there is a foresee-able loss of £30,000, a provision for this amount must be set up.

		£'000	£'000
DEBIT	Provision for losses (P/L)	30	
CREDIT	Provision for losses (B/S)		30

The provision for losses is set off against the balance of work-in-progress. The (excess) payments on account are then offset against the remaining balance of work-in-progress. The resultant credit balance is classified as payments on account under creditors. The approach is shown below.

Profit and loss account	£'000
Turnover	-
Cost of sales	-
Gross profit	-
Provision for loss on contract	30
Operating loss	(30)

	£'000
Debtors: amounts recoverable on contracts	
Included as turnover	-
Less payments on account	40
Excess payments on account, deduct from WIP	(40)
Therefore, debtors	nil

Work in progress	£'000
Costs incurred to date	50
Less transfer to profit and loss account	-
	50
Less provision for foreseeable losses	30
	20
Less excess payments on account	40
	(20)
Therefore, WIP	nil

Creditors: payments on account	20

It is arguable whether the credit balance of £20,000 is caused by payments on account being received in advance of work done or by the provision for losses. However, the view is taken in the standard that the provision for losses should be set off against costs incurred to date first and then excess payments on account should be deducted. This has the effect in this example that the credit balance is classified as 'payments on account'.

Chapter roundup

- Many commentators believe that the classification of a portion of long-term contract balances as debtors is misleading and incorrect. SSAP 9 has also been criticised for 'scattering' long-term contract balances around the balance sheet thus making it difficult for users of the financial statements to appreciate the full exposure of an entity to long-term contract activity. SSAP 9 does fail to tackle some issues, but on they whole it is comprehensive and consistent.

- At this stage of your studies the most likely aspect of SSAP 9 to be examined is the valuation and disclosure of long-term contracts. You must be able to calculate all the balances to be included in accounts and to discuss the reasons for SSAP 9's provisions, along with alternative possibilities.

- However, don't overlook the SSAP 9 and CA 1985 provisions on valuation and disclosure of stocks and short-term work in progress. You should by now be very familiar with these. Perhaps the most likely exam topic in this area is the valuation of stocks at net realisable value, so learn the definitions of cost and NRV and the circumstances when NRV is to be used.

Quick quiz

1   What categories of stock are identified in the statutory accounts formats of CA 1985? (see para 1.3)

2   How does SSAP 9 define a long-term contract? (2.1)

3   How does the standard define the attributable profit of a long-term contract? (2.5)

4   What are the main problems with the provisions of SSAP 9 concerning long-term contracts? (2.13 - 2.15)

Question to try	Level	Marks	Time
5	Exam	54	30 mins
6	Introductory	n/a	n/a

BPP PUBLISHING

Chapter 6

TAXATION IN COMPANY ACCOUNTS

Chapter topic list		Syllabus reference	Ability required
1	SSAP 8 and SSAP 5	9(a)	Skill
2	SSAP 15 *Accounting for deferred tax*	9(a)	Skill
3	Current issues: ASB discussion paper and FRED 18	9(a)	Knowledge

Introduction

You have met **SSAP 8** *The treatment of taxation under the imputation system in the accounts of companies* and **SSAP 5** *Accounting for value added tax* before, as well as the relevant provisions of the Companies Act 1985.

Students often have great difficulty tackling questions on taxation, particularly **deferred taxation**. Consequently, although you have met **SSAP 15** before, we will examine it in full again here. You should work through this chapter very carefully.

The ASB has recently published a **discussion paper** on deferred tax, which is covered in depth in Section 3.

1 SSAP 8 AND SSAP 5 5/96

1.1 You have come across both of these standards before, so only an outline is given here.

Exam focus point
Changes to tax legislation mean that companies no longer pay ACT on dividends paid after 6 April 1999. **With effect from May 1999 ACT should be ignored in any question involving the impact of dividends. The recovery of unrelieved surplus ACT will not be examined in this paper.**

SSAP 8

1.2 SSAP 8 deals mainly with presentational issues regarding advance corporation tax (ACT). The SSAP will presumably be amended in due course to reflect the abolition of ACT; indeed this is what is proposed in the new FRED 18, discussed in Section 3.

1.3 The effect of this is that the dividend tax credit, a feature of past questions, no longer applies.

> ### Knowledge brought forward from Paper 5
>
> *SSAP 8*
>
> Companies pay CT at 30%, usually 9 months after the year end.
>
> - **P&L a/c disclosure**
>   - ° Tax charge, made up and disclosed as follows.
>
> | | |
> |---|---|
> | UK corporation tax (at X% on taxable profit) | X |
> | Under/over provision in previous years | X |
> | Transfer to/from deferred taxation account | X |
> | | X |
>
>   - ° Dividends paid/proposed
>   - ° Dividends received/receivable
> - **Balance sheet disclosure**
>   - ° Proposed dividend, net: under creditors due < 1 year

SSAP 5 *Accounting for value added tax*

1.4 SSAP 5 *Accounting for value added tax* is one of the most straightforward of all the SSAPs. A summary of the provisions is given here, but you should make sure you understand how VAT operates.

> ### Knowledge brought forward from Paper 5
>
> *SSAP 5 Accounting for VAT*
>
> - **Turnover** shown in the P&L account should exclude VAT on taxable outputs. If gross turnover must be shown, then the VAT included in that figure must also be shown as a deduction in arriving at the turnover exclusive of VAT.
> - **Irrecoverable VAT** allocated to fixed assets and other items separately disclosed should be included in their cost where material and practical.
> - The **net amount due to or from Customs & Excise** should be included in the total for creditors or debtors, and need not be separately disclosed.
> - **CA 1985** also requires disclosure of the cost of sales figure in the published accounts. This amount should exclude VAT on taxable inputs.

Companies Act 1985 requirements on accounting for tax

1.5 The CA 1985 requires that the 'tax on profit or loss on ordinary activities' is disclosed on the face of the **P&L account** or in a note to the accounts. In addition, the notes to the P&L account must state the amounts of the charge for:

(a) UK corporation tax (showing separately the amount, if greater, of UK corporation tax before any double taxation relief);

(b) UK income tax;

(c) non-UK taxation on profits, income and capital gains.

1.6 In the **balance sheet,** CA 1985 requires disclosure of the amount for creditors in respect of taxation and social security costs (no analysis is required between corporation tax, VAT, PAYE, NIC etc.). It also requires disclosure by note of the amount included in each category of debtor which falls due after more than one year (deferred assets). This may

include recoverable ACT. Finally, the Act requires separate disclosure of the provision for deferred taxation, as already required by SSAP 15. All movements on provisions must be disclosed by way of note.

1.7 CA 1985 also requires disclosure by note of the treatment for taxation purposes of amounts credited or debited to the revaluation reserve. CA 1985 allows any deferred tax provision relating to a **revaluation surplus or deficit** to be taken to the revaluation reserve.

2 SSAP 15 ACCOUNTING FOR DEFERRED TAX   5/96, 5/97, 5/99

2.1 You may already be aware from your studies of taxation that accounting profits and taxable profits are not the same. There are several reasons for this but they may conveniently be considered under two headings.

(a) **Permanent differences** arise because certain expenditure, such as entertainment of UK customers, is not allowed as a deduction for tax purposes although it is quite properly deducted in arriving at accounting profit. Similarly, certain income (such as UK dividend income) is not subject to corporation tax, although it forms part of accounting profit.

(b) **Timing differences** arise because certain items are included in the accounts of a period which is different from that in which they are dealt with for taxation purposes.

KEY TERM

Deferred taxation is the tax attributable to timing differences.   *(SSAP 15)*

2.2 Deferred taxation is therefore a means of ironing out the tax inequalities arising from timing differences.

(a) In years when **corporation tax is saved** by timing differences such as accelerated capital allowances, a charge for deferred taxation is made in the P&L account and a provision set up in the balance sheet.

(b) In years when **timing differences reverse**, because the depreciation charge exceeds the capital allowances available, a deferred tax credit is made in the P&L account and the balance sheet provision is reduced.

Deferred tax is the subject of SSAP 15 *Accounting for deferred tax* and we will now look at the detailed requirements of the standard.

2.3 You should be clear in your mind that the tax actually payable to the Inland Revenue is the **corporation tax liability**. The credit balance on the deferred taxation account represents an estimate of tax saved because of timing differences but expected ultimately to become payable when those differences reverse.

2.4 SSAP 15 identifies the main categories in which timing differences can occur.

(a) **Short-term timing differences.** These arise because taxable profits are calculated on a receipts and payments basis, whereas accounting profits are calculated on an accruals basis. For example, a company may have a general provision for bad debts in the financial accounts which is not allowable for tax purposes until it crystallise into specific bad debts

(b) **Accelerated capital allowances.** When new assets are purchased, capital allowances may be available against taxable profits which exceed the amount of depreciation chargeable on the assets in the financial accounts for the year of purchase. These will not be very large now, compared to when 100% first year allowances were given.

(c) **Revaluation surpluses on fixed assets** for which a taxation charge does not arise until the fixed assets are eventually realised.

(d) **Surpluses on disposals of fixed assets** which are subject to rollover relief.

2.5 Deferred taxation is therefore an accounting convention which is introduced in order to apply the accruals concept to income reporting where timing differences occur. However, **deferred tax assets** are not included in accounts as a rule, because it would not be prudent, given that the recovery of the tax is uncertain.

Basis of provision

2.6 A comprehensive tax allocation system would be one in which deferred taxation is computed for every instance of timing differences: **full provision**. For reasons which will be explained later, a comprehensive system of accounting for deferred tax has been rejected. The opposite extreme would be the **nil provision** approach, where only the tax payable in the period would be charged to that period.

2.7 SSAP 15 rejects both these approaches and prescribes a middle course, called **partial provision**.

> 'Tax deferred or accelerated by the effect of timing differences should be accounted for to the extent that it is probable that a liability or asset will crystallise. Tax deferred or accelerated by the effect of timing differences should not be accounted for to the extent that it is probable that a liability or asset will not crystallise.'

2.8 The **probability** that a liability or asset will crystallise should be assessed by the directors on the basis of **reasonable assumptions**. They should take into account all relevant information available up to the date on which they approve the financial statements, and also their intentions for the future. Ideally, financial projections of future plans should be made for a number (undefined) of years ahead. The directors' judgement should be exercised with prudence.

2.9 If a company predicts, for example, that capital expenditure will **continue at the same rate** for the foreseeable future, so that capital allowances and depreciation will remain at the same levels, then no originating or reversing differences of any significance to the continuing trend of the tax charge will arise and so no change to the provision for deferred tax need be made (unless there are other significant timing differences).

2.10 An illustration of the three different bases will now be given, concentrating on the most common and important timing difference, **accelerated capital allowances**. This difference arises because depreciation spreads the cost of an asset over its life but is not allowable for tax, whereas capital allowances may be concentrated in the early years of an asset's life. An asset may be written off for tax purposes years before it is written off for accounting purposes.

(*Note.* This question is based on the tax system prior to the 1984 Finance Act. It illustrates the important effect of 100% FYAs.)

Question

Cuthbert Ltd buys a machine for £100,000 in 19X1. It is to be depreciated evenly over four years, has no scrap value, and will attract a 100% FYA. The company plans to buy a similar machine in 19X4 and its long term plans are for general expansion. Corporation tax is assumed to be 50% and pre-tax profit can be assumed to be £90,000 per annum before adjustments for tax in years 19X1-19X3. In 19X4 it will be £210,000. Calculate the figures for deferred tax for the years 19X1 to 19X4, using the nil, full and partial provision bases.

Answer

Nil provision would give rise to the following figures.

	19X1	19X2	19X3	19X4
	£'000	£'000	£'000	£'000
Pre-tax profit	90	90	90	210
Add depreciation	25	25	25	50
Less FYA	(100)	0	0	(100)
Taxable profit	15	115	115	160
Tax payable (50%)	7.5	57.5	57.5	80
Deferred tax charge	-	-	-	-
Tax charge in P & L a/c	7.5	57.5	57.5	80

Full provision of deferred tax requires that at each year end the deferred tax account in the balance sheet contains full provision for tax on all timing differences to date, which are equal to the excess of FYAs claimed over depreciation charged. The deferred tax calculations are as follows.

	19X1	19X2	19X3	19X4
	£'000	£'000	£'000	£'000
WDV of machines (tax)	-	-	-	-
NBV of machines (accounts)	75	50	25	75
Excess of NBV over WDV	75	50	25	75
(= accelerated capital allowances)				
Deferred tax provision (total) needed, at 50%	37.5	25	12.5	37.5
Deferred tax charge/(credit) for the year	37.5	(12.5)	(12.5)	25
(= movement required on provision)				
Tax payable (as above)	7.5	57.5	57.5	80
Deferred tax charge/(credit)	37.5	(12.5)	(12.5)	25
Tax charge in P & L a/c	45.0	45.0	45.0	105
Deferred tax provision in balance sheet	37.5	25.0	12.5	37.5

Note. The deferred tax figures could also be found as follows.

	FYA	Depreciation	Difference	Deferred tax charge/(credit) (50% of difference)
	£'000	£'000	£'000	£'000
19X1	100	25	75	37.5
19X2	-	25	(25)	(12.5)
19X3	-	25	(25)	(12.5)
19X4	100	50	50	25

Partial provision of deferred tax would involve making provision only for reversing differences foreseen. These must therefore be analysed. The deferred tax calculations are as follows.

	FYA	Depreciation	Originating/ (reversing) difference
	£'000	£'000	£'000
19X1	100	25	75
19X2	-	25	(25)
19X3	-	25	(25)
19X4	100	50	50

At the end of 19X1 reversing differences (excess of depreciation over FYAs) are foreseen for 19X2 and 19X3; therefore provision is made for them ($50\% \times 50 = 25$). This provision will reverse during 19X2 and 19X3. No provision is made in 19X4 as general expansion is foreseen.

	19X1	19X2	19X3	19X4
	£'000	£'000	£'000	£'000
Tax payable (as above)	7.5	57.5	57.5	80
Deferred tax charge/(credit)	25.0	(12.5)	(12.5)	-
Tax charge in P & L a/c	32.5	45.0	45.0	80
Deferred tax provision in balance sheet	25.0	12.5		

Method of computation

2.11 Where the **corporation tax rate** fluctuates from one year to another (unlike in the earlier example) a problem arises in respect of the amount of deferred taxation to be credited to the profit and loss account in later years. The amount could be calculated using either of two methods.

(a) The **deferral method** assumes that the deferred tax account is an item of 'deferred tax relief' which is credited to profits in the years in which the timing differences are reversed. Therefore the tax effects of timing differences are calculated using tax rates current when the differences **arise**.

(b) The **liability method** assumes that the tax effects of timing differences should be regarded as amounts of tax ultimately due by or to the company. Therefore deferred tax provisions are calculated at the rate at which it is estimated that tax will be paid (or recovered) when the timing differences **reverse**.

2.12 The deferral method involves extensive record keeping because the timing differences on each individual capital asset must be held. In contrast, under the liability method, the total originating or reversing timing difference for the year is converted into a deferred tax amount at the current rate of tax (and if any change in the rate of tax has occurred in the year, only a single adjustment to the opening balance on the deferred tax account is required). SSAP 15 insists on the **liability method**, because it is consistent with the aim of partial provision, which is to provide the deferred tax which it is probable will be payable or recoverable.

2.13 The following diagram will help you when dealing with deferred tax.

BPP PUBLISHING

Summary: deferred tax under partial provision

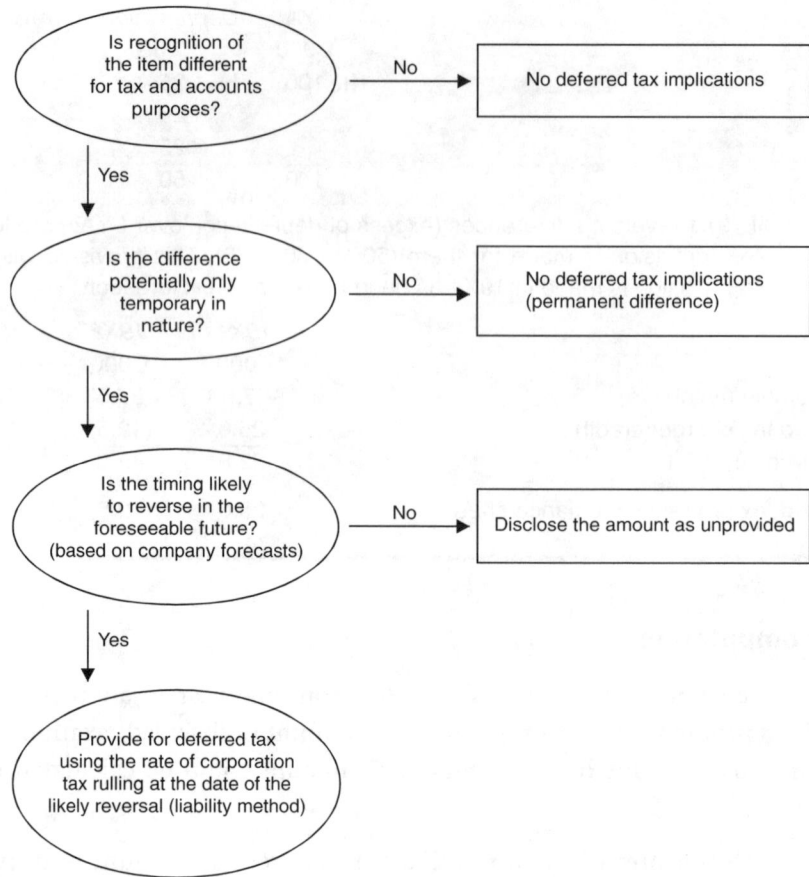

Standard accounting practice: deferred tax liabilities (credit balances)

2.14   A summary of the standard accounting practice is given here.

(a)   Deferred tax should be computed under the **liability method**.

(b)   Tax deferred or accelerated by the effect of timing differences should be accounted for to the extent that it is probable that a liability or asset will **crystallise**.

(c)   Tax deferred or accelerated by the effect of timing differences should not be accounted for to the extent that it is probable that a liability or asset will **not crystallise**.

(d)   The assessment of whether deferred tax liabilities or assets will or will not crystallise should be based upon **reasonable assumptions**.

(e)   The assumptions should take into account all **relevant information** available up to the date on which the financial statements are approved by the board of directors, and also the **intentions** of management. Ideally, this information will include financial plans or projections covering a period of years sufficient to enable an assessment to be made of the likely pattern of future tax liabilities. A prudent view should be taken in the assessment of whether a tax liability will crystallise, particularly where the financial plans or projections are susceptible to a high degree of uncertainty or are not fully developed for the appropriate period.

(f)   The provision for deferred tax liabilities should be reduced by any deferred tax **debit balances** arising from separate categories of timing differences and any **advance corporation tax** which is available for offset against liabilities.

1984 Finance Act

2.15 The 1984 Finance Act had a significant effect upon deferred tax calculations, changing not only the rates of corporation tax, but also the whole basis of the capital allowances system. There was a progressive reduction in the rates of corporation tax from 52% to 35% and first year allowances (previously 100%) on plant and machinery were phased out. Allowable capital expenditure now only qualifies for writing down allowances at 25% per annum on a reducing balance basis. The effect of the change in the allowances system was to reduce significantly the timing differences arising. This means that for many companies deferred tax became much less significant. The calculations above have been made based on the old 100% FYAs in order to give emphasis to the calculations. The same principles hold true under the current regime.

Deferred tax debit balances

2.16 While, in accordance with the accruals concept, debit deferred tax balances should be treated in the same way as credit balances, the concept of **prudence** requires that they should only be carried forward when there is a reasonable certainty of their recovery in future periods. The standard makes the point that most deferred tax net debit balances should not be carried forward as assets, except to the extent that they are expected to be **recoverable** without replacement by equivalent debit balances.

2.17 Debit deferred tax balances are most likely to arise from:

(a)   certain **short-term timing differences**, such as general bad debt and stock provisions;

(b)   **tax losses** (a special case, see below).

Tax losses

2.18 Deferred tax relating to **current trading losses** may be treated as recoverable when:

(a)   the loss results from an **identifiable** and **non-recurring cause**; *and*

(b)   the enterprise, or predecessor enterprise, has been **consistently profitable** over a considerable period, with any past losses being more than offset by income in subsequent periods; *and*

(c)   it is assured beyond reasonable doubt that **future taxable profits** will be sufficient to offset the current loss during the carry-forward period prescribed by tax legislation.

2.19 Deferred tax relating to **capital losses** may be treated as recoverable when:

(a)   a **potential chargeable gain** not expected to be covered by rollover relief is present in assets which have not been revalued in the financial statements to reflect that gain and which are not essential to the future operations of the enterprise; *and*

(b)   the enterprise has decided to **dispose of these assets** and thus realise the potential chargeable gain; *and*

(c)   the unrealised chargeable gain (after allowing for any possible loss in value before disposal) is sufficient to **offset the loss in question**, such that it is assured beyond reasonable doubt that a tax liability on the relevant portion of the chargeable gain will not crystallise.

2.20 A debit balance arising from one category of timing difference may be effectively carried forward by **setting it off** against a credit balance relating to another category. This process requires some care, however, and in particular:

(a) debits arising from **capital losses** should not normally be offset against credits arising from trading transactions as the law imposes restrictions limiting the extent to which capital losses may be offset against trading profits for tax purposes;

(b) debits and credits from **different trades** should not be offset unless there is reason to believe that the offset of the relevant reliefs and liabilities will be allowed at the time they crystallise (and see deferred tax and groups below).

2.21 Where losses *are* to be offset within the deferred tax account:

(a) **calculate the provision** required for other timing differences in the normal manner;

(b) **offset unrelieved trading losses** carried forward against the **appropriate elements** for the deferred tax balance in this provision.

The transfer to or from the P&L account in respect of deferred tax is the movement in this net balance.

2.22 EXAMPLE: TAX LOSSES

Petersen Ltd incurred a trading loss for taxation purposes of £2,000,000 for the accounting period ended 31 December 19X1. You may assume that the taxable profits, capital allowances and depreciation are expected to be as follows.

Year	Pre-tax profits £'000	Capital allowances £'000	Depreciation £'000
19X2	1,000	800	1,200
19X3	1,200	nil	1,400
19X4	3,000	600	1,500
Thereafter	Profit		Excess of capital allowances over depreciation

You may also assume that neither the trading loss nor capital allowances may be carried back and that the above forecasts, although uncertain at the time they were made, turn out to be accurate.

At 31 December 19X1, the company had claimed and utilised capital allowances that exceeded accumulated depreciation on the relevant assets by £2,700,000. At 31 December 19X0 there was no provision for deferred tax. Corporation tax is 33%.

You are required to show how the above will be reflected in the accounts of the company for the years 19X1 to 19X4.

2.23 SOLUTION

At 31 December 19X0 SSAP 15 requires that there should be a provision for deferred tax of £2,700,000 @ 33% = £891,000. Against this, however, may be set the trading loss of £2,000,000 @ 33% = £660,000. A net provision of £231,000 will, therefore, be required and this amount will constitute the whole of the taxation charge for the year ended 31 December 19X1.

	£'000	£'000
Corporation tax on results for the year @ 33%		nil
Transfer to deferred taxation account	891	
Offset of tax losses	660	
		231
Charge per profit and loss account		231

DEFERRED TAXATION ACCOUNT

		£'000			£'000
31.12.X1	P&L: trading losses offset	660	31.12.X1	P&L: accelerated	
	Balance c/f	231		capital allowances	891
		891			891

There will be no liability for corporation tax.

At 31 December 19X2, there will be a reversing timing difference of £400,000 (£1,200,000 – £800,000) on capital allowances. The net charge to the P&L account will be made up as follows.

	£'000
Corporation tax on profits for year (1,000 + 1,200 – 800 – losses (bal) 1,400)	nil
Transfer from deferred tax account re capital allowances (400 @ 33%)	(132)
Transfer from deferred tax account re losses utilised (1,400 @ 33%)	462
Charge per profit and loss account	330

The entries to the deferred tax account will be as follows.

DEFERRED TAXATION ACCOUNT

		£'000			£'000
31.12. X2	P&L: capital allowances	132	1.1.X2	Balance b/d	231
31.12. X2	Balance c/d	561	31.12.X2	P&L (trading loss utilised)	462
		693			693

The balance carried down of £561,000 comprises capital allowances £2,300,000 @ 33% = £759,000 net of unutilised losses £600,000 @ 33% = £198,000.

At 31 December 19X3, the reversing timing difference will be £1,400,000 on capital allowances. The net charge to the P&L account will be made up as follows.

	£'000
Corporation tax on profits for year (1,200 + 1,400 – losses 600*) @ 33%	660
Transfer from deferred tax account re capital allowances (1,400 @ 33%)	(462)
Transfer from deferred tax account re losses utilised (600 @ 33%)	198
Charge per profit and loss account	396
* Remainder of losses (2,000 – 1,400)	

The entries in the deferred taxation account will be:

DEFERRED TAXATION ACCOUNT

		£'000			£'000
31.12. X3	P&L: capital allowances	462	1.1.X3	Balance b/d	561
31.12. X3	Balance c/d	297	31.12.X3	P&L (trading loss utilised)	198
		759			759

At 31 December 19X4, the reversing timing difference will be £900,000 (£1,500,000 – £600,000). The net charge to the P&L account will be:

	£'000
Corporation tax on profits for the year (3,000 + 1,500 – 600) @ 33%	1,287
Transfer from deferred taxation account re capital allowances (900 @ 33%)	(297)
Charge per profit and loss account	990

The balance on the deferred tax account will be reduced to zero.

Groups and deferred tax

2.24 SSAP 15 makes the following points.

(a) Where a company is a member of a group, it should, in accounting for deferred tax, take account of any **group relief** which on reasonable evidence is expected to be

available and any charge which will be made for such relief. Assumptions made as to the availability of group relief and payment therefor should be stated.

(b) Deferred tax in respect of the remittance of **overseas earnings** should be accounted for in accordance with the provisions of this statement. Where deferred tax is not provided on earnings retained overseas, this should be stated.

2.25 The following points should be borne in mind when applying SSAP 15 to **group accounts**. (You may wish to return to this section after you have looked at group accounts later in this text.)

(a) There may be a need to consider making a provision for deferred tax when **intra group profits** are eliminated on consolidation (see example below).

(b) Provisions for deferred tax may need not be made because of the availability of **group relief**. For example, one company in a group may be foreseeing a reversal of timing differences which originated with accelerated capital allowances, whilst another expects to have trading losses for tax purposes, perhaps as a result of future capital allowances or stock relief. No liability may then arise because the second company will be able to surrender its losses to the first. The first company may not need to provide for deferred tax. This is acceptable although the following points should be considered.

(i) The management must be quite confident that suitable losses of sufficient amounts will arise in the appropriate accounting periods.

(ii) It must be legally possible for the group relief to be claimed.

(iii) The potential surrender of losses must be taken into account when considering the surrendering company's own deferred tax position.

(iv) Where the receiving company will be expected to pay for the losses, it may be necessary to provide for deferred tax (in whole or in part) as the payment for the relief will be equivalent to payment of the tax.

(c) **Offsetting debit and credit balances.** Some companies in a group may have potential debit deferred tax balances which are not carried forward in the accounts of the individual companies for reasons of prudence, whilst other companies have credit deferred tax balances. It may then be acceptable in the consolidated accounts to set up the debit balances and deduct them from the credit balances. This requires some care and should only be adopted when it is certain that the offset of the relevant relief and liabilities will be allowed at the time they crystallise.

2.26 EXAMPLE: DEFERRED TAX ON INTRA-GROUP TRANSACTIONS

Suppose that during the accounting period to 31 December 19X0, H Ltd sold some goods to its subsidiary, S Ltd, making a profit of £10,000. The goods were included in the trading stock of S Ltd at 31 December 19X0. The profit will be included in the taxable profits of H Ltd, for the year ended 31 December 19X0, but should be eliminated from the group P&L account. An adjustment may be made through the deferred tax account. If this was done what would the journal entry be?

2.27 SOLUTION

		£	£
DEBIT	Operating profit	10,000	
	Deferred tax account (@ 33%)	3,300	
CREDIT	Trading stock		10,000
	Deferred tax in P&L a/c		3,300

Whether the deferred tax account is actually debited will depend on the existence of a credit balance in respect of other timing differences or, in the absence of a credit balance, the degree of certainty that can be attached to the eventual realisation of the profit resulting from a sale to an outside customer.

Disclosure

2.28   SSAP 15 requires the following disclosure.

(a)   **Profit and loss account**

(i)   Deferred tax relating to the **ordinary activities** of the enterprise should be shown separately as part of the tax on profit or loss on ordinary activities, either on the face of the profit and loss account or in a note.

(ii)   Deferred tax relating to any **extraordinary items** (extremely rare) shown separately as part of the tax on extraordinary items either on the face of the P&L account or in a note.

(iii)   The amount of any **unprovided deferred tax** in respect of the period should be disclosed in a note, analysed into its major components.

(iv)   Adjustments to deferred tax arising from **changes in tax rates** and tax allowances should normally be disclosed separately as part of the tax charge for the period. SSAP 15 states that the effect of a change in the basis of taxation, or of a significant change in Government fiscal policy, should be treated as an extraordinary item where material. Under FRS 3, however, this is no longer possible.

(b)   **Balance sheet**

(i)   The **deferred tax balance**, and its major components, should be disclosed in the balance sheet or notes.

(ii)   **Transfers to and from** deferred tax should be disclosed in a note.

(iii)   Where amounts of deferred tax arise which relate to **movements on reserves** (for example resulting from the expected disposal of revalued assets) the amounts transferred to or from deferred tax should be shown separately as part of such movements.

(iv)   The total amount of any **unprovided deferred tax** should be disclosed in a note, analysed into its major components.

(v)   Where the **potential amount of deferred tax** on a revalued asset is not shown because the revaluation does not constitute a timing difference, the fact that it does not constitute a timing difference and that tax has therefore not been quantified should be stated.

(vi)   Where the **value of an asset** is shown in a note because it differs materially from its book amount, the note should also show the tax effects, if any, that would arise if the asset were realised at the balance sheet date at the noted value.

(c)   An **accounting policy note** is required, eg:

> '*Deferred tax* is calculated under the liability method and provision is made to the extent that it is considered probable a liability will crystallise. Deferred tax assets are not recognised in respect of provisions for post-retirement benefits.'

3   CURRENT ISSUES: ASB DISCUSSION PAPER AND FRED 18   5/97

Discussion paper

3.1   As mentioned above, there are various methods of accounting for deferred tax; SSAP 15 adopts the partial provision approach. SSAP 15 was singled out by the ASB as one of the standards most in need of review and in March 1995 a discussion paper, *Accounting for tax* was produced. This paper offers *very* tentative proposals for the **reform of deferred tax**, but it also offers a useful summary of the problems surrounding deferred tax.

Problems with SSAP 15

3.2   SSAP 15 is **conceptually inconsistent** with other standards in that it requires deferred tax to be recognised only where it is not expected to remain a permanent feature of the balance sheet. Other standards do not have this rule. For example, a liability for unfunded pension costs is recognised, even if it is never expected to reduce (because new liabilities will arise as old ones are settled). To deal with this inconsistency in the short term, the ASB issued *Amendment to SSAP 15* (see below) which allows deferred tax relating to post-employment benefits to be recognised in full. Without the amendment, companies would not normally be able to recognise the tax relief for post-employment benefits until these are actually paid. In the case of unfunded pensions, this may be decades after the costs are first recognised.

3.3   There are other disadvantages to SSAP 15, namely its inconsistency with **international practice** and the fact that it requires **estimation** of future transactions (which is against the *Statement of Principles,* see below).

The three different methods

3.4   The paper proposes that SSAP 15 should be replaced by a new FRS. It explores accounting for tax from first principles and discusses three methods - flow-through, full provision and partial provision - and **recommends adoption of full provision,** possibly modified by **discounting**. The paper emphasises that this is still a tentative position, offered as a basis for discussion rather than as a 'blueprint' for a future FRS.

3.5   Under the **flow-through method,** the tax liability recognised is the expected legal tax liability for the period (ie no provision is made for deferred tax). The main **advantages** of the method are that it is straightforward to apply and the tax liability recognised is closer to many people's idea of a 'real' liability than that recognised under either full or partial provision. The main **disadvantages** of flow-through are that it can lead to large fluctuations in the tax charge and that it does not allow tax relief for long-term liabilities to be recognised until those liabilities are settled. The method is not used internationally and the paper does not recommend its adoption.

3.6   The **full provision method** has the **advantage** that it is consistent with general international practice. It also recognises that each timing difference at the balance sheet date has an effect on future tax payments. If a company claims an accelerated capital allowance on an item of plant, future tax assessments will be bigger than they would have been otherwise. Future transactions may well affect those assessments still further, but that is not relevant in assessing the position at the balance sheet date. The **disadvantage** of full

provision is that, under certain types of tax system, it gives rise to large liabilities that may fall due only far in the future.

3.7   The **partial provision method** addresses this disadvantage by providing for deferred tax only to the extent that it is expected to be paid in the foreseeable future. This has an obvious intuitive appeal, but its effect is that deferred tax recognised at the balance sheet date includes the tax effects of future transactions that have not been recognised in the financial statements, and which the reporting company has neither undertaken nor even committed to undertake at that date. It is difficult to reconcile this with the ASB's draft *Statement of Principles*, which defines assets and liabilities as arising from past events.

3.8   As stated above, the discussion paper favours the full provision method. The apparent overstatement of the liability under the full provision method could be mitigated by **discounting**. The paper proposes that, for consistency, discounting deferred tax should be either required or prohibited, not merely permitted.

3.9   Whatever method is adopted must be reinforced by disclosure if it is to provide all the information that users of accounts require. Some new disclosures are proposed, in particular a reconciliation of the actual to the 'expected' tax charge (ie the profit before tax) multiplied by the UK corporation tax rate.

3.10   A FRED is awaited.

Deferred tax in practice

3.11   Although the moves discussed above towards full provision for deferred taxation have produced much adverse comment, it may not be as much cause for concern as first thought. Some companies, such as Shell and Unilever already provide in full on the basis of international harmonisation.

3.12   The UK is definitely 'out of sync' with international practice at present, but some would argue that the case for change has not yet been made.

- **Discounting** full provision liabilities may be unworkable.

- **Increases in deferred tax liabilities** from full provisioning will reduce distributable profits.

Exam focus point

You may be asked to discuss the different methods of providing for deferred tax, as happened in May 1997.

FRED 18 Current taxation

Exam focus point

Study this section only if you are taking the exam in May 2000 or later.

3.13   In June 1999 the ASB published FRED 18 *Current taxation*. A summary is given here.

3.14 The proposed accounting standard would replace the existing one, SSAP 8 *The treatment of taxation under the imputation system in the accounts of companies*, which was issued in 1974. In recent years there have been several changes to the UK tax system, notably the introduction in 1997 of restrictions on the reclaimability of tax credits and the **abolition in April this year of advance corporation tax**. As a result, the ASB has received approaches pressing for a review of SSAP 8. Of particular concern was the treatment of tax credits and withholding tax.

3.15 Under SSAP 8, **dividends received from UK companies** are at present required to be recognised in the profit and loss account with the addition of the tax credit. FRED 18 proposes that they should instead be included at the **net amount received**. The FRED distinguishes such dividends from other forms of income subject to a withholding tax, which would continue to be recognised by the recipient **before the deduction of withholding tax**. The FRED also invites comment on possible alternative treatments of tax credits and withholding taxes, under which both would be treated in the same way to reflect their similarity in economic effect.

3.16 Some had suggested that a **net-of-tax treatment** for dividends from UK companies should be applied only to dividends received after 5 April 1999, the date of the most recent changes to the tax credit. The FRED makes clear that its proposals would be applied from the start of an entity's financial year, thus avoiding a mixture of bases within the same accounting period.

3.17 The FRED also proposes to include in the new accounting standard the requirements of UITF Abstract 16 *Income and expenses subject to non-standard rates of tax* and to withdraw the abstract.

Chapter roundup

- You have met **SSAP 8** and **SSAP 5** before and should be familiar with their contents. Note that ACT has been abolished, which greatly simplifies matters.

- **SSAP 15** lays down complex provisions on calculating deferred tax. It is essential that you can both calculate a deferred tax balance and subsequent transfers to and from it, discuss critically the bases of your calculations, and describe the alternatives not permitted by the SSAP. Important aspects include the following.

  o Nil/full/partial provision
  o Deferral/liability methods
  o The treatment of tax losses and other debit balances
  o Group aspects

  It is not enough simply to learn the rules, however, you must have a sound understanding of the **principles** upon which deferred tax is based.

- You should be able to comment, though only in general terms, on the **ASB's new proposals** for deferred tax.

- You need a general overview of **FRED 18** which proposes to amend SSAP 8 to reflect, amongst other things, the **abolition of ACT**.

Quick quiz

1 Distinguish between permanent differences and timing differences. (see para 2.1)

2 Describe the three bases under which deferred tax can be computed: the nil provision basis, full provision basis and partial provision basis. (2.6, 2.7)

3 Describe the two methods under which deferred tax can be computed: the deferral method and the liability method. (2.11)

4 Which basis and method does SSAP 15 require to be used? (2.12)

5 Under what three circumstances are deferred tax debit balances likely to arise? (2.16)

6 When can deferred tax related to current trading losses be treated as recoverable? (2.18)

7 Describe the net basis and the nil basis for calculating earnings in an EPS calculation. (2.31)

8 What approach to deferred tax is suggested by the ASB's discussion paper? (3.4, 3.6)

9 What change would FRED 18 make to SSAP 8?

Question to try	Level	Marks	Time
7	Introductory	n/a	n/a

BPP PUBLISHING

Chapter 7

ACCOUNTING FOR PENSION COSTS

Chapter topic	Syllabus reference	Ability required
1 The nature of pension rights and costs	9(a)	Application
2 SSAP 24 *Accounting for pension costs*	9(a)	Application
3 Over- and under-funded schemes	9(a)	Application
4 ASB discussion papers	9(a)	Application

Introduction

An increasing number of companies now provide a **pension** as part of their employees' remuneration package. In view of this trend, it was important to standardise best practice for the way in which pension costs are **recognised and disclosed** in the accounts of sponsoring companies, and the way in which pension schemes themselves draw up sets of accounts. These are two completely separate issues, which are the subject of two different accounting publications. SORP 1 *Pension scheme accounts* covers the contents and format of pension scheme accounts (see Chapter 1). Accounting for pension costs affects the generality of companies, and so the accounting standard SSAP 24 *Accounting for pension costs* was issued.

The ASB has issued **discussion papers** on pension costs, in order to deal with some of the problems with SSAP 24, and these are discussed in Section 4.

1   THE NATURE OF PENSION RIGHTS AND COSTS

1.1   Before we look at SSAP 24, and to be absolutely clear as to how a pension scheme operates, let us examine a scheme in very simple terms. Consider the diagram below.

KEY TERM

A **pension scheme** is an arrangement (other than accident insurance) to provide pension and/or other benefits for members on leaving service or retiring and, after a member's death, for his/her dependants.   *(SSAP 24)*

1.2   The basic roles of the participants are as follows.

(a)   The **trustees** administer the scheme and safeguard its assets.

(b)   The **company** pays over both its own contributions and, in practice, those of its employees (if they are required to contribute), deducted from their salaries.

(c)   The trustees invest the contributions with a **fund manager,** who in turn invests in the stock market or other assets for the scheme. The return is either reinvested or paid back to the scheme.

BPP PUBLISHING

(d) The scheme pays out **pensions to employees** who have reached retirement age and also pays **transfer values** to other funds when employees leave.

(e) If allowed, the company contributions might be **refunded** to the company when the scheme is in surplus. Alternatively, the company's future contributions may be cut to use up a surplus.

(f) The role of the **actuary** is very important. He or she is responsible for determining the future contributions required from the company, based on the value of the fund, expected rate of growth, profile of employees and so on.

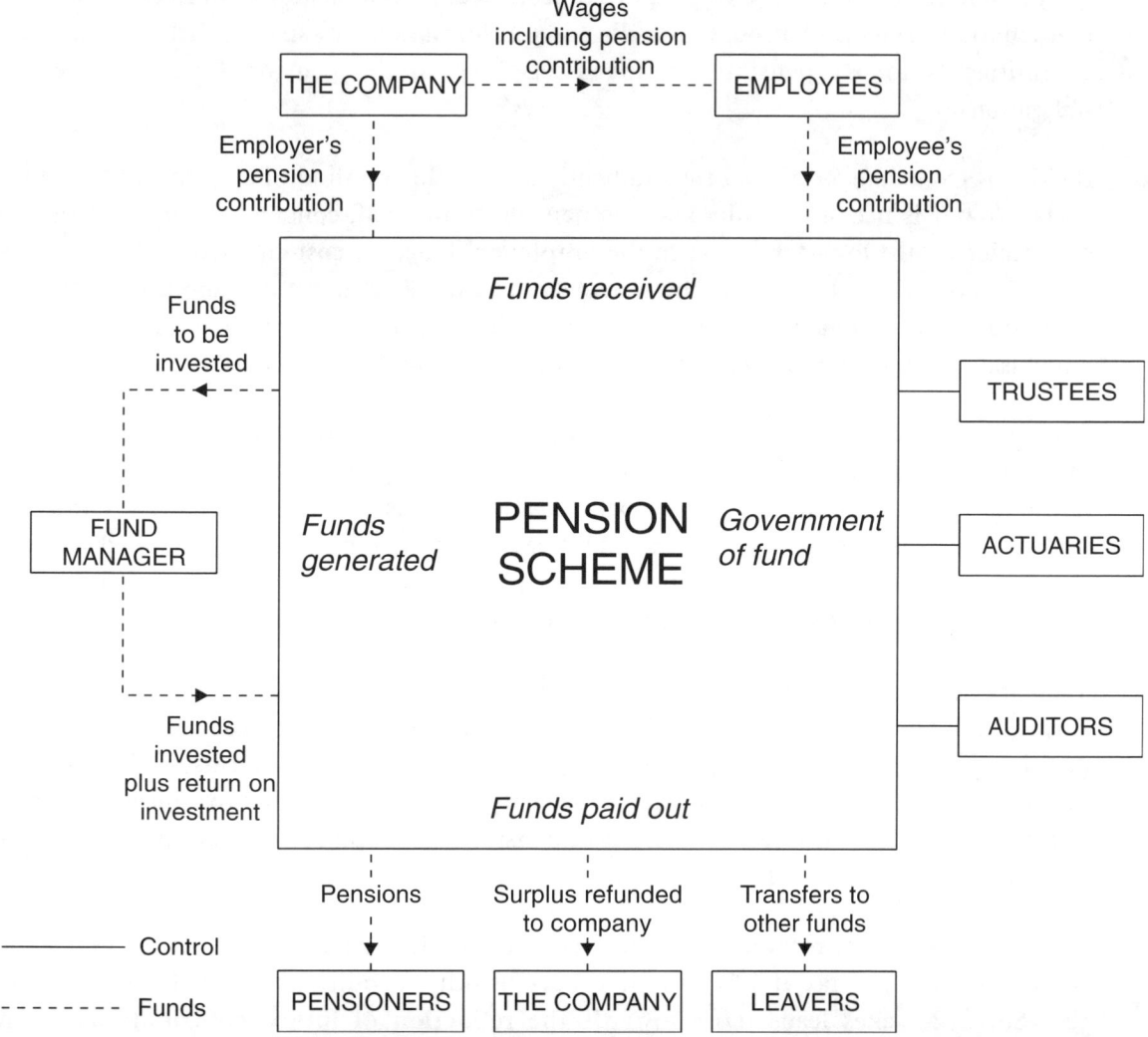

The conceptual nature of pension rights and costs

1.3 When a company employs a new worker and that worker is offered a chance to participate in the company's pension scheme, then the company is, in effect, saying that the contributions given by the employee and employer will secure an income in the future for the employee in the form of a **pension**.

1.4 The **cost of the pension** to the employer can be viewed in various ways. It could be described as a deferred salary to the employee. Alternatively, it is a deduction from the employee's true gross salary, used as a tax-efficient means of saving. The tax efficiency arises because the employer's contributions are not taxed on the employee, but they are a deduction from taxable profits for the employer. The income and capital gains made by the

BPP PUBLISHING

fund are tax free as well. It is only when the pension is received by the retired employee that the funds become taxable.

Accounting for pension costs

1.5 Accounting for pension costs is difficult. This is because of the **large amounts** involved, as well as the **long time scale, complicated estimates** and **uncertainty** surrounding the many assumptions which must be made. **Before SSAP 24,** the usual accounting practice was to charge the employer company's P&L account on the basis of the actual payments made to the pension fund. The company's reported profit was therefore subject to fluctuations as the contribution payments varied. Other disclosed information was sparse: little was said about commitments to pay pensions or any assets held in the pension funds to meet such obligations.

1.6 SSAP 24 *Accounting for pension costs* radically altered this method of accounting for pension costs. Now it is necessary to look at the pension fund itself, consider the state of the fund and decide on the **long-term cost to the employer.** Thus the cost charged in the accounts is based on actuarial valuations of the scheme and actuarial assumptions about its future. The standard requires changes in actuarial valuations to be recognised gradually, through amortisation, thus reducing the volatile effect of the yearly pension cost on profits.

1.7 The fundamental premise of SSAP 24 is that the pension fund is in effect a **vehicle of the employer company** and so any surplus on the fund represents an asset of the company (although it does not appear on the balance sheet). This is justified on the grounds that, under a final salary scheme, after the employee has made his or her fixed contribution, the company would have to make up any shortfall in the pension. If a shortfall (liability) belongs to the company, then an asset (surplus) should too.

1.8 This argument is certainly not accepted universally. Employees will often assert that any surplus belongs to them, the members of the scheme, on moral grounds. And the legal position may depend on the terms of the trust deed and the scheme itself. An additional problem was introduced by the Social Security Act 1990, which introduced mandatory requirements for the limited indexation of pensions, so surpluses in existing schemes must be used for indexation first.

1.9 Companies may take **refunds** from an over-funded scheme but it is difficult to do so, and there is a penalty of tax at 40% as well as various other conditions to satisfy. The approach that SSAP 24 takes leans more towards the **reduction of future contributions** when a pension is in surplus.

CA 1985 requirements

1.10 In the P&L account CA 1985 requires disclosure of staff costs showing separate totals for:

(a) wages and salaries;
(b) social security costs incurred by the company on behalf of employees;
(c) other pension costs so incurred.

Note that 'staff' includes directors.

1.11 The term 'pension costs' includes:

(a) contributions paid by the company to a pension fund or insurance company;
(b) amounts set aside to a provision for employee benefits;

(c) any amounts paid by the company in respect of pension payments without being set aside as under (b).

1.12 Particulars are also required of:

(a) any pension commitments included under any provision shown in the company's balance sheet; and

(b) any such commitment for which no provision has been made.

Further particulars are required of commitments relating to pensions payable to past directors of the company.

Directors' pensions

1.13 The requirements for the disclosure of directors' remuneration introduced by *The Company Accounts (Disclosure of Directors' Emoluments) Regulations 1997* have had an effect on the way amounts relating to directors' pensions are disclosed.

1.14 It is now generally accepted that, while contributions to money purchase schemes give a reasonable indication of the benefit to a director, contributions to defined benefit schemes may often not do so (these terms are defined below). CA 1985 now limits its disclosure requirements to the amount of company **contributions paid** or treated as paid to money purchase schemes, and the separate disclosure of the number of directors to whom **retirement benefits are accruing** under money purchase and under defined benefit schemes respectively. The only requirement that the Act now makes in respect of entitlement under defined benefit schemes relates to the disclosure of the highest paid director's emoluments.

1.15 If retirement benefits paid to or receivable by current or past directors are in **excess** of the ones they were entitled to when the benefits first became payable, or at 31 March 1997 (whichever is the later), the notes must disclose the aggregate of:

(a) the amount of the excess benefits paid to or receivable by **current** directors under pension schemes; and

(b) the amount of the excess benefits paid to or receivable by **past** directors, again under pension schemes.

2 SSAP 24 ACCOUNTING FOR PENSION COSTS   5/96

Types of scheme

2.1 SSAP 24 identifies the two usual forms of pension scheme.

> **KEY TERMS**
>
> - A **defined benefit scheme** is a pension scheme in which the rules specify the benefits to be paid and the scheme is financed accordingly.
>
> - A **defined contribution scheme** is a pension scheme in which the benefits are directly determined by the value of contributions paid in respect of each member. Normally the rate of contribution is specified in the rules of the scheme.
>
> *(SSAP 24)*

BPP PUBLISHING

(a) Under a **defined contribution scheme**, the employer will normally discharge his obligation by making agreed contributions to a pension scheme. The amount of pension ultimately payable to the employee is not guaranteed: it depends on the investment earnings of the funds contributed. Under this kind of scheme the cost to the employer is easily measured: it is simply the amount of the **contributions payable** in the period.

(b) Under a **defined benefit scheme** the eventual benefit payable to the employee is a predetermined amount, usually depending on the employee's salary immediately prior to retirement. In these circumstances it is impossible to be sure in advance that the regular contributions will generate a fund sufficient to provide the benefits. The employer may be obliged for legal reasons, or in the interests of maintaining good employee relations, to make good any deficiency in funding. This means that the **cost to the company is uncertain**.

Accounting objective

2.2 From the employer's point of view, a pension is part of the cost of obtaining an employee's services. The accounting objective is therefore that the employer should **recognise the cost** of providing a pension over the period during which he **derives benefit** from the employee's services. SSAP 24 deals with the method by which the allocation of this cost should be achieved. The standard is mainly concerned with defined benefit schemes because, as already mentioned, the cost of defined contribution schemes is easily established.

2.3 Defined benefit schemes usually make use of actuarial calculations to determine the pension cost to be charged each year. Most pension schemes undergo a **formal actuarial valuation** every three years, in which the actuary confirms that the present and future expected contribution levels are at least sufficient to provide for payment of the promised benefits. From his valuation, the actuary will recommend a **funding plan** to be followed by the company to enable future expected benefits to be paid.

2.4 The usual funding plan is a **level contribution rate**: a fixed proportion of each employee's pensionable pay is transferred to the pension scheme. In each case it is up to the **accountant** to confirm whether the actuary's funding plan is a satisfactory basis for allocating the pension costs to meet the accounting objective.

2.5 SSAP 24 does not attempt to specify a particular actuarial valuation method from the many in use, but it does require that the method selected should recognise the **effect of future increases** in earnings and in pensions where the employer has an expressed or implied commitment. The method selected should be **used consistently** and **disclosed**. In the very exceptional cases where there is a change of method the fact should be disclosed and the effect quantified.

Regular pension costs and variations from regular costs

2.6 SSAP 24 analyses the **total cost of pensions** in a year into two elements: regular costs and variations from regular cost.

> **KEY TERM**
>
> **Regular cost** is the consistent ongoing cost recognised under the actuarial method used.
>
> *(SSAP 24)*

2.7 **Variations from regular costs** may arise from revisions in the actuarial estimates of an employer's ultimate obligation; or from the retroactive effects of changes in assumptions, actuarial method, benefits or conditions for membership; or from increases to pensions currently being paid which have not previously been provided for.

2.8 The **regular cost** of pensions is adequately measured, in normal circumstances, by a **stable contribution rate** specified by an actuary and expressed as a percentage of pensionable earnings.

2.9 **Variations from regular costs** should normally be allocated over the **expected average remaining service lives of employees** in the scheme, unless prudence dictates that a shorter period should be used (see Section 3).

Disclosure requirements: defined contribution schemes

2.10 The following should be disclosed.

(a) Nature of the scheme (**defined contribution**)
(b) **Accounting policy**
(c) **Pension cost charge** for the period
(d) Any **outstanding or prepaid contributions** at the balance sheet date

Disclosure requirements: defined benefit scheme

2.11 The following disclosures should be made. Some of these will become clearer when you go through Section 3.

(a) Nature of scheme (**defined benefit**)

(b) Whether the scheme is **funded or unfunded**

(c) **Accounting policy** (and if different, funding policy)

(d) Whether the pension cost and liability (or asset) are assessed in accordance with the advice of a **professionally qualified actuary** and if so disclose:

(i) Date of most recent formal actuarial valuation or later review
(ii) If the actuary is an employee or officer of the company or group

(e) **Pension cost charge** for the period with explanations of significant changes from the previous period

(f) **Provisions or prepayments** (difference between costs recognised and funding amounts)

(g) Amount of **deficiency** on a current funding level basis, indicating the action, if any, being taken to deal with deficiency in the current and future financial statements

(h) Outline of results of most recent **formal actuarial valuation** or later review of funding of scheme on an ongoing basis:

(i) Actuarial method used and the main actuarial assumptions
(ii) Market value of scheme assets at the date of their valuation or review
(iii) Level of funding expressed in percentage terms
(iv) Comments on any material actuarial surplus or deficiency indicated by (iii)

(i) Expected effects on financial statements of commitments to make **additional payments** over a limited number of years

BPP PUBLISHING

(j)   Accounting treatment of a **refund** (which is subject to deduction of tax) where a credit appears in the financial statements in relation to it

(k)   Details of expected effects on future costs of any **material changes** in the group's and/or company's arrangements.

Effect of SSAP 24

2.12   SSAP 24 is orientated towards the **P&L account** rather than the balance sheet and seeks to even out the impact of pension contributions on earnings. As such, the asset or liability recorded in the balance sheet is a balancing figure, the cumulative difference between the P&L charge and the amount paid. It may be either a prepayment or an accrual, depending on whether contributions are in advance or arrears of 'cost' in P&L terms.

The balance can also be analysed as the combination of two figures:

(a)   the most recently reported **actuarial surplus or deficiency** in the fund (as adjusted for subsequent contributions and regular costs); and

(b)   the cumulative amount of **unamortised variations** awaiting recognition in the P&L account.

2.13   The **balance sheet disclosure** can cause some problems. Inclusion in accruals or prepayments has a great distorting effect on **performance ratios**, although full disclosure can be made by way of a note to provide proper figures for analysis. Another method used for disclosure is to show a prepayment separately from the rest of current assets, after the current asset sub-total.

2.14   Companies have also situated the pension fund prepayment or accrual *after* the net current assets figure. This is contrary to the Schedule 4 formats of CA 1985 and so a **true and fair override** is invoked. Other companies have included the prepayment as a fixed asset investment, but UITF Abstract 4 on long-term debtors held in current assets appears to clarify the situation: where long-term debtors in current assets are material then they should be disclosed separately on the face of the balance sheet, but still in current assets.

2.15   The standard's requirements on **measurement** are inevitably subjective because no single actuarial process is required and because actuarial calculations may themselves have an element of subjectivity. The standard's principal effect in achieving comparability between companies results from its extensive disclosure requirements.

UITF Abstract 6 *Accounting for post-retirement benefits other than pensions*

2.16   Abstract 6 gives guidance on both accounting treatment and disclosure. The UITF concluded that such benefits are liabilities that should be recognised in financial statements in accordance with the accruals and prudence concepts of SSAP 2 *Disclosure of accounting policies* and the Companies Act. The UITF also concluded that such benefits **share many of the characteristics** of pensions and that the principles of **SSAP 24** *Accounting for pensions costs* are **applicable.**

2.17   SSAP 24 has introduced, and UITF 6 will introduce in future, major changes in the way in which the long-term and somewhat uncertain obligations in respect of post-retirement benefits are treated. The obligations, particularly where they are not funded by a scheme financially independent of the company, carry very significant deferred tax implications.

UITF Abstract 18 - Pension costs following the 1997 tax changes in respect of dividend income

2.18 This abstract is concerned with the recognition in the financial statements of employers of the loss arising as a result of the Finance (No 2) Act 1997, whereby pension schemes are no longer able to reclaim a tax credit on dividend income. It states that this change to tax legislation does not, of itself, fall outside the normal scope of the actuarial assumptions as set out in paragraph 82 of SSAP 24 *Accounting for pension costs*. Hence, the **loss should be spread forward over the remaining service lives of current employees** in the scheme whatever the financial position of the scheme and regardless of any additional contributions that are made.

Pension costs and deferred tax

2.19 Wherever there are variations from regular cost, the total pensions paid in a given accounting period is unlikely to be the same as the amount charged to the P&L account. A **timing difference** arises because tax relief is given on the amount paid. The cumulative timing difference will be equivalent to the asset or liability in the balance sheet.

2.20 Deferred tax on pension costs is provided on a **full provision basis,** ie the amount of the timing difference is provided for in full irrespective of likely reversal in future accounting periods.

3   OVER- AND UNDER-FUNDED SCHEMES

3.1 As we have stated above, **defined contribution schemes** are simple to account for under SSAP 24. The employer has no obligation beyond payment of the contributions which he has agreed to make. The amount of these contributions defines the cost of providing pensions. Obviously, if the amount actually paid is less or more than that due, then an accrual or prepayment will be set up in the balance sheet, as for other expenses.

3.2 The accounting for **defined benefit schemes** is much more complicated since the employer's commitment is 'open-ended'. It is necessary to apply actuarial valuation techniques and a rather large number of assumptions must be made.

3.3 The **regular cost** must be determined and this is essentially the amount which the actuary would regard as a sufficient contribution to the scheme to provide the eventual pensions to be paid in respect of future service, provided present actuarial assumptions about the future were borne out in practice and there were no future changes in the terms of the scheme.

Variations from regular cost

3.4 SSAP 24 identifies **four** major categories of variations from regular cost.

   (a) **Experience surpluses or deficiencies** arise because the assumptions which were made at the time of the previous valuation have not been fully borne out by subsequent experience. They are discovered during an actuarial valuation.

   (b) The effects on the actuarial value of accrued benefits of **changes in actuarial assumptions** or method.

   (c) **Retroactive changes** in benefits or in conditions for membership.

   (d) **Increases to pensions** in payment or to deferred pensions for which provision has not previously been made.

3.5 As stated above, the **normal rule** will be to allocate the surplus or deficit over the average remaining service life of the current employees. There are some exceptions to this rule and these are explained below.

> ## KEY TERM
>
> The **average remaining service life** is a weighted average of the expected future service of the current members of the scheme up to their normal retirement dates or expected dates of earlier withdrawal or death in service.　　　　　*(SSAP 24)*

3.6 EXAMPLE: SPREADING TREATMENT

The actuarial valuation at 31 December 19X0 of the pension scheme of A Ltd showed a surplus of £260m. The actuary recommended that A Ltd eliminate the surplus by taking a contribution holiday in 19X1 and 19X2 and then paying contributions of £30m pa for eight years. After that the standard contribution would be £50m pa. The average remaining service life of employees in the scheme at 31 December 19X0 was 10 years. B Ltd's year end is 31 December.

3.7 SOLUTION

Assuming no change in circumstances, the annual charge in the P&L account for the years 19X1 to 19Y0 will be:

$$\text{Regular cost} - \frac{\text{Surplus}}{\text{Average remaining service life}} = £50m - \frac{£260m}{10} = £24m$$

The funding in these periods will be:

19X1 to X2	Nil
19X3 to Y0	£30m pa

The difference between the amounts funded and the amounts charged in the P&L account will be recognised as a provision as follows.

Year	Funded £m	Charged £m	(Provision) £m
19X1	-	24	(24)
19X2	-	24	(48)
19X3	30	24	(42)
19X4	30	24	(36)
19X5	30	24	(30)
19X6	30	24	(24)
19X7	30	24	(18)
19X8	30	24	(12)
19X9	30	24	(6)
19Y0	30	24	-

Subsequent actuarial valuations

3.8 Of course further actuarial valuations will occur during the 10 year period, probably every three years. A **new surplus or deficiency** may be discovered which requires adjustment to the charge and prepayment or provision in succeeding periods.

3.9 EXAMPLE: SUBSEQUENT ACTUARIAL VALUATION

Seringe plc prepares accounts to 31 December. On 1 January 19X6 an actuarial valuation of the company's defined benefit scheme revealed a surplus of £60m. At 31 December 19X5 there was an unamortised surplus of £18m from the previous actuarial valuation on 1 January 19X3. On both 1 January 19X3 and 19X6 the estimated remaining service lives of the employees covered by the scheme was 12 years. The actuary recommended a standard contribution of £30m in 19X3 and 19X6. How should the company account for the surplus in the year ended 31 December 19X6?

3.10 SOLUTION

It may appear at first sight that the company now has a surplus of £60m + £18m = £78m. This is not the case, however. The valuation on 1 January 19X3 anticipated a surplus at 1 January 19X6 of £24m calculated as:

$$\frac{£18m}{(12-3)\text{years}} \times 12 \text{ years} = £24m$$

because the company has maintained its normal contributions between 19X5 and 19X6. The new variation arising as a result of the actuarial valuation is therefore £60m – £24m = £36m.

As far as amortisation of both surpluses is concerned, they could *either*:

(a) be combined and amortised over 12 years; or
(b) £18m could be amortised over the remaining 9 years and £36m over 12 years.

Exceptions to the general spreading rule

3.11 SSAP 24 lists various exceptions to the general spreading rule.

Significant reduction in the number of employees: business segment closure

3.12 SSAP 24 (as revised by FRS 3) states that where a significant reduction in the number of employees is related to the sale or termination of an operation, the associated pension cost or credit should be **recognised immediately** to comply with the FRS 3. In all other cases where there is a significant reduction in employees, the reduction of contributions should be recognised as it occurs. The relevant part of FRS 3 states that:

> 'any consequential provision should reflect the extent to which obligations have been incurred that are not expected to be covered by the future profits of the operation or the disposal of its assets.'

3.13 This departure from the normal rule makes **common sense**. Why spread the effect over the working lives of remaining employees when it relates to those who have left?

3.14 The effect of these provisions of SSAP 24 and FRS 3 is that, in the case of the sale or termination of an operation, an entity must provide for the effects of that event, perhaps including the costs of redundancy programmes and so forth. If a variation of pension cost arises from such an event then it *appears* to be the case under the rules of FRS 3 that this should be **recognised as part of the overall effect of the closure**. It will therefore be taken into account in the year and this will be a departure from the normal spreading rule. The accounting effect is that the credit for the saving in pension costs can be offset against the exceptional provision for termination costs.

3.15 EXAMPLE: SIGNIFICANT REDUCTION IN THE NUMBER OF EMPLOYEES

The actuary advises that £50m out of the £260m surplus is attributable to the redundancy programme associated with the closure of a business segment which is treated as an exceptional item in 19X1. The accounting treatment in this instance will be to deal with this variation from regular cost immediately, as a credit to the exceptional cost of the closure, and to deal with the remaining £210m by amortising it over the working lives of the employees in the scheme.

3.16 SOLUTION

The effect of this amortisation on the amount charged will be as follows.

$$\text{Regular cost} - \frac{\text{Surplus}}{\text{Average remaining service life}} = £50m - \frac{£210m}{10} = £29m$$

The effect on the financial statements will therefore be as follows.

Year		Funded £m	Charged (Credited) £m	Prepayment (Provision) £m
19X1	ordinary charge	-	29	
	exceptional charge		(50)	
			(21)	21
19X2		-	29	(8)
19X3		30	29	(7)
19X4		30	29	(6)
19X5		30	29	(5)
19X6		30	29	(4)
19X7		30	29	(3)
19X8		30	29	(2)
19X9		30	29	(1)
19Y0		30	29	-

Significant reduction in the number of employees: no business segment closure

3.17   Reductions in the number of employees due to other reasons would be treated differently.

3.18 EXAMPLE: SIGNIFICANT REDUCTION/NO SEGMENT CLOSURE

The actuary advises that £50m out of a £260m surplus is attributable to a major redundancy programme occurring since the date of the last valuation. Accordingly the accounting treatment will be to deal with this variation from regular cost in line with the adjustments made to the funding programme, and deal with the remaining £210m by amortising it over the working lives of the employees in the scheme.

3.19 SOLUTION

The effect of this amortisation on the amount charged will again be as follows.

$$\text{Regular cost} - \frac{\text{Surplus}}{\text{Average remaining service life}} = £50m - \frac{£210m}{10} = £29m$$

However, it is still necessary to decide when to recognise the effect of the £50m which is attributable to the reduction of employees, because in reality the contributions have been

adjusted to eliminate the whole of the £260m surplus, not just the £50m. If the whole of the contribution holiday in the first year were designated as intended to deal with this part of the surplus, the effect would be as follows.

Year	Charged/ funded £m	Prepayment (Credited) £m	(Provision) £m
19X1	-	(21)	21
19X2	-	29	(8)
19X3	30	29	(7)
19X4	30	29	(6)
19X5	30	29	(7)
19X6	30	29	(8)
19X7	30	29	(3)
19X8	30	29	(2)
19X9	30	29	(1)
19Y0	30	29	-

3.20 The credit in 19X1 is calculated in the same way as in the example above, although the whole effect is shown as part of the ordinary pension cost in this case. In fact, the result is the same as in that example only because the contribution holiday in 19X1 is large enough to deal with the whole amount of the surplus arising from withdrawals.

3.21 This produces a rather **extreme and perhaps unfair result**. It would be possible to arrive at different results by attributing the changes in the contribution rates to their underlying reasons in a different way. For example, if the allocation were made in proportion to the changes in the contribution rate, the effect would be as follows.

Year	Funded £m	Charged £m	(Provision) £m
19X1	-	19.2	(19.2)
19X2	-	19.2	(38.4)
19X3	30	25.2	(33.6)
19X4	30	25.2	(28.8)
19X5	30	25.2	(24.0)
19X6	30	25.2	(19.2)
19X7	30	25.2	(14.4)
19X8	30	25.2	(9.6)
19X9	30	25.2	(4.8)
19Y0	30	25.2	-

3.22 The effect on the funding rate has been to reduce it by £50m in each of the first two years and by £20m in the remaining eight. Thus, the total surplus of £50m attributable to the redundancy programme has been apportioned over that period in the same way, to reduce the £29m charge (calculated as shown above) by £9.8m (50/260 × £50m, rounded up) in the first two years and by £3.8m (20/260 × £50m, rounded down) in the remaining eight years.

3.23 This seems to produce a more sensible and consistent charge, and may be regarded as preferable for that reason. Nevertheless either allocation, or indeed **any other reasoned allocation** would appear to be acceptable under the terms of the standard. After the first year, the difference between the two approaches is not very significant in terms of the profit and loss account, but the effect on the balance sheet remains quite different for some time.

Refunds subject to tax

3.24 Where a company receives a refund from the scheme, subject to deduction of tax, then an exception is allowed to the normal spreading rule. This is governed by tax anti-avoidance rules. SSAP 24 states that, where such refunds are taken, the company *may* **credit the**

refund to income in the year of receipt, rather than spreading the effects of the variations which have given rise to the surplus forward. In simple terms, a cash basis is allowed for such a refund. Full disclosure is required of the treatment used.

Material deficits may be recognised over a shorter period

3.25 In very limited circumstances, the standard provides for a more prudent approach, allowing the costs of making good a material deficit to be recognised over a shorter period than that normally used for amortisation. This is only allowed where **significant additional contributions** have been required *and* where the deficiency has arisen from an **external event** outside the normal scope of actuarial assumptions. SSAP 24 gives as an example the major mismanagement of the fund's assets. Major fraud seems to fit the requirements, and this was the case with the Mirror Group Newspapers' pension fund post-Maxwell. Part of a very long note on the pension scheme in the group's 1991 accounts stated:

> 'On the above basis, the actuarial liabilities exceed the market value of assets by £192.9m representing a funding level of 37.8%. £4.0m of this amount has been included in operating costs in respect of the regular cost of benefits for 1991. Provision has been made for the balance of £188.9m by a charge to extraordinary (now exceptional) items, the net impact of which is reduced due to the deferred taxation benefits of £62.3m.'

Discretionary and ex-gratia pension increases and ex-gratia pensions

KEY TERM

An **ex gratia pension** or **discretionary** or **ex gratia increase** in a pension is one which the employer has no legal, contractual or implied commitment to provide. *(SSAP 24)*

3.26 SSAP 24 states that allowance should be made for pension increases of all kinds, including those where **no contractual obligation exists**. Any subsequent increase in pensions which are different from those previously assumed will give rise to variations to be treated as stated above. Where previous assumptions have not been made, SSAP 24 requires that the **full capitalised value** of these increases must be provided in the year in which they are made, except to the extent that they are covered by an existing surplus.

3.27 The effect of the above is that, if there is a surplus in the scheme at the time the increases are granted, then the cost can be 'spread forward' as a reduction of a variation which would otherwise have reduced future pension costs. If there is no such surplus, or the surplus is insufficient, then the cost must be charged against current profits. It appears that the offset can be applied only when the surplus is in fact applied to meet the cost of the award *and* the offset is only permitted against an **unrecognised surplus**. Even then, it will be necessary to reduce the future variations being released to the P&L account by an equivalent amount.

Question

The directors of Richelieu plc have received a report from their actuaries dealing with each of the company's two non-contributory pension schemes, based upon data at 1 January 19X7. Extracts from the report are as follows.

'Works' Scheme

The closure of the Buckingham division (a material business segment) in June 19X7 will require an immediate contribution of £2m to ensure that the assets of the Scheme are sufficient to cover the liabilities in respect of the accrued benefits of the former employees at that location.

Other assets of the Scheme were insufficient to cover the liabilities in respect of the prospective benefits for continuing employees. The extent of the deficiency was some £5.5m. It is recommended that one lump sum payment of £3m be made on 31 December 19X7 followed by a payment of £2.7m on 31 December 19X8, and that contribution thereafter be at the rate of £1m pa until 31 December 19Y5 and £800,000 pa thereafter.

The average age of the continuing employees is 50 years, their average retirement age is 61 years and benefits are determined by pensionable salary at date of retirement.

Staff Scheme

A surplus in respect of prospective benefits of £2.2m has been disclosed by the valuation partly due to changes in the actuarial assumptions. It is recommended that a contribution holiday be taken in 19X7 and 19X8 and thereafter that contribution be £400,000 pa to 31 December 19Y0 and £750,000 pa thereafter. The age profile of this scheme is similar to that of the Works Scheme. Benefits are determined by pensionable salary at date of retirement.'

Required

On the assumption that the actuaries' recommendations are accepted, calculate the amounts to be included with respect to the pension schemes in the P&L account and balance sheet of Richelieu plc for the year ending 31 December 19X7 in order to comply with the provisions of SSAP 24.

Answer

Profit and loss account (extracts)

Regular pension cost £(800,000 + 750,000)	£1,550,000
Variations from regular cost £(500,000 – 200,000)	£300,000
Exceptional charge	£2,000,000

Balance sheet (extract)

Prepayment £(1,700,000 – 550,000	£1,150,000

Workings

1   *Works Scheme*

	Funding	Accounting	Prepayment
	£'000	£'000	£'000
19X7	3,000	800 + 500	1,700
19X8	2,700	800 + 500	3,100
19X9	1,000	800 + 500	2,800
19Y0	1,000	800 + 500	2,500
19Y1	1,000	800 + 500	2,200
19Y2	1,000	800 + 500	1,900
19Y3	1,000	800 + 500	1,600
19Y4	1,000	800 + 500	1,300
19Y5	1,000	800 + 500	1,000
19Y6	800	800 + 500	500
19Y7	800	800 + 500	-

Variation from regular cost = £5,500,000/11 = £500,000.

2   *Staff Scheme*

	Funding £'000	Accounting £'000	Prepayment £'000
19X7	-	750 – 200	550
19X8	-	750 – 200	1,100
19X9	400	750 – 200	1,250
19Y0	400	750 – 200	1,400
19Y1	750	750 – 200	1,200
19Y2	750	750 – 200	1,000
19Y3	750	750 – 200	800
19Y4	750	750 – 200	600
19Y5	750	750 – 200	400
19Y6	750	750 – 200	200
19Y7	750	750 – 200	-

Variation from regular cost = £2,200,000/11 = £200,000.

3.28   You should find the following summary diagram very useful.

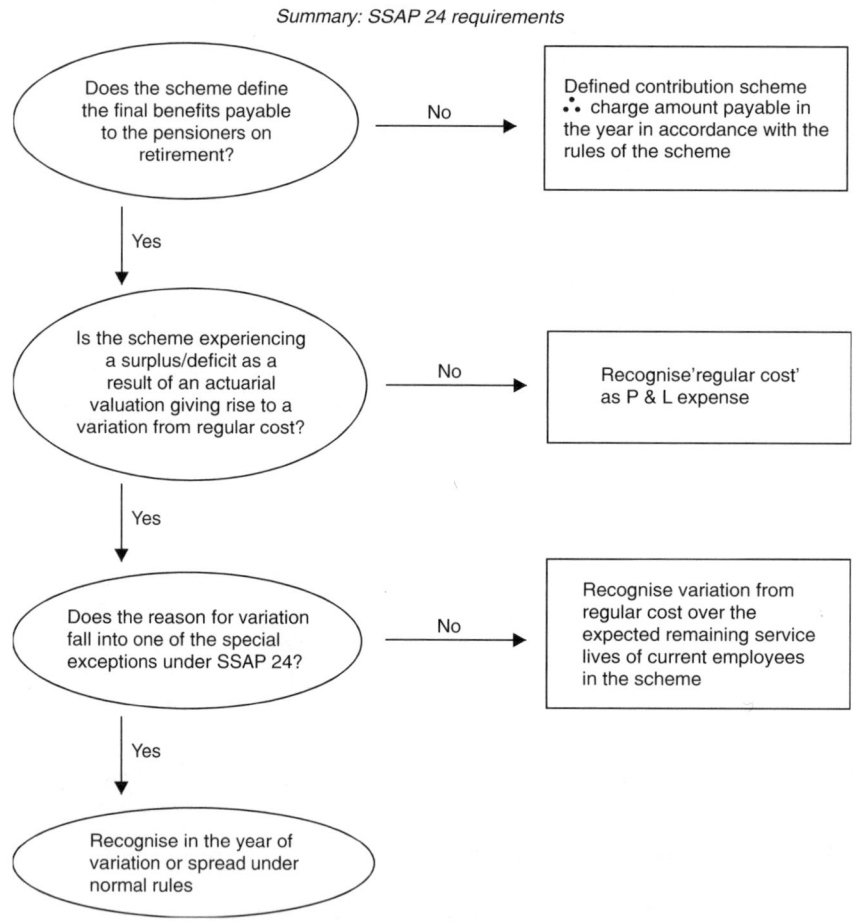

Summary: SSAP 24 requirements

Exam focus point
Questions could take the form of a discuss or a computation.

4   ASB DISCUSSION PAPERS

4.1   SSAP 24 has been **criticised** for two main reasons.

(a)   There is **too much scope** for employers to adjust the pension cost in the short term.

(b) The flexibility allowed by SSAP 24 is compounded by the fact that the **disclosure requirements** do not necessarily lead to an adequate explanation of the pension costs and related balances.

1995 Discussion Paper

4.2 To address the criticisms of existing practice, particularly in relation to accounting for final-salary defined benefit schemes, the ASB published a discussion paper *Pension costs in the employer's financial statements*, in June 1995. The ASB proposes a more **standardised approach** and **new disclosures**. As part of this review, the ASB examined current and developing international practice.

4.3 We discussed the difficulties associated with pension cost accounting in Section 1. The discussion paper rationalises the many choices into two approaches.

(a) The ASB's **chosen (actuarial) approach** would standardise practice following principles that are similar to SSAP 24.

(b) The **alternative (market-based) approach**, favoured by a minority of members of the ASB, would be to account for the obligation for pension benefits that exists now, based on current financial indicators such as market values of scheme investments.

Actuarial approach

4.4 The preferred actuarial approach includes the following proposals.

(a) An **accrued benefits actuarial method** should be used, which for a final salary scheme would mean the 'projected unit' method.

(b) The cost of real improvements to benefits for **former employees** should be accounted for in the year in which these awards are made.

(c) The cost of real improvements to benefits for **current employees** should be spread forward over their remaining service lives.

(d) An **experience surplus or deficiency** and the cost of past-service awards to current employees should be amortised on a straight-line basis.

4.5 The treatment of any changes in the surplus or deficiency is summarised by the paper as follows.

Cause of surplus or deficiency	Treatment in the gradual recognition approach
Measurement assumptions	
(a) Assumptions not fulfilled in practice (experience surpluses or deficiencies)	Recognise over future accounting periods as a component of a net pension cost in the P&L account
(b) Change in assumptions	
Changes in pension benefits	
(a) Real changes in benefits relating to past service of current employees (retroactive changes to benefits/a past service cost)	Recognise over future accounting periods as a component of a net pension cost in the P&L account

BPP PUBLISHING

Cause of surplus or deficiency	Treatment in the gradual recognition approach
(b) Real changes in benefits of former employees (a past service cost)	Immediately charge or credit to the P&L account the change in the liability resulting from these changes in pension benefits

4.6 The disclosures required by SSAP 24 can result in a **potentially confusing** array of information, some of which relates to pension cost, some to funding, and some to valuations assuming the scheme is wound up. Proposed new disclosures aim to explain more clearly the pension cost and how it has been determined. These specify the actuarial assumptions that should be disclosed and would require an **analysis of the pension cost or credit** into:

(a) normal pension cost;
(b) amortisation of the surplus;
(c) interest on the total recognised and unrecognised surplus or deficiency; and
(d) any post-service cost.

4.7 The paper also proposes there should be a **reconciliation** between the surplus or deficiency and the prepayment or liability for pensions in the balance sheet. This would also show the total of the scheme assets and liability for pension benefits at the balance sheet date. A further analysis would show the movements of the unrecognised surplus or deficiency.

4.8 The statement of total recognised gains and losses would include an item for the anticipated movements in the surplus or deficiency.

1998 Discussion paper

4.9 On 23 July the ASB published a Discussion Paper *Aspects of Accounting for Pension Costs*. The Discussion Paper comes at a time of far-ranging debates not only on the measurement of and accounting for pension costs but also on the more general issue of how financial performance should be presented.

4.10 The 1995 Paper and the comments received on its have provided the basis for the ASB's own project and also for the UK input to discussions in the International Accounting Standards Committee (IASC) which led, in March 1998, to the issue of a revised International Accounting Standard, IAS 19 *Employee benefits*.

Valuation of the assets

4.11 Most respondents to the 1995 Discussion Paper favoured preserving a traditional actuarial method of valuing the assets of a pension scheme by discounting their estimated future dividends at a long-term rate consistent with that used to discount the liabilities. IASC, however, came down firmly in favour of using market values, on the grounds that these gave the most objective and comparable information. Even in the UK many people now believe that the traditional method of discounting estimated future dividends will become increasingly subjective as companies use share buy-back schemes and other innovations, rather than dividends, as a means of providing a return to shareholders. **The Discussion Paper therefore proposes the use of market values as the basis of valuing scheme assets.**

The discount rate for the liabilities

4.12 A principal reason why the use of market values for pension scheme assets has been avoided in the UK is fear of the volatility that this could bring to the pension cost charged to the profit and loss account. However, the volatility of pension cost (often called 'actuarial gains and losses') is the result of the interaction of a number of factors. The Discussion Paper suggests that much of the volatility can be mitigated by the use of an **appropriate discount rate** in valuing the liabilities.

4.13 It opposes the rate adopted in IAS 19 (the rate on high quality, fixed rate corporate bonds or government bonds) and looks to the actuarial profession for guidance on appropriate rates for different classes of a liability. In particular, it expects that pensions based on final pay would be discounted at a rate that includes some element of expected equity return.

Accounting for actuarial gains and losses

4.14 Whatever methods are used to value the pension scheme assets and liabilities, it is inevitable that actuarial gains and losses, which in some cases can be very substantial, will occur, as actual experience departs from what had been assumed and as changes are made to actuarial assumptions. The Discussion Paper sets out arguments for and against each of four possible methods of treatment of actuarial gains and losses in the accounts.

   (a) The existing method required by SSAP 24 of amortisation over the average remaining service lives of employees (usually 10-15 years).

   (b) Charge in full to the profit and loss account, as the gain or loss arises, immediately below the level of operating profit.

   (c) Charge in full to the statement of total recognised gains and losses as the gain or loss arises.

   (d) Charge in full to the statement of total recognised gains and losses as the gain or loss arises but amortise from there to the profit and loss account over the average remaining service lives of employees.

Past service costs

4.15 Past service costs arise when improvements to benefits are awarded usually to current rather than past employees. For past employees such costs do not include the common adjustments to benefit in response to changes in the cost of living but only changes in the terms, such as extension of a pension to a spouse or dependants.

4.16 The Discussion Paper indicates that the majority ASB view favours **charging all past service costs to the profit and loss account when the improved benefits are awarded.** Two other possibilities on which views are sought are:

   (a) to recognise past service costs relating to former employees immediately and spread forward those relating to current employees; and

   (b) to offset past service costs against any surplus funding them and recognise as a cost only any excess amount.

Chapter roundup

- **Company pension schemes** have become more and more important as supplements to or replacements for the state pension, as a means of support after retirement. With an increasingly large pensioned population, the importance of this topic can only increase.

- **SSAP 24** is not an easy standard to follow.

  - Learn the SSAP 24 **disclosures** and **definitions**

  - Make sure that you understand the SSAP 24 **calculations**

  - You should be able to deal with an **experience surplus/deficit**.

  - Remember the treatments for those events which **provide exceptions to the general spreading rule**

- You should understand the **ASB's draft proposals on pension costs**.

Quick quiz

1 What does the actuary to a pension scheme do? (see para 1.2(f))

2 To whom does the surplus on a pension scheme belong? (1.7, 1.8)

3 What is the accounting objective in relation to pension costs in company accounts? (2.2)

4 What four major categories of variations from regular costs are identified by SSAP 24? (3.4)

5 How should a surplus arising on a subsequent actuarial valuation be treated? (3.9, 3.10)

6 What is the SSAP 24 required treatment for a variation due to a significant reduction in the number of employees and closure of a business segment? (3.12 - 3.18)

7 What is the more prudent approach allowed for material deficits as an alternative to amortisation? (3.27)

8 How should ESOP Trusts be accounted for and disclosed in the statements of the sponsoring company? (3.37)

9 What are the two approaches to accounting for pension costs given in the ASB's 1995 discussion paper? (4.4)

Question to try	Level	Marks	Time
8	Exam	25	45 mins

Chapter 8

OFF BALANCE SHEET FINANCE

Chapter topic	Syllabus reference	Ability required
1 Off balance sheet finance explained	9(a)	Application
2 Substance over form	9(a)	Application
3 FRS 5 *Reporting the substance of transactions*	9(a)	Application
4 Common forms of off balance sheet finance	9(a)	Application
5 Creative accounting	9(a)	Application

Introduction

This is a very topical area and there have been several recent examination questions involving FRS, so you must work through it carefully. Students with practical experience will have the advantage in thinking up or recognising examples of creative accounting.

There are important links between FRS 5 and **FRS 2** *Accounting for subsidiary undertakings* (Chapter 12), **FRS 3** *Reporting financial performance* (Chapters 2 and 22), and **SSAP 21** *Accounting for leases and hire purchase contracts* (Chapter 10).

1   OFF BALANCE SHEET FINANCE EXPLAINED

> **KEY TERM**
>
> **Off balance sheet finance** is the funding or refinancing of a company's operations in such a way that, under legal requirements and existing accounting conventions, some or all of the finance may not be shown on its balance sheet.

1.1 'Off balance sheet transactions' are transactions which meet the above objective. These transactions may involve the **removal of assets** from the balance sheet, as well as liabilities, and they are likely to have a significant impact on the P&L account.

Why off balance sheet finance exists

1.2 Why might company managers wish to enter into such transactions?

   (a) In the UK, companies have traditionally had a lower level of gearing than companies in other countries. Off balance sheet finance is used to **keep gearing low,** probably because of the views of some analysts and brokers.

   (b) A company may need to keep its gearing down in order to stay within the terms of **loan covenants** imposed by lenders.

BPP PUBLISHING

(c) A listed company with high borrowings is often expected (by analysts and others) to declare a **rights issue** in order to reduce gearing. This has an adverse effect on a company's share price and so off balance sheet financing is used to reduce gearing *and* the expectation of a rights issue.

(d) Analysts' short term views are a problem for companies **developing assets** which are not producing income during the development stage. Such companies will match the borrowings associated with such developing assets, along with the assets themselves, off balance sheet. They are brought back on balance sheet once income is being generated by the assets. This process keeps return on capital employed higher than it would have been during the development stage.

(e) Groups of companies have excluded **subsidiaries** from consolidation in an off balance sheet transaction because they carry out completely different types of business and have different characteristics. The usual example is a leasing company (in say a retail group) which has a high level of gearing.

Other examples are given in 4.1 below.

1.3 You can see from this brief list of reasons that the overriding motivation is to avoid **misinterpretation**. In other words, the company does not trust the analysts or other users to understand the reasons for a transaction and so avoids any effect such transactions might have by taking them off balance sheet. Unfortunately, the position of the company is then misstated and the user of the accounts is misled.

1.4 You must understand that not all forms of 'off balance sheet finance' are undertaken for cosmetic or accounting reasons. Some transactions are carried out to **limit or isolate risk**, to reduce interest costs and so on. In other words, these transactions are in the best interests of the company, not merely a cosmetic repackaging of figures which would normally appear in the balance sheet. Also, not all off balance sheet financing schemes derive from an intention to mislead. There may be genuine reasons for exclusion.

The off balance sheet finance problem

1.5 The result of the use of increasingly sophisticated off balance sheet finance transactions is a situation where the users of financial statements do not have a proper or clear view of the **state of the company's affairs**. The disclosures required by company law and accounting standards did not in the past provide sufficient rules for disclosure of off balance sheet finance transactions and so very little of the true nature of the transaction was exposed.

1.6 Whatever the purpose of such transactions, **insufficient disclosure** creates a problem. This problem has been debated over the years by the accountancy profession and other interested parties and some progress has been made (see the later sections of this chapter).

1.7 The main argument used for disallowing off balance sheet finance is that the true **substance** of the transactions should be shown, not merely the **legal form**, particularly when it is exacerbated by poor disclosure.

2   SUBSTANCE OVER FORM

KEY TERM

Substance over form: transactions and other events should be accounted for and presented in accordance with their substance and financial reality and not merely with their legal form.   *(IAS 1)*

2.1   This is a very important concept and, although it was not used directly by the ASC, it has been used to **determine accounting treatment** in financial statements through accounting standards and so prevent off balance sheet transactions. The following paragraphs give examples of where the principle of substance over form is enforced, particularly in accounting standards.

SSAP 21 *Accounting for leases and hire purchase* contracts

2.2   In SSAP 21, as we will see in the next chapter, there is an explicit requirement that if the lessor transfers substantially all the **risks and rewards of ownership** to the lessee then, even though the legal title has not passed, the item being leased should be shown as an asset in the balance sheet of the lessee and the amount due to the lessor should be shown as a liability.

FRS 8 *Related party disclosures*

2.3   FRS 8 requires financial statements to disclose fully material transactions undertaken with a related party by the reporting entity, **regardless of any price charged** (see Chapter 11).

SSAP 9 *Stocks and long-term contracts*

2.4   In SSAP 9 there is a requirement to account for **attributable profits** on long-term contracts under the accruals convention. However, there may be a problem with realisation, since it is arguable whether we should account for profit which, although attributable to the work done, may not have yet been invoiced to the customer. It is argued that the convention of substance over form is applied to justify ignoring the strict legal position.

FRS 2 *Accounting for subsidiary undertakings*

2.5   This is perhaps the most important area of off balance sheet finance which has been prevented by the application of the **substance over form** concept. The use of quasi-subsidiaries was very common in the 1980s.

KEY TERM

A **quasi-subsidiary** of a reporting entity is a company, trust, partnership or other vehicle that, though not fulfilling the definition of a subsidiary, is directly or indirectly controlled by the reporting entity and gives rise to benefits for that entity that are in substance no different from those that would arise were the vehicle a subsidiary. *(FRS 5)*

2.6   The main off balance sheet transactions involving quasi-subsidiaries were as follows.

(a) **Sale of assets.** The sale of assets to a quasi-subsidiary was carried out to remove the associated borrowings from the balance sheet and so reduce gearing; or perhaps so that the company could credit a profit in such a transaction. The asset could then be rented back to the vendor company under an operating lease (no capitalisation required by the lessee).

(b) **Purchase of companies or assets.** One reason for such a purchase through a quasi-subsidiary is if the acquired entity is expected to make losses in the near future. Post-acquisition losses can be avoided by postponing the date of acquisition to the date the holding company acquires the purchase from the quasi-subsidiary.

(c) **Business activities conducted outside the group.** Such a subsidiary might have been excluded through a quasi-subsidiary or not consolidated under the 'dissimilar activities' requirement in FRS 2. Exclusion from consolidation might be undertaken because the activities are high risk and have high gearing.

2.7 CA 1989 introduced a new definition of a subsidiary based on **control** rather than just ownership rights and this definition (along with other related matters) was incorporated into FRS 2, thus substantially reducing the effectiveness of this method of off-balance sheet finance (see Chapter 12). FRS 5 defines control of another entity as:

KEY TERM

Control of another entity is the ability to direct the financial and operating policies of that entity with a view to gaining economic benefit from its activities. *(FRS 5)*

2.8 The definition states that a subsidiary undertaking is one in which:

(a) the parent has a **majority of the voting rights**; *or*

(b) the parent is a member and can appoint or remove a **majority of the board**; *or*

(c) the parent is a member and controls voting rights **by agreement** with other members; *or*

(d) the parent can direct the operating and financial policies through the **memorandum and articles** or a **control contract**; *or*

(e) the parent has a **participating interest** and either exercises a **dominant influence** or manages both companies on a **unified basis**.

2.9 The main effects of this new definition on the use of quasi-subsidiaries were as follows.

(a) The use of 'voting rights' rather than 'equity shares' prevents the use of **company structures** which give the benefits of ownership to one class of shareholder without the appearance of doing so, eg a company has 100 'A' shares with 10 votes each and 900 'B' shares with one vote each.

(b) The right to appoint or remove a majority of the board now means those directors who control a majority of the voting rights at board meetings. This prevents control through **differential voting rights** at board meetings.

(c) The most important change is the introduction of the terms **participating interest** and **actual exercise of dominant influence**.

KEY TERMS

- A **participating interest** is an interest held by an undertaking in the shares of another undertaking which it holds on a long-term basis for the purpose of securing a contribution to its activities by the exercise of control or influence arising from or related to that interest.

  (a) A holding of 20% or more of the shares of an undertaking shall be presumed to be a participating interest unless the contrary is shown.

  (b) An interest in shares includes an interest which is convertible into an interest in shares, and includes an option to acquire shares or any interest which is convertible into shares.

  (c) An interest held on behalf of an undertaking shall be treated as held by that undertaking.

- The **actual exercise of dominant influence** is the exercise of an influence that achieves the result that the operating and financial polices of the undertaking influenced are set in accordance with the wishes of the holder of the influence and for the holder's benefit whether or not those wishes are explicit. The actual exercise of dominant influence is identified by its effect in practice rather than by the way in which it is exercised.

  (FRS 2)

2.10 CA 1989 and FRS 2 have curtailed drastically the use of quasi-subsidiaries for off balance sheet finance. More complex schemes are likely to be curtailed by FRS 5 *Reporting the substance of transactions* (see below).

FRS 9 Associates and joint ventures

2.11 FRS 9 is considered in Chapter 17. The aspect which is relevant to substance over form is the required treatment for joint arrangements which are not entities . The section of the standard dealing with such arrangements is headed 'a structure with the form but not the substance of a joint venture'. Such structures are **not** to be accounted for as joint ventures.

2.12 You may also hear the term **creative accounting** used in the context of reporting the substance of transactions. This can be defined simply as the manipulation of figures for a desired result. Remember, however, that it is very rare for a company, its directors or employees to manipulate results for the purpose of fraud. The major consideration is usually the effect the results will have on the company's share price. Some areas open to abuse (although some of these loopholes have been closed) are given below and you should by now understand how these can distort a company results.

  (a) Income recognition and cut-off
  (b) Use of merger accounting
  (c) Treatment of purchased goodwill
  (d) Manipulation of reserves
  (e) Exceptional/extraordinary items
  (f) Revaluations and depreciation
  (g) Window dressing
  (h) Changes in accounting policy

Question 1

Creative accounting, off balance sheet finance and related matters (in particular how ratio analysis can be used to discover these practices) often come up in articles in, for example, the *Financial Times* and *The Economist*. Find a library, preferably a good technical library, which can provide you with copies of back issues of such newspapers or journals and look for articles on creative accounting. In particular, you might look at three articles in the April and May 1998 editions of the *CIMA Student*. The first two look at the *techniques* of creative accounting, which you should know about. The third examines in depth the *motivation* behind it - all is not as it seems.

3   FRS 5 REPORTING THE SUBSTANCE OF TRANSACTIONS   11/97, 11/98

3.1   There has been a long debate on this issue, with two ASC exposure drafts and an ASB FRED leading up to FRS 5. There is also a major overlap with the *Statement of Principles,* Chapter 4 of which defines assets and liabilities and also lays out criteria for their recognition and derecognition in the financial statements. Those matters will be discussed in Chapter 22 in the section on the *Statement of Principles* and they are almost exactly the same as in FRS 5.

FRS 5 *Reporting the substance of transactions*

3.2   FRS 5 *Reporting the substance of transactions* is a daunting document, running to well over 100 pages, although the standard section itself is relatively short. The overriding principle of FRS 5 is that transactions should be accounted for according to their **substance rather than their legal form**, as we discussed above.

3.3   As stated in Chapter 3 of the *Statement of Principles*, accounting for items according to substance and economic reality and not merely legal form is a key determinant of reliable information.

   (a)   For the majority of transactions there is **no difference** between the two and therefore no issue.

   (b)   For other transactions **substance and form diverge** and the choice of treatment can give different results due to non-recognition of an asset or liability even though benefits or obligations result.

   FRS 5 makes clear that full disclosure is not enough: all transactions must be **accounted for** correctly, with full disclosure of related details as necessary to give the user of accounts a full understanding of the transactions.

Scope and exclusions

3.4   FRS 5 applies to all entities whose accounts are intended to give a true and fair view, with **no exemptions** for any particular type or size of companies. However, it **excludes a number of transactions** from its scope, unless they are part of a larger series of transactions that is within the scope of the standard. These exclusions are mainly financing transactions which the ASB will consider separately, such as forward contracts and futures, foreign exchange and interest rate swaps etc. Employment contracts are also excluded.

Relationship to other standards

3.5   The interaction of FRS 5 **with other standards and statutory requirements** is also an important issue; whichever rules are the more specific should be applied. Leasing provides

a good example (as we will see in the next chapter): straightforward leases which fall squarely within the terms of SSAP 21 should continue to be accounted for without any need to refer to FRS 5, but where their terms are more complex, or the lease is only one element in a larger series of transactions, then FRS 5 comes into play. In addition, the standard requires that its general principle of substance over form should apply in the application of other existing rules.

Basic principles

3.6 As stated above, FRS 5's fundamental principle is that the substance of an entity's transactions should be reflected in its accounts. The key considerations are whether a transaction has **given rise to new assets and liabilities**, and whether it has **changed any existing assets and liabilities**.

3.7 The characteristics of transactions whose substance is not readily apparent are as follows.

(a) The **legal title** to an item is separated from the ability to enjoy the principal benefits, and the exposure to the main risks associated with it.

(b) The transaction is **linked to one or more others** so that the commercial effect of the transaction cannot be understood without reference to the complete series.

(c) The transaction includes **one or more options**, under such terms that it makes it highly likely that the option(s) will be exercised.

Definitions of assets and liabilities

> **KEY TERMS**
>
> - **Assets** are rights or other access to future economic benefits controlled by an entity as a result of past transactions or events.
>
> - **Liabilities** are an entity's obligations to transfer economic benefits as a result of past transactions or events.   *(FRS 5)*

3.8 Identification of **who has the risks** relating to an asset will generally indicate **who has the benefits** and hence **who has the asset**. If an entity is, in certain circumstances unable to avoid an **outflow of benefits**, this will provide evidence that it has a liability. The various risks and benefits relating to particular assets and liabilities are discussed in the application notes (see Section 4). Other important definitions are given by the standard in relation to assets and liabilities.

> **KEY TERMS**
>
> - **Control in the context of an asset** is the ability to obtain the future economic benefits relating to an asset and to restrict the access of others to those benefits.
>
> - **Risk** is uncertainty as to the amount of benefits. The term includes both potential for gain and exposure to loss.   *(FRS 5)*

Recognition

> ### KEY TERM
>
> **Recognition** is the process of incorporating an item into the primary financial statements with the appropriate headings. It involves depiction of the items in words and by a monetary amount and inclusion of that amount in the statement totals. *(FRS 5)*

3.9   The next key question is deciding **when** something which satisfies the definition of an asset or liability has to be recognised in the balance sheet. The standard seeks to answer this by saying that:

> 'where a transaction results in an item that meets the definition of an asset or liability, that item should be recognised in the balance sheet if:
>
> (a)   there is sufficient evidence of the existence of the item (including, where appropriate, evidence that a future inflow or outflow of benefit will occur), and
>
> (b)   the item can be measured at a monetary amount with sufficient reliability.'

Derecognition

3.10   As the name suggests, derecognition is the opposite of recognition. It concerns the question of when to **remove from the balance sheet** the assets and liabilities which have previously been recognised. FRS 5 addresses this issue only in relation to assets, not liabilities, and its rules are designed to determine one of three outcomes.

(a)   **Complete derecognition**
(b)   **No derecognition**
(c)   The in-between case, **partial derecognition**

3.11   The issue of derecognition is perhaps one of the most common aspects of off balance sheet transactions: **has an asset been sold or has it been used to secure borrowings**? The concept of partial derecognition and attempts to deal with the in-between situation of where sufficient benefits and risks have been transferred to warrant at least some derecognition of an asset.

Complete derecognition

3.12   In the simplest case, where a transaction results in the transfer to another party of all the **significant benefits and risks** relating to an asset, the entire asset should cease to be recognised. In this context, the word 'significant' is explained further: it should not be judged in relation to all the conceivable benefits and risks that could exist, but only in relation to those that are **likely to occur in practice**. This means that the importance of the risk retained must be assessed in relation to the magnitude of the total realistic risk which exists.

No derecognition

3.13   At the other end of the spectrum, where a transaction results in **no significant change** to the benefits or to the risks relating to the asset in question, no sale can be recorded and the entire asset should continue to be recognised. Retaining **either** the benefits or the risks is sufficient to keep the asset on the balance sheet. This means that the elimination of risk by financing the asset on a **non-recourse basis** (ie finance secured only on the asset in question) will not remove it from the balance sheet; it would be necessary to dispose of the

upside as well in order to justify recording a sale. A further possible treatment, the special case of a 'linked presentation', is discussed below.

3.14 The standard says that any transaction that is **in substance a financing** will not qualify for derecognition; the item will therefore stay on the balance sheet, and the finance will be introduced as a liability.

Partial derecognition

3.15 As can be seen, the above criteria are relatively restrictive. The standard therefore goes on to deal with circumstances where, although not all significant benefits and risks have been transferred, the transaction is more than a mere financing and has transferred enough of the benefits and risks to warrant at least some derecognition of the asset. It addresses three such cases.

(a) **Where an asset has been subdivided**

Where an identifiable part of an asset is separated and sold off, with the remainder being retained, the asset should be split and a partial sale recorded. Examples include the sale of a proportionate part of a loan receivable, where all future receipts are shared equally between the parties, or the stripping of interest payments from the principal of a loan instrument.

(b) **Where an item is sold for less than its full life**

The seller retains a residual value risk by offering to buy the asset back at a predetermined price at a later stage in the asset's life. Such an arrangement is sometimes offered in relation to commercial vehicles, aircraft, and so on. In such cases the original asset will have been replaced by a residual interest in the asset together with a liability for its obligation to pay the repurchase price.

(c) **Where an item is transferred for its full life but some risk or benefit is retained**

This may arise, for example, where a company gives a warranty or residual value guarantee in relation to the product being sold. This does not prevent the recording of the sale so long as the exposure under the warranty or guarantee can be assessed and provided for if necessary. Companies may also sometimes retain the possibility of an upward adjustment to the sale price of an asset based on its future performance, eg when a business is sold subject to an earn-out clause, but again this should not prevent the recognition of the sale.

3.16 In all of these cases of partial disposals, the amount of the initial profit or loss may be **uncertain**. The normal rules of prudence should be applied, but also that the uncertainty should be disclosed if it could have a material effect on the accounts.

Linked presentation

3.17 A 'linked presentation' requires **non-recourse finance** to be shown on the face of the balance sheet as a deduction from the asset to which it relates (rather than in the liabilities section of the balance sheet), provided certain **stringent criteria** are met. This is really a question of how, rather than whether, to show the asset and liability in the balance sheet, so it is not the same as derecognition of these items, although there are some similarities in the result.

3.18 Linked presentation should be used when an asset is financed in such a way that:

BPP PUBLISHING

(a) the finance will be repaid only from **proceeds generated by the specific item** it finances and there is no possibility whatsoever of a claim on the entity being established other than against funds generated by that item; *and*

(b) there is no provision whereby the entity may either **keep the item** on repayment of the finance or **reacquire** it at any time.

There are also several more specific conditions which elaborate on these principles.

3.19 An obvious example where linked presentation applies is when **debts are factored**. Debt factoring is discussed in more detail in the next section, but in simplified terms such a transaction would appear as follows.

Current assets	£'000
Debtors	500
Less non-returnable amounts received on sale of debtor	(425)
	75

In this case 85% of the debtor balances are received on a non-returnable basis.

Question 2

The managing director of your company has read an article about FRS 5 relating to linked presentation. The company is seeking to structure a financing of its head office in such a way that the asset and the funding could be 'linked' on the balance sheet.

As the company's finance director, draft a reply to the managing director, stating whether this treatment is possible.

Answer

The 'linked presentation' is a layout that shows the amount of borrowing or proceeds raised that has been deducted from the original asset amount, on the assets side of the balance sheet. It was developed in response to the ASB's difficulties in settling an appropriate accounting treatment for securitisations, but the criteria for its use are expressed in general terms; it is not reserved solely for securitisations.

Nevertheless, the provisions of FRS 5 relating to linked presentation are drawn extremely strictly. And even though companies should in general interpret FRS 5 in terms of its spirit and reasoning, the ASB's intention in the case of linked presentation was to limit its application by requiring the criteria to be met 'to the letter' before a linked presentation could be adopted.

It is a question of fact whether the proposed financial transaction meets the criteria in FRS 5, although, apart from some securitisations and factoring arrangements, the transactions it does apply to are likely to be very rare. The main criteria are that the finance that is shown as linked should be non-recourse, ie secured only on the asset in question, and that the company must not keep the asset when the finance is paid off, or reacquire it at any time.

In this case, the transaction is unlikely to be effective, as presumably the company will want to continue to use its head office after the finance is repaid.

Offset

3.20 FRS 5 makes it clear that assets and liabilities which qualify for recognition should be accounted for individually, rather than netted off. Offset is allowed by the standard only where the debit and credit balances are **not really separate assets and liabilities**, eg where there are amounts due to and from the same third party and there is a legal right of set-off. The key consideration is whether the entity can **enforce** a right of set-off so that there is no possibility of having to pay the creditor balance without recovering the debtor amount.

3.21 The detailed criteria which permit offset and **all of which must apply** are set out in FRS.

(a) The parties owe each other **determinable monetary amounts**, denominated either in the same currency or in different but freely convertible currencies.

(b) The reporting entity has the ability to insist on a **net settlement**, which can be enforced in all situations of default by the other party.

(c) The reporting entity's ability to insist on a net settlement is **assured beyond doubt**. This means that the debit balance must be receivable no later than the credit balance requires to be paid, otherwise the entity could be required to pay the other party and later find that it was unable to obtain payment itself. It also means that the ability to insist on a net settlement would survive the insolvency of the other party (which may require detailed examination in group situations).

Consolidation of other entities

3.22 As we saw in Section 2, the Companies Act and FRS 2 definition of a 'subsidiary undertaking' means that the consolidation of other entities is based largely on *de facto* control. FRS 5 takes the view that this is not conclusive in determining which entities are to be included in consolidated accounts. It envisages that there will be occasions where the need to give a true and fair view will require the inclusion of **quasi-subsidiaries** as defined above.

3.23 The key feature of this definition is **control**, which means the ability to direct the vehicle's financial and operating policies with a view to gaining economic benefit from its activities. Control is also indicated by the ability to prevent others from exercising those policies or from enjoying the benefits of the vehicle's net assets. A 'deadlock' 50:50 **joint venture** will still be off balance sheet for both parties, provided the two parties concerned are genuine equals in terms of both their ability to control the venture and their interests in its underlying assets.

3.24 FRS 5 requires that when quasi subsidiaries are included in consolidated accounts, the fact of their inclusion should be **disclosed**, together with a summary of their own financial statements.

Disclosure

3.25 FRS 5 has a general requirement to disclose transactions in sufficient detail to enable the reader to understand their **commercial effect**, whether or not they have given rise to the recognition of assets and liabilities. This means that where transactions or schemes give rise to assets and liabilities which are *not* recognised in the accounts, disclosure of their nature and effects still has to be considered in order to ensure that the accounts give a true and fair view.

3.26 A second general principle is that an explanation should be given where there are any assets or liabilities whose **nature is different** from that which the reader might expect of assets or liabilities appearing in the accounts under that description. There are specific disclosures in relation to the use of the linked presentation, the inclusion of quasi-subsidiaries in the accounts, and the various transactions dealt with in the application notes (see below).

Question 3

Explain the proposed accounting treatment and disclosure requirements for off balance sheet finance.

Answer

In the past neither accounting standards nor company law provided fully effective means for outlawing all off balance sheet practices either by specifying an accounting treatment or by adequate disclosure. Some may consider that the requirement for accounts to provide a true and fair view implies that disclosure is required of the existence and financial effect of, say, a controlled non-subsidiary. On the other hand, it was common practice to rely on the letter of the law to avoid this.

The ASB (carrying on the work of the ASC) has strengthened the principle of 'substance over form' by introducing new definitions of assets and liabilities that require recognition of most forms of off balance sheet financing. FRS 5 requires recognition of the true economic and commercial effects of such transactions regardless of the form that they take.

In addition, individual laws or standards outlaw specific practices. For example, the 1989 Companies Act, which implements the EC 7th Directive on consolidated accounts, amended the Companies Act 1985 so that it now applies tests regarding control over, rather than ownership of another company to determine whether or not it should be consolidated. This deals with the above situation, where control is exercised even in the absence of majority ownership. These changes were incorporated into SSAP 1 and FRS 2 by the ASB.

These moves indicate that there is decreasing sympathy in the accounting profession and in the business community for off balance sheet financing. Thus, we can expect the auditors to take a firmer line on this topic than in the past and the investment community and the financial press pay more attention to it.

Exam focus point

Examination questions to date have asked for calculations, accounting treatment and disclosure for a variety of transactions, including sale and leaseback transactions and debt factoring agreements. A question on FRS 5 has been combined with one on FRS 4 (see Chapter 9). Question practice in this area is very worthwhile.

Private finance initiative

3.27 In 1999 the ASB published a new *Application Note to FRS 5 Reporting the substance of transactions*.

3.28 The accounting treatment of PFI has become the subject of much debate. To fulfil a PFI contract, a private sector 'operator' typically constructs a capital asset (eg a road, bridge, hospital, prison, computer system or school) and uses that asset to provide services to a public sector 'purchaser'. The key accounting question is:

- whether the purchaser has an asset of the property used to provide the contracted services together with a corresponding liability to pay the operator for it; or, alternatively

- whether the operator has an asset of the property used to provide the contracted services or a financial asset being a debt due from the purchaser.

3.29 FRS 5 has a two-stage test.

Stage 1: Exclude any separable elements of the contract that relate only to services (such as cleaning, laundry, catering etc), rather than to the capital asset. Any such **service** elements are not relevant to determining which party has the **asset** and should be ignored.

Stage 2: Assess what remains to see if the leasing standard (SSAP 21) or FRS 5 should be applied.

Accounting treatment for the recognition of assets and liabilities

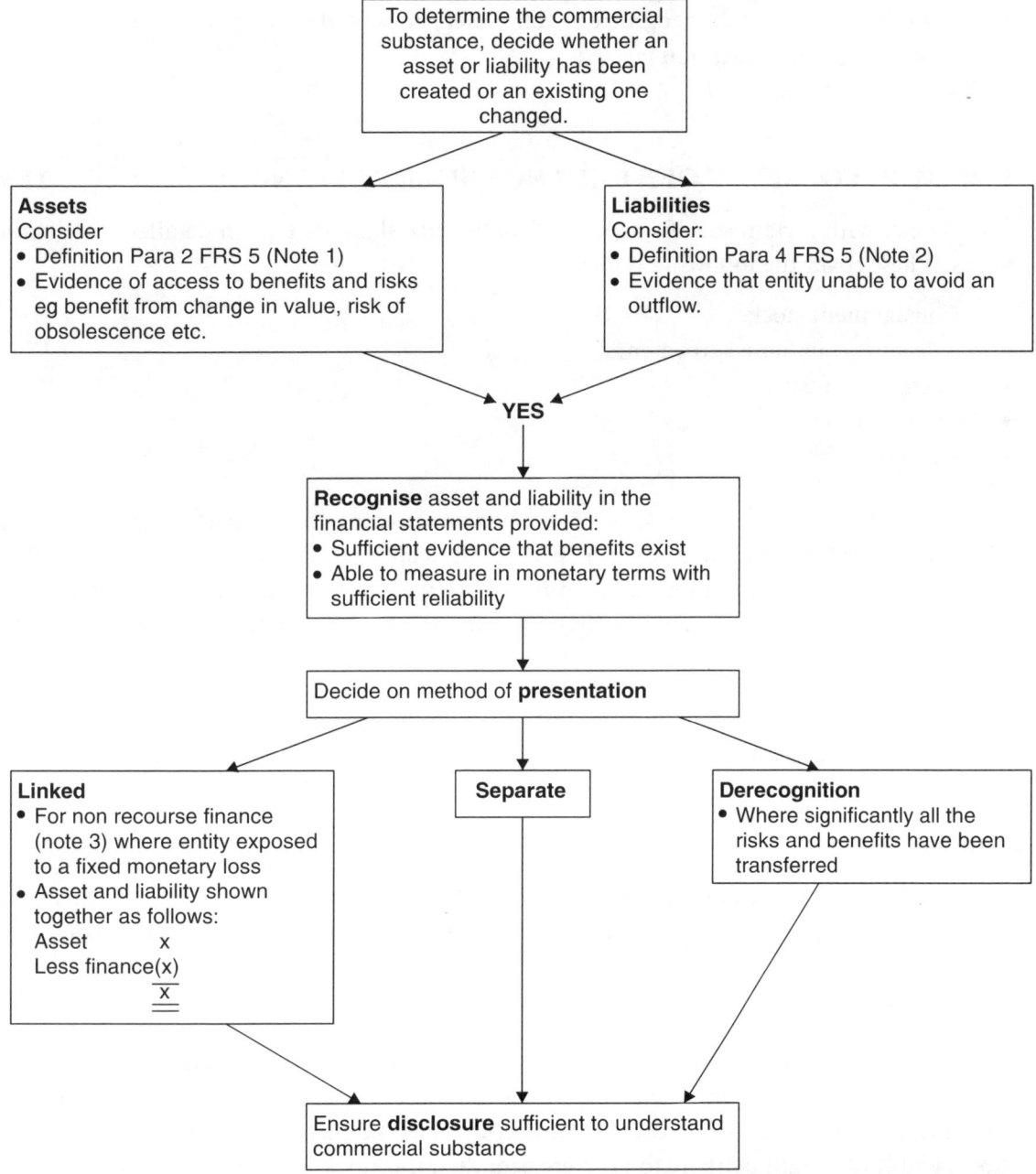

To determine the commercial substance, decide whether an asset or liability has been created or an existing one changed.

Assets
Consider
- Definition Para 2 FRS 5 (Note 1)
- Evidence of access to benefits and risks eg benefit from change in value, risk of obsolescence etc.

Liabilities
Consider:
- Definition Para 4 FRS 5 (Note 2)
- Evidence that entity unable to avoid an outflow.

YES

Recognise asset and liability in the financial statements provided:
- Sufficient evidence that benefits exist
- Able to measure in monetary terms with sufficient reliability

Decide on method of **presentation**

Linked
- For non recourse finance (note 3) where entity exposed to a fixed monetary loss
- Asset and liability shown together as follows:
Asset   x
Less finance(x)
              $\underline{\underline{x}}$

Separate

Derecognition
- Where significantly all the risks and benefits have been transferred

Ensure **disclosure** sufficient to understand commercial substance

Notes

1   *Assets*: rights or other access to future economic benefits controlled by an entity as a result of past transactions or events.

2   *Liabilities*: an entity's obligations to transfer future economic benefits as a result of past transactions or events.

3   *Non-recourse finance*: there is no (or limited) recourse to the seller for losses.

3.30 Section summary

The diagram should help to explain a sensible approach to FRS 5 in examination questions. Important points to remember are:

- **Substance over form**
- Definitions of **assets** and **liabilities**
- Definition of **recognition**
- Different degrees of **derecognition**: complete, partial and none
- When **linked presentation** is used
- When **offset** is allowed

4 COMMON FORMS OF OFF BALANCE SHEET FINANCE 11/96

4.1 FRS 5 deals with certain specific aspects of off balance sheet finance in detailed **application notes**. These cover the following topics.

- Consignment stock
- Sale and repurchase agreements
- Factoring of debts
- Securitised assets
- Loan transfers

4.2 The application notes explain how to apply the standard to the particular transactions which they describe, and also contain specific disclosure requirements in relation to those transactions. The application notes are **not exhaustive** and they do not override the general principles of the standard itself, but they are regarded as authoritative insofar as they assist in interpreting it.

4.3 Note that in *all* cases **full disclosure** of the transaction should be given, whatever its accounting treatment. This will particularly hold where a **linked presentation** is used.

Consignment stock

4.4 Consignment stock is an arrangement where stock is held by one party (say a distributor) but is owned by another party (for example a manufacturer or a finance company). Consignment stock is common in the motor trade and is similar to goods sold on a 'sale or return' basis.

4.5 To identify the correct treatment, it is necessary to identify the point at which the distributor or dealer acquired the benefits of the asset (the stock) rather than the point at which legal title was acquired. If the manufacturer has the right to require the return of the stock, and if that right is likely to be exercised, then the stock is *not* an asset of the dealer. If the dealer is rarely required to return the stock, then this part of the transaction will have little commercial effect in practice and should be ignored for accounting purposes. The potential liability would need to be disclosed in the accounts.

Summary of indications of asset status

4.6 The following analysis is given in FRS 5.

Indications that the stock is *not an asset* of the dealer at delivery	Indications that the stock *is an asset* of the dealer at delivery
Manufacturer can require dealer to **return stock** (or transfer stock to another dealer) without compensation; or	Manufacturer cannot require dealer to **return or transfer stock**; or

Indications that the stock is *not an asset* of the dealer at delivery	Indications that the stock *is an asset* of the dealer at delivery
Penalty paid by the dealer to prevent returns/transfers of stock at the manufacturer's request.	**Financial incentives** given to persuade dealer to transfer stock at manufacturer's request.
Dealer has unfettered **right to return stock** to the manufacturer without penalty and actually exercises the right in practice.	Dealer has **no right to return stock** or is commercially compelled not to exercise its right of return.
Manufacturer bears **obsolescence risk**, eg: (a) obsolete stock is returned to the manufacturer without penalty; or (b) financial incentives given by manufacturer to prevent stock being returned to it (eg on a model change or if it becomes obsolete).	Dealer bears **obsolescence risk**, eg: (a) penalty charged if dealer returns stock to manufacturer; or (b) obsolete stock cannot be returned to the manufacturer and no compensation is paid by manufacturer for losses due to obsolescence.
Stock **transfer price** charged by manufacturer is based on manufacturer's list price at date of transfer of legal title.	Stock **transfer price** charged by manufacturer is based on manufacturer's list price at date of delivery.
Manufacturer bears **slow movement risk**, eg: transfer price set independently of time for which dealer holds stock, and there is no deposit.	Dealer bears **slow movement risk**, eg: (a) dealer is effectively charged interest as transfer price or other payments to manufacturer vary with time for which dealer holds stock; or (b) dealer makes a substantial interest-free deposit that varies with the levels of stock held.

Required accounting

4.7 Where it is concluded that the stock **is in substance an asset** of the dealer:

(a) the stock should be recognised as such on the dealer's balance sheet, together with a corresponding liability to the manufacturer;

(b) any deposit should be deducted from the liability and the excess classified as a trade creditor;

(c) full disclosure should be given in the notes to the financial statements.

4.8 Where it is concluded that the stock is **not in substance an asset** of the dealer:

(a) the stock should not be included on the dealer's balance sheet until the transfer of title has crystallised;

(b) any deposit should be included under 'other debtors';

(c) full disclosure should be given in the notes to the financial statements.

Question 4

Daley Motors Ltd owns a number of car dealerships throughout Essex. The terms of the arrangement between the dealerships and the manufacturer are as follows.

(a)   Legal title passes when the cars are either used by Daley Ltd for demonstration purposes or sold to a third party.

(b)   The dealer has the right to return vehicles to the manufacturer without penalty. (Daley Ltd has rarely exercised this right in the past.)

(c)   The transfer price is based on the manufacturer's list price at the date of delivery.

(d)   Daley Ltd makes a substantial interest-free deposit based on the number of cars held.

Should the asset and liability be recognised at the date of delivery?

Answer

(a)   Legal form is irrelevant.
(b)   Yes: only because rarely exercised (otherwise 'no').
(c)   Yes: per FRS 5.
(d)   Yes: the dealership is effectively forgoing the interest which could be earned on the cash sum.

Sale and repurchase agreements

4.9   These are arrangements under which the company sells an asset to another person on terms that allow the company to **repurchase the asset** in certain circumstances. A common example is the sale and repurchase of maturing whisky stocks. The key question is whether the transaction is a **straightforward sale**, or whether it is, in effect, a **secured loan**. It is necessary to look at the arrangement to determine who has the rights to the economic benefits that the asset generates, and the terms on which the asset is to be repurchased.

4.10   If the seller has the right to the benefits of the **use of the asset,** and the repurchase terms are such that the **repurchase is likely** to take place, the transaction should be accounted for as a **loan.**

Summary of indications of the sale of the asset

4.11   FRS 5 gives the following summary

Indications of *sale* of original asset to buyer (nevertheless, the seller may retain a different asset)	Indications of *no sale* of original asset to buyer (secured loan)
	Sale price does not equal **market value** at date of sale.
No commitment for **seller to repurchase** asset, eg call option where there is a real possibility the option will fail to be exercised.	Commitment for **seller to repurchase** asset, eg: • put and call option with the same exercise price; • either a put or a call option with no genuine commercial possibility that the option will fail to be exercised; or • seller requires asset back to use in its business, or asset is in effect the only source of seller's future sales.
Indications of *sale* of original asset to buyer (nevertheless, the seller may retain a different asset)	Indications of *no sale* of original asset to buyer (secured loan)

Indications of *sale* of original asset to buyer (nevertheless, the seller may retain a different asset)	Indications of *no sale* of original asset to buyer (secured loan)
Risk of **changes in asset value** borne by buyer such that buyer does not receive solely a lender's return, eg both sale and repurchase price equal market value at date of sale/repurchase	Risk of **changes in asset value** borne by seller such that buyer receives solely a lender's return, eg: • repurchase price equals sale price plus costs plus interest; • original purchase price adjusted retrospectively to pass variations in the value of the asset to the seller; • seller provides residual value guarantee to buyer or subordinated debt to protect buyer from falls in the value of the asset.
Nature of the asset is such that it will be used over the life of the agreement, and seller has no rights to **determine its use**. Seller has no rights to determine asset's development or future sale.	Seller retains right to **determine asset's use**, development or sale, or rights to profits therefrom.

Required accounting

4.12 Where the substance of the transaction is that of a **secured loan**:

    (a) the seller should continue to recognise the original asset and record the proceeds received from the buyer as a liability;

    (b) interest, however designated, should be accrued;

    (c) the carrying amount of the asset should be reviewed and provided against if necessary;

    (d) full disclosure should be made in the notes to the financial statements.

4.13 Where the transaction is a **sale and leaseback,** no profit should be recognised on entering in to the arrangement and no adjustment made to the carrying value of the asset. As stated in the guidance notes to SSAP 21, this represents the substance of the transactions, 'namely the raising of finance secured on an asset that continues to be held and that is not disposed of'.

4.14 Where the **seller has a new asset or liability** (eg merely a call option to repurchase the original asset), it should recognise or disclose that new asset or liability on a prudent basis in accordance with the provisions of SSAP 18. In particular, the seller should recognise (and not merely disclose) a liability for any kind of unconditional obligation it has entered into. Where doubts exist regarding the amount of any gain or loss arising, full provision should be made for any expected loss; but recognition of any gain, to the extent that it is in doubt, should be deferred until it is realised.

Question 5

A construction company, Mecanto plc, agrees to sell to Hamlows Bank some of the land within its landbank. The terms of the sale are as follows.

(a) The sales price is to be at open market value.

(b) Mecanto plc has the right to develop the land on the basis that it will pay all the outgoings on the land plus an annual fee of 5% of the purchase price.

(c) Mecanto has the option to buy back the land at any time within the next five years. The repurchase price is based on:

    (i)   original purchase price;
    (ii) expenses relating to the purchase;
    (iii) an interest charge of base rate + 2%;
    (iv) less amounts received from Mecanto by Hamlows.

(d) At the end of five years Hamlows Bank may offer the land for sale generally. Any shortfall on the proceeds relative to the agreed purchase price agreed with Mecanto has to be settled by Mecanto in cash.

Should the asset continue to be recognised and the sales proceeds treated as a loan?

Answer

(a) No: the sales price is as for an arms' length transaction.

(b) Yes: Mecanto has control over the asset.
    Yes: Mecanto has to pay a fee based on cash received.

(c) Yes: interest is charged on the proceeds paid to Mecanto.
    Yes: the repurchase price is based on the lender's return

(d) Yes: options ensure that Mecanto bears all the risk (both favourable and unfavourable) of changes in the market value of the land.

Factoring of debts

4.15 Where debts are factored, the original creditor **sells the debts to the factor**. The sales price may be fixed at the outset or may be adjusted later. It is also common for the factor to offer a credit facility that allows the seller to draw upon a proportion of the amounts owed.

4.16 In order to determine the correct accounting treatment it is necessary to consider whether the benefit of the debts has been passed on to the factor, or whether the factor is, in effect, providing a loan on the security of the debtors. If the seller has to **pay interest** on the difference between the amounts advanced to him and the amounts that the factor has received, and if the seller bears the **risks of non-payment** by the debtor, then the indications would be that the transaction is, in effect, a loan. Depending on the circumstances, either a linked presentation or separate presentation may be appropriate.

Summary of indications of appropriate treatment

4.17 FRS 5 gives the following summary of indicators of the appropriate treatment.

Indications that derecognition is appropriate (debts are *not an asset* of the seller)	Indications that a *linked presentation* is appropriate	Indications that a separate presentation is appropriate (debts are an *asset* of the seller)
Transfer is for **a single non-returnable fixed sum**.	Some **non-returnable proceeds** received, but seller has rights to further sums from the factor (or vice versa) whose amount depends on whether or when debtors pay.	**Finance cost varies** with speed of collection of debts, eg: • by adjustment to consideration for original transfer; or • subsequent transfers priced to recover costs of earlier transfers.

Indications that derecognition is appropriate (debts are *not an asset* of the seller)	Indications that a *linked presentation* is appropriate	Indications that a separate presentation is appropriate (debts are an *asset* of the seller)
There is **no recourse** to the seller for losses.	There is either **no recourse** for losses, or such recourse has a fixed monetary ceiling.	There is **full recourse** to the seller for losses.
Factor is paid **all amounts** received from the factored debts (and no more). Seller has no rights to further sums from the factor.	Factor is paid only out of **amounts collected** from the factored debts, and seller has no right or obligation to repurchase debts.	Seller is required to **repay** amounts received from the factor on or before a set date, regardless of timing or amounts of collections from debtors.

Required accounting

4.18 **Derecognition**. Where the seller has retained no significant benefits and risks relating to the debts and has no obligation to repay amounts received from the factors, the debtors should be removed from its balance sheet and no liability shown in respect of the proceeds received from the factor. A profit or loss should be recognised, calculated as the difference between the carrying amount of the debts and the proceeds received.

4.19 **Linked presentation**. Where the conditions for a linked presentation are met, the proceeds received, to the extent they are non-returnable, should be shown deducted from the gross amount of the factored debts (after providing for bad debts, credit-protection charges and any accrued interest) in the face of the balance sheet. The interest element of the factor's charges should be recognised as it accrues and included in the P&L account with other interest charges.

4.20 **Separate presentation**. Where neither derecognition nor a linked presentation is appropriate, a separate presentation should be adopted: a gross asset (equivalent in amount to the gross amount of the debts) should be shown on the balance sheet of the seller within assets, and a corresponding liability in respect of the proceeds received from the factor should be shown within liabilities. The interest element of the factor's charges should be recognised as it accrues and included in the P&L account with other interest charges. Other factoring costs should be similarly accrued and included in the P&L account within the appropriate caption.

Securitised assets

4.21 Securitisation is very common in the financial services industry, and the assets that are most commonly securitised are mortgages and credit card accounts, although hire purchase loans, trade debts and even property and stocks are sometimes securitised. **Blocks of assets** are thus financed, rather than the company's general business.

4.22 The normal procedure is for the assets to be transferred by the person who held them (the originator) to a special purpose company (the issuer) in exchange for cash. The issuer will use the proceeds of an issue of debentures or loan notes to pay for the assets. The shares in the issuer are usually held by a third party so that it does not need to be consolidated. The issuer will usually have a very small share capital, and so most of the risk will be borne by the people who lent it the money through the debentures to pay for the assets. For this reason there is usually some form of insurance taken out on the assets to give some security for the lenders.

Summary of indications as to accounting treatment

4.23 FRS 5 gives the following summary of indications of the appropriate treatment.

Indications that derecognition is appropriate (securitised assets are *not an asset* of the seller)	Indications that a *linked presentation* is appropriate	Indications that a separate presentation is appropriate (securitised assets are *assets* of the originator)
Originator's individual financial statements		
Transaction price is **arm's length price** for an outright sale.	Transaction price **is not arm's length price** for an outright sale.	Transaction price is **not arm's length price** for an outright sale.
Transfer is for a **single, non-returnable fixed sum**.	Some **non-returnable proceeds** received, but originator has rights to further sums from the issuer, the amount of which depends on the performance of the securitised assets.	Proceeds received are **returnable**, or there is a provision whereby the originator may keep the securitised assets on repayment of the loan notes or re-acquire them.
There is **no recourse** to the originator for losses.	There is either **no recourse** for losses, or such recourse has a fixed monetary ceiling.	There is or may be **full recourse** to the originator for losses, eg: <ul><li>originator's directors are unable or unwilling to state that it is not obliged to fund any losses;</li><li>noteholders have not agreed in writing that they will seek repayment only from funds generated by the securitised assets.</li></ul>
Originator's consolidated financial statements		
Issuer is owned by an **independent third party** that made a substantial capital investment, has control of the issuer, and has the benefits and risks of its net assets.	Issuer is a **quasi-subsidiary** of the originator, but the conditions for a linked presentation are met from the point of view of the group.	Issuer is a **subsidiary** of the originator.

Required accounting: originator's financial statements

4.24 **Derecognition.** Where the originator has retained no significant benefits and risks relating to the securitised assets and has no obligation to repay the proceeds of the note issue, the asset should be removed from its balance sheet, and no liability shown in respect of the proceeds of the note issue. A profit or loss should be recognised, calculated as the difference between the carrying amount of the assets and the proceeds received.

4.25 **Linked presentation.** Where the conditions for a linked presentation are met, the proceeds of the note issue (to the extent they are non-returnable) should be shown deducted from the securitised assets on the face of the balance sheet within a single asset caption. Profit should be recognised and presented in the manner set out in FRS 5. The disclosure requirements are extensive, including a description of the securitised assets and all relevant terms, income and expenses, claims on proceeds, etc.

4.26 **Separate presentation.** Where neither derecognition nor a linked presentation is appropriate, a separate presentation should be adopted, ie a gross asset (equal in amount to the gross amount of the securitised assets) should be shown on the balance sheet of the originator within assets, and a corresponding liability in respect of the proceeds of the note issue shown within liabilities. No gain or loss should be recognised at the time the securitisation is entered into (unless adjustment to the carrying value of the asset independent of the securitisation is required).

Required accounting: issuer's financial statements

4.27 The requirements set out in the paragraphs above for the originator's individual financial statements also apply to the issuer's financial statement. In most cases the issuer will be required to adopt a **separate presentation**, in which case the provisions of Paragraph 4.26 will apply.

Loan transfers

4.28 These are arrangements where a loan is transferred to a transferee from an original lender. This will usually be done by the **assignment of rights and obligations** by the lender, or the **creation of a new agreement** between the borrower and the transferee. The same principles apply to loan transfers as to debt factoring and securitised assets.

Summary of indications of appropriate treatment

4.29 FRS 5 gives the following summary.

Indications that *derecognition* is appropriate (off lender's balance sheet	Indications that a *linked presentation* is appropriate	Indications that a *separate presentation* is appropriate (on lender's balance sheet
Transfer is for a **single, non-returnable fixed sum**.	Some **non-returnable proceeds received**, but lender has rights to further sums whose amount depends on whether or when the borrowers pay.	The proceeds received are **returnable** in the event of losses occurring on the loans.
There is **no recourse** to the lender for losses from any cause.	There is either **no recourse** for losses, or such recourse has a fixed monetary ceiling.	There is **full recourse** to the lender for losses.
Transferee is paid **all amounts received** from the loans (and no more), as and when received. Lender has no rights to further sums from the loans or the transferee.	Transferee is paid only **out of amounts received** from the loans, and lender has no right or obligation to repurchase them.	Lender is required to **repay amounts received** from the transferee on or before a set date, regardless of the timing or amount of payments by the borrowers.

BPP PUBLISHING

Required accounting

4.30 **Derecognition.** Where the lender has retained no significant benefits and risks relating to the loans and has no obligation to repay the transferee, the loans should be removed from its balance sheet and no liability shown in respect of the amounts received from the transferee. A profit or loss may arise for the lender. Where the profit or loss is realised in cash it should be recognised, calculated as the difference between the carrying amount of the loans and the cash proceeds received. Where, however, the lender's profit or loss is not realised in cash and there are doubts as to its amount, full provision should be made for any expected loss but recognition of any gain, to the extent it is in doubt, should be deferred until cash has been received.

4.31 **Linked presentation.** Where the conditions for a linked presentation are met, the proceeds received, to the extent they are non-returnable, should be shown deducted from the gross amount of the loans on the face of the balance sheet. Profit should be recognised and presented as set out in FRS 5.

4.32 **Separate presentation.** Where neither derecognition not a linked presentation is appropriate, a separate presentation should be adopted, ie a gross asset (equivalent in amount to the gross amount of the loans) should be shown on the balance sheet of the lender within assets, and a corresponding liability in respect of the amounts received from the transferee should be shown within creditors. No gain or loss should be recognised at the time of the transfer (unless adjustment to the carrying value of the loan independent of the transfer is required).

> **Exam focus point**
> In spite of FRS 5 and its application notes, there are *still* opportunities to manipulate results.

4.33 FRS 5 is counted as one of the ASB's successes. However, it is not without its critics. It is very long, dense and in places difficult to understand. Moreover, the linked presentation requirement is controversial, and some commentators think it is wrong.

5 CREATIVE ACCOUNTING

5.1 Creative accounting, the **manipulation of figures for a desired result,** takes many forms. Off balance sheet finance is a major type of creative accounting and it probably has the most serious implications. Before we look at some of the other types of creative accounting, we should consider some important points.

5.2 Firstly, it is **very rare** for a company, its directors or employees to manipulate results for the purpose of **fraud.** The major consideration is usually the effect the results will have on the share price of the company If the share price falls, the company becomes vulnerable to takeover. Analysts, brokers and economists, whose opinions affect the stock markets, are often perceived as having an outlook which is both short-term and superficial. Consequently, companies will attempt to produce the results the market expects or wants. The companies will aim for steady progress in a few key numbers and ratios and they will aim to meet the market's stated expectation.

5.3 Another point to consider, particularly when you approach this topic in an examination, is that the number of methods available for creative accounting and the determination and imagination of those who wish to perpetrate such acts are **endless.** It has been seen in the past that, wherever an accounting standard or law closes a loophole, another one is found.

This has produced a change of approach in regulators and standard setters, towards general principles rather than detailed rules.

5.4   Let us now examine some **examples** of creative accounting, the reaction of the standard setters and possible actions in the future which may halt or change such practices. Remember that this list is not comprehensive and that the frequency and materiality of the use of each method will vary a great deal. Remember also that we have already covered several methods in our examination of off balance sheet finance.

Income recognition and cut-off

5.5   Manipulation of cut-off is relatively straightforward. A company may issue invoices before the year end and inflate sales for the year when in fact they have not received firm orders for the goods. Income recognition can be manipulated in a variety of ways. One example is where a company sells software under contract. The sales contracts will only be realised in full over a period of time, but the company might recognise the full sales value of the contract once it has been secured, even though some payments from clients will fall due over several years. This is clearly imprudent, but the company might justify it by pointing to the irrevocable nature of the contract. But what if a customer should go in to liquidation? No income would be forthcoming from the contract under such circumstances.

Merger accounting

5.6   The rules which allow companies to use merger accounting rather than acquisition accounting are stringent, as we will see in a later chapter. The main advantages of merger accounting are that no undistributable share premium account must be created and there is no purchased goodwill on acquisition. Also, the results of the merged group are shown as if the companies had always been merged, affecting both current year results and prior year comparisons.

5.7   The criteria for merger accounting are based on a share-for-share exchange. Many shareholders are not happy to receive new shares for their old ones for a variety of reasons.

(a)   The shares in the take-over company might be riskier than those in the target company, for example they might be quoted on the AIM rather than the full market.

(b)   The shareholder may want to invest elsewhere and so wants cash rather than shares when the merger or take-over takes place.

5.8   In answer to this problem, and before such stringent restrictions were put into place, creative accounting experts came up with **vendor placings**. A vendor placing involved the basic principles of merger accounting. The acquiring company made an offer for the target company in the form of shares. The acquiring company then arranged for some or all of its shares to be placed, usually with institutional investors. This was arranged by the acquiring company's financial advisers and the number of shares placed depended on the number of shareholders who passed their shares in the acquiring company in return for the money raised from the placing.

5.9   Objections were made to such schemes by the smaller existing shareholders in the acquiring company because their interest was being diluted and institutional investors were gaining a greater concentration of the shares. This problem was overcome by using **vendor rights**, an extension of a **vendor placing**. Rather than placing the shares with an institutional investor,

BPP PUBLISHING

the financial adviser offered these new shares to existing shareholders on a ratio determined by their existing holding.

5.10 Previously, neither of the schemes outlined above broke the rules on merger accounting and yet they in no way followed the spirit of the relevant accounting standard (SSAP 23) because they did not constitute true share-for-share exchanges. The ASB has now outlawed these practices by producing stringent criteria, based on *general principles* for merger accounting under FRS 6 *Acquisitions and mergers* (see Chapter 19).

Other creative accounting techniques

5.11 The examples given above are some of the major 'abuses' in accounting over recent years. A few more are mentioned here and you should aim to think up as many examples of each as you can. You may also know of other creative accounting techniques which we have not mentioned here.

(a) **Window dressing**. This is where transactions are passed through the books at the year end to make figures look better, but in fact they have not taken place and are often reversed after the year end. An example is where cheques are written to creditors, entered in the cash book, but not sent out until well after the year end.

(b) **Taxation**. It has been known for some companies to decide how much they want to pay in taxes for the year and state their profits accordingly! Although the relationship between taxable profits and accounting profits is not straightforward, there is a direct effect on the accounts.

(c) **Change of accounting policies**. This tends to be a last resort because companies which change accounting policies know they will not be able to do so again for some time. The effect in the year of change can be substantial and prime candidates for such treatment are depreciation, stock valuation, changes from current cost to historical cost (practised frequently by privatised public utilities) and foreign currency losses.

(d) **Manipulation of accruals, prepayments and contingencies**. These figures can often be very subjective, particularly contingencies. In the case of impending legal action, for example, a contingent liability is difficult to estimate, the case may be far off and the solicitors cannot give any indication of likely success, or failure. In such cases companies will often only disclose the possibility of such a liability, even though the eventual costs may be substantial. The new FRS 12 should go some way towards eliminating abuses.

Exam focus point
You should keep an eye on the financial press for examples of creative accounting and its consequences.

Chapter roundup

*   The subject of **off balance sheet finance** is a complex one which has plagued the accountancy profession. In practice, off balance sheet finance schemes are often very sophisticated and they are beyond the range of this syllabus.

*   Make sure that you have memorised the definitions for **assets and liabilities** and the criteria for their **recognition and derecognition** given in FRS 5.

*   You also need to understand the methods of presentation described in FRS 5, particularly *offset* and **linked presentation**.

*   The major types of off balance sheet finance are discussed in the **application notes** to FRS 5.

*   **Creative accounting**, of which off balance sheet finance is one type, can be used in many different areas. Reading the financial and accountancy press will help you to keep up to date with any new controversies.

Quick quiz

1   Why do companies want to use off balance sheet finance? (see para 1.2)

2   How does IAS 1 describe substance over form? (key term)

3   What is a quasi subsidiary? (key term)

4   What are the common features of transactions whose substance is not readily apparent? (3.7)

5   What does 'recognition' mean in the context of FRS 5? (key term)

6   When should a transaction be recognised? (3.9)

7   In which three circumstances does FRS 5 allow partial derecognition? (3.15)

8   Describe 'linked presentation' and 'offset' as set out in FRS 5. (3.17, 3.18)

9   Summarise the indications of appropriate treatment for:

    (a) consignment stock (4.6)
    (b) sale and purchase agreements (4.11)
    (c) securitised assets (4.23)
    (d) loan transfers (4.29)

10 Name some creative accounting techniques. (5.11)

Question to try	Level	Marks	Time
9	Introductory	n/a	n/a

BPP PUBLISHING

Chapter 9

CAPITAL INSTRUMENTS

Chapter topic	Syllabus reference	Ability required
1 FRS 4 *Capital instruments*	9(a)	Skill
2 The treatment of certain capital instruments	9(a)	Skill
3 FRS 13 *Derivatives and other financial instruments: disclosures*	9(a)	Skill

Introduction

Capital instruments and **derivatives** are often extremely complex in business but in the exam there is a limit to how difficult a question can be asked. You are more likely to be asked about the general approach of the documents in this chapter, rather than any complicated calculations.

FRS 4 *Capital instruments* requires most attention here. You do not need to memorise these different types of capital instrument, but you should attempt to **understand** the accounting treatment in each case.

1 FRS 4 CAPITAL INSTRUMENTS   5/95, 11/98

1.1 **Capital instruments** are instruments which are issued to raise finance. There are many different types. FRS 4 addresses how issuers should account for capital instruments. The standard covers all capital instruments **except** leases, options or warrants granted under employee share schemes and equity shares issued in a business combination accounted for as a merger.

> **KEY TERM**
>
> • **Capital instrument:** all instruments that are issued by reporting entities as a means of raising finance, including shares, debentures, loans and debt instruments, options and warrants that give the holder the right to subscribe for or obtain capital instruments. In the case of consolidated financial statements the term includes capital instruments issued by subsidiaries except those that are held by another member of the group included in the consolidation.   *(FRS 4)*

1.2 Other important **definitions** are given in FRS 4.

KEY TERMS

- **Debt:** capital instruments that are classified as liabilities.

- **Equity shares**: shares other than non-equity shares.

- **Finance costs**: the difference between the net proceeds of an instrument and the total amount of the payments (or other transfer of economic benefits) that the issuer may be required to make in respect of the instrument.

- **Issue costs**: the costs that are incurred directly in connection with the issue of a capital instrument, that is, those costs that would not have been incurred had the specific instrument in question not been issued.

- **Net proceeds**: the fair value of the consideration received on the issue of a capital instrument after deduction of issue costs.

- **Non-equity shares**: shares possessing any of the following characteristics.

  (a) Any of the rights of the shares to receive payments (whether in respect of dividends, in respect of redemption or otherwise) are for a limited amount that is not calculated by reference to the company's assets or profits or the dividends on any class of equity share.

  (b) Any of their rights to participate in a surplus in a winding up are limited to a specific amount that is not calculated by reference to the company's assets or profits and such limitation had a commercial effect in practice at the time the shares were issued or, if later, at the time the limitation was introduced.

  (c) The shares are redeemable either according to their terms, or because the holder, or any party other than the issuer, can require their redemption.

- **Participating dividend**: a dividend (or part of a dividend) on a non-equity share that, in accordance with a company's memorandum and articles of association is always equivalent to a fixed multiple of the dividend payable on an equity share.

- **Share**: share in the share capital of the reporting company (or, in the context of consolidated financial statements, the holding company of a group) including stock.

- **Shareholders' funds**: the aggregate of called up share capital and all reserves, excluding minority interests.

- **Term (of a capital instrument)**: the period from the date of issue of the capital instrument to the date at which it will expire, be redeemed, or be cancelled.

  If either party has the option to require the instrument to be redeemed or cancelled and, under the terms of the instrument, it is uncertain whether such an option will be exercised, the term should be taken to end on the earliest date at which the instrument would be redeemed or cancelled on exercise of such an option.

  If either party has the right to extend the period of an instrument, the term should not include the period of the extension if there is a genuine commercial possibility that the period will not be extended.

- **Warrant**: an instrument that requires the issuer to issue shares (whether contingently or not) and contains no obligations for the issuer to transfer economic benefits.

(FRS 4)

Scope

1.3   The standard applies to all financial statements intended to give a true and fair view of a reporting entity's financial position and profit or loss (or income and expenditure). **No exemptions** have been given on the grounds of size, ownership or industry. Comparative figures may require restatement where the effect on prior years is material.

Distinguishing between debt and equity

1.4   One of the key users' ratios is the **gearing ratio,** ie the measure of the proportion of debt to equity. In order for this measure to be meaningful there must be consistency in the allocation of financial instruments between these two categories. (Minority interests in consolidated financial statements represent a minor category, discussed below.)

1.5   Capital instruments should be included in one of two categories in the balance sheet: **liabilities** or **shareholders' funds.** The rules for distinguishing between debt and equity are based on the accounting model being developed in the ASB's *Statement of Principles.* They require:

(a)   a company's **shares** to remain in **shareholders' funds;**

(b)   **capital instruments** to be reported as **liabilities** if they contain an 'obligation to transfer economic benefits'; and

(c)   **capital instruments** to be reported as **shareholders' funds** if they do not contain an 'obligation to transfer economic benefits'.

1.6   Some capital instruments have features of **both debt and equity.** The common example of such 'hybrid' instruments is convertible debt, which is economically equivalent to conventional debt plus a warrant to acquire shares in the future.

(a)   If the individual components of such instruments are **physically separable,** the FRS requires that they should be **accounted for separately.**

(b)   Where the components are **inseparable,** the instrument should be accounted for as a **single instrument,** eg a convertible bond should not be notionally 'split' into debt and an option to acquire shares.

1.7   The rule for determining whether a capital instrument is a **liability** is widely drawn. An 'obligation to transfer economic benefits' means any requirement to make cash payments (usually) or transfer other kinds of property (more rarely) even if the requirement is only contingent. Hence, convertible debt instruments are usually liabilities.

1.8   The standard says that the effect of applying these criteria is that the classification of capital instruments will be consistent with their **substance,** rather than their **legal form.** (A number of observers have said exactly the opposite.)

Disclosure: general

1.9   A fundamental part of FRS 4's approach on hybrid instruments and other less conventional forms of finance is that their issuers must make **considerable disclosures.**

1.10   In order to distinguish shares with debt characteristics from other share capital, the FRS contains a definition of **non-equity shares.** Broadly speaking, these are shares that contain preferential rights to participate in the company's profits or assets (for example preference shares) or are redeemable.

1.11 The main new disclosure requirement is the analysis of the following items in the balance sheet.

Item	Analysed between	
Shareholders' funds	Equity interests	Non-equity interests
Minority interests in subsidiaries	Equity interests in subsidiaries	Non-equity interests in subsidiaries
Liabilities	Convertible liabilities	Non-convertible liabilities

Such analysis is usually to be given on the **face of the balance sheet**. Dividends to shareholders and the minority interests' share of the results for the year should be analysed similarly in the P&L account. Considerable disclosure is also required about the rights and terms of each class of non-equity share and convertible debt.

1.12 The overall effect is to provide the users of financial statements with quite a **detailed analysis of shareholders' funds** showing the amounts pertaining to each separate class of share and a summary of the rights of the holders.

Question 1

A company issues a convertible instrument which does not pay a coupon and is mandatorily convertible into shares of the issuer after 3 years. The holder is compensated through the conversion rights attached to the instrument. Although it is mandatorily convertible, the holders will rank as creditors in the event of insolvency of the issuer.

How should the instrument be classified?

Answer

Under FRS 4, this instrument should be classified in shareholders' funds as there is no 'obligation to transfer economic benefits'. Hence, this will be accounted for like a 'fully-paid' warrant. Its impact will be to dilute shareholders' interests in the future.

(Source: *Capital Instruments: A Guide to FRS 4*, Ernst & Young)

Accounting for debt instruments

1.13 Debt should be recorded in the balance sheet at the **fair value** of the consideration received less **costs incurred** directly in connection with the issue of the instrument. Such issue costs are narrowly defined and sometimes have to be written off immediately, but otherwise are spread over the life of the debt.

1.14 The carrying amount of debt should be **increased by the finance cost** in respect of the reporting period and **reduced by payments** made in respect of the debt in that period.

1.15 The **finance cost** of debt is the difference between the **total payments** required to be made and the **initial carrying value of the debt** (that is the interest cost or the dividends plus any premium payable on redemption or other payments). This should be charged to the profit and loss account over the term of the instrument at a **constant rate of interest** on the outstanding amount of the debt. The effective rate of interest implicit in the debt instrument will be required for that purpose.

1.16 Note that under s 130 CA 1985 **discounts** on the issue of debentures may be taken against the share premium account. This would be shown as a transfer in reserves.

BPP PUBLISHING

Question 2

On 1 January 19X4, an entity issued a fixed rate debt instrument and received £900,000. Interest is payable annually in arrears at a rate of 5% on the stated principal amount of £1,000,000. The instrument has a 5 year term and the stated principal will be repaid at maturity. Issue costs of £50,000 were incurred.

State the disclosure of the instrument in the profit and loss account and the balance sheet for each year of the term.

Answer

The net proceeds of this issue are £850,000. The finance cost of this instrument is £400,000, being the difference between the total future payments (ie £1,250,000, see column (a) below) and the net proceeds from the issue.

The effective rate of interest implicit in this instrument is the discount rate which equates the present value of future cash flows to the net proceeds received. This is calculated as 8.84% by applying the NPV formula (use interpolation).

The interest charge for the year (column (b) below) is calculated by applying this rate to the carrying value of the debt in the balance sheet during the year.

	(a)	(b)	(c)
			Carrying value
	Cash	Interest	in the balance
	flows	charge	sheet
	£'000	£'000	£'000
At January 19X4	(850)		850.0
At 31 December 19X4	50	75.1	875.1
At 31 December 19X5	50	77.4	902.5
At 31 December 19X6	50	79.8	932.3
At 31 December 19X7	50	82.4	964.7
At 31 December 19X8	1,050	85.3	-
Total	400	400.0	

(Source: *Capital Instruments: A Guide to FRS 4, Ernst & Young*)

1.17 If debt is **repurchased** or **settled** before its maturity, any gains or losses should be recognised immediately in the P&L account.

Convertible debt

1.18 FRS 4 requires that **conversion of debt** should *not* be anticipated but rather reported in liabilities with the finance cost calculated on the assumption that the debt will *never* be converted. When the debt is converted, the amount of consideration recognised in respect of the shares should be the amount of the liability for the debt at the date of conversion.

Disclosure: debt

1.19 (a) **Maturity of debt**. The financial statements or notes should include an analysis of the maturity of debt showing amount falling due:

    (i)   in one year or less, or on demand;
    (ii)   in more than one year but not more than two years;
    (iii) in more than two years, but not more than five years;
    (iv) in more than five years.

The maturity of the debt should be determined by reference to the **earliest date** on which the lender can demand repayment.

(b) **Convertible debt** should be stated separately from other liabilities. The following details must be given:

    (i)   the date of redemption;

    (ii)   the amount payable on redemption;

    (iii) the number and class of shares into which the debt may be converted;

    (iv) the period in which the conversion may take place; and

    (v)   whether conversion is at the option of the issuer or holder.

Repurchase of own debt

1.20 Any profits or losses arising on the repurchase of debt should be recognised in the **year of repurchase**. This applies to debt repurchased or settled early. Gains or losses should be separately disclosed in the P&L account within, or adjacent to, 'interest payable and similar charges'.

1.21 This is consistent with the treatment previously required by UITF Abstract 8 *Repurchase of own debt* (which FRS 4 replaced), although the wording in the standard makes it clear that this treatment should be applied to debt that is settled early as well as debt that is repurchased. Abstract 8 stated that there were **two circumstances** where it would not be appropriate to recognise any gain or loss on the repurchase of debt:

(a) where the transaction was **not undertaken at a fair value,** but there were other relevant terms to the total transaction (which would often imply, but not require, that the transaction had taken place with a party connected with the company in some way); and

(b) where the debt was **replaced with new debt** on virtually identical terms, except for a difference in the rate of finance cost.

1.22 The basic text of FRS 4 ignores these issues, although they are mentioned in the notes on the development of the standard. The notes mention that such situations may need to be considered in the light of FRS 5 *Reporting for substance of transactions*. Under FRS 5, the transactions would need to be treated as linked, and accounted for as a whole rather than individually. Although not quite as specific or clear as UITF Abstract 8, this is usually likely to arrive at the same result. The apparent profit or loss would need to be considered together with all the other implications of the group of transactions, and it seems likely that this would often lead to deferral of the gain or loss.

Accounting for shares

1.23 Share issues should be recorded at the **fair value** of the consideration received less **issue costs**. Issue costs should be written off directly to reserves and should not be reported in the STRGL, ie those relating directly to the issue of the instrument should be accounted for as a reduction in the proceeds of a capital instrument.

Question 3

A company issues 100 £1 ordinary shares at par. Issue costs of £2 are incurred.

State how this transaction should be recorded and disclosed.

Answer

If there is a share premium account in existence, the share issue may be recorded by increasing share capital by £100 and setting off the issue costs against share premium account. In the analysis of total shareholders' funds, the equity interests will have increased by £98.

If there is no share premium account, share capital will be increased by £100 but the issue costs would be deducted from another reserve (usually profit and loss account reserve) subject to the provisions of the company's articles. Prior to FRS 4, companies in this situation had to charge the issue costs to the P&L account. The equity interest within shareholders' funds also increases by £98 in this case.

(Source: *Capital Instruments: A Guide to FRS 4, Ernst & Young*)

1.24 As stated above, under FRS 4 the balance sheet should show the amount of **shareholders' funds attributable** to equity interests and the amount attributable to non-equity interests.

1.25 The **finance cost** of non-equity shares should be calculated on the same basis as for debt instruments. Dividends in respect of non-equity shares have to be accounted for on an accruals basis. The only exception is where there are insufficient distributable profits and the dividend rights are non-cumulative. Arrears of preference dividends must therefore be provided for rather than simply disclosed.

Warrants

1.26 Warrants should be included in shareholders' funds at the **net proceeds** of the issue. If the warrant **lapses unexercised**, the amount paid for it becomes a gain and should be taken to the STRGL. If the warrant is **exercised**, the shares issued should be recorded at the aggregate of the net proceeds received when the warrant was issued and the fair value of the consideration received on exercise less issue costs of the shares.

Scrip dividends

1.27 If **shares are issued in lieu of dividends**, the value of the shares issued, being equal to the value of the dividend payable, should be reflected in the P&L account as an appropriation of profit.

Disclosure: shares

1.28 The following disclosures should be made.

(a) **Analysis of shares** between equity and non-equity interests.

(b) The **rights of each class** of shares should be summarised detailing:

    (i)   the rights to dividends;

    (ii)   the dates at which shares are redeemable and the amounts payable in respect of redemption;

    (iii) their priority and amounts receivable on a winding up; and

    (iv) their voting rights.

(c) Where **warrants or convertible debt** are in issue that may require the company to issue shares of a class not currently in issue the details in (b) above must be given.

(d) The **aggregate dividends** for each class of shares should be disclosed.

Minority interests

1.29 In consolidated financial statements, shares of subsidiary companies which are not owned by the group are accounted for as minority interests (either equity or non-equity). There is **one exception to this rule**. In some situations (for example where the parent or another group company has guaranteed their dividends or redemption), such shares become **liabilities** from the perspective of the group and therefore have to be reported as such on consolidation. For other capital instruments of a subsidiary, if the subsidiary has classified a capital instrument as debt, then the consolidated accounts will also do so.

1.30 Section summary

FRS 4 is technically extremely complex. You should be able to discuss the main provisions of the standard.
- **Definitions**, particularly of capital instruments, debt, equity/non-equity shares and shareholders' funds
- **General disclosure**: shareholders' funds, minority interests and liabilities
- Accounting for **debt instruments**
- Accounting for **shares**
- **Minority interests**

2 TREATMENT OF CERTAIN CAPITAL INSTRUMENTS

2.1 The application notes of FRS 4 contain guidance on the treatment of **specific types** of capital instrument. The list is not exhaustive and each complex capital instrument must be assessed on its individual terms and features.

Auction Market Preferred Shares (AMPS)

2.2 AMPS are **preference shares** that are entitled to dividends determined in accordance with an auction process in which a panel of investors participates, the shares being transferred at a fixed price to the investor who will accept the lowest dividend. If the auction process fails, for example because no bids are received, the shares remain in the ownership of the former holder and the dividend is increased to a rate, known as the default rate, that is calculated in accordance with a prescribed formula.

Analysis and required accounting

2.3 As AMPS are shares, dividends cannot be paid in respect of them except out of distributable profits, nor can they be redeemed unless the redemption is financed out of distributable profits or by a fresh issue of shares. Because they are redeemable at a fixed amount and because the dividend rights are limited, AMPS constitute **non-equity shares**.

2.4 AMPS should be reported within shareholders' funds as non-equity shares and included in the amount attributable to non-equity shares. The **finance cost** for each period should be the dividend rights accruing in respect of the period.

Capital contributions

2.5 Capital contributions are sometimes made by a holding company to its wholly-owned subsidiary in order to provide the finance necessary for the subsidiary, where it is not desired that this should be by way of debt and there would be adverse consequences (for example, tax consequences) arising from a subscription for new shares. Whilst a capital

contribution enhances the value of the holding company's investment in its subsidiary, there is no requirement for the subsidiary to bear any servicing cost, nor can it be required to repay the contribution.

Analysis and required accounting

2.6   From the standpoint of the subsidiary, a capital contribution does not contain an obligation to transfer economic benefits. In accordance with FRS 4 it should be reported within **shareholders' funds**. In the year in which the capital contribution is made, it should be reported in the reconciliation of movements in shareholders' funds.

Convertible capital bonds

2.7   The detailed provisions of convertible capital bonds vary but the following are typical. Convertible capital bonds are debt instruments on which interest is paid periodically, issued by a special purpose subsidiary incorporated outside the UK. Prior to maturity they my be exchanged for shares of the subsidiary which, at the option of the bondholder, are either immediately redeemed or immediately exchanged for ordinary shares of the parent. The bonds and payments in respect of the shares of the subsidiary are guaranteed by the parent. The parent has the right to issue convertible redeemable preference shares of its own in substitution for the bonds should it wish to do so.

Analysis and required accounting

2.8   From the standpoint of the **subsidiary**, convertible capital bonds are clearly debt since the obligation to pay interest is an obligation to transfer economic benefits. In addition, FRS 4 requires that conversion of debt should *not* be anticipated. In the subsidiary's financial statements the bonds should therefore be accounted for as **debt**.

2.9   From the standpoint of the **group** they are also **liabilities**. Even though the parent has the option to issue convertible preference shares in substitution for the bonds, the requirements of FRS 4 again entail that such conversion should *not* be anticipated. Whilst non-equity shares have a particular legal status that justifies their inclusion in shareholders' funds, this does not justify reporting within shareholders' funds an instrument that does not have that status and may never be converted into one that does.

2.10   Since the liabilities are convertible, the amount attributable to convertible capital bonds should be included in the amount of **convertible debt**, which should be stated separately from other liabilities.

Convertible debt with a premium put option

2.11   Convertible debt with a premium put option contains an option for the holder to demand redemption (either at the maturity of the debt or at some earlier date) for an amount that is in excess of the amount originally received for the debt. At the time the debt is issued, it is uncertain whether the debt will be converted before the redemption option my be exercised, and hence whether the premium on redemption will be paid.

Analysis and required accounting

2.12   The premium put option provides a higher guaranteed return to the holder of the debt that would be received on identical debt without such a put option. Often this higher return corresponds to that which the holder would have expected to receive on non-convertible

debt. The holder's decision as to whether to exercise the option will depend on the relative values of the shares to which he would be entitled on conversion and the cash receivable, including the premium, on exercise of the option.

2.13 The term of convertible debt with a premium put option should be considered to end on the **earliest date** at which the holder has the option to require redemption. The **premium** payable on exercise of the premium put option should be included in the calculation of the finance costs for the debt.

On conversion, the proceeds of the shares issued should be deemed to be the carrying amount of the debt, including accrued premium, immediately prior to conversion.

Convertible debt with enhanced interest

2.14 As an alternative to the premium put structure discussed above, convertible debt may contain an undertaking that the interest will be increased at a date in the future. At the time the debt is issued, it is uncertain whether the debt will be converted before the enhanced interest is payable.

Analysis and required accounting

2.15 The enhanced rate of interest increases the guaranteed return to the holder. Often this higher return corresponds to that which the holder would have expected to receive on non-convertible debt. The holders' decision as to whether to convert the debt will take into account the interest forgone by such a decision.

2.16 The interest for the **full term** of the convertible debt should be taken into account in the allocation of finance costs, which should be allocated at a **constant rate**.

2.17 EXAMPLE: CONVERTIBLE DEBT WITH ENHANCED INTEREST

Convertible debt is issued on 1 January 2000 for £1,000 and is redeemable at the same amount on 31 December 2014. It carries interest of £59 a year (a nominal rate of 5.9%) for the first five years, after which the rate rises to £141 a year (a nominal rate of 14.1%).

2.18 The finance costs should be allocated to accounting periods at the rate of 10% a year. The movement on the carrying amount over the term of the debt would be as follows.

Year ending	*Balance at beginning of year*	*Finance costs for year (10%)*	*Cash paid during year*	*Balance at end of year*
	£	£	£	£
31.12.2000	1,000	100	(59)	1,041
31.12.2001	1,041	104	(59)	1,086
31.12.2002	1,086	109	(59)	1,136
31.12.2003	1,136	113	(59)	1,190
31.12.2004	1,190	119	(59)	1,250
31.12.2005	1,250	125	(141)	1,234
31.12.2006	1,234	124	(141)	1,217
31.12.2007	1,217	122	(141)	1,198
31.12.2008	1,198	120	(141)	1,177
31.12.2009	1,177	118	(141)	1,154
31.12.2010	1,154	116	(141)	1,129
31.12.2011	1,129	113	(141)	1,101
31.12.2012	1,101	110	(141)	1,070
31.12.2013	1,070	107	(141)	1,036
31.12.2014	1,036	105*	(141 + 1,000)	-

BPP PUBLISHING

* Increased by £1 rounding difference.

Debt issued with warrants

2.19 Debt is sometimes issued with warrants. The issue is often made for the par value of the debt and the debt will be redeemed at the same amount. The warrants and the debts are capable of being transferred separately.

Analysis and required accounting

2.20 The proceeds of the issue should be allocated between the **debt** and the **warrants**. As a result, the amount of the proceeds deemed to relate to the debt will be less than par value. The discount on issue should be treated as **finance costs** and apportioned to accounting periods so that the total finance costs on the debt will have a constant relationship to the outstanding obligation.

2.21 Accounting for warrants is discussed above in Section 1.26.

2.22 EXAMPLE: DEBT ISSUED WITH WARRANTS

Debt and warrants are issued together for £1,250. The debt is redeemable at the same amount. The term of the debt is five years from 1 January 2000 and it carries interest at 4.7% (£59 a year). It is determined (for example by reference to the market values for the debt and the warrants immediately after issue) that the fair value of the debt and the warrants are respectively £1,000 and £250.

2.23 The debt would initially be recognised at £1,000. The finance cost of the debt is the difference between the payments required by the debt which total £1,545 ((5 × £59) + £1,250) and the deemed proceeds of £1,000, that is £545. In order to allocate these costs over the term of the debt at a constant rate on the carrying amount they must be allocated at the rate of 10%. The movements on the carrying amount of the debt over its term would be as follows.

Year ending	Balance at beginning of year £	Finance costs for year (10%) £	Cash paid during year £	Balance at end of year £
31.12.2000	1,000	100	(59)	1,041
31.12.2001	1,041	104	(59)	1,086
31.12.2002	1,086	109	(59)	1,136
31.12.2003	1,136	113	(59)	1,190
31.12.2004	1,190	119	(1,250 + 59)	-

Deep discount bonds

2.24 Deep discount bonds are bonds that carry a low nominal rate of interest and accordingly are issued at a discount to the value at which they will be redeemed. In the extreme case where no interest at all is payable they are sometimes referred to as **zero coupon bonds**.

Analysis and required accounting

2.25 The cost to the borrower of issuing a deep discount bond comprises the discount on issue as well as any interest payments. It is clear that deep discount bonds represent **liabilities** of the issuer since they contain an obligation to make cash payments. The **finance costs** will constitute the difference between the net proceeds and the total payments that the issuer

may be required to make in respect of the instrument and will be allocated to periods at a constant rate on the carrying amount, with the result that the carrying amount of the bond immediately prior to redemption will equate to the amount at which it is to be redeemed. The discount should *not* be treated as an asset.

2.26 The example shown above under debt issued with warrants illustrates the accounting treatment of a deep discount bond.

Income bonds

2.27 The distinctive feature of income bonds is that interest is payable only in the event that the issuer has sufficient reported profits (after allowing for interest on other kinds of debt) to make the payment. If profits are insufficient the issuer is not in default and no additional rights accrue to the holder of the bond, although interest payments may be redeemed by the issuer at a fixed amount on a specific date.

Analysis and required accounting

2.28 The requirement to redeem the bonds is an obligation to transfer economic benefits. The bonds must therefore be accounted for as a **liability**.

Index linked loans

2.29 Sometimes loan agreements do not state a specific amount for the payments: instead they include a formula to be used for their calculation. For example, in the case of floating rate loans, the amount of periodic payments of interest will be calculated by reference to a basic rate, eg LIBOR + 2%. Another example is that of index linked loans which may be redeemable at the principal amount multiplied by an index.

Analysis and required accounting

2.30 **Finance costs** contingent on uncertain events such as changes in an index should be adjusted to reflect those events only once they have occurred. The effect is that the initial carrying amount will take no account of those events but the carrying amount at each subsequent balance sheet date will be recalculated to take account of the changes occurring in that reporting period. The resulting change in carrying amount is accounted for as an increase or decrease in finance costs for the period.

2.31 **EXAMPLE: INDEX LINKED LOAN**

A loan of £1,250 is issued on 1 January 2000 on which interest of 4% (£50) is paid annually and the principal amount is repayable based on an index. The balance at the end of each year is found by multiplying the original principal amount by the index at the end of the year: the change in the amount is treated as additional finance costs.

Year ending	Balance at beginning of year	Finance costs for year (10%)	Cash paid during year	Balance at end of year	Index at end of year
	£	£	£	£	
31.12.2000	1,250	125	(50)	1,325	106
31.12.2001	1,325	10	(50)	1,375	110
31.12.2002	1,375	75	(50)	1,400	112
31.12.2003	1,400	150	(50)	1,500	120
31.12.2004	1,500	175	(1,625 + 50)	-	130

BPP PUBLISHING

Limited recourse debt

Features

2.32 Sometimes debt is raised on terms that the lender's recourse is limited. Although the borrower is expected to meet the obligations of the debt out of his general resources, in the event of default the lender can obtain repayment only by enforcing his rights against the particular security that is identified in the loan agreement. If the proceeds of the security are insufficient to repay the loan, the lender must bear the loss and has no further rights against the borrower.

Analysis and required accounting

2.33 Limited recourse debt constitutes an obligation on the part of the borrower to repay, and hence should be accounted for as a *liability*. The borrower will normally have all the benefits of the security (including the right to receive the sale proceeds) and will have to meet the obligation to repay the debt in order to preserve these rights. If the security declines in value the borrower may be able to elect to hand it over to the lender and thus avoid any further liability in respect of the debt. However, such an eventuality would be unusual, and therefore should not be reflected in the accounting until the asset is transferred.

2.34 Limited recourse debt is one of the kinds of debt envisaged in FRS 4 in that its **legal nature** differs from that usually associated with debt. A brief description of its nature should be given.

Participating preference shares

2.35 Participating preference shares are similar to other familiar kinds of preference shares except that they are entitled, in addition to a fixed dividend for each accounting period, to a proportion of the dividends paid on equity shares.

Analysis and required accounting

2.36 Because participating preference shares contain an entitlement to share in profits that is of a restricted amount and has priority over the other classes of shares, they are *non*-**equity shares** and their interest in **shareholders' funds** should be presented in the balance sheet within the aggregate amount attributable to non-equity shares. The fixed and participating elements of the dividend will be disclosed separately.

Perpetual debt

2.37 Perpetual debt is debt in respect of which the issuer has neither the right nor the obligation to repay the principal amount of the debt. Usually, interest is paid at a constant rate, or at a fixed margin over a benchmark rate such as LIBOR.

Analysis and required accounting

2.38 Sometimes it is suggested that as the principal amount will never be repaid there is no need for the balance sheet to reflect a liability in respect of the debt. However, the obligation to pay interest is an obligation to transfer economic benefits and hence the instrument is a **liability**. As there are no repayments of principal the burden of this liability never diminishes.

2.39 FRS 4 is based on the principle that debt should be accounted for having regard to all the payments required by the debt, irrespective of their legal description, in the determination of the appropriate finance charge and capital repayment for each accounting period. In the case of perpetual debt where interest is paid at a constant rate, or at a fixed margin over a benchmark, the correct **finance charge** will be equal to the coupon payable for each period. Hence no part of the repayments will reduce the carrying amount of net proceeds.

Repackaged perpetual debt

2.40 Sometimes perpetual debt is issued that carries interest at a relatively high rate for a number of years ('the primary period'), and then bears no further interest, or only a nominal amount. As the debt cannot be required to be redeemed, its value after the primary period has expired is negligible and, in practice, there will usually be arrangements to transfer it to a party friendly to the issuer or to enable the issuer to elect, in effect, to redeem the debt for a token amount.

Analysis and required accounting

2.41 The substance of such an arrangement is that the debt is repaid over the primary period. The payments required by the debt should be apportioned between a finance charge for each accounting period and the effective reduction of the principal amount. It would be necessary to make full disclosure of the arrangement in the financial statements.

2.42 The **finance costs** of the debt will be the difference between the net proceeds and the payments which the issuer is required to make. This will be allocated to periods over the primary period at a constant rate on the carrying amount.

2.43 EXAMPLE: REPACKAGED PERPETUAL DEBT

On 1 January 2000 a company borrows £1,250 which is stated to be irredeemable and to carry interest of 16.275% for the first ten years after which no further payments are required. The annual payments would be £203. The substance of the arrangement is that the ten payments of £203 would repay the amount borrowed and the finance charge would be allocated using a rate of 10 per cent. The accounting would be as follows.

Year ending	Balance at beginning of year	Finance costs for year (10%)	Cash paid during year	Balance at end of year
	£	£	£	£
31.12.2000	1,250	125	(203)	1,172
31.12.2001	1,172	117	(203)	1,086
31.12.2002	1,086	108	(203)	991
31.12.2003	991	99	(203)	887
31.12.2004	887	88	(203)	772
31.12.2005	772	77	(203)	646
31.12.2006	646	64	(203)	507
31.12.2007	507	50	(203)	354
31.12.2008	354	35	(203)	186
31.12.2009	186	17*	(203)	-

* Reduced by £1 rounding difference.

Stepped interest bonds

2.44 The stated rate of interest payable in respect of stepped interest bonds increases progressively over the period of issue.

Analysis and required accounting

2.45 In the case of stepped interest bonds, the stated rate of interest for each accounting period does not reflect the true economic cost of borrowing in any period during the time the bond is outstanding, since low rates of interest in one period are compensated for by higher rates in another.

2.46 The pattern of the interest payments does not affect the **allocation of finance costs**. The payments required by the debt should be apportioned between a finance charge for each accounting period at a constant rate on the outstanding obligation and a reduction of the carrying amount. The effect of this accounting on a stepped interest bond is that the overall effective interest cost will be charged in each accounting period: an accrual will be made in addition to the cash payments in earlier periods and will reverse, partially offsetting the higher cash payments, in later periods. It would be necessary to make full disclosure of the arrangement in the financial statements.

2.47 EXAMPLE: STEPPED INTEREST BOND

A loan of £1,250 is entered into on 1 January 2000 under which interest is payable according to the following schedule.

Year ending	Rates of interest (as a % nominal amount)	Balance at beginning of year
	£	£
31.12.2000	6.0	75
31.12.2001	8.0	100
31.12.2002	10.0	125
31.12.2003	12.0	150
31.12.2004	16.4	205

2.48 The overall effective rate can be found to be 10%. The movement on the loan over its period in issue would be as follows.

Year ending	Balance at beginning of year	Finance costs for year (10%)	Cash paid during year	Balance at end of year
	£	£	£	£
31.12.2000	1,250	125	(75)	1,300
31.12.2001	1,300	130	(100)	1,330
31.12.2002	1,330	133	(125)	1,338
31.12.2003	1,338	134	(150)	1,322
31.12.2004	1,322	133	(1,250 + 205)	-

Subordinated debt

2.49 Subordinated debt is debt under which the rights of the lender are not as great as those of other creditors of the issuer. The methods of subordination vary widely. One method of subordination is a prohibition on repayment of the debt whilst other creditors remain unpaid.

Analysis and required accounting

2.50 Irrespective of the means of subordination that is used, the lender on subordinated terms does not forgo the right to be repaid: he simply accepts that under certain conditions repayment will be postponed. It follows that, despite the subordination, the company has an obligation to repay (that it, an obligation to transfer economic benefits) and therefore subordinated debt should be accounted for as a **liability**.

2.51 Subordinated debt is one of the kinds of debt envisaged in FRS 4 in that its **legal nature** differs from that usually associated with debt. A brief description of its nature should be given.

2.52 Section summary

There is no need for you to learn all the descriptions and treatments given above. They are provided only as illustrations of the more common types of capital investments. You should read about each type carefully and try to understand *why* the relevant treatments are required in relation to the analysis given of FRS 4 in the previous section.

Exam focus point

Remember that, in an exam, you should judge each instrument on its individual terms.

3 FRS 13 DERIVATIVES AND OTHER FINANCIAL INSTRUMENTS: DISCLOSURES

3.1 FRS 13 appeared in September 1998. Although the measurement and hedging issues discussed above will take a long time to resolve, the disclosure of derivatives and other financial instruments is much less controversial.

Objectives

3.2 The objective of FRS 13 is to ensure that reporting entities falling within its scope provide in their financial statements disclosure necessary to enable users to assess:

   (a) the **risk profile** of the entity for each of the main risks that arise in connection with financial instruments, commodity contracts with similar characteristics; and

   (b) the **significance** of such instruments and contracts, regardless of whether they are on balance sheet (recognised) or off balance sheet (unrecognised), to an entity's reported financial position, performance and cash flows.

Scope

3.3 FRS 13 applies to an entity that:

   (a) has any of its capital instruments **listed** or **publicly traded** on a stock exchange or market; and

   (b) prepares financial statements that are intended to give a true and fair view of the entity's financial position and profit or loss (or income and expenditure) for a period.

3.4 The FRS is in three parts:

   (a) **Reporting entities other than financial institutions** and financial institution groups
   (b) **Banks,** banking groups and similar institutions
   (c) **Other financial institutions** and financial institution groups

We will concentrate on Part (a) as this is more relevant to your syllabus.

3.5 There are various **exclusions** encompassing all interests in group companies (except where held exclusively for resale) pensions, share options, obligations under operating leases (see

SSAP 21), insurance contracts, equity shares and warrants and options on equity shares issued by the entity.

Definitions

3.6   The following important definitions are given in FRS 13 (among others).

> ### KEY TERMS
>
> - **Borrowings**: an entity's borrowings are its debt (as defined in FRS 4) together with its obligations under finance leases (as defined in SSAP 21).
>
> - **Capital instruments**: defined as in FRS 4.
>
> - **Derivative financial instrument**: a financial instrument that derives its value from the price or rate of some underlying item.
>
> - **Equity instrument:** any instrument that evidences an ownership interest in an entity, ie a residual interest in the assets of the entity after deducting all of its liabilities.
>
> - **Fair value:** The amount at which an asset or liability could be exchanged in an arm's length transaction between informed and willing parties, other than in a forced or liquidation sale.
>
> - **Financial asset**: any asset that is:
>
>   (a)   cash;
>
>   (b)   a contractual right to receive cash or another financial asset from another entity;
>
>   (c)   a contractual right to exchange financial instruments with another entity under conditions that are potentially favourable; or
>
>   (d)   an equity instrument of another entity.
>
> - **Financial instrument**: a financial instrument is any contract that gives rise to both a financial asset of one entity and a financial liability or equity instrument of another entity.
>
> - **Financial liability**: any liability that is a contractual obligation:
>
>   (a)   to deliver cash or another financial asset to another entity; or
>
>   (b)   to exchange financial instruments with another entity under conditions that are potentially unfavourable.
>
> - **Functional currency**: the currency of the primary economic environment in which an entity operates and generates net cash flows.
>
> - **Short term debtors and creditors**: Financial assets and liabilities which meet all the following criteria.
>
>   (a)   They would be included under one of the following balance sheet headings if the entity was preparing its financial statements in accordance with Schedule 4 to the Companies Act 1985:
>
>   (i)   debtors;
>
>   (ii)   prepayments and accrued income;

KEY TERMS

  (iii) creditors: amounts falling due within one year, other than items that would be included under the 'debenture loans' and 'bank loans and overdrafts' subheadings;

  (iv) provisions for liabilities and charges; or

  (v) accruals and deferred income.

 (b) They mature or become payable within 12 months of the balance sheet date.

 (c) They are not a derivative financial instrument.

- **Trading in financial assets and financial liabilities**: Buying, selling, issuing or holding financial assets and financial liabilities in order to take advantage of short-term changes in market prices or rates or, in the case of financial institutions and financial institution groups, in order to facilitate customer transactions. *(FRS 13)*

Instruments to be dealt with in the disclosures

3.7 The FRS applies to all financial assets and financial liabilities, except those mentioned in Paragraph 3.5 above. Note also:

 (a) Short-term debtors and creditors - **either all** of those should be included in the disclosures **or none of these**.

 (b) **All non-equity** shares should be dealt with in the disclosures in the same way as financial liabilities except they should be **disclosed separately**.

Types of risks arising from financial instruments

3.8 This FRS is all about the disclosure of risk, so the different aspects of risk are analysed in some depth.

3.9 The two most familiar risks arising from financial instruments are credit risk and liquidity risk.

KEY TERMS

- **Credit risk**: the possibility that a loss may occur from the failure of another party to perform according to the terms of a contract.

- **Liquidity risk** (also referred to as funding risk): the risk that an entity will encounter difficulty in realising assets or otherwise raising funds to meet commitments associated with financial instruments. *(FRS 13)*

3.10 These are **familiar** and they tend to be the types of risk disclosed in financial statements, eg debtors' provisions indicate credit risk; borrowing conditions, current ratio and quick ratio indicate liquidity risk.

3.11 Financial instruments, however, entail two other important types of risk: **cash flow risk** and **market price risk**.

 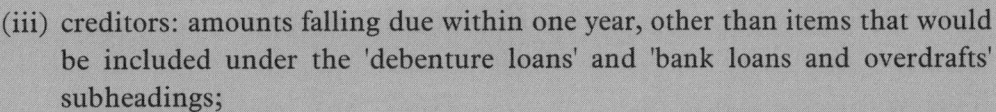

KEY TERMS

- **Cash flow risk**: the risk that future cash flows generated by a monetary financial instrument will fluctuate in amount.

- **Market price risk**: the possibility that future changes in market prices may change the value, or the burden, of a financial instrument. *(FRS 13)*

3.12 The main components of **market price risk** likely to affect most entities are also defined.

KEY TERMS

- **Interest rate risk**: the risk that the value of a financial instrument will fluctuate because of changes in market interest rates.

- **Currency risk**: the risk that the value of a financial instrument will fluctuate because of changes in foreign exchange rates.

- **Other market price risk**: the risk that the value of a financial instrument will fluctuate as a result of changes in market prices caused by factors other than interest rates or currencies. This category includes risk stemming from commodity prices and share prices. *(FRS 13)*

3.13 Until now information on these types of risk has been 'scant and often lacking in focus'. The fact that market price risk and cash flow risk are **diametrically opposed** is rarely mentioned; but the relationship between them has a significant impact on the risk profile. This can be illustrated as follows.

Financial instrument	Market price risk	Cash flow risk
Fixed rate interest-earning asset	Exposure	No exposure
Floating rate interest-earning asset	No exposure	Exposure

3.14 Depending on **management's attitude** to these particular risks, transactions may be undertaken to reduce one of the risks at the expense of increasing the other. Consequently, the choice of which risk it seeks to reduce will have an important bearing on the entity's financial position, financial results and cash flows.

Summary of requirements

3.15 FRS 13 requires entities that have any of their capital instruments listed or publicly traded on a domestic or foreign stock market, and all other banks and insurance companies, to disclose in their financial statements certain information, including information about **risk** on the derivatives and other financial instruments that they hold or have issued. This is to enable users to understand the major aspects of the risk profile that might affect the entity's performance and financial condition and how this risk profile is being managed.

3.16 The FRS requires **narrative disclosures** that put into context the entity's chosen risk profile. These narrative disclosures set the scene for, and are supplemented by, a range of **numerical disclosures** that show how the entity's objectives and policies were implemented in the period and provide supplementary quantitative information for evaluating significant or potentially significant exposures. Together, these disclosures will provide a broad

overview of the financial instruments held or issued and of the risk position created by them, focusing on those risks and instruments that are of greatest significance.

3.17 The **extent** of information disclosed will vary according to the nature of an entity's activities and the relative importance and complexity of transactions involving financial instruments. The vast majority of companies are not involved in complex transactions. The FRS also encourages an appropriate degree of **aggregation** to avoid excessively detailed disclosures.

Narrative disclosures

3.18 An entity is required to provide an explanation of the role of financial instruments in **creating or changing the risks** faced by an entity during the period. This discussion should also include a description of the entity's objectives, policies and strategies for holding and issuing derivatives and other financial instruments. The disclosures may be summarised as follows.

   (a) An explanation of the **objectives and policies** of holding financial instruments

   (b) **Significant changes** in these objectives or policies

   (c) An explanation of how the period end **numerical disclosures reflect the policies** and explanations presented

3.19 Although this disclosure is mandatory, the FRS permits the information to be given in a statement other than the financial statements, eg the **operating and financial review (OFR)**, provided that it is incorporated into the financial statements by reference.

3.20 The FRS offers the following **example** of discursive disclosure, which would probably be given in the OFR.

> 'The Group's financial instruments, other than derivatives, comprise borrowings, some cash and liquid resources, and various items, such as trade debtors, trade creditors etc, that arise directly from its operations. The main purpose of these financial instruments is to raise finance for the Group's operations.
>
> The Group also enters into derivatives transactions (principally interest rate swaps and forward foreign currency contracts). The purpose of such transactions is to manage the interest rate and currency risks arising from the Group's operations and its sources of finance.
>
> It is, and has been throughout the period under review, the Group's policy that no trading in financial instruments shall be undertaken.
>
> The main risks arising from the Group's financial instruments are interest rate risk, liquidity risk and foreign currency risk. The Board reviews and agrees policies for managing each of these risks and they are summarised below. These policies have remained unchanged since the beginning of 19X0.
>
> *Interest rate risk*
>
> The Group finances its operations through a mixture of retained profits and bank borrowings. The Group borrows in the desired currencies at both fixed and floating rates of interest and then uses interest rate swaps to generate the desired interest profile and to manage the Group's exposure to interest rate fluctuations. The Group's policy is to keep between 50 per cent and 65 per cent of its borrowings at fixed rates of interest. At the year-end, 62 per cent of the Group's borrowings were at fixed rates after taking account of interest rate swaps.
>
> *Liquidity risk*
>
> As regards liquidity, the Group's policy has throughout the year been that, to ensure continuity of funding, at least 50 per cent of its borrowings should mature in more than five years. At the year-end, 57 per cent of the Group's borrowings were due to mature in more than five years.
>
> Short-term flexibility is achieved by overdraft facilities.

Foreign currency risk

The Group has one significant overseas subsidiary - Foreign - which operates in the USA and whose revenues and expenses are denominated exclusively in US dollars. In order to protect the Group's sterling balance sheet from the movements in the US dollar/sterling exchange rate, the Group finances its net investment in this subsidiary by means of US dollar borrowings.

About one-third of the sales of the Group's UK businesses are to customers in continental Europe. These sales are priced in sterling but invoiced in the currencies of the customers involves. The Group's policy is to eliminate all currency exposures on sales at the time of sale through forward currency contracts. All the other sales of the UK businesses are denominated in sterling.'

Numerical disclosures

3.21   The FRS requires specific numerical disclosures. So they do not become so detailed that their message is obscured, the FRS encourages, and in some cases requires, a high degree of aggregation. The required disclosures are as follows.

   (a) **Interest rate risk**. The carrying amount of financial liabilities should be analysed to show those liabilities at fixed interest rates and those at floating rates. Under this heading, operating entities will need to provide:

   (i)   The weighted average interest rate for fixed debt
   (ii)   The weighted average period for which interest rates are fixed
   (iii)   A benchmark for determining floating rate interest charges (eg LIBOR)

   (b) **Currency risk**. Monetary assets and liabilities should be analysed by principal currency (ignoring those assets and liabilities denominated in the entity's functional currency)

   (c) **Liquidity risk**. Disclose:

   (i)   The maturity profile of the carrying amount of financial liabilities
   (ii)   The maturity profile of undrawn committed borrowing facilities

   (d) **Fair values** and book values of financial assets and liabilities must be disclosed, along with an indication of how the fair value was ascertained (eg discounting cash flows, market price)

   (e) **Financial instruments used for trading**. Disclose:

   (i)   The net gain or loss included in the P&L, analysed by type of financial instrument, business activity or risk

   (ii)   Their period end value, including the average fair value where this is untypical.

   (f) **Financial instruments used for hedging**. Disclose:

   (i)   The cumulative aggregate gains and losses that are unrecognised at the balance sheet date

   (ii)   The cumulative aggregate gains and losses carried forwards at the balance sheet date pending their recognition in the profit and loss account

   (iii)   The extent to which (i) and (ii) are expected to be recognised in the profit and loss account in the next accounting period

   (iv)   Amounts of gains and losses included in the period's profit and loss account that arose in previous years and were unrecognised and carried forward

   (g) Certain **commodity contracts**

   (h) **Market price risk** (encouraged, not required)

Question 4

Why do you think FRS 13 requires disclosure of the following?

(a) The maturity profile of the carrying amount of financial liabilities

(b) The maturity profile of undrawn committed borrowing facilities

(c) The carrying amount of financial liabilities analysed to show those liabilities at fixed interest rates and those at floating rates

Answer

(a) This will tell us about patterns of cash flow in the foreseeable future - will we have to pay a big loan off soon; how great is our exposure to debt?

(b) An example of 'undrawn committed borrowing facilities' might be an overdraft facility whose limit is, say, three times our actual overdraft. Such a facility provides a **cushion** against other risks, and gives us flexibility, or, in the words of the *Statement of Principles* 'financial adaptability'.

(c) Again, this is about risk - a floating interest rate liability will be more risky than a fixed rate one, although this risk can go in our favour.

3.22 The FRS gives **examples** of numerical disclosures, as follows.

'*Interest rate risk profile of financial assets and financial liabilities*

Financial assets

The Group has no financial assets, other than short-term debtors and an immaterial amount of cash at bank.

Financial liabilities

After taking into account the various interest rate swaps and forward foreign currency contracts entered into by the Group, the interest rate profile of the Group's financial liabilities at 31 December 19X1 was:

Currency	Total	*Floating rate financial liabilities*	*Fixed rate financial liabilities*	*Financial liabilities on which no interest is paid*
	£m	£m	£m	£m
Sterling	415	150	250	15
US dollar	200	80	120	-
Total	615	230	370	15

	Fixed rate financial liabilities		*Financial liabilities on which no interest is paid*
Currency	*Weighted average interest rate*	*Weighted average period for which rate is fixed*	*Weighted average period until maturity*
	%	Years	Years
Sterling	10	5	1.4
US dollar	7	8	-
Total	-	6	1.4

The floating rate financial liabilities comprise:

- Sterling denominated bank borrowings and overdrafts that bear interest at rates based on the six-month LIBOR; and

- US dollar denominated bank borrowings that bear interest at rates based on the US Prime rate.

Currency exposures

As at 31 December 19X1, after taking into account the effects of forward foreign exchange contracts the Group had no currency exposures.

Maturity of financial liabilities

The maturity profile of the Group's financial liabilities at 31 December 19X1 was as follows.

	£m
In one year or less, or on demand	200
In more than one year but not more than two years	15
In more than two years but not more than five years	60
In more than five years	340
	615

Borrowing facilities

The Group has various undrawn committed borrowing facilities. The facilities available at 31 December 19X1 in respect of which all conditions precedent had been met were as follows.

	£m
Expiring in one year or less	40
Expiring in more than one year but not more than two years	7
Expiring in more than two years	3
	50

Fair values of financial assets and financial liabilities

Set out below is a comparison by category of book values and fair values of the Group's financial assets and liabilities as at 31 December 19X1.

	Book value £m	Fair value £m
Primary financial instruments held or issued to finance the Group's operations:		
Short-term financial liabilities and current portion of long-term borrowings	(215)	(223)
Long-term borrowings	(400)	(370)
Financial assets	7	8
Derivative financial instruments held to manage the interest rate and currency profile:		
Interest rate swaps	-	15
Forward foreign currency contracts	-	(5)

The fair values of the interest rate swaps, forward foreign currency contracts and sterling denominated long-term fixed rate debt with a carrying amount of £250 million have been determined by reference to prices available from the markets on which the instruments involved are traded. All the other fair values shown above have been calculated by discounting cash flows at prevailing interest rates.

Gains and losses

The Group enters into forward foreign currency contracts to eliminate the currency exposures that arise on sales denominated in foreign currencies immediately those sales are transacted. It also uses interest rate swaps to manage its interest rate profile. Changes in the fair value of instruments used as hedges are not recognised in the financial statements until the hedged position matures. An analysis of these unrecognised gains and losses is as follows:

	Gains £m	Losses £m	Total net gains/(losses) £m
Unrecognised gains and losses on hedges at 1.1.X1	9	12	(3)
Gains and losses arising in previous years that were recognised in 19X1	8	9	1
Gains and losses arising before 1.1.X1 that were not recognised in 19X1	1	3	(2)
Gains and losses arising in 19X1 that were not recognised in 19X1	18	6	12
Unrecognised gains and losses on hedges at 31.12.X1	19	9	10
Of which:			
Gains and losses expected to be recognised in 19X2	12	6	6
Gains and losses expected to be recognised in 19X3 or later	7	3	4

Market price risk

The Group's exposure to market price risk comprises interest rate and currency risk exposures. It monitors these exposures primarily through a process known as sensitivity analysis.

On the basis of the Group's analysis, it is estimated that a rise of one percentage point in all interest rates would have reduced 19X1 profit before tax by approximately 1.5 per cent and that a three percentage point increase would have reduced such profits by 4.2 per cent. This is well within the ranges that the Group regards as acceptable.'

Criticisms of FRS 13

3.23 As a disclosure standard applying only to quoted companies, banks and similar institutions, FRS 13 would not appear to present too many implementation problems. However, some criticisms have been voiced about the detail of the disclosures.

(a) Not all companies will have systems which enable the data on hedging to be easily collected.

(b) The requirement to fair-value financial assets and liabilities will involve extra time and costs.

(c) Not all the disclosures are particularly meaningful.

3.24 Section summary

Concentrate on getting an overall picture of the FRS 13 disclosures.

- **Definitions**: financial instruments, derivatives, financial assets/liabilities
- **Risk**: understand market price risk and cash flow risk and their relationship
- **Disclosure**: overall narrative and numerical disclosure requirements

Chapter roundup

- FRS 4 *Capital instruments* is a complex standard. It has been issued to halt abuses in the accounting for **debt** and **equity**.

- The important things to remember in relation to **FRS 4** are:
  - Definitions
  - Accounting treatment
  - Disclosure

- Although the **application notes** to FRS 4 examine the treatment of certain capital instruments, each one must be judged on its own terms.

- **Disclosure matters** relating to derivatives have already been developed in **FRS 13**. You should understand the major definitions and the different types of risk.

Quick quiz

1 How should debt and equity be distinguished under FRS 4? (see para 1.5)

2 How should hybrid instruments be disclosed according to FRS 4? (1.6)

3 At what value should debt be recorded in the balance sheet? (1.14)

4 How should the finance costs of debt be allocated under FRS 4? (1.15)

5 What disclosures should be made in relation to debt? (1.20)

6 Summarise the accounting treatment required in the application notes to FRS 4 for:

(a) convertible capital bonds (2.8 - 2.10)
(b) deep discount bonds (2.25)
(c) index linked loans (2.30)
(d) participating performance shares (2.36)
(e) perpetual debt (2.38, 2.39)

7 What are the objectives of FRS 13? (3.2)

8 Define a derivative financial instrument. (key term)

9 Which two types of risk are associated particularly with financial instruments? (3.9)

10 What two types of disclosure are required by FRS 13? (3.16)

11 What are the main numerical disclosures required by FRS 13? (3.21)

Question to try	Level	Marks	Time
10	Introductory	n/a	n/a

Chapter 10

HIRE PURCHASE AND LEASING

Chapter topic	Syllabus reference	Ability required
1 Forms of lease	9(a)	Application
2 Lessee accounting	9(a)	Application
3 Lessor accounting	9(a)	Application
4 A criticism of SSAP 21	9(a)	Application

Introduction

Leasing transactions are externally common in business and you will often come across them in both your business and personal capacity. You should be familiar with the more straightforward aspects of this topic from your earlier studies, but we will go through these aspects in full as leasing can be very complicated. The first section of this chapter goes over some of that basic groundwork, before the chapter moves on to more complicated aspects, including the **actuarial method after tax** for lessor accounting.

Leasing is strongly associated with **off balance sheet finance** and you should therefore bear the contents of the previous chapter in mind. Leasing is the most common example given of off balance sheet finance.

1 FORMS OF LEASE
11/95, 5/99

KEY TERM

A **lease** is a contract between a lessee for the hire of a specific asset. The lessor retains ownership of the asset but conveys the right of the use of the asset to the lessee for an agreed period of time in return for the payment of specified rentals. The term 'lease' also applies to other arrangements in which one party retains ownership of an asset but conveys the right to the use of the asset to another party for an agreed period of time in return for specified payments.
(SSAP 21)

1.1 Leasing can be considered, to be, like hire purchase, a form of instalment credit. Leases of this type are referred to as **finance leases.** Although there are many variations, in general a finance lease will have the following characteristics.

(a) The lease term will consist of a **primary period and a secondary period**. The primary period, which is usually for three, four or five years, will be non-cancellable or cancellable only under certain conditions, for example on the payment of a heavy settlement figure. The secondary period is usually cancellable at any time at the lessee's option.

BPP PUBLISHING

(b) The rentals payable during the primary period will be sufficient to **repay to the lessor** the cost of the equipment plus interest thereon.

(c) The rentals during the secondary period will be of a **nominal amount**.

(d) If the lessee wishes to **terminate the lease** during the secondary period, the equipment will be sold and substantially all of the sale proceeds will be paid to the lessee as a rebate of rentals.

(e) The lessee will be responsible for the **maintenance** and **insurance** of equipment throughout the lease.

(f) At no time may the lessee acquire the **legal title** to the equipment.

1.2 It can be seen from the above that, from the point of view of the lessee, leasing an asset is very **similar to purchasing** it using a loan repayable over the primary period. The lessee has all of the benefits and responsibilities of ownership except for the capital allowances.

1.3 Other leases are of a very different nature. For example, a businessman may decide to hire (lease) a car whilst his own is being repaired. A lease of this nature is for a short period of time compared with the car's useful life and the lessor will expect to lease it to many different lessees during that life. Furthermore, the lessor rather than the lessee will be responsible for maintenance. Agreements of this type are usually called **operating leases**.

1.4 **SSAP 21** *Accounting for leases and hire purchase contracts* requires that different accounting treatments should be adopted for finance and operating leases. In distinguishing between them, SSAP 21 makes the following definitions.

KEY TERMS

- A **finance lease** is a lease that transfers substantially all the risks and rewards of ownership of an asset to the lessee. It should be presumed that such a transfer of risks and rewards occurs if at the inception of a lease the present value of the minimum lease payments, including any initial payment, amounts to substantially all (normally 90% or more) of the fair value of the leased asset. The present value should be calculated by using the interest rate implicit in the lease. If the fair value of the asset is not determinable, an estimate thereof should be used.

  Notwithstanding the fact that a lease meets the conditions in (the above) paragraph, the presumption that it should be classified as a finance lease may in exceptional circumstances be rebutted if it can be clearly demonstrated that the lease in question does not transfer substantially all the risks and rewards of ownership (other than legal title) to the lessee. Correspondingly, the presumption that a lease which fails to meet the conditions in (the above) paragraph is not a finance lease may in exceptional circumstances be rebutted.

- An **operating lease** is a lease other than a finance lease. *(SSAP 21)*

2 LESSEE ACCOUNTING   5/99

Finance leases

2.1 From the lessee's point of view there are two main **accounting problems**:

(a) whether the asset should be **capitalised** as if it had been purchased; and

(b) how the **lease charges** should be allocated between different accounting periods.

2.2 SSAP 21 requires that the following should take place.

(a) A finance lease should be recorded in the balance sheet of a lessee as an asset and as an obligation to pay future rentals. At the inception of the lease the sum to be recorded both as an asset and as a liability should be the **present value of the minimum lease payments,** derived by discounting them at the interest rate implicit in the lease.

(b) In practice in the case of a finance lease the **fair value** of the asset will often be a sufficiently close approximation to the present value of the minimum lease payments and may in these circumstances be substituted for it.

(c) The combined benefit to a lessor of regional development and other **grants** together with **capital allowances,** which reduce tax liabilities, may enable the minimum lease payments under a finance lease to be reduced to a total which is less than the fair value of the asset. In these circumstances, the amount to be capitalised and depreciated should be restricted to the **minimum lease payments**. A negative finance charge should not be shown.

(d) **Rentals payable** should be apportioned between the finance charge and a reduction of the outstanding obligation for future amounts payable. The total finance charge under a finance lease should be allocated to accounting periods during the lease term so as to produce a **constant periodic rate of charge** on the remaining balance of the obligation for each accounting period, or a reasonable approximation thereto.

(e) An asset leased under a finance lease should be **depreciated** over the shorter of the lease term or its useful life. However, in the case of a hire purchase contract which has the characteristics of a finance lease, the asset should be depreciated over its useful life.

2.3 In interpreting the above these definitions from SSAP 21 should be borne in mind.

KEY TERMS

- **Fair value** is the price at which an asset could be exchanged in an arm's length transaction less, where applicable, any grants receivable towards the purchase or use of the asset.

- **Finance charge** is the amount borne by the lessee over the lease terms, representing the difference between the total of the minimum lease payments (including any residual amounts guaranteed by him) and the amount at which he records the leased asset at the inception of the lease.

- The **interest rate implicit in a lease** is the discount rate which at the inception of the lease, when applied to the amounts which the lessor expects to receive and retain produces an amount (the present value) equal to the fair value of the leased asset. The amounts which the lessor expects to receive and retain comprise:

  (a) the minimum lease payments to the lessor (as defined below); *plus*
  (b) any unguaranteed residual value; *less*
  (c) any part of (a) and (b) for which the lessor will be accountable to the lessee.

  If the interest rate implicit in the lease is not determinable, it should be estimated by reference to the rate which a lessee would be expected to pay on a similar lease.

> **KEY TERMS**
>
> - The **lease term** is the period for which the lessee has contracted to lease the asset and any further term for which the lessee has the option to continue to lease the asset, with or without further payment, which option it is reasonably certain at the inception of the lease that the lessee will exercise.
>
> - The **minimum lease payments** are the minimum payments over the remaining part of the lease term (excluding charges for services and taxes to be paid by the lessor) and:
>
>   (a) in the case of the lessee, any residual amounts guaranteed by him or by a party related to him; or
>
>   (b) in the case of the lessor, any residual amounts guaranteed by the lessee or by an independent third party.
>
> - The **inception of a lease** is the earlier of the time the asset is brought into use or the date from which rentals first accrue.   *(SSAP 21)*

2.4 We have seen that the main argument in favour of capitalisation is substance over form. The main arguments **against** capitalisation are as follows.

(a) **Legal position.** The benefit of a lease to a lessee is an intangible asset, not the ownership of the equipment. It may be misleading to users of accounts to capitalise the equipment when a lease is legally quite different from a loan used to purchase the equipment. Capitalising leases also raises the question of whether other executory contracts should be treated similarly, for example contracts of employment.

(b) **Complexity.** Many small businesses will find that they do not have the expertise necessary for carrying out the calculations required for capitalisation.

(c) **Subjectivity.** To some extent, capitalisation is a somewhat arbitrary process and this may lead to a lack of consistency between companies.

(d) **Presentation.** The impact of leasing can be more usefully described in the notes to financial statements. These can be made readily comprehensible to users who may not understand the underlying calculations.

2.5 There are two main ways of **allocating the finance charge** between accounting periods:

(a) the actuarial method (before tax); and
(b) the sum of the digits method.

Each of these is illustrated in an example later in this chapter. The actuarial method is to be preferred as it most exactly reflects the way in which the finance charges are incurred. The sum of the digits method produces a reasonable approximation to the actuarial method.

Operating leases

2.6 SSAP 21 requires that the **rentals** under operating leases should be written off as an expense on a **straight line basis** over the lease term even if the payments are not made on such a basis, unless another systematic and rational basis is justified by the circumstances.

Hire purchase contracts

2.7   Assets acquired under hire purchase agreements should be **capitalised** in the same way as those under finance leases if the HP contracts are of a financing nature. Otherwise (eg, if the option to purchase is not to be taken up) they should be accounted for on a basis similar to that used for operating leases.

Disclosure requirements: lessees

2.8   SSAP 21 requires lessees to disclose the following information.

(a)   The gross amounts of **assets held under finance leases*** together with the related accumulated depreciation, analysed by class of asset must be shown. This information may be consolidated with the corresponding information for owned assets, and not shown separately. In that case, the net amount of assets held under finance leases* included in the overall total should also be disclosed.

(b)   The amounts of **obligations related to finance leases*** (net of finance charges allocated to future periods) should be disclosed. These should be shown separately from other obligations and liabilities and should be analysed between amounts payable in the next year, amounts payable in the second to fifth years inclusive from the balance sheet date and the aggregate amounts payable thereafter.

(c)   The **aggregate finance charges** allocated for the period in respect of finance leases must appear.

(d)   Disclosure should be made of the amount of any **commitments** existing at the balance sheet date in respect of finance leases which have been entered into but whose inception occurs after the year end.

(e)   The total of **operating lease rentals** charged as an expense in the profit and loss account should be disclosed, analysed between amounts payable in respect of hire of plant and machinery and in respect of other operating leases.

(f)   In respect of **operating leases**, the lessee should disclose the payments which he is **committed** to make during the next year, analysed between those in which the commitment expires within that year, in the second to fifth years inclusive and over five years from the balance sheet date, showing separately the commitments in respect of leases of land and buildings and other operating leases.

*   Including the equivalent information in respect of **hire purchase contracts**.

> **Exam focus point**
> Rather than learn this list by heart, take a look at a set of company accounts and see how those disclosures work in practice.

2.9   EXAMPLE: ACTUARIAL AND SUM OF DIGITS METHODS

A lessee enters a leasing agreement on 31 December 19X3 for a piece of equipment costing £47,460. The lease requires the payment of an annual rental of £13,610 payable in advance. The primary period of the lease is for four years. After the end of the primary period, the lessee has the right to extend the lease indefinitely on payment of a nominal annual rental. The lessee believes that the equipment will last for four years and will have no scrap value at the end of that period. The lessee depreciates assets of this type using the straight line basis. Both the lessor and the lessee have accounting periods ending on 31 December.

2.10 SOLUTION: ACTUARIAL METHOD

Under the actuarial method, the first problem is to find the implied rate of interest in the lease. To do this the following steps should be followed.

Step 1   Establish the amount of money that has been advanced. This will be equal to the cost of the equipment less any deposit and/or rental payable at the start of the lease.

	£
Cost	47,460
Initial rental	13,610
Amount advanced	33,850

Step 2   Divide the amount advanced by the period rental to give the annuity (or cumulative discount) factor.

$$\text{Annuity factor} = \frac{33,850}{13,610} = 2.487$$

Step 3   Establish how many rentals are payable excluding, if appropriate, that payable at the start of the lease. Here it is 3 rentals.

Step 4   Inspect the annuity table for the number of periods equal to the number of rentals found in Step 3. The implied rate will have the same annuity factor as that found in Step 2.

From the table reproduced towards the end of this Study Text it can be seen that a rate of 10% has an annuity factor of 2.487.

In some cases it will be found that the annuity factor calculated in Step 2 does not equate exactly to one in the table. It will then be necessary to find the implied rate by interpolation.

Note. This calculation assumes that the secondary period rental is nominal and ignores the residual value of the equipment.

In the present case, the purchase cost is known to the lessee. The liability and the value of the machine will, therefore, be recorded at £47,460 at the start of the lease. The liability will of course be reduced immediately by the first rental. Since the lease started on the last day of the lessee's accounting period to 31 December 19X3, there will be no finance charge in respect of that year.

It is now possible to establish the amount of the finance charges in each period.

Period	Liability at start of period £	Rental payment £	Liability during period £	Finance charge = 10% of liability during period £	Liability at end of period £
1	47,460	13,610	33,850	3,385	37,235
2	37,235	13,610	23,625	2,362	25,987
3	25,987	13,610	12,377	1,233	13,610
4	13,610	13,610			

Notes

(a)   The periods (1 - 4) are years under the lease rather than accounting periods (see below).

(b)   The format of the table would obviously need to be adjusted if the rentals were payable in arrears.

(c)   As suggested in the standard the allocation 'produces a constant periodic rate of return (10%) on the remaining balance of the liability'.

(d)   Payment in arrears would be calculated differently.

Charges to the P&L account

Year ending 31 December	Finance charge £	Depreciation £	Total £
19X3	-	-	-
19X4	3,385	11,865	15,250
19X5	2,362	11,865	14,227
19X6	1,233	11,865	13,098
19X7	-	11,865	11,865
	6,980	47,460	54,440

Note that the total charge to the P&L account over the life of the machine is equal to the total rentals paid (£13,610 × 4 = £54,440).

Balance sheet presentation

	As at 31 December				
	19X3 £	19X4 £	19X5 £	19X6 £	19X7 £
Assets					
Equipment acquired under finance leases	47,460	47,460	47,460	47,460	47,460
Less accumulated depreciation	-	11,865	23,730	35,595	47,460
	47,460	35,595	23,730	11,865	-
Liabilities					
Obligations under finance leases					
Within 2 - 5 years	23,625	12,377	-	-	-
Within 1 year	10,225	11,248	12,377	-	-
	33,850	23,625	12,377	-	-

Note that the obligations under the lease can be found from the main table constructed above. It is, of course, necessary to ensure that the finance charges are allocated to the correct accounting periods.

SSAP 21 also permits this alternative analysis.

Leasing commitments: finance leases

The future minimum lease payments under finance leases to which the company is committed as at 31 December 19X3 are as follows.

Year ending 31 December	£	
19X4	13,610	
19X5	13,610	
19X6	13,610	
19X7	-	) This part of the table has been included
19X8	-	) for illustrative purposes as the standard
19X9 and after	-	) suggests that the figures for the next
	40,830	five years should be shown separately and those thereafter in aggregate.
Less finance charged allocated to future periods	6,980	
	33,850	This figure will be the same as that in the balance sheet

2.11 SOLUTION: SUM OF THE DIGITS METHOD

The sum of the digits (or rule of 78) method gives an acceptable approximation to the actuarial method and, because of its relative simplicity, has been more popular in practice. Although you should already be familiar with the technique, it is as well to revise the main steps.

BPP PUBLISHING

Step 1   Calculate the total finance charges. This will be equal to the total rentals less the value of the equipment.

	£
Cost	54,440
Initial rental	47,460
Amount advanced	6,980

Step 2   Establish how many rentals are payable excluding if appropriate, that payable at the start of the lease (see note below). Here it is 3 rentals

Step 3   Calculate the sum of the digits. For large numbers it is best to use the formula below where n is the number found in Step 2.

$$\text{Sum of digits} = \frac{n(n+1)}{2}$$

$$1 + 2 + 3 = 6 \quad \frac{3(3+1)}{2} = 6$$

Step 4   Calculate the appropriate proportion of the finance charges starting with the number obtained in Step 2 for the first period of the lease.

Period	Finance charges
1	3/6 × £6,980 = £3,490
2	2/6 × £6,980 = £2,327
3	1/6 × £6,980 = £1,163

Note. In the present case, although the primary period of the lease is four years, the liability under the lease will be discharged after three years (and one day) as all four rentals will then have been paid. For this reason, the finance charges will be allocated to the accounting periods 19X4, 19X5 and 19X6 (as under the actuarial method) and no charge will arise in the final year of the primary period, 19X7. If the rentals had been payable in arrears, it would have been necessary to calculate a finance charge for each year of the primary period and the sum of the digits would be 10 (1 + 2 + 3 + 4).

Charges to the P&L account

Year ending 31 December	Finance charge £	Depreciation £	Total £
19X4	3,490	11,865	15,355
19X5	2,327	11,865	14,192
19X6	1,163	11,865	13,028
19X7	-	11,865	11,865
	6,980	47,460	54,440

The balance sheet presentation for the asset will be the same as under the actuarial method. The obligation under the lease could be arrived at by preparing a table similar to that used before. In this case, however, let us consider the entries in the liability account.

OBLIGATIONS UNDER FINANCE LEASE

Date		£	Date		£
31.12.X3	Cash	13,610	31.12.X3	Fixed assets	47,460
31.12.X3	Balance c/f	33,850			
		47,460			47,460
31.12.X4	Cash	13,610	1.1.X4	Balance b/f	33,850
31.12.X4	Balance c/f	23,730	31.12.X4	Finance charge: P&L	3,490
		37,340			37,340
31.12.X5	Cash	13,610	1.1.X5	Balance b/f	23,730
31.12.X5	Balance c/f	12,447	31.12.X5	Finance charge: P&L	2,327
		26,057			26,057

Date		£	Date		£
31.12.X6	Cash	13,610	1.1.X6	Balance b/f	12,447
			31.12.X6	Finance charge: P&L	1,163
		13,610			13,610

Summary

2.12   The two main methods of allocating the finance charges are summarised below.

	Actuarial	*Sum of the digits*
	£	£
19X4	3,385	3,490
19X5	2,362	2,327
19X6	1,233	1,163
	6,980	6,980

UITF Abstract 12 *Lessee accounting for reverse premiums and similar incentives*

2.13   This Abstract requires benefits received and receivable by a lessee as an **incentive** to sign a lease to be spread on a **straight-line basis** over the lease term, or, if shorter than the full lease term, over the period to the review date on which the rent is first expected to be adjusted to the prevailing market rate. This treatment is based on the presumption that an incentive (however structured) is in substance part of the market return which the lessor is for the time being prepared to accept in order to let a particular property.

2.14   The UITF believes that the presumption referred to above can be **rebutted** only where, exceptionally, adoption of the standard treatment required by the Abstract would be misleading. In such circumstances another systematic and rational basis may be used, with various disclosures as set out in the Abstract. The Abstract also recognises that a spreading method other than straight-line may be appropriate in exceptional circumstances: eg where it is expected that market rents will rise, but will exceed the initial rent payable under the lease only at the second rent review rather than the first, the spreading method used should take account of this, rather than being straight-line, so that the P&L charge in each year corresponds as closely as possible to the expected market rent.

Question 1

On 31 December 19X3 Cradlebrake Ltd entered into a leasing arrangement with Heathcliffe Finance for a large packaging machine. The terms of the lease require quarterly payments in arrears for four years of £1,107.24. Cradlebrake depreciates all plant and machinery on a straight line basis. The engineering manager estimates that the packaging machine will last 4 years and will have no scrap value. The rate of interest implicit in the lease is 5% per quarter. The company intends to capitalise the machine and show as a liability the outstanding rentals (excluding interest).

You are required to calculate the relevant P&L account and balance sheet figures for incorporation in the annual accounts for the accounting periods ending 30 September 19X4, 19X5, 19X6, 19X7 and 19X8.

Answer

	Balance sheet		P&L account	
	Leased assets	*Leasing creditor*	*Depreciation charge*	*Interest*
Year ending	£	£	£	£
30.9.X4	9,750	10,401	2,250	1,723
30.9.X5	6,750	7,870	3,000	1,898
30.9.X6	3,750	4,794	3,000	1,353
30.9.X7	750	1,055	3,000	690
30.9.X8	-	-	750	53

Working

Using the table towards the end of the Study Text, the present value of the payments under the lease is equal to £1,107.24 × 10.838 = £12,000 at the start of the lease.

Period	Liability at start of period £	Finance charge £	Rental payment £	Liability at end of period £
1	12,000.00	600.00	(1,107.24)	11,492.76
2	11,492.76	574.64	(1,107.24)	10,960.16
3	10,960.16	548.01	(1,107.24)	10,400.93
4	10,400.93	520.05	(1,107.24)	9,813.74
5	9,813.74	490.69	(1,107.24)	9,197.19
6	9,197.19	459.86	(1,107.24)	8,549.81
7	8,549.81	427.49	(1,107.24)	7,870.06
8	7,870.06	393.50	(1,107.24)	7,156.32
9	7,156.32	357.82	(1,107.24)	6,406.90
10	6,406.90	320.34	(1,107.24)	5,620.00
11	5,620.00	281.00	(1,107.24)	4,793.76
12	4,793.76	239.69	(1,107.24)	3,926.21
13	3,926.21	196.31	(1,107.24)	3,015.28
14	3,015.28	150.76	(1,107.24)	2,058.80
15	2,058.80	102.94	(1,107.24)	1,054.50
16	1,054.50	52.74	(1,107.24)	Nil

The finance charges for each year can be found by adding together those for the appropriate quarters.

Where a large number of payments are involved, it is probably simpler to look at accounting periods rather than the periods within the lease. The liability at any point of the lease is equal to the present value of payments due thereafter. Thus the liability at 30.9.X4 when there are 13 instalments outstanding will be £1,107.24 × 9.394 (see cumulative discount table) = £10,401. The finance charge can then be found as follows.

	£
Rentals paid to 30.9.X4 (£1,107.24 × 3)	3,322
Capital repayment (reduction in liability)	
£12,000 − £10,401	1,599
Finance charge	1,723

The calculations for the remaining periods are shown below.

Year ending 30.9.X5

Liability at 30.9.X5 with 9 instalments to pay:
       £1,107.24 × 7.108 = £7,870; £10,401 − £7,870 = £2,531;
Interest = (4 × £1,107.24) − £2,531 = £1,898

Year ending 30.9.X6

Liability at 30.9.X6 with 5 instalments to pay:
       £1,107.24 × 4.329 = £4,794; £7,870 − £4,794 = £3,076
Interest = (4 × £1,107.24) − £3,076 = £1,353

Year ending 30.9.X7

Liability at 30.9.X7 with 1 instalment to pay:
       £1,107.24 × 0.952 = £1,055; £4,794 − £1,055 = £3,739
Interest = (4 × £1,107.24) − £3,739 = £690

Year ending 30.9.X8

Interest = £1,107.24 − £1,055 = £52

3 LESSOR ACCOUNTING

3.1 The following SSAP 21 definitions are relevant to lessor accounting.

KEY TERMS

- **Initial direct costs** are those costs incurred by the lessor that are directly associated with negotiating and consummating leasing transactions, such as commissions, legal fees, costs of credit investigations and costs of preparing and processing documents for new leases acquired.

- **Gross earnings** comprise the lessor's gross finance income over the lease term, representing the difference between his gross investment in the lease and the cost of the leased asset less any grants receivable towards the purchase or use of the asset.

- The **gross investment** in a lease at a point in time is the total of the minimum lease payments and any unguaranteed residual value accruing to the lessor.

- The **net investment** in a lease at a point in time comprises:

  (a) the gross investment in a lease (as defined above);
  (b) less gross earnings allocated to future periods.

- The **net cash investment** in a lease at a point in time is the amount of funds invested in a lease by a lessor, and comprises the cost of the asset plus or minus the following related payments or receipts:

  (a) government/other grants receivable towards the purchase or use of the asset;
  (b) rentals received;
  (c) taxation payments and receipts, including the effect of capital allowances;
  (d) residual values, if any, at the end of the lease term;
  (e) interest payments (where applicable);
  (f) interest received on cash surplus;
  (g) profit taken out of the lease. *(SSAP 21)*

3.2 EXAMPLE: GROSS INVESTMENT

Willco Ltd has just purchased a lorry from Drogon Trucks Ltd for £50,000. The lorry has been leased to Newton Freight Ltd on a two year lease requiring annual payments in arrears of £13,500. Drogon Trucks have agreed to buy the truck back at open market value at the end of the lease. Newton Freight Ltd have guaranteed that the value of the lorry after two years will be not less than £30,000. A realistic estimate of its value at that time is £33,000, ie the unguaranteed residual value is £3,000.

What is the gross investment in the lease at the start of the lease?

3.3 SOLUTION

At the start of the lease the 'minimum lease payments' will be the rentals due of £27,000 plus the guaranteed residual of £30,000 giving £57,000. The gross investment in the lease will be the minimum lease payments of £57,000 plus the unguaranteed residual of £3,000 (£33,000 – £30,000) giving £60,000.

It will be apparent from the definition of net investment above that when any residual amount receivable by the lessor is insignificant (as is usually the case in normal full payout

leases) the net investment in the lease will be equal to the cost of the equipment less any grant receivable.

Standard accounting practice for lessors

3.4 The requirements of SSAP 21 for accounting by lessors are as follows.

(a) The **amount due from the lessee** under a finance lease should be recorded in the balance sheet of a lessor as a *debtor* at the amount of the **net investment in the lease** after making provisions for items such as bad and doubtful rentals receivable.

(b) The **total gross earnings** under a finance lease should normally be allocated to accounting periods to give a **constant rate of return** on the lessor's net cash investment in the lease in each period. In the case of a hire purchase contract which has characteristics similar to a finance lease, allocation of gross earnings so as to give a constant periodic rate of return on the finance company's net investment will in most cases be a suitable approximation to allocation based on the net cash investment.

In arriving at the constant periodic rate of return, a reasonable approximation may be made.

(c) As an alternative to (b) above, an **allocation** may first be made out of gross earnings of an amount equal to the lessor's estimated cost of finance included in the net cash investment calculation, with the balance being recognised on a systematic basis.

(d) **Tax free grants** which are available to the lessor against the purchase price of assets acquired for leasing should be spread over the period of the lease and dealt with by treating the grant as non-taxable income (see below).

(e) An **asset** held for use in operating leases by a lessor should be recorded as a fixed asset and depreciated over its useful life.

(f) **Rental income from an operating lease**, excluding charges for services such as insurance and maintenance, should be recognised on **a straight-line basis** over the period of the lease, even if the payments are not made on such a basis, unless another systematic and rational basis is more representative of the time pattern in which the benefit from the leased asset is receivable.

(g) **Initial direct costs** incurred by a lessor in arranging a lease may be apportioned over the period of the lease on a systematic and rational basis.

Amendment to SSAP 21

3.5 Until recently, SSAP 21 allowed an alternative treatment for the **tax free grants** mentioned in Paragraph 3.4(d) above. Such tax free grants were still spread over the period of the lease, but could be dealt with by grossing up the grant and including the grossed-up amount in arriving at profit before tax. Where this treatment was adopted, the lessor had to disclose the amount by which the profit before tax and the tax charge had been increased as a result of grossing up the grant. This treatment was outlawed by an *Amendment to SSAP 21* published in 1997; it arose as a direct result of UITF Abstract 16.

UITF Abstract 16 *Income and expenses subject to non-standard rates of tax*

3.6 This abstract is concerned with transactions which depend for their **overall profitability** on some or all of the income or expenditure being either **non-taxable or taxable** at a lower (or higher) rate than the standard rate (including some leasing transactions). In some cases the

transaction may, after taking account of the cost of financing, result in a pre-tax loss and an after-tax profit.

3.7 A special accounting treatment has sometimes been adopted for these transactions. This treatment entails changing the pre-tax profit and the tax charge by the same amount, so that a **standard rate of tax** is reported. Such an adjustment is sometimes referred to as a **'grossing up' adjustment** (an example of which was given above).

3.8 This assists the **comparison** of the pre-tax results with those of other kinds of businesses, and of profits of different periods where a company changes the nature of the transactions in which it engages. However, the grossing up, because it is notional, fails to reflect the **true nature** of the transactions that have occurred in the period.

3.9 The UITF concluded that a transaction that provides a tax benefit but yields a low pre-tax profit (or a pre-tax loss) does not, in substance, yield the same pre-tax result and have the same tax consequences as a transaction that is taxed on a normal basis. Rather, both the form and the substance of the transaction are that it **bears tax at a non-standard rate**, and it should therefore be reported in those terms, in order to achieve a faithful presentation. This view is consistent with generally accepted practice in accounting for items such as expenditure that is not allowable for tax, where no adjustment is usually made.

UITF consensus

3.10 The UITF reached a consensus that income and expenses subject to non-standard rates of tax should be included in the pre-tax results on the basis of the **income or expenses actually receivable or payable**, without any adjustment to reflect a notional amount of tax that would have been paid or relieved in respect of the transaction if it had been taxable, or allowable for tax purposes, on a different basis.

This Abstract takes effect at the same time as the amendment to SSAP 21 above.

3.11 EXAMPLE: NET INVESTMENT

Consider again the example first given in Paragraph 2.9, this time from the point of view of the lessor.

3.12 SOLUTION

	Years ending 31 December				
	19X3	*19X4*	*19X5*	*19X6*	*Total*
	£	£	£	£	£
Rentals receivable	13,610	13,610	13,610	13,610	54,440
Capital repayment	13,610	10,225	11,248	12,377	47,460
Finance charge	-	3,385	2,362	1,233	6,980
Average sum outstanding during period		33,850	23,625	12,377	
Finance charge expressed as a % return on the average sum outstanding in the period		10%	10%	10%	

As suggested in the standard, this return is constant.

The lessor's balance sheet and notes will include the following amounts for each year.

BPP PUBLISHING

		As at 31 December		
		19X3	*19X4*	*19X5*
		£	£	£
Debtors				
Net investment in finance lease		33,850	23,625	12,377
Of which the following is due in				
more than one year		23,625	12,377	-

3.13 Note that under the assumptions of this question the total net investments shown above are the same as the obligations shown in the lessee's balance sheet. This would not have been the case had the lessee based its disclosure on a present value found using its cost of borrowing rather than the implied rate in the lease.

3.14 The best methods of obtaining a **constant periodic rate of return** on the lessor's net *cash* investment are:

(a) the actuarial method *after* tax; and

(b) the investment period method (IPM).

3.15 The **main difference** between these two methods and the methods discussed above (actuarial method before tax and sum of the digits) is that the former methods take into account the impact of tax relief on the lessor's cash flow. All four possible methods give very similar results when applied to the current tax regime (only a 25% writing down allowance is available and the top CT rate is 33%).

Question 2

Lockhart plc entered into a leasing agreement on 1 January 19X1 to lease to Mossford Ltd a machine costing £40,000. The lease requires the payment for four years of rentals of £7,000 per half year payable in advance. Corporation tax is 35% and writing down allowances are available at 25% per annum. Profit is to be taken out of the lease at 7.87% per half year. Corporation tax is payable on 1 January 12 months after each 31 December year-end.

Answer: actuarial method after tax

The first step is to draw a table that will enable us to calculate:

(a) the net cash investment for each period;

(b) the amount of profit taken out of the lease each period.

Period	NCI b/f	Capital cost	Rentals	Tax	Average NCI during period	Profit taken out of lease	NCI c/f
	£	£	£	£	£	£	£
1	-	(40,000)	7,000	-	(33,000)	(2,597)	(35,597)
2	(35,597)	-	7,000	-	(28,597)	(2,251)	(30,848)
3	(30,848)	-	7,000	-	(23,848)	(1,877)	(25,725)
4	(25,725)	-	7,000	-	(18,725)	(1,474)	(20,199)
5	(20,199)	-	7,000	(1,400)	(14,599)	(1,149)	(15,748)
6	(15,748)	-	7,000	-	(8,748)	(688)	(9,436)
7	(9,436)	-	7,000	(2,275)	(4,711)	(371)	(5,082)
8	(5,082)	-	7,000	-	1,918	151	2,069
9	2,069	-	-	(2,931)	(862)	(68)	(930)
10	(930)	-	-	-	(930)	(73)	(1,003)
11	(1,003)	-	-	1,006	3		

Notes

(a) The table has been constructed to show periods relating to the lease: six-monthly periods beginning on 1 January 19X1.

(b) The tax figures have been computed as below.

	Rentals £	WDA £	Taxable profits £	CT @ 35% £
19X1	14,000	10,000	4,000	1,400
19X2	14,000	7,500	6,500	2,275
19X3	14,000	5,625	8,375	2,931
19X4	14,000	16,875	(2,875)	(1,006)

For convenience, the entire capital allowances of the remaining £16,875 (£40,000 − £10,000 − £7,500 − £5,625) have been allocated to 19X4.

(c) Profits taken out of the lease are computed as 7.87% of the average NCI for each period.

(d) The average NCI at the end of the table should be zero, but is 3 because of roundings and because the 7.87% profit rate is not entirely accurate.

It is now possible to construct the P&L accounts for each period.

PROFIT AND LOSS ACCOUNTS FOR THE YEARS ENDING 31 DECEMBER

	19X1 £	19X2 £	19X3 £	19X4 £
Rental (given)	14,000	14,000	14,000	14,000
Less capital repayment (balancing figure)	(6,542)	(8,845)	(11,174)	(13,662)
Profit before tax (100%)	7,458	5,155	2,826	338
Taxation (given)	(1,400)	(2,275)	(2,931)	1,006
	6,058	2,880	(105)	1,344
Deferred tax (balancing figure)	(1,210)	471	1,942	(1,124)
Profit after tax (given: 65%)	4,848	3,351	1,837	220
	(2,597+ 2,251)	(1,877+ 1,474)	(1,149 + 688)	(371 − 151)

Start by filling in the figures you know. Then work out the profit before tax (for example £4,848 × $^{100}/_{65}$ = £7,458). Then you can calculate the remaining balancing figures.

In the balance sheets, the net investment in the finance lease can be found by deducting the figures for capital repayments from the original cost.

BALANCE SHEETS AS AT 31 DECEMBER

	19X1 £	19X2 £	19X3 £	19X4 £
Net interest in finance lease *	33,458	24,613	13,439	-

*after eliminating the rounding errors.

Answer: investment period method

In the above table we arrived at figures for the profit taken out of the lease (eg £33,000 × 7.87% = £2,597) and, under the actuarial method after tax, we built up the P&L account from these. In the IPM the same table is used, and the total finance charges are then allocated to periods before the cash surplus has arisen in proportion to the NCI at the end of each period. (Sometimes the average or opening NCI is used.)

In our example, there is a net cash investment in the lease from periods 1 to 7. The total finance charges of £16,000 ((8 × £7,000) − £40,000) are therefore split in proportion to the NCI at the end of these periods compared with the total NCI (ie £142,635).

Period	NCI at end of period £	Proportion £	Finance charge allocation £
1	35,597	$\dfrac{35,597}{142,635}$	3,993
2	30,848	$\dfrac{30,848}{142,635}$	3,460
3	25,725	$\dfrac{25,725}{142,635}$	2,886
4	20,199	$\dfrac{20,199}{142,635}$	2,266
5	15,748	$\dfrac{15,748}{142,635}$	1,767
6	9,436	$\dfrac{9,436}{142,635}$	1,058
7	5,082	$\dfrac{5,082}{142,635}$	570
	142,635		16,000

The P&L accounts under the IPM can then be drawn up in a similar method to that above.

PROFIT AND LOSS ACCOUNTS FOR THE YEARS ENDING 31 DECEMBER

	19X1 £	19X2 £	19X3 £	19X4 £
Rental (given)	14,000	14,000	14,000	14,000
Less capital repayment (balancing figure)	(6,547)	(8,848)	(11,175)	(13,430)
Profit before tax (= finance charge allocation for the year, as above)	7,453	5,152	2,825	570
Taxation (given)	1,400)	(2,275)	(2,931)	1,006
	6,053	2,877	(106)	1,576
Deferred tax (balancing figure)	(1,209)	472	1,942	(1,206)
Profit after tax (65% of profit before tax)	4,844	3,349	1,836	370

Exam focus point

The calculations above for the post-tax actuarial method and the IPM may appear rather complicated. Remember that it is the actuarial method after tax which gives a constant return on the lessor's net cash investment during the investment period as required by SSAP 21. Note also that without first year allowances, pre-tax and post-tax methods will give very similar answers, so it will usually be acceptable to use a pre-tax method unless you are specifically told otherwise.

Disclosure requirements: lessors

3.16 The disclosure requirements of SSAP 21 are as follows.

(a) The **net investment** in (i) finance leases and (ii) hire purchase contracts at each balance sheet date should be disclosed.

(b) The **gross amounts of assets** held for use in operating leases★, and the related accumulated depreciation charges, should be disclosed.

(c) Disclosure should be made of:

  (i) the **policy adopted** for accounting for operating leases★ and finance leases★ and, in detail, the policy for accounting for finance lease income★;

  (ii) the **aggregate rentals receivable** in respect of an accounting period in relation to (i) finance leases★ and (ii) operating leases★; and

(iii)   the **cost of assets acquired**, whether by purchase or finance leases*, for the purpose of letting under finance leases*.

* Including the equivalent information in respect of **hire purchase contracts** which have characteristics similar to that type of lease.

Selling profit

3.17   A manufacturer or dealer lessor should not recognise a selling profit under an operating lease. The selling profit under a finance lease should be **restricted** to the excess of the fair value of the asset over the manufacturer's or dealer's cost less any grants receivable by the manufacturer or dealer towards the purchase, construction or use of the asset.

Sale and leaseback transactions

3.18   These should be dealt with as follows.

(a)   **Accounting by the seller/lessee**

(i)   In a sale and leaseback transaction which results in a **finance lease**, any apparent profit or loss (that is, the difference between the sale price and the previous carrying value) should be deferred and amortised in the financial statements of the seller/lessee over the shorter of the lease term or the useful life of the asset.

(ii)   If the leaseback is an **operating lease**:

(1)   any profit or loss should be recognised immediately, provided it is clear that the transaction is established at a **fair value;**

(2)   the **sale price is below fair value**, any profit or loss should be recognised immediately except that if the apparent loss is compensated by future rentals at below market price it should to that extent be deferred and amortised over the remainder of the lease term (or, if shorter, the period during which the reduced rentals are chargeable);

(3)   if the **sale price is above fair value**, the excess over fair value should be deferred and amortised over the shorter of the remainder of the lease term and the period to the next rent review (if any).

(b)   **Accounting by the buyer/lessor**

A buyer/lessor should account for a sale and leaseback in the same way as he accounts for other leases.

Note the effect of FRS 5 on accounting for sale and leaseback transactions (Chapter 8).

> ### Exam focus point
> A leasing question may be connected to off balance sheet finance in general. In particular, you may be asked to discuss the links between SSAP 21 and FRS 5.

UITF Abstract 4 *Presentation of long-term debtors in current assets*

3.19   Where the figure of debtors due after more than one year is **material** in the context of the total net current assets then it should be **disclosed on the face of the balance sheet**, rather than just by way of a note (as has been the practice in the past where long-term debtors were included in current assets). The figure would be material in relation to net current assets if

its non-disclosure on the balance sheet would cause readers to misinterpret the accounts. This is of relevance mainly to lessors.

4 A CRITICISM OF SSAP 21

4.1 SSAP 21 has not been without its critics. Although it closed many loopholes in the treatment of leases, it is still open to abuse and manipulation. A great deal of this topic is tied up in the off balance sheet finance and creative accounting debate discussed in the last chapter.

Unguaranteed residual value

KEY TERM

Unguaranteed residual value is that portion of the residual value of the leased asset (estimated at the inception of the lease), the realisation of which by the lessor is not assured or is guaranteed solely by a party related to the lessor. *(SSAP 21)*

4.2 As we have already seen, to qualify as a finance lease the risks and rewards of ownership must be transferred to the lessee. One reward of ownership is any **residual value** in the asset at the end of the primary period. If the asset is returned to the lessor then it is he who receives this reward of ownership, not the lessee. This might prevent the lease from being a finance lease if this reward is significant (SSAP 21 allows insubstantial ownership risks and rewards not to pass).

4.3 SSAP 21 states that it should normally be presumed that a transfer of substantially all the risks and rewards of ownership occurs if, at the beginning of the lease, the present value of the minimum lease payments amounts to 90% or more of the fair value of the leased asset. This is an application of **discounting principles** to financial statements. The discounting equation is:

Present value of minimum lease payment	+	Present value of unguaranteed residual amount accruing to lessor	=	Fair value of leased asset

Note. Any **guaranteed residual amount** accruing to the lessor will be included in the minimum lease payments.

4.4 If there is an unguaranteed residual amount due to the lessor, it can be seen that its present value must be **less than 10% of the fair value** of the leased asset if the lease is to qualify as a finance lease, since only then will the present value of the minimum lease payments amount to 90% or more of that fair value under the 90% rule.

4.5 You should now be able to see the **scope for manipulation** involving lease classification. Whether or not a lease is classified as a finance lease can hinge on the size of the unguaranteed residual amount due to the lessor, and that figure will only be an estimate. A lessor might be persuaded to estimate a larger residual amount than he would otherwise have done and cause the lease to fail the 90% test, rather than lose the business. While the test is only intended to be presumptive and does not provide a precise mathematical definition of a finance lease, it would be a brave auditor who would contend that a lease which failed the test was still a finance lease.

4.6 EXAMPLE: UNGUARANTEED RESIDUAL VALUE

A company enters into two leasing agreements.

	Lease A £'000	Lease B £'000
Fair value of asset	210	120
Estimated residual value (due to lessor)	21	30
Minimum lease payments	238	108

How should each lease be classified?

4.7 SOLUTION

You should note that it is unnecessary to perform any calculations for discounting in this example.

Lease A: it is obvious that the present value of the unguaranteed lease payments is less than £21,000, and therefore less than 10% of the fair value of the asset. This means that the present value of the minimum lease payments is over 90% of the fair value of the asset. Lease A is therefore a finance lease.

Lease B: the present value of the minimum lease payments is obviously less than £108,000 and therefore less than 90% of the fair value of the asset. Lease B is therefore an operating lease.

Implicit interest rate

4.8 It will often be the case that the lessee does not know the unguaranteed residual value placed on the asset by the lessor and he is therefore unaware of the interest rate implicit in the lease. In such a case, SSAP 21 allows the lessee to provide his **own estimate**, to calculate the implicit interest rate and perform the 90% test. It is obviously very easy to estimate a residual amount which fails the test. This situation would also lead to different results for the lessee and the lessor.

Chapter roundup

- SSAP 21's requirements are not as tricky as they seem at first reading. There are four common methods to **allocate interest/finance charges**.

  - Sum of the digits
  - Actuarial (pre-tax)
  - Actuarial (post-tax)
  - Investment period method

  Remember that the last two are the best methods of obtaining a constant periodic rate of return on the lessor's net cash investment in finance leases. You should be able to define this term and also gross and net investments in finance leases.

- As usual, as well as being able to make calculations, you must be able to **comment critically** on the differences between methods.

- You should understand the reasons why an **Amendment to SSAP 21** was required, as well as **UITF Abstract 16.**

- You must also have a sound grasp of the **disclosure requirements** of SSAP 21 for both lessors and lessees in respect of finance leases, operating leases and HP contracts.

- You must be able to discuss the distinction between **different types of leases**, the difference between **leasing and HP**, and the arguments for and against **capitalisation** of finance leased assets.

BPP PUBLISHING

Quick quiz

1 Distinguish between a finance lease and an operating lease. (see key term)

2 What are the arguments both for and against lessees capitalising leased assets? (2.4)

3 List the disclosure requirements for lessees. (2.8)

4 How should reverse premiums and similar incentives to lessees be treated? (2.13, 2.14)

5 What is the lessor's net cash investment in a lease? (key term)

6 What is the standard accounting practice for lessors? (3.4)

7 What does UITF Abstract 16 say about the treatment of income and expenses subject to non-standard rates of tax? (3.10)

8 List the disclosure requirements for lessors. (3.16)

9 How can the unguaranteed residual value cause problems under SSAP 21? (4.2 - 4.5)

Question to try	Level	Marks	Time
11	Exam	15	27 mins

Chapter 11

MISCELLANEOUS STANDARDS

Chapter topic	Syllabus reference	Ability required
1 FRS 8 *Related party disclosures*	9(a)	Application
2 Post balance sheet events	9(a)	Application
3 Provisions, contingent liabilities and contingent assets	9(a)	Application

Introduction

The contents of this chapter represents a variety of disclosure matters and accounting treatments. **SSAP 17** is straightforward, but nonetheless still important. It is summarised here as you have studied it at Stage 2.

FRS 8 is highly examinable. It is concerned almost entirely with disclosure.

FRS 12 is a new, important and controversial standard.

1 FRS 8 RELATED PARTY DISCLOSURES   11/96, 5/99

1.1   The ASB has produced its most recent FRS on related parties. FRS 8 *Related party disclosures* makes it clear why a standard was required on this subject.

> 'In the absence of information to the contrary, it is assumed that a reporting entity has independent discretionary power over its resources and transactions and pursues its activities independently of the interests of its individual owners, managers and others. Transactions are presumed to have been undertaken on an arm's length basis, ie on terms such as could have obtained in a transaction with an external party, in which each side bargained knowledgeably and freely, unaffected by any relationship between them.
>
> These assumptions may not be justified when related party relationships exist, because the requisite conditions for competitive, free market dealings may not be present. Whilst the parties may endeavour to achieve arm's length bargaining the very nature of the relationship may preclude this occurring.'

1.2   FRS 8 can be summarised as follows.

(a)   FRS 8 *Related party disclosures* requires the disclosure of:

    (i)   **information** on related party transactions; and

    (ii) the **name of the party controlling** the reporting entity and, if different, that of the ultimate controlling party whether or not any transactions between the reporting entity and those parties have taken place.

Aggregated disclosures are allowed subject to certain restrictions.

Related parties are defined below.

(b)   **No disclosure** is required in consolidated financial statements of **intragroup transactions** and balances eliminated on consolidation. A parent undertaking is not

BPP PUBLISHING

required to provide related party disclosures in its own financial statements when those statements are presented with consolidated financial statements of its group.

(c) Disclosure is not required in the financial statements of subsidiary undertakings, 90% or more of whose voting rights are controlled within the group, of transactions with entities that are part of the group or investees of the group qualifying as related parties provided that the consolidated financial statements in which that subsidiary is included are publicly available.

FRS 8 is not long and the more detailed requirements are as follows.

Objective

1.3 The objective of FRS 8 is to ensure that financial statements contain the disclosures necessary to draw attention to the possibility that the reported financial position and results may have been affected by the existence of related parties and by material transactions with them. In other words, this is a standard which is primarily concerned with *disclosure*.

Definitions

1.4 The definitions given in FRS 8 are fundamental to the effect of the standard.

> **KEY TERMS**
>
> - **Close family**. Close members of the family of an individual are those family members, or members of the same household, who may be expected to influence, or be influenced by, that person in their dealings with the reporting entity.
>
> - **Control**. The ability of an entity to direct the operating and financial policies of another entity with a view to gaining economic benefits from its activities.
>
> - **Key management**. Those persons in senior positions having authority or responsibility for directing or controlling the major activities and resources of the reporting entity.
>
> - **Persons acting in concert**. Persons who, pursuant to an agreement or understanding (whether formal or informal), actively co-operate, whether by the ownership by any of them of shares in an undertaking or otherwise, to exercise control or influence over that undertaking.
>
> *FRS 8*

1.5 The most important definitions are of **related parties** and **related party transactions**.

> **KEY TERMS**
>
> **Related parties**
>
> (a) Two or more parties are related parties when at any time during the financial period:
>
>   (i) one party has direct or indirect control of the other party; or
>
>   (ii) the parties are subject to common control from the same source; or

KEY TERMS (cont)

(iii) one party has influence over the financial and operating policies of the other party to an extent that that other party might be inhibited from pursuing at all times its own separate interests; or

(iv) the parties, in entering a transaction, are subject to influence from the same source to such an extent that one of the parties to the transaction has subordinated its own separate interests.

(b) For the avoidance of doubt, the following are related parties of the reporting entity:

    (i) its ultimate and intermediate parent undertakings, subsidiary undertakings, and fellow subsidiary undertakings;

    (ii) its associates and joint ventures;

    (iii) the investor or venturer in respect of which the reporting entity is an associate or a joint venture;

    (iv) directors* of the reporting entity and the directors of its ultimate and intermediate parent undertakings; and

    (v) pension funds for the benefit of employees of the reporting entity or of any entity that is a related party of the reporting entity;

[* Directors include shadow directors, which are defined in companies legislation as persons in accordance with whose directions or instructions the directors of the company are accustomed to act.]

(c) and the following are presumed to be related parties of the reporting entity unless it can be demonstrated that neither party has influenced the financial and operating policies of the other in such a way as to inhibit the pursuit of separate interests:

    (i) the key management of the reporting entity and the key management of its parent undertakings or undertakings;

    (ii) a person owning or able to exercise control over 20 per cent or more of the voting rights of the reporting entity, whether directly or through nominees;

    (iii) each person acting in concert in such a way as to be able to exercise control or influence [in terms of part (a)(iii) of the definition of related party transitions, above] over the reporting entity; and

    (iv) an entity managing or managed by the reporting entity under a management contract.

(d) Additionally, because of their relationship with certain parties that are, or are presumed to be, related parties of the reporting entity, the following are also presumed to be related parties of the reporting entity:

    (i) members of the close family of any individual falling under parties mentioned in (a) - (c) above; and

    (ii) partnerships, companies, trusts or other entities in which any individual or member of the close family in (a) - (c) above has a controlling interest.

Sub-paragraphs (b), (c) and (d) are not intended to be an exhaustive list of related parties.

KEY TERMS (CONT)

Related party transaction

The transfer of assets or liabilities or the performance of services by, or for a related party irrespective of whether a price is charged.'

1.6 The most important point is in paragraph (a) of the definition of related parties because it defines in **general terms** what related party transactions are; the succeeding paragraphs of definition only add **some specifics**.

Scope

1.7 FRS 8 applies to all financial statements that are intended to give a true and fair view but it **excludes** some transactions; it does **not** require disclosure:

(a) in consolidated financial statements, of any **transactions or balances between group entities** that have been eliminated on consolidation;

(b) in a **parent's own financial statements** when those statements are presented together with its **consolidated financial statements**;

(c) in the **financial statements of subsidiary undertakings**, 90% per cent or more of whose voting rights are controlled within the group, of transactions with entities that are part of the group or investees of the group qualifying as related parties, provided that the consolidated financial statements in which that subsidiary is included are publicly available;

(d) of **pension contributions** paid to a pension fund; and

(e) of **emoluments** in respect of services as an **employee** of the reporting entity.

Reporting entities taking advantage of the exemption in (c) above are required to state that fact.

1.8 Further types of transaction are also excluded as the FRS does not require disclosure of the relationship and transactions between the reporting entity and the parties listed in (a) to (d) below simply as a result of their role as:

(a) providers of finance in the course of their business in that regard;
(b) utility companies;
(c) government departments and their sponsored bodies,

even though they may circumscribe the freedom of action of an entity or participate in its decision-making process; and

(d) a customer, supplier, franchiser, distributor or general agent with whom an entity transacts a significant volume of business.

1.9 FRS 8 then states the disclosures it requires, under two headings:

(a) disclosure of control; and
(b) disclosure of transactions and balances.

Disclosure of control

1.10 When the reporting entity is controlled by another party, there should be disclosure of the related party relationship and the name of that party and, if different, that of the ultimate controlling party. If the controlling party or ultimate controlling party of the reporting entity is not known, that fact should be disclosed. This information should be disclosed **irrespective of whether any transactions have taken place** between the controlling parties and the reporting entity.

Disclosure of transactions and balances

1.11 Financial statements should disclose material transactions undertaken by the reporting entity with a related party. Disclosure should be made **irrespective of whether a price is charged.** The disclosure should include:

(a) the names of the transacting parties;

(b) a description of the relationship between the parties;

(c) a description of the transactions;

(d) the amounts involved;

(e) any other elements of the transactions necessary for an understanding of the financial statements;

(f) the amounts due to or from related parties at the balance sheet date and provisions for doubtful debts due from such parties at that date; and

(g) amounts written off in the period in respect of debts due to or from related parties.

Transactions with related parties may be disclosed on an aggregated basis (aggregation of similar transactions by type of related party) unless disclosure of an individual transaction, or connected transactions, is necessary for an understanding of the impact of the transactions on the financial statements of the reporting entity or is required by law.

1.12 Further points of interest are made in the explanatory notes, particularly those on applying the definition of 'related party' given above.

(a) **Common control** is deemed to exist when both parties are subject to control from boards having a controlling nucleus of directors in common.

(b) The difference between control and **influence** is that control brings with it the ability to cause the controlled party to subordinate its separate interests whereas the outcome of the exercise of influence is less certain. Two related parties of a third entity are not necessarily related parties of each other.

1.13 Examples of such a situation of 'influence' rather than 'control' are given:

(a) where two companies are associates of the same investor;

(b) when one party is subject to control and another party is subject to influence from the same source; and

(c) where two parties have a director in common;

then these two parties would not normally be treated as related parties.

1.14 The **explanatory notes** also give examples of related party transactions which would require disclosure:

(a) purchases or sales of goods (finished or unfinished);

(b) purchases or sales of property and other assets;

(c) rendering or receiving of services;

(d) agency arrangements;

(e) leasing arrangements;

(f) transfer of research and development;

(g) licence agreements;

(h) provision of finance (including loans and equity contributions in cash or in kind);

(i) guarantees and the provision of collateral security; and

(j) management contracts.

1.15 The **materiality** of related party transactions is also an important question because only **material** related party transactions must be disclosed. You should be familiar with the general definition of materiality, that transactions are material when disclosure might reasonably be expected to influence decisions made by the users of general purpose financial statements. In the case of related party transactions, materiality:

'is to be judged, not only in terms of their significance to the reporting entity, but also in relation to the other related party when that party is:

(a) a director, key manager or other individual in a position to influence, or accountable for stewardship of, the reporting entity; or

(b) a member of the close family of any individual mentioned in (a) above; or

(c) an entity controlled by any individual mentioned in (a) or (b) above.'

Question 1

Which transactions are *excluded* by FRS 8?

Answer

See Paragraphs 1.7 and 1.8.

Current CA 1985 and Stock Exchange requirements

1.16 Some types of related party transactions are covered by existing statutory or Stock Exchange requirements, such as the provisions of the Companies Act 1985 covering transactions by directors and connected persons and 'Class IV' circulars which listed companies are required to send to shareholders when an acquisition or disposal of assets is made from or to a director, substantial shareholder or associate.

2 POST BALANCE SHEET EVENTS

2.1 SSAP 17 should be very familiar to you by this stage in you studies. The most important aspects are highlighted in the summary below.

Knowledge brought forward from Paper 5

SSAP 17 Accounting for post balance sheet events

- **Post balance sheet event (PBSEs)** are events, both favourable and unfavourable, which occur between the B/S date and the date on which the financial statements are approved by the board of directors.

- **Adjusting events are PBSEs** which provide additional evidence of conditions existing at the B/S date, and therefore need to be incorporated into the financial statements.

- **Non-adjusting events are PBSEs** which concern conditions which did *not* exist at the B/S date.

- **Window dressing** is the arranging of transactions, the substance of which is primarily to alter the appearance of the B/S: it is *not* falsification of accounts. SSAP 17 does allow window dressing but *disclosure* should be made of such transactions

3 FRS 12 PROVISIONS, CONTINGENT LIABILITIES AND CONTINGENT ASSETS

3.1 As we have seen with regard to post balance sheet events, financial statements must include **all the information necessary for an understanding of the company's financial position**. Provisions, contingent liabilities and contingent assets are 'uncertainties' that must be accounted for consistently if are to achieve this understanding.

Objective

3.2 FRS 12 *Provisions, contingent liabilities and contingent assets* aims to ensure that appropriate **recognition criteria** and **measurement bases** are applied to provisions, contingent liabilities and contingent assets and that **sufficient information** is disclosed in the **notes** to the financial statements to enable users to understand their nature, timing and amount.

Provisions

3.3 You will be familiar with provisions for depreciation and doubtful debts from your earlier studies. The sorts of provisions addressed by FRS 12 are, however, rather different.

3.4 Before FRS 12, there was no accounting standard dealing with provisions. Companies wanting to show their results in the most favourable light used to make large **'one off' provisions** in years where a high level of underlying profits was generated. These provisions, often known as **'big bath'** provisions, were then available to shield expenditure in future years when perhaps the underlying profits were not as good.

3.5 In other words, **provisions were used for profit smoothing**.

IMPORTANT

The key aim of FRS 12 is to ensure that **provisions are made only where there are valid grounds for them**.

3.6 FRS 12 views a provision as a **liability**.

> ### KEY TERMS
>
> A **provision** is a **liability** of uncertain timing or amount.
>
> A **liability** is an obligation of an entity to transfer economic benefits as a result of past transactions or events. *(FRS 12)*

3.7 The FRS distinguishes provisions from other liabilities such as trade creditors and accruals. This is on the basis that for a provision there is **uncertainty** about the timing or amount of the future expenditure. Whilst uncertainty is clearly present in the case of certain accruals the uncertainty is generally much less than for provisions.

Recognition

3.8 FRS 12 states that a provision should be **recognised** as a liability in the financial statements when:

- An entity has a **present obligation** (legal or constructive) as a result of a past event

- It is probable that a **transfer of economic benefits** will be required to settle the obligation

- A **reliable estimate** can be made of the obligation

Meaning of obligation

3.9 It is fairly clear what a legal obligation is. However, you may not know what a **constructive obligation** is.

> ### KEY TERM
>
> FRS 12 defines a **constructive obligation** as
>
> 'An obligation that derives from an entity's actions where:
>
> - by an established pattern of past practice, published policies or a sufficiently specific current statement the entity has indicated to other parties that it will accept certain responsibilities; and
>
> - as a result, the entity has created a valid expectation on the part of those other parties that it will discharge those responsibilities.

Question 2

In which of the following circumstances might a provision be recognised?

(a) On 13 December 19X9 the board of an entity decided to close down a division. The accounting date of the company is 31 December. Before 31 December 19X9 the decision was not communicated to any of those affected and no other steps were taken to implement the decision.

(b) The board agreed a detailed closure plan on 20 December 19X9 and details were given to customers and employees.

(c) A company is obliged to incur clean up costs for environmental damage (that has already been caused).

(d) A company intends to carry out future expenditure to operate in a particular way in the future.

Answer

(a) No provision would be recognised as the decision has not been communicated.

(b) A provision would be made in the 19X9 financial statements.

(c) A provision for such costs is appropriate.

(d) No present obligation exists and under FRS 12 no provision would be appropriate. This is because the entity could avoid the future expenditure by its future actions, maybe by changing its method of operation.

Probable transfer of economic benefits

3.10 For the purpose of the FRS, a transfer of economic benefits is regarded as **'probable'** if the event is **more likely than not** to occur. This appears to indicate a probability of more than 50%. However, the standard makes it clear that where there is a number of similar obligations the probability should be based on considering the population as a whole, rather than one single item.

3.11 EXAMPLE: TRANSFER OF ECONOMIC BENEFITS

If a company has entered into a warranty obligation then the probability of transfer of economic benefits may well be extremely small in respect of one specific item. However, when considering the population as a whole the probability of some transfer of economic benefits is quite likely to be much higher. If there is a **greater than 50% probability** of some transfer of economic benefits then a **provision** should be made for the **expected amount**.

Measurement of provisions

IMPORTANT

The amount recognised as a provision should be the best estimate of the expenditure required to settle the present obligation at the balance sheet date.

3.12 The estimates will be determined by the **judgement** of the entity's management supplemented by the experience of similar transactions.

3.13 Allowance is made for **uncertainty**. Where the provision being measured involves a large population of items, the obligation is estimated by weighting all possible outcomes by their discounted probabilities, ie **expected value**.

Question 3

Parker plc sells goods with a warranty under which customers are covered for the cost of repairs of any manufacturing defect that becomes apparent within the first six months of purchase. The company's past experience and future expectations indicate the following pattern of likely repairs.

% of goods sold	Defects	Cost of repairs £m
75	None	-
20	Minor	1.0
5	Major	4.0

What is the expected cost of repairs?

Answer

The cost is found using 'expected values' (75% × £nil) + (20% × £1.0m) + (5% × £4.0m) = £400,000.

3.14 Where the effect of the **time value of money** is material, the amount of a provision should be the **present value** of the expenditure required to settle the obligation. An appropriate **discount** rate should be used.

3.15 The discount rate should be a **pre-tax rate** that reflects current market assessments of the time value of money. **The discount rate(s) should not reflect risks for which future cash flow estimates have been adjusted.**

3.16 The **unwinding of the discount** should be included as a financial item adjacent to interest but it should be **shown separately** from other interest either on the face of the profit and loss account or in a note.

Future events

3.17 **Future events** which are reasonably expected to occur (eg new legislation, changes in technology) may affect the amount required to settle the entity's obligation and should be taken into account.

Expected disposal of assets

3.18 Gains from the expected disposal of assets should not be taken into account in measuring a provision.

Reimbursements

3.19 Some or all of the expenditure needed to settle a provision may be expected to be recovered form a third party. If so, the **reimbursement should be recognised only when it is virtually certain that reimbursement will be received if the entity settles the obligation.**

- The reimbursement should be treated as a separate asset, and the amount recognised should not be greater than the provision itself.

- The provision and the amount recognised for reimbursement may be netted off in the profit and loss account.

Changes in provisions

3.20 Provisions should be renewed at each balance sheet date and adjusted to reflect the current best estimate. If it is no longer probable that a transfer of economic benefits will be required to settle the obligation, the provision should be reversed.

Use of provisions

3.21 **A provision should be used only for expenditures for which the provision was originally recognised**. Setting expenditures against a provision that was originally recognised for another purpose would conceal the impact of two different events.

Recognising an asset when recognising a provision

3.22 Normally the setting up of a provision should be charged immediately to the profit and loss account. But **if the incurring of the present obligation recognised as a provision gives access to future economic benefits an asset should be recognised.**

3.23 EXAMPLE: RECOGNISING AN ASSET

An obligation for decommissioning costs is incurred by commissioning an oil rig. At the same time, the commissioning gives access to oil reserves over the years of the oil rig's operation. Therefore an asset representing future access to oil reserves is recognised at the same time as the provision for decommissioning costs.

Future operating losses

3.24 **Provisions should not be recognised for future operating losses.** They do not meet the definition of a liability and the general recognition criteria set out in the standard.

Onerous contracts

3.25 If an entity has a contract that is onerous, the present obligation under the contract **should be recognised and measured** as a provision. An example might be vacant leasehold property.

> **KEY TERM**
>
> • An **onerous contract** is a contract entered into with another party under which the unavoidable costs of fulfilling the terms of the contract exceed any revenues expected to be received from the goods or services supplied or purchased directly or indirectly under the contract and where the entity would have to compensate the other party if it did not fulfil the terms of the contract.

3.26 EXAMPLES OF POSSIBLE PROVISIONS

It is easier to see what FRS 12 is driving at if you look at examples of those items which are possible provisions under this standard. Some of these we have already touched on.

(a) **Warranties**. These are argued to be genuine provisions as on past experience it is probable, ie more likely than not, that some claims will emerge. The provision must be estimated, however, on the basis of the class as a whole and not on individual claims. There is a clear legal obligation in this case.

(b) **Major repairs**. In the past it has been quite popular for companies to provide for expenditure on a major overhaul to be accrued gradually over the intervening years between overhauls. Under FRS 12 this will no longer be possible as FRS 12 would argue that this is a mere intention to carry out repairs, not an obligation. The entity can always sell the asset in the meantime. The only solution is to treat major assets

such as aircraft, ships, furnaces etc as a series of smaller assets where each part is depreciated over shorter lives. Thus any major overhaul may be argued to be replacement and therefore capital rather than revenue expenditure.

(c) **Self insurance**. A number of companies have created a provision for self insurance based on the expected cost of making good fire damage etc instead of paying premiums to an insurance company. Under FRS 12 this provision would no longer be justifiable as the entity has no obligation until a fire or accident occurs. No obligation exists until that time.

(d) **Environmental contamination**. If the company has an environment policy such that other parties would expect the company to clean up any contamination or if the company has broken current environmental legislation then a provision for environmental damage must be made.

(e) **Decommissioning or abandonment costs**. When an oil company initially purchases an oilfield it is put under a legal obligation to decommission the site at the end of its life. Prior to FRS 12 most oil companies applied the SORP on *Accounting for abandonment costs* published by the Oil Industry Accounting Committee and they built up the provision gradually over the field so that no one year would be unduly burdened with the cost.

FRS 12, however, insists that a legal obligation exists on the initial expenditure on the field and therefore a liability exists immediately. This would appear to result in a large charge to profit and loss in the first year of operation of the field. However, the FRS takes the view that the cost of purchasing the field in the first place is not only the cost of the field itself but also the costs of putting it right again. Thus all the costs of abandonment may be capitalised.

(f) **Restructuring**. This is considered in detail below.

Provisions for restructuring

3.27 One of the main purposes of FRS 12 was to target abuses of provisions for restructuring. Accordingly, FRS 12 lays down **strict criteria** to determine when such a provision can be made.

KEY TERM

FRS 12 defines a **restructuring** as:

A programme that is planned and is controlled by management and materially changes either:

- the scope of a business undertaken by an entity; or
- the manner in which that business is conducted.

3.28 The FRS gives the following **examples** of events that may fall under the definition of restructuring.

- The **sale or termination** of a line of business
- The **closure of business locations** in a country or region or the **relocation** of business activities from one country region to another
- **Changes in management structure**, for example, the elimination of a layer of management

- **Fundamental reorganisations** that have a material effect on the **nature and focus** of the entity's operations

3.29 The question is whether or not an entity has an obligation - legal or constructive - at the balance sheet date.

- An entity must have a **detailed formal plan** for the restructuring.

- It must have **raised a valid expectation** in those affected that it will carry out the restructuring by starting to implement that plan or announcing its main features to those affected by it

> **IMPORTANT**
>
> **A mere management decision is not normally sufficient.** Management decisions may sometimes trigger off recognition, but only if earlier events such as negotiations with employee representatives and other interested parties have been concluded subject only to management approval.

3.30 Where the restructuring involves the **sale of an operation** then FRS 12 states that no obligation arises until the entity has entered into a **binding sale agreement**. This is because until this has occurred the entity will be able to change its mind and withdraw from the sale even if its intentions have been announced publicly.

Costs to be included within a restructuring provision

3.31 The FRS states that a restructuring provision should include only the **direct expenditures** arising from the restructuring, which are those that are both:

- **Necessarily entailed** by the restructuring; and
- Not associated with the **ongoing activities** of the entity.

3.32 The following costs should specifically **not** be included within a restructuring provision.

- **Retraining** or relocating continuing staff
- **Marketing**
- **Investment in new systems** and distribution networks

Disclosure

3.33 Disclosures for provisions fall into two parts.

- Disclosure of details of the **change in carrying value** of a provision from the beginning to the end of the year

- Disclosure of the **background** to the making of the provision and the uncertainties affecting its outcome

Contingent liabilities

3.34 Now you understand provisions it will be easier to understand contingent assets and liabilities.

> ### KEY TERM
>
> FRS 12 defines a **contingent liability** as:
>
> - A possible obligation that arises from past events and whose existence will be confirmed only by the occurrence or non-occurrence of one or more uncertain future events not wholly within the entity's control; or
>
> - A present obligation that arises from past events but is not recognised because:
>
>   o It is not probable that a transfer of economic benefits will be required to settle the obligation; or
>
>   o The amount of the obligation cannot be measured with sufficient reliability.

3.35   As a rule of thumb, probable means more than 50% likely. **If an obligation is probable, it is not a contingent liability** - instead, a **provision is needed**.

Treatment of contingent liabilities

3.36   Contingent liabilities **should not be recognised in financial statements** but they **should be disclosed**. The required disclosures are:

- A brief description of the nature of the contingent liability
- An estimate of its financial effect
- An indication of the uncertainties that exist
- The possibility of any reimbursement

Contingent assets

> ### KEY TERM
>
> FRS 12 defines a **contingent asset** as:
>
> A possible asset that arises from past events and whose existence will be confirmed by the occurrence of one or more uncertain future events not wholly within the entity's control.

3.37   **A contingent asset must not be recognised.** Only when the realisation of the related economic benefits is **virtually certain** should recognition take place. At that point, **the asset is no longer a contingent asset!**

Disclosure: contingent liabilities

3.38   A **brief description** must be provided of all material contingent liabilities unless they are likely to be remote. In addition, provide

- An estimate of their **financial effect**
- Details of **any uncertainties**

3.39 *Disclosure: contingent assets*

Contingent assets must only be disclosed in the notes if they are **probable**. In that case a brief description of the contingent asset should be provided along with an estimate of its likely financial effect.

'Let out'

3.40 FRS 12 permits reporting entities to avoid disclosure requirements relating to provisions, contingent liabilities and contingent assets if they would be expected to **seriously prejudice** the position of the entity in dispute with other parties. However, this should only be employed in **extremely rare** cases. Details of the general nature of the provision/contingencies must still be provided, together with an explanation of why it has not been disclosed.

3.41 You must practise the questions below to get the hang of FRS 12. But first, study the flow chart, taken from FRS 12, which is a good summary of its requirements.

Exam focus point

If you learn this flow chart you should be able to deal with most of the questions you are likely to meet in an exam.

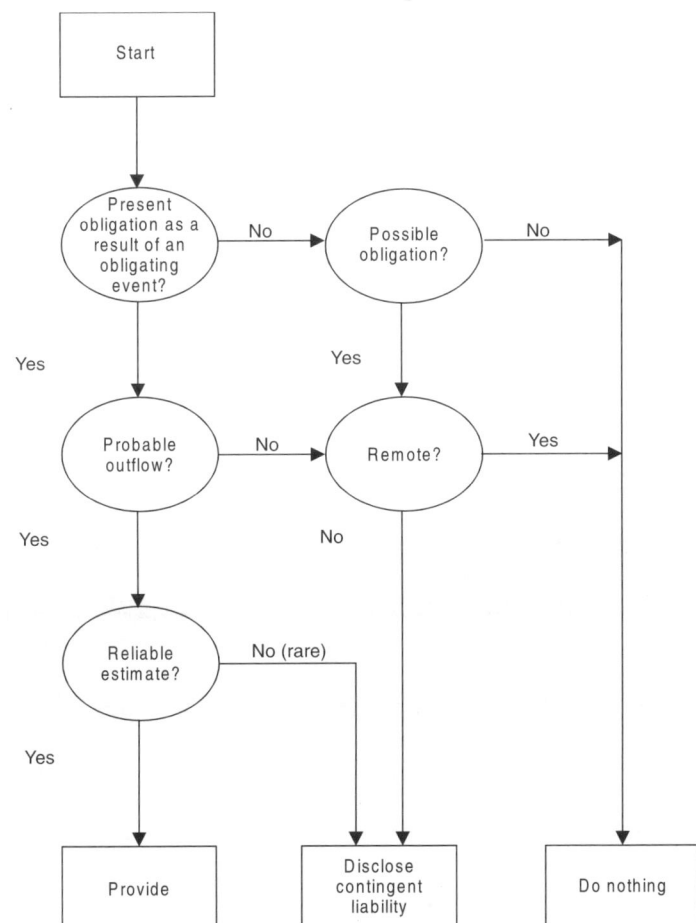

BPP
PUBLISHING

Question 4

During 19X9 Smack Ltd gives a guarantee of certain borrowings of Pony Ltd, whose financial condition at that time is sound. During 19Y0, the financial condition of Pony Ltd deteriorates and at 30 June 19Y0 Pony Ltd files for protection from its creditors.

What accounting treatment is required:

(a)   at 31 December 19X9; and
(b)   at 31 December 19Y0?

Answer

(a)   At 31 December 19X9

There is a present obligation as a result of a past obligating event. The obligating event is the giving of the guarantee, which gives rise to a legal obligation. However, at 31 December 19X9 no transfer of economic benefits is probable in settlement of the obligation.

No provision is recognised. The guarantee is disclosed as a contingent liability unless the probability of any transfer is regarded as remote.

(b)   At 31 December 19Y0

As above, there is a present obligation as a result of a past obligating event, namely the giving of the guarantee.

At 31 December 19Y0 it is probable that a transfer of economic events will be required to settle the obligation. A provision is therefore recognised for the best estimate of the obligation.

Question 5

Warren Ltd gives warranties at the time of sale to purchasers of its products. Under the terms of the warranty the manufacturer undertakes to make good, by repair or replacement, manufacturing defects that become apparent within a period of three years from the date of the sale. Should a provision be recognised?

Answer

Warren Ltd **cannot avoid** the cost of repairing or replacing all items of product that manifest manufacturing defects in respect of which warranties are given before the balance sheet date, and a provision for the cost of this should therefore be made.

Warren Ltd is obliged to repair or replace items that fail within the entire warranty period. Therefore, in respect of **this year's sales**, the obligation provided for at the balance sheet date should be the cost of making good items for which defects have been notified but not yet processed, **plus** an estimate of costs in respect of the other items sold for which there is sufficient evidence that manufacturing defects **will** manifest themselves during their remaining periods of warranty cover.

Question 6

After a wedding in 2000 ten people died, possibly as a result of food poisoning from products sold by Callow Ltd. Legal proceedings are started seeking damages from Callow but it disputes liability. Up to the date of approval of the financial statements for the year to 31 December 2000, Callow's lawyers advise that it is probable that it will not be found liable. However, when Callow prepares the financial statements for the year to 31 December 2001 its lawyers advise that, owing to developments in the case, it is probable that it will be found liable.

What is the required accounting treatment:

(a)   at 31 December 2000;
(b)   at 31 December 2001?

Answer

(a) *At 31 December 2000*

On the basis of the evidence available when the financial statements were approved, there is no obligation as a result of past events. No provision is recognised. The matter is disclosed as a contingent liability unless the probability of any transfer is regarded as remote.

(b) *At 31 December 2001*

On the basis of the evidence available, there is a present obligation. A transfer of economic benefits in settlement is probable.

A provision is recognised for the best estimate of the amount needed to settle the present obligation.

Section summary

3.42 • The objective of FRS 12 is to ensure that **appropriate recognition criteria** and measurement bases are applied to **provisions and contingencies** and that **sufficient information** is disclosed.

• The FRS seeks to ensure that provisions are **only recognised** when a **measurable obligation** exists. It includes detailed rules that can be used to ascertain when an obligation exists and how to measure the obligation.

• It attempts to **eliminate** the 'profit smoothing' which went on before it was issued.

Chapter roundup

• **FRS 8** is primarily a disclosure statement. It is concerned to improve the quality of information provided by published accounts and also to strengthen their stewardship role.

• Under **FRS 12**, a **provision** should be recognised
   o When an entity has a **present obligation**, legal or constructive
   o It is probable that a **transfer of economic benefits** will be required to settle it
   o A **reliable estimate** can be made of its amount

• An entity **should not recognise a contingent asset or liability**, but they **should be disclosed**.

Quick quiz

1 Summarise the requirements of FRS 8 (1.2)

2 How does FRS 8 define related parties? (1.5 (a))

3 Which parties are *deemed* to be related parties of the reporting entity? (1.5 (b)-(d))

4 What are the disclosure requirements of FRS 8? (1.10, 1.11)

5 How does FRS 12 define a provision? (key term)

6 According to FRS 12 when, and only when, can a provision be recognised? (3.8)

7 What are the general rules to be applied when discounting a provision? (3.15)

8 Can a provision ever be made for future operating losses? (3.24)

9 How does FRS 12 define a contingent liability? (key term)

10 When should a contingent liability be recognised? (3.37)

Question to try	Level	Marks	Time
12	Exam	20	36 mins

Chapter 12

CONSTITUTION OF A GROUP

Chapter topic		Syllabus reference	Ability required
1	Definitions	9(a)	Application
2	Exclusion of subsidiary undertakings from group accounts	9(a)	Application
3	Exemption from the requirement to prepare group accounts	9(a)	Application
4	Content of group accounts	9(a)	Application
5	Group structure	9(a)	Application

Introduction

This is the first time you have faced group accounts and consolidation. it is an extremely important area of your Paper 9 syllabus as you are almost certain to face a large compulsory consolidation question in the examination.

In the Syllabus Guidance Notes the examiner states the following in relation to group accounts.

> 'Candidates may be required to demonstrate an ability to prepare consolidated financial statements for a UK parent undertaking and discuss the underlying theoretical issues involved. One or more of the four primary statements could be involved. The group could typically contain associated undertakings in addition to subsidiary undertakings and one or more of the investee undertakings could be an overseas undertaking. Questions may involve a change in the group structure during the year.'

You will probably know that many large companies actually consist of several companies controlled by one central or administrative company. Together these companies are called 'a group'. The controlling company, called the parent or holding company, will own some or all of the shares in the other companies, called subsidiary and associated companies. There are many reasons for businesses to operate as groups; for the goodwill associated with the names of the subsidiaries, for tax or legal purposes and so forth. Company law requires that the results of a group should be presented as a whole. Unfortunately, it is not possible simply to add all the results together and this chapter and those following will teach you how to 'consolidate' all the results of companies within a group.

The key to consolidation questions in the examination is to adopt a logical approach and to practise as many questions as possible.

1 DEFINITIONS

11/95

1.1 There are many reasons for businesses to operate as groups; for the goodwill associated with the names of the subsidiaries, for tax or legal purposes and so forth. Company law requires that the results of a group should be presented as a whole. Unfortunately, it is not possible simply to add all the results together and this chapter and those following will teach you how to **consolidate** all the results of companies within a group.

1.2 **In traditional accounting terminology, a group of companies consists of a holding company (or parent company) and one or more subsidiary companies which are controlled by the holding company.** The CA 1989 widened this definition. (The Act amended the CA 1985 and references below are to the amended sections.) As a result, FRS 2 *Accounting for subsidiary undertakings* was published in July 1992 by the ASB, incorporating the CA 1989 changes.

Exam focus point
If you are revising, go straight to the summary at the end of this section.

1.3 There are **two definitions of a group in company law. One** uses the terms 'holding company' and 'subsidiary' and applies **for general purposes. The other** is wider and applies **only for accounting purposes.** It **uses the terms 'parent undertaking' and 'subsidiary undertaking'.** The purpose of this widening of the group for accounting purposes was to curb the practice of structuring a group in such a way that not all companies or ventures within it had to be consolidated. This is an example of off balance sheet financing and has been used extensively to make consolidated accounts look better than is actually justified (see Chapter 8).

1.4 We are only really interested in the accounting definitions of parent and subsidiary undertaking here: they automatically include 'holding companies' and 'subsidiaries' under the general definition.

Parent and subsidiary undertakings: definition

1.5 FRS 2 states that an undertaking is the **parent undertaking** of another undertaking (**a subsidiary undertaking**) if any of the following apply.

PARENT UNDERTAKING

(a) It holds a **majority of the voting rights** in the undertaking.

(b) It **is a member of the undertaking and has the right to appoint or remove directors** holding a majority of the voting rights at meetings of the board on all, or substantially all, matters.

(c) **It has the right to exercise a dominant influence over the undertaking:**

　(i) by virtue of provisions contained in the undertaking's memorandum or articles; or

　(ii) by virtue of a control contract (in writing, authorised by the memorandum or articles of the controlled undertaking, permitted by law).

(d) **It is a member of the undertaking and controls alone,** under an agreement with other shareholders or members, **a majority of the voting rights in the undertaking.**

(e) It **has a participating interest in the undertaking** and:

　(i) it actually exercises a dominant influence over the undertaking; or
　(ii) it and the undertaking are managed on a unified basis.

(f) A parent undertaking is **also treated as the parent undertaking of the subsidiary undertakings of its subsidiary undertakings.**

1.6   This replaced the previous criterion of owning a majority of equity with one of holding a majority of voting rights. **Also, the board is considered to be controlled if the holding company has the right to appoint directors with a majority of the voting rights on the board** (not just to appoint a simple majority of the directors, regardless of their voting rights).

> ### Exam focus point
> The above definition is extremely important and you may be asked to apply it to a given situation in an exam. It depends in turn, however, on the definition of various terms which are included in Paragraph 1.6.

Participating interest

> ### KEY TERM
> FRS 2 states that a **participating interest is an interest held by an undertaking in the shares of another undertaking which it holds on a long-term basis for the purpose of securing a contribution to its activities by the exercise of control or influence** arising from or related to that interest.
>
> (a)   A holding of **20% or more** of the shares of an undertaking is **presumed** to be a participating interest unless the contrary is shown.
>
> (b)   An interest in shares includes an interest which is convertible into an interest in shares, and includes an option to acquire shares or any interest which is convertible into shares.
>
> (c)   An interest held on behalf of an undertaking shall be treated as held by that undertaking (ie all group holdings must be aggregated to determine if a subsidiary exists).

1.7   A 'participating interest', like an investment in a 'subsidiary undertaking', **need not be in a company,** because an 'undertaking' means:

(a)   a body corporate; or

(b)   a partnership; or

(c)   an unincorporated association carrying on a trade or business, with or without a view to profit.

1.8   **'Shares'** therefore **means**:

(a)   **allotted** shares; **or**

(b)   for undertakings without share capital, **the right to share in the capital and profits and the corresponding liability to meet losses and debts on winding up.**

Dominant influence

> **KEY TERM**
>
> FRS 2 defines **dominant influence** as influence that can be exercised to achieve the operating and financial policies desired by the holder of the influence, notwithstanding the rights or influence of any other party.

1.9 The standard then distinguishes between the two different situations involving dominant influence.

(a) In the context of Paragraph 1.6(c) above, **the right to exercise a dominant influence** means that the holder has **a right to give directions** with respect to the operating and financial policies of another undertaking with which its directors are obliged to comply, whether or not they are for the benefit of that undertaking.

(b) **The actual exercise of dominant influence** is the exercise of an influence that achieves the result that the operating and financial policies of the undertaking influenced are set in accordance with the wishes of the holder of the influence and for the holder's benefit whether or not those wishes are explicit. The actual exercise of dominant influence is identified by its effect in practice rather than by the way in which it is exercised.

1.10 There are four other important definitions.

(a) **Control** is the ability of an undertaking to direct the financial and operating policies of another undertaking with a view to gaining economic benefits from its activities.

(b) An **interest held on a long-term basis** is an interest which is held other than exclusively with a view to subsequent resale.

(c) An **interest held exclusively with a view to subsequent resale** is either:

(i) an interest for which a purchaser has been identified or is being sought, and which is reasonably expected to be disposed of within approximately one year of its date of acquisition; or

(ii) an interest that was acquired as a result of the enforcement of a security, unless the interest has become part of the continuing activities of the group or the holder acts as if it intends the interest to become so.

(d) **Managed on a unified basis:** two or more undertakings are managed on a unified basis if the whole of the operations of the undertakings are integrated and they are managed as a single unit. Unified management does not arise solely because one undertaking manages another.

Other definitions from the standard will be introduced where relevant over the next few chapters.

The requirement to consolidate

1.11 FRS 2 requires a parent undertaking to prepare consolidated financial statements for its group unless it uses one of the exemptions available in the standard (see Section 2).

> ## KEY TERM
>
> **Consolidation** is defined as: 'The process of adjusting and combining financial information from the individual financial statements of a parent undertaking and its subsidiary undertaking to prepare consolidated financial statements that present financial information for the group as a single economic entity.'

Associated undertakings

1.12 Another important definition, which applies only for the purposes of preparing group accounts, is that of an 'associated undertaking'. This is not defined by FRS 2, but as CA 1985 (and FRS 9: see Chapter 17).

> ## KEY TERM
>
> 'An "**associated undertaking**" means an undertaking in which an undertaking included in the consolidation has a participating interest and over whose operating and financial policy it exercises a significant influence, and which is not:
>
> (a) a subsidiary undertaking of the parent company; or
> (b) a joint venture'. (s 20(1) Sch 4A, CA 1985)
>
> 'Where an undertaking holds 20% or more of the voting rights in another undertaking, it shall be presumed to exercise such an influence over it unless the contrary is shown.'
>   (s 20(2) Sch 4A, CA 1985)

1.13 The importance of this definition is that **parent companies are required by law to use equity accounting to account for holdings in 'associated undertakings'**. However, holdings in 'associated companies' (FRS 9 definition: see Chapter 17) are **already accounted for in this way to comply with the SSAP.**

1.14 **Participating interests,** on the other hand, which are not in 'associated undertakings' **have to be disclosed separately from other investments but do not have to be accounted for by the equity method.** Participating interests must be disclosed both in group accounts and in individual company accounts. If you refer back to the statutory accounts formats in Chapter 2, you will see the captions in both the balance sheet and the profit and loss account which refer to 'participating interests'.

1.15 However, in **group accounts** these formats must be amended if necessary as follows.

    (a) Income from interests in associated undertakings   X
        Income from other participating interests   X

        should replace the captions at 8 (format 1) and 10 (format 2) 'Income from participating interests' in the profit and loss account.

    (b) Interests in associated undertakings   X
        Other participating interests   X

        should replace item BIII 3 'Participating interests' in the balance sheet.

1.16 An undertaking **S is a subsidiary undertaking of H if:**

(a) H is a member of S and *either* holds or **controls > 50% of the voting rights** *or* controls the board; *OR*

(b) S is a **subsidiary** of H (ie S is a sub-subsidiary); *OR*

(c) H has the right to exercise a **dominant influence** over S (laid down in the memorandum or articles or a control contract); *OR*

(d) H has a **participating interest** in S **and** either **actually** exercises a **dominant influence** over S *or* H and S are managed on a unified basis.

∴ **Special treatment: consolidate**

1.17 An undertaking A is an **associated undertaking** of H if:

(a) H and/or one or more of its subsidiary undertakings have a **participating interest** in A and **either** hold more than **20%** of the voting rights **or** can otherwise be demonstrated to exercise a **significant** influence over A's operating and financial policy; *AND*

(b) A is not a subsidiary undertaking of H nor is it a joint venture.

∴ **Special treatment: equity accounting**

1.18 An investment in an undertaking P is a **participating interest** of H if:

(a) the H group owns **more than 20%** of P's share capital; *OR*

(b) the H group has a shareholding or equivalent interest in P **for the long term** and for the purpose of securing a contribution to its activities.

∴ **Special treatment: separate disclosure**

2 EXCLUSION OF SUBSIDIARY UNDERTAKINGS FROM GROUP ACCOUNTS

2.1 S 229 CA 1985 (as amended by the CA 1989) provides that a **subsidiary may be omitted** from the consolidated accounts of a group **if:**

(a) in the opinion of the directors, its inclusion 'is **not material** for the purpose of giving a true and fair view; but two or more undertakings may be excluded only if they are not material taken together'; or

(b) there are **severe long-term restrictions** in exercising the parent company's rights eg civil war in the country of an overseas subsidiary; or

(c) the holding is **exclusively for resale**; or

(d) the information cannot be obtained 'without **disproportionate expense** or undue delay'

2.2 If in the opinion of the directors, a subsidiary undertaking's consolidation is undesirable because the **business of the holding company and subsidiary are so different that they cannot reasonably be treated as a single undertaking, then that undertaking** *must* **be excluded.**

> 'This .... does not apply merely because some of the undertakings are industrial, some commercial and some provide services, or because they carry on industrial or commercial activities involving different products or provide different services.'

2.3 FRS 2 states that a **subsidiary must be excluded** from consolidation if:

(a) **Severe long-term restrictions are substantially hindering the exercise of the parent's rights** over the subsidiary's assets or management.

(b) The group's interest in the subsidiary undertaking is **held exclusively with a view to subsequent resale and** the subsidiary has **not been consolidated previously.**

(c) The subsidiary undertaking's **activities are so different** from those of other undertakings to be included in the consolidation **that its inclusion would be incompatible with the obligation to give a true and fair view.**

The FRS requires the circumstances in which subsidiary undertakings are to be excluded from consolidation to be interpreted **strictly.**

2.4 Where a subsidiary is excluded from group accounts, FRS 2 lays down supplementary provisions on the disclosures and accounting treatment required.

2.5 Where a subsidiary is excluded on grounds of **dissimilar activities** (which should be exceptional), the group accounts should **include separate financial statements for that subsidiary including:**

(a) A note of the **holding company's interest.**

(b) Details of **intra-group balances.**

(c) The **nature of its transactions** with the rest of the group.

(d) A **reconciliation of the subsidiary's results** (as shown separately) with the value in the consolidated accounts for the 'group's investment in the subsidiary'.

In the consolidated accounts, the excluded subsidiary **should be accounted for by the equity method** of accounting (as though it were an associated company). This is explained in Chapter 17 on accounting for associated companies.

2.6 Subsidiary undertakings **excluded** from consolidation **because of severe long-term restrictions** are to be **treated as fixed asset investments.** They are to be included at their carrying amount when the restrictions came into force, and no further accruals are to be made for profits or losses of those subsidiary undertakings, unless the parent undertaking still exercises significant influence. In the latter case they are to be treated as associated undertakings.

2.7 The following information should be **disclosed** in the group accounts:

(a) Its **net assets.**

(b) Its **profit or loss** for the period.

(c) Any amounts included in the **consolidated profit and loss account** in respect of:

(i) **Dividends received** by the holding company from the subsidiary.
(ii) **Writing down the value of the investment.**

2.8 If control is temporary (the investment is **held purely for resale**), the temporary investment **should be included under current assets** in the consolidated balance sheet at the lower of cost and net realisable value.

2.9 In all cases given above, FRS 2 states that the consolidated accounts should show:

(a) The **reasons** for exclusion.
(b) The **names** of subsidiaries excluded.
(c) The **premium or discount on acquisition** not written off.
(d) **Anything else required** by the Companies Acts.

2.10 The CA 1985 requires that when consolidated group accounts are not prepared, or if any subsidiaries are excluded from the group accounts (for any of the reasons given above), **a note to the accounts should be given:**

(a) to explain the reasons why the subsidiaries are not dealt with in group accounts;

(b) to disclose any auditors' qualifications in the accounts of the excluded subsidiaries.

A note to the (holding) company's accounts (or the consolidated accounts, if any) should also state, for subsidiaries which are not consolidated in group accounts, the aggregate value of the total investment of the holding company in the subsidiaries, by way of the 'equity method' of valuation.

2.11 Section summary

The following table summaries the rules relating to exclusion of a subsidiary.

Reason	Accounting treatment
• Severe long-term restrictions hindering exercise of parent's rights	B/S: equity method up to date of severe restrictions less amounts written off if permanent fall in value
	P&L a/c: dividends received only
• Held exclusively for subsequent resale; has never been consolidated	Current asset at the lower of cost and net realisable value
• Dissimilar activities	Equity method (see Chapter 17)

3 EXEMPTION FROM THE REQUIREMENT TO PREPARE GROUP ACCOUNTS

3.1 The CA 1989 introduced a completely new provision exempting some groups from preparing consolidated accounts. There are two grounds.

(a) **Smaller groups** can claim exemptions on grounds of size (see below).

(b) **Parent companies** (*except* for listed companies) **whose immediate parent is established in an EU member country** need not prepare consolidated accounts. The accounts must give the name and country of incorporation of the parent and state the fact of the exemption. In addition, a copy of the audited consolidated accounts of the parent must be filed with the UK company's accounts. Minority shareholders can, however, require that consolidated accounts are prepared.

FRS 2 adds that exemption may be gained if all of the parent's subsidiary undertakings gain exemption under s 229 CA 1985 (see Paragraph 2.1).

3.2 The **exemption** from preparing consolidated accounts is **not available to:**

(a) Public companies.

(b) Banking and insurance companies.

(c) Authorised persons under the Financial Services Act 1986.

(d) Companies belonging to a group containing a member of the above classes of undertaking.

3.3 Any two of the following **size criteria** for small and medium-sized groups must be met.

	Small	**Medium-sized**
Aggregate turnover	≤ £2.8 million net/ £3.36 million gross	≤ £11.2 million net/ £13.44 million gross
Aggregate gross assets	≤ £1.4 million net/ £1.68 million gross	≤ £5.6 million net/ £6.72 million gross
Aggregate number of employees (average monthly)	≤ 50	≤ 250

3.4 The aggregates can be calculated either before (gross) or after (net) consolidation adjustments for intra-group sales, unrealised profit on stock and so on (see following chapters). The qualifying conditions **must be met**:

(a) **in the case of the parent's first financial year, in that year; and**
(b) **in the case of any subsequent financial year, in that year and the preceding year.**

If the qualifying conditions were met in the preceding year but not in the current year, the exemption can be claimed. If, in the subsequent year, the conditions are met again, the exemption can still be claimed, but if they are not met, then the exemption is lost until the conditions are again met for the second of two successive years.

3.5 When the exemption is claimed, but the auditors believe that the company is not entitled to it, then they must state in their report that the company is in their opinion not entitled to the exemption and this report must be attached to the individual accounts of the company (ie no report is required when the company *is* entitled to the exemption).

4 CONTENT OF GROUP ACCOUNTS

4.1 The information contained in the individual accounts of a holding company and each of its subsidiaries does not give a picture of the group's activities as those of a single entity. To do this, a separate set of accounts can be prepared from the individual accounts. *Note.* **Remember that a group has no separate (legal) existence, except for accounting purposes.**

4.2 There is more than one way of amalgamating the information in the individual accounts into a set of group accounts, but the most common way (and now the legally required way) is to prepare consolidated accounts. **Consolidated accounts are one form of group accounts which combines the information contained in the separate accounts of a holding company and its subsidiaries as if they were the accounts of a single entity.** 'Group accounts' and 'consolidated accounts' are often used synonymously, and now that UK law *requires* group accounts to be consolidated accounts, this tendency will no doubt increase.

4.3 In simple terms a set of consolidated accounts is prepared by **adding together** the assets and liabilities of the holding company and each subsidiary. The **whole of the assets and liabilities of each company** are included, **even though some subsidiaries may be only partly owned**. The 'capital and reserves' side of the balance sheet will indicate how much of the net assets are attributable to the group and how much to outside investors in partly owned subsidiaries. These **outside investors** are known as **minority interests**.

4.4 The CA 1985 requires that group accounts should be prepared whenever a company:

(a) is a parent company at the end of its financial year; and

(b) is not itself a wholly owned subsidiary of a company incorporated in Great Britain.

4.5 Most parent companies present their own individual accounts and their group accounts in a single **package**. The package typically comprises a:

(a) **Parent company balance sheet**, which will include 'investments in subsidiary undertakings' as an asset.

(b) **Consolidated balance sheet**.

(c) **Consolidated profit and loss** account.

(d) **Consolidated cash flow statement**.

It is not necessary to publish a parent company profit and loss account (s 230 CA 1985), provided the consolidated profit and loss account contains a note stating the profit or loss for the financial year dealt with in the accounts of the parent company and the fact that the statutory exemption is being relied on.

Exam focus point
If you are in a hurry skim or skip the rest of Section 4.

Co-terminous accounting periods

4.6 S 223 (5) CA 1985 requires that the directors of the holding company **should ensure that the financial year of each of the subsidiaries in the group shall coincide with the financial year of the holding company.** This is to prevent any possible 'window dressing' (although financial years need not coincide if the directors hold the opinion that there are reasons against it).

4.7 If the financial year end of a subsidiary does not coincide with the financial year of the holding company, the appropriate results to include in the group accounts for the subsidiary will be those for its year ending before the year end of the holding company; or if this ended more than three months previously, from interim accounts prepared as at the holding company's year end (s 2(2) Sch 4A CA 1985). These two provisions are included in FRS 2.

4.8 Additionally, FRS 2 requires that a note to the group accounts should disclose the:

(a) Reasons why the directors consider that coinciding dates are not appropriate.

(b) Name(s) of the subsidiary(ies) concerned.

(c) Accounting date and length of the accounting period of each relevant subsidiary.

Disclosure of subsidiaries

4.9 The CA 1985 requires that a parent company disclose, by note:

(a) The name of each subsidiary undertaking.

(b) Its country of incorporation (or, if unincorporated, address of principal place of business).

(c)   The identity and proportion of the nominal value of each class of shares held (distinguishing between direct and indirect holdings).

(d)   The reason for treating a subsidiary undertaking as such *unless* a majority of the voting rights are held and the proportion is the same as that of shares held.

FRS 2 confirms these provisions and also requires that the nature of each subsidiary's business should be indicated.

(*Note*. A subsidiary company must show, in its own accounts, its ultimate holding company's name and country of incorporation.)

Further provisions of FRS 2

4.10   FRS 2 also requires the following.

(a)   **Uniform accounting policies should be applied by all companies in the group,** or if this is not done, appropriate adjustments should be made in the consolidated accounts to achieve uniformity. (If, in exceptional cases, such adjustments are impractical, the different accounting policies used, the effect of the difference on the results and net assets, and the reason for the different treatment should all be disclosed). This is also required by the CA 1985.

(b)   **Where there are material additions to the group there should be disclosure of the extent to which the results of the group are affected by profits and losses** of subsidiaries brought in for the first time. This is also now required by the CA 1985.

(c)   **Outside or minority interests in the share capital and reserves of companies consolidated should be disclosed separately in the consolidated balance sheet** (also required by the CA 1985). Debit balances should be shown only if there is a binding obligation on minority shareholders to make good any losses. Similarly, the profits and losses of such companies attributable to outside interests should be shown separately in the consolidated profit and loss account after arriving at group profit or loss after tax but before extraordinary items. Minority interests in extraordinary items should be deducted from the relevant amounts.

(d)   Changes in membership of a group occur on the date control passes, whether by a transaction or other event. **Changes in the membership of the group during the period should be disclosed.**

(e)   When a subsidiary undertaking is acquired the FRS requires its **identifiable assets and liabilities to be brought into the consolidation at their fair values at the date that undertaking becomes a subsidiary** undertaking, even if the acquisition has been made in stages. When a group increases its interest in an undertaking that is already its subsidiary undertaking, the identifiable assets and liabilities of that subsidiary undertaking should be calculated by reference to that fair value. This revaluation is not required if the difference between fair values and carrying amounts of the identifiable assets and liabilities attributable to the increase in stake is not material.

(f)   The effect of consolidating the parent and its subsidiary undertakings may be that aggregation obscures useful information about the different undertakings and activities included in the consolidated financial statements. Parent undertakings are encouraged to give **segmental analysis to provide** readers of consolidated financial statements with **useful information on the different risks and rewards, growth and prospects of the different parts of the group.** The specification of such analysis, however, falls outside the scope of the FRS.

Further provisions of the Companies Act 1985

4.11 For each material acquisition in the period, in addition to the above disclosures, a note must state:

(a) The composition and **fair value** of the consideration given.

(b) The name of the undertaking (of the parent undertaking in the case of a newly acquired group).

(c) Whether acquisition or merger accounting has been used (see Chapter 19).

4.12 If **acquisition accounting** was used, a table of the book values and *fair values* as at acquisition of each class of assets and liabilities of the undertaking or group acquired is to be given, including a statement of the amount of any goodwill or negative consolidation difference arising and an explanation of any significant adjustments made.

4.13 If **merger accounting** is used, then an explanation is to be given of any significant adjustments made together with a statement of adjustments to consolidated reserves.

4.14 For each **material disposal** in the period, the name of the subsidiary must be disclosed, along with the FRS 2 requirements (see Section 2).

4.15 Finally, the CA 1985 requirement to disclose cumulative goodwill written off has been amended recently to exclude goodwill written off through the profit and loss account. Consequently, only the **cumulative goodwill that has been written off direct to reserves** in the current year or past years need now be disclosed. Note that negative goodwill does not require disclosure.

5 GROUP STRUCTURE

5.1 With the difficulties of definition and disclosure dealt with, let us now look at group structures. The simplest are those in which a holding company has only a direct interest in the shares of its subsidiary companies. For example:

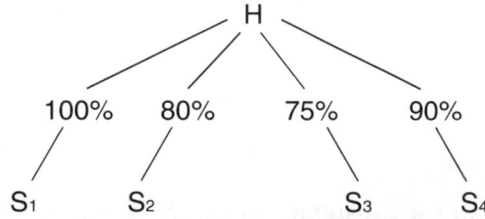

S_1 Ltd is a wholly owned subsidiary of H Ltd. S_2 Ltd, S_3 Ltd and S_4 Ltd are partly owned subsidiaries; a proportion of the shares in these companies is held by outside investors.

5.2 Often a holding company will have indirect holdings in its subsidiary companies. This can lead to more complex group structures.

(a)

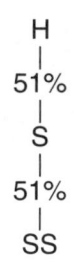

H Ltd owns 51% of the equity shares in S Ltd, which is therefore its subsidiary. S Ltd in its turn owns 51% of the equity shares in SS Ltd. SS Ltd is therefore a subsidiary of S Ltd and consequently a subsidiary of H Ltd. SS Ltd would describe S Ltd as its **parent** (or holding) company and H Ltd as its **ultimate parent** (or holding) company.

Note that although H Ltd can control the assets and business of SS Ltd by virtue of the chain of control, its interest in the assets of SS Ltd is only 26%. This can be seen by considering a dividend of £100 paid by SS Ltd: as a 51% shareholder, S Ltd would receive £51; H Ltd would have an interest in 51% of this £51 = £26.01.

(b)

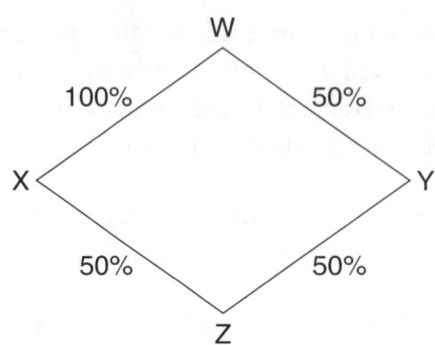

W Ltd owns 100% of the equity of X Ltd and 50% of the equity of Y Ltd. X Ltd and Y Ltd each own 50% of the equity of Z Ltd. Assume that:

(i)   W Ltd does not control the composition of Y Ltd's board; and

(ii)   W Ltd does not hold or control more than 50% of the *voting rights* in Y Ltd; and

(iii)   W Ltd does not have the right to exercise a dominant influence over Y Ltd by virtue of its memorandum, articles or a control contract; and

(iv)   W Ltd and Y Ltd are not managed on a unified basis; and

(v)   W Ltd does not actually exercise a dominant influence over Y Ltd; and

(vi)   none of the above apply to either X Ltd's or Y Ltd's holdings in Z Ltd.

In other words, because W Ltd is not in co-operation with the holder(s) of the other 50% of the shares in Y Ltd, neither Y nor Z can be considered subsidiaries.

In that case:

(i)   X Ltd is a subsidiary of W Ltd;

(ii)   Y Ltd is not a subsidiary of W Ltd;

(iii)   Z Ltd is not a subsidiary of either X Ltd or Y Ltd. Consequently, it is not a subsidiary of W Ltd.

If Z Ltd pays a dividend of £100, X Ltd and Y Ltd will each receive £50. The interest of W Ltd in this dividend is as follows.

	£
Through X Ltd (100% × £50)	50
Through Y Ltd (50% × £50)	25
	75

Although W Ltd has an interest in 75% of Z Ltd's assets, Z Ltd is not a subsidiary of W Ltd.

(c)

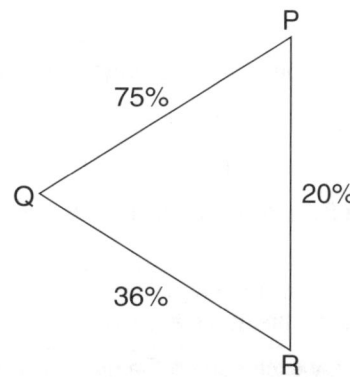

Q Ltd is a subsidiary of P Ltd. P Ltd therefore has indirect control over 36% of R Limited's equity. P Ltd also has direct control over 20% of R Limited's equity. R Ltd is therefore a subsidiary of P Ltd, although P Limited's interest in R Limited's assets is only $20\% + (75\% \times 36\%) = 47\%$.

Examples (b) and (c) illustrate an important point in company law: in deciding whether a company A holds more than 50% of the equity (or equivalent) of an undertaking B it is necessary to aggregate:

(i)   shares (or equivalent) in B held directly by A; and

(ii)   shares (or equivalent) in B held by undertakings which are subsidiaries of A.

Question

During the time until your examination you should obtain as many sets of the published accounts of top quoted companies as possible. Examine the accounting policies in relation to subsidiary and associated companies and consider how these policies are shown in the accounting and consolidation treatment. Consider the effect of any disposals during the year. Also, look at all the disclosures made relating to fair values, goodwill etc and match them to the disclosure requirements outlined in this chapter and in subsequent chapters on FRSs 6 and 7.

Alternatively (or additionally) you should attempt to obtain such information from the financial press.

Exam focus point

You should have absorbed and understood **all** of this chapter. It is a crucial foundation for your later studies.

Chapter roundup

*   This chapter has explained the concept of a **group** and introduced several important definitions.

*   The principal **regulations** governing the preparation of group accounts have been explained. Many of these are hard to understand and you should re-read this chapter after you have completed your study of this section of the text.

*   A number of possible **group structures** have been illustrated to show that a company may hold an interest in the net assets of another company which exceeds 50%, without conferring control of the other company. The converse is also true.

Quick quiz

1   What is the FRS 2 definition of a 'subsidiary'? (see para 1.5)

2   What is a 'participating interest'? (1.7)

3   What is a 'dominant influence'? (1.9)

4   How must investments in associated undertakings be treated in a parent company's own accounts? (1.13)

5   Under what circumstances *may* subsidiary undertakings be excluded under the CA 1985? (2.1) When *must* an undertaking be excluded? (2.3)

6   How should a subsidiary excluded on the grounds of temporary control be accounted for in the consolidated balance sheet? (2.8)

7   What are the size criteria for exemption from preparing group accounts under the CA 1985? (3.3)

8   What is the profit which a parent company must disclose if it wishes to claim exemption under s 230 CA 1985 from publishing its own profit and loss account? (4.5)

9   What must be disclosed in the notes to the consolidated accounts in respect of all newly acquired subsidiary undertakings (if material to the group)? (4.10(b), 4.11) What extra disclosures are required depending on the consolidation method adopted? (4.12, 4.13)

Question to try	Level	Marks	Time
13	Introductory	n/a	n/a

Chapter 13

CONSOLIDATED BALANCE SHEET: BASIC PRINCIPLES

Chapter topic	Syllabus reference	Ability required
1 Cancellation and part cancellation	9(a)	Application
2 Minority interests	9(a)	Application
3 Dividends payable by a subsidiary	9(a)	Application
4 Goodwill arising on consolidation	9(a)	Application
5 A technique of consolidation	9(a)	Application
6 Inter-company trading	9(a)	Application
7 Inter-company sales of fixed assets	9(a)	Application
8 Summary: consolidated balance sheet		

Introduction

This chapter introduces the **basic procedures** required in consolidation and gives a formal step plan for carrying out a balance sheet consolidation. This step procedure should be useful to you as a starting guide for answering any question, but remember that you cannot rely on it to answer the question for you.

Each question must be approached and answered on its own merits. Examiners often put small extra or different problems in because, as they are always reminding students, it is not possible to 'rote-learn' consolidation.

The method of consolidation shown here uses schedules for workings (reserves, minority interests etc) rather than the ledger accounts used in some other texts. This is because we believe that ledger accounts lead students to 'learn' the consolidation journals without thinking about what they are doing - always a dangerous practice in consolidation questions.

There are plenty of questions in this chapter - work through **all** of them carefully.

1 CANCELLATION AND PART CANCELLATION   5/95, 11/96

1.1   The preparation of a consolidated balance sheet, in a very simple form, consists of two procedures.

(a)   Take the individual accounts of the holding company and each subsidiary and **cancel out items which appear as an asset in one company and a liability in another.**

(b)   **Add together all the uncancelled assets** and liabilities throughout the group.

1.2   **Items requiring cancellation** may include the following.

(a)   The asset **'shares in subsidiary companies'** which appears in the parent company's accounts will be matched with the liability 'share capital' in the subsidiaries' accounts.

(b) There may be **inter-company trading** within the group. For example, S Ltd may sell goods to H Ltd. H Ltd would then be a debtor in the accounts of S Ltd, while S Ltd would be a creditor in the accounts of H Ltd.

1.3 EXAMPLE: CANCELLATION

H Ltd regularly sells goods to its one subsidiary company, S Ltd. The balance sheets of the two companies on 31 December 19X6 are given below.

H LIMITED
BALANCE SHEET AS AT 31 DECEMBER 19X6

	£	£	£
Fixed assets			
Tangible assets			35,000
40,000 £1 shares in S Ltd at cost			40,000
			75,000
Current assets			
Stocks		16,000	
Debtors: S Ltd	2,000		
Other	6,000		
		8,000	
Cash at bank		1,000	
		25,000	
Current liabilities			
Creditors		14,000	
			11,000
			86,000
Capital and reserves			
70,000 £1 ordinary shares			70,000
Reserves			16,000
			86,000

S LIMITED
BALANCE SHEET AS AT 31 DECEMBER 19X6

	£	£	£
Fixed assets			
Tangible assets			45,000
Current assets			
Stocks		12,000	
Debtors		9,000	
		21,000	
Current liabilities			
Bank overdraft		3,000	
Creditors: H Ltd	2,000		
Other	2,000		
		4,000	
		7,000	
			14,000
			59,000
Capital and reserves			
40,000 £1 ordinary shares			40,000
Reserves			19,000
			59,000

Prepare the consolidated balance sheet of H Ltd.

1.4 SOLUTION

The cancelling items are:

(a) H Ltd's asset 'investment in shares of S Ltd' (£40,000) cancels with S Ltd's liability 'share capital' (£40,000);

(b) H Ltd's asset 'debtors: S Ltd' (£2,000) cancels with S Ltd's liability 'creditors: H Ltd' (£2,000).

The remaining assets and liabilities are added together to produce the following consolidated balance sheet.

H LIMITED
CONSOLIDATED BALANCE SHEET AS AT 31 DECEMBER 19X6

	£	£
Fixed assets		
Tangible assets		80,000
Current assets		
Stocks	28,000	
Debtors	15,000	
Cash at bank	1,000	
	44,000	
Current liabilities		
Bank overdraft	3,000	
Creditors	16,000	
	19,000	
		25,000
		105,000
Capital and reserves		
70,000 £1 ordinary shares		70,000
Reserves		35,000
		105,000

Notes on the example

1.5 (a) H Ltd's bank balance is not netted off with S Ltd's bank overdraft. To offset one against the other would be less informative and would conflict with the statutory principle that assets and liabilities should not be netted off.

(b) The share capital in the consolidated balance sheet is the share capital of the parent company alone. This must *always* be the case, no matter how complex the consolidation, because the share capital of subsidiary companies must *always* be a wholly cancelling item.

Part cancellation

1.6 **An item may appear in the balance sheets of a parent company and its subsidiary, but not at the same amounts.**

(a) **The parent company may have acquired shares in the subsidiary at a price greater or less than their nominal value.** The asset will appear in the parent company's accounts at cost, while the liability will appear in the subsidiary's accounts at nominal value. **This raises the issue of goodwill**, which is dealt with later in this chapter.

(b) Even if the parent company acquired shares at nominal value, it **may not have acquired all the shares of the subsidiary** (so the subsidiary may be only partly owned). This **raises the issue of minority interests,** which are also dealt with later in this chapter.

(c) The inter-company trading balances may be out of step because of **goods or cash in transit.**

(d) One company may have **issued loan stock of which a proportion only is taken up** by the other company.

1.7 The following example illustrates the techniques needed to deal with the second two items. The procedure is to **cancel as far as possible. The remaining uncancelled amounts will appear in the consolidated balance sheet.**

(a) Uncancelled loan stock will appear as a liability of the group.

(b) Uncancelled balances on inter-company accounts represent goods or cash in transit, which will appear in the consolidated balance sheet.

Question 1

The balance sheets of H Ltd and of its subsidiary S Ltd have been made up to 30 June. H Ltd has owned all the ordinary shares and 40% of the loan stock of S Ltd since its incorporation.

H LIMITED
BALANCE SHEET AS AT 30 JUNE

	£	£
Fixed assets		
Tangible assets		120,000
Investment in S Ltd, at cost		
80,000 ordinary shares of £1 each		80,000
£20,000 of 12% loan stock in S Ltd		20,000
		220,000
Current assets		
Stocks	50,000	
Debtors	40,000	
Current account with S Ltd	18,000	
Cash	4,000	
	112,000	
Creditors: amounts falling due within one year		
Creditors	47,000	
Taxation	15,000	
	62,000	
Net current assets		50,000
		270,000
Creditors: amounts falling due after more than one year		
10% loan stock		75,000
		195,000
Capital and reserves		
Ordinary shares of £1 each, fully paid		100,000
Reserves		95,000
		195,000

S LIMITED
BALANCE SHEET AS AT 30 JUNE

	£	£
Tangible fixed assets		100,000
Current assets		
Stocks	60,000	
Debtors	30,000	
Cash	6,000	
	96,000	
Creditors: amounts falling due within one year		
Creditors	16,000	
Taxation	10,000	
Current account with H Ltd	12,000	
	38,000	
		58,000
		158,000
Creditors: amounts falling due after more than one year		
12% Loan stock		50,000
		108,000
Capital and reserves		
80,000 ordinary shares of £1 each, fully paid		80,000
Reserves		28,000
		108,000

The difference on current account arises because of goods in transit. Prepare the consolidated balance sheet of H Ltd.

Answer

H LIMITED
CONSOLIDATED BALANCE SHEET AS AT 30 JUNE

	£	£
Tangible fixed assets		220,000
Current assets		
Stocks	110,000	
Goods in transit	6,000	
Debtors	70,000	
Cash	10,000	
	196,000	
Creditors: amounts falling due within one year		
Creditors	63,000	
Taxation	25,000	
	88,000	
		108,000
		328,000
Creditors: amounts falling due after more than one year		
10% loan stock	75,000	
12% loan stock	30,000	
		105,000
		223,000
Capital and reserves		
Ordinary shares of £1 each, fully paid		100,000
Reserves		123,000
		223,000

Note especially how:

(a)   the uncancelled loan stock in S Ltd becomes a liability of the group;

(b)   the goods in transit is the difference between the current accounts (£18,000 – £12,000).

BPP PUBLISHING

2   MINORITY INTERESTS

2.1   It was mentioned earlier that the total assets and liabilities of subsidiary companies are included in the consolidated balance sheet, even in the case of subsidiaries which are only partly owned. A proportion of the net assets of such subsidiaries in fact belongs to investors from outside the group (minority interests).

> ### KEY TERM
>
> FRS 2 defines **minority interest** in a subsidiary undertaking as the 'interest in a subsidiary undertaking included in the consolidation that is attributable to the shares held by or on behalf of persons other than the parent undertaking and its subsidiary undertakings'.

In the consolidated balance sheet it is necessary to distinguish this proportion from those assets attributable to the group and financed by shareholders' funds.

2.2   The net assets of a company are financed by share capital and reserves. The consolidation procedure for dealing with partly owned subsidiaries is to **calculate the proportion of ordinary shares, preference shares and reserves attributable to minority interests.**

2.3   EXAMPLE: MINORITY INTERESTS

H Ltd has owned 75% of the share capital of S Ltd since the date of S Ltd's incorporation. Their latest balance sheets are given below.

H LIMITED - BALANCE SHEET

	£
Fixed assets	
Tangible assets	50,000
30,000 £1 ordinary shares in S Ltd at cost	30,000
	80,000
Net current assets	25,000
	105,000
Capital and reserves	
80,000 £1 ordinary shares	80,000
Reserves	25,000
	105,000

S LIMITED
BALANCE SHEET

	£
Tangible fixed assets	35,000
Net current assets	15,000
	50,000
Capital and reserves	
40,000 £1 ordinary shares	40,000
Reserves	10,000
	50,000

Prepare the consolidated balance sheet.

2.4   SOLUTION

All of S Ltd's net assets are consolidated despite the fact that the company is only 75% owned. The amount of net assets attributable to minority interests is calculated as follows.

	£
Minority share of share capital (25% × £40,000)	10,000
Minority share of reserves (25% × £10,000)	2,500
	12,500

Of S Ltd's share capital of £40,000, £10,000 is included in the figure for minority interest, while £30,000 is cancelled with H Ltd's asset 'investment in S Limited'.

The consolidated balance sheet can now be prepared.

H GROUP
CONSOLIDATED BALANCE SHEET

	£
Tangible fixed assets	85,000
Net current assets	40,000
	125,000
Share capital	80,000
Reserves £(25,000 + (75% × 10,000))	32,500
Shareholders' funds	112,500
Minority interest	12,500
	125,000

2.5 In this example we have shown minority interest on the 'capital and reserves' side of the balance sheet to illustrate how some of S Ltd's net assets are financed by shareholders' funds, while some are financed by outside investors. You may see minority interest as a deduction from the other side of the balance sheet. The second half of the balance sheet will then consist entirely of shareholders' funds. The Companies Act 1985 permits either of the above presentations, but **FRS 4 seems to require the disclosure shown above**.

Exam focus point

In more complicated examples the following technique is recommended for dealing with minority interests.

Step 1 Cancel common items in the draft balance sheets. If there is a minority interest, the subsidiary company's share capital will be a partly cancelled item. Ascertain the proportion of ordinary shares and the proportion (possibly different) of preference shares held by the minority.

Step 2 Produce a working for the minority interest. Add in the amounts of preference and ordinary share capital calculated in step 1: this completes the cancellation of the subsidiary's share capital.

Add also the minority's share of each reserve in the subsidiary company. Reserves belong to equity shareholders; the proportion attributable to minority interests therefore depends on their percentage holding of *ordinary* shares.

Step 3 Produce a separate working for each reserve (capital, revenue etc) found in the subsidiary company's balance sheet. The initial balances on these accounts will be taken straight from the draft balance sheets of the parent and subsidiary company.2.6

Step 4 The closing balances in these workings can be entered directly onto the consolidated balance sheet.

Question 2

Set out below are the draft balance sheets of H Ltd and its subsidiary S Ltd. You are required to prepare the consolidated balance sheet.

H LIMITED

	£	£
Fixed assets		
Tangible assets		31,000
Investment in S Ltd		
12,000 £1 ordinary shares at cost	12,000	
4,000 £1 preference shares at cost	4,000	
£4,000 10% debentures at cost	4,000	
		20,000
		51,000
Net current assets		11,000
		62,000
Capital and reserves		
Ordinary shares of £1 each		40,000
Revenue reserve		22,000
		62,000

S LIMITED

	£
Tangible fixed assets	34,000
Net current assets	22,000
	56,000
Long-term liability	
10% debentures	10,000
	46,000
Capital and reserves	
Ordinary shares of £1 each	20,000
Preference shares of £1 each	16,000
Capital reserve	6,000
Revenue reserve	4,000
	46,000

Answer

Partly cancelling items are the components of H Ltd's investment in S Ltd, ie ordinary shares, preference shares and loan stock. Minorities have an interest in 75% (12,000/16,000) of S Ltd's preference shares and 40% (8,000/20,000) of S Ltd's equity, including reserves.

You should now product workings for minority interests, capital reserve and revenue reserve as follows.

Workings

1   *Minority interests*

	£
Ordinary share capital (40% of 20,000)	8,000
Reserves: capital (40% $\times$ 6,000)	2,400
revenue (40% $\times$ 4,000)	1,600
	12,000
Preference share capital (75% $\times$ 16,000)	12,000
	24,000

2   *Capital reserve*

	£
H Ltd	-
Share of S Ltd's capital reserve (60% $\times$ 6,000)	3,600
	3,600

3   *Revenue reserve*

	£
H Ltd	22,000
Share of S Ltd's revenue reserves (60% × 4,000)	2,400
	24,400

The results of the workings are now used to construct the consolidated balance sheet (CBS).

H GROUP
CONSOLIDATED BALANCE SHEET

	£
Tangible fixed assets	65,000
Net current assets	33,000
	98,000
Long-term liability	
10% debentures	6,000
	92,000
Capital and reserves	
Ordinary shares of £1 each	40,000
Capital reserve	3,600
Revenue reserve	24,400
Shareholders' funds	68,000
Minority interests	24,000
	92,000

Notes

(a)   S Ltd is a subsidiary of H Ltd because H Ltd owns 60% of its equity capital. It is unimportant how little of the preference share capital is owned by H Ltd.

(b)   As always, the share capital in the consolidated balance sheet is that of the parent company alone. The share capital in S Ltd's balance sheet was partly cancelled against the investment shown in H Ltd's balance sheet, while the uncancelled portion was credited to minority interest.

(c)   The figure for minority interest comprises the interest of outside investors in the share capital and reserves of the subsidiary. The uncancelled portion of S Ltd's loan stock is not shown as part of minority interest but is disclosed separately as a liability of the group.

---

3   DIVIDENDS PAYABLE BY A SUBSIDIARY   5/95, 11/96

3.1   When a subsidiary company pays a dividend during the year the accounting treatment is not difficult. Suppose S Ltd, a 60% subsidiary of H Ltd, pays a dividend of £1,000 on the last day of its accounting period. Its total reserves before paying the dividend stood at £5,000.

(a)   £400 of the dividend is paid to minority shareholders. The cash leaves the group and will not appear anywhere in the consolidated balance sheet.

(b)   The holding company receives £600 of the dividend, debiting cash and crediting profit and loss account.

(c)   The remaining balance of reserves in S Ltd's balance sheet (£4,000) will be consolidated in the normal way. The group's share (60% × £4,000 = £2,400) will be included in group reserves in the balance sheet; the minority share (40% × £4,000 = £1,600) is credited to the minority interest account.

3.2   More care is needed when dealing with **proposed dividends** not yet paid by a subsidiary. The **first step** must be to **ensure that the draft accounts of both subsidiary and parent company are up-to-date and reflect the proposed dividend.**

3.3   If neither company has accrued for the proposed dividend you will need to make appropriate adjustments to the draft balance sheets.

(a)   If the subsidiary has not yet accrued for the proposed dividend, the adjustment is:

> DEBIT   Revenue reserves
> CREDIT   Dividends payable

with the full amount of the dividend payable in the subsidiary's books, whether it is due to the parent company or to minority shareholders.

(b)   If the parent company has not yet accrued for its share of the proposed dividend, the adjustment is:

> DEBIT   Debtors (dividend receivable)
> CREDIT   Revenue reserves

with the *parent company's share* of the dividend receivable in the parent's books.

3.4   **On consolidation, the dividend payable in S Ltd's accounts will cancel with the dividend receivable in H Ltd's accounts.** If S Ltd is a wholly owned subsidiary, there will be complete cancellation; if S Ltd is only partly owned, there will be only part cancellation. The uncancelled portion will be the amount of dividend payable to minority shareholders and this will appear in the consolidated balance sheet as a current liability.

3.5   **When preparing the workings for reserves and minority interest, the relevant reserves figures for both companies are the figures *after* adjusting for the proposed dividend.**

3.6   EXAMPLE: DIVIDENDS

Set out below are the draft balance sheets of Hug Ltd and its subsidiary Bug Ltd. Hug Ltd has not yet taken account of the dividend proposed by Bug Ltd.

You are required to prepare the consolidated balance sheet.

HUG LIMITED

	£	£
Fixed assets		
Tangible assets		1,350
Investment in Bug Ltd: 1,500 shares at cost		1,500
		2,850
Current assets	700	
Current liabilities		
Creditors	400	
		300
	–	3,150
Capital and reserves		£
Ordinary shares of £1 each		1,000
Revenue reserves		2,150
		3,150

BUG LIMITED

	£	£
Tangible fixed assets		2,500
Current assets	900	
Current liabilities		
Creditors	200	
Proposed dividend	200	
		500
		3,000
Capital and reserves		
Ordinary shares of £1 each		2,000
Revenue reserves		1,000
		3,000

3.7 SOLUTION

The first step is to bring Hug Ltd's balance sheet up to date by accruing for its share of the dividend receivable from Bug Ltd. Hug Ltd owns 75% (1,500/2,000) of the shares in Bug Ltd. Its share of the proposed dividend is therefore 75% × £200 = £150. Hug Ltd's draft balance sheet should be adjusted as follows.

DEBIT	Debtors: dividend receivable	£150	
CREDIT	Revenue reserves		£150

3.8 Next deal with cancellation. There are two part-cancelling items, the shares of Bug Ltd and the dividend receivable/payable.

3.9 The workings may now be produced. Notice how the relevant reserves figures are the figures after adjusting for the proposed dividend. Because Bug Ltd's accounts are up-to-date, and reflect the proposed figure, the correct reserves figure (£1,000) can be taken straight from the draft balance sheet. In the case of Hug Ltd, it is the adjusted reserves figure (£2,150 + £150 = £2,300) which is used.

Workings

		£
1	*Minority interests*	
	Share capital (25% × 2,000)	500
	Revenue reserves (25% × 1,000)	250
		750
2	*Revenue reserves*	
		£
	Hug Ltd (as adjusted)	2,300
	Share of Bug Ltd's revenue reserves (1,000 × 75%)	750
		3,050

HUG GROUP
CONSOLIDATED BALANCE SHEET

	£	£
Tangible fixed assets		3,850
Current assets	1,600	
Current liabilities		
Creditors	600	
Minority proposed dividend	50	
		950
		4,800

BPP PUBLISHING

Capital and reserves	£
Ordinary shares of £1 each	1,000
Revenue reserves	3,050
Shareholders' funds	4,050
Minority interests	750
	4,800

3.10 If there is a proposed *preference dividend* payable by the subsidiary the same procedure should be applied. Again, the first step is to bring both companies' balance sheets up to date, and again the workings accounts will deal with reserves figures *after* adjusting for the proposed dividends.

3.11 EXAMPLE: PROPOSED PREFERENCE DIVIDEND

Set out below are the draft balance sheets of H Ltd and S Ltd. Neither company has yet provided for any dividend, but you should now provide for:

(a) the preference dividend of S Ltd;

(b) a proposed ordinary dividend of 10% by S Ltd;

(c) a proposed ordinary dividend of 20% by H Ltd.

You are required to prepare the consolidated balance sheet.

H LIMITED

	£	£
Fixed assets		
Tangible assets		72,000
Investment in S Ltd		
30,000 £1 ordinary shares at cost	30,000	
6,000 £1 7% preference shares at cost	6,000	
		36,000
		108,000
Current assets	73,000	
Current liabilities	21,000	
		52,000
		160,000
Capital and reserves		
Ordinary shares of £1 each		100,000
Revenue reserves		60,000
		160,000

S LIMITED

	£	£
Tangible fixed assets		40,000
Current assets	51,700	
Current liabilities	19,000	
		32,700
		72,700
Capital and reserves		
Ordinary shares of £1 each		40,000
7% preference shares of £1 each		10,000
		50,000
Revenue reserves		22,700
		72,700

3.12 SOLUTION

The draft balance sheet of S Ltd must be adjusted by the following entries.

DEBIT	Revenue reserves	£4,700		
CREDIT	Proposed dividends			
	Preference (7% × £10,000)		£700	
	Ordinary (10% × £40,000)		£4,000	

The adjusted balance on S Ltd's revenue reserves is now £(22,700 − 4,700)=£18,000.

H Ltd's share in these dividends is:

	£
Preference (60%)	420
Ordinary (75%)	3,000
	3,420

H Ltd's balance sheet must therefore be adjusted as follows.

DEBIT	Debtors: dividends receivable	£3,420	
CREDIT	Revenue reserves		£3,420

A further adjustment to H Ltd's balance sheet is necessary in respect of the company's own proposed dividend of 20% × £100,000 = £20,000.

DEBIT	Revenue reserves	£20,000	
CREDIT	Proposed dividend		£20,000

The adjusted balance on H Ltd's revenue reserve is now £(60,000 + 3,420 − 20,000) = £43,420.

3.13 After S Ltd's share capital and the dividends payable/receivable have been part-cancelled, the workings can be drawn up.

Workings

1 *Minority interests*

	£
Ordinary share capital (25% × 40,000)	10,000
Revenue reserves (25% × 18,000)	4,500
	14,500
Preference share capital (40% × 10,000)	4,000
	18,500

2 *Revenue reserves*

	£
H Ltd's (adjusted balance)	43,420
Share of S Ltd's revenue reserve (75% × 18,000)	13,500
	56,920

H LIMITED CONSOLIDATED BALANCE SHEET

	£	£
Tangible fixed assets		112,000
Current assets	124,700	
Current liabilities		
Sundry	40,000	
Proposed dividend	20,000	
Minority proposed dividend (25% × £4,000) + (40% × £700)	1,280	
		63,420
		175,420
Capital and reserves		
Ordinary shares of £1 each		100,000
Revenue reserves		56,920
Shareholders' funds		156,920
Minority interests		18,500
		175,420

4 GOODWILL ARISING ON CONSOLIDATION

4.1 In the examples we have looked at so far the cost of shares acquired by the parent company has always been equal to the nominal value of those shares. This is seldom the case in practice and we must now consider some more complicated examples. To begin with, **we will examine the entries made by the parent company in its own balance sheet when it acquires shares.**

4.2 When a company H Ltd wishes to **purchase shares** in a company S Ltd it must pay the previous owners of those shares. The most obvious form of payment would be in **cash**. Suppose H Ltd purchases all 40,000 £1 shares in S Ltd and pays £60,000 cash to the previous shareholders in consideration. The entries in H Ltd's books would be:

DEBIT	Investment in S Ltd at cost	£60,000	
CREDIT	Bank		£60,000

4.3 However, the previous shareholders might be prepared to accept some other form of consideration. For example, they might accept an agreed number of **shares** in H Ltd. H Ltd would then issue new shares in the agreed number and allot them to the former shareholders of S Ltd. This kind of deal might be attractive to H Ltd since it avoids the need for a heavy cash outlay. The former shareholders of S Ltd would retain an indirect interest in that company's profitability via their new holding in its parent company.

4.4 Continuing the example, suppose the shareholders of S Ltd agreed to accept one £1 ordinary share in H Ltd for every two £1 ordinary shares in S Ltd. H Ltd would then need to issue and allot 20,000 new £1 shares. How would this transaction be recorded in the books of H Ltd?

4.5 The simplest method would be as follows.

DEBIT	Investment in S Ltd	£20,000	
CREDIT	Share capital		£20,000

However, if the 40,000 £1 shares acquired in S Ltd are thought to have a value of £60,000 this would be misleading. The former shareholders of S Ltd have presumably agreed to accept 20,000 shares in H Ltd because they consider each of those shares to have a value of £3. This view of the matter suggests the following method of recording the transaction in H Ltd's books.

DEBIT	Investment in S Ltd		£60,000
CREDIT	Share capital	£20,000	
	Share premium account	£40,000	

The second method is the one which the Companies Act 1985 requires should normally be used in preparing consolidated accounts.

4.6 The amount which H Ltd records in its books as the cost of its investment in S Ltd may be more or less than the book value of the assets it acquires. Suppose that S Ltd in the previous example has nil reserves, so that its share capital of £40,000 is balanced by net assets with a book value of £40,000. For simplicity, assume that the book value of S Ltd's assets is the same as their market or fair value.

4.7 Now when the directors of H Ltd agree to pay £60,000 for a 100% investment in S Ltd they must believe that, in addition to its tangible assets of £40,000, S Ltd must also have intangible assets worth £20,000. This amount of £20,000 paid over and above the value of the tangible assets acquired is called **goodwill arising on consolidation** (sometimes **premium on acquisition**).

4.8 Following the normal cancellation procedure the £40,000 share capital in S Ltd's balance sheet could be cancelled against £40,000 of the 'investment in S Limited' in the balance sheet of H Ltd. This would leave a £20,000 debit uncancelled in the parent company's accounts and this £20,000 would appear in the consolidated balance sheet under the caption 'Intangible fixed assets. Goodwill arising on consolidation' (although see below for FRS 10's requirements on this type of goodwill).

Goodwill and pre-acquisition profits

4.9 Up to now we have assumed that S Ltd had nil reserves when its shares were purchased by H Ltd. Assuming instead that S Ltd had earned profits of £8,000 in the period before acquisition, its balance sheet just before the purchase would look as follows.

	£
Net tangible assets	48,000
Share capital	40,000
Reserves	8,000
	48,000

4.10 If H Ltd now purchases all the shares in S Ltd it will acquire net tangible assets worth £48,000 at a cost of £60,000. Clearly in this case S Ltd's intangible assets (goodwill) are being valued at £12,000. It should be apparent that **any reserves earned by the subsidiary prior to its acquisition by the parent company must be incorporated in the cancellation process so as to arrive at a figure for goodwill arising on consolidation.** In other words, not only S Ltd's share capital, but also its pre-acquisition reserves, must be cancelled against the asset 'investment in S Ltd' in the accounts of the parent company. The uncancelled balance of £12,000 appears in the consolidated balance sheet.

4.11 The consequence of this is that any pre-acquisition reserves of a subsidiary company are not aggregated with the parent company's reserves in the consolidated balance sheet. **The figure of consolidated reserves comprises the reserves of the parent company plus the post-acquisition reserves only of subsidiary companies. The post-acquisition reserves are simply reserves at the consolidation date less reserves at acquisition.**

4.12 EXAMPLE: GOODWILL AND PRE-ACQUISITION PROFITS

Sing Ltd acquired the ordinary shares of Wing Ltd on 31 March when the draft balance sheets of each company were as follows.

SING LIMITED
BALANCE SHEET AS AT 31 MARCH

	£
Fixed assets	
Investment in 50,000 shares of Wing Ltd at cost	80,000
Net current assets	40,000
	120,000
Capital and reserves	
Ordinary shares	75,000
Revenue reserves	45,000
	120,000

WING LIMITED
BALANCE SHEET AS AT 31 MARCH

	£
Net current assets	60,000
Share capital and reserves	
50,000 ordinary shares of £1 each	50,000
Revenue reserves	10,000
	60,000

Prepare the consolidated balance sheet as at 31 March.

4.13 SOLUTION

The technique to adopt here is to produce a new working: 'Goodwill'. A proforma working is set out below.

Goodwill

	£	£
Cost of investment		X
Share of net assets acquired as represented by:		
Ordinary share capital	X	
Share premium	X	
Reserves on acquisition	X	
Group share	a%	(X)
		X
b% preference shares		(X)
Goodwill		X

4.14 Applying this to our example the working will look like this.

	£	£
Cost of investment		80,000
Share of net assets acquired as represented by:		
Ordinary share capital	50,000	
Revenue reserves on acquisition	10,000	
	60,000	
Group share 100%		60,000
Goodwill		20,000

SING LIMITED
CONSOLIDATED BALANCE SHEET AS AT 31 MARCH

	£
Fixed assets	
Goodwill arising on consolidation	20,000
Net current assets	100,000
	120,000
Capital and reserves	
Ordinary shares	75,000
Revenue reserves	45,000
	120,000

FRS 10 *Goodwill and intangible assets*

4.15 Goodwill arising on consolidation is one form of **purchased goodwill**, and is therefore governed by FRS 10. As explained in an earlier chapter FRS 10 requires that purchased goodwill should be capitalised and classified as an asset on the balance sheet. It is then eliminated from the accounts by **amortisation** through the profit and loss account.

4.16 **A consolidation adjustment** will be required each year as follows.

DEBIT   Consolidated P&L account
CREDIT   Provision for amortisation of goodwill

The **unamortised portion** will be included in the consolidated balance sheet under **fixed assets**.

4.17 Goodwill arising on consolidation is the difference between the cost of an acquisition and the value of the subsidiary's net assets acquired. This difference can be **negative**: the aggregate of the fair values of the separable net assets acquired may exceed what the holding company paid for them. This 'negative goodwill', also sometimes called 'discount arising on consolidation', is required by FRS 10 to be disclosed in the intangible fixed assets category, directly under positive goodwill, ie as a 'negative asset'

4.18 The standard contains a presumption that the useful life of the goodwill is less than 20 years. The presumption may be rebutted. If it is greater than 20 years, it must still be amortised. If it is indefinite, it should not be amortised, but a full impairment review should be performed each year. An impairment review should, in any case, be performed at the end of the first full year after acquisition.

> **Exam focus point**
> Do not worry too much about this. The question will tell you the period over which to amortise any goodwill.

5 A TECHNIQUE OF CONSOLIDATION

5.1 We have now looked at the topics of cancellation, minority interests and goodwill arising on consolidation. It is time to set out an approach to be used in tackling consolidated balance sheets. The approach we recommend consists of five stages.

Stage 1   Update the draft balance sheets of subsidiaries and parent company to take account of any proposed dividends not yet accrued for.

Stage 2   Agree inter-company current accounts by adjusting for items in transit.

Stage 3   Cancel items common to both balance sheets.

Stage 4   Produce working for minority interests as shown in Paragraph 2.4.

Stage 5   Produce a goodwill working as shown in Paragraph 4.13 above. Then produce a working for capital and revenue reserves.

5.2   You should now attempt to apply this technique to the following question.

Question 3

The draft balance sheets of Ping Ltd and Pong Ltd on 30 June 19X4 were as follows.

PING LIMITED
BALANCE SHEET AS AT 30 JUNE 19X4

	£	£
Fixed assets		
Tangible assets	50,000	
20,000 ordinary shares in Pong Ltd at cost	30,000	
		80,000
Current assets		
Stock	3,000	
Debtors (including £4,000 dividend proposed by Pong Ltd)	20,000	
Cash	2,000	
	25,000	
Creditors: amounts falling due within one year		
Owed to Pong Ltd	8,000	
Trade creditors	10,000	
	18,000	
Net current assets		7,000
		87,000
Capital and reserves		
Ordinary shares of £1 each		45,000
Capital reserves		12,000
Revenue reserves		30,000
		87,000

PONG LIMITED
BALANCE SHEET AS AT 30 JUNE 19X4

	£	£
Tangible fixed assets		40,000
Current assets		
Stock	8,000	
Owed by Ping Ltd	10,000	
Debtors	7,000	
	25,000	
Creditors: amounts falling due within one year		
Trade creditors	7,000	
Proposed dividends	5,000	
	12,000	
Net current assets		13,000
		53,000
Capital and reserves		£
Ordinary shares of £1 each		25,000
Capital reserves		5,000
Revenue reserves		23,000
		53,000

Ping Ltd acquired its investment in Pong Ltd on 1 July 19X1 when the revenue reserves of Pong Ltd stood at £6,000. There have been no changes in the share capital or capital reserves of Pong Ltd since that date. At 30 June 19X4 Pong Ltd had invoiced Ping Ltd for goods to the value of £2,000 which had not been received by Ping Ltd.

Goodwill is deemed to have an indefinite useful life and is therefore to remain in the balance sheet.

Prepare the consolidated balance sheet of Ping Ltd as at 30 June 19X4.

Answer

Stage 1. Ensure parent company and subsidiary balance sheets have correctly taken account of the proposed dividends.

Ping Ltd has £4,000 included in debtors for its share (80%) of Pong Ltd's proposed dividend, so there is no adjustment to make. Similarly, Pong Ltd has correctly accounted for its dividend payable.

Stage 2. Agree current accounts.

Ping Ltd has stock in transit of £2,000 making its total stock £3,000 + £2,000 = £5,000 and its liability to Pong Ltd £8,000 + £2,000 = £10,000.

Stage 3. Cancel common items: these are the current accounts between the two companies of £10,000 each and the dividends payable by Pong to Ping. This leaves a creditor for the dividend owed to the minority in Pong.

Stage 4. Calculate the minority interest.

Minority interest

	£
Ordinary share capital (20% × 25,000)	5,000
Capital reserves (20% × 5,000)	1,000
Revenue reserves (20% × 23,000)	4,600
	10,600

Note. In this particular case, where there are no preference shares or adjustments to Pong Ltd's revenue reserves, the minority interest figure may simply be calculated as 20% of Pong Ltd's net assets, ie 20% × £53,000. Because, however, such adjustments and complications often arise, it is a good idea to get into the habit of producing the working as shown.

Stage 5. Calculate goodwill and reserves.

Goodwill

	£	£
Cost of investment		30,000
Share of assets acquired as represented by:		
Ordinary share capital	25,000	
Capital reserves on acquisition	5,000	
Revenue reserves on acquisition	6,000	
	36,000	
Group share 80%		28,800
Goodwill		1,200

Consolidated capital reserves

	£
Ping Ltd	12,000
Share of Pong Ltd's post acquisition capital reserve	-
	12,000

Consolidated revenue reserves

	£
Ping Ltd	30,000
Share of Pong Ltd's post acquisition revenue reserves: 80%(23,000 - 6,000)*	13,600
	43,600

*Note. Post acquisition reserves of Pong Ltd are simply reserves now less reserves at acquisition. The consolidated balance sheet may now be written out.

BPP PUBLISHING

PING LIMITED
CONSOLIDATED BALANCE SHEET AS AT 30 JUNE 19X4

	£	£
Fixed assets		
Intangible fixed assets: goodwill		1,200
Tangible assets (£50,000 + £40,000)		90,000
		91,200
Current assets		
Stocks (£5,000 + £8,000)	13,000	
Debtors (£16,000 + £7,000)	23,000	
Cash	2,000	
	38,000	
Creditors: amounts falling due within one year		
Trade creditors (£10,000 + £7,000)	17,000	
Minority dividends	1,000	
	18,000	
Net current assets		20,000
		111,200
Capital and reserves		
Ordinary shares of £1 each		45,000
Capital reserves		12,000
Revenue reserves		43,600
Shareholders' funds		100,600
Minority interests		10,600
		111,200

Exam focus point

A consolidated balance sheet will come up as regularly as clockwork. There will nearly always be an adjustment for inter-company trading.

6 INTER-COMPANY TRADING

5/95, 11/95

6.1 We have already come across cases where one company in a group engages in trading with another group company. Any debtor/creditor balances outstanding between the companies are cancelled on consolidation. No further problem arises if all such intra-group transactions are undertaken at cost, without any mark-up for profit.

6.2 However, each company in a group is a separate trading entity and may wish to treat other group companies in the same way as any other customer. In this case, a company (say A Ltd) may buy goods at one price and sell them at a higher price to another group company (B Ltd). The accounts of A Ltd will quite properly include the profit earned on sales to B Ltd; and similarly B Ltd's balance sheet will include stocks at their cost to B Ltd at the amount at which they were purchased from A Ltd.

6.3 This gives rise to **two problems.**

(a) Although A Ltd makes a profit as soon as it sells goods to B Ltd, the group does not make a sale or achieve a profit until an outside customer buys the goods from B Ltd.

(b) Any purchases from A Ltd which remain unsold by B Ltd at the year end will be included in B Ltd's stock. Their balance sheet value will be their cost to B Ltd, which is not the same as their cost to the group.

6.4 The objective of consolidated accounts is to present the financial position of several connected companies as that of a single entity, the group. This means that **in a consolidated balance sheet the only profits recognised should be those earned by the group** in providing goods or services to outsiders; and similarly, stock in the consolidated balance sheet should be valued at cost to the group.

6.5 Suppose that a holding company H Ltd buys goods for £1,600 and sells them to a wholly owned subsidiary S Ltd for £2,000. The goods are in S Ltd's stock at the year end and appear in S Ltd's balance sheet at £2,000. In this case, H Ltd will record a profit of £400 in its individual accounts, but from the group's point of view the figures are:

Cost	£1,600
External sales	nil
Closing stock at cost	£1,600
Profit/loss	nil

6.6 If we add together the figures for retained reserves and stock in the individual balance sheets of H Ltd and S Ltd the resulting figures for consolidated reserves and consolidated stock will each be overstated by £400. A **consolidation adjustment** is therefore necessary as follows.

DEBIT	**Group reserves**
CREDIT	**Group stock (balance sheet)**

with the amount of profit unrealised by the group.

Question 4

H Ltd acquired 80% of the shares in S Ltd when the reserves of S Ltd stood at £10,000. Draft balance sheets for each company are as follows.

	H Ltd		S Ltd	
	£	£	£	£
Fixed assets				
Tangible assets		80,000		40,000
Investment in S Ltd at cost		46,000		
		126,000		
Current assets	40,000		30,000	
Current liabilities	21,000		18,000	
		19,000		12,000
		145,000		52,000
Capital and reserves				
Ordinary shares of £1 each		100,000		30,000
Reserves		45,000		22,000
		145,000		52,000

During the year H Ltd sold goods to S Ltd for £50,000, the profit to H Ltd being 20% of selling price. At the balance sheet date, £15,000 of these goods remained unsold in the stocks of S Ltd. At the same date, S Ltd owed H Ltd £12,000 for goods bought and this debt is included in the creditors of S Ltd and the debtors of H Ltd.

Note. Goodwill is deemed to have an indefinite useful life and is therefore to remain in the balance sheet.

Required

Prepare a draft consolidated balance sheet for H Ltd.

Answer

1 Goodwill

	£	£
Cost of investment		46,000
Share of net assets acquired as represented by		
Share capital	30,000	
Reserves	10,000	
	40,000	
Group share (80%)		(32,000)
		14,000

2 Reserves

	£
H Ltd per question	45,000
Less unrealised profit (20% × £15,000)	(3,000)
	42,000
Share of S Ltd's post acquisition retained reserves	3,000
80% £(22,000 − 10,000)	9,600
	51,600

3 Minority interest

	£
Share capital (20% × £30,000)	6,000
Reserves (20% × £22,000)	4,400
	10,400

H LIMITED
CONSOLIDATED BALANCE SHEET

	£	£
Intangible fixed assets: goodwill		14,000
Tangible fixed assets		120,000
		134,000
Current assets (W1)	55,000	
Current liabilities (W2)	27,000	
		28,000
		162,000
Capital and reserves		
Ordinary shares of £1 each		100,000
Reserves		51,600
		151,600
Minority interest		10,400
		162,000

Workings

1 Current assets

	£	£
In H Ltd's balance sheet		40,000
In H Ltd's balance sheet	30,000	
Less H Ltd's current account with H Ltd cancelled	12,000	
		18,000
		58,000
Less unrealised profit excluded from stock valuation		3,000
		55,000

2 Current liabilities

	£
In H Ltd's balance sheet	21,000
Less H Ltd's current account with H Ltd cancelled	12,000
	9,000
In H Ltd's balance sheet	18,000
	27,000

Unrealised inter-company profits on sales made by the subsidiary

6.7 A further problem occurs where a subsidiary company which is not wholly owned is involved in inter-company trading within the group. If a subsidiary S Ltd is 75% owned and sells goods to the holding company for £16,000 cost plus £4,000 profit, ie for £20,000 and if these stocks are unsold by H Ltd at the balance sheet date, the 'unrealised' profit of £4,000 earned by S Ltd and charged to H Ltd will be partly owned by the minority interest of S Ltd. As far as the minority interest of S Ltd is concerned, their share (25% of £4,000) amounting to £1,000 of profit on the sale of goods would appear to have been fully realised. It is only the group that has not yet made a profit on the sale.

6.8 The ASB has stated that the minority should be charged or credited with its share of all consolidation adjustments where the adjustment is made in respect of partly owned subsidiaries' profits. If the parent company has made the unrealised profit or loss, then the minority interest is not affected. The whole of the profit loading must always be eliminated from stock. The double entry is therefore as follows.

ENTRIES TO LEARN

DEBIT	Group reserves
DEBIT	Minority interest
CREDIT	Group stock (balance sheet)

Exam focus point

A useful technique for exam purposes is to note the adjustments on the face of the question against stock and the profit and reserve (of the selling company). This should ensure that you remember to deal with the adjustment when you pick up the relevant figures for the reserves and minority interests workings.

6.9 EXAMPLE: MINORITY INTERESTS AND INTER-COMPANY PROFITS

H Ltd has owned 75% of the shares of S Ltd since the incorporation of that company. During the year to 31 December 19X2, S Ltd sold goods costing £16,000 to H Ltd at a price of £20,000 and these goods were still unsold by H Ltd at the end of the year. Draft balance sheets of each company at 31 December 19X2 were as follows.

	H Limited		S Limited	
Fixed assets	£	£	£	£
Tangible assets		125,000		120,000
Investment: 75,000 shares in S Ltd at cost		75,000		-
		200,000		120,000
Current assets				
Stocks	50,000		48,000	
Trade debtors	20,000		16,000	
	70,000		64,000	
Creditors	40,000		24,000	
		30,000		40,000
		230,000		160,000
Capital and reserves				
Ordinary shares of £1 each fully paid		80,000		100,000
Reserves		150,000		60,000
		230,000		160,000

Required

Prepare the draft consolidated balance sheet of H Ltd.

6.10 SOLUTION

The profit earned by S Ltd but unrealised by the group is £4,000 of which £3,000 (75%) is attributable to the group and £1,000 (25%) to the minority.

Remove the whole of the profit loading, charging the minority with their proportion; this is the treatment used here, as required by the ASB.

Reserves	£
H Ltd	150,000
Share of S Ltd's post-acquisition retained reserves	
£(60,000 − 4,000) × 75%	42,000
	192,000

Minority interest	£
Share capital (25% × £100,000)	25,000
Reserves £(60,000 − 4,000) × 25%	14,000
	39,000

H LIMITED
CONSOLIDATED BALANCE SHEET AS AT 31 DECEMBER 19X2

	£	£
Tangible fixed assets		245,000
Current assets		
Stocks £(50,000 + 48,000 − 4,000)	94,000	
Trade debtors	36,000	
	130,000	
Creditors	64,000	
Net current assets		66,000
		311,000
Capital and reserves		
Ordinary shares of £1 each		80,000
Reserves		192,000
Shareholders' funds		272,000
Minority interest		39,000
		311,000

7 INTER-COMPANY SALES OF FIXED ASSETS

7.1 As well as engaging in trading activities with each other, **group companies may on occasion wish to transfer fixed assets. In their individual accounts the companies concerned will treat the transfer just like a sale between unconnected parties:** the selling company will record a profit or loss on sale; while the purchasing company will record the asset at the amount paid to acquire it, and will use that amount as the basis for calculating depreciation.

7.2 **On consolidation, the usual 'group entity' principle applies.** The consolidated balance sheet must show assets at their cost to the group, and any depreciation charged must be based on that cost. **Two consolidation adjustments** will usually be needed to achieve this.

(a) An **adjustment to alter reserves and fixed assets cost so as to remove any element of unrealised profit or loss**. This is similar to the adjustment required in respect of unrealised profit in stock.

(b) An **adjustment to alter reserves and accumulated depreciation** is made so that consolidated depreciation is based on the asset's cost to the group.

7.3 **The double entry is as follows.**

(a) *Sale by holding company*

DEBIT   Group reserves
CREDIT   Fixed assets

with the profit on disposal.

DEBIT   Fixed assets
CREDIT   Group reserves (H's share)
CREDIT   Minority interest (MI's share)

with the additional depreciation.

(b) *Sale by subsidiary*

DEBIT   Group reserves (H's share)
DEBIT   Minority interest (MI's share)
CREDIT   Fixed assets

with the profit on disposal.

DEBIT   Fixed assets
CREDIT   Group reserves

with the additional depreciation.

7.4 EXAMPLE: INTER-COMPANY SALE OF FIXED ASSETS

H Ltd owns 60% of S Ltd and on 1 January 19X1 S Ltd sells plant costing £10,000 to H Ltd for £12,500. The companies make up accounts to 31 December 19X1 and the balances on their revenue reserves at that date are:

H Ltd	after charging depreciation of 10% on plant	£27,000
S Ltd	including profit on sale of plant	£18,000

Required

Show the revenue reserves account.

7.5 SOLUTION

Revenue reserves

	£
H Ltd	27,000
Share of S Ltd's post-acquisition retained reserves	
£(18,000 – 2,500) × 60%	9,300
Depreciation on plant (10% × £2,500)	250
	36,550

Notes

1   The minority interest in the revenue reserves of S Ltd 40% × £(18,000 – 2,500) = £6,200.

2   The asset is written down to cost and depreciation on the 'profit' element is removed. The group profit and loss account for the year is thus reduced by a net ((£2,500 × 60%) – £250) = £1,250.

8 SUMMARY: CONSOLIDATED BALANCE SHEET

Purpose	To show the net assets which H controls and the ownership of those assets.
Net assets	Always 100% H plus 100% S providing H holds a majority of voting rights.
Share capital	H only.
Reason	Simply reporting to the holding company's shareholders in another form.
Reserves	100% H plus group share of post-acquisition retained reserves of S less consolidation adjustments.
Reason	To show the extent to which the group actually owns net assets included in the top half of the balance sheet.
Minority interest	MI share of S's consolidated net assets.
Reason	To show the extent to which other parties own net assets that are under the control of the holding company.

Chapter roundup

- This chapter has covered the mechanics of preparing simple **consolidated balance sheets**. In particular, procedures have been described for dealing with
  - Cancellation
  - Calculation of minority interests
  - Calculation of goodwill arising on consolidation

- A five-stage drill has been described and exemplified in a comprehensive example.

- The stages are as follows.
  - Update the draft balance sheets to take account of proposed dividends not accrued for
  - Agree intercompany current accounts by adjusting for items in transit
  - Cancel items common to both balance sheets
  - Minority interests
  - Goodwill

- We have examined the consolidation adjustments necessary when group companies trade **with or sell fixed assets to each** other.
  - The guiding principle is that the consolidated balance sheet must show assets at their cost to the group.
  - Any profit arising on intra-group transactions must be eliminated from the group accounts unless and until it is realised by a sale outside the group.

- It is important that you have a clear understanding of the material in this chapter before you move on to more complicated aspects of consolidation.

Quick quiz

1 What are the components making up the figure of minority interest in a consolidated balance sheet? (see para 2.2)

2 What adjustment is necessary before consolidation in cases where a holding company has not accrued for dividends receivable from a subsidiary? (3.3)

3 What is 'goodwill arising on consolidation'? (4.6, 4.7) How is it calculated? (4.10)

4 How should 'negative goodwill' be disclosed in the consolidated balance sheet? (4.18)

5 What consolidation problems arise when trading takes place between two companies within the same group? (6.3)

6 What is the basic principle of consolidation that determines the accounting treatment of inter-company trading? (6.4)

7 What are the three possible methods of accounting for minority interests in unrealised inter-company profits? (6.8)

8 What two consolidation adjustments are necessary to account for fixed assets transferred between two companies within the same group? (7.2)

To get you started, the question recommended is rather easier than you could expect in an exam

Question to try	Level	Marks	Time
14	Introductory	n/a	n/a

BPP PUBLISHING

Chapter 14

ACQUISITION OF SUBSIDIARIES

Chapter topic		Syllabus reference	Ability required
1	Acquisition of a subsidiary during its accounting period	9(a)	Application
2	Dividends and pre-acquisition profits	9(a)	Application
3	FRS 7 *Fair values in acquisition accounting*	9(a)	Application

Introduction

This chapter deals with the problems associated with the consolidation of a subsidiary acquired during the accounting period (a fairly common occurrence).

You will not understand the rest of the chapters on consolidation, particularly Chapters 15 and 18, unless you grasp the principles laid out in this chapter. You should pay particular attention to the determination of pre- and post-acquisition profits and the effect of dividends in Section 2.

The major topic of merger accounting vs acquisition accounting is covered in Chapter 19, along with the consolidated profit and loss account and accounting for associated undertakings.

You should note the interaction of FRS 7 with FRS 2 *Accounting for subsidiary undertakings* (Chapter 12) and FRS 6 *Acquisitions and mergers* (Chapter 19).

1 ACQUISITION OF A SUBSIDIARY DURING ITS ACCOUNTING PERIOD
11/96

1.1 When a holding company acquires a subsidiary **during its accounting period the only** accounting **entries will be those recording the cost of acquisition in the holding company's books.** As we have already seen, **at the end of the accounting year** it will be necessary to **prepare consolidated accounts**.

1.2 The subsidiary company's accounts to be consolidated will show the subsidiary's profit or loss for the whole year. **For consolidation** purposes, however, it will be necessary to **distinguish between:**

(a) **profits earned before acquisition;** and
(b) **profits earned after acquisition.**

1.3 In practice, a subsidiary company's profit may not accrue evenly over the year; for example, the subsidiary might be engaged in a trade, such as toy sales, with marked seasonal fluctuations. Nevertheless, statute permits the **assumption** to be made **that profits accrue evenly** whenever it is impracticable to arrive at an accurate split of pre- and post-acquisition profits.

1.4 Once the amount of pre-acquisition profit has been established the appropriate consolidation workings (goodwill, reserves) can be produced, as shown in Chapter 13.

1.5 Bear in mind that **in calculating minority interests the distinction between pre- and post-acquisition profits is irrelevant.** The minority shareholders are simply credited with their share of the subsidiary's total reserves at the balance sheet date.

1.6 It is worthwhile to summarise what happens on consolidation to the reserves figures extracted from a subsidiary's balance sheet. Suppose the accounts of S Ltd, a 60% subsidiary of H Ltd, show reserves of £20,000 at the balance sheet date, of which £14,000 were earned prior to acquisition. The figure of £20,000 will appear in the consolidated balance sheet as follows.

	£
Minority interests working: their share of total reserves at balance sheet date (40% × £20,000)	8,000
Goodwill working: group share of pre-acquisition profits (60% × £14,000)	8,400
Consolidated reserves working: group share of post-acquisition profits (60% × £6,000)	3,600
	20,000

Question 1

Hinge Ltd acquired 80% of the ordinary shares of Singe Ltd on 1 April 19X5. On 31 December 19X4 Singe Ltd's accounts showed a share premium account of £4,000 and revenue reserves of £15,000. The balance sheets of the two companies at 31 December 19X5 are set out below. Neither company has paid or proposed any dividends during the year.

You are required to prepare the consolidated balance sheet of Hinge Ltd at 31 December 19X5.

Note. Goodwill is to be amortised over 25 years. A full year's amortisation is charged in the year of acquisition.

HINGE LIMITED
BALANCE SHEET AS AT 31 DECEMBER 19X5

	£
Fixed assets	
Tangible assets	32,000
16,000 ordinary shares of 50p each in Singe Ltd	50,000
	82,000
Net current assets	65,000
	147,000
Capital and reserves	
Ordinary shares of £1 each	100,000
Share premium account	7,000
Revenue reserves	40,000
	147,000

SINGE LIMITED
BALANCE SHEET AS AT 31 DECEMBER 19X5

	£
Tangible fixed assets	30,000
Net current assets	23,000
	53,000
Capital and reserves	
20,000 ordinary shares of 50p each	10,000
Share premium account	4,000
Revenue reserves	39,000
	53,000

Answer

Singe Ltd has made a profit of £24,000 (£39,000 − £15,000) for the year. In the absence of any direction to the contrary, this should be assumed to have arisen evenly over the year; £6,000 in the three months to 31 March and £18,000 in the nine months after acquisition. The company's pre-acquisition revenue reserves are therefore as follows.

	£
Balance at 31 December 19X4	15,000
Profit for three months to 31 March 19X5	6,000
Pre-acquisition revenue reserves	21,000

The balance of £4,000 on share premium account is all pre-acquisition.

The consolidation workings can now be drawn up.

1 Minority interest

	£
Ordinary share capital (20% × £10,000)	2,000
Revenue reserves (20% × £39,000) (pre-acquisition)	7,800
Share premium (20% × £4,000)	800
	10,600

2 Goodwill

	£	£
Cost of investment		50,000
Share of net assets acquired represented by		
Ordinary share capital	10,000	
Revenue reserves (pre-acquisition)	21,000	
Share premium	4,000	
	35,000	
Group share (80%)		28,000
Goodwill		22,000

3 Revenue reserves

	£
Hinge Ltd	40,000
Share of Singe Ltd's post acquisition retained reserves £(39,000 − 21,000) × 80%	14,400
	54,400
Less: goodwill amortised on consolidation (22,000 ÷ 25)	(880)
	53,520

4 Share premium account

	£
Hinge Ltd	7,000
Share of Singe Ltd's post acquisition retained reserve	-
	7,000

HINGE LIMITED
CONSOLIDATED BALANCE SHEET AS AT 31 DECEMBER 19X5

	£
Intangible fixed assets: goodwill	21,120
Tangible fixed assets	62,000
Net current assets	88,000
	171,120

	£
Capital and reserves	
Ordinary shares of £1 each	100,000
Reserves	
Share premium account	7,000
Revenue reserves	53,520
Shareholders' funds	160,520
Minority interest	10,600
	171,120

1.7 EXAMPLE: PRE-ACQUISITION LOSSES OF A SUBSIDIARY

As an illustration of the entries arising when a subsidiary has pre-acquisition *losses*, suppose H Ltd acquired all 50,000 £1 ordinary shares in S Ltd for £20,000 on 1 January 19X1 when there was a debit balance of £35,000 on S Ltd's revenue reserves. In the years 19X1 to 19X4 S Ltd makes profits of £40,000 in total, leaving a credit balance of £5,000 on revenue reserves at 31 December 19X4. H Ltd's reserves at the same date are £70,000. Any goodwill is deemed to have an indefinite useful life and should be held in the balance sheet.

1.8 The consolidation workings would appear as follows.

1 *Goodwill*

	£	£
Cost of investment		20,000
Share of net assets acquired		
as represented by		
Ordinary share capital	50,000	
Revenue reserves	(35,000)	
	15,000	
Group share (100%)		15,000
Goodwill		5,000

2 *Revenue reserve*

	£
H Ltd	70,000
Share of S Ltd's post-acquisition	
retained reserves	40,000
Group reserves	110,000

2 DIVIDENDS AND PRE-ACQUISITION PROFITS

2.1 **A further problem in consolidation occurs when a subsidiary pays out a dividend soon after acquisition.** The holding company, as a member of the subsidiary, is entitled to its share of the dividends paid but it is necessary to decide whether or not these dividends come out of the pre-acquisition profits of the subsidiary.

2.2 **If the dividends come from post-acquisition profits** there is no problem. **The holding company simply credits the relevant amount to its own profit and loss account,** as with any other dividend income. The double entry is **quite different,** however, **if the dividend is paid from pre-acquisition profits,** being as follows.

DEBIT Cash
CREDIT Investment in subsidiary

The holding company's balance sheet would then disclose the investment as 'Investment in subsidiary at cost less amounts written down'.

2.3 It is **very important that you are clear about the reason for this**. Consider the following balance sheets of S_1 Ltd and S_2 Ltd as at 31 March 19X4.

	S_1 Ltd £	S_2 Ltd £
Current assets	30,000	30,000
Current liabilities	10,000	10,000
Ordinary shareholders' funds	20,000	20,000

Both companies have goodwill, not reflected in the books, valued at £5,000 and are identical in every respect, except that the current liabilities of S_1 Ltd are trade creditors while the current liabilities of S_2 Ltd are a proposed ordinary dividend.

2.4 H_1 Ltd, a prospective purchaser of S_1 Ltd, is willing to pay £25,000 for 100% of S_1, including goodwill. H_2 Ltd, a prospective purchaser of S_2 Ltd, will clearly be willing to pay £35,000 for the acquisition of that company in the knowledge that £10,000 of the cost will immediately be 'refunded' by way of dividend.

2.5 Assume that the two purchases are completed on 31 March 19X4 and on 1 April 19X4 S_1 Ltd and S_2 Ltd pay off their current liabilities as appropriate. H_1 and H_2 will then own identical investments, each consisting of £20,000 of current assets plus £5,000 of goodwill, and it is clearly appropriate that the investment figures in their own balance sheets should be identical. This will be the case if H_2 Ltd sets off the £10,000 dividend receivable against the £35,000 cost of the acquisition, disclosing the investment in S_2 at a net cost of £25,000.

2.6 The point to grasp is that H_2 Ltd cannot credit the dividend to profit because no profit has been made. The correct way of looking at it is to say that H_2 Ltd was willing to pay 'over the odds' for its investment in the presumption that a part of its cost would immediately be repaid. When the dividend is paid, this presumption must be pursued to its conclusion by treating the dividend as a reduction of the cost of the investment.

2.7 **This accounting treatment** used to be a legal requirement but is not *required* by the CA 1985 (or any current SSAP or FRS). However, it **must be considered best practice.**

2.8 EXAMPLE: DIVIDENDS AND PRE-ACQUISITION PROFITS

Hip Ltd acquired 8,000 of the 10,000 £1 ordinary shares of Sip Ltd on 1 January 19X5 for £25,000. Sip Ltd's balance sheet at 31 December 19X4 showed a proposed ordinary dividend of £4,000 and retained reserves of £12,000. The balance sheets of the two companies at 31 December 19X5 are given below.

HIP LIMITED
BALANCE SHEET AS AT 31 DECEMBER 19X5

	£
Fixed assets	
Tangible assets	35,000
Investment in Sip Ltd at cost less	
amounts written down	21,800
	56,800
Net current assets	27,000
	83,800
Capital and reserves	
Ordinary shares of £1 each	50,000
Retained reserves	33,800
	83,800

SIP LIMITED
BALANCE SHEET AS AT 31 DECEMBER 19X5

	£
Tangible fixed assets	14,500
Net current assets	12,500
	27,000
Capital and reserves	
Ordinary shares of £1 each	10,000
Retained reserves	17,000
	27,000

Required

Prepare the consolidated balance sheet of Hip Ltd at 31 December 19X5.

Note. Goodwill is deemed to have a useful life of 10 years and is therefore to be amortised over that period.

2.9 SOLUTION

During the year Sip Ltd has paid the £4,000 proposed dividend in its 19X4 balance sheet. Hip Ltd's share (80% × £4,000 = £3,200) has been correctly credited by that company to its 'investment in Sip Ltd' account. That account appears in the books of Hip Ltd as follows.

INVESTMENT IN SIP LIMITED

	£		£
Bank: purchase of 8,000		Bank: dividend received from	
£1 ordinary shares	25,000	pre-acquisition profits	3,200
		Balance c/f	21,800
	25,000		25,000

If Hip Ltd had incorrectly credited the pre-acquisition dividend to its own profit and loss account, it would have been necessary to make the following adjustments in Hip Ltd's accounts before proceeding to the consolidation.

DEBIT	Retained reserves	£3,200	
CREDIT	Investment in Sip Ltd		£3,200

This procedure is sometimes necessary in examination questions.

The consolidation workings can be drawn up as follows.

1   *Minority interest*

	£
Share capital (20% × £10,000)	2,000
Reserves (20% × £17,000)	3,400
	5,400

2   *Goodwill*

	£	£
Cost of investment		25,000
Less share of pre-acquisition dividend (80% × £4,000)		3,200
		21,800
Share of net assets acquired as represented by		
Ordinary share capital	10,000	
Reserves	12,000	
	22,000	
Group share (80%)		17,600
Goodwill		4,200

BPP PUBLISHING

3   *Reserves*

	£
Hip Ltd	33,800
Share of Sip Ltd's post acquisition retained reserves	
£(17,000 – 12,000) × 80%	4,000
	37,800
Goodwill amortised on consolidation (4,200 × 1/10)	(420)
	37,380

HIP LIMITED
 CONSOLIDATED BALANCE SHEET AS AT 31 DECEMBER 19X5

	£
Intangible fixed assets	3,780
Tangible fixed assets	49,500
Net current assets	39,500
	92,780
Capital and reserves	
Ordinary shares of £1 each	50,000
Retained reserves	37,380
Shareholders' funds	87,380
Minority interest	5,400
	92,780

2.10   The example above included an ordinary dividend paid from pre-acquisition profits. The treatment would be exactly the same if a **preference dividend** had been paid from pre-acquisition profits. Any share of such a preference dividend received by the holding company would be credited not to profit and loss account, but to the investment in subsidiary account.

Is the dividend paid from pre-acquisition profits?

2.11   We need next to consider how it is decided whether a dividend is paid from pre-acquisition profits. In the example above there was no difficulty: Hip Ltd acquired shares in Sip Ltd on the first day of an accounting period and the dividend was in respect of the previous accounting period. Clearly, the dividend was paid from profits earned in the period before acquisition.

2.12   **The position is less straightforward if shares are acquired during the subsidiary's accounting period.** An example will illustrate the point.

2.13   EXAMPLE: ACQUISITION DURING SUBSIDIARY'S ACCOUNTING PERIOD

H Ltd and S Ltd each make up their accounts to 31 December. H Ltd buys 80,000 of the 100,000 £1 ordinary shares of S Ltd for £175,000 on 1 October 19X1. S Ltd's revenue reserves (after deducting proposed dividends) stood at £50,000 on 31 December 19X0. S Ltd's profits after tax for the year to 31 December 19X1 were £20,000. In January 19X2 S Ltd declared a first and final dividend for 19X1 of £10,000. At 31 December 19X1, H Ltd's reserves stood at £110,000; this does not include any adjustment for dividends receivable from S Ltd.

Required

Prepare consolidation workings for revenue reserves, minority interest and cost of control as at 31 December 19X1.

2.14 SOLUTION

The problem is to decide how much of the dividend paid by S Ltd comes from pre-acquisition profits. There are several possible ways of doing this but the method we recommend is based on time-apportionment. The 19X1 dividend eventually declared by S Ltd is deemed to have accrued evenly over the year.

Note. Of the £8,000 dividend receivable by H Ltd, £6,000 is deemed to have come from pre-acquisition profits and is credited to 'Investment in S Ltd'. £2,000 comes from post-acquisition profits and is added to reserves.

1   *Minority interest*

	£
Share capital (20% × £100,000)	20,000
Revenue reserves (20% × £60,000)	12,000
	32,000

The minority also has an interest (£2,000) in the proposed dividend payable by S Ltd. This will appear as a current liability in the consolidated balance sheet.

2   *Goodwill*

	£	£
Cost of investment		175,000
Less pre-acquisition dividend		
£10,000 × ⁹/₁₂ × 80%		6,000
		169,000
Share of net assets acquired as represented by		
Ordinary share capital	100,000	
Revenue reserves		
£(50,000 + 15,000 − 7,500)	57,500	
	157,500	
Group share (80%)		126,000
Goodwill		43,000

3   *Revenue reserves*

	£
H Ltd	110,000
Dividend receivable	2,000
	112,000
Share of S Ltd's post acquisition retained reserves £(60,000 − 57,500) × 80%	2,000
Group reserves	114,000

2.15   It has been argued by some that the question as to whether a dividend from a subsidiary to the holding company is available for onward distribution by the holding company depends on whether receipt of the dividend can be regarded as giving rise to a **realised profit** in the financial statements of the holding company and not simply whether it derives from the pre- or post-acquisition profits of the subsidiary.

2.16   In other words if the subsidiary **recovers in value** after the distribution, the **loss in value is temporary** and need not be deducted from the cost of the investment (only permanent diminutions should be provided).

2.17   Where the investment is carried at fair value, however, it is likely that a dividend which represents a return of pre-acquisition profits would give rise to a **diminution in the value** of investment and thus should be applied in reducing the cost (carrying value) of that investment.

2.18   If this **diminution is not permanent**, this treatment is **not mandatory**. Thus companies could distribute all the subsidiary's pre-acquisition profits as long as the subsidiary could replace them in the future.

2.19   This practice may be legal but it offends good accounting practice. The pre-acquisition dividend is a return of the purchase price and it seems right to deduct it from the cost of the investment.

> **Exam focus point**
> Candidates were required to discuss the arguments in paragraphs 2.15 - 2.19 in the December 1996 paper.

3   FRS 7 FAIR VALUES IN ACQUISITION ACCOUNTING

3.1   FRS 10 *Goodwill and intangible assets* **defines goodwill as the difference between the purchase consideration paid by the acquiring company and the aggregate of the 'fair values' of the identifiable assets and liabilities acquired.** The balance sheet of a subsidiary company at the date it is acquired may not be a guide to the fair value of its net assets. For example, the market value of a freehold building may have risen greatly since it was acquired, but it may appear in the balance sheet at historical cost less accumulated depreciation.

Fair value adjustment calculations   5/95, 11/96

3.2   Until now we have calculated goodwill as the difference between the cost of the investment and the **book value** of net assets acquired by the group. If this calculation is to comply with the definition in FRS 10 we **must ensure that the book value of the subsidiary's net assets is the same as their fair value.**

3.3   There are **two possible ways** of achieving this.

(a)   **The subsidiary company might incorporate any necessary revaluations in its own books of account.** In this case, we can proceed directly to the consolidation, taking asset values and reserves figures straight from the subsidiary company's balance sheet.

(b)   **The revaluations may be made as a consolidation adjustment without being incorporated in the subsidiary company's books.** In this case, we must make the necessary adjustments to the subsidiary's balance sheet as a working. Only then can we proceed to the consolidation.

Note. Remember that when depreciating assets are revalued there may be a corresponding alteration in the amount of depreciation charged and accumulated.

3.4   EXAMPLE: FAIR VALUE ADJUSTMENTS

H Ltd acquired 75% of the ordinary shares of S Ltd on 1 September 19X5. At that date the fair value of S Ltd's fixed assets was £23,000 greater than their net book value, and the balance of retained profits was £21,000. The balance sheets of both companies at 31 August 19X6 are given below. S Ltd has not incorporated any revaluation in its books of account.

H LIMITED
BALANCE SHEET AS AT 31 AUGUST 19X6

	£
Fixed assets	
Tangible assets	63,000
Investment in S Ltd at cost	51,000
	114,000
Net current assets	62,000
	176,000
Capital and reserves	
Ordinary shares of £1 each	80,000
Retained profits	96,000
	176,000

S LIMITED
BALANCE SHEET AS AT 31 AUGUST 19X6

	£
Tangible fixed assets	28,000
Net current assets	33,000
	61,000
Capital and reserves	
Ordinary shares of £1 each	20,000
Retained profits	41,000
	61,000

If S Ltd had revalued its fixed assets at 1 September 19X5, an addition of £3,000 would have been made to the depreciation charged in the profit and loss account for 19X5/X6.

Required

Prepare H Ltd's consolidated balance sheet as at 31 August 19X6.

Note: goodwill is deemed to have a useful life of 5 years and is to be amortised over that period.

3.5 SOLUTION

S Ltd has not incorporated the revaluation in its draft balance sheet. Before beginning the consolidation workings we must therefore adjust the company's balance of profits at the date of acquisition and at the balance sheet date.

S Ltd adjusted balance of retained profits

	£	£
Balance per accounts at 1 September 19X5		21,000
Consolidation adjustment: revaluation surplus		23,000
∴ Pre-acquisition profits for consolidation purposes		44,000
Profit for year ended 31 August 19X6		
Per draft accounts £(41,000 – 21,000)	20,000	
Consolidation adjustment: increase in depreciation charge	(3,000)	
		17,000
Adjusted balance of retained profits at 31 August 19X6		61,000

In the consolidated balance sheet, S Ltd's fixed assets will appear at their revalued amount: £(28,000 + 23,000 – 3,000) = £48,000. The consolidation workings can now be drawn up.

1 *Minority interest*

	£
Share capital (25% × £20,000)	5,000
Revenue reserves (25% × £61,000)	15,250
	20,250

2   *Goodwill*

	£	£
Cost of investment		51,000
Share of net assets acquired as represented by		
Ordinary share capital	20,000	
Revenue reserves		
£(21,000 + 23,000)	44,000	
	64,000	
Group share (75%)		48,000
Goodwill		3,000

3   *Revenue reserves*

	£
H Ltd	96,000
Share of S Ltd's post acquisition retained reserves	
£(41,000 – 21,000 – 3,000) × 75%	12,750
Goodwill amortised on consolidation	(600)
Group reserves	108,150

H LIMITED CONSOLIDATED BALANCE SHEET AS AT 31 AUGUST 19X6

	£
Intangible fixed assets: goodwill	2,400
Tangible fixed assets £(63,000 + 48,000)	111,000
Net current assets	95,000
	208,400
Capital and reserves	
Ordinary shares of £1 each	80,000
Retained profits	108,150
Shareholders' funds	188,150
Minority interest	20,250
	208,400

Question 2

An asset is recorded in S Ltd's books at its historical cost of £4,000. On 1 January 19X1 P Ltd bought 80% of S Ltd's equity. Its directors attributed a fair value of £3,000 to the asset as at that date. It had been depreciated for two years out of an expected life of four years on the straight line basis. There was no expected residual value. On 30 June 19X1 the asset was sold for £2,600. What is the profit or loss on disposal of this asset to be recorded in S Ltd's accounts and in P Ltd's consolidated accounts for the year ended 31 December 19X1?

Answer

S Ltd: NBV at disposal (at historical cost) = £4,000 × 1½/4 = £1,500

∴ Profit on disposal = £1,100 (depreciation charge for the year = £500)

P Ltd: NBV at disposal (at fair value) = £3,000 × 1½/2 = £2,250

∴ Profit on disposal for consolidation = £350 (depreciation for the year = £750). The minority would be credited with 20% of both items as part of the one line entry in the profit and loss account.

FRS 7 *Fair values in acquisition accounting*

3.6   FRS 7 and FRS 6 *Acquisitions and mergers* were published together in September 1994 in order to reform both acquisition and merger accounting practices. Merger accounting and FRS 6 are both discussed in Chapter 19.

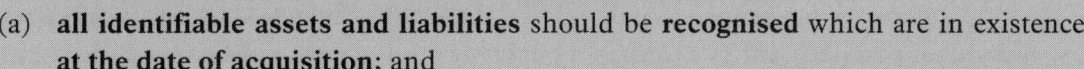

IMPORTANT!

The basic principles stated by FRS 7 are that:

(a) **all identifiable assets and liabilities** should be **recognised** which are in existence **at the date of acquisition**; and

(b) such recognised assets and liabilities should be **measured at fair values** which reflect the conditions existing at the date of acquisition.

Fair values should not reflect either the acquirer's intentions or events subsequent to the acquisition.

3.7 In addition any **changes** to the acquired assets and liabilities, and the resulting gains and losses, that arise **after control** of the acquired entity has passed to the acquirer should be reported as part of the **post-acquisition profits** of the group.

3.8 FRS 7 also sets out specific rules on how fair values should be determined for the main categories of asset and liability. The underlying principle remains that **fair values should reflect the price at which an asset or liability could be exchanged in an arm's length transaction.** For long-term monetary assets and liabilities, fair values may be derived by discounting.

3.9 The standard also describes how the value attributed to the consideration given for the acquisition should be determined, and the acquisition expenses that may be included as part of the cost.

Definitions

3.10 The following definitions are given by FRS 7. They are self explanatory except for the highlighted terms.

(a) Acquisition
(b) Business combination
(c) Date of acquisition
(d) **Fair value**
(e) Identifiable assets and liabilities
(f) **Recoverable amount**
(g) **Value in use**

KEY TERMS

(a) In particular note the definition of **fair value**.

'The amount at which an asset or liability could be exchanged in an arm's length transaction between informed and willing parties, other than in a forced or liquidation sale.'

(b) **Recoverable amount** is the greater of the net realisable value of an asset and, when appropriate, the amount recoverable from its further use.

(c) **Value in use** is the present value of the future cash flows obtainable as a result of an asset's continued use, including those resulting from the ultimate disposal of the asset.

Scope

3.11 FRS 7 applies to all financial statements that are intended to give a true and fair view. Although the FRS is framed in terms of the acquisition of a subsidiary undertaking by a parent company that prepares consolidated financial statements, it **also applies where an individual company entity acquires a business other than a subsidiary undertaking**. This last point means that companies cannot avoid the provisions of FRS 7 when taking over an unincorporated entity or joint venture vehicle.

Determining the fair values of identifiable assets and liabilities acquired

3.12 Most importantly, the FRS lists those **items which do not affect fair values** at the date of acquisition, and **which are therefore to be treated as post-acquisition items**:

(a) Changes resulting from the **acquirer's intentions or future actions.**

(b) **Impairments** or other changes, resulting from events subsequent to the acquisition.

(c) **Provisions or accruals for future operating losses** or for reorganisation and integration costs expected to be incurred as a result of the acquisition, whether they relate to the acquired entity or to the acquirer.

Assessing fair value of major categories

3.13 In general terms, fair values should be determined in accordance with the acquirer's accounting policies for similar assets and liabilities. The standard does, however, go on to describe how the major categories of assets and liabilities should be assessed for fair values.

(a) **Tangible assets: fair value based on:**

　(i)　**market value,** if similar assets are sold on the open market; or
　(ii)　**depreciated replacement cost,** reflecting normal business practice.

　However, **fair value ≤ replacement cost.**

(b) **Intangible assets,** where recognised: **fair value should be based on replacement costs,** which will normally be estimated market value.

(c) **Stocks and work in progress**

　(i)　For stocks which are replaced by purchasing in a **ready market** (commodities, dealing stock etc), the fair value is **market value.**

　(ii)　For other stocks, with **no ready market** (most manufacturing stocks), fair value is represented by the **current cost** to the acquired company of reproducing the stocks.

(d) **Quoted investments:** value at **market price,** adjusted where necessary for unusual price fluctuations or the size of the holding.

(e) **Monetary assets and liabilities:** fair values should take into account the **amounts expected to be received or paid** and their timing. Reference should be made to market prices (where available) or to the current price if acquiring similar assets or entering into similar obligations, or to the discounted present value.

(f) **Contingencies: reasonable estimates** of the expected outcome may be used.

(g) **Pensions and other post-retirement benefits:** the **fair value of a deficiency, a surplus** (to the extent it is expected to be realised) or accrued obligation should be **recognised** as an asset/liability of the acquiring group. Any changes on acquisition should be treated as post-acquisition items.

(h) **Deferred taxation:** deferred tax assets and liabilities should be considered **in terms of the whole group**. The benefit to the group of any tax losses attributable to an acquired entity should be valued according to SSAP 15.

Business sold or held with a view to subsequent resale

3.14 The fair value exercise for such an entity, 'sold as a single unit, within approximately one year of acquisition', should be carried out on the basis of a **single asset investment**.

> 'Its fair value should be based on the **net proceeds of the sale**, **adjusted for the fair value of any assets or liabilities transferred** into or out of the business, unless such adjusted net proceeds are demonstrably different from the fair value at the date of acquisition as a result of a post-acquisition event.'

Any relevant part of the business can be treated in this way if it is separately identifiable, ie it does not have to be a separate subsidiary undertaking.

3.15 Where the first financial statements after the date of acquisition come for approval, but the business has not been sold, the above treatment can still be applied if:

(a) a purchaser has been identified or is being sought; *and*

(b) the disposal is expected to occur within one year of the date of acquisition.

3.16 The interest (or its assets) should be shown in current assets. On determination of the sales price, the original estimate of fair value should be adjusted to reflect the actual sales proceeds.

Investigation period and goodwill adjustments

3.17 FRS 7 states that:

> 'The recognition and measurement of assets and liabilities acquired should be completed, if possible, by the date on which the first post-acquisition financial statements of the acquirer are approved by the directors.'

Where this has not been possible, provisional valuations should be made, amended if necessary in the next financial statements with a corresponding adjustment to goodwill. Such adjustments should be incorporated into the financial statements in the full year following acquisition. After that, any adjustments (except for the correction of fundamental errors by prior year adjustment) should be recognised as profits or losses as they are identified.

Determining the fair value of purchase consideration

3.18 The cost of acquisition is the amount of cash paid and the fair value of other purchase consideration given by the acquirer, together with the expenses of the acquisition. Where a subsidiary undertaking is acquired in stages, the cost of acquisition is the total of the costs of the interests acquired, determined as at the date of each transaction.

3.19 The main likely components of purchase consideration are as follows.

(a) *Ordinary shares*

 (i) **Quoted shares** should be valued at **market price** on the date of acquisition.

 (ii) Where there is **no suitable market**, estimate the value using:

  (1) the value of **similar quoted securities**; *or*

  (2) the **present value of the future cash** flows of the instrument used; *or*

(3) any **cash alternative** which was offered.

(b) **Other securities:** the value should be based on similar principles to those given in (a).

(c) **Cash or monetary amounts:** value at the **amount paid or payable**.

(d) **Non-monetary assets:** value at **market price,** estimated realisable value, independent valuation or based on other available evidence.

(e) **Deferred consideration: discount** the amounts calculated on the above principles (in (a) to (d)). An appropriate discount rate is that which the acquirer could obtain for a similar borrowing.

(f) **Contingent consideration:** use the **probable** amount. When the actual amount is known, it should be recorded in the financial statements and goodwill adjusted accordingly.

3.20 **Acquisition cost** (the fees and expenses mentioned above) should be **included in the cost of the investment**. Internal costs and the costs of issuing capital instruments should *not* be capitalised, according to the provisions of FRS 4, ie they must be written off to the profit and loss account.

UITF Abstract 22 The acquisition of a Lloyd's business

3.21 This Abstract, which was issued in June 1998, interprets FRS 7 in the context of the acquisition of a Lloyd's business and requires that the estimated results of periods before the acquisition for which the accounts are not yet closed should be reflected in the assets and liabilities that are acquired.

Summary and assessment

3.22 **The most important effect of FRS 7 is the ban it imposes on making provisions for future trading losses** of acquired companies and the costs of any related rationalisation or reorganisation, unless outgoing management had already incurred those liabilities. This is a controversial area, demonstrated by the dissenting view of one member of the ASB.

3.23 **Some commentators argued that the ASB's approach ignores the commercial reality of the transaction** by treating as an expense the costs of reorganisation that the acquirer regards as part of the capital cost of the acquisition; and that within defined limits a provision for planned post-acquisition expenditure should be permitted to be included in the net assets acquired.

Case example

The Hundred Group of finance directors gave an example. If you buy a house for, say £100,000 that you know needs £50,000 spent on it to bring it into good condition and make it equivalent to a property that sells for £150,000, then you would treat the £50,000 renovation expense as part of the cost of the house and not as part of ordinary outgoings. The group states that FRS 7 goes beyond standards set in other countries, including the US. It also recommends that abuses in this area should be dealt with by tightening existing accounting standards and through 'proper policing' by external auditors (the standard is seen to undermine the professional judgement of the auditor) and 'not by distorting accounting concepts'.

3.24 The ASB rejected this view, saying that an intention to incur revenue expenditure subsequent to the acquisition could not properly be regarded as a liability of the acquired business at the date of acquisition.

> 'Acquisition accounting should reflect the business that is acquired as it stands at the date of acquisition and ought not to take account of the changes that an acquirer might intend to make subsequently. Nor could the ASB accept the proposition that some of the inadequacies of the present system could be met by better disclosure. In the ASB's view deficient accounting cannot be put right by disclosure alone.'

3.25 This is still an open area of debate and you should keep track of the arguments in the financial and accountancy press.

Question 3

Tyzo plc prepares accounts to 31 December. On 1 September 19X7 Tyzo plc acquired 6 million £1 shares in Kono plc at £2.00 per share. The purchase was financed by an additional issue of loan stock at an interest rate of 10%. At that date Kono plc produced the following interim financial statements.

	£m		£m
Tangible fixed assets (note 1)	16.0	Trade creditors	3.2
Stocks (note 2)	4.0	Taxation	0.6
Debtors	2.9	Bank overdraft	3.9
Cash in hand	1.2	Long-term loans (note 6)	4.0
		Share capital (£1 shares)	8.0
		Profit and loss account	4.4
	24.1		24.1

Notes

1 The following information relates to the tangible fixed assets of Kono plc at 1 September 19X7.

	£m
Gross replacement cost	28.4
Net replacement cost	16.6
Economic value	18.0
Net realisable value	8.0

The fixed assets of Kono plc at 1 September 19X7 had a total purchase cost to Kono plc of £27.0 million. They were all being depreciated at 25% per annum pro rata on that cost. This policy is also appropriate for the consolidated financial statements of Tyzo plc. No fixed assets of Kono plc which were included in the interim financial statements drawn up as at 1 September 19X7 were disposed of by Kono plc prior to 31 December 19X7. No fixed asset was fully depreciated by 31 December 19X7.

2 The stocks of Kono plc which were shown in the interim financial statements at cost to Kono plc of £4 million would have cost £4.2 million to replace at 1 September 19X7 and had an estimated net realisable value at that date of £4.8 million. Of the stock of Kono plc in hand at 1 September 19X7, goods costing Kono plc £3.0 million were sold for £3.6 million between 1 September 19X7 and 31 December 19X7.

3 The long-term loan of Kono plc carries a rate of interest of 10% per annum, payable on 31 August annually in arrears. The loan is redeemable at par on 31 August 2001. The interest cost is representative of current market rates. The accrued interest payable by Kono plc at 31 December 19X7 is included in the trade creditors of Kono plc at that date.

4 On 1 September 19X7 Tyzo plc took a decision to rationalise the group so as to integrate Kono plc. The costs of the rationalisation (which were to be borne by Tyzo plc) were estimated to total £3.0 million and the process was due to start on 1 March 19X8. No provision for these costs has been made in any of the financial statements given above.

Required

Compute the goodwill on consolidation of Kono plc that will be included in the consolidated financial statements of the Tyzo plc group for the year ended 31 December 19X7, explaining your treatment of the items mentioned above. You should refer to the provisions of relevant accounting standards.

Answer

Goodwill on consolidation of Kono Ltd

	£m	£m
Consideration (£2.00 × 6m)		12.0
Group share of fair value of net assets acquired		
Share capital	8.0	
Pre-acquisition reserves	4.4	
Fair value adjustments		
Tangible fixed assets (16.6 – 16.0)	0.6	
Stocks (4.2 – 4.0)	0.2	
	13.2	
Group share	75%	9.9
Goodwill		2.1

Notes on treatment

(a)   It is assumed that the market value (ie fair value) of the loan stock issued to fund the purchase of the shares in Kono plc is equal to the price of £12.0m. FRS 2 *Accounting for subsidiary undertakings* requires goodwill to be calculated by comparing the fair value of the consideration given with the fair value of the separable net assets of the acquired business or company.

(b)   Share capital and pre-acquisition profits represent the book value of the net assets of Kono plc at the date of acquisition. Adjustments are then required to this book value in order to give the fair value of the net assets at the date of acquisition. For short-term monetary items, fair value is their carrying value on acquisition.

(c)   FRS 7 *Fair values in acquisition accounting* states that the fair value of tangible fixed assets should be determined by market value or, if information on a market price is not available (as is the case here), then by reference to depreciated replacement cost, reflecting normal business practice. The net replacement cost (ie £16.6m) represents the gross replacement cost less depreciation based on that amount, and so further adjustment for extra depreciation is unnecessary.

(d)   FRS 7 also states that stocks which cannot be replaced by purchasing in a ready market (eg commodities) should be valued at current cost to the acquired company of reproducing the stocks. In this case that amount is £4.2m.

(e)   The fair value of the loan is the present value of the total amount payable, ie on maturity and in interest. If the quoted interest rate was used as a discount factor, this would give the current par value.

(f)   The rationalisation costs must be reported in post-acquisition results under FRS 7 *Fair values in acquisition accounting*, so no adjustment is required in the goodwill calculation.

Chapter roundup

- In this chapter we have looked at certain problems involved in distinguishing between **pre-acquisition** and **post-acquisition profits** of subsidiary companies.

- When a subsidiary is acquired **during its accounting period**, its **pre-acquisition profits** will include a **proportion of its total profits** for the accounting period.

- In the absence of information to the contrary, the profits earned during the period may be assumed to have **accrued evenly** and should be allocated accordingly.

- **Dividends** paid by a subsidiary to its parent company may only be **credited to the parent's profit and loss account** to the extent that they are paid from **post-acquisition profits**.

- **Dividends** received by the holding company **from pre-acquisition profits** should be credited to 'investment in subsidiary' account and treated as **reducing the cost of the shares** acquired.

- **Goodwill arising on consolidation** is the difference between the purchase consideration and the fair value of net assets acquired.

- **Goodwill** should be calculated **after revaluing** the subsidiary company's assets.

- If the subsidiary does not incorporate the revaluation in its own accounts, it should be done as a **consolidation adjustment**.

- The accounting requirements and disclosures of the **fair value exercise** are covered by **FRS 7**, which is controversial as it outlaws the use of provisions for future losses and for reorganisation costs on acquisition of a subsidiary.

Quick quiz

1   A holding company can assume that, for a subsidiary acquired during its accounting period, profits accrue evenly during the year. True or false? (see para 1.3)

2   What entries are made in the consolidated workings accounts to record the pre-acquisition losses of a subsidiary? (1.8)

3   What entries are made in the holding company's accounts to record a dividend received from a subsidiary's pre-acquisition profits? (2.2)

4   Describe the requirement of FRS 10 in relation to the revaluation of a subsidiary company's assets. (3.2)

5   How may this requirement be achieved in practice? (3.3)

6   What are the basic principles in determining the fair value of identifiable assets and liabilities? (3.6)

7   How is 'fair value' defined by FRS 7? (3.10, *Glossary*)

8   Which items does FRS 7 state *must* be treated as post-acquisition? (3.12)

9   How should businesses which are held for resale be treated in the fair value exercise? (3.14)

10 For how long can fair values be adjusted after acquisition? (3.17)

Question to try	Level	Marks	Time
15	Introductory	n/a	n/a

Chapter 15

MULTI-COMPANY STRUCTURES

Chapter topic	Syllabus reference	Ability required
1 Multi-company structures	9(a)	Application
2 Consolidating sub-subsidiaries	9(a)	Application
3 Direct holdings in sub-subsidiaries	9(a)	Application

Introduction

This chapter introduces the first of several more complicated consolidation topics. The best way to tackle these questions is to be logical and to carry out the consolidation on a **step by step** basis.

In questions of this nature, it is very helpful to sketch a **diagram of the group structure**, as we have done. This clarifies the situation and it should point you in the right direction: always sketch the group structure as your first working and double check it against the information in the question.

1   MULTI-COMPANY STRUCTURES

1.1   In this section we shall consider how the principles of balance sheet consolidation may be applied to more complex structures of companies within a group.

(a) **Several subsidiary companies**

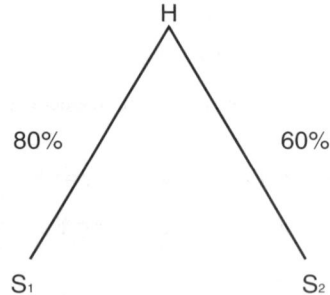

You have already seen this type of structure in your previous studies.

(b) **Sub-subsidiaries**

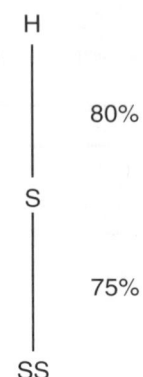

H holds a controlling interest in S which in turn holds a controlling interest in SS. SS is therefore a subsidiary of a subsidiary of H; in other words, a *sub-subsidiary* of H.

(c) **Direct holdings in sub-subsidiaries: 'D' shaped groups**

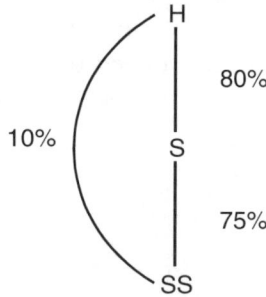

In this example, SS is a sub-subsidiary of H with additional shares held directly by H.

In practice, groups are usually larger, and therefore more complex, but the procedures for consolidation of large groups will not differ from those we shall now describe for smaller ones.

A holding company which has several subsidiaries

1.2 Where a company H has several subsidiaries S_1, S_2, S_3 and so on, the technique for consolidation is exactly as described already. **Cancellation** is from the holding company, which has assets of investments in subsidiaries S_1, S_2, S_3, to each of the several subsidiaries.

1.3 The consolidated balance sheet will show:

(a) a single figure for **minority interest**; and
(b) separate totals for **goodwill** arising.

A single working should be used for each of the constituents of the consolidated balance sheet: one working for goodwill, one for minority interest, one for revenue reserves, and so on, but on the consolidated balance sheet itself the separate portions of goodwill arising must each be accounted for in compliance with FRS 10.

Sub-subsidiaries   11/95

1.4 A slightly different problem arises when there are sub-subsidiaries in the group, which is how should we **identify the minority interest** in the reserves of the group? Suppose H owns 80% of the equity of S, and that S in turn owns 60% of the equity of SS.

1.5 It would appear that in this situation:

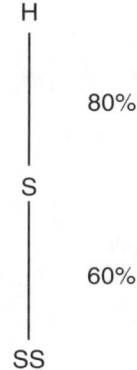

(a) H owns 80% of 60% = 48% of SS;
(b) the minority interest in S owns 20% of 60% = 12% of SS;
(c) the minority interest in SS itself owns the remaining 40% of the SS equity.

SS is nevertheless a **sub-subsidiary** of H, because it is a subsidiary of S which in turn is a subsidiary of H. The chain of control thus makes SS a sub-subsidiary of H which owns only 48% of its equity.

1.6 The total minority in SS may be checked by considering a **dividend** of £100 paid by SS where S then distributes its share of this dividend in full to its own shareholders.

		£
S will receive	£60	
H will receive	80% × £60 =	48
Leaving for the total minority in SS		52
		100

Date of effective control

1.7 The date the sub-subsidiary comes under the **control of the holding company** is either:

(a) the date H acquired S if S already holds shares in SS; or

(b) if S acquires shares in SS later, then that later date.

2 CONSOLIDATING SUB-SUBSIDIARIES   11/95, 5/98

2.1 The basic consolidation method is as follows.

(a) **Net assets**: show what the group controls.

(b) **Capital and reserves**: show who owns the net assets included in the top half of the balance sheet. Reserves, therefore, are based on **effective holdings**.

2.2 As indicated earlier, the major problem on consolidation is to identify the minority interest share of the reserves of S and (especially) SS. There are **two techniques**.

(a) The two-stage (or indirect) method
(b) The single-stage (or direct) method.

2.3 The two stage method is used **in practice** (where there are sub-sub-subsidiary companies it would be a three-stage method). The single-stage method is useful **in examinations**, because it is quicker and acceptable to examiners.

2.4 EXAMPLE: SINGLE STAGE DIRECT METHOD OF CONSOLIDATION

The draft balance sheets of H Ltd, S Ltd and SS Ltd on 30 June 19X7 were as follows.

	H Ltd £	H Ltd £	S Ltd £	S Ltd £	SS Ltd £	SS Ltd £
Fixed assets						
Tangible assets		105,000		125,000		180,000
Investments, at cost						
80,000 shares in S Ltd		120,000		-		-
60,000 shares in SS Ltd		-		110,000		-
Current assets	80,000		70,000		60,000	
Creditors	30,000		35,000		25,000	
		50,000		35,000		35,000
		275,000		270,000		215,000
Capital and reserves						
Ordinary shares of £1 each		80,000		100,000		100,000
Reserves		195,000		170,000		115,000
		275,000		270,000		215,000

H Ltd acquired its shares in S Ltd when the reserves of S Ltd stood at £40,000; and S Ltd acquired its shares in SS Ltd when the reserves of SS Ltd stood at £50,000.

For the moment, we will assume that both acquisitions occurred on the same date.

Required

Prepare the draft consolidated balance sheet of H Group, using the single stage method.

Note. Goodwill should be capitalised, but amortisation can be ignored.

2.5 SOLUTION

Having calculated the minority interest and the H group interest (see Paragraph 1.5 above), the workings can be constructed. You should, however, note the following.

(a) **Minority interest working**: bring in the total minority interests in S Ltd's share capital and reserves (20%), and the total minority interests in SS Ltd's share capital and reserves (52%). Bring in the goodwill arising on S Ltd's acquisition of SS Ltd.

(b) **Goodwill working**: compare the costs of investments with the effective group interests acquired (80% of S Ltd and 60% of SS Ltd).

(c) **Reserves working**: bring in the share of S Ltd's and SS Ltd's post-acquisition reserves in the normal way.

1   *Minority interests*

	£	£
S Ltd		
Share capital (20% × £100,000)		20,000
Reserves (20% × £170,000)		34,000
Goodwill on acquisition of SS Ltd (20% × 20,000)		4,000
Investment in SS Ltd (20% × £110,000)		(22,000)
		36,000
SS Ltd		
Share capital (52% × £100,000)	52,000	
Reserves (52% × £115,000)	59,800	
		111,800
		147,800

Note. The rationale behind the treatment of goodwill is that on consolidation all assets are consolidated gross and minority interests shown separately. Goodwill is just another asset and should be treated in the same way.

2   *Goodwill*

	£	£	£
S Ltd			
Cost of investment			120,000
Share of net assets acquired			
as represented by			
Ordinary share capital		100,000	
Reserves		40,000	
		140,000	
Group share (80%)			112,000
Goodwill c/d			8,000

	£	£	£
Goodwill b/f			8,000
SS Ltd			
Cost of investment		110,000	
Share of net assets acquired			
Ordinary share capital	100,000		
Reserves	50,000		
	150,000		
SS share (60%)		90,000	
Goodwill			20,000
Net goodwill			28,000

3   *Reserves*

	£
H Ltd	195,000
Share of S Ltd's post acquisition retained reserves £(170,000 – 40,000) × 80%	104,000
Share of SS Ltd's post acquisition retained reserves £(115,000 – 50,000) × 48%	31,200
	330,200

H LIMITED
CONSOLIDATED BALANCE SHEET AT 30 JUNE 19X7

	£	£
Fixed assets		
Goodwill		28,000
Tangible assets		410,000
Current assets	210,000	
Creditors	90,000	
		120,000
		558,000
Capital and reserves		
Ordinary shares of £1 each fully paid		80,000
Reserves		330,200
3		410,200
Minority interest		147,800
		558,000

Question 1

The balance sheets of Antelope Ltd, Yak Ltd and Zebra Ltd at 31 March 19X4 are summarised as follows.

	Antelope Ltd		Yak Ltd		Zebra Ltd	
Fixed assets	£	£	£	£	£	£
Freehold property		100,000		100,000		-
Plant and machinery		210,000		80,000		3,000
		310,000		180,000		3,000
Investments in subsidiaries						
Shares, at cost	80,000		2,200			-
Loan account	-		3,800			-
Current accounts	10,000		12,200			-
		90,000		18,200		3,000
Current assets						
Stocks	200,000		24,500		15,000	
Debtors	140,000		50,000		1,000	
Cash at bank	60,000		16,500		4,000	
	400,000		91,000		20,000	
Creditors						
Trade creditors	130,000		40,200		800	
Due to Antelope Ltd	-		12,800		600	
Due to Yak Ltd	-		-		12,600	
Taxation	40,000		7,000		-	
Unclaimed dividends	400		-		-	
Proposed dividends	50,000		-		-	
	220,400		60,000		14,000	
Net current assets		179,600		31,000		6,000
		579,600		229,200		9,000
Capital and reserves						
Ordinary share capital		200,000		100,000		10,000
Reserves		379,600		129,200		(1,000)
		579,600		229,200		9,000

Antelope Ltd acquired 75% of the shares of Yak Ltd in 19X1 when the credit balance on the reserves of that company was £40,000. No dividends have been paid since that date. Yak Ltd acquired 80% of the shares in Zebra Ltd in 19X3 when there was a debit balance on the reserves of that company of £3,000. Subsequently £500 was received by Zebra Ltd and credited to its reserves, representing the recovery of a bad debt written off before the acquisition of Zebra's shares by Yak Ltd. During the year to 31 March 19X4 Yak Ltd purchased stock from Antelope Ltd for £20,000 which included a profit mark-up of £4,000 for Antelope Ltd. At 31 March 19X4 one half of this amount was still held in the stocks of Yak Ltd. Group accounting policies are to make a full provision for unrealised inter-company profits, and to treat goodwill in accordance with FRS 10.

Prepare the draft consolidated balance sheet of Antelope Ltd at 31 March 19X4.

Answer

The loan account and current accounts of the three companies are self-cancelling assets and liabilities. The minority interests are as follows.

Direct minority interest in Yak Ltd		25%
Direct minority interest in Zebra Ltd	20%	
Indirect minority interest in Zebra Ltd (25% of 80%)	20%	
Total minority interest in Zebra Ltd		40%

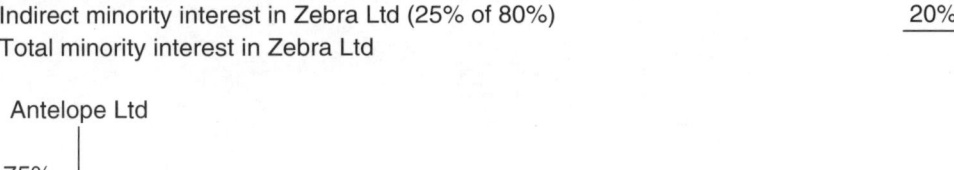

Antelope Ltd

75%

Yak Ltd ——— Minority Interest (direct) 25%

80%

Zebra Ltd ——— Minority Interest (direct) 20%

The group therefore owns a 75% interest in Yak Ltd and a 60% interest in Zebra Ltd.

BPP PUBLISHING

Part A: Company and group accounts

1   Minority interests

	£	£
Yak Ltd		
Share capital (25% × £100,000)		25,000
Reserves (25% × £129,200)		32,300
Negative goodwill on acquisition of Zebra (3,800 × 25%)		(950)
Investment in Zebra Ltd (25% × £2,200)		(550)
		55,800
Zebra Ltd		
Share capital (40% × £10,000)	4,000	
Reserves (40% × £(1,000))	(400)	
		3,600
		59,400

2   Goodwill

	£	£	£
Yak Ltd			
Cost of investment			80,000
Share of net assets acquired as represented by			
Share capital		100,000	
Reserves		40,000	
		140,000	
Group share (75%)			105,000
Negative goodwill			(25,000)
Zebra Ltd			
Cost of investment		2,200	
Share of net assets acquired as represented by			
Share capital	10,000		
Reserves (£3,000) + £500	(2,500)		
	7,500		
Yak's share (80%)		6,000	
Negative goodwill			(3,800)
Total negative goodwill			(28,800)

3   Reserves

	£
Antelope Ltd	379,600
Unrealised profit on stocks (£4,000 × ½)	(2,000)
Share of Yak Ltd's post acquisition retained reserves	
£(129,200 − 40,000) × 75%	66,900
Share of Zebra Ltd's post acquisition retained reserves	
£(−1,000 − (−2,500)) × 60%	900
Reserves	445,400

ANTELOPE LIMITED
CONSOLIDATED BALANCE SHEET AS AT 31 MARCH 19X4

	£	£
Fixed assets		
Negative goodwill		(28,800)
Freehold property		200,000
Plant and machinery		293,000
		464,200
Current assets		
Stocks £(239,500 – 2,000)	237,500	
Debtors	191,000	
Cash and bank	80,500	
	509,000	
Creditors: amounts falling due within one year		
Trade creditors	171,000	
Taxation	47,000	
Unclaimed dividends	400	
Proposed dividends	50,000	
	268,400	
Net current assets		240,600
		704,800
Capital and reserves		
Ordinary share capital		200,000
Reserves		445,400
Shareholders' funds		645,400
Minority interests		59,400
		704,800

2.6 Section summary

You should follow this **step by step approach** in all questions using the single-stage method. This applies to Section 3 below as well.

Step 1   Sketch the **group structure** and check it to the question

Step 2   **Add details** to the sketch of dates of acquisition, holdings acquired (percentage and nominal values) and cost

Step 3   **Minority interest working**: total MI in subsidiary plus total MI in sub-subsidiary

Step 4   **Goodwill working**: compare costs of investment with the **effective** group interests acquired. Check the question: how is goodwill to be treated? If the sub-subsidiary has already been acquired by the subsidiary, goodwill should be calculated by comparing the cost of the investments to the consolidated separable net assets of the subsidiary (net of all goodwill). If the sub-subsidiary is acquired post acquisition, include goodwill arising in the consolidated balance sheet.

Step 5   **Reserves working**: group share of subsidiary and sub-subsidiary post-acquisition reserves (effective holdings again)

Step 6   Prepare the **consolidated balance sheet** (and P&L account if required).

Exam focus point

The May 1998 paper contained a complex consolidation involving a 'conventional' subsidiary, a sub-subsidiary and a minority investment which is consolidated as a subsidiary because of the ability of the parent to exercise dominant influence.

3 DIRECT HOLDINGS IN SUB-SUBSIDIARIES

3.1 Consider the following structure, sometimes called a **'D-shaped' group**.

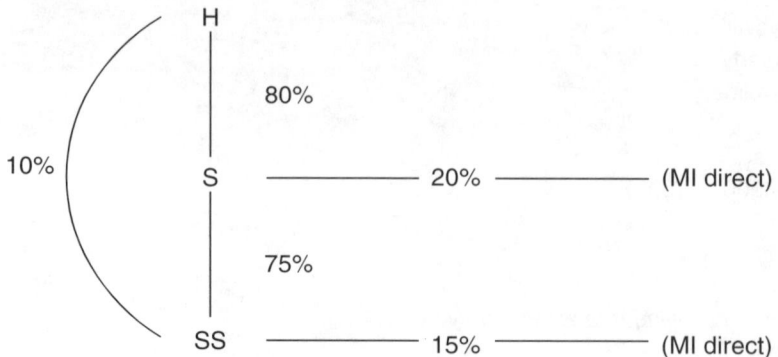

3.2 In practice several consolidations might be carried out, using procedures which are the same as in the **'two-stage' method** of consolidation for sub-subsidiaries:

(a) S with SS;

(b) H with the S group;

(c) H with SS (for the direct holding of 10%).

3.3 In an examination however, the **single-stage method** is recommended as it will save you valuable time. In the structure above, there is:

(a) a **direct** minority in S of		20%
(b) a **direct** minority in SS of	15%	
(c) an **indirect** minority in SS of 20% × 75% =	15%	
		30%

3.4 Once again, you could check a **dividend distribution** of £100 from SS.

	£
S will receive £75	
H will receive 80% of £75 =	60
H will receive 10% of £100 =	10
	70
Leaving for the total minority in SS	30

3.5 Having ascertained the structure and minority interests, proceed as for a typical sub-subsidiary situation by the single-stage method.

Question 2

The draft balance sheets of Hulk Ltd, Molehill Ltd and Pimple Ltd as at 31 May 19X5 are as follows.

	Hulk Ltd		Molehill Ltd		Pimple Ltd	
	£	£	£	£	£	£
Fixed assets						
Tangible assets		90,000		60,000		60,000
Investments in subsidiaries at cost						
Shares in Molehill Ltd	90,000		-		-	
Shares in Pimple Ltd	25,000		42,000		-	
		115,000		42,000		-
		205,000		102,000		60,000
Current assets	40,000		50,000		40,000	
Creditors due within one year						
Proposed dividends	30,000		20,000		10,000	
Other creditors	20,000		20,000		15,000	
	50,000		40,000		25,000	
Net current assets (liabilities)		(10,000)		10,000		15,000
		195,000		112,000		75,000
Creditors (falling due after one year)						
12% loan stock		-		10,000		-
		195,000		102,000		75,000

	Hulk Ltd	Molehill Ltd	Pimple Ltd
	£	£	£
Capital and reserves			
Ordinary shares of £1, allotted and fully paid	100,000	50,000	50,000
Share premium account	50,000	20,000	-
Profit and loss reserves	45,000	32,000	25,000
	195,000	102,000	75,000

(a) Hulk Ltd acquired 60% of the shares in Molehill on 1 January 19X3 when the balance on that company's profit and loss reserves was £8,000 (credit) and there was no share premium account.

(b) Hulk acquired 20% of the shares of Pimple Ltd and Molehill acquired 60% of the shares of Pimple Ltd on 1 January 19X4 when that company's profit and loss reserves stood at £15,000.

(c) There has been no payment of dividends by either Molehill or Pimple since they became subsidiaries.

(d) The proposed dividends have not yet been recorded in the books of the shareholding companies as dividends receivable.

(e) Goodwill arising on consolidation is assumed to have an indefinite life and is therefore capitalised in the balance sheet.

Required

Prepare the consolidated balance sheet of Hulk Ltd as at 31 May 19X5 using the single-stage method.

Answer

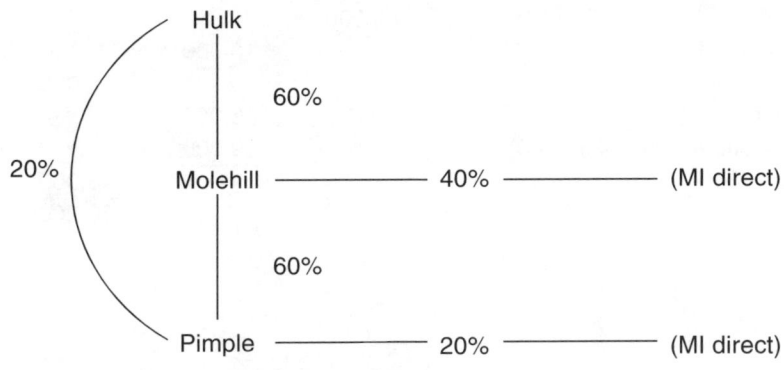

The direct minority interest in Molehill Ltd is		40%
The direct minority interest in Pimple Ltd is	20%	
The indirect minority interest in Pimple Ltd is (40% of 60%)	24%	
The total minority interest in Pimple Ltd is		44%

Part A: Company and group accounts

The group share of Molehill Ltd is 60% and of Pimple Ltd is (100 − 44)% = 56%

Dividends receivable

In Molehill Ltd's books:
DEBIT   Dividends receivable   £6,000
CREDIT Profit and loss reserves   £6,000

Being 60% of Pimple Ltd's proposed dividend

In Hulk Ltd's books:
DEBIT   Dividends receivable   £14,000
CREDIT Profit and loss reserves   £14,000

Being 20% of Pimple Ltd's proposed dividend plus 60% of Molehill Ltd's proposed dividend

1   Minority interests

	£	£
Molehill Ltd		
Share capital (40% × £50,000)		20,000
Share premium (40% × £20,000)		8,000
Reserves (40% × £(32,000 + 6,000))		15,200
Goodwill on acquisition of Pimple (40% × 3,000)		1,200
Investment in Pimple (40% × £42,000)		(16,800)
		27,600
Pimple Ltd		
Share capital (44% × £50,000)	22,000	
Reserves (44% × £25,000)	11,000	
		33,000
		60,600

2   Goodwill

	£	£	£
Molehill Ltd			
Cost of investment			90,000
Share of net assets acquired represented by			
Share capital		50,000	
Reserves		8,000	
		58,000	
Group share (60%)			34,800
Goodwill			55,200
Pimple Ltd			
Cost of direct holding		25,000	
Share of net assets acquired represented by			
Share capital	50,000		
Reserves	15,000		
	65,000		
Group share (direct interest - 20%)		13,000	
Goodwill			12,000
Cost of indirect holding		42,000	
Share of net assets acquired (60% × 65,000)		39,000	
			3,000
Total goodwill			70,200

3   *Reserves*

	£
Hulk Ltd	45,000
Dividends receivable	14,000
	59,000

Share of Molehill's post-acquisition retained reserves
£(32,000 − 8,000 + 6,000) × 60%   18,000
Share of Pimple's post acquisition retained reserves
£(25,000 − 15,000) × 56%   5,600
       82,600

4   *Share premium account*

	£
Hulk Ltd	50,000
Molehill Ltd: all post-acquisition (£20,000 × 60%)	12,000
	62,000

HULK LIMITED
CONSOLIDATED BALANCE SHEET AT 31 MAY 19X5

	£	£
Fixed assets		
Intangible asset: goodwill		70,200
Tangible assets		210,000
Current assets	130,000	
Creditors: amounts falling due within one year		
Minority proposed dividend	10,000	
Proposed dividend	30,000	
Other creditors	55,000	
	95,000	
Net current assets		35,000
Creditors: amounts falling due after more than one year		
12% loan stock		10,000
		305,200
Capital and reserves		
Ordinary shares of £1 allotted and fully paid		100,000
Share premium		62,000
Profit and loss reserves		82,600
Shareholders' funds		244,600
Minority interests		60,600
		305,200

Chapter roundup

- When a holding company has **several subsidiaries**, the consolidated balance sheet shows a single figure for minority interests and for goodwill arising on consolidation. There may also be a figure for 'capital reserve arising on consolidation'. In cases where there are several subsidiary companies the technique is to open up a single minority interest working and a single goodwill working.

- When dealing with **sub-subsidiaries**, there are two possible consolidation techniques. For examination purposes, the greater simplicity of the single-stage method makes it preferable to the two-stage method.

- The **date of acquisition** is important when dealing with sub-subsidiaries. Renumber that it is the post-acquisition reserves from a **group perspective** which are important.

Quick quiz

1   B Ltd owns 60% of the equity of C Ltd which owns 75% of the equity of D Ltd. What is the total minority interest in D Ltd? (see para 1.5)

2   What is the basic consolidation method for sub-subsidiaries? (2.1)

3   What are the two techniques available for consolidating a subsidiary? (2.2)

4   P Ltd owns 20% of R Ltd's equity and 75% of Q Ltd's equity. Q Ltd owns 40% of R Ltd's equity. What is the total minority interest in R Ltd? (3.3)

Question to try	Level	Marks	Time
16	Exam	20	36 mins

Chapter 16

THE CONSOLIDATED PROFIT AND LOSS ACCOUNT

Chapter topic	Syllabus reference	Ability required
1 First principles	9(a)	Application
2 Inter-company trading	9(a)	Application
3 Inter-company dividends	9(a)	Application
4 Pre-acquisition profits	9(a)	Application
5 Disclosure requirements	9(a)	Application

Introduction

Generally speaking, the preparation of the consolidated profit and loss account is **more straightforward** than the preparation of the consolidated balance sheet.

Complications do arise, however, usually in the form of **inter-company transactions** and **accounting for pre-acquisition profits**. These areas are covered in Sections 2, 3 and 4.

The consolidated profit and loss account will appear again in the next chapter when we consider the treatment of associated companies.

You should refer to the material on FRS 3 in Chapter 2 for disclosure purposes, and that in Chapter 18, which covers disposals of subsidiaries.

1 FIRST PRINCIPLES 11/95

1.1 As always, the source of the consolidated statement is the individual accounts of the separate companies in the group. It is customary in practice to prepare a working paper (known as a **consolidation schedule**) on which the individual profit and loss accounts are set out side by side and totalled to form the basis of the consolidated profit and loss account.

Exam focus point

In an examination it is very much quicker not to do this. Use workings to show the calculation of complex figures such as the minority interest and show the derivation of others on the face of the profit and loss account, as shown in our examples.

1.2 CONSOLIDATED PROFIT AND LOSS ACCOUNT: SIMPLE EXAMPLE

H Ltd acquired 75% of the ordinary shares of S Ltd on that company's incorporation in 19X3. The summarised profit and loss accounts of the two companies for the year ending 31 December 19X6 are set out below.

	H Ltd £	S Ltd £
Turnover	75,000	38,000
Cost of sales	30,000	20,000
Gross profit	45,000	18,000
Administrative expenses	14,000	8,000
Profit before taxation	31,000	10,000
Taxation	10,000	2,000
Retained profit for the year	21,000	8,000
Retained profits brought forward	87,000	17,000
Retained profits carried forward	108,000	25,000

Required

Prepare the consolidated profit and loss account.

1.3 SOLUTION

H LIMITED
CONSOLIDATED PROFIT AND LOSS ACCOUNT
FOR THE YEAR ENDED 31 DECEMBER 19X6

	£
Turnover (75 + 38)	113,000
Cost of sales (30 + 20)	50,000
Gross profit	63,000
Administrative expenses (14 + 8)	22,000
Profit before taxation	41,000
Taxation (10 + 2)	12,000
Profit after taxation	29,000
Minority interest (25% × £8,000)	2,000
Group retained profit for the year	27,000
Retained profits brought forward (group share only: 87 + (17 × 75%))	99,750
Retained profits carried forward	126,750

1.4 **Notice how the minority interest is dealt with.**

(a) **Down to the line 'profit after taxation' the whole of S Ltd's results is included without reference to group share or minority share. A one-line adjustment is then inserted to deduct the minority's share of S Ltd's profit after taxation.**

(b) **The minority's share (£4,250) of S Ltd's retained profits brought forward is excluded.** This means that the carried forward figure of £126,750 is the figure which would appear in the balance sheet for group retained reserves.

1.5 This last point may be clearer if we revert to our balance sheet technique and construct the working for group reserves.

Group reserves

	£
H Ltd	108,000
Share of S Ltd's PARR (75% × £25,000)	18,750
	126,750

The minority share of S Ltd's reserves comprises the minority interest in the £17,000 profits brought forward plus the minority interest (£2,000) in £8,000 retained profits for the year. (*Note*. PARR = Post acquisition retained reserves.)

1.6 Notice that a consolidated profit and loss account links up with a consolidated balance sheet exactly as in the case of an individual company's accounts: the figure of retained profits

carried forward at the bottom of the profit and loss account appears as the figure for retained profits in the balance sheet.

1.7 We will now look at the **complications introduced by inter-company trading, inter-company dividends and pre-acquisition profits in the subsidiary.**

2 INTER-COMPANY TRADING   11/95

2.1 Like the consolidated balance sheet, the consolidated profit and loss account should deal with the results of the group as those of a single entity. When one company in a group sells goods to another an identical amount is added to the turnover of the first company and to the cost of sales of the second. Yet as far as the entity's dealings with outsiders are concerned no sale has taken place.

The consolidated figures for turnover and cost of sales should represent sales to, and purchases from, outsiders. An adjustment is therefore necessary to reduce the turnover and cost of sales figures by the value of inter-company sales during the year.

2.2 We have also seen in an earlier chapter that any **unrealised profits on inter-company trading should be excluded from the figure of group profits.** This will occur whenever goods sold at a profit within the group remain in the stock of the purchasing company at the year end. The best way to deal with this is to **calculate the unrealised profit on unsold stocks at the year end and reduce consolidated gross profit** by this amount. Cost of sales will be the balancing figure

2.3 EXAMPLE: INTER-COMPANY TRADING

Suppose in our earlier example that S Ltd had recorded sales of £5,000 to H Ltd during 19X6. S Ltd had purchased these goods from outside suppliers at a cost of £3,000. One half of the goods remained in H Ltd's stock at 31 December 19X6.

2.4 SOLUTION

The consolidated profit and loss account for the year ended 31 December 19X6 would now be as follows.

	Group £
Turnover (75 + 38 − 5)	108,000
Cost of sales (balancing figure)	46,000
Gross profit (45 + 18 − 1*)	62,000
Administrative expenses	(22,000)
Profit before taxation	40,000
Taxation	(12,000)
	28,000
Minority interest (25% × (£8,000 − £1,000*))	1,750
Group retained profit for the year	26,250
Retained profits brought forward	99,750
Retained profits carried forward	126,000

*Provision for unrealised profit: ½ × (£5,000 − £3,000)

A provision will be made for the unrealised profit against the stock figure in the consolidated balance sheet, as explained in Chapter 13.

3 INTER-COMPANY DIVIDENDS 11/95

3.1 In our example so far we have assumed that S Ltd retains all of its after-tax profit. It may be, however, that S Ltd distributes some of its profits as dividends. As before, the minority interest in the subsidiary's profit should be calculated immediately after the figure of after-tax profit. For this purpose, **no account need be taken of how much of the minority interest is to be distributed by S Ltd as dividend**.

3.2 A complication may arise if the subsidiary has preference shares and wishes to pay a preference dividend as well as an ordinary dividend. In such a case great care is needed in calculating the minority interest in S Ltd's after-tax profit.

> **Exam focus point**
>
> In an exam question on the consolidated profit and loss account it is certain that you will get inter-company transactions such as the above.

3.3 EXAMPLE: INTER-COMPANY DIVIDENDS

Sam Ltd's capital consists of 10,000 6% £1 preference shares and 10,000 £1 ordinary shares. On 1 January 19X3, the date of Sam Ltd's incorporation, Ham Ltd acquired 3,000 of the preference shares and 7,500 of the ordinary shares. The profit and loss accounts of the two companies for the year ended 31 December 19X6 are set out below.

	Ham Ltd	Sam Ltd
	£	£
Turnover	200,000	98,000
Cost of sales	90,000	40,000
Gross profit	110,000	58,000
Administrative expenses	35,000	19,000
Profit before tax	75,000	39,000
Taxation	23,000	18,000
Profit after tax	52,000	21,000
Dividends proposed: preference	-	600
ordinary	14,000	2,000
Retained profit for the year	38,000	18,400
Retained profits brought forward	79,000	23,000
	117,000	41,400

Ham Ltd has not yet accounted for its share of the dividends receivable from Sam Ltd.

Prepare Ham Ltd's consolidated profit and loss account.

3.4 SOLUTION

To calculate the minority interest in Sam Ltd's after-tax profit it is necessary to remember that the first £600 of such profits goes to pay the preference dividend. The balance of after-tax profits belongs to the equity shareholders. The calculation is as follows.

	Total		Minority share
	£		£
Profits earned for preference shareholders	600	(70%)	420
Balance earned for equity shareholders	20,400	(25%)	5,100
Total profits after tax	21,000		5,520

It is irrelevant how much of this is distributed to the minority as dividends: the whole £5,520 must be deducted in arriving at the figure for group profit. The dividends receivable

by Ham Ltd, calculated below would cancel with the dividends payable by Sam Ltd to its holding company.

	£
Preference dividend (30% × £600)	180
Ordinary dividend (75% × £2,000)	1,500
	1,680

3.5   HAM LIMITED
        CONSOLIDATED PROFIT AND LOSS ACCOUNT
        FOR THE YEAR ENDED 31 DECEMBER 19X5

	Group
	£
Turnover (200 + 98)	298,000
Cost of sales (90 + 40)	130,000
Gross profit	168,000
Administrative expenses (35 + 19)	54,000
Profit before tax	114,000
Taxation (23 + 18)	41,000
Profit after tax	73,000
Minority interest (as above)	5,520
Group profit for the year	67,480
Dividend proposed (parent company only)	14,000
Retained profit for the year	53,480
Retained profits brought forward	
(group share only: 79 + (23 × 75%))	96,250
Retained profits carried forward	149,730

4   PRE-ACQUISITION PROFITS

4.1   As explained above, the figure for retained profits at the bottom of the consolidated profit and loss account must be the same as the figure for retained profits in the consolidated balance sheet. We have seen in previous chapters that **retained profits in the consolidated balance sheet comprise**:

(a)   **the whole of the parent company's retained profits; plus**

(b)   a **proportion** of the subsidiary company's retained profits. The proportion **is the group's share of post-acquisition retained profits** in the subsidiary. From the total retained profits of the subsidiary we must therefore exclude both the minority's share of total retained profits *and* the group's share of pre-acquisition retained profits.

4.2   **A similar procedure is necessary in the consolidated profit and loss account** if it is to link up with the consolidated balance sheet. Previous examples have shown how the minority share of profits is excluded in the profit and loss account: their share of profits for the year is deducted from profit after tax; while the figure for profits brought forward in the consolidation schedule includes only the group's proportion of the subsidiary's profits.

4.3   In the same way, when considering examples which include pre-acquisition profits in a subsidiary, the figure for profits brought forward should include only the group's share of the post-acquisition retained profits. If the subsidiary is acquired *during* the accounting year, it is therefore necessary to apportion its profit for the year between pre-acquisition and post-acquisition elements. There are two approaches which may be used for this in the consolidated profit and loss account: the whole-year method and the part-year method.

4.4 With the **whole-year method**, the whole of the subsidiary's turnover, cost of sales and so on is included and a deduction is then made lower down to exclude the profit accruing prior to acquisition.

4.5 With the **part-year method**, the entire profit and loss account of the subsidiary is split between pre-acquisition and post-acquisition proportions. Only the post-acquisition figures are included in the profit and loss account. This method is **more usual** than the whole-year method and is the one which will be used in this Study Text.

Question 1

H Ltd acquired 60% of the equity of S Ltd on 1 April 19X5. The profit and loss accounts of the two companies for the year ended 31 December 19X5 are set out below.

	H Ltd	S Ltd	S Ltd ($^9/_{12}$)
	£	£	£
Turnover	170,000	80,000	60,000
Cost of sales	65,000	36,000	27,000
Gross profit	105,000	44,000	33,000
Administrative expenses	43,000	12,000	9,000
Profit before tax	62,000	32,000	24,000
Taxation	23,000	8,000	6,000
Profit after tax	39,000	24,000	18,000
Dividends (paid 31 December)	12,000	6,000	
Retained profit for the year	27,000	18,000	
Retained profits brought forward	81,000	40,000	
Retained profits carried forward	108,000	58,000	

H Ltd has not yet accounted for the dividends received from S Ltd.

Prepare the consolidated profit and loss account.

Answer

The shares in S Ltd were acquired three months into the year. Only the post-acquisition proportion (9/12ths) of S Ltd's P & L account is included in the consolidated profit and loss account. This is shown above for convenience.

H LIMITED CONSOLIDATED PROFIT AND LOSS ACCOUNT
FOR THE YEAR ENDED 31 DECEMBER 19X5

	£
Turnover (170 + 60)	230,000
Cost of sales (65 + 27)	92,000
Gross profit	138,000
Administrative expenses (43 + 9)	52,000
Profit before tax	86,000
Taxation (23 + 6)	29,000
Profit after tax	57,000
Minority interest (40% × £18,000)	7,200
Group profit for the year	49,800
Dividends (H Ltd only)	12,000
Retained profit for the year	37,800
Retained profits brought forward*	81,000
Retained profits carried forward	118,800

* All of S Ltd's profits brought forward are pre-acquisition.

5   DISCLOSURE REQUIREMENTS

5.1   S 230 CA 1985 allows a parent company to dispense with the need to publish its own individual profit and loss account.

(a) Companies taking advantage of this dispensation are obliged to state in their consolidated profit and loss account how much of the group's profit for the financial year is dealt with in the parent company's own profit and loss account.

(b) For internal purposes, of course, it will still be necessary to prepare the parent company's profit and loss account and the profit or loss shown there is the figure to be shown in the note to the group accounts.

(c) This is a point which has been clarified by the CA 1989. In the example above, H Ltd should disclose its own profit after adjustment for its share of the S Ltd dividend (from post-acquisition profits - remember that the pre-acquisition element should be credited to the cost of H's investment in S Ltd).

5.2   In the extremely unlikely event that there are **extraordinary** items in the profit and loss account of a group company, the **group share only** of such items should be included, *after* minority interest and the adjustment for inter-company dividends but *before* dividends payable by the parent company.

5.3   If you are required to prepare a consolidated profit and loss account in statutory form, you may need to disclose a figure for **directors' emoluments**. The figure should represent the emoluments of **parent company directors only,** whether those emoluments are paid by the parent company or by subsidiary companies. The emoluments of directors of subsidiary companies should be excluded, unless they are also directors of the parent company.

5.4   The movement of reserves statement may be required to show a transfer from the profit and loss account to other reserves. Where this transfer occurs in a subsidiary, only the group's (post-acquisition) share of the transfer will be recorded in the movement of reserves statement. Any minority interest or pre-acquisition profits would be excluded.

MOVEMENT OF RESERVES

	£
Profit and loss account brought forward	X
Add retained profit for the year	X
	X
Less transfer to reserves (all of parent company transfers plus the group share of transfers in a subsidiary)	(X)
Profit and loss account carried forward	X

Question 2

The following information relates to the Brodick group of companies for the year to 30 April 19X7.

	Brodick plc £'000	Lamlash Ltd £'000	Corrie Ltd £'000
Turnover	1,100	500	130
Cost of sales	630	300	70
Gross profit	470	200	60
Administrative expenses	105	150	20
Dividend from Lamlash Ltd	24	-	-
Dividend from Corrie Ltd	6	-	-
Profit before tax c/f	395	50	40

	Brodick plc	Lamlash Ltd	Corrie Ltd
	£'000	£'000	£'000
Profit before tax b/f	395	50	40
Taxation	65	10	20
Profit after tax	330	40	20
Interim dividend	50	10	-
Proposed dividend	150	20	10
Retained profit for the year	130	10	10
Retained profits brought forward	460	106	30
Retained profits carried forward	590	116	40

Additional information

(a)   The issued share capital of the group was as follows.

Brodick plc: 5,000,000 ordinary shares of £1 each.
Lamlash Ltd: 1,000,000 ordinary shares of £1 each.
Corrie Ltd: 400,000 ordinary shares of £1 each.

(b)   Brodick plc purchased 80% of the issued share capital of Lamlash Ltd in 19X0. At that time, the retained profits of Lamlash amounted to £56,000.

(c)   Brodick plc purchased 60% of the issued share capital of Corrie Ltd in 19X4. At that time, the retained profits of Corrie amounted to £20,000.

(d)   Brodick plc recognises dividends proposed by other group companies in its profit and loss account.

Required

Insofar as the information permits, prepare the Brodick group of companies' consolidated profit and loss account for the year to 30 April 19X7 in accordance with the Companies Act 1985 and related statements of accounting practice.

Note. Notes to the profit and loss account are not required but you should append a statement showing the make up of the 'retained profits carried forward', and your workings should be submitted.

Answer

You are not asked for notes, but you should know that Brodick would have to state in the notes that it had taken advantage of the provisions of s 230 CA and was not publishing its own profit and loss account. It would then show its own profit for the year, which the Act now states clearly should be the profit shown in its own books (in this case, including dividends received and receivable from Lamlash and Corrie). Brodrick's profit for the financial year is £330,000, as shown in the question. An analysis of reserves would also be given as a note to the balance sheet, showing movements on both company and consolidated reserves.

CONSOLIDATED PROFIT AND LOSS ACCOUNT
FOR THE YEAR TO 30 APRIL 19X7

	£'000
Turnover (1,100 + 500 + 130)	1,730
Cost of sales (630 + 300 + 70)	1,000
Gross profit	730
Administrative expenses (105 + 150 + 20)	275
Profit on ordinary activities before taxation	455
Tax on profit on ordinary activities (65 + 10 + 20)	95
Profit on ordinary activities after taxation	360
Minority interests (W1)	16
Profit for the financial year	344
Dividends paid and proposed (parent only)	200
Retained profit for the year	144
Retained profit brought forward 1 May 19X6 (W2)	506
Retained profit carried forward 30 April 19X7	650

Workings

1   *Minority interests*

		£
In Lamlash (20% × profit after tax)		8,000
In Corrie (40% × profit after tax)		8,000
		16,000

2   *Retained profits brought forward*

	£
Brodick plc	460,000
Group share of post-acquisition retained profits brought forward	
Lamlash 80% × £(106,000 – 56,000)	40,000
Corrie 60% × £(30,000 – 20,000)	6,000
	506,000

M.1 (handwritten note)

Reserve (handwritten note)

FRS 3 *Reporting financial performance*

5.5   As you may recall from Chapter 2, FRS 3 requires certain disclosures in relation to acquisitions and disposals. In particular, it requires the profit and loss account to be shown in a layered format, showing the results of acquired operations and those which have been sold or discontinued. To remind yourself, look again at the profit and loss account and notes formats required by FRS 3 in Chapter 2. We will look at the FRS 3 implications of disposals in Chapter 18.

Summary: consolidated P & L account

Purpose	To show the results of the group for an accounting period as if it were a single entity.
Turnover to profit after tax	100% H + 100% S (excluding dividend receivable from subsidiary and adjustments for inter-company transactions).
Reason	To show the results of the group which were controlled by the holding company.
Inter-company sales Unrealised profit on inter-company sales	Strip out inter-company activity from both turnover and cost sales. (a) *Goods sold by H Ltd.* Increase cost of sales by unrealised profit. (b) *Goods sold by S Ltd.* Increase cost of sales by full amount of unrealised profit and decrease minority interest by their share of unrealised profit.
Depreciation	If the value of S Ltd's fixed assets have been subjected to a fair value uplift then any additional depreciation must be charged in the consolidated profit and loss account. The minority interest will need to be adjusted for their share.
Transfer of fixed assets	Expenses must be increased by any profit on the transfer and reduced by any additional depreciation arising from the increased carrying value of the asset.

Minority interests	S's profit after tax (PAT)	X
	Less: * unrealised profit	(X)
	* profit on disposal of fixed assets	(X)
	additional depreciation following FV uplift	(X)
	Add: ** additional depreciation following	
	disposal of fixed assets	$\underline{X}$
		$\underline{\underline{X}}$
	MI%	X
	* Only applicable if sales of goods and fixed assets made by subsidiary.	
	** Only applicable if sale of fixed assets made by holding company.	
Reason	To show the extent to which profits generated through H's control are in fact owned by other parties.	
Dividends	H's only.	
Reason	S's dividend is due (a) to H; and (b) to MI.	
	H has taken in its share by including the results of S in the consolidated P & L a/c. The MI have taken their share by being given a proportion of S's PAT. Remember: PAT = dividends + retained profit.	
Retained reserves	As per the balance sheet calculations.	

Chapter roundup

- This chapter has explained how to prepare a consolidated profit and loss account by combining the profit and loss accounts of each group company.

- Adjustments must be made:

  - to reduce turnover by the amount of any intra-group trading, and to deduct from consolidated gross profit any unrealised profit on stocks thus acquired which are held at the year end. Cost of sales will be the balancing figure;

  - to reduce stock values by the amount of any unrealised profit on intra-group trading;

  - to calculate the minority interest in subsidiary companies' results for the year;

  - to account for intra-group dividends;

  - to eliminate pre-acquisition profits.

Quick quiz

1   Describe the preparation of a consolidated profit and loss account in its simplest form. (see para 1.1)

2   At what stage in the consolidated profit and loss account does the figure for minority interests appear? (1.4)

3   What adjustments are made to the consolidated profit and loss account in respect of inter-company trading? (2.4)

4   Describe the whole-year and part-year methods for dealing with pre- and post-acquisition reserves in the consolidated P & L account. (4.4, 4.5)

5   What dispensation is granted to a parent company by s 230 CA 1985? (5.1)

6   Describe the make-up of the figure for directors' emoluments in a consolidated profit and loss account. (5.3)

Question to try	Level	Marks	Time
17	Exam	40	72 mins

BPP PUBLISHING

Chapter 17

ASSOCIATES AND JOINT VENTURES

Chapter topic	Syllabus reference	Ability required
1 Equity accounting	9(a)	Application
2 FRS 9 *Associates and joint ventures*	9(a)	Application
3 Associates	9(a)	Application
4 Joint ventures and joint arrangements	9(a)	Application
5 Disclosures for associates and joint ventures	9(a)	Application

Introduction

Some investments which do not satisfy the criteria for classification as subsidiaries may nevertheless be much more than trade investments. The most important of these are associates and joint ventures which are the subject of this chapter and of one of the ASB's recent standards FRS 9 *Associates and joint ventures.*

1   EQUITY ACCOUNTING

1.1   In the 1960s it became increasingly common for companies to trade through companies in which a **substantial but not a controlling interest** was held. Traditionally such companies were accounted for in the same way as trade investments. In other words the income from associated companies was only included in the investing company's accounts to the extent of the dividends received and receivable up to its balance sheet date. However, it was felt that this treatment did not reflect the reality of the investment, not least because the investor could in many cases influence the investee's dividend policy. The need thus arose for an **intermediate form of accounting for those investments which lie between full subsidiary and trade investment status**.

Equity accounting

1.2   The intermediate form of accounting developed for this purpose is known as **equity accounting.** The full, up-to-date (FRS 9) definition of equity accounting will be given later in this chapter. For now, think of it as follows.

> **KEY TERM**
>
> **Equity accounting** is a modified form of consolidation of the results and assets of the investee where the investor has exercise significant influence but not control. Rather than full, line by line consolidation, it involves incorporating the investor's share of the profit/loss and assets of the investee **in one line** in the investor's profit and loss account and balance sheet.

2 FRS 9 ASSOCIATES AND JOINT VENTURES   5/99

2.1 FRS 9 *Associates and joint ventures* was issued in November 1997. It sets out the definition and accounting treatments for associates and joint ventures, two types of interests that a reporting entity may have in other entities. The FRS also deals with joint arrangements that are not entities. The definitions and treatments prescribed have been developed to be consistent with the Accounting Standards Board's approach to accounting for subsidiaries (dealt with in FRS 2 *Accounting for subsidiary undertakings*). The requirements are consistent with companies legislation.

Objective

2.2 The objective of FRS 9 is to reflect the effect on an investor's financial position and performance of its interest in two special kinds of investments - **associates** and **joint ventures**. The investor is partly accountable for the activities of these investments because of the closeness of its involvement.

(a) It is closely involved in **associates** as a result of its **participating interest** and **significant influence**.

(b) Its close involvement with **joint ventures** arises as a result of its **long-term interest** and **joint control**.

2.3 The FRS also deals with **joint arrangements** that do not qualify as associates or joint ventures because they are not entities.

Scope

2.4 The FRS applies to **all financial statements** intending to give a true and fair view.

> **Exam focus point**
> - At this stage, read through the summary and example **for overview only**. Do not expect to understand everything you read.
> - **At the end of the chapter**, when you have worked through the detailed sections on associates and joint ventures, **come back to this section to put it in context**.
> - When you come to **revise**, look at this section as it contains a clear summary of the requirements of the FRS.

Summary

2.5 The table below, taken from the FRS, describes the **different sorts of interest that a reporting entity may have in other entities or arrangements**. The sections marked with an asterisk (*) are covered by the FRS. The defining relationships described in the table form the basis for the definitions used in the FRS.

Entity/ arrangement	Nature of relationship	Description of the defining relationship - the full definitions are given in the FRS
Subsidiary	Investor controls its investee	Control is the ability of an entity to direct the operating and financial policies of another entity with a view to gaining economic benefits from its activities. To have control an entity must have both: (a) the ability to deploy the economic resources of the investee or to direct it; and (b) the ability to ensure that any resulting benefits accrue to itself (with corresponding exposure to losses) and to restrict the access of others to those benefits.
★ Joint arrangement that is not an entity	Entities participate in an arrangement to carry on part of their own trades or businesses	A joint arrangement, whether or not subject to joint control, does not constitute an entity unless it carries on a trade or business of its own.
★ Joint venture	Investor holds a long-term interest and shares control under a contractual arrangement	The joint venture agreement can override the rights normally conferred by ownership interests with the effect that: • acting together, the venturers can control the venture and there are procedures for such joint action • each venturer has (implicitly or explicitly) a veto over strategic policy decisions. There is usually a procedure for settling disputes between venturers and, possibly, for terminating the joint venture.
★ Associate	Investor holds a participating interest and exercises significant influence	The investor has a long-term interest and is actively involved, and influential, in the direction of its investee through its participation in policy decisions covering the aspects of policy relevant to the investor, including decisions on strategic issues such as: (i) the expansion or contraction of the business, participation in other entities or changes in products, markets and activities of its investee; and (ii) determining the balance between dividend and reinvestment.
Simple investment		The investor's interest does not quality the investee as an associate, a joint venture or a subsidiary because the investor has limited influence or its interest is not long-term.

2.6 The table below, also taken from the FRS, sets out the **treatments in consolidated financial statements** for the different interests that a reporting entity may have in other entities and for joint arrangements that are not entities - the sections marked with an asterisk (★) are covered by the FRS.

Type of investment	Treatment in consolidated financial statements
Subsidiaries	The investor should consolidate the assets, liabilities, results and cash flows of its subsidiaries.
* Joint arrangements that are not entities	Each party should account for its own share of the assets, liabilities and cash flows in the joint arrangement, measured according to the terms of that arrangement, for example pro rata to their respective interests.
Joint ventures	The venturer should use the gross equity method showing in addition to the amounts included under the equity method, on the face on the balance sheet, the venturer's share of the gross assets and liabilities of its joint ventures, and, in the profit and loss account, the venturer's share of their turnover distinguished from that of the group. Where the venturer conducts a major part of its business through joint ventures, it may show fuller information provided all amounts are distinguished from those of the group.
Associates	The investor should include its associates in its consolidated financial statements using the equity method. In the investor's consolidated profit and loss account the investor's share of its associates' operating results should be included immediately after group operating results. From the level of profit before tax, the investor's share of the relevant amounts for associates should be included within the amounts for the group. In the consolidated statement of total recognised gains and losses the investor's share of the total recognised gains and losses of its associates should be included, shown separately under each heading, if material. In the balance sheet the investor's share of the net assets of its associates should be included and separately disclosed. The cash flow statement should include the cash flows between the investor and its associates. Goodwill arising on the investor's acquisition of its associates, less any amortisation or write-down, should be included in the carrying amount for the associates but should be disclosed separately. In the profit and loss account the amortisation or write-down of such goodwill should be separately disclosed as part of the investor's share of its associates' results.
Simple investments	The investor includes its interests as investments at either cost or valuation.

2.7   EXAMPLE: CONSOLIDATED FINANCIAL STATEMENTS

The following example of consolidated financial statements is taken from Appendix IV of FRS 9. Study it for an overview and come back to it when you have finished the chapter.

2.8   The format is illustrative only. The amounts shown for 'Associates' and 'joint ventures' are subdivisions of the item for which the statutory prescribed heading is 'Income from interests in associated undertakings'. The subdivisions may be shown in a note rather than on the face of the profit and loss account.

CONSOLIDATED PROFIT AND LOSS ACCOUNT

	£m	£m
Turnover: group and share of joint ventures	320	
Less: share of joint ventures' turnover	(120)	
Group turnover		200
Cost of sales		(120)
Gross profit		80
Administrative expenses		(40)
Group operating profit		40
Share of operating profit in		
Joint ventures	30	
Associates	24	
		54
		94
Interest receivable (group)		6
Interest payable		
Group	(26)	
Joint ventures	(10)	
Associates	(12)	
		(48)
Profit on ordinary activities before tax		52
Tax on profit on ordinary activities★		(12)
Profit on ordinary activities after tax		40
Minority interests		(6)
Profit on ordinary activities after taxation and minority interest		34
Equity dividends		(10)
Retained profit for group and its share of associates and joint ventures		24

★Tax relates to the following:	Parent and subsidiaries	(5)
	Joint ventures	(5)
	Associates	(2)

CONSOLIDATED BALANCE SHEET

	£m	£m	£m
Fixed assets			
Tangible assets		480	
Investments			
Investments in joint ventures:			
Share of gross assets	130		
Share of gross liabilities	(80)		
		50	
Investments in associates		20	
			550
Current assets			
Stock		15	
Debtors		75	
Cash at bank and in hand		10	
		100	
Creditors (due within one year)		(50)	
Net current assets			50
Total assets less current liabilities			600
Creditors (due after more than one year)			(250)
Provisions for liabilities and charges			(10)
Equity minority interest			(40)
			300
Capital and reserves			
Called up share capital			50
Share premium account			150
Profit and loss account			100
Shareholders' funds (all equity)			300

Notes

In the example, there is no individual associate or joint venture that accounts for more than 25 per cent of any of the following for the investor group (excluding any amount for associates and joint ventures).

- Gross assets
- Gross liabilities
- Turnover
- Operating results (on a three-year average)

Additional disclosures for joint ventures (which in aggregate exceed the 15 per cent threshold)

	£m	£m
Share of assets		
Share of fixed assets	100	
Share of current assets	30	
		130
Share of liabilities		
Liabilities due within one year or less	(10)	
Liabilities due after more than one year	(70)	
		(80)
Share of net assets		50

Additional disclosures for associates (which in aggregate exceed the 15 per cent threshold)

	£m	£m
Share of turnover of associates		90
Share of assets		
Share of fixed assets	4	
Share of current assets	28	
		32
Share of liabilities		
Liabilities due within one year or less	(3)	
Liabilities due after more than one year	(9)	
		(12)
Share of net assets		20

3 ASSOCIATES   5/95, 11/96

3.1 Associated undertakings should be included by an entity in its consolidated financial statements using the **equity method**. In the investor's individual statements, the interest in associates is shown as a **fixed asset investment,** at cost (less any amounts written off) or valuation.

3.2 The most important definitions relate to the **identification** of associates.

> **KEY TERMS**
>
> - **Associate**: an entity (other than a subsidiary) in which another entity (the investor) has a participating interest and over whose operating and financial policies the investor exercises a significant influence.
>
> - **Control** the ability of an entity to direct the operating and financial policies of another entity with a view to gaining economic benefits from its activities.
>
> - **Entity**: a body corporate, a partnership or an unincorporated association carrying on a trade or business with or without a view to profit.   *(FRS 9)*

Participating interest

3.3 FRS 9 defines 'participating interest' in the same way as FRS 2.

> **KEY TERM**
>
> **Participating interest**: an interest held in the shares of another entity on a long-term basis for the purpose of securing a contribution to the investor's activities by the exercise of control or influence arising from or related to that interest.   *(FRS 9)*

3.4 The investor's interest must be **beneficial**, the benefits linked to the exercise of significant influence. An interest convertible to an interest in shares and an option to acquire shares also qualify.

3.5 A participating interest is a **continuing relationship** and the interest does not cease only because the investor sells its interest in the associate.

Long-term interest

3.6 This definition relates to a participating interest.

> **KEY TERM**
>
> **Interest held on a long-term basis**: an interest that is held other than exclusively with a view to subsequent resale. An interest held exclusively with a view to subsequent resale is:
>
> - an interest for which a purchaser has been identified or is being sought, and which is reasonably expected to be disposed or within approximately one year of its date of acquisition; or
>
> - an interest that was acquired as a result of the enforcement of a security, unless the interest has become part of the continuing activities of the group or the holder acts as if it intends the interest to become so.   *(FRS 9)*

3.7 This definition is extremely important.

> **KEY TERM**
>
> **Exercise of significant influence**: the exercise of a degree of influence by an investor over the operating and financial policies of its investee that results in the following conditions being fulfilled.
>
> (a) The investor is actively involved and is influential in the direction of its investee through its participation in policy decisions covering all aspects of policy relevant to the investor, including decisions on strategic issues such as:
>
>   (i) the expansion or contraction of the business, participation in other entities, changes in products, markets and activities of its investee; and

> **KEY TERM (cont)**
>
> (ii) determining the balance between dividend and reinvestment.
>
> (b) Over time, the investee generally implements policies that are consistent with the strategy of the investor and avoids implementing policies that are contrary to the investor's interests. *(FRS 9)*

3.8 Significant influence is usually wielded through nomination to the **board of directors**, although it may be achieved in other ways. It presupposes an agreement (formal or informal) between the investor and investee.

3.9 The **20% rule** given in SSAP 1 is followed here, so that a holding of 20% or more of the voting rights suggests (but does not guarantee) that the investor exercises significant influence. At 20% the presumption of the exercise of significant influence can be rebutted if the criteria above are not fulfilled. The holdings of both parent and subsidiaries in the entity should be taken into account.

Accounting for associates

3.10 Following FRS 9, a reporting entity that prepares **consolidated financial statements** should include its associates in those statements using the **equity method in all the primary statements**. In the investor's **individual financial statements**, its interests in associates should be treated as **fixed asset investments** and shown either **at cost less any amounts written off or at valuation**.

3.11 The equity method is discussed here in more detail with regard to each of the primary statements.

Consolidated profit and loss account

3.12 FRS 9 stipulates the following.

(a) The investor's **share of its associates' operating results** should be included **immediately after group operating result** (but after the investor's share of the results of its joint ventures, if any).

(b) Any **amortisation** or write-down of **goodwill** arising on acquiring the associates should be **charged at this point** and disclosed.

(c) The **investor's share of any exceptional items** included after operating profit (paragraph 20 of FRS 3) or of interest should be **shown separately** from the amounts for the group.

(d) **At and below the level of profit before tax**, the investor's share of the relevant amounts for associates should be **included within the amounts for the group**, although for items below this level, such as taxation, the amounts relating to associates should be disclosed.

(e) Where it is helpful to give an indication of the size of the business as a whole, a **total** combining the investor's share of its **associates' turnover with group turnover** may be shown as a **memorandum item** in the profit and loss account but the investor's share of its associates' turnover should be clearly distinguished from group turnover.

BPP PUBLISHING

(f) Similarly, the **segmental analysis of turnover and operating profit** (if given) should clearly **distinguish** between that of the **group** and that of **associates**.

Consolidated balance sheet

3.13 FRS 9 requires the following.

(a) The investor's **consolidated balance sheet** should include as a **fixed asset investment the investor's share of the net assets of its associates** shown as a separate item.

(b) **Goodwill** arising on the investor's acquisition of its associates, less any amortisation or write-down, should be **included in the carrying amount for the associates but should be disclosed separately**.

Consolidated cash flow statement

3.14 Cash flow statements are covered in Chapter 24. FRS 9 amends the revised version of FRS 1 to reflect the following.

(a) The consolidated cash flow statement should include **dividends received from associates as a separate item** between operating activities and returns on investments and servicing of finance.

(b) Any other cash flows between the investor and its associates should be included under the appropriate cash flow heading for the activity giving rise to the cash flow. None of the other cash flows of the associates should be included.

Consolidated statement of total recognised gains and losses

3.15 The statement of total recognised gains and losses is discussed in Chapter 10 which deals with FRS 3. FRS 9 requires the **investor's share of the total recognised gains and losses of its associates to be included**. If the amounts included are material they should be shown separately under each heading, either in the statement or in a note that is referred to in the statement.

3.16 EXAMPLE: ASSOCIATED COMPANY IN INVESTOR'S OWN ACCOUNTS

H Ltd, a company with subsidiaries, acquires 25,000 of the 100,000 £1 ordinary shares in A Ltd for £60,000 on 1 January 19X0. A Ltd meets the FRS 9 definitions of an associate. In the year to 31 December 19X0, A Ltd earns profits after tax of £24,000, from which it declares a dividend of £6,000.

How will A Ltd's results be accounted for in the individual and consolidated accounts of H Ltd for the year ended 31 December 19X0?

3.17 SOLUTION

In the individual accounts of H Ltd, the investment will be recorded on 1 January 19X0 at cost. Unless there is a permanent diminution in the value of the investment, this amount will remain in the individual balance sheet of H Ltd permanently. The only entry in H Ltd's individual profit and loss account will be to record dividends received. For the year ended 31 December 19X0, H Ltd will:

DEBIT	Cash	£1,500	
CREDIT	Income from shares in associated companies		£1,500

Consolidated profit and loss account

3.18 A consolidation schedule may be used to prepare the consolidated profit and loss account of a group with associates. The treatment of the associate's profits in the following example should be studied carefully.

3.19 EXAMPLE: ASSOCIATE COMPANY IN CONSOLIDATED ACCOUNTS

The following consolidation schedule relates to the H Ltd group, consisting of the holding company, an 80% owned subsidiary (S Ltd) and an associate (A Ltd) in which the group has a 30% interest.

CONSOLIDATION SCHEDULE

	Group	*H Ltd*	*S Ltd*		*A Ltd*
	£'000	£'000	£'000		£'000
Turnover	1,400	600	800		300
Cost of sales	770	370	400		120
Gross profit	630	230	400		180
Distribution costs and administrative expenses (including depreciation, directors' emoluments etc)	290	110	180		80
Group operating profit	340	120	220		100
Share of operating profit in associate	30	-	-	30%	30
	370	120	220		30
Interest receivable (group)	30	30	-		-
	400	150	220		30
Interest payable (group)	(20)	-	(20)		-
Profit on ordinary activities before tax	380	150	200		30
Taxation					
H Ltd	(150)	(60)	(90)		
Associate	(12)	-	-		(12)
Profit after taxation	218	90	110		18
Minority interest	(22)		(22)		
	196	90	88		18
Inter-company dividends	-	20	(18)		(2)
Group profit	196	110	70		16
Dividends paid and proposed	(45)	(45)	-		-
Retained profits for the financial year	151	65	70		16
Retained profits brought forward	45	30	10		5
Retained profits carried forward	196	95	80		21

Notes

(a) **Group turnover, group gross profit and costs** such as depreciation etc **exclude** the turnover, gross profit and costs etc of **associates**.

(b) The **group share** of the associate's **operating profit is credited** to the group profit and loss account (here, 30% of £100,000 = £30,000). If the associated company has been acquired during the year, it would be necessary to deduct the pre-acquisition profits.

(c) **Taxation** consists of:

    (i) taxation on the **holding company** and subsidiaries in total;

    (ii) only the **group's share of the tax charge of the associated company**; A Ltd tax would be £40,000, so that the group share is £40,000 × 30% = £12,000.

(d) The **minority interest** will **only** ever apply to **subsidiary companies**.

(e) **Inter-company dividends** from subsidiaries and associated companies should **all be recorded**.

BPP
PUBLISHING

(f) **Dividends** paid and proposed relate to the **holding company only**.

Pro-forma consolidated profit and loss account

3.20 The following is a **suggested layout** (using the figures given in the illustration above) for a profit and loss account for a company having subsidiaries as well as associates. It follows the FRS 9 example given in Section 2 of this chapter.

	£'000	£'000
Turnover		1,400
Cost of sales		770
Gross profit		630
Distribution costs and administrative expenses		290
Group operating profit		340
Share of operating profit in associate		30
		370
Interest and similar income receivable (group)		30
		400
Interest payable and similar charges (group)		(20)
Profit on ordinary activities before tax		380
Tax on profit on ordinary activities★		162
Profit after taxation		218
Minority interest (in the current year post tax profits of subsidiary)		(22)
Profit for the financial year attributable to the group		196
Dividends (of the holding company)		
Paid	20	
Proposed	25	
		45
		151
Earnings per share		Xp
Retained profits for the year		£'000
Holding company		66
Subsidiary		70
Associated company		15
		151
★Tax relates to the following:		
Parent and subsidiaries	150	
Associate	12	

Consolidated balance sheet

3.21 As explained earlier, the consolidated balance sheet will contain an **asset 'Investment in associates'**. FRS 9 requires the investment in associated companies to be measured and analysed as:

(a) Group share of associate's net assets

(b) Goodwill arising on acquisition of associate less any amortisation or write down is included in (a) but disclosed separately

3.22 EXAMPLE: CONSOLIDATED BALANCE SHEET

On 1 January 19X6 the net tangible assets of A Ltd amount to £220,000, financed by 100,000 £1 ordinary shares and revenue reserves of £120,000. H Ltd, a company with subsidiaries, acquires 30,000 of the shares in A Ltd for £75,000. During the year ended 31

December 19X6 A Ltd's profit after tax is £30,000, from which dividends of £12,000 are paid.

Show how H Ltd's investment in A Ltd would appear in the consolidated balance sheet at 31 December 19X6.

3.23 SOLUTION

CONSOLIDATED BALANCE SHEET
AS AT 31 DECEMBER 19X6 (extract)

	£
Fixed assets	
Investment in associate	
Share of net assets	71,400
Unamortised goodwill	9,000
	80,400

3.24 An important point to note is that this figure of £80,400 can be arrived at in a completely different way. It is the sum of:

(a) the group's share of A Ltd's net assets at 31 December 19X6; and

(b) the premium paid over net book value for the shares acquired.

3.25 This is calculated as follows.

	£	£
(a) A Ltd's net assets at 31 December 19X6		
Net assets at 1 January 19X6	220,000	
Retained profit for year	18,000	
Net assets at 31 December 19X6	238,000	
Group share (30%)		71,400
(b) Premium on acquisition		
Net assets acquired by group on 1 Jan 19X6		
(30% × £220,000)	66,000	
Price paid for shares	75,000	
Premium on acquisition		9,000
Investment in associate per balance sheet		80,400

3.26 Fair values should be attributed to the associate's underlying assets and liabilities. These will provide the basis for subsequent depreciation. Both the consideration paid in the acquisition and the goodwill arising should be calculated in the same way as on the acquisition of a subsidiary. The associate's assets should not include any goodwill earned in the balance sheet of the associate.

3.27 The goodwill should be treated in accordance with the provisions of FRS 10 *Goodwill and intangible assets*. The usual treatment would therefore be to capitalise and amortise. (Our example assumes for simplicity that the goodwill has an indefinite life and there is no amortisation.)

Question 1

How should a holding company treat the following items in the financial statements for an associated company, when preparing group accounts:

(a) turnover;

(b) inter-company profits;

(c) goodwill?

Answer

(a) The holding company should not aggregate the turnover of an associated company with its own turnover.

(b) Wherever the effect is material, adjustments similar to those adopted for the purpose of presenting consolidated financial statements should be made to exclude from the investing group's consolidated financial statements such items as unrealised profits on stocks transferred to or from associated companies.

(c) The investing group's balance sheet should disclose 'interest in associated companies'. The amount disclosed under this heading should include both the investing group's share of any goodwill in the associated companies' own financial statements and any premium paid on acquisition of the interests in the associated companies in so far as it has not already been written off or amortised.

Minority interests

3.28 FRS 9 dose not specifically address the situation where an investment in an associate is held by a subsidiary. However, the FRS does stipulate that in calculating the amounts to be included in the consolidated financial statements the same principles should be applied as are applied in the consolidation of subsidiaries. This implies that the **group accounts should include the 'gross' share of net assets, operating profit, interest payable and receivable (if any) and tax, accounting for the minority interest separately.** For example, we will suppose that H Ltd owns 60% of S Ltd which owns 25% of A Ltd, an associate of H Ltd. The relevant amounts for inclusion in the consolidated financial statements would be as follows.

CONSOLIDATED PROFIT AND LOSS ACCOUNT
Operating profit (H 100% + S 100%)
Share of operating profit of associate (A 25%)
Interest receivable (group) (H 100% + S 100% + A 25%)
Interest payable (H 100% + S 100% + A 25%)
Exceptional items (H 100% + S 100% + A 25%)
Tax (H 100% + S 100% + A 25%)
Minority interest (S 40% + A 10%)
Retained profits (H 100% + S 60% + A 15%)

CONSOLIDATED BALANCE SHEET
Investment in associated company (figures based on 25% holding)
Minority interest ((40% × shareholders' funds of S) + (10% × post-acquisition reserves of A))
Group profit and loss account ((100% × H) + (60% × post-acquisition of S) + (15% × post-acquisition reserves of A)

4 JOINT VENTURES AND JOINT ARRANGEMENTS

Joint ventures

4.1 Joint ventures are another form of entity which, while not giving the investor control as with a subsidiary, gives it considerable influence.

4.2 There are three important definitions here.

KEY TERMS

*   **Joint venture**: an entity in which the reporting entity holds an interest on a long-term basis and is **jointly controlled** by the reporting entity and one or more other venturers under a contractual arrangement.

*   **Joint control**: a reporting entity jointly controls a venture with one or more other entities if none of the entities alone can control that entity but all together can do so and decisions on financial and operating policy essential to the activities, economic performance and financial position of that venture require each venturer's consent.

(FRS 9)

4.3 Joint control is exercised by the venturers for their **mutual benefit**, each conducting its part of the contractual arrangement with a view to its own advantage. It is possible within the definition for one venturer to manage the joint venture, provided that the venture's principal operating and financial policies are collectively agreed by the venturers and the venturers have the power to ensure that those policies are followed.

4.4 High-level strategic decisions require the consent of each venturer. In effect, each venturer has a veto on such decisions.

Question 2

How is this situation different from that of a minority shareholder in a company? (Think back to your law studies.)

Answer

A minority shareholder has no veto and is subject to majority rule: *Foss v Harbottle 1843*, except in very limited circumstances.

FRS 9 treatment

4.5 FRS 9 emphasises the special nature of joint control by identifying joint ventures as a **single class of investments wholly separate from associates** to be included by a special method of accounting - the **gross equity method**.

KEY TERM

Gross equity method: a form of equity method under which the investor's share of the aggregate gross assets and liabilities underlying the net amount included for the investment is shown on the face of the balance sheet and, in the profit and loss account, the investor's share of the investee's turnover is noted.

(FRS 9)

4.6 The gross equity method is like the equity method except with regard to the following.

(a) In the **consolidated profit and loss** account the investor's share of **joint ventures' turnover** is shown, but not as part of group turnover. For example:

	£m	£m
Turnover: group and share of joint ventures	560	
Less: share of joint ventures' turnover	130	
Group turnover		430

(b) In the segmental analysis the investor's share of its joint ventures' turnover should also be distinguished from the turnover of the group.

(c) In the **consolidated balance sheet, the investor's share of the gross assets and liabilities** underlying the net equity amount included for joint ventures should be shown in amplification of that amount. For example:

	£m	£m	£m
Fixed assets			
Tangible assets			700
Investments			
Investments in joint ventures:			
Share of gross assets	250		
Share of gross liabilities	(120)		
		130	
Investment in associates		80	
			910

(d) In both the profit and loss account and the balance sheet any supplemental information given for joint ventures must be shown clearly separate from amounts for the group and must not be included in the group totals. An exception is made for items below profit before tax in the profit and loss account.

4.7 In the investor's individual financial statements, investments in joint ventures should be treated as fixed asset investments and shown at cost, less any amounts written off, or at valuation.

Further aspects of FRS 9 applying to both joint ventures and associates

Principles of consolidation

4.8 As has been mentioned, when calculating the amounts to be included in the investor's consolidated financial statements, whether using the equity method for associates or the gross equity method for joint ventures, the **same principles should be applied as are applied in the consolidation of subsidiaries**. This has the following implications.

(a) **Fair values** are to be attributed to assets and liabilities on acquisition. Goodwill should be treated as per FRS 10. This point was dealt with in connection with associates in Paragraphs 3.27 and 3.28. The same applies to joint ventures.

(b) In arriving at the amounts to be included by the equity method, the same **accounting policies** as those of the investor should be applied.

(c) The financial statements of the investor and the associate or joint venture should be prepared to the **same accounting date** and for the **same accounting period**; associates/joint ventures can prepare three months before if necessary with appropriate adjustments and disclosure.

(d) Profits or losses resulting from **transactions between the investor and its associate/joint venture** may be included in the carrying amount of assets in either party. Where this is the case, the part relating to the **investor's share should be eliminated**. Any impairment of those or similar assets must be taken into account if evidence of it is given by the transactions in question.

Investor is a group

4.9 Where the investor is a group, it share of its associate or joint venture is the aggregate of the holdings of the parent and its subsidiaries in that entity. The holdings of any of the group's

other associates or joint ventures should be ignored for this purpose. Where an associate or joint venture itself has subsidiaries, associates or joint ventures, the results and net assets to be taken into account by the equity method are those reported in that investee's consolidated financial statements (including the investee's share of the results and net assets of its associates and joint ventures), after any adjustment necessary to give effect to the investor's accounting policies.

Options, convertibles and non-equity shares

4.10   The investor may hold options, convertibles or non-equity shares in its associate or joint venture. In certain circumstances, the conditions attaching to such holdings are such that the investor should take them into account in reflecting its interest in its investee under the equity or gross equity method. In such cases, the costs of exercising the options or converting the convertibles, or future payments in relation to the non-equity shares, should also be taken into account.

Impairment

4.11   In cases where there is impairment in any goodwill attributable to an associate or joint venture the **goodwill should be written down** and the amount written off in the accounting period separately disclosed.

Commencement and cessation of relationship

4.12   The following points apply with regard to commencement or cessation of an associate or joint venture relationship.

   (a)   An investment **becomes an associate** on the date on which the investor begins:

   (i)   to hold a **participating interest**;
   (ii)   to exercise **significant influence**.

   (b)   An investment **ceases to be an associate** on the date when it **ceases to fulfil** either of the above.

   (c)   An investment **becomes a joint venture** on the date on which the investor begins to **control it jointly** with other investors, provided it has a long-term interest.

   (d)   On the date when an investor **ceases to have joint control**, the investment **ceases to be a joint venture**.

   (e)   The **carrying amount** (percentage of investment retained) should be reviewed and, if necessary, written down to the **recoverable amount**.

Joint arrangements that are not entities

4.13   A reporting entity may operate through a structure that has the appearance of a joint venture but not the reality. It may thus be a separate entity in which the participants hold a long-term interest and exercise joint management, but there may be no common interest because each venturer operates independently of the other venturers within that structure. The framework entity acts merely as an agent for the ventures with each venturer able to identify and control its share of the assets, liabilities and cash flows arising within the entity. **Such arrangements have the form but not the substance of a joint venture.**

BPP PUBLISHING

> The accounting treatment for such joint arrangements required by FRS 9 is that **each venturer should account directly for its share of the assets, liabilities and cash flows held within that structure.** This treatment reflects the substance rather than the form of the arrangement.

Investors that do not prepare consolidated accounts

4.14 A reporting entity may have an associate or joint venture, but no subsidiaries. It will thus not prepare group accounts. In such cases it should present the relevant amounts for associates and joint ventures, as appropriate, by preparing a **separate set of financial statements** or by showing the relevant amounts, together with the effects of including them, as additional information to its own financial statements. Investing entities that are exempt from preparing consolidated financial statements, or would be exempt if they had subsidiaries, are exempt from this requirement.

Question 3

Ross plc is a long established business in office supplies. The nature of its business has expanded and diversified to take account of technological changes which have taken place in recent years. Now in addition to stationery and office furniture, it also supplies photocopiers, fax machines and more recently new computer based technologies. The expansion has occurred organically but also through acquisition of existing companies and joint ventures. Ross plc's investments are as follows.

(a) *Joey Ltd.* Ross has a 40% interest in the issued share capital of Joey Ltd and representation on the board. Joey Ltd manufactures office furniture and a large proportion of what it produces is sold to Ross. Ross is therefore actively involved in decisions regarding product ranges, designs and pricing to ensure they get the products they want.

(b) *Rachel NRG.* Rachel NRG is a joint venture company which commenced operations on 1 June 19X7. The joint venturers in Rachel are Ross plc and Monica Inc, a company also in office automation, specialising in computer products. The purpose of the joint venture was to distribute their products to Asia Pacific where the demand for office automation is growing rapidly. Ross and Monica have an equal interest in Rachel.

(c) *Phoebe Ltd.* Phoebe Ltd's principal activities is the supply and fitting of bathroom suites. Its managing director is Mrs Janice Chandler, wife of Mr Paul Chandler, a director of Ross plc. Ross plc has a 25% interest in the share capital of Phoebe and the remaining shares are held by various members of the Chandler family. Mr Chandler is on the board of Phoebe as a non-executive director and this was approved at the last AGM by all the voting members of the Chandler family. The activities of Phoebe and Ross are in totally different markets, the share interest is there for historic reasons and Ross has not exercised its voting rights for several years. During the year Ross plc sold one of the company's executive cars to Phoebe Ltd for an agreed open market value of £30,000.

The following are extracts from the financial statements of Joey, Rachel and Phoebe for the year ended 31 March 19X8.

	Joey £'000	Rachel £'000	Phoebe £'000
Turnover	4,068	17,720	7,640
Operating costs	3,872	16,834	6,980
Operating profit	196	886	660
Interest payable	-	280	30
Profit before tax	196	606	630
Tax	40	152	200
Profit after tax	156	454	430
Fixed assets	360	1,720	260
Current assets	2,940	2,130	834
Creditors falling due within one year	(2,214)	(710)	(252)
Creditors falling due after one year	(26)	(1,810)	(400)
	1,060	1,330	442
Cost of investment	600	500	400

Sales of office furniture from Joey to Ross amounted to £160,000 during the year. 10% of the goods remain in the closing stock of Ross. These goods had been sold at a mark up of 25% on cost.

Required

Produce extracts from the consolidated profit and loss account and balance sheet of Ross for the year ended 31 March 19X8 indicating clearly the treatments for Joey, Rachel and Phoebe and where each item would appear.

Answer

EXTRACTS FROM THE CONSOLIDATED PROFIT AND LOSS ACCOUNT
FOR THE YEAR ENDED 31 MARCH 19X8

	£'000	£'000
Turnover	X	
Less share of joint ventures' turnover	(8,860)	
Group turnover		X
Group operating profit		X
Share of operating profit in		
Joint ventures	443	
Associates (W1)	77.2	
Interest payable		
Group	X	
Joint ventures	(140)	
Profit before tax		X
Tax (see below)		X
Profit after tax		X
Tax relates to		
Parent and subsidiary		X
Joint ventures		76
Associates		16

EXTRACTS FROM THE CONSOLIDATED BALANCE SHEET AS AT 31 MARCH 19X8

	£'000	£'000
Fixed assets		
Investments		
Investments in joint ventures		
Share of gross assets	1,925	
Share of gross liabilities	1,260	
		665.0
Investments in associates (W2)		422.8
Other investments		400.0

Workings

1   *Share of associate company profit*

	£'000
Profit of Joey per question	196.0
Less PUP (160,000 × 10% × $^{25}/_{125}$)	3.2
	192.8
Group share (40%) (rounded)	77.2

2   *Investment in associates*

	£'000
Net assets per question	1,060.0
Less PUP (W1)	(3.2)
	1,056.8
Group share (40%) (rounded)	422.8

5   DISCLOSURES FOR ASSOCIATES AND JOINT VENTURES

5.1   The disclosures required by FRS 9 are extensive. Some are required for all associates and joint ventures and other additional disclosures are required if certain thresholds are exceeded. These disclosures are to be made in addition to the amounts required on the face of the financial statements under the equity method or the gross equity method.

> **Exam focus point**
>
> If you are in a hurry or revising, go to the summary in Paragraph 5.10.

All associates and joint ventures

5.2   The financial statements of the investing group must show the **names** of the main associates and joint ventures. For each associate and joint venture the following must be shown.

   (a)   The **proportion of the issued shares** in each class held by the investing group, indicating any special rights or constraints attaching to them

   (b)   The **accounting period or date** of the financial statements used if they differ from those of the investing group

   (c)   An indication of the **nature of its business**

5.3   There may be notes relating to the financial statements of associates or joint ventures that are material to understanding the effect on the investor of its investments. There may also be matters that should have been noted had the investor's accounting policies been applied that are similarly material to understanding. Such matters should be disclosed, in particular noting the investor's share in contingent liabilities incurred jointly with other venturers or investors and its share of the capital commitments of the associates and joint ventures themselves.

5.4   The extent must be indicated of any **significant statutory, contractual or exchange control restrictions on the ability of an associate or joint venture to distribute its reserves.** (This does not apply to non-distributable reserves.)

5.5   The **amounts owing and owed between an investor and its associates or joint ventures** should be analysed between loans and trading balances. These disclosures may be combined with those in FRS 8 *Related party disclosures*.

5.6   As explained earlier, there is a presumption that an investor holding **20% or more of the shares** of another entity has a **participating interest** and that an investor holding **20% or more of the voting rights** of another entity **exercises significant influence** over the operating and financial policies of that entity. The facts of any particular case may **rebut** this presumption, but if so a **note should explain why**.

Additional disclosures at 15% and 25% thresholds

15% threshold

5.7   If the investor's aggregate share of its associate's gross assets, gross liabilities, turnover or (on an three-year average) operating results exceeds 15% of the corresponding group figure

(excluding the share of associates), an additional note needs to be given to disclose the investor's share in the following.

- Turnover (unless already included as a memorandum item)
- Fixed assets
- Current assets
- Liabilities due within one year
- Liabilities due after one year or more

5.8 If the investor's share in its joint ventures' gross assets, gross liabilities, turnover or three year average operating results exceeds 15% of any of the investing group, the investor's aggregate share of each of the following should be shown.

- Fixed assets
- Current assets
- Liabilities due within one year
- Liabilities due after one year or more

25% threshold

5.9 If the investor's share in any individual associate or joint venture exceeds 25% of the corresponding group figure (excluding the share of associates), the **name** of the associate needs to be noted and a further note should disclose the investor's share in the following items for that associate.

- Turnover
- Profit before tax
- Taxation
- Profit after tax
- Fixed assets
- Current assets
- Liabilities due within one year
- Liabilities due after one year or more

5.10 These disclosures are quite tricky to remember. The table below may help.

FRS 9: Summary of disclosure requirements

All associates and joint ventures	15% threshold*	25% threshold*
• Names of principal associates/joint venture	• Turnover (associates only)	• Turnover
• Proportion of shares held	• Fixed assets	• Profit before tax
• Accounting date if different	• Current assets	• Taxation
• Nature of business	• Liabilities due within one year	• Profit after tax
• Material differences in accounting policies	• Liabilities due after one year or more	• Fixed assets
• Restrictions on distributions		• Current assets
• Intercompany balances		• Liabilities due within one year
• Reason for rebutting 20% presumption of participating interest/ significant influence		• Liabilities due after one year or more

*Threshold refers to investor's aggregate share of gross assets, gross liabilities, turnover or three year average operating result of investee as compared with the corresponding group figure.

Exam focus point

Look back to the summary and example in Section 2 of this chapter. Then try the following question.

Question 4

Comic plc, the holding company of the Comic Group, acquired 25% of the ordinary shares of Strip plc on 1 September 19X0 for £54 million. Strip plc carried on business as a property investment company. The draft accounts as at 31 August 19X1 are as follows.

PROFIT AND LOSS ACCOUNTS FOR THE YEAR ENDED 31 AUGUST 19X1

	Comic Group £m	Strip plc £m
Sales	175.0	200
Profit before interest and tax	90.0	80
Exceptional profit on sale of property	20.0	-
Interest	(2.0)	(20)
	108.0	60
Taxation	(23.2)	(20)
	84.8	40
Proposed dividends	(61.0)	-
	23.8	40

BALANCE SHEETS AS AT 31 AUGUST 19X1

	Comic Group	*Strip plc*
	£m	*£m*
Fixed assets		
Tangible fixed assets	135	200
Investment in Strip plc	54	-
Current assets		
Stock	72	210
Debtors	105	50
Current liabilities		
Creditors	(95)	(20)
Overdraft	(14)	(100)
Net current assets	68	140
	257	340
Capital and reserves		
Ordinary shares of £1 each	135	50
Reserves	122	90
10% loan	-	200
	257	340

On 1 September 19X0 Comic plc sold a property with a book value of £40 million to Strip plc at its market value of £60 million. The tax suffered on this gain was £7 million. Strip plc obtained the funds to pay the £60 million by raising a loan which is included in the 10% loan that appears in its balance sheet at 31 August 19X1.

Premiums on acquisition are amortised over 5 years.

Required

Prepare:

(a) the consolidated profit and loss account of the Comic Group for the year ended 31 August 19X1 and a consolidated balance sheet as at that date; and

(b) relevant notes to comply with the requirements of FRS 9 *Associates and joint ventures*.

Answer

(a) COMIC GROUP
CONSOLIDATED PROFIT AND LOSS ACCOUNT
FOR THE YEAR ENDED 31 AUGUST 19X1

	£m	£m
Group turnover		175.00
Group operating profit (90 – 5.8)		84.20
Share of operating profit in associate		20.00
		104.20
Profit on sales of property		15.00
Interest payable		
Group	2	
Associate	5	
		(7.00)
		112.20
Taxation		
Group	21.45	
Associate	5.00	
		(26.45)
		85.75
Dividends		(61.00)
Retained profit for the year		24.75

COMIC GROUP
CONSOLIDATED BALANCE SHEET
AS AT 31 AUGUST 19X1

	Notes	£m	£m
Fixed assets			
Tangible assets			135.00
Interest in associated company	2, 5		54.95
			189.95
Current assets			
Stock		72	
Debtors		105	
		177	
Current liabilities			
Creditors		95	
Bank overdraft		14	
		109	
Net current assets			68.00
			257.95
Capital and reserves			
Ordinary shares £1 each			135.00
Reserves	4		122.95
			257.95

(b) NOTES TO THE ACCOUNTS

1   *Retained profit*

	£m
Retained by Comic and its subsidiaries	14.75
Retained by Strip plc	10.00
	24.75

2   *Interest in associate*

	£m
Group's share of net assets (25% × (340 − 200))	35.00
Less unrealised profit (25% × 13)	(3.25)
Unamortised goodwill (29 − 5.8)	23.20
	54.95

Additional disclosures for associates

The group has one associate, Strip plc, in which the group's share exceeds 25 per cent with respect to the group.

	£m	£m
Share of turnover of associate		50
Share of assets		
Share of fixed assets (W5)		45
Share of current assets		65
		110
Share of liabilities		
Liabilities due within one year or less (W6)	(28.25)	
Liabilities due after more than one year	(50.00)	
		(78.25)
		31.75

Workings

1   *Premium on acquisition*

	£m
Share capital	50
Reserves at date of acquisition (90 − 40)	50
	100

		£m
Group share (25%)		25
Cost		54
Premium on acquisition		29
Amortisation (29,000 ÷ 5)		5.8

2   *Reserves*

	£m
Comic reserves per question	122.00
Less: amortisation	(5.80)
Group share of post acquisition reserves of Strip	
(40 × 25%)	10.00
	126.20
	(3.25)
	122.95

3   *Working: exceptional profit*

	£m
Profit per Comic's profit and loss account	20
Less unrealised profit	
(25% × 20)	(5)
	15

4   *Group tax charge*

	£m
Comic per question	23.20
Less tax on unrealised element of exceptional profit	
(7 × 25%)	(1.75)
	21.45

5   *Share of Strip's fixed assets*

		£m
Strip fixed assets per question		200
Unrealised profit		(20)
		180
	× 25%	45

6   *Share of Strip's liabilities within one year*

		£m
Strip liabilities per question		120
Tax element of unrealised profit		(7)
		113
	× 25%	28.25

Chapter roundup

- **Associates** and **joint ventures** are entities in which an investor holds a **substantial but not controlling interest**.

- They are the subject of an accounting standard: **FRS 9** *Associates and joint ventures.*

- **Associates** are to be included in the investor's consolidated financial statements using the **equity method**.

  o The investor's share of its associates' results should be included immediately after group operating profit.

  o The investor's share of its associates' turnover may be shown as a memorandum item.

- **Joint ventures** are to be included in the venturer's consolidated financial statements by the **gross equity method**.

  o This requires, in addition to the amounts included under the equity method, disclosure of the venturer's share of its joint ventures' turnover, gross assets and gross liabilities.

- Other **joint arrangements**, such as cost-sharing arrangements and one-off construction projects, are to be included in their participants' individual and consolidated financial statements by **each participant including directly** its share of the assets, liabilities and cash flows arising from the arrangements.

Quick quiz

1 What types of interest does FRS 9 identify? (2.6)

2 How does FRS 9 define associate? (3.2)

3 What is meant by 'participating interest'? (3.3)

4 What is meant by 'exercise of significant influence'? (3.7)

5 How should associates be treated in the consolidated profit and loss account? (3.12)

6 What is the correct treatment in situations where the investment in an associate is held by a subsidiary? (3.28)

7 What is a joint venture? (4.2)

8 What is the 'gross equity method'? (4.5)

9 What treatment does FRS 9 prescribe for joint arrangements that are not entities? (4.13)

10 What disclosures are required when the '25% threshold' is exceeded? (5.9)

Question to try	Level	Marks	Time
18	Exam	20	36 mins

Chapter 18

OTHER CHANGES IN THE COMPOSITION OF A GROUP

Chapter topic	Syllabus reference	Ability required
1 Piecemeal acquisitions	9(a)	Application
2 Bonus issues and capital reductions	9(a)	Application
3 Disposals	9(a)	Application
4 Changes in direct ownership	9(a)	Application
5 Demergers	9(a)	Application
6 FRS 3 *Reporting financial performance*	9(a)	Application

Introduction

You should refer back to Chapter 2 when you reach Section 6 of this chapter to remind yourself of the provisions of FRS 3. Here, we consider the effect of disposals on the profit and loss account.

Complex consolidation issues are very likely to come up in this, the final stage of your studies on financial accounting. Your approach should be the same as for more simple consolidation questions: **methodical and logical**.

Remember that all the undertakings are limited companies unless stated otherwise.

1   PIECEMEAL ACQUISITIONS   11/95

1.1   A holding company may acquire a controlling interest in the shares of a subsidiary as a result of **several successive share purchases**, rather than by purchasing the shares all on the same day. For the purpose of consolidation, it is necessary to decide which reserves of the subsidiary are pre-acquisition profits; but since the acquisition has occurred in several stages, it is not immediately clear how to decide what they are.

1.2   If a controlling interest is achieved by means of a build-up of share acquisitions over a period of time, so that the present reserves include elements which are **pre-acquisition** as regards some blocks of shares held, but **post-acquisition** as regards other blocks of shares, the problem faced in deciding how much of the present reserves belongs to the goodwill calculation is really one of **interpretation**.

The basic question is: **What is meant by pre-acquisition?** Acquisition of what? Acquisition of shares or acquisition of control?

1.3   The general rule is that the pre-acquisition and post-acquisition reserves and profits should be established at each purchase of shares, if it can be assumed that each purchase is substantial and there is an objective of **gaining ultimate control**. When these assumptions

are not present, the pre- and post-acquisition profits should only be established when control has been gained.

1.4 The significance of the assumption made lies in the different procedures adopted for consolidation when the partly-bought company eventually **becomes a subsidiary**. The exercise involves looking back at previous share purchases to decide on how to consolidate now that a subsidiary status (controlling interest) has been achieved.

1.5 EXAMPLE: PIECEMEAL ACQUISITION

Suppose that X Ltd bought 20,000 ordinary £1 shares in Y Ltd in 19X1 when the reserves of Y Ltd stood at £27,000 and a further 20,000 shares in 19X2 when the reserves of Y Ltd were £42,000. Finally, a purchase of 30,000 shares in 19X3 when the reserves of Y Ltd were £60,000 gave X Ltd a controlling interest over the 100,000 shares of Y Ltd. The cost of the shares purchased was £30,000 in 19X1, £34,000 in 19X2 and £56,000 for the final 30,000 shares in 19X3.

What are the pre-acquisition and post-acquisition profits of the group in Y Ltd, and what is the goodwill arising on consolidation at the date of the final acquisition in 19X3? Assume that no dividends were paid in these three years.

1.6 SOLUTION: INTENTION TO ACQUIRE CONTROL

Purchase	*% of shares in Y Ltd bought*	*% of shares in Y Ltd now held*
19X1	20%	20%
19X2	20%	40%
19X3	30%	70% (controlling interest)

Each block of shares purchased is regarded as substantial (a subjective judgement).

If we assume that X Ltd intended ultimately to acquire control of Y Ltd, we would use the **step-by-step method**. This method calculates pre-acquisition profits by computing the proportion of reserves attaching to the shares at the time of **each individual purchase**.

		£
19X1	Pre-acquisition profits of 20,000 shares (20% of £27,000)	5,400
19X2	Pre-acquisition profits of next 20,000 shares (20% of £42,000)	8,400
19X3	Pre-acquisition profits of final 30,000 shares (30% of £60,000)	18,000
	Total pre-acquisition profits	31,800

Note that post-acquisition profits would be:

		£
(a)	on shares bought in 19X1:	
	20% of profits since 19X1 = 20% of £(60,000 – 27,000) =	6,600
(b)	on shares bought in 19X2:	
	20% of profits since 19X2 = 20% of £(60,000 – 42,000) =	3,600
	(since no dividends were paid out on profits in this time)	10,200

Reserve working: share of Y Ltd's post acquisition retained reserves = (£60,000 × 70%) – £31,800 = £10,200.

This step-by-step calculation is only required when the company (Y Ltd) becomes a subsidiary in 19X3 and subsequent years.

Goodwill arising on consolidation would be the excess of the cost of the shares bought over their called-up value, less pre-acquisition profits: £(120,000 – 70,000 – 31,800) = £18,200.

1.7 SOLUTION: NO INTENTION TO ACQUIRE CONTROL

If we had made the alternative assumption that X Ltd did not intend to acquire a controlling interest when it bought the shares of Y Ltd in 19X1 and 19X2, but only intended to gain control when it made its final purchase in 19X3, the pre-acquisition profits would be calculated on the basis of reserves at the date of acquisition of control, ie in our example on the basis of reserves of £60,000 at the date of acquisition in 19X3.

Reserve working: share of Y Ltd's pre-acquisition retained reserves = £60,000 × 70% = £42,000.

Goodwill on consolidation would be the excess of the cost of shares over their called-up value, less pre-acquisition profits = £(120,000 – 70,000 – 42,000) = £8,000.

Suggested method

1.8 The decisive factor is whether or not there is an intention, when a minority holding of shares is bought, to **acquire control ultimately**. A rule-of-thumb approach to piecemeal acquisitions might be suggested as follows.

(a) Ignore share purchases which keep the buying company's share of equity **below 20%**: make no step-by-step method calculations before the bought company becomes an associated company. This is on the rough and ready assumption that an intention to obtain control does not exist until associated company status is reached for the partly-bought company.

(b) When the purchase of shares first takes a company's **holding above 20% (and up to 50%)**, treat all the shares purchased up to this date as a single block of purchases for the purpose of calculating pre-acquisition profits.

(c) For **future (significant) purchases** up to the time when control is eventually acquired, the step-by-step method should be applied.

Question 1

A Ltd acquired shares in Z Ltd, which has issued and fully paid share capital of 100,000 £1 ordinary shares, on three separate dates.

Date	Number of shares bought in the purchase	Cost £	Reserves of Z Ltd at date of purchase £
1 February 19X0	10,000	16,000	40,000
1 November 19X0	25,000	42,000	60,000
1 April 19X1	20,000	40,000	80,000

Required

Calculate the pre-acquisition profits of the A group in Z Ltd when Z Ltd eventually became a subsidiary on 1 April 19X1.

Answer

Step	Date	% of shares bought	% of total holding	
1	1 February 19X0	10%	10%	Ignore
2	1 November 19X0	25%	35%	Z Ltd achieves associated company status
3	1 April 19X1	20%	55%	Z Ltd becomes a subsidiary

A step-by-step calculation of pre-acquisition profits, using our assumptions stated earlier, would regard the first step as the purchase of shares which made Z Ltd an associated company: step 2.

	£
Pre-acquisition profits	
35% of reserves at 1 November 19X0 (35% of £60,000)	21,000
Plus 20% of reserves at 1 April 19X1 (20% of £80,000)	16,000
Total pre-acquisition profits	37,000
The minority interest at 1 April 19X1 is 45% of £80,000 =	£36,000
Post-acquisition profits are therefore £(80,000 – 37,000 – 36,000) =	£7,000

Piecemeal acquisition of a sub-subsidiary

1.9 Care may be needed in deciding the group's share of **pre-acquisition profits** when shares in a sub-subsidiary are acquired on several dates.

1.10 EXAMPLE 1: PIECEMEAL ACQUISITION OF A SUB-SUBSIDIARY

Suppose H Ltd buys 60% of the shares of S Ltd on 1 April 19X3 and 20% of the shares of SS Ltd on 1 October 19X3. S Ltd bought 70% of the shares of SS Ltd on 1 January 19X3.

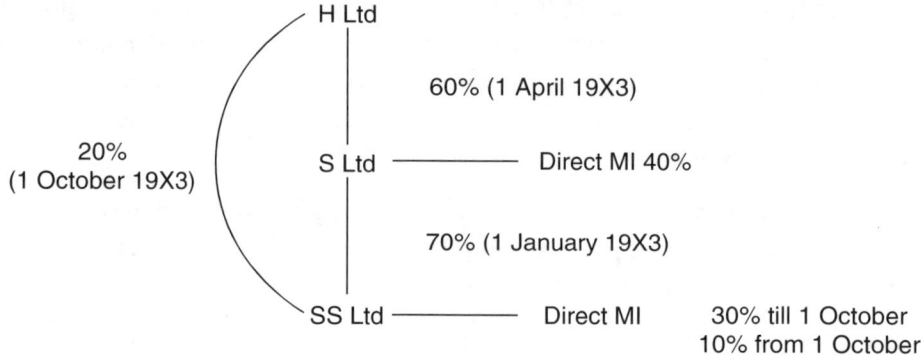

1.11 SOLUTION

Pre-acquisition profits of H Ltd in SS Ltd would be calculated as follows, by the single-stage method of consolidation:

(a) 60% × 70% = 42% of the reserves of SS Ltd at 1 April 19X3 (when the indirect minority is 40% × 70% = 28% and the total minority interest is 58%); *plus*

(b) 20% of the reserves of SS Ltd at 1 October 19X3 when the additional shares are bought.

1.12 EXAMPLE 2: PIECEMEAL ACQUISITION OF A SUB-SUBSIDIARY

Suppose instead that H Ltd buys 80% of the shares of S Ltd on 1 April 19X4 and 30% of the shares of SS Ltd on 1 November 19X4. S Ltd bought 40% of the shares of SS Ltd on 1 January 19X4.

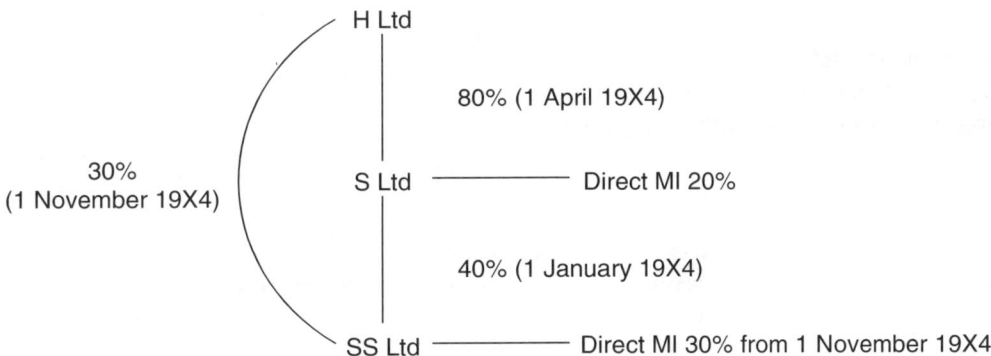

1.13 SOLUTION

In this example, SS Ltd does not come under the control of the group until 1 November 19X4 and an intention by H Ltd to acquire control before 1 November is unlikely (since the original shares were bought by S Ltd before it became a subsidiary of H Ltd). The most appropriate assumption would be to calculate the pre-acquisition reserves in SS Ltd on the basis of reserves at the date of acquiring control, 1 November 19X4, so that the pre-acquisition profits in SS Ltd would be 62% of the reserves at that date.

(The indirect minority interest in SS Ltd is 20% of 40% = 8%. Therefore, the total minority interest is 38% and the group interest is 62%.)

Question 2

Juniper plc made the following share purchases in gaining control of Berry plc.

	Voting rights and
Date	shares acquired
1.4.X2	20%
1.4.X3	25%
1.4.X4	10%

The reserves of Berry plc were as follows.

Date	Reserves plc
	£'000
31.3.X2	300
31.3.X3	1,200
31.3.X4	1,500
31.3.X5	1,800

Berry plc has paid no dividends since 19X2.

Required

(a)   Calculate the post-acquisition reserves for the consolidated accounts as at 31 March 19X5.
(b)   Calculate the pre-acquisition reserves.
(c)   Calculate the minority interest.

Answer

Year ended	% of shares held	Year-end reserves £'000	Post-acquisition £'000	
31.3.X2	-	300	-	
31.3.X3	20%	1,200	180	(20% × 900)
31.3.X3	45%	1,500	135	(45% × 300)
31.3.X5	55%	1,800	165	(55% × 300)
			480	

	£'000
Minority interest 45% × 1,800	810
Post-acquisition reserves, as above	480
Remainder, being pre-acquisition reserves	510
	1,800

Check

Year ended	Year-end reserves £'000	Increase in reserves £'000	Pre-acquisition	Pre-acquisition reserves £'000
31.3.X2	300		55%	165
31.3.X3	1,200	900	35% (55% – 20%)	315
31.3.X4	1,500	300	10% (55% – 45%)	30
Pre-acquisition reserves, as above				510

Note. This 'piecemeal acquisition' method is suitable only where the purchases of shares are made over a period of time with a view to ultimately gaining control.

1.14 Section summary

Where there is a build up of share acquisitions over time:

- What are the **pre-acquisition** profits?
- If the objective is to **gain ultimate control** use the step-by-step method.
- If it is not, use reserves at the **date control is achieved.**
- Use the same principles for piecemeal acquisitions of **sub-subsidiaries**.

2 BONUS ISSUES AND CAPITAL REDUCTIONS

Bonus issues

2.1 A bonus issue is simply a **capitalisation of reserves** and therefore there is no alteration in the percentage holding of any party. When calculating goodwill, it is easiest to ignore the effect of the bonus issue and simply use the reserves and share capital as at acquisition.

Capital reductions

2.2 A capital reduction will involve a **reduction in the nominal value of shares in issue**. In acquisition accounting, we are using calculations which show the net assets acquired (as represented by pre-acquisition reserves and share capital), so any change in the nominal value of the shares at a later date is irrelevant and should be ignored.

3 DISPOSALS   11/97

3.1 A holding company may dispose of a subsidiary in total, or reduce the holding to the level of an associate or an investment.

Effective date of disposal

3.2 FRS 2 defines the effective date of disposal in terms of **when control passes**: 'the date for accounting for an undertaking ceasing to be a subsidiary undertaking is the date on which its former parent undertaking relinquishes its control over that undertaking'. **FRS 3** requires that the results of discontinued operations should be shown separately in the P&L account in the year of disposal (see Section 6 of this chapter and Chapter 2). **FRS 2** states that the consolidated P&L account should include the results of a subsidiary undertaking

up to the date of its disposal. We are not concerned with FRS 3 disclosure in this section, only the FRS 2 calculations.

Goodwill

3.3   When a subsidiary is disposed of, the group needs to deal with any goodwill (positive or negative) which arose when the subsidiary was purchased. If the goodwill was **written off to reserves**, it could by-pass the P&L account, thus causing a misstatement of the profit or loss on disposal.

UITF Abstract 3 *Treatment of goodwill on disposal of a business*

3.4   Consider the following situation. Cod plc purchased Chips plc on 1 January 19X4 for £15m and sold the company for £24m on 1 January 19X7. In between, the Chips plc had earned £6m profit. On acquisition the fair value of its net assets was £10.5m. The goodwill of £4.5m had been written off to reserves. The calculation of the **profit of loss on disposal** can be made in two ways.

	Option A		Option B	
	£m	£m	£m	£m
Sales proceeds		24.0		24.0
Carrying value				
Fair value of assets	10.5		10.5	
Retained profits	6.0		6.0	
		16.5		16.5
		7.5		7.5
Less goodwill previously written off to reserves		-		4.5
Gain on sale reported		7.5		3.0

3.5   It is clear that option B gives the **true picture** of the gain made by the company. UITF Abstract 3 outlawed the practice in option A and this was incorporated into FRS 2. Note that comparative figures should be restated where possible.

3.6   The treatment in option B may not be easy if the subsidiary has been absorbed into the group or restructured. In such cases the goodwill which was acquired is not necessarily being sold as the company is in a different form. However, CA 1985 and SSAP 22 require **records to be kept** on goodwill on acquisition, and so some sort of apportionment should be possible. Where it is not, full disclosure should be made and the reasons given. Note that the gross goodwill figure should be used: there should be no adjustment for notional amortisation.

> ### Exam focus point
> Now that FRS 10 has outlawed immediate write off of goodwill to reserves, this situation will be less common in practice. However, the FRS says that goodwill previously eliminated against reserves may remain thus eliminated until the business is disposed of, so the treatment explained here is still valid.

Disposals and partial disposals

3.7   When only part of an investment is sold, but an **associate or subsidiary status** is retained, then it is necessary to decide how to account for the disposal.

Disposal: subsidiary, status retained

3.8   If the holding is still a subsidiary then it must still be **consolidated line by line**. The consolidated accounts are only adjusted in reserves and in the minority interest. A comparison of the sale proceeds and the consolidated net asset value attributable to the shares sold at the date of disposal will give the profit or loss on disposal.

3.9   EXAMPLE: PARTIAL DISPOSALS

Chalk plc bought 100% of the voting share capital of Cheese plc on 1 January 19X2 for £160,000. Cheese plc earned and retained £240,000 from that date until 31 December 19X7. At that date the balance sheets of the company and the group were as follows.

	Chalk plc £'000	Cheese plc £'000	Consolidated £'000
Investment in Cheese	160	-	-
Other net assets	800	400	1,200
	960	400	1,200
Share capital	400	160	400
Reserves	560	240	800
	960	400	1,200

On 1 January 19X8 Chalk plc sold 40% of its shareholding in Cheese plc for £280,000. The profit on disposal (ignoring tax) is calculated as follows.

	Holding company £'000	Group £'000
Sale proceeds	280	280
40% of investment/net assets	64	160
Gain on sale	216	120

3.10   SOLUTION: SUBSIDIARY STATUS

The balance sheets immediately after the sale will appear as follows.

	Chalk plc £'000	Cheese plc £'000	Consolidated £'000
Investment in Cheese	96	-	-
Other net assets	1,080	400	1,480
	1,176	400	1,480
Minority interest			(160)
			1,320
Share capital	400	160	400
Reserves	776	240	920
	1,176	400	1,320

Disposal: subsidiary to associate status

3.11   The only difference when a subsidiary becomes an associate is that the balance sheet only carries the underlying asset on **one line**. Otherwise, the same principles apply.

3.12   SOLUTION: ASSOCIATE STATUS

Using the above example, assume that Chalk plc sold 60% of its holding in Cheese plc for £440,000. The gain or loss on disposal would be calculated as follows.

	Holding company	Group
	£'000	£'000
Sale proceeds	440	440
60% of investment/net assets	96	240
Profit on sale	344	200

The balance sheets would now appear as follows.

	Chalk plc	Cheese plc	Consolidated
	£'000	£'000	£'000
Investment in Cheese	64	-	160
Other net assets	1,240	400	1,240
	1,304	400	1,400
Share capital	400	160	400
Reserves	904	240	1,000
	1,304	400	1,400

Disposal: subsidiary to investment status

3.13 In these circumstances dividend income only is shown in the P&L account after the date of disposal. The investment should be left in the balance sheet at the **equity valuation at the date of disposal**. Consider whether any write down is required.

Summary of accounting treatment

3.14 Calculate the gain or loss on disposal.

(a) **In holding company**

	£
Sale proceeds	X
Less cost of investment	X
Profit/(loss): (taxable)	X/(X)

(b) **In group accounts**

(i) *Either*:

	£	£
Sale proceeds		X
Less: net assets now disposed of	X	
goodwill not yet w/off through P & L a/c	X	
		X
Profit/(loss)		X/(X)

(ii) *Or*:

	£
Profit/(loss) per holding company	X
Less post-acquisition retained reserves now disposed of	(X)
	X
Add goodwill previously written off through P & L a/c	X
	X

3.15 For a **full disposal**, apply the following treatment.

(a) **P&L account**

(i) Consolidate results to the date of disposal.

(ii) Show the group gain or loss as an exceptional item after operating profit and before interest.

(b) **Balance sheet**

There will be no minority interest and no consolidation as there is no subsidiary at the date the balance sheet is being prepared.

3.16 For **partial disposals,** use the following treatments.

(a) **Subsidiary to subsidiary**

(i) The **minority interest in the P&L account** will be based on percentage before and after disposal, ie time apportion.

(ii) The **minority interest in the balance sheet** is based on the year end percentage.

(b) **Subsidiary to associate**

(i) **P&L account**

(1) Treat the undertaking as a subsidiary up to the date of disposal, ie consolidate for the correct number of months and show the minority interest in that amount.

(2) Treat as an associate thereafter.

(ii) **Balance sheet**: use an equity valuation based on the year end holding.

(c) **Subsidiary to trade investment**

(i) **P&L account**

(1) Treat the undertaking as a subsidiary up to the date of disposal.
(2) Show dividend income only thereafter.

(ii) **Balance sheet**: leave the investment valued at its equity valuation at the date of disposal but consider whether any write-down is required.

3.17 The following comprehensive exercise should help you get to grips with disposal problems. Try to complete the whole exercise without looking at the solution, and then check your answer very carefully. Give yourself at least an hour.

Question 3

Smith Ltd bought 80% of the share capital of Jones Ltd for £324,000 a number of years ago. At that date Jones Ltd's P&L account balance stood at £180,000. The balance sheets at 30 September 19X8 and the summarised P&L accounts to that date are given below.

	Smith Ltd	Jones Ltd
	£'000	£'000
Fixed assets	360	270
Investment in Jones Ltd	324	-
Net current assets	270	270
	954	540
Share capital and reserves		
£1 ordinary shares	540	180
Profit and loss account	414	360
	954	540

	Smith Ltd	Jones Ltd
	£'000	£'000
Profit before tax	153	126
Tax	45	36
Retained profit	108	90
Retained profit b/f	306	270
Retained profit c/f	414	360

No entries have been made in the accounts for any of the following transactions.

Assume that profits accrue evenly throughout the year and that any goodwill has been fully amortised.

Ignore taxation.

Required

Prepare the consolidated balance sheet and P&L account at 30 September 19X8 in each of the following circumstances.

(a)   Smith Ltd sells its entire holding in Jones Ltd for £650,000 on 30 September 19X8.

(b)   Smith Ltd sells its entire holding in Jones Ltd for £650,000 on 30 June 19X8.

(c)   Smith Ltd sells one quarter of its holding in Jones Ltd for £160,000 on 30 June 19X8.

(d)   Smith Ltd sells one half of its holding in Jones Ltd for £340,000 on 30 June 19X8, and the remaining holding is to be dealt with:

> (i)   as an associate;
> (ii)   as a trade investment.

Answer

(a)   *Complete disposal at year end*

CONSOLIDATED BALANCE SHEET
AS AT 30 SEPTEMBER 19X8

	£'000
Fixed assets	360
Net current assets (270 + 650)	920
	1,280
Share capital and reserves	
£1 ordinary shares	540
Profit and loss account (W3)	740
	1,280

CONSOLIDATED PROFIT AND LOSS ACCOUNT
FOR THE YEAR ENDED 30 SEPTEMBER 19X8

	£'000	£'000
Profit before tax (153 + 126)		279
Exceptional item (W1)		218
Tax (45 + 36)		81
		416
Minority interest (20% × 90)		18
Profit attributable to members of Smith Ltd		398
Retained profit brought forward		342
Retained profit carried forward (W3)		740

Workings

1   *Profit on disposal in Jones Ltd*

	£'000
Sales proceeds	650
Cost	324
Profit in Smith Ltd	326
Profit on consolidation	
Per above working	326
Less post acquisition profits now sold	
(360 − 180) × 80%	144
Add goodwill previously amortised (note)	136
	218

Alternative calculation of group profit on disposal

	£'000	£'000
Sales proceeds		650
Less: net assets of Jones now sold (540 × 80%)		432
		218

Note: goodwill	£'000
Cost	324
Acquired 80% × (180 + 180)	288
	36

2   *Retained profit brought forward*

	£'000
Smith	306
Jones: 80% × (270 – 180)	72
Goodwill fully amortised (W1)	(36)
	342

3   *Retained profit carried forward*

	£'000
Smith	414
Profit on disposal (W1)	326
	740

(b)   *Complete disposal mid-year*

CONSOLIDATED BALANCE SHEET
AS AT 30 SEPTEMBER 19X8

	£'000
Fixed assets	360
Net current assets (270 + 650)	920
	1,280
Share capital and reserves	
£1 ordinary shares	540
Profit and loss account (W3)	740
	1,280

CONSOLIDATED PROFIT AND LOSS ACCOUNT
FOR THE YEAR ENDED 31 SEPTEMBER 19X8

	£'000	£'000
Profit before tax (153 + (9/12 × 126))		247.5
Exceptional item (W1)		236.0
Tax (45 + (36 × 9/12))		72.0
Profit after tax		411.5
Minority interest		
(20% × 90 × 9/12)		13.5
Profit attributable to members of Smith Ltd		398.0
Retained profit brought forward (W2)		342.0
		378.0
Retained profit carried forward (W3)		740.0

Workings

1   *Profit on disposal in Smith Ltd*

	£'000
Sale proceeds	650
Cost	324
Profit in Smith Ltd	326

Profit on consolidation	
Per above working	326
Less post-acquisition profits now sold	
80% × (270 + (90 × 9/12) – 180)	126
Add: goodwill previously amortised (note)	36
	236

Alternative calculation of group profit on disposal

	£'000	£'000
Sale proceeds		650
Less: net assets of Jones now sold		
$((540 - 90) + (^9/_{12} \times 90)) \times 80\%$		414
		236

2   *Retained profit brought forward*

	£'000
Smith	306
Jones: $80\% \times (270 - 180)$	72
Goodwill fully amortised	(36)
	342

3   *Retained profit carried forward*

	£'000
Smith	414
Profit on disposal (W1)	326
	740

(c)   *Partial disposal: subsidiary to subsidiary*

CONSOLIDATED BALANCE SHEET AS AT 30 SEPTEMBER 19X8

	£'000
Fixed assets (360 + 270)	630
Net current assets (270 + 160 + 270)	700
	1,330
Share capital and reserves	
£1 ordinary shares	540
Profit and loss account (W3)	574
	1,114
Minority interest (40% × 540)	216
	1,330

CONSOLIDATED PROFIT AND LOSS ACCOUNT
FOR THE YEAR ENDED 30 SEPTEMBER 19X8

	£'000	£'000
Profit before tax (153 +126)		279.0
Exceptional item (W1)		56.5
Tax (45 + 36)		81.0
Profit after tax		254.5
Minority interest		
$20\% \times 90 \times ^9/_{12}$	13.5	
$40\% \times 90 \times ^3/_{12}$	9.0	
		22.5
Profit attributable to members of Smith Ltd		232.0
Retained profit brought forward (W2)		342.0
Retained profit carried forward (W3)		574.0

Workings

1   *Profit on disposal in Smith Ltd*

	£'000
Sale proceeds	160
Cost (324 × 25%)	81
Profit in Smith Ltd	79
Profit on consolidation	
Per above working	79.0
Less post-acquisition profits now sold	
$(270 + (90 \times ^9/_{12}) - 180) \times 20\%$	31.5
Add goodwill previously amortised	9.0
	56.5

Alternative calculation of group profit on disposal

	£'000	£'000
Sale proceeds		160.0
Less: net assets of Jones now sold		
20% × ((540 − 90) + (9/12 × 90))		103.5
		56.5

2 *Retained profit brought forward*

	£'000
Smith	306
Jones: 80% × (270 − 180)	72
Goodwill fully amortised	(36)
	342

3 *Retained profit carried forward*

	£'000
Smith	414
Profit on disposal (W1)	79
Jones 60% × (360 − 180)	108
Goodwill fully amortised	(27)
	574

(d) (i) *Partial disposal: subsidiary to associate*

CONSOLIDATED BALANCE SHEET AS AT 30 SEPTEMBER 19X8

	£'000
Fixed assets	360
Investment in associated undertaking (40% × 540)	216
Net current assets (270 + 340)	610
	1,186
Share capital and reserves	
£1 ordinary shares	540
Profit and loss account (W3)	646
	1,186

CONSOLIDATED PROFIT AND LOSS ACCOUNT
FOR THE YEAR ENDED 30 SEPTEMBER 19X8

	£'000	£'000
Profit before tax*		
(153 + (9/12 × 126)) + (3/12 × 126 × 40%)		260.1
Exceptional item (W1)		133.0
Tax (45 + (9/12 × 36)) + (3/12 × 36 × 40%)		75.6
Profit after tax		317.5
Minority interest (20% × 90 × 9/12)		13.5
Profit attributable to members of Smith Ltd		304.0
Retained profit brought forward (W2)		342.0
Retained profit carried forward (W3)		646.0

*Note. Per FRS 9 *Associates and joint ventures* disclosure should be made of group's share of associate's operating profit. However, PBT is used here for the sake of simplicity.

Workings

1 *Profit on disposal in Smith Ltd*

	£'000
Sales proceeds	340
Cost (50% × 324,000)	162
Profit in Smith Ltd	178
Profit on consolidation	
Per above working	178
Less post-acquisition profits now sold	
40% × (270 + (90 × 9/12) − 180)	63
Add goodwill previously amortised (36 × 50%)	18
	133

Alternative calculation of group profit on disposal

	£'000	£'000
Sale proceeds		340
Less: net assets of Jones now sold		
$40\% \times ((540 - 90) + (9/12 \times 90))$		207
		133

2   *Retained profit brought forward*

	£'000
Smith	306
Jones $80\% \times (270 - 180)$	72
Goodwill fully amortised	(36)
	342

3   *Retained profit carried forward*

	£'000
Smith	414
Profit on disposal (W1)	178
Jones $40\% \times (360 - 180)$	72
Goodwill fully amortised	(18)
	646

(ii)   Partial disposal: subsidiary to trade investment

CONSOLIDATED BALANCE SHEET
AS AT 30 SEPTEMBER 19X8

	£'000
Fixed assets	360
Investment $(40\% \times (180 + 270 + (9/12 \times 90)))$	207
Net current assets	610
	1,177

Share capital and reserves

	£'000
£1 ordinary shares	540
Profit and loss account	637
	1,177

CONSOLIDATED PROFIT AND LOSS ACCOUNT
FOR THE YEAR ENDED 30 SEPTEMBER 19X8

	£'000	£'000
Profit before tax $(153 + (9/12 \times 126))$		247.5
Exceptional item (See (d)(i) above)		133.0
Tax $(45 + (9/12 \times 36))$		72.0
Profit after tax		308.5
Minority interest		13.5
Profit attributable to members of Smith Ltd		+295.0
Retained profit brought forward		342.0
Retained profit carried forward (W)		637.0

Working

Retained profit carried forward

	£'000
Smith	414
Profit on disposal	178
Jones $40\% \times (270 + (9/12 \times 90)) - 180$	63
Goodwill fully amortised	(18)
	637

Dividends

3.18   The retained reserves/net assets at the date of disposal of the subsidiary should be calculated deducting only those dividends to which the **holding company is entitled,** in other words

dividends paid up to the date of disposal and dividends proposed if the shares are sold *ex-dividend*.

3.19   At the date of disposal this would be as follows.

	£
Retained profits brought forward	X
Profits after tax and extraordinary items to date of disposal	X
Dividends paid/proposed at date of disposal	(X)
	X

Disclosure requirements

3.20   The following disclosure requirements should be made when a disposal has taken place.

(a)   **Results for the year**: for any material disposals the consolidated financial statements should contain significant information to enable the shareholders to appreciate the effect on the consolidated results.

(b)   FRS 3 *Reporting financial performance* requires the results of **discontinued operations** to be analysed separately.

(c)   The following should be disclosed in respect of each material disposal of a previously acquired business or business segment:

   (i)   the **profit or loss** on the disposal;

   (ii)   the amount of purchased **goodwill attributable** to a disposal and how it has been treated in determining the profit or loss on disposal;

   (iii) the accounting treatment adopted and the amount of the proceeds in situations where no profit or loss is recorded on a disposal because the proceeds have been accounted for as a **reduction in the cost** of the acquisition.

3.21   Section summary

Disposals occur occasionally in FRP consolidation questions.

- The effective date of disposal is when **control passes**.
- Treatment of **goodwill** is according to UITF 3 (and FRS 2).
- Disposals may be **full** or **partial,** to subsidiary, associate or investment status.
- **Gain or loss** on disposal is calculated for the holding company and the group.
- **FRS 3** disclosure requirements are important.

4   CHANGES IN DIRECT OWNERSHIP

4.1   Groups will reorganise on occasions for a variety of reasons.

(a)   A group may want to float a business to **reduce the gearing** of the group. The holding company will initially transfer the business into a separate company.

(b)   Companies may be transferred to another business during a **divisionalisation** process.

(c)   The group may 'reverse' into another company to obtain a **stock exchange quotation**.

(d)   Internal reorganisations may create efficiencies of group structure for **tax purposes.**

4.2   Such reorganisations involve a restructuring of the relationships within a group. Companies may be transferred to another business during a divisionalisation process. There is generally no effect on the consolidated financial statements, *provided that* no minority interests are affected, because such reorganisations are only internal. The impact on the individual

companies within the group, however, can be substantial. A variety of different transactions are described here, **only involving 100% subsidiaries**.

New top holding company

4.3 A new top holding company might be needed as a vehicle for flotation or to improve the co-ordination of a diverse business. The new company, H, will issue its own shares to the holdings of the shares in S. This type of transaction will qualify as a **merger** under FRS 6 (see Chapter 19).

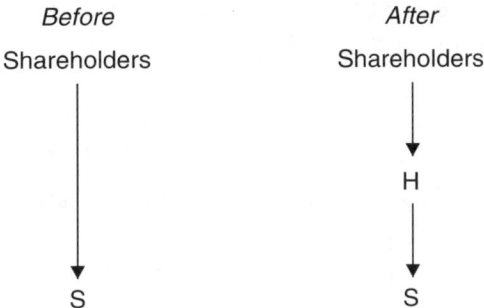

Subsidiary moved up

4.4 This transaction is shown in the diagram below. It might be carried out to allow S_1 to be **sold** while S_2 is retained, or to **split diverse businesses**.

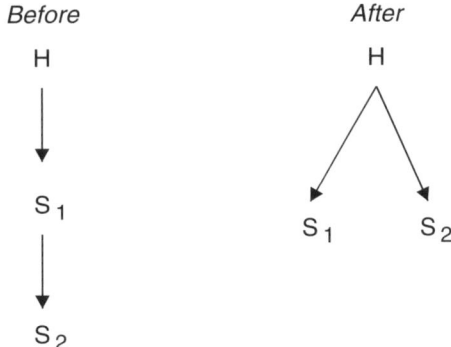

4.5 S_1 could transfer its investment in S_2 to H as a dividend *in specie* or by H paying cash. A share for share exchange is not possible because an allotment by H to S_1 is void. A **dividend in specie** is simply a dividend paid other than in cash.

4.6 S_1 must have sufficient **distributable profits** for a dividend *in specie*. If the investment in S_2 has been revalued then that can be treated as a realised profit for the purposes of determining the legality of the distribution. For example, suppose the balance sheet of S_1 is as follows.

	£m
Investment in S_2 (cost £100m)	900
Other net assets	100
	1,000
Share capital	100
Revaluation reserve	800
Profit and loss account	100
	1,000

4.7 It appears that S_1 cannot make a distribution of more than £100m; if, however, S_1 makes a distribution in kind of its investment in S_2, then the **revaluation reserve** can be treated as realised.

4.8 It is not clear how H should account for the transaction. The carrying value to S_2 might be used, but there is **no legal rule**. H will need to write down its investment in S_1 at the same time. A transfer for cash is probably easiest, but there are still legal pitfalls as to what is distributable, depending on how the transfer is recorded.

4.9 There will be **no effect** on the group financial statements as the group has stayed the same: it has made no acquisitions or disposals.

Subsidiary moved along

4.10 This is a transaction which is treated in a very similar manner to that described above.

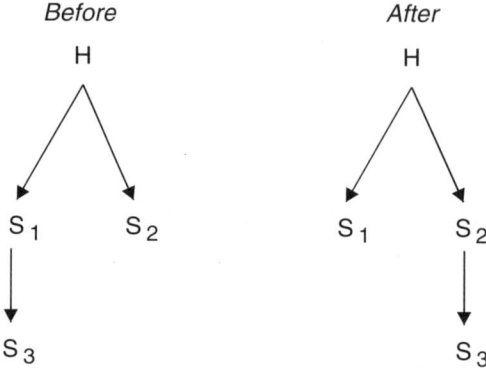

4.11 The problem of an effective distribution does not arise here because the holding company did not buy the subsidiary. There may be problems with **financial assistance** if S_2 pays less than the fair value to purchase S_3 as a prelude to S_1 leaving the group.

Subsidiary moved down

4.12 This situation could arise if H is foreign and S_1 and S_2 are UK companies. A **UK tax group** can be formed out of such a restructuring.

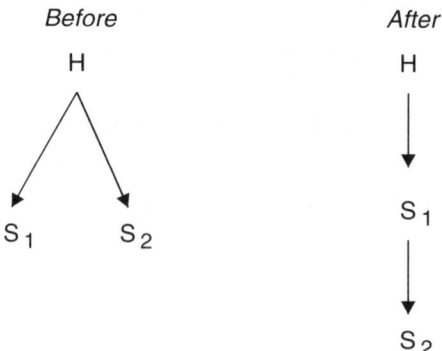

4.13 If S_1 paid cash for S_2, the transaction would be straightforward (as described above). The law is again unclear on the issue of whether H should recognise a gain or loss on the sale if S_2 is sold for more or less than carrying value. S_1 would only be deemed to have made a distribution only if the **price was excessive**.

4.14 A share for share exchange would be affected by s 132 CA 1985 which gives partial relief against the need to create a **share premium account**. A share premium account must be set up with a 'minimum premium value'. This is the amount by which the book value of the shares (or lower cost) exceeds the nominal value of the shares issued. This preserves the book value of the investment.

4.15 EXAMPLE: MINIMUM PREMIUM VALUE

Hop plc has two 100% subsidiaries, Skip and Jump. The balance sheets at 31 December 19X5 are as follows.

	Hop plc £'000	Skip Ltd £'000	Jump Ltd £'000	Group £'000
Investment in Skip	1,000	-	-	-
Investment in Jump	500	-	-	-
Net assets	1,500	1,375	1,500	4,375
	3,000	1,375	1,500	4,375
Share capital	2,500	1,000	500	2,500
P & L account	500	375	1,000	1,875
	3,000	1,375	1,500	4,375

4.16 SOLUTION

Skip Ltd issues 250,000 £1 shares in exchange for Hop plc's investment in Jump Ltd. The minimum premium value is £500,000 (carrying value) – £250,000 = £250,000. The balance sheets are now as follows.

	Hop plc £'000	Skip Ltd £'000	Jump Ltd £'000	Group £'000
Investment in Skip	1,500	-	-	-
Investment in Jump	-	500	-	-
Net assets	1,500	1,375	1,500	4,375
	3,000	1,875	1,500	4,375
Share capital	2,500	1,250	500	2,500
Share premium	-	250	-	-
P & L account	500	375	1,000	1,875
	3,000	1,875	1,500	4,375

Divisionalisation

4.17 This type of transaction involves the **transfer of businesses** from subsidiaries into just one company. The businesses will all be similar and this is a means of rationalising and streamlining. The savings in administration costs can be quite substantial. The remaining shell company will leave the cash it was paid on an inter-company balance as it is no longer trading. The accounting treatment is generally straightforward.

5 DEMERGERS

5.1 A demerger will usually involve **splitting up an existing group** into two or more separate groups. This is usually done to separate different types of trade, particularly when it is intended to sell one of the resulting parts.

5.2 There are a number of ways to carry out such a transaction.

(a) H transfers shares in S_1 to its **shareholders** as a dividend *in specie*.

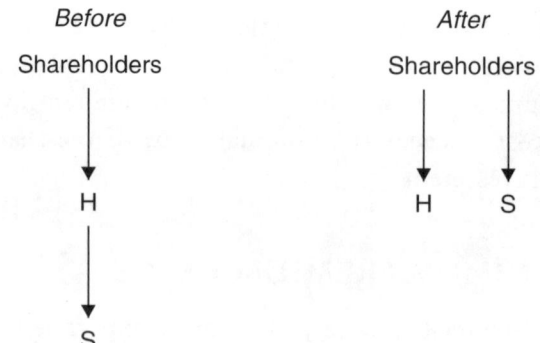

(b) H transfers a trade to **another company** S, often formed for the purpose, and in exchange S issues shares to its shareholders.

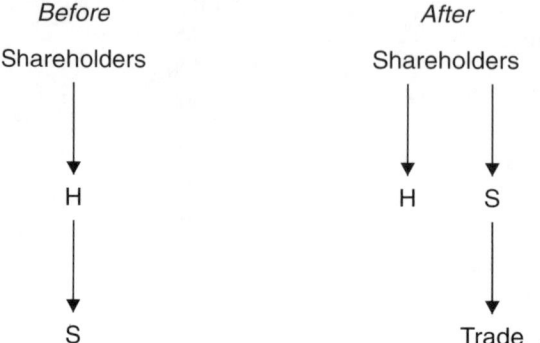

(c) H transfers shares in S_1 to **another company** S_2, who in return issues shares to the shareholders in H.

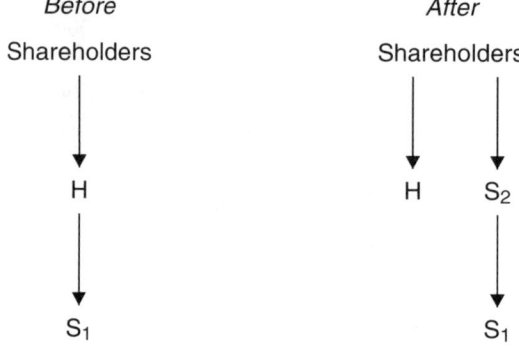

5.3 Most importantly, you should note that the transaction will *always* involve a **distribution by H to its shareholders**, even though this point may seem obscure at times.

5.4 EXAMPLE: DEMERGER

Guinevere Ltd, a subsidiary of Arthur plc, is to be demerged from the group. A new company, Lancelot Ltd, is to be created and it will issue its shares to the shareholders of Arthur in return for the investment in Guinevere. The balance sheets on the day before the demerger were as follows.

	Arthur plc £'000	Guinevere Ltd £'000	Arthur Group £'000
Investment in Guinevere	3,000	-	-
Other net assets	7,200	4,800	12,000
	10,200	4,800	12,000
Share capital	6,000	3,000	6,000
P & L account	4,200	1,800	6,000
	10,200	4,800	12,000

In exchange for Arthur's holding in Guinevere, Lancelot plc issues 3 million £1 shares to Arthur plc's shareholders.

5.5 SOLUTION

In effect this is a distribution by Arthur to its shareholders. The net assets of the company are reduced by £3m and the net assets of the group are reduced by £4.8m, the value of Guinevere. It is usual to show such treatment as movements on retained earnings.

	Company	*Group*
	£'000	£'000
Profit and loss account		
Balance at 1.1.19X5	4,200	6,000
Demerger of Guinevere	(3,000)	(4,800)
Profit for the year	2,100	2,100
Balance at 31.12.19X5	3,300	3,300

Lancelot's shares have been issued at a premium and so share premium relief ought to be taken because the transaction is in effect a merger between Guinevere and Lancelot.

6 FRS 3 REPORTING FINANCIAL PERFORMANCE 5/96, 11/97

6.1 As you may recall from Chapter 2, **FRS 3** requires certain **disclosures** in relation to **acquisitions and disposals**. In particular, it requires the profit and loss account to be shown in a layered format, showing the results of acquired operations and those which have been sold or discontinued.

6.2 The question of disposals under FRS 3 is not necessarily straightforward. The standard requires discontinued operations to be disclosed, but questions arise as to *when* an operation can be considered to be discontinued. This problem is considered in the next few paragraphs.

When is an operation discontinued?

6.3 The question of what constitutes a discontinued operation is proving to be a point of contention; **true** discontinued operations are probably **rather rare in practice**. FRS 3 lays down several conditions, all of which have to be satisfied if an operation is to be regarded as discontinued.

(a) The sale or termination must have been **completed** before the **earlier of 3 months after the year end** or **the date the financial statements are approved**. (Terminations not completed by this date may be disclosed in the notes.)

(b) Former activity must have **ceased permanently**.

(c) The sale or termination has a **material effect** on the nature and focus of the entity's operations and represents a material reduction in its operating facilities resulting either from:

    (i) its withdrawal from a particular market (class of business or geographical): or from

    (ii) a material reduction in turnover in its continuing markets.

(d) The assets, liabilities, results of operations and activities are **clearly distinguishable**, physically, operationally and for financial reporting purposes.

In addition, the explanation section of the standard requires the sale or termination to have resulted from a strategic decision by the company to withdraw from a market or to curtail materially its presence in a continuing market, if it is to be classified as discontinued. The following points and examples cover a number of the more subjective tests.

'Ceased permanently'

6.4   A common problem likely to be encountered is where a company has wound down an operation but still retains the building or factory in which it was carried out. Whether such an operation has ceased permanently will depend on the **fungibility** of the building or factory.

(a)   If it can be used for a variety of purposes, particularly if the company had used it for differing purposes in the past, then it seems likely that the ownership of the factory can be separated from the operation in question and the operation can therefore be treated as discontinued.

(b)   If the property was designed for a specific purpose and could only be used for that purpose, and the operation has effectively been 'mothballed', then the operation is not discontinued. Similarly, if the building is to be disposed of as a consequence of ceasing the activity, the activity cannot be treated as fully discontinued until the property is sold.

Material effect on the nature and focus of a company's operations

6.5   FRS 3 **does not require** that an operation must be a **separate business** segment, for the purposes of SSAP 25 (see Chapter 28), if it is to be classified as discontinued. FRS 3 illustrates the requirement for a change in nature and focus by using the example of a hotel company that switches from the lower end of the market to a chain of luxury hotels. By the same justification, a company that ran hotels in both ends of the market, but which decided to sell the 'budget' chain would be able to treat it as a discontinued operation even though both chains were 'bundled' under one category in the segmental results analysis required by SSAP 25.

6.6   EXAMPLE: NATURE AND FOCUS

A company in the business of manufacturing and selling office furniture carried out an assessment of its manufacturing process and came to the conclusion that it would be cost-effective in the long term to subcontract manufacturing. The company ceased manufacturing office furniture prior to the year end, but continued to sell to the same customer base using supplies from subcontractors. Does this constitute a material effect on the nature and focus of operations?

6.7   SOLUTION

This example illustrates a situation that is *not* a material change in nature and focus even though there has been a substantial change in the way in which the company concerned carries out its business.

6.8   The fact that a company ceases manufacturing goods does not necessarily mean that there has been a change in the nature and focus of operations. The ultimate purpose of producing the office furniture was the generation of profits by selling them to customers. In this example these activities are still continuing, but the company has found it more cost-

effective to employ a third party to manufacture the goods in future. In this case, the cessation of manufacturing does not constitute a discontinued activity.

Material reduction in operating facilities

6.9 A material reduction in operating facilities results either from a company withdrawing from a particular market (whether class of business or geographical) or from a material reduction in turnover in its continuing markets, as the following example demonstrates.

6.10 EXAMPLE: MATERIAL REDUCTION IN OPERATING FACILITIES

During the current year a company closed one of its two plant hire depots. The staff were all made redundant but the assets were transferred to the other depot and it is expected that there will be no overall reduction in the customer base. Is there a material reduction in operating facilities?

6.11 SOLUTION

The closure is not expected to lead to a material reduction in turnover in the continuing market and thus does not meet the conditions in FRS 3. The operations of the closed depot are not, therefore, discontinued. If the costs are material they may need to be separately disclosed. They do not appear to fall into one of the categories listed in the standard, as there is no material effect on the nature and focus of the reporting entity's operations. Therefore the costs would be charged in arriving at operating profit.

Provisions as a consequence of a decision to sell or terminate an operation

6.12 Under FRS 3, **provision** should be made for the **losses arising as a consequence of a decision** to sell or terminate an operation only where the company is '**demonstrably committed**' to the sale or termination. This requirement applies irrespective of whether the operation falls to be treated as discontinued in the current period. This is reinforced in FRS 12 *Provisions, contingent assets and contingent liabilities*, discussed in Chapter 11.

6.13 The term 'demonstrably committed' is not defined by the FRS but it does indicate that for a termination evidence is given by:

(a) a detailed formal plan for termination from which the company cannot realistically withdraw;

(b) public announcement of plans, commencement of implementation; or

(c) other circumstances obliging the entity to complete the termination.

6.14 Similarly, for a sale, evidence is given by a binding sale agreement (possibly entered into after the period end, provided the decision to sell was clearly taken before the period end) or other circumstances obliging the entity to complete the sale.

6.15 In the event that an entity is 'demonstrably committed', provision should be made for the direct costs of the sale or termination and the operating loss of the operation up to the date of termination or sale. This provision should be made net of any future profits arising from the operation or the disposal of its assets. In addition, provision should be made for any permanent diminution in asset values irrespective of whether an entity is 'demonstrably committed' to the sale or termination. This is illustrated in the following table.

Nature of provision	Demonstrably committed to disposal or termination	Not demonstrably committed to disposal or termination
Direct costs of the sale or termination	Provision required	Do not provide
Operating loss of the operation up to the date of termination or sale	Provision required	Do not provide
Permanent diminution in asset values	Provision required	Provision required

6.16   Where a company is *not* demonstrably committed, the provisions required are demonstrated in the following example.

6.17 EXAMPLE: DECISION TO SELL

Company P's board has taken a decision (on 25 September 19X3) to close an operation that is lossmaking. At the company's year end (30 September 19X3) it is estimated that it will take one year to close the operation and that it will lose a further £2.75m over that time. Fixed assets with a book value of £2.0m are expected to have a recoverable amount not exceeding £1.3m as a result of the closure decision. Implementation of the decision had not commenced at the balance sheet date and no public announcements had been made. What costs should be provided for at 30 September 19X3?

6.18 SOLUTION

The company is clearly not demonstrably committed to the termination and therefore the only provision that should be made is the £0.7m to reduce fixed assets to their recoverable amount. The operation is not discontinued and thus the provisions should be classified as continuing operations.

Chapter roundup

- Transactions of the type described in this chapter can be very complicated and certainly look rather daunting. Remember and apply the **basic techniques** and you should find such questions easier than you expected.

- **Piecemeal acquisitions** can lead to a company becoming a fixed asset investment, an associate and then a subsidiary over time. Make sure you can deal with each of these situations.

- In piecemeal acquisitions, use the rule-of-thumb in Paragraph 1.9 to decide whether the **step-by-step method** or the **one-computation-at-the-date-of-control method** is more appropriate.

- **Disposals** can drop a subsidiary holding to associate status, fixed asset investment status and to zero, or a the parent might still retain a subsidiary undertaking with a reduced holding. Once again, you should be able to deal with all these situations. Remember particularly how to deal with goodwill.

- **Changes in direct ownership** (ie internal group reorganisations) can take many forms. Apart from divisionalisation, all other internal reorganisations will not affect the consolidated financial statements, but they will affect the accounts of individual companies within the group.

- **Demergers** are not unusual in practice and are not difficult to account for. Concentrate on the substance of the transactions undertaken.

- The **FRS 3 criteria** for discontinued operations **must** be applied carefully.

Quick quiz

1   What is the general rule in determining pre- and post-acquisition reserves in a piecemeal acquisition? (see para 1.3)

2   What effect does a bonus issue have on the calculation of goodwill on consolidation? (2.1)

3   How does FRS 2 define the effective date of disposal of shares in an investment? (3.2)

4   How should goodwill previously written off be treated as disposal of the related shares? (3.4, 3.5)

5   Why might a group undertake an internal reconstruction? (4.1)

6   What is a dividend *in specie*? (4.5)

7   Why might a subsidiary be moved down? (4.12)

8   What is a demerger? (5.1)

9   What conditions does FRS 3 lay down for determining whether an operation is discontinued? (6.3)

10 What would count as a material reduction in operating facilities according to FRS 3? (6.9)

11 What provisions are required by FRS 3 when a business is *not* demonstrably committed to the sale of an operation? (6.15, table)

Questions to try	Level	Marks	Time
19	Introductory	n/a	n/a

BPP PUBLISHING

Chapter 19

MERGER ACCOUNTING

Chapter topic	Syllabus reference	Ability required
1 The accounting problem with business combinations	9(a)	Application
2 FRS 6 *Acquisitions and mergers*	9(a)	Application
3 Further practical issues and merger relief	9(a)	Application

Introduction

The debate about merger and acquisition accounting relates directly to the topics covered in Chapter 14 and you should refer back to that chapter where necessary.

Merger accounting is a very contentious area at the moment. FRS 6 has drawn criticism for its approach and it is likely to remain controversial for some time. In the future, the use of merger accounting (for 'true' mergers) could be very rare.

The distinction between merger accounting and merger relief is an important one. Make sure you can accurately describe both concepts.

In relation to FRS 6 and merger accounting, the examiner has said that complex consolidations involving the merger method will not be set, but candidates could still be required to prepare a relatively straightforward balance sheet using the merger method of consolidation.

1   THE ACCOUNTING PROBLEM WITH BUSINESS COMBINATIONS

1.1   FRS 6 *Acquisitions and mergers* deals with the accounting treatment of business combinations which arise when one or more companies become subsidiaries of another company. Two different methods of accounting for such combinations have evolved in practice.

(a) **Acquisition accounting** is the traditional method of accounting for business combinations and is the method which has been described in the previous chapters. A company acquires shares in another company (or companies) and either pays for them in cash or issues its own shares or loan stock in exchange for them. If much of the purchase price is paid in cash, there may be a significant outflow of assets from the group.

(b) **Merger accounting** is a method of preparing consolidated accounts which may be regarded as appropriate in cases where a business combination is brought about without any significant outflow of funds from the group. This might happen, for example, where one company acquires shares in another company and issues its own shares as consideration for the purchase, rather than paying cash.

1.2   You should be clear in your mind that the term **merger accounting** refers to a method of preparing **consolidated accounts**. FRS 6 hardly mentions the problems of how to account for share acquisitions in the individual accounts of the acquiring company. This is a problem to which statutory provisions are relevant; we will discuss it later in this chapter.

1.3 The main problem with using the acquisition method concerns the effect on the holding company's **distributable profits**. Suppose that H Ltd acquires all the shares of S Ltd on day 1 and on day 2 S Ltd pays a dividend equal to the entire amount of its distributable profits. Using the conventional techniques of acquisition accounting described in earlier chapters, H Ltd would not credit the dividend received to its own P&L account, so as to increase its own distributable profits; instead, the dividend would be applied to reduce the cost of the investment in S Ltd. The profits available for distribution to members of H Ltd would be unchanged from what they were before the combination.

1.4 If the shares in S Ltd were **purchased for cash**, this might seem reasonable: cash has been paid out as well as received and so net assets have not increased. The amount of profits available to distribute to the original shareholders of H Ltd remains unchanged, being the distributable profits shown in H Ltd's own individual accounts. On this assumption, conventional acquisition accounting seems to achieve a fair result.

1.5 But what happens if the shareholders in S Ltd are not bought out for cash? This would be the case if H Ltd paid for the shares in S Ltd by, say, an **issue of new shares** in H Ltd. This would mean that members of S Ltd would exchange their shares in that company for a share of the newly-formed group. The number of shareholders of H Ltd would now be greatly increased. But using acquisition accounting there would be no corresponding increase in the distributable profits of H Ltd.

1.6 This result can be avoided if merger accounting principles are used. We will come later to the detailed criteria of CA 1985 and FRS 6, but broadly speaking a business combination may be accounted for as a merger if payment for the shares acquired is by means of a **share exchange**; if payment is by cash, conventional acquisition accounting must be used.

1.7 EXAMPLE: ACQUISITION V MERGER ACCOUNTING

John Smith and Fred Jones run electrical wholesaling businesses of identical size. Both businesses are incorporated as limited liability companies, the shareholders of which are Smith, Jones and their respective wives.

In 19X1, Smith and Jones decide to combine their businesses and for this purpose they form a new company Smith and Jones Ltd. It is agreed that the new company will acquire all of the shares of John Smith Ltd and Fred Jones Ltd, the consideration in each case being the issue of equal numbers of shares in the new company. The balance sheets of John Smith Ltd and Fred Jones Ltd as at 31 December 19X1 are set out below.

	John Smith Ltd	*Fred Jones Ltd*
	£'000	£'000
Net assets	100	100
Share capital	20	20
Profit and loss account	80	80
	100	100

The fair value of each business is considered to be £160,000.

1.8 SOLUTION: ACQUISITION ACCOUNTING

Using normal acquisition accounting principles, the balance sheet of Smith and Jones Ltd after the share transfers will be as follows.

	Smith and Jones Ltd £'000
Investment in John Smith Ltd	160
Investment in Fred Jones Ltd	160
	320
Share capital	40
Share premium *(160 + 120)*	280
	320

The balance on the share premium account is the difference between the nominal value of the shares issued and the value of the assets acquired.

Assuming that the net assets of John Smith Ltd and Fred Jones Ltd are already stated at their fair value, the difference between the book value of the assets (£100,000 in each case) and the fair value of the business (£160,000 in each case) will be goodwill.

The consolidated balance sheet at the date of transfer will therefore be as follows.

	£'000
Goodwill arising on consolidation *(320 – 200)*	120
Net assets	200
	320
Share capital	40
Share premium *(160 + 120)*	280
	320

1.9 From the above, it can be seen that the new company will have **no distributable reserves** at the date of the transfer. Smith and Jones may well consider that this situation is highly unsatisfactory, as from their point of view there is no real change of ownership, merely a pooling of interests. Furthermore there has been no change in the underlying net assets, even though their balance sheet values have increased.

1.10 It is in the kind of situation outlined above that **merger accounting** may be appropriate. In merger accounting, the emphasis is on the **continuity** of the amalgamated businesses.

1.11 The single most important feature of merger accounting is that when a holding company issues shares in consideration for the transfer to it of shares in another company, the shares issued are accounted for at their **nominal value** only. (Under acquisition accounting the shares must be accounted for at their **market value**.) The other features of merger accounting are demonstrated below.

1.12 SOLUTION: MERGER ACCOUNTING

If we apply merger accounting in the above example, the entry in the books of Smith and Jones Ltd will be:

		£'000	£'000
DEBIT	Investment in John Smith Ltd	20	
	Investment in Fred Jones Ltd	20	
CREDIT	Share capital		40

The investment in the subsidiaries is therefore recorded as the nominal value of the consideration given.

Under the merger method, the balance sheet of Smith and Jones Ltd would be:

	Smith & Jones Ltd £'000
Investment in John Smith Ltd	20
Investment in Fred Jones Ltd	20
	40
Share capital	40

Consolidation would involve cancellation of the 'investment in subsidiary' with the subsidiary's share capital and aggregation of the net assets. The resulting consolidated balance sheet would be:

	£'000
Net assets	200
Share capital	40
Profit and loss account	160
	200

1.13 A comparison of the merger balance sheet with the acquisition balance sheet will demonstrate the following features of merger accounting.

(a) Assets can be recorded at their **previous values,** as there is no obligation to record them at fair value.

(b) **No share premium account** will arise in the books of the holding company, as shares issued are recorded at their nominal value only.

(c) A **premium on acquisition** (ie goodwill) will never arise under merger accounting.

(d) Previously distributable reserves of the individual companies may remain **distributable** as there is no enforced freezing of pre-acquisition reserves.

(e) It is **simpler** than acquisition accounting.

1.14 Point (a) above means that a **ROCE** based on a merger balance sheet is usually higher than one based on an acquisition balance sheet. This, together with point (d), has contributed greatly to the popularity enjoyed by merger accounting.

2 FRS 6 ACQUISITIONS AND MERGERS

2.1 Before we look at FRS 6, which was published in September 1994, let us briefly examine the Companies Act requirements for merger accounting.

Companies Act 1985

2.2 CA 1985 lays down the following conditions for accounting for acquisition as a merger (s 10 Sch 4A CA 1985).

(a) **At least 90%** of the nominal value of the 'relevant shares'* in the undertaking acquired must be held by the group.

(b) This must be achieved as a result of an arrangement providing for the issue of **equity shares** by the parent company (or one or more of its subsidiaries).

(c) The **fair value** of any consideration other than equity shares **must not exceed 10% of the nominal value** of the equity shares issued.

(d) Adoption of the merger method must accord with **generally accepted accounting principles** or standards.

*'Relevant shares' are 'those carrying unrestricted rights to participate both in distributions and in the assets of the undertaking upon liquidation': usually these will be equity shares.

2.3 These requirements are very similar to those in **SSAP 23** *Accounting for acquisitions and mergers*, the forerunner of FRS 6. Previously, if any or all of these conditions were not met, the business combination was an acquisition and acquisition accounting had to be used. Even if all the conditions were met, SSAP 23 only said that merger accounting principles *could* be used. The investing company could still choose to use acquisition accounting.

2.4 You should be clear that the CA 1985 requirements still exist. FRS 6, although it encompasses the CA 1985 requirements, has tightened the requirements for merger accounting by concentrating on the **spirit of the transaction**, rather than on mechanical aspects, such as levels of shareholding.

Criticisms and abuses of merger accounting

2.5 The following criticisms were made about merger accounting, although some of these can be rebutted.

(a) **Creation of instant earnings** by combining the results of the companies in both the year of merger and the corresponding year figures. This is no real criticism when a genuine merging of interests takes place as the same shareholders have interests in the same earnings both before and after the merger.

(b) **Creation of instant distributable reserves**. Again, this criticism is not valid as the same shareholders have the same access to the same reserves both before and after the merger.

(c) **Assets understated** as no fair value exercise is undertaken. However, this was the situation before the merger as well and there is no reason why a revaluation should not take place anyway.

(d) **Holding company profitability**. Dividends paid by the acquired company out of pre-acquisition profits could be credited to the holding company's P&L account, distorting profitability. These dividends, however, will be eliminated on consolidation and disclosure of such dividends by way of a note could clarify the situation.

(e) **Exceptional gains** can arise by selling off assets or investments owned by one of the combining companies. Any profit was mostly accrued pre-merger as the assets were brought into the accounts at historical cost, and thus the operating profit of the group is distorted, particularly as FRS 3 would presumably treat such events as exceptional, where previously they would be treated as extraordinary.

2.6 The **general criticism** of SSAP 23 given by the ASB was:

'Inappropriate use of merger accounting to enhance the acquiring group's earnings by including the results of the acquired company for the whole of the year rather than just from the date of acquisition.'

2.7 The ASB sees FRS 6 as a remedy to this problem.

'FRS 6 restricts the use of merger accounting to very rare cases of mergers that cannot properly be viewed as the takeover of one company by another; all other business combinations must be accounted for by using acquisition accounting.'

'FRS 6 sets out disclosure requirements, for both acquisitions and mergers, to ensure that full explanation of the effect of the combination is disclosed in the financial statements. It also encourages further voluntary disclosure of the acquirer's intended expenditure on the acquired business.'

FRS 6 *Acquisitions and mergers*

2.8   In general terms FRS 6 aims to prevent the use of merger accounting for anything other than **'true' mergers**, where a partnership is formed, on an equal footing. Where there is an identifiable 'acquirer', then acquisition accounting *must* be used.

Objective

2.9   The objective of FRS 6 is:

(a)   to ensure that **merger accounting** is used only for those business combinations that are not, in substance, the acquisition of one entity by another but the formation of a new reporting entity as a **substantially equal partnership** where no party is dominant;

(b)   to ensure the use of **acquisition accounting** for all other business combinations; and

(c)   to ensure that in either case the financial statements provide **relevant information** concerning the effect of the combination.

Definitions

2.10   The following definitions are given by the standard, which also defines **acquisitions** and **business combinations** which are already shown under FRS 7, which we looked at earlier in this Study Text.

> ### KEY TERMS
>
> - **Equity shares**: shares other than non-equity shares.
>
> - **Group reconstruction**: any of the following arrangements:
>
>   (a)   the transfer of a shareholding in a subsidiary undertaking from one group company to another;
>
>   (b)   the addition of a new parent company to a group;
>
>   (c)   the transfer of shares in one or more subsidiary undertakings of a group to a new company that is not a group company but whose shareholders are the same as those of the group's parent;
>
>   (d)   the combination into a group of two or more companies that before the combination had the same shareholders.
>
> - **Merger**: a business combination that results in the creation of a new reporting entity formed from the combining parties, in which the shareholders of the combining entities come together in a partnership for the mutual sharing of the risks and benefits of the combined entity, and in which no party to the combination in substance obtains control over any other, or is otherwise seen to be dominant, whether by virtue of the proportion of its shareholders' rights in the combined entity, the influence of its directors or otherwise.

> **KEY TERMS**
>
> • **Non-equity shares**: shares possessing any of the following characteristics:
>
> (a) any of the rights of the shares to receive payments (whether in respect of dividends, in respect of redemption or otherwise) are for a limited amount that is not calculated by reference to the company's assets or profits or the dividends on any class of equity share;
>
> (b) any of their rights to participate in a surplus in a winding up are limited to a specific amount that is not calculated by reference to the company's assets or profits and such limitations had a commercial effect in practice at the time the shares were issued, or, if later, at the time the limitation was introduced;
>
> (c) the shares are redeemable, either according to their terms or because the holder, or any party other than the issuer, can require their redemption. *(FRS 6)*

Scope

2.11 FRS 6 applies to all financial statements that are intended to give a true and fair view. Although the FRS is framed in terms of an entity becoming a subsidiary undertaking of a parent company that prepares consolidated financial statements, it also applies where an **individual company** or other reporting entity combines with a business other than a subsidiary undertaking, ie an unincorporated entity.

Use of merger accounting

2.12 Merger accounting should be used when:

(a) the use of merger accounting is **not prohibited** by companies legislation; and
(b) the **five specific criteria** for a merger laid out in FRS 6 are satisfied.

Point (a) means that the CA 1985 criteria for merger accounting given in Paragraph 2.2 *must* still be met.

2.13 The criteria for determining whether the definition of a merger is met are as follows. Note that convertible share or loan stock should be regarded as equity to the extent that it is converted into equity **as a result of the business combination**.

Criterion 1 Neither party is portrayed, by either its management or any other party, as either acquirer or acquired.

Criterion 2 All parties take part in setting up a management structure and selecting personnel for the combined entity on the basis of consensus rather than purely by exercise of voting rights.

Criterion 3 The relative sizes of the parties are not so disparate that one party dominates the combined entity by virtue of its relative size.

Criterion 4 A substantial part of the consideration for equity shareholdings in each party will comprise equity shares; conversely, non-equity shares or equity shares with reduced voting rights will comprise only an 'immaterial' part of the consideration.

This criterion also covers existing shareholdings. Where one of the combining entities has, within the period of two years before the combination acquired shares in another of the combining entities, the consideration for this acquisition should be taken into account in determining whether this criterion has been met.

This criterion states in general terms what is laid out in CA 1985 in terms of specific shareholdings.

Criterion 5 No equity shareholders of any of the combining entities retains any material interest in the future performance of only part of the combined equity.

> ### Exam focus point
> It is almost inconceivable that you would be asked about FRS 6 and mergers without having to discuss the five criteria here. In the December 1996 exam, you were asked to analyse a proposed transaction to decide whether it was a merger; the framework for your solution to such a question must be the five criteria, so you must learn them. In December 1997 you had to analyse and describe the criteria under various headings.

2.14 Note that, for the purpose of Criterion 4, the consideration should *not* include:

(a) an interest in a **peripheral part** of the business of the entity in which they were shareholders and which does not form part of the combined entity; or

(b) the **proceeds of the sale** of such a business, or loan stock representing such proceeds.

A peripheral part of the business is one that can be disposed of without having a material effect on the nature and focus of the entity's operations.

Group reconstructions, new parents etc

2.15 Despite the strict criteria which must be met before merger accounting can be used, FRS 6 does allow the use of merger accounting in various other, slightly unusual situations.

(a) In **group reconstructions**, provided:

(i) the use of merger accounting is not prohibited by companies legislation;

(ii) the ultimate shareholders remain the same, and the rights of each such shareholders, relative to the others, are unchanged; and

(iii) no minority's interest in the net assets of the group is altered by the transfer.

(b) In a combination effected by using a **new parent company**, where a direct combination of the parties concerned would have met the FRS 6 criteria for merger accounting. If there *is* an 'acquirer', then the acquirer and new parent should first be combined using merger accounting, then other parties combined using acquisition accounting.

(c) In **various structures of business combination** the FRS should be applied to other transactions which achieve the same results.

Merger accounting

2.16 The main accounting provisions of the merger method are listed by the FRS as follows and these match the accounting treatment we looked at in Section 1.

(a) **No fair value** exercise is required, but appropriate adjustments to achieve uniformity of accounting policies should be made.

(b) In the group accounts in the year of merger, results should be shown as if the entities **had always been combined,** in both that year and the previous year as shown in the corresponding figures.

(c) Differences between the nominal value of the shares issued plus the fair value of any other consideration given, and the nominal value of any shares received in exchange should be shown as a **movement on other reserves** in the consolidated financial statements.

(d) Any existing balance on the new subsidiary's share premium account or capital **redemption reserve** should be shown as a movement on other reserves. The transactions in (c) and (d) should be shown in the reconciliation of movements in shareholders' funds.

(e) **Merger expenses** should be charged to the P&L account of the combined entity at the date of the merger (ie *not* as a movement on reserves) in accordance with FRS 3.

These provisions contrast directly with the requirements of acquisition accounting.

Disclosure

2.17 The disclosure requirements of FRS 6 are lengthy and substantial. The following information should be disclosed for both acquisitions and mergers in the accounts of the acquirer or issuing entity, for each combination in the period.

(a) The **names** of the combining entities (other than the reporting entity)
(b) Whether the combination has been accounted for as an **acquisition or a merger**
(c) The **date** of the combination

2.18 In effect, full disclosure is required of all material factors relating to both acquisitions and mergers. Under **merger accounting** the main results of each party should be given, plus major adjustments to asset values and details of the consideration. In relation to **acquisitions,** details of the consideration should be given and you should also consider:

(a) **FRS 10** on goodwill (Chapter 4):

(b) **FRS 3** (Chapters 2 and 22) on:

   (i) acquisition as a component of continuing operations; and
   (ii) exceptional profits and losses relating to fair values;

(c) **FRS 1** and the impact of acquisitions on cash flows (Chapter 24);

(d) **FRS 12** on *Provisions, contingent assets and contingent liabilities* (Chapter 11).

2.19 In relation to FRS 3 and provisions, FRS 6 makes it very clear that any **costs incurred post-acquisition** for reorganising, restructuring and integrating the acquisition should be shown in the P&L account of that period (ie post-acquisition). Such costs are described as those that:

(a) would not have been incurred had the acquisition not taken place; and

(b) relate to a project identified and controlled by management as part of a reorganisation or integration programme set up at the time of acquisition or as a direct consequence of an immediate post-acquisition review.

In other words, such costs *cannot* be treated as movements on reserves.

2.20 **Movements on provisions and accruals** made in relation to the acquisition should be disclosed and analysed between the amounts used for the specific purpose for which they were created and the amounts released unused.

Substantial acquisitions

2.21 Extra information should be disclosed for 'substantial acquisitions', which are defined as each business combination accounted for by using **acquisition accounting** where:

(a) for listed companies, the combination is a Class I or Super Class I transaction under the Stock Exchange Listing Rules (see below);

(b) for other entities, either:

(i) the net assets or operating profits of the acquired entity exceed 15% of those of the acquiring entity; or

(ii) the fair value of the consideration given exceeds 15% of the net assets of the acquiring entity;

and should also be made in other exceptional cases where an acquisition is of such significance that the disclosure is necessary in order to give a true and fair view.

2.22 The extra information requiring **disclosure** is a summarised P&L account, and STRGL of the acquired entity from the beginning of the period to the date of acquisition. The profit after tax and minority interests for the acquired entity's previous financial year should also be disclosed.

UITF Abstract 15 *Disclosure of substantial acquisitions*

2.23 In relation to Paragraph 2.21(a) above, in August 1995 the Stock Exchange revised its Listing Rules and they no longer refer to Class 1 transactions.

2.24 The Stock Exchange Listing Rules classify transactions by **assessing their size** relative to that of the company proposing to make the transaction. It does this by ascertaining whether any of a number of ratios (eg the net assets of the target to the net assets of the offeror) exceeds a given percentage. Class 1 transactions used to be those where the percentage exceeded 15%. Super Class 1 are those where the percentage exceeds 25%. FRS 6 uses the 15% criterion for non-listed entities.

2.25 The UITF reached a consensus that, in order to retain the ASB's original intentions for FRS 6, the reference to Class 1 transactions should be interpreted as meaning those transactions in which any of the ratios set out in the London Stock Exchange Listing Rules defining Super Class 1 transactions **exceeds 15%.**

2.26 Section summary

FRS 6 represents a major revision of the principles and practices of merger accounting.

- **CA 1985** lays down specific rules restricting merger, included in FRS 6.

- Merger accounting was **criticised** as it was open to abuse.

- FRS 6 restricts the use of merger accounting by imposing **five criteria.**

- FRS 6 also covers various **group reconstructions.**

• There are many disclosures required by FRS 6, including extra disclosure for **substantial acquisitions.**

Question 1

List the criteria for merger accounting given by FRS 6.

Answer

See Paragraph 2.13.

---

3 FURTHER PRACTICAL ISSUES AND MERGER RELIEF

Merger: NV shares ≠ NV shares acquired

3.1 The Smith and Jones example in Section 1 above involved a share for share exchange where the **nominal value** of the shares issued was equal to the nominal value of the shares acquired. Where this is not the case, or where there is additional consideration in some form other than equity shares, the basic method needs some modification.

Question 2

America plc has decided to combine with Europe plc and has made a successful one for one offer to the ordinary shareholders of Europe plc. Ordinary shares in America plc are quoted on the Stock Exchange at £2.20. The balance sheets of the two companies are set out below.

	America plc £	Europe plc £
Fixed assets	2,800	2,400
Net current assets	1,400	800
	4,200	3,200
Ordinary shares of £1 each	3,000	2,000
Reserves (realised)	1,200	1,200
	4,200	3,200

Required

Prepare a consolidated balance sheet on a merger basis for America plc:

(a)   using the information given above;

(b)   assuming the offer had been 3 shares in America plc for every 2 shares in Europe plc;

(c)   assuming the offer had been 1 share in America plc for every 2 shares in Europe plc;

(d)   assuming that America plc had paid 25p per share for Europe plc as well as giving a one for one share exchange.

Answer

The investment in Europe plc shown in the accounts of America plc will be as follows.

Under (a)	£2,000
Under (b)	£3,000
Under (c)	£1,000
Under (d) (£2,000 + £500)	£2,500

CONSOLIDATED BALANCE SHEETS

	(a) £	(b) £	(c) £	(d) £
Fixed assets	5,200	5,200	5,200	5,200
Net current assets	2,200	2,200	2,200	1,700
	7,400	7,400	7,400	6,900
Ordinary shares of £1 each	5,000	6,000	4,000	5,000
Unrealised reserve	-	-	1,000	-
Realised reserves	2,400	1,400	2,400	1,900
	7,400	7,400	7,400	6,900

The balance sheet in (a) shows no change in the total realised reserves. This is because the nominal value of the shares acquired exactly matches the nominal value of the shares issued.

The balance sheet in (b) reflects the fact that America plc has issued 3,000 shares, whose nominal value is £1,000 more than the nominal value of the shares taken over. The difference is deducted from realised reserves, since the group has no unrealised reserves.

The balance sheet in (c) includes an unrealised reserve, created because the nominal value of the shares issued is £1,000 less than the nominal value of the shares acquired.

The (d) balance sheet shows net current assets reduced by £500, the amount of cash paid. The difference between America's investment in subsidiary (£2,500) and the nominal value of the shares acquired (£2,000) is again deducted from realised reserves on consolidation.

3.2 It should be obvious from the above that the total net assets figure never changes (unless part of the consideration is cash). Under merger accounting consolidated reserves become in effect a **balancing figure**.

Profit and loss account

3.3 Interest in merger accounting generally focuses on the balance sheet. The P&L account aspect is really extremely simple: it involves aggregation of the individual company's figures, with normal consolidation adjustments but no attempt to distinguish between pre- and post-merger profits in the year of merger. All **comparatives are restated** as though the companies had always been merged. Note the effects of FRS 3.

Minority interest

3.4 Any minority interest (which **will never exceed 10%** under CA 1985, and under FRS 6 will be *very* rare) is accounted for in the usual way, namely:

(a) the minority interest in the subsidiary's shareholders' funds is a deferred liability;

(b) their share of any proposed dividend is a current liability;

(c) their share of the subsidiary's profits after tax is deducted in the consolidated P&L account.

Merger relief

3.5 Although this section of the text is concerned with group accounts it is worthwhile to consider here the way in which a holding company records a share acquisition in its **own individual accounts**. We are mainly concerned with s 131 CA 1985.

3.6 S 131 CA 1985 provides that **no share premium account** need be created on an issue of shares provided that:

(a) the shares are issued as part of an arrangement to **acquire shares** in another company; and

(b) the investing company, after the issue, has managed to secure **at least 90%** of the equity shares in the other company. Any shares held by the investing company prior to the new issue may be counted towards the 90% but the relief under s 131 will *only* apply to the shares issued as part of the arrangement.

3.7 The exemption granted by s 131 is often referred to as **merger relief**. This has often led to confusion between two quite different things. You should be clear in your mind that the statutory provisions relate to the recording of a share issue in the **individual accounts of an investing company**; whereas merger accounting is concerned only with methods of preparing consolidated accounts.

3.8 A company taking advantage of merger relief has a **choice of accounting methods** when recording the share issue for purposes of its own (not its consolidated) accounts. Assuming an issue of shares with a nominal value of £50,000 and a market value of £220,000, the choices are as follows.

(a) DEBIT   Investment in subsidiary   £50,000
      CREDIT   Ordinary share capital   £50,000

This method has the disadvantage that it disguises the true value of the investment acquired. The individual balance sheet will be misleading.

(b) DEBIT   Investment in subsidiary   £220,000
      CREDIT   Ordinary share capital   £50,000
                Share premium account   £170,000

This is a most unlikely option in practice. To show a more realistic balance sheet, the company foregoes the relief available under s 131 and creates an unwelcome share premium account.

(c) DEBIT   Investment in subsidiary   £220,000
      CREDIT   Ordinary share capital   £50,000
                Merger reserve   £170,000

This is perhaps the most likely choice. To record the investment at its 'true' cost, the company shows the share issue at its market value by setting up a reserve account; but the restrictions attaching to a share premium account are avoided by labelling the reserve a 'merger reserve'.

3.9 The method chosen from these three options will not affect the decision on the **method of consolidation** to be adopted. That decision must be taken in the light of the CA 1985 and FRS 6 criteria.

3.10 EXAMPLE: MERGER RELIEF

Comic plc acquired a 95% holding in Strip plc on 1 January 19X7 for £1,000,000 satisfied through the issue of 400,000 £1 ordinary shares in Comic plc. On 1 January 19X7 the balance sheets of the two companies were as follows (the acquisition has not yet been accounted for).

	Comic plc	Strip plc
	£'000	£'000
Net assets	3,000	800
Share capital	2,000	500
Profit and loss account	1,000	300
	3,000	800

Prepare the consolidated balance sheet as at 1 January 19X8 under the acquisition method, assuming merger relief is available. Goodwill is written off to reserves and the carrying value of the net assets of Strip plc approximate to their fair value.

3.11 SOLUTION

CONSOLIDATED BALANCE SHEET
AS AT 1 JANUARY 19X7

	£'000
Net assets	3,800
Share capital (2,000 + 400)	2,400
Merger reserve (1,000 – 400)	600
Profit and loss account (W2)	760
Shareholders' funds	3,760
Minority interest (W3)	40
	3,800

Workings

1 *Goodwill*

	£'000
Fair value of consideration	1,000
Net assets acquired (95% × 800)	760
Goodwill	240

2 *Profit and loss account*

	£'000
Comic plc	1,000
Strip plc: no post-acquisition retained reserves	-
Goodwill written off	240
	760

3 *Minority interests*

	£'000
Share of net assets (5% × 800)	40

Question 3

You are given the following information.

(a) On 30 June 19X7 Stepney plc obtained acceptance by 100% of the ordinary shareholders of Brennan plc of its offer of one new ordinary share in Stepney plc for every one ordinary share in Brennan plc. The offer was also declared unconditional on 30 June 19X7 and arrangements were made for the share exchange to take place within the next few days. On 30 June 19X7 the ordinary shares of Stepney plc had a market value of £8.50 each. The newly-formed group became known as the Stepney Group plc.

(b) It may be assumed that profits before extraordinary items of both companies accrue evenly over the year. The extraordinary charge in the accounts of Stepney plc relates to an event occurring in March 19X7.

(c) Stepney plc uses the average cost method of stock valuation while Brennan plc has used the FIFO method in preparing its 19X7 financial statements. The directors of the new group have agreed to standardise accounting practice by using average cost throughout the group. This change would have affected Brennan plc's stock values as shown below.

Stock values (Brennan plc)	FIFO basis	Average cost basis
	£'000	£'000
Stock (31 December 19X6)	2,748	2,528
Stock (31 December 19X7)	3,826	3,014

(d) SUMMARISED BALANCE SHEETS AT 31 DECEMBER 19X7

	Stepney plc £'000	Brennan plc £'000
Fixed assets	61,376	24,299
Investment in Brennan plc	2,000	-
Current assets	22,685	8,623
	86,061	32,922
Current liabilities	12,472	5,461
Ordinary share capital	15,000 *	1,000 **
Retained profits	58,589	26,461
	86,061	32,922

* called-up share capital in ordinary shares of £1.00 each
** called-up share capital in ordinary shares of £0.50 each.

(e) SUMMARISED PROFIT AND LOSS ACCOUNTS
FOR THE YEAR ENDED 31 DECEMBER 19X7

	Stepney plc £'000	Brennan plc £'000
Turnover	41,456	15,396
Cost of sales	18,221	5,492
Gross profit	23,235	9,904
Administration expenses	2,694	1,063
Selling and distribution costs	4,143	1,824
Exceptional loss	3,904	-
Profit on ordinary activities before taxation	12,494	7,017
Taxation	3,952	2,076
Profit on ordinary activities after taxation	8,542	4,941
Dividend	2,000	-
Retained profit for year	6,542	4,941
Retained profits at 1 January 19X7	52,047	21,520
Retained profits at 31 December 19X7	58,589	26,461

You are required to prepare, on a merger accounting basis, the consolidated balance sheet at 31 December 19X7 and the consolidated P&L account for the year ended 31 December 19X7 of the Stepney Group plc. Assume that the merger requirements of FRS 6 have been met.

Answer

STEPNEY PLC
CONSOLIDATED BALANCE SHEET AS AT 31 DECEMBER 19X7

	£'000	£'000
Fixed assets		85,675
Current assets (W1)	30,496	
Current liabilities	17,933	
Net current assets		12,563
Total assets less current liabilities		98,238
Capital and reserves		
Share capital		15,000
Profit and loss account		83,238
		98,238

CONSOLIDATED PROFIT AND LOSS ACCOUNT
FOR THE YEAR ENDED 31 DECEMBER 19X7

	£'000	£'000
Turnover		56,852
Cost of sales (W3)		24,305
Gross profit		32,547
Distribution costs		5,967
Administrative expenses		3,757
Exceptional loss		3,904
Profit on ordinary activities before taxation		18,919
Tax on profit on ordinary activities		6,028
Profit on ordinary activities after taxation		12,891
Dividend		2,000
		10,891
Merger adjustment (W2)		(1,000)
Retained profit for the financial year		9,891
Retained profits brought forward		
As previously reported (52,047 + 21,520)	73,567	
Prior year adjustment (2,748 – 2,528)	(220)	
As restated		73,347
Retained profits carried forward		83,238

Workings

1 *Current assets*

	£'000	£'000
Stepney		22,685
Brennan		8,623
		31,308
Adjustment in respect of Brennan's closing stock		
FIFO cost	3,826	
Average cost	3,014	
		(812)
		30,496

2 *Merger adjustment*

	£'000
Nominal value of shares issued by Stepney	2,000
Nominal value of shares acquired by Stepney	1,000
Difference to be deducted from group reserves	1,000

3 *Cost of sales*

	£'000	£'000
Stepney		18,221
Brennan		
Unadjusted	5,492	
Adjustment in respect of stock valuation		
(3,826 – 3,014) – (2,748 – 2,528)	592	
		6,084
		24,305

BPP PUBLISHING

Chapter roundup

- Make sure you know the **criteria** for **merger accounting** under FRS 6 and CA 1985. You should be able to discuss the **criticisms** of merger accounting. Make sure also that you can clearly differentiate acquisitions from mergers and that you can prepare accounts using both acquisition and merger accounting.

- You should also be able to explain s 131 CA 1985 **merger relief** and distinguish it clearly from merger accounting.

- **FRS 6** represents a major step in restricting the practice of businesses who use merger accounting in non-merger situations and therefore distort the true picture of their affairs.

Quick quiz

1   Describe the effect of acquisition accounting on the distributable profits of a company. (see para 1.3)

2   What is the most important feature of the mechanics of merger accounting? (1.11)

3   What entries are made in the holding company's accounts to record a dividend received from a subsidiary's pre-acquisition profits? (2.8)

4   When can a business combination be treated as a merger under CA 1985? (2.2)

5   How does FRS 6 define a merger? (2.10)

6   When should merger accounting be used? (2.12)

7   How is a minority dealt with in merger accounting? (3.4)

8   Which section of CA 1985 deals with merger relief? (3.5) and what is it? (3.8)

Questions to try	Level	Marks	Time
20	Introductory	n/a	n/a

Chapter 20

FOREIGN SUBSIDIARIES AND FOREIGN BRANCHES

Chapter topic		Syllabus reference	Ability required
1	Foreign currency translation	9(a)	Application
2	The individual company stage	9(a)	Application
3	The consolidated financial statements stage	9(a)	Application
4	Foreign borrowings	9(a)	Application
5	Disclosure and other matters	9(a)	Application
6	Foreign branches	9(a)	Application

Introduction

This is almost the last major consolidation topic in this Study Text, apart from consolidated cash flow statements which are covered in Chapter 24.

Students have always found accounting for foreign currency difficult but, as with most financial accounting topics, you only need to adopt a logical approach and to practise plenty of questions.

It is important that you learn the definitions associated with foreign currency and when each of the different methods of translation are applicable, otherwise you will not know how to tackle each question.

1 FOREIGN CURRENCY TRANSLATION

1.1 SSAP 20 *Foreign currency translation* standardises the accounting treatment of foreign currency transactions. It explains the background and the objectives of translation as follows.

> 'The translation of foreign currency transactions and financial statements should produce results which are generally compatible with the effects of rate changes on a **company's cash flows and its equity** and should ensure that the financial statements present a true and fair view of the results of management actions. Consolidated statements should reflect the financial results and relationships as measured in the foreign currency financial statements prior to translation.'

1.2 We can distinguish between two terms here to avoid confusion.

(a) **Conversion** is the physical exchange of currencies.
(b) **Translation** is the expression of one currency in the value of another.

1.3 SSAP 20 considers the procedures which should be adopted when accounting for foreign operations in **two stages**, namely:

(a) the preparation of the financial statements of an individual company; and

(b)   the preparation of consolidated financial statements.

2   THE INDIVIDUAL COMPANY STAGE

Monetary and non-monetary items

2.1   First of all, it is worth highlighting the difference between **monetary** and **non-monetary items** as defined by SSAP 20. This is necessary because the accounting treatments for each is different.

> ### KEY TERMS
>
> - **Monetary items**: are money held and amounts to be received or paid in money and should be categorised as either short-term or long-term. Short-term monetary items are those which fall due within one year of the balance sheet date. Examples include debtors, creditors, loans and bank balances.
>
> - **Non-monetary items**: are the reverse: items which are *not* money held or amounts to be received or paid in money, eg fixed assets, investments and stock.   *(SSAP 20)*

Accounting practice

2.2   SSAP 20 lays out the following accounting practice for the individual company stage.

During the period

2.3   (a)   Translate each transaction at the exchange rate ruling on the date the transaction occurred, ie at the **historical rate**.

       (b)   Where exchange rates do not fluctuate significantly, the **average rate** for the period may be used as an approximation.

       (c)   Where the transaction is to be settled at a **contracted rate**, that rate should be used.

       (d)   Where a trading transaction is covered by a related or matching **forward contract** the forward rate *may* by used.

> ### KEY TERM
>
> - A **forward contract** is an agreement to exchange different currencies at a specified future date and at a specified rate. The difference between the specified rate and the spot rate ruling on the date the contract was entered into is the discount or premium on the forward contract.   *(SSAP 20)*

2.4   Where the transaction is settled during the period, the exchange difference is a **realised gain or loss** and is reported in the P&L account for the year.

At the balance sheet date

2.5   (a)   **Non-monetary assets** should not be restated, but should remain at historical rate.

       (b)   **Monetary assets and liabilities** (including long-term items) should be restated at the closing rate (or contract/forward rate as above).

Treatment of exchange differences

2.6 Exchange differences are part of the profit or loss on ordinary activities for the year. Include exchange gains or losses:

(a) under 'other operating income or charges' for **trading transactions**; or

(b) under 'other interest receivable/payable and similar income/charges' for **financing transactions**.

Commentary

2.7 Exchange differences are **recorded separately** rather than being used to adjust the purchases figure because they result from an event (a rate change) that is separate from the original purchase or sale transaction. The exchange difference can be attributed to the delay in payment and could have been minimised or avoided, for example by denominating the purchase in sterling or by negotiating a forward exchange contract. The treatment of exchange differences under SSAP 20 is comparable to the universal treatment of bad debts or settlement discounts, in that they are dealt with separately rather than netted against sales or purchases.

Treatment of short-term monetary items

2.8 Exchange profits on unsettled short-term monetary items should be **included in profit**, although not realised in cash form. The justification for including such 'unrealised' gains in profit is twofold.

(a) The items involved are short term and will be realised soon after the year end.
(b) It provides symmetry of treatment with unrealised short-term losses.

The fact that a loss is realised in the subsequent year is irrelevant: the loss arises from exchange rate movements *after* the year end. **SSAP 17** gives as an example of a non-adjusting post balance sheet event 'changes in rates of foreign exchange'.

2.9 The above discussion illustrates yet again the problem of **defining realised profits**. The ASC decided to take the view that exchange gains on short-term monetary items such as the above are realised in accordance with SSAP 2: they are 'realised in the form of other assets, the ultimate realisation of which can be assessed with reasonable certainty'.

Treatment of long-term monetary items

2.10 SSAP 20 takes the view that it is appropriate that exchange gains and losses on long-term monetary items should also be **recognised in the P&L account** for the sake of symmetry. This is despite the prudence difficulties of recognising unrealised gains. The convertibility and marketability of the currency should be taken into account.

2.11 Where **unrealised gains on unsettled long-term monetary items** are taken to the P&L account this may constitute a departure from the CA 1985 requirement that only realised profits should be included in the P&L account. SSAP 20 makes it clear that such a departure would be justified by the need to give a true and fair view. This being the case, particulars of the departure, the reasons for it and its effect should be given in a note.

Question 1

White Cliffs Ltd, whose year end is 31 December, buys some goods from Mid West Inc of the USA on 30 September. The invoice value is $40,000 and is due for settlement in equal instalments on 30 November and 31 January. The exchange rate moved as follows.

	$ = £1
30 September	1.60
30 November	1.80
31 December	1.90
31 January	1.85

Required

State the accounting entries in the books of White Cliffs Ltd.

Answer

The purchase will be recorded in the books of White Cliffs Ltd using the rate of exchange ruling on 30 September.

		£	£
DEBIT	Purchases	25,000	
CREDIT	Trade creditors		25,000

Being the sterling cost of goods purchased for $40,000 ($40,000 ÷ $1.60/£1)

On 30 November, White Cliffs must pay $20,000. This will cost $20,000 ÷ $1.80/£1 = £11,111 and the company has therefore made an exchange gain of £12,500 - £11,111 = £1,389.

		£	£
DEBIT	Trade creditors	12,500	
CREDIT	Exchange gains: P & L account		1,389
	Cash		11,111

On 31 December, the balance sheet date, the outstanding liability will be recalculated using the rate applicable to that date: $20,000 ÷ $1.90/£1 = £10,526. A further exchange gain of £1,974 has been made and will be recorded as follows.

		£	£
DEBIT	Trade creditors	1,974	
CREDIT	Exchange gains: P & L account		1,974

The total exchange gain of £3,363 will be included in the operating profit for the year ending 31 December.

On 31 January, White Cliffs must pay the second instalment of $20,000. This will cost them £10,811 ($20,000 ÷ $1.85/£1).

		£	£
DEBIT	Trade creditors	10,526	
	Exchange losses: P & L account	285	
CREDIT	Cash		10,811

3 THE CONSOLIDATED FINANCIAL STATEMENTS STAGE 5/96, 11/98

3.1 The following SSAP 20 definitions are relevant at this stage.

KEY TERMS

- A **foreign enterprise** is a subsidiary, associated company or branch whose operations are based in a country other than that of the investing company or whose assets and liabilities are denominated mainly in a foreign currency.

- A **foreign branch** is either a legally constituted enterprise located overseas or a group of assets and liabilities which are accounted for in foreign currencies. *(SSAP 20)*

3.2 In order for a UK holding company or company with a foreign branch to prepare its group accounts or final accounts for the year, the financial statements of its foreign enterprises must first be **translated into sterling**. Two main methods have been evolved, all of them involving one or both of the following types of exchange rate:

KEY TERMS

- The **closing rate** is the rate for spot transactions ruling at the balance sheet date and is the mean of the buying and selling rates at the close of business on the day for which the rate is to be ascertained.

- An **historical rate** is the rate of exchange ruling at the time a relevant transaction (or possibly revaluation) was effected. *(SSAP 20)*

3.3 The two different methods are as follows.

(a) **The temporal method**. Under this method:

   (i) non-monetary items that are recorded in the foreign currency financial statements on a historical cost basis are translated at the historical rates ruling when the relevant transactions occurred;

   (ii) non-monetary items that have been revalued in the foreign currency financial statements are translated at the rates that existed on the dates of their revaluations;

   (iii) monetary items are translated at the closing rate.

(b) **The closing rate method** under which all assets and liabilities are translated at the closing rate.

Under (a), reserves will be calculated as a balancing figure.

3.4 The **temporal** and the **closing rate methods** have been the most widely used in the UK and the US and feature in SSAP 20. A brief illustration may be helpful at this stage.

3.5 EXAMPLE: TEMPORAL METHOD AND CLOSING RATE METHOD

A UK company, Stone Ltd, set up a US subsidiary on 30 June 19X1. Stone subscribed $24,000 for share capital when the exchange rate was $2 = £1. The subsidiary, Brick Inc, borrowed $72,000 in the US and bought a non-monetary asset for $96,000. Stone Ltd prepared its accounts on 31 December 19X1 and by that time the exchange rate had moved to $3 = £1. As a result of highly unusual circumstances, Brick Inc sold its asset early in 19X2 for $96,000. It repaid its loan and was liquidated. Stone's capital of $24,000 was repaid in February 19X2 when the exchange rate was $3 = £1.

Required

Account for the above transactions using both the closing rate and temporal methods.

3.6 SOLUTION

From the above it can be seen that Stone Ltd will record its initial investment at £12,000 which is the starting cost of its shares. The balance sheet of Brick Inc at 31 December 19X1 is summarised below.

	$'000
Non-monetary asset	96
Share capital	24
Loan	72
	96

This may be translated using the temporal and closing rate methods as follows.

	Temporal method £'000	*Closing rate method* £'000
Non-monetary asset		
($2 = £1)	48	
($3 = £1)		32
Share capital and reserves (balancing figure)	24	8
Loan ($3 = £1)	24	24
	48	32
Exchange gain/(loss) for 19X1	12	(4)

The exchange gain and loss are the differences between the value of the original investment (£12,000) and the total of share capital and reserves as disclosed by the above balance sheets.

On liquidation, Stone Ltd will receive £8,000 ($24,000 converted at $3 = £1). The accounts of Stone Ltd will therefore need to show a loss of £16,000 (£24,000 – £8,000) in 19X2 if the temporal method is being used. No gain or loss will arise in 19X2 if the closing rate method is being used.

3.7 The figures in the above example reveal the following points.

(a) The exchange rate movement was such as to cause a loss to a UK company investing in the US. (If Stone Ltd had held $24,000 in cash throughout the period it would have lost £4,000.) The temporal method, however, shows an exchange gain in the accounts to 31 December 19X1. This gain is solely attributable to the loan.

	£'000
Loan translated at $2 = £1	36
Loan translated at $3 = £1	24
Exchange gain (reduction in liability)	12

The closing rate method also recognises a loss on holding the non-monetary asset.

	£'000
Asset translated at $2 = £1	48
Asset translated at $3 = £1	32
Exchange loss (fall in value of asset)	(16)
Exchange gain on loan as before	12
Net exchange loss	(4)

After taking into account the loss of £16,000 arising in 19X2 under the temporal method, the net position under the two methods will be the same. It may be argued that the closing rate method is more in line with the economic reality as it recognises the loss of £4,000 in 19X1 which is the year in which the rate change occurred. It can be seen that the closing rate method, in effect, accrues the loss caused by the exchange rate change. Whilst this may be considered acceptable and even desirable on the basis of prudence, a strict application of historical cost accounting would not allow the accrual of the unrealised gain that would have resulted had the exchange rate movement been in the opposite direction.

(b) Despite the comments made in (a) above, it is worth pointing out that the temporal method achieves its aim of representing the transactions as if they had been undertaken by the parent. The position would then have been:

	£'000
19X1 Exchange gain on loan	12
19X2 Loss on sale of asset	(16)
Net loss	(4)

(c) Under the closing rate method, the gearing ratio in the sterling accounts at 31 December 19X1 will be the same as that in the dollar accounts. This is not true for the accounts prepared under the temporal method.

The SSAP 20 approach: net investment (closing rate) vs temporal

3.8 Except in certain specified circumstances, SSAP 20 requires that the **closing rate method** of translation should be used.

(a) Exchange differences arising from the retranslation of the opening net investment in a foreign enterprise at the closing rate should be recorded as a **movement on reserves**.

(b) The P&L account of a foreign enterprise accounted for under the closing rate/net investment method should be translated at the **closing rate** *or* at an **average rate** for the period.

3.9 SSAP 20 takes the view that in most circumstances the foreign enterprise should be seen as a single entity operating semi-independently and as a **single business unit**. The interest of the UK company should be regarded as a 'net investment' rather than as an investment in its many separate individual assets, liabilities and transactions. In other words, since the foreign enterprise is a single unit, its P&L account and balance sheet should each be translated at a single rate. This support for the net investment concept explains the preference given to the **closing rate method** over the temporal method by SSAP 20.

> ### KEY TERM
>
> The **net investment** which a company has in a foreign enterprise is its effective equity stake and comprises its proportion of such foreign enterprise's net assets; in appropriate circumstances, intra-group loans and other deferred balances may be regarded as part of the effective equity stake. *(SSAP 20)*

3.10 The vast majority of foreign enterprises are thought to fall into the category of 'net investments' and thus to necessitate use of the closing rate method. The temporal method may only be used where the enterprise trades as a **direct extension** of the investing company, rather than as a separate entity. Amongst the factors to be taken into account will be:

(a) the extent to which the **cash flows** of the enterprise have a direct impact upon those of the investing company;

(b) the extent to which the **functioning** of the enterprise is dependent directly upon the investing company;

(c) the **currency** in which the majority of the trading transactions are denominated;

(d) the **major currency** to which the operation is exposed in its financing structure.

3.11 Examples of situations where the **temporal method** may be appropriate are where the foreign enterprise:

(a) acts as a **selling agency** receiving stocks of goods from the investing company and remitting the proceeds back to the company;

(b) produces a raw material or manufactures parts or sub-assemblies which are then shipped to the investing company for **inclusion in its own products**;

(c) is located overseas for tax, exchange control or similar reasons to act as a **means of raising finance** for other companies in the group.

In other words, in those circumstances where the trade of the foreign enterprise is more dependent on the economic environment of the investing company's currency than that of its own reporting currency, the temporal method should be used.

The closing rate method in more detail

3.12 Under the closing rate method the following treatments are used.

(a) The **assets and liabilities** shown in the foreign enterprise's balance sheet are translated at the rate of exchange ruling at the (closing) balance sheet date, regardless of the date on which those items originated. The balancing figure on the translated balance sheet represents the head office net investment in the enterprise.

(b) Amounts in the **P&L account** should be translated at either:

(i) the closing rate; or

(ii) an average rate for the accounting period (calculated in an appropriate manner).

The method chosen should be applied **consistently** from one year to the next. Where the average rate is used and this differs from the closing rate, there will be an exchange difference (gain or loss) which should be dealt with in **reserves** and not in the P&L account for the year.

(c) Exchange differences arising from the re-translation at the end of each year of the holding company's net investment should be reported through **reserves**, not through the P&L account for the year.

The temporal method in more detail

3.13 The mechanics of this method are identical with those used in preparing the accounts of an individual company.

(a) The **P&L account** is translated using actual rates where known (an average for the period tends to be used in practice) and historical rates for non-monetary items such as opening and closing stock and depreciation.

(b) Any exchange differences are reported as **part of profit** for the year.

Some practical points

3.14 The following points apply to *both* methods.

(a) For consolidation purposes calculations are simpler if a subsidiary's share capital is translated at the **historical rate** (the rate when the investing company acquired its interest) and reserves are found as a balancing figure.

(b) **Dividends proposed** by a subsidiary should always be translated at the **closing rate** in the P&L account and at the actual rate on the date of payment. This is because the investing company will record the items at these rates in its own books.

These are both points of detail, not mentioned in SSAP 20.

Methods compared

3.15 A summary of the translation methods is given below, which shows the main steps to follow in the consolidation process.

	Closing rate method	Temporal method
Step 1 Translate the **closing balance sheet** (net assets/shareholders' funds) and use this for preparing the consolidated balance sheet in the normal way.	Under **closing rate** at the year end for all items (see note).	Use the **closing rate** at the year end for monetary items and the appropriate **historical rates** for non-monetary items. Shareholders' funds should be treated as the balancing figure (see note).
Step 2 Translate the **P&L account.** (In all cases, dividends should be translated at the rate ruling when the dividend was paid or, in the case of proposed dividends, the closing rate at the year end.)	Use the **average rate** or the **closing rate** for the year for all items (but see comment on dividends). The figures obtained can then be used in preparing the consolidated P&L a/c.	In most examination questions, translate all items apart from depreciation at the **average rate** for the year and translate depreciation at the rates ruling when the relevant fixed assets were **acquired** (or **revalued**). If however, the information is available, use the temporal rates specific to opening and closing stocks. At this stage it is not possible to prepare the consolidated P&L a/c. It may be necessary to break down costs of sales to get the translation of opening/closing sales.

BPP PUBLISHING

	Closing rate method	Temporal method
Step 3		
Translate the **shareholders' funds** (net assets) at the beginning of the year.	Use the **closing rate** at the beginning of the year (the opening rate for the current year).	Use the **closing rate** at the beginning of the year for monetary items and the appropriate **historical rates** for non-monetary items. In many questions it is necessary to reconstruct the **opening balance sheet.**
Step 4		
Calculate the **total exchange difference** for the year as follows.	This stage will be **unnecessary** unless you are asked to state the total exchange differences or are asked to prepare a statement of the movement on reserves, where the exchange difference will be shown.	After finding the exchange differences it will be possible to prepare the **consolidated P&L a/c.** The exchange differences should be included before tax.

For the Closing rate method, Step 4 table:

	£
Closing net assets at closing rate (Step 1)	X
Less opening net assets at opening rate (Step 3)	X̲
	X
Less retained profit per translated P&L a/c (Step 2)	X
Exchange differences	X̲
Group share (%)	X

It may be necessary to adjust for any profits or losses taken direct to reserves during the year.

For the Temporal method, Step 4 column continued:

For **exam purposes** you can translate the closing shareholders' funds as follows.

(a) Share capital + pre-acquisition reserves at historical rate.

(b) Post-acquisition reserves as a balancing figure.

As mentioned above, the share capital may be translated at the historical rate (under both methods). The reserves will then be the balancing figure. The advantage of this method is that it simplifies the 'cancellation' of the share capital on consolidation.

Question 2

The abridged balance sheets and P&L account of Darius Ltd and its foreign subsidiary, Xerxes Inc, appear below.

DRAFT BALANCE SHEET AS AT 31 DECEMBER 19X1

	Darius Ltd		Xerxes Inc	
Fixed assets	£	£	$	$
Plant at cost	600		500	
Less depreciation	(250)		(200)	
		350		300
100 $1 shares in Xerxes		25		-
		375		300
Current assets				
Stocks	225		200	
Debtors	150		100	
	375		300	
Current liabilities	100		110	
Net current assets		275		190
		650		490
Loans		50		110
		600		380
Capital and reserves				
Ordinary capital £1/$1 shares		300		100
Retained profit		300		280
		600		380

PROFIT AND LOSS ACCOUNTS
FOR THE YEAR ENDED 31 DECEMBER 19X1

	Darius Ltd	Xerxes Inc
	£	$
Profit before tax	200	160
Tax	100	80
Profit after tax, retained	100	80

The following further information is given.

(a) Darius Ltd has had its interest in Xerxes Inc since the incorporation of the company.

(b) Depreciation is 8% per annum on cost.

(c) There have been no loan repayments or movements in fixed assets during the year. The opening stock of Xerxes Inc was $120. Assume that stock turnover times are very short.

(d) Exchange rates: $4 to £1 when Xerxes Inc was incorporated
                            $2.5 to £1 when Xerxes Inc acquired its fixed assets
                            $2 to £1 on 31 December 19X0
                            $1.6 to £1 average rate of exchange year ending 31 December 19X1
                            $1 to £1 on 31 December 19X1.

Required

Prepare the summarised consolidated financial statements of Darius Ltd using:

(a) the closing rate/net investment method;
(b) the temporal method.

Answer: closing rate/net investment method

Step 1. The balance sheet of Xerxes Inc at 31 December 19X1 should be translated at $1 = £1.

SUMMARISED BALANCE SHEET AT 31 DECEMBER 19X1

	£	£
Fixed assets (net book value)		300
Current assets		
Stock	200	
Debtors	100	
	300	
Current liabilities	110	
Net current assets		190
		490
Loan		110
Net assets (= shareholders' funds)		380

387

Since Darius Ltd acquired the whole of the issued share capital on incorporation, the post-acquisition reserves including exchange differences will be the value of shareholders' funds arrived at above, less the original cost to Darius Ltd of £25. Post-acquisition reserves = £380 − £25 = £355.

SUMMARISED CONSOLIDATED BALANCE SHEET AS AT 31 DECEMBER 19X1

		£	£
Fixed assets (net book value)	£(350 + 300)		650
Current assets			
Stock	£(225 + 200)	425	
Debtors	£(150 + 100)	250	
		675	
Current liabilities	£(100 + 110)	210	
Net current assets			465
			1,115
Loans	£(50 + 110)		160
			955
Capital and reserves			
Ordinary £1 shares (Darius Ltd only)			300
Reserves	£(300 + 355)		655
			955

Note. It is quite unnecessary to know the amount of the exchange differences when preparing the consolidated balance sheet.

Step 2. The P&L account should be translated at average rate ($1.6 = £1).

SUMMARISED PROFIT AND LOSS ACCOUNT
FOR THE YEAR ENDED 31 DECEMBER 19X1

	£
Profit before tax	100
Tax	50
Profit after tax, retained	50

SUMMARISED CONSOLIDATED PROFIT AND LOSS ACCOUNT
FOR THE YEAR ENDED 31 DECEMBER 19X1

		£
Profit before tax	£(200 + 100)	300
Tax	£(100 + 50)	150
Profit after tax, retained	£(100 + 50)	150

Step 3. The equity interest at the beginning of the year can be found as follows.

	$
Equity value at 31 December 19X1	380
Retained profit for year	80
Equity value at 31 December 19X0	300
Translated at $2 = £1, this gives	£150

Step 4. The exchange difference can now be calculated.

	£
Equity interest at 31 December 19X1 (step 1)	380
Equity interest at 1 January 19X1 (step 3)	150
	230
Less retained profit (step 2)	50
Exchange gain	180

CONSOLIDATED STATEMENT OF MOVEMENTS ON RESERVES
FOR THE YEAR ENDED 31 DECEMBER 19X1

	£
Consolidated reserves at 31 December 19X0	325
Exchange gains arising on consolidation	180
Retained profit for the year	150
Consolidated reserves at 31 December 19X1	655

(*Note*. The post-acquisition reserves of Xerxes Inc at the beginning of the year must have been £150 – £25 = £125 and the reserves of Darius Ltd must have been £300 – £100 = £200. The consolidated reserves must therefore have been £325.)

Answer: temporal method

Step 1

SUMMARISED BALANCE SHEET AS AT 31 DECEMBER 19X1

	Rate	£	£
Fixed assets at NBV	$2.5 = £1		120
Current assets			
Stock	Assumed to be $1 = £1	200	
Debtors	$1 = £1	100	
		300	
Current liabilities	$1 = £1	110	
Net current assets			190
			310
Loans	$1 = £1		110
Net assets (= Shareholders' funds)	Balancing figure		200

In arriving at the consolidated balance sheet the same comments apply as in stage 1 for the closing rate method. The post-acquisition reserves of Xerxes Inc will be £200 – £25 = £175.

SUMMARISED CONSOLIDATED BALANCE SHEET AS AT 31 DECEMBER 19X1

		£	£
Fixed assets at NBV	£(350 + 120)		470
Current assets			
Stocks	£(225 + 200)	425	
Debtors	£(150 + 100)	250	
		675	
Current liabilities	£(100 + 110)	210	
			465
			935
Loans	£(50 + 110)		160
			775
Capital and reserves			
Ordinary £1 shares			300
Reserves	£(300 + 175)		475
			775

Note. As with the closing rate method, it has been quite unnecessary to know the amount of the exchange differences when preparing the consolidated balance sheet.

Step 2. The following rates should be used for the P&L account.

	Rate
Depreciation	$2.5 = £1
Opening stock	$2.0 = £1
Closing stock	$1.0 = £1
All other items	$1.6 = £1

SUMMARISED PROFIT AND LOSS ACCOUNT FOR THE YEAR ENDED 31 DECEMBER 19X1

	$	$	Rate	£	£
Profit before tax, depreciation and increase in stock value		120	$1.6 = £1		75
Opening stock	120		$2.0 = £1	60	
Closing stock	200		$1.0 = £1	200	
Increase in stock value		80			140
		200			215
Depreciation (8% × $500)		40	$2.5 = £1		16
Profit before tax		160			199
Tax		80	$1.6 = £1		50
Profit after tax, retained		80			149

Step 3. Since there were no movements in fixed assets or loan repayments, the opening balance sheet in dollars can be summarised as shown below. This has been translated at $2.5 = £1 for fixed assets and at $2.0 = £1 for monetary items and stocks.

SUMMARISED BALANCE SHEET AS AT 31 DECEMBER 19X0

	$	Rate	£
Fixed assets NBV $(300 + 40)	340	$2.5 = £1	136
Stocks	120	$2.0 = £1	60
Net current monetary liabilities (balancing figure)	50	$2.0 = £1	25
	410		171
Loans	110	$2.0 = £1	55
	300		116
Shareholders' funds $(380 - 80)	300	Balancing figure	116

Step 4. The exchange difference can be calculated.

	£
Shareholders' funds at 31 December 19X1	200
Less shareholders' funds at 31 December 19X0	116
	84
Less retained profit before exchange differences	149
Exchange loss	(65)

SUMMARISED CONSOLIDATED PROFIT AND LOSS ACCOUNT
FOR THE YEAR ENDED 31 DECEMBER 19X1

	£
Profit before tax £(200 + 199 − 65)	334
Tax £(100 + 50)	150
Profit after tax, retained	184
Shareholders' funds at 31 December 19X0	116
Less cost of shares	25
Post-acquisition reserves in Xerxes Inc at 31 December 19X0	91
Reserves of Darius Ltd at 31 December 19X0	200
Consolidated reserves at 31 December 19X0	291

CONSOLIDATED STATEMENT OF MOVEMENTS ON RESERVES
FOR THE YEAR ENDED 31 DECEMBER 19X1

	£
Consolidated reserves at 31 December 19X0	291
Retained profit for the year	184
Consolidated reserves at 31 December 19X1	475

Exam focus point

You could get either method in the exam, possibly with an explanation of when you would use which method.

Analysis of exchange differences

3.16 Under both the closing rate and the temporal methods, the exchange differences in the above exercise could be reconciled by splitting them into their component parts. (Such a split is not required by SSAP 20, nor is it required in your exam, but it may help your understanding of the subject.

(a) **Closing rate method**

Using the opening balance sheet reconstructed for the temporal method and translating at $2 = £1 and $1 = £1 gives the following.

	$2 = £1	$1 = £1	Difference
	£	£	£
Fixed assets at NBV	170	340	170
Stocks	60	120	60
Net current monetary liabilities	(25)	(50)	(25)
	205	410	205
Shareholders' funds	150	300	150
Loans	55	110	55
	205	410	205

Translating the P&L account arrived at for the temporal method using $1.60 = £1 and $1 = £1 gives the following results.

	$1.60 = £1	$1 = £1	Difference
	£	£	£
Profit before tax, depreciation and increase in stock values	75	120	45
Increase in stock values	50	80	30
	125	200	75
Depreciation	(25)	(40)	(15)
	100	160	60
Tax	(50)	(80)	(30)
Profit after tax, retained	50	80	30

The overall position is then:

	£	£
Gain on fixed assets (£170 – £15)		155
Loss on loan		(55)
Gain on stocks (£60 + £30)	90	
Loss on net monetary current assets/ liabilities (all other differences) (£45 – £30 – £25)	(10)	
		80
Net exchange gain: as above		180

(b) **Temporal method**

Under the temporal method there will be no gains on fixed assets or stocks so the overall position will be:

	£
Loss on net current monetary items	10
Loss on loan	55
Net exchange loss (as above)	65

Minority interests

3.17 In problems involving minority interests the following points should be noted.

(a) The figure for **minority interests in the balance sheet** will be the appropriate proportion of the translated share capital and reserves of the subsidiary. In addition, it may be necessary to show the proposed dividend payable to the minorities as a liability. The proposed dividend should be translated at the closing rate for this purpose.

(b) The **minority interest in the P&L account** will be the appropriate proportion of sterling profits available for distribution. In the case of the temporal method, this profit will be arrived at *after* charging or crediting the exchange differences.

3.18 EXAMPLE: MINORITY INTERESTS

The summarised accounts of Camrumite Inc are shown below.

BALANCE SHEET AS AT 31 DECEMBER 19X3

	Fr
Fixed assets	10,000
Net monetary assets	5,000
	15,000
Ordinary share capital and reserves	15,000

PROFIT AND LOSS ACCOUNT FOR THE YEAR ENDED 31 DECEMBER 19X3

	Fr
Profit after tax	3,080
Proposed final dividend	1,680
Retained profit	1,400

60% of the issued capital of Camrumite Inc is owned by Bates Ltd, a UK company.

There have been no movements in fixed assets during the year. The depreciation charge for the year was 560 Fr.

The exchange rate has moved as follows.

Date on which fixed assets were acquired	8 Fr = £1
1 January 19X3	5 Fr = £1
Average for the year ended 31.12.X3	7 Fr = £1
31 December 19X3	8 Fr = £1

You are required to calculate the figures for minority interests to be included in the consolidated accounts of Bates Ltd using:

(a) the closing rate/net investment method;
(b) the temporal method.

Show the movements on the minority interest accounts during the year.

3.19 SOLUTION: CLOSING RATE METHOD

Translating the shareholders' funds using the closing rate as at 31 December 19X3 gives 15,000 Fr ÷ 8 = £1,875. The minority interest in the balance sheet will be 40% × £1,875 = £750.

The proposed dividend translated at the closing rate is 1,680 Fr ÷ 8 = £210. The amount payable to the minority shareholders is 40% × £210 = £84.

The profit after tax translated at the average rate is 3,080 Fr ÷ 7 = £440. The minority interest in the P&L account is therefore 40% × £440 = £176.

At the beginning of the year the share capital and reserves must have been 15,000 Fr – 1,400 Fr = 13,600 Fr. Translating this at the rate ruling on 1 January 19X3 gives 13,600 Fr ÷ 5 = £2,720. The minority interest at 1 January 19X3 was 40% × £2,720 = £1,088.

	£	£
Shareholders' funds as at 1 January 19X3		2,720
Add: profit for year	440	
less dividends	210	
		230
		2,950
Less shareholders' funds at 31 December 19X3		1,875
Exchange loss		1,075
Minority interest therein £1,075 × 40%		430

The minority interest can be summarised as follows.

		£
Balance at 1 January 19X3		1,088
Minority interest in profit for the year		176
Minority interest in exchange losses		(430)
		834
Balance at 31 December 19X3		750
Dividend payable to minority		84
		834

3.20 SOLUTION: TEMPORAL METHOD

Shareholders' funds at 31 December 19X3

		£
Fixed assets	10,000 Fr ÷ 8	1,250
Net monetary assets	5,000 Fr ÷ 8	625
		1,875
Minority interest therein £1,875 × 40%		750

The profit after tax but before depreciation and exchange differences is 3,640 Fr. The translated P&L account before dividends will be as follows.

		£
Profit after tax but before depreciation	3,640 Fr ÷ 7	520
Depreciation	560 Fr ÷ 8	70
		450
Minority interest therein £450 × 40%		180

Shareholders' funds at 1 January 19X3

		£
Fixed assets	10,560 Fr ÷ 8	1,320
Net monetary assets (balancing figure)	3,040 Fr ÷ 5	608
Shareholders' funds	13,600 Fr	1,928
Minority interest therein £1,928 × 40%		771

	£	£
Shareholders' funds at 1 January 19X3		1,928
Add: profit for year before exchange differences	450	
less dividend	210	
		240
		2,168
Less shareholders' funds at 31 December 19X3		1,875
Exchange loss		293
Minority interest therein £293 × 40%		117

The minority interest account can be summarised as follows.

	£
Balance at 1 January 19X3	771
Minority interest in profit for the year £(180 − 117)	63
	834
Balance at 31 December 19X3	750
Dividend payable to minority	84
	834

Goodwill arising on consolidation

3.21 The calculation of goodwill should be based on the exchange rates ruling at the **date of acquisition**. It will not be altered by subsequent exchange rate changes. In other words, exchange rate differences occurring after acquisition are adjusted through post-acquisition reserves and do not affect the translation of pre-acquisition reserves. Similarly, **pre-acquisition exchange differences** are dealt with through pre-acquisition reserves.

3.22 This means that, when using the **temporal method** for translating the results of a subsidiary company acquired as a going concern, the temporal rates for non-monetary assets owned by the subsidiary at the date of acquisition will be the rate ruling on that date rather than rates ruling when the assets were originally acquired by the subsidiary and that goodwill will be the same whether the closing rate method or the temporal method is used subsequent to acquisition.

Deferred tax

3.23 Obviously, before preparing consolidated accounts it will be necessary to ensure that the accounts of foreign subsidiaries are prepared (or adjusted) in accordance with **SSAP 15**.

When the accounts of foreign subsidiaries are translated using the closing rate method, the closing rate will be used for deferred tax balances. When the temporal method is used for deferred tax balances the position is not so clear cut. If the deferred tax balance is viewed as a liability, then it would seem appropriate to use the closing rate.

Foreign associated undertakings

3.24 Foreign associates will be companies with substantial autonomy from the group and so the **closing rate/net investment method** will be used when translating net assets into sterling.

3.25 Section summary

The main points to remember in this section relate to when and how to use the closing rate/net investment method or the temporal method.

- **Closing rate/net investment**
  - Use for independent subsidiary
  - Translate assets and liabilities at closing rate
  - Translate P&L account at average/closing rate
  - Exchange differences through reserves

- **Temporal**
  - Use for direct extensions of the investing company
  - Translate assets and liabilities at closing rate (monetary items) and historical rate (non-monetary)
  - Translate P&L account at actual (average) rate and historical rate (non-monetary items)
  - Exchange differences are part of profit

4 FOREIGN BORROWINGS

4.1 A special case exists where foreign equity investments are financed by foreign borrowings.

Individual company accounts

4.2   The normal treatment for exchange differences on foreign currency borrowings would be to include them in the P&L account for the year. Equally, foreign equity investments (whether in subsidiaries or not) are regarded as **non-monetary items**, which are not normally retranslated at the year end and which therefore do not give rise to any exchange differences.

4.3   There is an argument, however, that where a foreign equity investment is financed by a foreign currency loan, so that the company is **hedging the exchange risk**, gains or losses on the loan should be **offset** against losses or gains on the investment, the latter being retranslated at the closing rate. This argument is particularly strong where the loan and the investment are in the same foreign currency, since a loss on the loan will automatically be accompanied by a gain on the investment, and *vice versa*, and the company's exposure to exchange risks may be much reduced.

4.4   Where such hedging takes place SSAP 20 allows the equity investments to be translated at the **closing rate** and the exchange differences taken to **reserves**. The exchange gains or losses on the foreign currency borrowings should then offset these exchange differences as a reserve movement. The following conditions apply.

   (a)   In any accounting period, exchange gains or losses arising on the borrowings may be offset **only to the extent** of exchange differences arising on the equity investments.

   (b)   The foreign currency borrowings, whose exchange gains or losses are used in the offset process, should not exceed, in the aggregate, the **total amount of cash** that the investments are expected to be able to generate, whether from profits or otherwise.

   (c)   The accounting treatment adopted should be **applied consistently** from period to period.

   (d)   The borrowing and the investment need *not* be denominated in the **same foreign currency**.

Consolidated accounts

4.5   Companies are permitted to offset exchange differences on foreign currency loans and foreign equity investments in the consolidated accounts, just as they can be offset in the individual company accounts. The additional requirement that the **closing rate method must be used** is logical since under the temporal method differences go through the P&L account in *all* circumstances.

4.6   The rule is that, where foreign currency borrowings have been used to finance, or to provide a hedge against, group equity investments in foreign enterprises, exchange gains or losses on the borrowings, which would otherwise have been taken to the P&L account, may be offset as reserve movements against exchange differences arising on the retranslation of the net investments provided that:

   (a)   the relationship between the investing company and the foreign enterprises concerned **justify the use** of the closing rate method for consolidation purposes;

   (b)   in any accounting period, the exchange gains and losses arising on foreign currency borrowings are offset **only to the extent** of the exchange differences arising on the net investments in foreign enterprises;

(c) the foreign currency borrowings, whose exchange gains or losses are used in the offset process, should not exceed, in the aggregate, the **total amount of cash** that the net investments are expected to be able to generate, whether from profits or otherwise; and

(d) the accounting treatment is **applied consistently** from period to period.

4.7 Where the provisions of Paragraph 4.4 have been applied in the investing company's financial statements to a foreign equity investment which is neither a subsidiary nor an associated company, the same offset procedure may be applied in the consolidated financial statements.

5 DISCLOSURE AND OTHER MATTERS

Disclosure

5.1 The disclosure requirements of SSAP 20 are as follows.

(a) The **methods used** in the translation of the financial statements of foreign enterprises and the treatment accorded to exchange differences should be disclosed in the financial statements (as an accounting policy note).

(b) The following information should also be disclosed in the financial statements:

(i) for all companies or groups of companies, the net amount **of exchange gains and losses** on foreign currency borrowings less deposits, identifying separately:

(1) the amount offset in reserves; and
(2) the net amount charged/credited to the P&L account;

(ii) for all companies or groups of companies, the net **movement on reserves** arising from exchange differences.

5.2 Disclosure of the **basis** on which foreign currencies have been translated into sterling is also a requirement of CA 1985.

5.3 Under SSAP 20, exchange gains arising on **long-term monetary items** (ie falling due after more than one year) are deemed to be 'unrealised', and therefore the following treatment and disclosure is appropriate.

(a) Where there are doubts as to the **convertibility** of a currency, consider on the grounds of prudence whether to restrict the amount of the gain to be recognised in the P&L account.

(b) Where gains on long-term monetary items are included in the P&L account, this represents a departure from paragraph 12 Sch 4 CA 1985 and the following is a **specimen note** to comply with CA 1985.

> 'The P&L account includes £X of exchange gains on long-term monetary items which represents a departure from the accounting principle in the Companies Act 1985 that only realised profits should be recognised. This departure has been made in accordance with SSAP 20 in order to show a true and fair view of the results of the business.'

This covers particulars, reasons and the effect of the departure.

Criticisms of SSAP 20

5.4 Although SSAP 20 is an improvement over the previous situation, it is still criticised.

Translation of the P&L account: closing rate vs average rate

5.5 Under the closing rate method either the closing rate or the average rate may be used to translate the P&L account. This is a weakness of SSAP 20 and the problem of a **lack of comparability** between companies is exacerbated.

5.6 Arguments for the use of the **closing rate** include the following.

(a) The use of the closing rate is simpler as it avoids the need to find an average rate weighted by the volume of transactions.

(b) The use of the closing rate will preserve the relationships in the foreign currency financial statements between P&L account items and balance sheet items. (This is stated as one of the reasons for choosing the closing rate method at all.)

(c) Many UK companies prefer the closing rate, have used it for some years and would object to a change.

5.7 On the other hand, the **average rate** method has the following advantages.

(a) Profits accrue over a whole period, so the average rate will reflect the true events.
(b) There is no need to restate interim results.
(c) It is less volatile than the closing rate method.
(d) It gives greater comparability between companies with overlapping accounting periods.

Forward contracts

5.8 Two criticisms are made in relation to forward contracts and similar vehicles (currently swaps, options).

(a) There is **insufficient guidance** in the standard on accounting for such contracts, particularly the discount or premium.

(b) The use of forward rates is **optional** and so companies can ignore a related forward contract if they wish and this leads to inconsistency.

Cover method

5.9 The cover method describes where there is an **offset** of exchange differences on foreign currency loans and foreign equity investments. Again, there are several criticisms in this area.

(a) The use of the cover method is **optional,** so companies can choose not to use the cover method provisions. Again, this leads to a lack of comparability. The same applies to exchange differences in consolidated financial statements, which *may* be offset as reserve movements.

(b) Since there is no requirement that borrowings should be in the same currency as the investment, cover may not exist, in other words exchange risk is **not being hedged** unless loan *and* investment are in the same currency.

(c) Allowing borrowings to be in different currencies from the investments means that exchange differences on the borrowings will not necessarily be treated the same **each year** (some years taken to reserves, some to the P&L account).

Reserve accounting

5.10 The criticism here is that exchange differences on net investments and borrowings which are a hedge never pass through the P&L account. However, exchange differences will ultimately be reflected in **cash flows** when dividends are received from the investments or when the investments are ultimately sold. No provisions are contained in SSAP 20 as to what should happen to the cumulative exchange differences which have arisen on the investments when the investments are sold or dividends are received. As a result, the exchange differences are usually not reflected in the P&L account at any time, even when the investment is sold.

5.11 Similarly, exchange differences on borrowings which have financed or provided a hedge against equity investments are normally taken to reserves even although they will have an impact on the **cash flows** of the company. It is therefore possible for the borrowings to have been completely repaid and none of the exchange differences thereon taken through the P&L account.

5.12 The problems associated with reserve accounting have been partly overcome by the greater prominence given to reserve movements by the **STRGL.**

Realised profits in individual companies: exchange losses

5.13 Where exchange losses have arisen, it would seem that s 275 CA 1985 is applicable. This requires that provisions should be treated as **realised losses** for the purposes of determining distributable profits. Realised losses will include those on:

(a) settled transactions;
(b) unsettled short-term monetary items; and
(c) long-term monetary items (to be prudent).

5.14 However, a problem exists in the case of losses on **long-term overseas borrowings** taken directly to the reserves of an individual company which uses the offset procedure in its own accounts. The question arises as to whether such losses should be treated as realised.

5.15 The cash flows can be considered where the loan **has been repaid**; in other words, where the exchange losses taken for offset to reserves relate to borrowings which have been repaid then they are **realised**. The cash flow situation where borrowings have not been repaid will be affected by the level of **dividends received** from the foreign investment before the borrowings are due to be repaid.

(a) If dividends received are sufficient, then a hedge exists and the loss on the borrowings can be treated as unrealised.

(b) If insufficient dividends are received before the borrowings are repaid, there is no hedge and the losses should be treated as realised.

5.16 This last criticism is perhaps the most serious, although the first four are bad enough as they allow a great deal of manipulation. The solution would to be an amendment to SSAP 20, taking account of the above criticisms. However, foreign currency transactions are not very high on the ASB's agenda and so revision is probably some way off.

UITF Abstract 9 *Accounting for operations in hyper-inflationary economies*

5.17 This UITF Abstract is relevant to SSAP 20 requirements: see Chapter 23.

UITF Abstract 19 *Tax on gains and losses on foreign currency borrowing that hedge an investment in a foreign enterprise*

5.18   This abstract formalises the view expressed two years ago, following changes to the tax treatment of certain exchange differences, that where exchange differences are reported in the statement of total recognised gains and losses, the related tax should also be reported in that statement.

5.19   The abstract also specifies how tax should be taken into account in applying the restrictions contained in SSAP 20 *Foreign currency translation* on the treatment of gains and losses on borrowings that finance or hedge a foreign net investment and clarifies the necessary disclosures.

5.20   Section summary

- **Disclosure**: remember the true and fair departure note for gains on long-term monetary items

- **Criticisms**: the main ones are:

    ○   Closing rate vs average rate arguments

    ○   Forward contracts: optional and insufficient guidance

    ○   Cover method: optional and no real hedge

    ○   Reserve accounting: hides results (but STRGL)

    ○   Realised profits/losses on long-term overseas borrowings

6   FOREIGN BRANCHES

6.1   Questions on foreign branch accounts might present you with a **trial balance** for the head office in sterling and a trial balance for the branch in the foreign currency. You are then required to produce (normally in the usual columnar form) draft accounts in sterling for the head office, the branch and the combined entity.

6.2   Such problems should be tackled as follows.

Step 1   Translate the branch trial balance into sterling using the closing rate or temporal method as appropriate

(a)   Translate all items in the given trial balance except for the head office current account balance. The actual sterling figure for the current account, to be found in the head office books, is used.

(b)   Make any required year end adjustments in respect of depreciation, closing stocks, accruals and so on in the foreign currency (by extending the trial balance) and then translate these items at appropriate rates into sterling.

(c)   Enter the difference on the branch sterling trial balance as the profit or loss on exchange.

Step 2   Combine the branch results, now in sterling, with the results of the head office exactly as in the case with a UK branch. The profit or loss on exchange, recorded through the branch current account in the head office books, is shown in the P&L account (if the temporal method has been used) or as a movement on reserves (if the closing rate method has been used).

BPP PUBLISHING

6.3 EXAMPLE: CLOSING RATE METHOD IN FOREIGN BRANCH ACCOUNTS

Wilde Ltd operates a branch in Beastland. At 1 January 19X1, when the exchange rate was 10 grunts (the local currency) to £1 sterling, the summarised branch balance sheet was as follows.

	Grs
Fixed assets	50,000
Net current assets	10,000
	60,000
Head office current account	60,000

The summarised branch P&L account for the year ended 31 December 19X1 was as follows.

	Grs
Sales	270,000
Less cost of sales	180,000
Gross profit	90,000
Less sundry expenditure (including £10,000 depreciation)	72,000
Net profit	18,000

The balance sheet at 31 December 19X1, when the rate of exchange was 8 grunts to £1 sterling, was as follows.

	Grs
Fixed assets (less depreciation)	40,000
Net current assets	38,000
	78,000
Head office current account	
Opening balance	60,000
Profit for the year	18,000
	78,000

For the purposes of preparing combined accounts of the business in respect of the year ended 31 December 19X1, redraft the branch trading and P&L account and balance sheet in £ sterling, using the closing rate method of translation. Show the treatment of any exchange rate differences.

6.4 SOLUTION

BRANCH BALANCE SHEET AS AT 31 DECEMBER 19X1

	Grs	*Rate of exchange*	£
Net fixed assets	40,000	8	5,000
Net current assets	38,000	8	4,750
	78,000		9,750
Head office current account			
Balance at 1.1.19X1	60,000	10	6,000
Increase in the year	18,000	balancing figure	3,750
Balance at 31.12.19X1	78,000		9,750

Since the profits or losses on currency translation are attributable to the current year, the opening balance on the head office current account is translated at the opening rate. The profit for the year is inserted in the £ sterling balance sheet as the balancing figure.

TRADING, AND PROFIT AND LOSS ACCOUNT
FOR THE YEAR ENDED 31 DECEMBER 19X1

	Grs	Rate of exchange	£
Sales	270,000	9	30,000
Less cost of sales	180,000	8	20,000
Gross profit	90,000		10,000
Less expenditure	72,000	9	8,000
Net profit	18,000		2,000

Note. 9 grunts to the £ is the average rate.

The total gain on exchange of £1,750 (£3,750 increase in head office net investment less the £2,000 profit for the year) may be explained as follows.

(a) The £1,500 exchange gain on the opening net investment is due to the increase in the value of the £ between the opening and closing balance sheet dates (60,000 Grs @ 10 less 60,000 Grs @ 8 = £1,500).

(b) The £250 exchange gain arises because 18,000 Grs profit for the year has been translated at 9 Grs to the £, while the increase in net assets (resulting from the profit) has been translated at 8 Grs to the £ (£2,250 – £2,000 = £250).

When Wilde Ltd prepares the combined accounts, the translated results of the branch are added to the head office results. The exchange gain would be shown as a movement on reserves, which in the case of Wilde Ltd (in respect of the branch) would be:

	£	£
Opening capital (net investment)		6,000
Profit for the year to 31.12.19X1	2,000	
Movement on reserves in respect of foreign currency exchange gains	1,750	
		3,750
Closing capital (net investment)		9,750

6.5 EXAMPLE: TEMPORAL METHOD IN FOREIGN BRANCH ACCOUNTS

Drak Ltd opened a foreign branch in Uland on 1 January 19X1 supplying necessary funds on that date. Fixed assets costing 80,000 Ules and stock costing 36,000 Ules were purchased on 1 January 19X1, leaving the branch with a cash balance of 24,000 Ules. The trial balance of the branch at 31 December 19X1 is given below. No provision has yet been made for depreciation on the fixed assets, which have an estimated useful life of 10 years and a residual value of nil. The closing stock of the branch is valued at 54,000 Ules. The exchange rate has moved as follows.

1 January 19X1	8 Ules to £1
31 December 19X1	10 Ules to £1
Average for the year	9 Ules to £1
Rate applicable to closing stock	9.6 Ules to £1

BPP PUBLISHING

DRAK LIMITED
BRANCH TRIAL BALANCE AT 31 DECEMBER 19X1

	Ules	Ules
Head office current account		140,000
Fixed assets: cost	80,000	
accumulated depreciation		-
Sales		540,000
Purchases	450,000	
Opening stock	36,000	
Expenses	81,000	
Debtors	45,000	
Creditors		33,000
Cash	21,000	
	713,000	713,000

Required

You are required to prepare the branch trading and P&L account and balance sheet in sterling ready for consolidation with head office results, using the temporal method.

6.6   SOLUTION

DRAK LTD: BRANCH TRADING AND P&L ACCOUNT
FOR THE YEAR ENDED 31 DECEMBER 19X1

	Ules	Ules	*Rate*	£	£
Sales		540,000	9		60,000
Opening stock	36,000		8	4,500	
Purchases	450,000		9	50,000	
	486,000			54,500	
Closing stock	54,000		9.6	5,625	
Cost of sales		432,000			48,875
Gross profit		108,000			11,125
Expenses	81,000		9	9,000	
Depreciation	8,000		8	1,000	
		89,000			10,000
Net profit		19,000			1,125

BRANCH BALANCE SHEET AS AT 31 DECEMBER 19X1

	Ules	Ules	*Rate*	£	£
Fixed assets		72,000	8		9,000
Current assets					
Stocks	54,000		9.6	5,625	
Debtors	45,000		10	4,500	
Cash	21,000		10	2,100	
	120,000			12,225	
Less creditors	33,000		10	3,300	
		87,000			8,925
		159,000			17,925
Head office current account					
Balance at 1.1.19X1		140,000	8		17,500
Profit for year		19,000			1,125
		159,000			18,625
Loss on exchange (balancing figure)		-			(700)
		159,000			17,925

The loss on exchange of £700 would be an item in the combined P&L account of head office and branch.

Question 3

A company operates an airline engaged in the UK charter trade. It has a number of aircraft that have been financed by US dollar loans. The aircraft earn income in sterling. At the year end there are exchange losses on the loans which are material. The company proposes to defer the exchange losses and amortise them over the life of the loans. Is the proposed treatment acceptable?

Answer

Under SSAP 20 *Foreign currency translation*, the aircraft would be translated from US dollars to sterling at the rate of exchange at the date of transaction (ie at the date(s) of purchase, not at the date(s) of payment) and this carrying value is not retranslated for subsequent changes in the rate of exchange. Exchange gains and losses on the borrowing would be taken to the P&L account each year, but no corresponding gain or loss on the 'value' of the asset will be recognised.

One exception to the above rule is where a company has used foreign currency borrowing to finance or provide a hedge against its foreign currency investment. SSAP 20 recognises that in such situations a company may be covered in economic terms against any movements in exchange rates, and states that it would be inappropriate in such cases to record an accounting profit or loss when exchange rates change.

Accordingly, where certain conditions are satisfied, the equity investment may be denominated in the appropriate foreign currency and retranslated at each year end at closing rates. Where this is done, the resulting exchange differences may be taken to reserves and the exchange gains or losses on the foreign currency borrowing should then be offset, as a reserve movement, against these exchange differences.

It should be noted that the offset treatment is also applicable to foreign branches. The standard's definition of a foreign branch includes a group of asset and liabilities that are accounted for in foreign currencies. This was further elaborated in the statement by the Accounting Standards Committee on the publication of SSAP 20 (TR 504). TR 504 includes an example of a branch comprising a ship or aircraft purchased in US dollars with a US dollar loan and which earns revenue and incurs expenses in US dollars to be accounted for under the closing rate/net investment method.

Therefore, it would be acceptable treat the aircraft as a foreign branch if they are purchased in foreign currencies and earn income in that currency.

This is not the case here, however, as the aircraft, although purchased in US dollars, do not earn income in dollars. As the aircraft fail to qualify as a foreign branch and the offset option is not open, the exchange loss should be taken to the P&L account as it arises. The company's proposed treatment is therefore not acceptable.

Chapter roundup

- Questions on foreign currency translation have always been popular with examiners. In general you are required to prepare **consolidated accounts** for a group which includes a foreign subsidiary.

- You may have to make the decision yourself as to which method of currency translation to use, **temporal** or **closing rate**, and on whether to translate the P&L account at **average or closing rate**.

- You must be able to calculate **exchange differences** etc and also to explain the differences between the methods. You should be able to discuss the treatment of **foreign currency borrowings** to finance overseas investment.

- **Practising** examination questions is the best way of learning this topic.

- **SSAP 20** is criticised for a variety of reasons and a revision may be forthcoming in the future.

BPP PUBLISHING

Quick quiz

1 Define 'monetary' and 'non-monetary' items. (see para 2.1)

2 Summarise the accounting treatment of foreign currency transactions in an individual company's accounts. (2.3 - 2.5)

3 How will the resulting exchange differences be treated? (2.6)

4 How should the exchange gains or losses on long-term monetary items be treated in an individual company's accounts according to SSAP 20? (2.10)

5 What are the four possible methods for translating a foreign enterprise's accounts into sterling? (3.3)

6 Does SSAP 20 require that the closing rate method or the temporal method should normally be used to consolidate foreign enterprises? (3.8)

7 When would the *other* method be appropriate? (3.11)

8 State the three conditions which must hold before the hedging provisions of SSAP 20 can be invoked in an individual company's accounts, so that an equity investment can be retranslated at a balance sheet rate. (4.4)

9 Summarise the main disclosure requirements of SSAP 20. (5.1 - 5.3)

10 Under the closing rate method, should the P&L account be translated at the closing rate, the average rate, or is either acceptable? (5.5 - 5.7)

Question to try	Level	Marks	Time
21	Introductory	n/a	n/a
22	Exam	25	45 mins

Chapter 21

CAPITAL REDUCTIONS, RECONSTRUCTIONS AND AMALGAMATIONS

Chapter topic		Syllabus reference	Ability required
1	Purchase and redemption of own shares	9(a)	Skill
2	Capital reduction	9(a)	Skill
3	Schemes of arrangement	9(a)	Skill
4	Company reconstruction	9(a)	Skill

Introduction

The transactions discussed in this chapter have been put together because they represent upheavals in a company, generally involving how the company is financed and its capital structure.

Most of these transactions are quite rare; most companies will never undertake any of them unless they get into financial trouble. The purchase and redemption of own shares is more widespread, particularly in large companies.

The Examiner states in the Guidance Notes that you will not be expected to design a scheme of reducing, or otherwise reconstructing, the capital structure of an undertaking, ie you will only have to implement a scheme given in the exam.

1   PURCHASE AND REDEMPTION OF OWN SHARES

1.1   Shares and debentures are sources of long-term finance for a company, but the term of their issue need not be infinite. Debentures are nearly always 'redeemable'; the loan must eventually be repaid. Some shares, too, may be issued as redeemable shares. This has long been possible in the case of preference shares, but the Companies Act 1985 permits companies, if they wish, to issue redeemable ordinary shares as well.

1.2   When companies come to redeem shares they are reducing the **creditors' buffer**. For this reason, a company which redeems shares must comply with statutory regulations which are designed to ensure that creditors' rights are not prejudiced. The creditors' buffer consists of:

- Share capital; plus
- Non-distributable reserves.

1.3   If a company wishes to issue redeemable shares it must already have in issue **some** shares which are **not redeemable**. Otherwise it could happen that, after redeeming the redeemable shares, the company might be left with no issued share capital at all.

1.4 When the time comes to redeem the shares the company will **pay the agreed amount** (not necessarily nominal value) to the shareholders. The company will then own the shares itself and **must** proceed to **cancel** them.

1.5 With similar restrictions, a company may purchase its own shares. For example, a listed company may buy its own shares on the Stock Exchange, just as it might purchase shares in any other company. However, such shares must not be held as an investment. They must immediately be cancelled.

1.6 The reasons why a company may wish to purchase its own shares include the following.

(a) To buy out a **dissident shareholder**

(b) To retain **family control**

(c) To **encourage investment by a third party** in an **unlisted company**, where a contract to purchase the shares at a future date is part of the agreement to invest (this is particularly relevant in the case of a management buy-out funded by external financiers)

(d) To allow shares issued under an **employees' share scheme** to be purchased when employees leave the company's employment

(e) To provide a means of using **surplus cash** advantageously

1.7 The following legal formalities apply.

(a) The transaction must authorised by the **articles**.

(b) The company must have some **non-redeemable shares** in issue after redemption/purchase as noted above.

(c) Shares must be **fully paid**.

(d) In general, shares must be redeemed/purchased either out of **distributable profits or proceeds of fresh issue**.

(e) For **purchase of shares only**

(i) *Off-market purchase*: the contract must be approved by *special resolution* prior to purchase.

(ii) *Market purchase*: by *ordinary resolution* (may be a general authority but must specify maximum number of shares, maximum/minimum price and can only give authority for maximum of 18 months).

1.8 EXAMPLE: REDEMPTION OF SHARES

Alpha Ltd has in issue 20,000 £1 ordinary shares redeemable at par on 31 December 19X6. What accounting entries will be made by the company on that date?

1.9 SOLUTION

The shares are redeemable 'at par'. This means the redemption price payable by the company is the nominal value of the shares. The redemption would be recorded as follows.

		£	£
DEBIT	Ordinary share capital	20,000	
CREDIT	Ordinary share redemption account		20,000

Being entry on declaration of redemption

		£	£
DEBIT	Ordinary share redemption account	20,000	
CREDIT	Bank		20,000

Being redemption of shares

Alternatively, these two journals could be amalgamated:

		£	£
DEBIT	Ordinary share capital	20,000	
CREDIT	Bank		20,000

1.10 Notice that the **share capital** account must be **debited** with the **nominal value** of the shares redeemed (or purchased); this reflects the cancellation of the shares. It would not be permissible to debit an asset account 'investment in own shares'.

1.11 The effect of this is to reduce the creditors' buffer by £20,000 because £20,000 of the company's fixed capital (share capital plus undistributable reserves) has been paid out to shareholders. This is not permissible under companies legislation and must be rectified by reclassifying £20,000 of the company's distributable reserves as a non-distributable reserve, called the **Capital Redemption Reserve** (CRR).

1.12 The following entry is therefore necessary in addition to those above.

DEBIT	Profit and loss account (or any other distributable reserve)	£20,000	
CREDIT	Capital redemption reserve		£20,000

Undistributable share capital has now been replaced with an undistributable reserve and the creditors' buffer has been restored to its original level.

1.13 Two other rules should be studied before we look at a more complicated example.

(a) If the shares are redeemable at a premium (for example 50p shares redeemable at 60p) the amount of the premium paid must be debited to profit and loss account.

(b) If a new issue of shares is made to provide funds for the redemption, any proceeds, (including share premium) of the new issue are an increase in the creditors' buffer. The amount which must be transferred to CRR is reduced accordingly and perhaps eliminated entirely.

1.14 Two examples will now be given. In the first, the redemption is funded entirely from existing distributable profits of the company; in the second, the redemption is partly funded from the proceeds of a new issue.

1.15 EXAMPLE: REDEMPTION FUNDED BY DISTRIBUTABLE PROFITS

The share capital of A Ltd consists of 150,000 ordinary shares of £1 each fully paid and 50,000 redeemable preference shares of £1 each fully paid, redeemable at a premium of 10p per share. The company has a credit balance of £63,000 on its profit and loss account.

The company has resolved to redeem the preference shares wholly from distributable profits.

You are required to show:

(a) the journal entries necessary to record the above transactions; and

(b) the share capital and reserves of A Ltd as they would appear in the balance sheet after redemption.

BPP PUBLISHING

1.16 SOLUTION

(a) JOURNAL ENTRIES

		£	£
DEBIT	Preference share capital	50,000	
CREDIT	Preference share redemption account		50,000

Being entry on declaration of redemption

		£	£
DEBIT	Profit and loss account	5,000	
CREDIT	Preference share redemption account		5,000

Being premium payable on redemption

		£	£
DEBIT	Preference share redemption account	55,000	
CREDIT	Bank		55,000

Being redemption of preference shares

		£	£
DEBIT	Profit and loss account	50,000	
CREDIT	Capital redemption reserve		50,000

Being required transfer to capital redemption reserve

(b) BALANCE SHEET EXTRACTS

	£
Called up share capital	
Ordinary shares of £1 each	150,000
Capital redemption reserve	50,000
Profit and loss account £(63,000 – 5,000 – 50,000)	8,000
	208,000

1.17 Note that the creditors' buffer is the same in total as before the redemption.

	Before	After
	£	£
Ordinary shares	150,000	150,000
Preference shares	50,000	-
Capital redemption reserve	-	50,000
	200,000	200,000

1.18 EXAMPLE: REDEMPTION PARTLY FUNDED BY NEW SHARE ISSUE

Suppose that A Ltd in the first example had decided to redeem the preference shares partly from the proceeds of a new share issue and to that end an issue of 20,000 ordinary shares of £1 each were made at a premium of 20%. What would the journal entries and balance sheet extract then be?

1.19 SOLUTION

(a) JOURNAL ENTRIES

		£	£
DEBIT	Bank	24,000	
CREDIT	Application and allotment account		24,000

Being amount received on the issue of new shares

		£	£
DEBIT	Application and allotment account	24,000	
CREDIT	Ordinary share capital		20,000
	Share premium account		4,000

Being the allotment of new shares issued

		£	£
DEBIT	Preference share capital	50,000	
CREDIT	Preference share redemption account		50,000

Being entry on declaration of redemption

		£	£
DEBIT	Profit and loss account	5,000	
CREDIT	Preference share redemption account		5,000

Being premium payable on redemption

		£	£
DEBIT	Preference share redemption account	55,000	
CREDIT	Bank		55,000

Being redemption of preference shares

		£	£
DEBIT	Profit and loss account	26,000	
CREDIT	Capital redemption reserve		26,000

Being required transfer to capital redemption reserve
£(50,000 – 24,000)

(b) BALANCE SHEET EXTRACTS

	£
Capital and reserves	
Called up share capital	
Ordinary shares of £1 each	170,000
Share premium account	4,000
Capital redemption reserve	26,000
Profit and loss account £(63,000 – 5,000 – 26,000)	32,000
	232,000

Again, the creditors' buffer is unchanged: £(170,000 + 4,000 + 26,000) = £200,000.

Redemption of shares issued at a premium

1.20 It was stated earlier that when shares are redeemed at a premium, the amount of the premium must be debited to profit and loss account. There is one exception to this rule which relates to the redemption of **shares originally issued at a premium** (s 160 (2) CA 1985).

1.21 Any premium payable on the redemption of such shares may be paid out of the proceeds of a fresh issue of shares made for the purpose of the redemption, up to an amount equal to the premium on the original issue (or the current balance on the share premium account, if lower: in other words, the **share premium account must not end up with a debit balance**).

1.22 The premium is therefore debited to the share premium account as far as possible instead of to distributable profits. Thus, the **maximum** debit to share premium is the lowest of:

- The proceeds of the fresh issue
- The premium on redemption
- The premium on the original issue
- The balance on the share premium account (*including* any premium on new issue)

Question

The share capital of B Ltd consists of 100,000 ordinary shares of £1 each fully paid and 50,000 redeemable ordinary shares of £1 each fully paid and redeemable at £1.20. The redeemable shares had been issued at a premium of 10%. The company has credit balances of £80,000 on its profit and loss account and £20,000 on its share premium account. The company has resolved:

(a) to redeem the redeemable ordinary shares;

(b) to issue 30,000 ordinary shares of £1 each at £1.05 per share in order to provide part of the funds for the redemption.

Required

(a) Show the necessary journal entries.
(b) Produce the relevant balance sheet extract after the redemption.

Answer

The balance on share premium account after the new issue is as follows.

	£
Balance before new issue	20,000
Premium on new issue (30,000 × 5p)	1,500
Balance after new issue	21,500

The share premium which arose on the original issue of the redeemable shares was 50,000 × 10% = £5,000. The premium payable on redemption is 50,000 × 20p = £10,000.

Of this £10,000 the amount debited to share premium account must be the lowest of £31,500 (proceeds of fresh issue); or £10,000; or £5,000; or £21,500. In other words, the maximum debit to share premium account is £5,000. The remaining £5,000 premium on redemption must be debited to profit and loss account.

The transfer to CRR is calculated as follows.

	£
Nominal value of shares redeemed	50,000
Less proceeds of new issue	31,500
	18,500

(a) JOURNAL ENTRIES

		£	£
DEBIT	Bank	31,500	
CREDIT	Ordinary share capital		30,000
	Share premium account		1,500
Being proceeds of fresh issue			
DEBIT	Redeemable ordinary share capital	50,000	
	Share premium account	5,000	
	Profit and loss account	5,000	
CREDIT	Bank		60,000
Being redemption of redeemable ordinary shares			

(b) BALANCE SHEET EXTRACT

	£
Capital and reserves	
Called up share capital	
Ordinary shares of £1 each	130,000
Share premium account	16,500
Capital redemption reserve	18,500
Profit and loss account	56,500
	221,500

Note. The creditors' buffer has fallen by £5,000: the premium on redemption is a permitted use of the share premium account (s 170) and therefore this is a permitted reduction in capital.

Redemption or purchase of own shares from capital

1.23 So far we have looked at cases where a company is able to redeem or purchase its own shares either from distributable profits or from the proceeds of a new share issue. What happens if these sources of finance are unavailable, or insufficient to meet the cost of the redemption?

1.24 The answer is that in the case of a **public company** the redemption **cannot** normally take place. But a **private company** is allowed **in certain circumstances** to redeem or purchase its own shares from *capital*. The company's articles must contain authorisation for this procedure and a special resolution is also necessary. In addition, certain declarations must be made by the directors and auditors concerning the company's ability to meet its debts after the capital payment has been made. Protection is given to members or creditors by allowing them to apply to the court for cancellation of the special resolution.

1.25 Assuming that these formalities have been completed, the procedure is straightforward. The company must first of all exhaust all the proceeds of any new share issue and all its distributable profits; any redemption cost still to be financed is known as the *Permissible Capital Payment* (PCP). If the PCP (plus the proceeds of any new share issue) is less than the nominal amount of shares redeemed or purchased, the difference is transferred to the capital redemption reserve.

1.26 EXAMPLE: REDEMPTION OR PURCHASE OF OWN SHARES FROM CAPITAL

The capital and reserves of C Ltd at 31 December 19X3 are as follows.

	£
Ordinary shares of £1 each, fully paid	100,000
Redeemable ordinary shares of £1 each, fully paid	70,000
Share premium account	10,000
Capital and non-distributable reserves	180,000
Distributable profits	30,000
	210,000

On the same date C Ltd issues 30,000 £1 ordinary shares at £1.20 each to provide part of the funding for redeeming all the redeemable ordinary shares at a premium of 10%.

Required

(a) Calculate the permissible capital payment.
(b) Show the capital and reserves of C Ltd after the redemption.

1.27 SOLUTION

(a)

	£	£
Price of redemption		77,000
Less: proceeds of fresh issue	36,000	
distributable profits	30,000	
		66,000
Permissible capital payment		11,000

(b)

		£
Ordinary shares of £1 each fully paid		130,000
Share premium account		16,000
Capital redemption reserve*		23,000
Capital and non-distributable reserves		169,000
Distributable profits		-
		169,000
* Nominal amount of shares redeemed		70,000
Less: PCP	11,000	
proceeds of fresh issue	36,000	
		47,000
Transfer to capital redemption reserve		23,000

BPP
PUBLISHING

Note that capital and non-distributable reserves have fallen from £180,000 to £169,000, the difference of course being equal to the permissible capital payment of £11,000.

2 CAPITAL REDUCTION

2.1 A company trading and incurring **heavy losses** over a period of time will diminish its resources and probably end up with a **debit on its profit and loss reserve**. A tenet of company law is that the issued share capital provides a fund to which creditors can look for payment of their debts. But as losses increase (and the profit and loss reserve becomes a debit balance) the share capital will not be fully represented by the net assets.

2.2 It may be possible, if market and trading conditions are suitable, to **reconstruct the company** in some way in order to give it a **fresh start**. Provided that all the parties concerned (the shareholders, debenture holders, creditors) can come to some agreement to adjust their claims on the company and thereby to write off (together) fictitious and overvalued assets, the company might be placed in a position from which to trade successfully.

2.3 This process may be achieved by either of **two principal methods**.

(a) **Reduce and reorganise** the company's capital structure, with the company continuing to trade after the re-organisation.

(b) Reconstruct the company by **selling the old enterprise** to a **new company** formed especially for that purpose.

2.4 The **reduction of capital** is **tightly controlled by the CA 1985**, in order to protect the rights of creditors. S 135 allows such a reduction if it is authorised by the articles, a special resolution of the company, and confirmation by the High Court (with an opportunity for creditors to object).

(a) A company may extinguish or reduce the members' liability on any unpaid capital. This does not involve any accounting double entry, merely a change in the designation of the share capital (for example, 'ordinary shares of £1 each, 80p paid' become 'ordinary shares of 80p each, fully paid'.

(b) A company may repay to the members any paid up share capital which is in excess of the company's requirements. In this way excess cash may be returned to the subscribers.

(c) A company may cancel any paid up capital which is lost or not represented by available assets. This acknowledges that capital has been lost and that a debit balance exists on the profit and loss reserve, but in itself does not reduce the likelihood of creditors being paid. However, as long as revenue reserves are in debit, investors cannot benefit (in the form of dividends) and so:

(i) losses should be written off; and
(ii) overvalued or intangible assets should be adjusted;

against the capital reserves and equity capital. This is the most common form of reduction.

2.5 EXAMPLE: CAPITAL REDUCTION

If there is only one class of shares in existence the scheme of reduction will be straightforward. For example, suppose that the balance sheet of Flip Ltd at 31 December 19X0 was as follows.

	£
Assets	280,000
Creditors	80,000
Net assets	200,000
Ordinary shares: 1,000,000 25p shares allotted and fully paid	250,000
Share premium account	100,000
Profit and loss account	(150,000)
	200,000

The company wishes to extinguish the deficit on its profit and loss account. This may be achieved by writing off the £150,000 deficit against the ordinary capital and share premium leaving a balance of £200,000 which will be Flip Ltd's new capital. If the nominal value per share is to remain at 25p then Flip Ltd's new capital will consist of 800,000 25p shares. For every 5 original shares in issue, 1 share will be cancelled. The balance sheet after the reduction will be:

	£
Net assets	200,000
Ordinary shares: 800,000 25p shares allotted and fully paid	200,000

Preference shareholders and creditors

2.6 If there are two classes of shares in issue, say ordinary shares and preference shares, then the scaling down of capital has to take into account the rights of both parties. These rights will be laid down in the company's articles.

2.7 Contrary to popular belief, preference shares do *not* carry any priority to return of capital in a liquidation *unless* the memorandum or articles or terms of issue confer it on them. Such a provision is, however, a common one and where it is made the preference shares will not have any right to participate in the distribution of the surplus assets.

2.8 It must also be borne in mind that any alteration in the rights attached to a class of shares has to be made within the ambit of s 127 CA 1985. This section provides that holders of not less than 15% in aggregate of the class of shares in question may apply to the court to have the variation cancelled. The decision of the court on any such application is final, which bars any appeal.

2.9 In light of the above, the scaling down of capital will normally have to be weighted against the ordinary shareholders, so if a profit and loss account deficit of £5,000 has to be cancelled against capital consisting of 10,000 £1 ordinary shares and 10,000 £1 preference shares it will be the ordinary shares which bear the brunt; the capital after the reduction will consist of 5,000 £1 ordinary shares and 10,000 £1 preference shares.

Any arrears of dividend on cumulative preference shares should also be allowed for (in full or in part) in a capital reduction scheme.

3 SCHEMES OF ARRANGEMENT 5/97

3.1 A capital reduction under s 135 is limited in scope as a compromise or **scheme of arrangement** with creditors is not permitted. Companies are far more likely to reorganise

their structure under s 425 CA 1985 which permits a company to enter into a type of scheme regarding either its creditors or its shareholders as long as the scheme does not conflict with general law or any particular statutory provision.

3.2   Where a compromise or arrangement is proposed between a company and its creditors or members, the court may, on the application of the company or any creditor, or member, or liquidator, order separate meetings of the debenture holders, creditors, or members. The scheme document is considered at the meetings, together with a statement explaining:

(a)   the effects of the scheme;

(b)   the material interests of the directors;

(c)   the effect of the scheme on the directors;

(d)   in the case of debentures secured by a trust deed, how the trustees of the deed will be affected.

3.3   If a majority in number representing three-quarters in value of the creditors or members present and voting either in person or by proxy at each meeting agrees to the scheme, it is then submitted to the court for approval. If the court, having considered any objections, approves the scheme, it becomes binding on all parties once an office copy of the court order has been delivered to the registrar.

3.4   For a reorganisation under s 425 (often referred to as a reconstruction scheme) to be considered worthwhile, the business must be expected to have reasonable prospects of a return to profitability. It is difficult to get agreement between unsecured creditors and secured creditors and the shareholders and, if possible, the unsecured creditors should be paid in full (thus dispensing with the need for their consent). If this is not possible the creditors may have to accept loss, or a delay in payment, in preference to losing more (or all) on a liquidation. When devising a scheme to scale down the claims of creditors, debenture holders and shareholders it must be borne in mind that fairness to all parties will make the chance of a successful operation more likely.

3.5   EXAMPLE: SCHEME OF ARRANGEMENT

Flap Ltd has been making losses for several years. The draft balance sheet at 31 December 19X0 showed the following.

	£	£
Fixed assets		
Plant		40,000
Current assets		
Stock	10,000	
Debtors	20,000	
	30,000	
Current liabilities		
Creditors	40,000	
		(10,000)
		30,000
Debentures (secured)		50,000
		(20,000)
Capital and reserves		
£1 ordinary shares		50,000
Profit and loss account		(70,000)
		(20,000)

On a liquidation the assets would realise the following amounts.

	£
Plant	15,000
Stock	6,000
Debtors	18,000
	39,000

If the company continues to trade it is estimated that annual profits of £10,000 (after charging annual depreciation of £10,000) can be earned.

Assuming that there would be no surplus cash to repay the creditors and debenture holders until after four years and that stock and debtors could then be realised at their book values, you are required to prepare a reconstruction scheme. (Ignore taxation).

3.6 SOLUTION

If liquidation took place immediately only £39,000 would be raised. This would be given to the debenture holders, leaving them with a deficiency of £11,000, and there would be nothing for the creditors and shareholders.

However, if trading continues for the next four years and estimated results are achieved the cash available would be as follows.

	£
Profits	40,000
Depreciation (4 years @ £10,000 per annum)	40,000
Stock and debtors: full value	30,000
	110,000

£110,000 would enable the debenture holders and creditors to be paid in full leaving £20,000 available for the ordinary shareholders. Everyone will be better off if the company is allowed to continue trading, but since the debenture holders probably have the right to appoint a receiver they would insist on some compensation for not enforcing that right. The creditors might also expect something for having to wait four years before receiving some payment.

The reconstruction scheme should be favourably weighted towards the debenture holders, creditors and ordinary shareholders in that order, if agreement is to be reached. Although there can be no one solution to such a question, one that might be acceptable may require the debenture holders and creditors to waive all or part of the amounts owed to them in exchange for ordinary shares, so that they will have full participation in the future profitability of the company. Terms of such an exchange (requiring an increase in the share capital) *might* be:

(a) 37,500 £1 ordinary shares to the debenture holders (three £1 ordinary shares for every £4 of debentures);

(b) 20,000 £1 ordinary shares to the creditors (one £1 ordinary share for every £2 due)

(c) 12,500 £1 ordinary shares to the old ordinary shareholders (one £1 ordinary share for every four of the old £1 ordinary shares).

After the reconstruction, the summarised balance sheet of Flap Ltd would be as follows.

	£	£
Fixed assets		
Plant		40,000
Current assets		
Stock	10,000	
Debtors	20,000	
		30,000
		70,000
Capital: £1 ordinary shares		70,000

Alternatively, new loan stock could be issued to cover all (or part) of the amounts due to the old debenture holders and creditors. If preference shares had been in issue, any unpaid arrears of preference dividends might also be covered by the issue of loan stock.

Examination problems

3.7   In examination questions the examiner will set out the terms of the reorganisation and the bookkeeping entries should be made through a *capital reduction and reorganisation account* (also referred to as a *capital reduction and reconstruction account*).

The procedure to adopt is illustrated in the journal entries below.

JOURNAL

			£	£
(a)	DEBIT	Share capital (old)	X	
		Share premium/CRR etc	X	
	CREDIT	Capital reduction account		X
		Removing the old share capital and capital reserves		
(b)	DEBIT	Capital reduction account	X	
	CREDIT	Share capital (new)		X
		Introducing the new share capital		
(c)	DEBIT	Capital reduction account	X	
	CREDIT	Intangible assets (for example goodwill)		X
		Profit and loss account (Debit balance)		X
		Writing off intangible assets etc		
(d)	DEBIT	Capital reduction account	X	
	CREDIT	Tangible assets, investments etc		X
		Reducing assets to agreed values		
(e)	DEBIT	Debenture holders/creditors	X	
	CREDIT	Capital reduction account		X
		Adjusting liabilities as necessary according to the scheme of arrangement		

Any profit arising as a direct result of the scheme should be transferred to the capital reduction account, any balance remaining being transferred to a capital reserve. (In most examination questions the scheme is usually devised in such a way that no balance remains on the capital reduction account.)

3.8   As with all such adjustment accounts, in the capital reduction and reorganisation account you have the choice of either:

(a)   entering existing book values and withdrawing new book values; or
(b)   displaying the net effect of each adjustment.

It is also useful to remember that if the terms of the scheme (as laid down by the examiner) reduce the new share capital to below its authorised amount, new shares may be allotted to bring the issued capital up to the amount of the authorised capital (even if the question does not specifically request this).

3.9   EXAMPLE: REDUCTION AND REORGANISATION ACCOUNT

Flop Ltd prepared its draft balance sheet at 31 December 19X0.

	£
Goodwill	30,000
Development costs	20,000
Tangible fixed assets	70,000
	120,000
9% debentures	50,000
	70,000
Capital and reserves	
£1 ordinary shares, fully paid	100,000
Profit and loss account	(30,000)
	70,000

A capital reconstruction scheme is designed in which the ordinary shares will be reduced to a nominal value of 10p each. The fixed assets are to be reduced to £65,000 book value and all other debit balances are to be written off. After protracted discussions the debenture holders agree to take 55 new ordinary shares, fully paid, for every £5 of debentures held. Show the effect of these transactions in a reduction and reorganisation account.

3.10 SOLUTION

Reference is made, in the suggested solution, to the journal entries illustrated in Paragraph 3.7 above.

REDUCTION AND REORGANISATION ACCOUNT

	£		£
Fixed assets (d)	70,000	Ordinary shares of £1 (a)&(b)	100,000
Goodwill (c)	30,000	9% debentures (e)&(b)	50,000
Development costs (c)	20,000	Fixed assets (d)	65,000
Profit and loss account (c)	30,000		
Former debenture holders			
550,000 10p shares (b)&(e)	55,000		
Therefore existing shareholders			
100,000 10p shares (b)&(a)	10,000		
	215,000		215,000

3.11 The balance sheet after the reconstruction would be:

	£
Fixed assets	65,000
10p ordinary shares fully paid	65,000

Notice that the shareholders merely receive what is left after the debenture holders have agreed their terms. It is likely that the debentures would be secured, probably on the fixed assets, so that some arrangement with the debenture holders is vital if the company is not to be put into the hands of a receiver and liquidator.

3.12 As suggested previously the new shares may be issued to the old shareholders, requiring them to subscribe for these shares. If the authorised share capital of the company is £100,000, another 350,000 10p shares may be allotted to the old shareholders, so raising £35,000 cash for company operations. The balance sheet would then be:

	£
Fixed assets	65,000
Cash	35,000
	100,000
10p ordinary shares, fully paid	100,000

3.13 The advantages of a scheme of arrangement are:

BPP
PUBLISHING

(a) flexibility;

(b) only three-quarters majority of votes cast is required; and

(c) the scheme is implemented (without need for other action) by the court order.

4 COMPANY RECONSTRUCTION

4.1 Although the above examples have illustrated a capital reduction and reorganisation within the books of the existing company, the court may make orders for the transfer of all the company's assets and liabilities and for its dissolution. The scheme may provide for the formation of a **new company** to take over the undertaking of the old company, or an amalgamation, to acquire the undertakings of a number of companies, the members and creditors of which accept shares or debentures in the new company in exchange for their former rights. The bookkeeping entries in respect of a sale of an existing undertaking to a new company are dealt with below in the context of a company reconstruction under s 110 Insolvency Act 1986 (members' voluntary winding up).

4.2 Under the Insolvency Act 1986 a company may go into voluntary liquidation so that its liquidator may sell all or part of its assets to another company in exchange for shares in the new company to be issued to members of the old company. It is a method of reconstruction by which the business of one company (A) is transferred to another (usually newly formed) company (B) of which the former members of A become shareholders. There is no change in the ultimate ownership of the business as it is owned by the same shareholders through shareholdings of a different company.

4.3 The advantage of using s 110 Insolvency Act 1986 is that the sanction of the court is not required (as it is under s 427 Companies Act 1985), since the new company must be solvent so that any creditors who object to the scheme can be paid out in full. The members of the company must approve the scheme (to liquidate the old company and to form a new one) by special resolution, but a creditors' meeting need not be held. In *practice*, this procedure is not often used, as the new company will not have the cash to pay off its creditors, but it may come up in the *examination*.

4.4 EXAMPLE: COMPANY RECONSTRUCTION

The draft balance sheet of Sink Ltd on 31 December 19X0, was as follows.

	£
Fixed and current assets	23,000
Current liabilities	10,000
	13,000
10% debentures	5,000
	8,000
£1 ordinary shares, fully paid	10,000
Profit and loss account	(2,000)
	8,000

Swim Ltd was to be incorporated to take over the assets and liabilities of Sink Ltd as at 31 December 19X9 for the following considerations:

(a) the ordinary shareholders of Sink Ltd to receive 5,000 £1 ordinary shares in Swim Ltd;

(b) the debenture holders of Sink Ltd to receive 3,000 £1 ordinary shares in Swim Ltd and £3,000 of 15% debentures in Swim Ltd;

(c) the creditors of Sink Ltd to receive £10,000 of 15% debentures in Swim Ltd.

Swim Ltd values the assets of Sink Ltd at £21,000.

Required

You are required to show the balance sheet of Swim Ltd on 1 January 19X1.

4.5 SOLUTION

SWIM LIMITED
BALANCE SHEET AS AT 1 JANUARY 19X1

	£
Fixed and current assets	21,000
15% debentures	(13,000)
	8,000
£1 ordinary shares, fully paid	8,000

4.6 Although the change of company name may be minimised (for example Rolls Royce Ltd becoming Rolls Royce (1971) Ltd) the legal fact is that a new company has bought all, or part of the undertaking from the old one, which is then dissolved. The approach to be taken, therefore, is to:

(a) close off the ledger accounts in the books of the old company; and then

(b) open the ledger accounts in the books of the new company.

4.7 The ledger accounts are closed off, as far as possible, through a realisation account, while a purchase of business account is normally used to open the accounts in the new company's books.

> **Exam focus point**
> In an exam you may have to implement such a scheme but not to suggest one, ie the terms of the scheme would be given to you. You may have to comment on the viability of the scheme.

Closing the books of the old company

4.8 There are, unfortunately, **several methods** which could be used to close off the books of a company in liquidation, the principal difference being in the interpretation of the term purchase consideration. This may be considered as:

(a) the total amount in money or money's worth (such as shares or debentures) which the new company pays to the old company for the total assets taken over (this will be the total amount payable by the new company in respect of the acquisition); or

(b) the amount in money or money's worth which is paid to the *members* of the old company (excluding the amounts due to creditors and debenture holders and others, as these are not members).

Note. Both methods lead to the same final result. For examination purposes, we recommend the first method, which is the one more likely to be used in practice.

4.9 EXAMPLE: CLOSING THE BOOKS

The draft balance sheets of Trip Ltd and Slip Ltd at 31 December 19X0 were as follows.

	Trip Ltd £	Slip Ltd £
Sundry assets	21,000	13,000
Cash	1,000	-
	22,000	13,000
Creditors	3,000	4,000
10% debentures	5,000	-
	14,000	9,000
£1 ordinary shares	10,000	10,000
Reserves	4,000	(1,000)
	14,000	9,000

Stumble Ltd is formed to amalgamate the two concerns on the following terms.

(a) In the case of Trip Ltd the net purchase consideration payable in cash is £24,000. Stumble Ltd also agrees to issue £6,000 14% debentures to the 10% debenture holders and to discharge the creditors (these were ultimately settled for £2,900). The ordinary shareholders accepted one new £1 ordinary share in Stumble Ltd for each £1 ordinary share in Trip Ltd.

(b) In the case of Slip Ltd, Stumble Ltd agreed to acquire the net assets for a consideration of £8,000 payable in ordinary shares of £1 each at par.

Required

Close the books of Trip Ltd and Slip Ltd.

4.10 SOLUTION

If purchase consideration is considered to be the amount payable by the new company for the total assets the procedure will be as follows.

(a) Transfer assets taken over by the new company to the debit of the realisation account at book value.

(b) Transfer share capital, reserves, profit and loss balances, intangible assets written off and so on, to a sundry members account in which a separate column is maintained for each class of shares. (*Note.* Preference shareholders are not normally entitled to surpluses nor do they have to bear losses on realisation. They may, however, be entitled to arrears of preference dividend.)

(c) Transfer the liabilities (including debentures) which are to be settled by the new company to the credit of a new company account at book value. (*Note.* The realisation account may be debited with any 'new' liabilities not shown in the original accounts, for example, cost of reconstruction.)

(d) Pay any liabilities (debit creditors; credit bank) which have to be cleared by the old company. (Similarly, any assets not taken over by the new company would be dealt with separately, any profit/loss being transferred to the sundry members).

(e) Calculate the purchase consideration (the amount payable to acquire the assets of the old company) and debit new company account; credit realisation account with this amount.

(f) Transfer the profit or loss on realisation (balance on the realisation account) to the sundry members account.

(g) Close the remaining ledger accounts by making the appropriate entries (for example, debit sundry members account; credit new company account) in respect of shares, debentures and so on issued by the new company. (*Note.* Any cash settlement may be passed through the company bank account.)

Trip Limited

REALISATION ACCOUNT

	£		£
Sundry assets (a)	22,000	Stumble Ltd: purchase	
Sundry members: profit (f)	20,000	consideration (e)	42,000
	42,000		42,000

SUNDRY MEMBERS ACCOUNT

	£		£
Stumble Ltd: shares (g)	10,000	Share capital (b)	10,000
Bank (g)	24,000	Reserves (b)	4,000
		Realisation account (f)	20,000
	34,000		34,000

STUMBLE LTD ACCOUNT

	£		£
Realisation account (e)	42,000	6% debentures (c)	5,000
		Creditors (c)	3,000
		Sundry members (g)	10,000
		Bank (g)	24,000
	42,000		42,000

BANK ACCOUNT

	£		£
Stumble Ltd (g)	24,000	Sundry members (g)	24,000

Slip Limited

REALISATION ACCOUNT

	£		£
Sundry assets (a)	13,000	Stumble Ltd: purchase	
		consideration (e)	12,000
		Sundry members: loss (f)	1,000
	13,000		13,000

SUNDRY MEMBERS ACCOUNT

	£		£
Reserves (b)	1,000	Share capital (b)	10,000
Realisation account (f)	1,000		
Stumble Ltd shares (g)	8,000		
	10,000		10,000

STUMBLE LTD ACCOUNT

	£		£
Realisation account	12,000	Creditors (c)	4,000
		Sundry members (g)	8,000
	12,000		12,000

Opening the books in the new company

4.11 When the books of the old company are closed off, care must be taken to ensure that the future (new) valuations of assets are ignored. However, as far as the new company is concerned it is starting afresh and all accounts must be opened at the new agreed values. Usually a purchase of business account is used to introduce the assets and liabilities into the ledger.

4.12 The purchase of business account is:

(a) credited with assets acquired, at their agreed valuation;

(b) debited with liabilities in the amount and form assumed (including cost of reconstruction if these are to be borne by the new company);

(c) debited with the share capital, debentures, cash and so on which is 'paid' to the shareholders of the old company.

4.13 If the total purchase consideration reflects the net assets acquired at their new valuation there will be no remaining balance on the purchase of business account. However, if this is not the case (as often happens) any debit balance on the account represents goodwill while any credit balance represents share premium or capital reserve.

4.14 EXAMPLE: OPENING THE BOOKS

The purchase of business account for Stumble Ltd (assuming that the new company values the total assets of Trip Ltd at £42,000 and those of Slip Ltd at £12,000) would be:

PURCHASE OF BUSINESS ACCOUNT

	£		£
Creditors: re Trip Ltd	3,000	Assets at valuation	
re Slip Ltd	4,000	Re Trip Ltd: bank	1,000
14% debentures		other	41,000
Re 10% debenture holders	6,000	Re Slip Ltd	12,000
Ordinary shares: re Trip Ltd	10,000	Balance: goodwill	1,000
re Slip Ltd	8,000		
Bank re Trip Ltd	24,000		
	55,000		55,000

4.15 When the liabilities are paid (£6,900) a profit of £100 is made on the payment and the overdraft is increased. If such action was taken the draft balance sheet would then be:

	£
Sundry assets (including £1,000 goodwill)	54,000
Bank overdraft	29,900
	24,100
14% debentures	6,000
	18,100
Ordinary £1 shares	18,000
Profit and loss account	100
	18,100

If necessary, the bank overdraft might be cleared by the issue (for cash) of more ordinary shares or by the issue of new debentures.

Chapter roundup

- Companies may issue *redeemable securities*, either shares or debentures.

- Share capital forms part of a *buffer fund* which by law must be kept intact to meet the claims of external creditors. It follows that when shares are redeemed the buffer fund must be boosted by a compensating amount. This may be done by a new issue of shares or by reclassifying distributable reserves as a non-distributable capital redemption reserve; a combination of the two is also possible.

- Any *premium* payable on the redemption of shares must normally be charged against distributable reserves. A limited exception to this rule is available when redeeming shares originally issued at a premium.

- In the examination you may encounter *two principal types* of reduction and reconstruction problems. You will be given all the necessary information in respect of the proposed scheme, and all that you have to do is to put it into effect in the company books. Remember that if the reconstruction is to take place:

  o within the existing company, a capital reduction and reconstruction (or re-organisation account) should be used to write down assets, write off losses and so on;

  o by the formation of a new company to take over the undertaking:

    - the old company books must be closed off (at old values) and any distributions and so on made to the shareholders; and

    - the new company books must be opened up (usually through a purchase of business account) with assets and liabilities introduced at their new (agreed) valuation or amounts payable.

Quick quiz

1   What are the legal formalities for the redemption or purchase of own shares? (see para 1.7)

2   What is a 'capital redemption reserve'? Is it distributable? (1.11)

3   In what circumstances may a premium payable on the redemption of shares be debited to the share premium account? (1.20, 1.21)

4   Public companies are forbidden from redeeming their own shares from capital. True or false? (1.24)

5   List the three schemes of capital reduction available to a company under s 135 CA 1985. (2.4)

6   Preference shares carry a priority right to return of capital in a liquidation. True or false? (2.7)

7   Name one advantage of using s 110 Insolvency Act 1986 rather than s 427 CA 1985 in a scheme of reconstruction. (4.3)

Question to try	Level	Marks	Time
23	Exam	35	63 mins

Part B
Income and value measurement

Chapter 22

ASSET VALUATION AND PROFIT MEASUREMENT

Chapter topic		Syllabus reference	Ability required
1	Profit, capital maintenance and asset valuation	9(b)	Application
2	Realised and distributable profits	9(b)	Application
3	ASB *Statement of Principles*	9(b)	Application
4	FRS 3 *Reporting financial performance*	9(b)	Application
5	Environmental accounting issues	9(b)	Knowledge
6	Discounting	9(b)	Knowledge

Introduction

The issues introduced in this chapter should cause you to reflect on all aspects of the **valuation of assets**, including intangible assets. In particular you should go back and look at the chapters on fixed assets (Chapter 3), intangible fixed assets (Chapter 4), stocks (Chapter 5) and leases and hire purchase contracts (Chapter 9). You should also look at how minority interests are treated in consolidated accounts.

In the case of all of the above topics, you should consider the different aspects of their valuation as they are discussed here.

The connection between parts A and B of the syllabus (and this Study Text) are highlighted by the examiner in the Syllabus Guidance Notes.

> 'These two sections of the syllabus have been grouped together deliberately in line with the philosophy of requiring reflection and application side by side in the examination. The two sections together could be said to encompass the theoretical and practical issues surrounding the preparation of financial reports for UK undertakings.'

Once again we will discuss aspects of **FRS 3** *Reporting financial performance* in this chapter and this underlines the importance of the standard. You should go back to Chapter 2 to remind yourself of the basic provisions of FRS 3.

Environmental accounting is an emerging accounting issue and you should read up on the subject as much as possible in the financial and accounting press. The ASB has also just produced a working paper on discounting in financial reporting which is discussed briefly in Section 6.

1 PROFIT, CAPITAL MAINTENANCE AND ASSET VALUATION

The meaning of profit

1.1 A useful starting point in the definition of profit is the work of economists, most notably Sir John Hicks, on the meaning of personal income. Hicks' conclusions on personal income can be adapted to the measurement of a company's profit. Note that in this chapter the term 'income' is used in preference to 'profit' in order to compare economic and accounting theories. 'Income' is not intended here to mean 'revenue'.

1.2   Hicks defined income (in *Value and capital*, 1946).

> ### KEY TERM
>
> **Income:** 'the maximum value which an individual can consume during a week and still expect to be as well off at the end of the week as he was at the beginning.'

When a committee (the Sandilands Committee) reported in 1975 on the problems of accounting during periods of inflation, they adapted Hicks' definition to provide a definition of accounting profit:

> ### KEY TERM
>
> 'A company's **profit** for the year is the maximum value which the company can distribute during the year, and still expect to be as well off at the end of the year as it was at the beginning.'

In other words, if a company can maintain its well-offness (its opening capital) any excess value created over and above this is profit.

1.3   This view of profit corresponds with a view of the balance sheet as the primary accounting statement (and this view is held by the ASB in its *Statement of Principles*, as we will see below). This is because once the opening balance sheet and the closing balance sheet for a period have been drawn up, profit emerges as merely a balancing figure between the capital values shown by the two balance sheets. (Of course, adjustments would need to be made for any capital injected or withdrawn during the period).

1.4   An alternative view might be taken by those who regard the profit and loss account as the primary accounting statement (and the new draft *Statement of Principles* has been criticised by those who hold this view). In double-entry bookkeeping any occurrence leading to an increase in the value of a business (such as a sale being made) is recorded at once as a revenue item. Costs incurred in earning the revenue are recorded as debit entries. The primary accounting exercise is then to allocate credits against matching debits so as to produce an appropriate transfer to profit and loss account. In this view, it is the balance sheet which is residual, in that it is merely a collection of unallocated debits and credits.

Question 1

Write down the definitions of income produced by Hicks and the Sandilands Committee.

Answer

See Paragraph 1.2.

Capital maintenance

1.5   There are different views of capital maintenance.

Financial capital maintenance

1.6 Under historical cost accounting (HCA), the amount maintained is the capital sum put into the business by the owner and this is financial capital maintenance.

1.7 Focusing on the equity ownership of the company is often referred to as the **proprietary concept of capital**: if we pay all profits out as dividends and inflation exists then in future our business will gradually run down, as our cash will become insufficient to buy replacement stock.

Operating capital maintenance

1.8 Under this concept, capital is looked at as the capacity to maintain a level of assets, alternatively referred to as the **physical capacity capital maintenance concept**, or the **entity concept**: by using **replacement cost** for our cost of sales we will set aside enough cash to buy replacement assets.

Asset valuation

1.9 Entry and exit values are examples of current value accounting which attempt to find an alternative accounting convention which combines the advantages of objective reporting with the use of realistic values for assets.

Entry values

1.10 Under this concept, **non-monetary assets** are converted to current replacement cost.

1.11 The **advantages** of using entry values are as follows.

(a) It ensures operating capital maintenance by recognising operating profit.

(b) It separates operational from holding gains, so we can distinguish gains under the control of management.

(c) It produces a realistic value of capital employed.

1.12 There are **disadvantages,** as follows.

(a) It is based on the historical cost convention.
(b) Replacement costs may not always be available.
(c) It is subjective.

Exit values

1.13 Using exit values, income is determined as closing capital valued at exit price less opening capital at exit price. Exit prices are the amounts at which **non-monetary assets** could be sold in an orderly realisation.

1.14 The **advantages** of using exit values are as follows.

(a) It is based on the concept of opportunity cost.
(b) Most people understand realisable values.
(c) It shows creditors the amounts available on a winding up.

1.15 Once again, there are **disadvantages**.

(a) It is not based upon the **going concern concept**.

(b) The valuation of assets is subjective.

(c) The assumption of orderly realisation of assets in their existing state may be misleading.

(d) It does not ensure operating capability.

1.16 **Deprival values** are another example of current value accounting which we will look at under CCA later.

Inflation accounting

1.17 We can use historical cost maintenance concepts to show 'profits' and balance sheet values, but if the 'profit' gained by holding assets over time is given by way of dividend, the company's operating capacity will decline.

1.18 To prevent this situation occurring we could:

(a) alter accounts for the general rate of inflation to reflect the decreasing purchasing power of money; or

(b) alter the accounts to reflect specific rates of inflation on the business assets: this is the operating capital maintenance concept.

The now defunct SSAP 16 covered these possibilities: Current Purchasing Power (CPP), and Current Cost Accounting (CCA), covered in the next chapter.

2 REALISED AND DISTRIBUTABLE PROFITS

2.1 The definitions and significance of realised profits and distributable profits are closely related. The importance of realised profits lies in the fact that company law does not allow the distribution of unrealised profits. This fact means that the implications of realised profits underlie a great deal of financial accounting regulation. Some of those implications relate to group accounts.

Realised profits

2.2 A definition of 'realised profits' is provided in the Companies Act 1985, but it is unclear and badly worded. Similarly, it was thought that the definition of 'distributable' profits needed more clarification. In October 1982, in response to the need for definitions, the Consultative Committee of Accountancy Bodies (CCAB) issued two statements of guidance, about the determination of realised profits and of distributable profits.

2.3 The term 'realised' profits was introduced into UK law by the Companies Acts of 1980 and 1981 (both now consolidated into the 1985 Act):

(a) the 1980 Act prohibited the distribution of unrealised profits to shareholders;

(b) the 1981 Act stated that:

(i) 'only profits **realised** at the balance sheet date shall be **included in the profit and loss account**';

(ii) similarly, **transfers from a revaluation reserve** to the profit and loss account are **only** permitted if they represent a transfer of **realised profits**.

2.4 S 262(3) states that:

'references to realised profits and realised losses, in relation to a company's accounts, are to such profits or losses of the company as fall to be treated as realised in accordance with principles generally accepted, at the time when the accounts are prepared, with respect to the determination for accounting purposes of realised profits or losses.'

2.5 However, this definition of realised profits is inexact, and the CCAB guidance note attempts an interpretation. This interpretation is not definitive, and might be altered by new or revised accounting standards, and even more significantly the interpretation might be overturned by a judicial decision in a court of law. 'Interpretation of the law rests ultimately with the courts'.

2.6 The CCAB suggests that the framework for defining 'realised profits' should be Schedule 4 and statements of standard accounting practice (and FRSs), notably SSAP 2.

2.7 However, since the 1985 Act states that there is an overriding requirement to give a true and fair view, the directors may include an unrealised profit in the profit and loss account where there are special reasons for doing so. However, if unrealised profits are thus recognised in the profit and loss account, particulars of this departure from the statutory accounting principle, the reasons for it and its effect are required to be given in a note to the accounts.

2.8 The CCAB gave examples of how some SSAPs help to establish generally accepted principles for determining realised profits.

   (a) **FRS 9** (see Chapter 17) states that if a company does not prepare group accounts, but holds an interest in an associated company:

      (i)   the profit and loss account of the holding company may include dividends received from the associate (out of the associate's profits) but must not include retained earnings by the associate, because these earnings are only realised by the holding company when (and if) the associate pays them out as a dividend;

      (ii)   however, a failure to report the retained profits of an associate would prevent a true and fair view from being obtained, and FRS 9 therefore requires a separate or supplementary statement in the company's accounts to report the profits of its associated company.

   (b) **SSAP 9** states that turnover and profits should be recognised on long-term contracts as soon as their outcome is foreseeable with reasonable certainty. With the introduction of the Companies Act 1985, there was some doubt as to whether this practice should be allowed to continue, on the grounds that 'attributable' profit might not be 'realised'. However, the CCAB takes the view that since attributable profits in SSAP 9 are based on the principle of *reasonable certainty*, they may be regarded as *realised* profits within the context of the 1985 Act.

Distributable profits

2.9 A *distribution* is defined by s 263(2) CA 1985.

KEY TERM

Distribution: every description of distribution of a company's assets to members (shareholders) of the company, whether in cash or otherwise, with the exceptions of:

(a) an issue of bonus shares;

(b) the redemption or purchase of the company's own shares out of capital (including the proceeds of a new issue) or out of unrealised profits;

(c) the reduction of share capital by:

  (i)   reducing the liability on shares in respect of share capital not fully paid up;
  (ii) paying off paid up share capital;

(d) a distribution of assets to shareholders in a winding up of the company.

2.10 Companies must not make a distribution except out of profits available for the purpose (ie 'distributable profits'). These available profits are:

(a) **its accumulated realised profits**, insofar as these have not already been used for an earlier distribution or for 'capitalisation';

(b) **minus its accumulated realised losses**, insofar as these have not already been written off in a reduction or reconstruction scheme.

Capital profits and revenue profits (if realised) are taken together and capital losses and revenue losses (if realised) are similarly grouped together. **Unrealised profits** cannot be distributed (for example profit on the revaluation of fixed assets); nor must a company apply unrealised profits to pay up debentures or any unpaid amounts on issued shares.

2.11 Capitalisation of realised profits is the use of profits:

(a) to issue bonus shares; or
(b) as a transfer to the capital redemption reserve.

2.12 As a point of detail, s 275(2) allows that any **excess depreciation** on a revalued fixed asset above the amount of depreciation that would have been charged on its historical cost can be treated as a realised profit for the purpose of distributions. This is to avoid penalising companies that make an unrealised profit on the revaluation of an asset, and must then charge depreciation on the revalued amount.

2.13 For example, suppose that a company buys an asset at a cost of £20,000. It has a life of 4 years and a nil residual value. If it is immediately revalued to £30,000, an unrealised profit of £10,000 would be credited to the revaluation reserve. Annual depreciation must be based on the revalued amount, in this case, ¼ of £30,000 or £7,500. This exceeds depreciation which would have been charged on the asset's cost (£5,000 pa) by £2,500 per annum. This £2,500 can be treated as a distributable profit under s 275(2).

2.14 S 264 imposes further restrictions on the distributions of **public companies**. A public company cannot make a distribution if at the time:

(a) the amount of its net assets is less than the combined total of its called-up share capital plus its undistributable reserves; or

(b) the distribution will reduce the amount of its net assets to below the combined total of its called-up share capital plus its undistributable reserves.

> **KEY TERM**
>
> 'Undistributable reserves' are:
>
> (a) the share premium account;
>
> (b) the capital redemption reserve;
>
> (c) any accumulated surplus of unrealised profits over unrealised losses;
>
> (d) any other reserve which cannot be distributed, whether by statute, or the company's memorandum or articles of association.

2.15 The key feature of s 264 is that **all accumulated distributable profits,** both **realised and unrealised, must exceed the accumulated realised and unrealised losses** of the company before any distribution can be made. The difference between the profits and losses is the maximum possible distribution.

2.16 In contrast with s 263, s 264 includes consideration of *unrealised* profits and losses, so that if unrealised losses exceed unrealised profits, the amount of distributions which can be made will be reduced by the amount of the 'deficit'.

2.17 EXAMPLE: PRIVATE COMPANY V PUBLIC COMPANY DISTRIBUTIONS

Huddle Ltd is a private company and Publimco plc is a public limited company. Both companies have a financial year ending on 31 December. On 31 December 19X5, the balance sheets of the companies, by a remarkable coincidence, were identical, as follows.

	Huddle Ltd		Publimco plc	
	£'000	£'000	£'000	£'000
Net assets		365		365
Share capital		300		300
Share premium account		60		60
Unrealised losses on asset revaluations		(25)		(25)
Realised profits	50		50	
Realised losses	(20)		(20)	
		30		30
		365		365

What is the maximum distribution that each company can make?

2.18 SOLUTION

(a) S 263 restricts the distributable profits of Huddle Ltd to £30,000.

(b) S 264 further restricts the distributable profits of Publimco plc to £30,000 – £25,000 = £5,000 (or alternatively, £365,000 – £300,000 – £60,000 = £5,000. This is the surplus of net assets over share capital plus undistributable reserves, which in this example are represented by the share premium account).

Distributable profits and realised profits

2.19 The Companies Act 1985 states that unrealised profits may not be distributed to shareholders. However, there is no legal requirement to distinguish between distributable and non-distributable profits in a published balance sheet. As a general guideline:

(a) profits reported in the profit and loss account should be realised profits (1985 Act);

(b) unrealised profits will be credited direct to a reserve and will not be taken through the profit and loss account (such as revaluation surpluses);

(c) however, some realised profits may be included in reserves.

2.20 The concept of distributable profits does not strictly apply to group accounts. For example, if a holding company H Ltd has three wholly-owned subsidiaries S_1, S_2 and S_3, the group profits will be the combined profits of all four companies. The profits of S_1, S_2 and S_3 may only be distributed to their own shareholders (to the holding company) and may not be paid directly to the holding company's shareholders. The holding company receives dividends from its subsidiaries, and may distribute profits from dividends received; the holding company cannot distribute profits retained by subsidiaries as dividends to its own shareholders.

2.21 Although the concept of distributable profits does not therefore properly apply to group accounts, it should nevertheless be the case that the realised profits of subsidiaries are distributable to the holding company.

2.22 The CCAB's guidance note on distributable profits attempts to make some clarification about how distributable profits (realised profits less realised losses) should be determined. The following points were included in the note.

2.23 If an asset is revalued, the surplus is unrealised profit and is not taken through the profit and loss account. The double entry is:

DEBIT   Asset account
CREDIT   Revaluation reserve

with the amount of the increase in valuation. However, when the asset is sold, this unrealised profit becomes realised.

2.24 The 1985 Act states that certain *provisions* are to be considered as realised losses. These provisions are specified as:

'any amount written off by way of providing for depreciation or diminution in value of assets'

'any amount retained as reasonably necessary for the purpose of providing for any liability or loss which is likely to be incurred, or certain to be incurred but uncertain as to amount or as to the date on which it will arise.'

2.25 Development costs are realised losses in the year in which the costs are incurred, unless the costs are capitalised (in accordance with SSAP 13 and the Companies Act 1985) in which case the development costs are written off as realised losses over a number of years.

The relevant accounts

2.26 S 270 defines the 'relevant accounts' which should be used to determine the distributable profits. These are the most recent audited annual accounts of the company, prepared in compliance with the Companies Acts. If the accounts are qualified by the auditors, the auditors must state in their report whether they consider that the proposed distribution would contravene the Act.

2.27 Companies may also base a distribution on **interim accounts**, which need not be audited. However, in the case of a **public** company, such interim accounts must be properly prepared and comply with:

(a) s 228(2) (accounts to give a true and fair view); and

(b) s 238 (directors to sign the company's balance sheet).

A copy of the interim accounts should be delivered to the Registrar.

Investment and insurance companies

2.28   S 265 makes a special provision for investment companies which are public companies. Investment companies may make a distribution out of realised revenue profits (insofar as they have not already been utilised or capitalised) less its realised and unrealised revenue losses (insofar as these have not already been written off in a capital reduction or reconstruction) provided that its assets equal at least one and a half times the aggregate amount of its liabilities.

2.29   S 268 refers to insurance companies which have long-term business. Any surplus of assets over liabilities on long-term business which has been properly transferred to the company's profit and loss account should be regarded as a *realised* profit. (This section makes a specific point of clarification, and is therefore relatively minor in importance.)

Distributions to employees

2.30   S 309 CA 1985 states that the directors of a company must have regard to the interests of the company's employees in general, as well as to the interests of shareholders. This is a duty which is owed by directors to the company alone.

2.31   This section appears on its own, and its full significance, if any, has yet to emerge. It was intended to be seen in connection with s 719, which gives a company power to provide for employees in the event of a shutdown of the company or a take-over, even if it is not in the best interests of a company or its members. In the case of *Parke v Daily News Limited 1962* it had been held that a company was not entitled to distribute £1.5 million out of £2 million from the proceeds of selling off most of the company's assets to provide redundancy payments to its employees. S 719, coupled with s 309, has overturned the case decision by statute, and directors now have the power to make such payments in the event of a shutdown or take-over, if they so wish (and probably also if sanctioned by an ordinary resolution of the company).

Question 2

The following balances and notes were included in the accounts of Uppercross at 31 December 19X5.

BPP PUBLISHING

Part B: Income and value measurement

	£m	£m
Assets		170.0
Liabilities		76.5
		93.5
Reserves		
Revaluation reserve		11.0
Share premium account		6.2
Merger reserve		3.5
Profit and loss account		
Brought forward	(1.3)	
19X5	12.1	
Carried forward		10.8
Total reserves		31.5
Share capital		62.0
		93.5

Further information is given in the notes to the account and this is summarised here.

(a)   Revaluation reserve

The company's office furniture was revalued on 1 January 19X5 and was found to be worth £1.8m less than its book value. This deficit was taken to the revaluation reserve.

The company's plant and machinery was also revalued on 1 January 19X5. The surplus on revaluation was £14m, from which £1,200,000 was transferred to the profit and loss account. This figure represented the depreciation on the surplus.

Uppercross has other assets carried at historic cost which will probably be revalued at a later date.

(b)   Share premium account

This amount arose on the issue of share capital on 1 January 19X3.

(c)   Merger reserve

On 1 January 19X5 Uppercross acquired the entire share capital of Kelynch. The consideration consisted entirely of shares in Uppercross and the transaction qualified as a merger under the provisions of the Companies Act 1985. The premium on the shares issued was £9.0m, from which was deducted £5.5m goodwill. This goodwill arose from a completely different event and is estimated to have a useful life of 10 years.

(d)   Profit and loss account for 19X5

The following transactions have been passed through the profit and loss account for the year.

(i)   The depreciation amount of £1.2m mentioned in Note (a) above was transferred to the profit and loss account.

(ii)   A provision of £7.3m had been made in respect of Wentworth Ltd, a subsidiary. This provision is because of a permanent diminution in value.

(iii)   A loan taken out by the company on 1 January 19X5 is denominated in Deutschmarks but the funds are used in the UK. At the year end an exchange gain of £240,000 was credited to the profit and loss account.

(iv)   An unincorporated business, Harville, was purchased on 1 January 19X5 and the acquired goodwill, which has an estimated useful life of 8 years, was £2.4m. This entire amount was written off in the profit and loss account.

Required

Assuming that Uppercross is:

(a)   a public company; and
(b)   an investment company;

calculate the distributable profit for 19X5 in each case.

Answer

(a) Profits available for distribution by a public company are defined as the accumulated realised retained profits less accumulated realised losses.

	£m
Share capital and undistributable reserves	
Share capital	62.00
Share premium	6.20
Merger reserve (3.5 + 5.5)	9.00
	77.20
Unrealised reserves	
Revaluation of plant (capital)	12.80
Foreign currency difference (revenue)	0.24
	13.04
Realised profits less realised losses	
Realised loss brought forward	(1.30)
Profit for 19X5	12.10
Amortisation of goodwill	
From merger reserve transaction (5.5m × 10%)	(0.55)
From Harville (2.4m × 12.5%)	(0.30)
Add back unrealised goodwill: Harville	2.40
Foreign exchange difference	(0.24)
Total realised revenue profits	12.11
Revaluation of office (capital)	(1.80)
Realised profits	10.31
Total assets (170 + 5.5 - 0.55 + 2.4 – 0.3)	177.05
Total liabilities	76.50
	100.55
Capital and reserves: total (77.20 + 13.04 + 10.31)	100.55

The distributable profits of the public limited company are the total realised profits of £10.31m.

(b) For an investment company, a distribution may be made out of its accumulated realised revenue profits, less its accumulated revenue losses (whether realised *or* unrealised) *only if* both before and after the distribution, the amount of its assets is at least equal to one and a half times the aggregate of its liabilities.

	£m
Realised revenue profits	13.41
Realised revenue losses	(1.30)
Unrealised revenue losses	-
	12.11

	Before	After
Assets	177.50	177.50
Less maximum distribution		12.11
		165.39
Liabilities	76.50	76.50
Liabilities × 1.5	114.75	114.75

The distributable profits of the investment company are therefore £12.11m.

---

3   ASB STATEMENT OF PRINCIPLES   11/96

3.1   The Accounting Standards Board (ASB) published (in November 1995) an exposure draft of its *Statement of Principles for Financial Reporting*. In March 1999, the text was substantially revised with particular attention being given to the clarity of expression. The ASB issued with the revised draft an introductory booklet and a technical supplement. Together these documents respond to the criticisms raised on the 1995 version by exploding myths, rebutting arguments and making technical changes.

3.2 The statement consists of eight chapters.

    (1) The objective of financial statements
    (2) The reporting entity
    (3) The qualitative characteristics of financial information
    (4) The elements of financial statements
    (5) Recognition in financial statements
    (6) Measurement in financial statements
    (7) Presentation of financial information
    (8) Accounting for interests in other entities

Purpose of the *Statement of Principles*

3.3 The following are the main reasons why the Accounting Standards Board (ASB) developed the *Statement of Principles*.

    (a) To assist the ASB by providing a basis for reducing the number of alternative accounting treatments permitted by accounting standards and company law

    (b) To provide a framework for the future development of accounting standards

    (c) To assist auditors in forming an opinion as to whether financial statements conform with accounting standards

    (d) To assist users of accounts in interpreting the information contained in them

    (e) To provide guidance in applying accounting standards

    (f) To give guidance on areas which are not yet covered by accounting standards

    (g) To inform interested parties of the approach taken by the ASB in formulating accounting standards

The role of the *Statement* can thus be summed up as being to provide **consistency, clarity and information**.

Chapter 1 The objective of financial statements

3.4 The main points raised here are as follows.

    (a) 'The objective of financial statements is to provide information about the reporting entity's **performance and financial position** that is useful to a wide range of users for assessing the stewardship of management and for making economic decisions.'

    (b) It is acknowledged that while all not all the information needs of users can be met by financial statements, there are needs that are common to all users. Financial statements that meet the needs of providers of risk capital to the enterprise will also meet most of the needs of other users that financial statements can satisfy.

    Users of financial statements other than investors include the following.

        (i) Investors
        (ii) Lenders
        (iii) Suppliers and other creditors
        (iv) Employees
        (v) Customers
        (vi) Government and their agencies
        (vii) The public

    (c) The limitations of financial statements are emphasised as well as the strengths.

(d) Investors are the defining choice of user because they focus on the entity's cash-generation ability or financial adaptability.

(d) The information required by investors relates to:

   (i)   financial performance
   (ii)   financial position
   (iii) generation and use of cash
   (iv)   financial adaptability

The exposure draft discusses the importance of each of these elements and why they are disclosed in the financial statements.

Chapter 2 The reporting entity

3.5   This chapter makes the point that it is important that entities that ought to prepare financial statements, in fact do so. The entity must be a cohesive economic unit. It has a determinable boundary and is held to account for all the things it can control. For this purpose, first direct control and secondly direct plus indirect control are taken into account.

> **KEY TERM**
>
> **Control** means two things:
>
> (a)   The ability to deploy the economic resources involved; and
> (b)   the ability to benefit (or to suffer) from their deployment.
>
> An entity will have control of a second entity if it has the ability to direct that entity's operating and financial policies with a view to gaining economic benefit from its activities.

Control must be distinguished from **management**, where the entity is not exposed to the benefits arising from or risks inherent in the activities of the second entity.

Chapter 3 Qualitative characteristics of financial information

3.6   The ED gives a diagrammatic representation of the discussion, shown below.

(a) Qualitative characteristics that relate to **content** are **relevance** and **reliability**.

(b) Qualitative characteristics that relate to **presentation** are **comparability** and **understandability**.

The diagram shown here is reasonably explanatory.

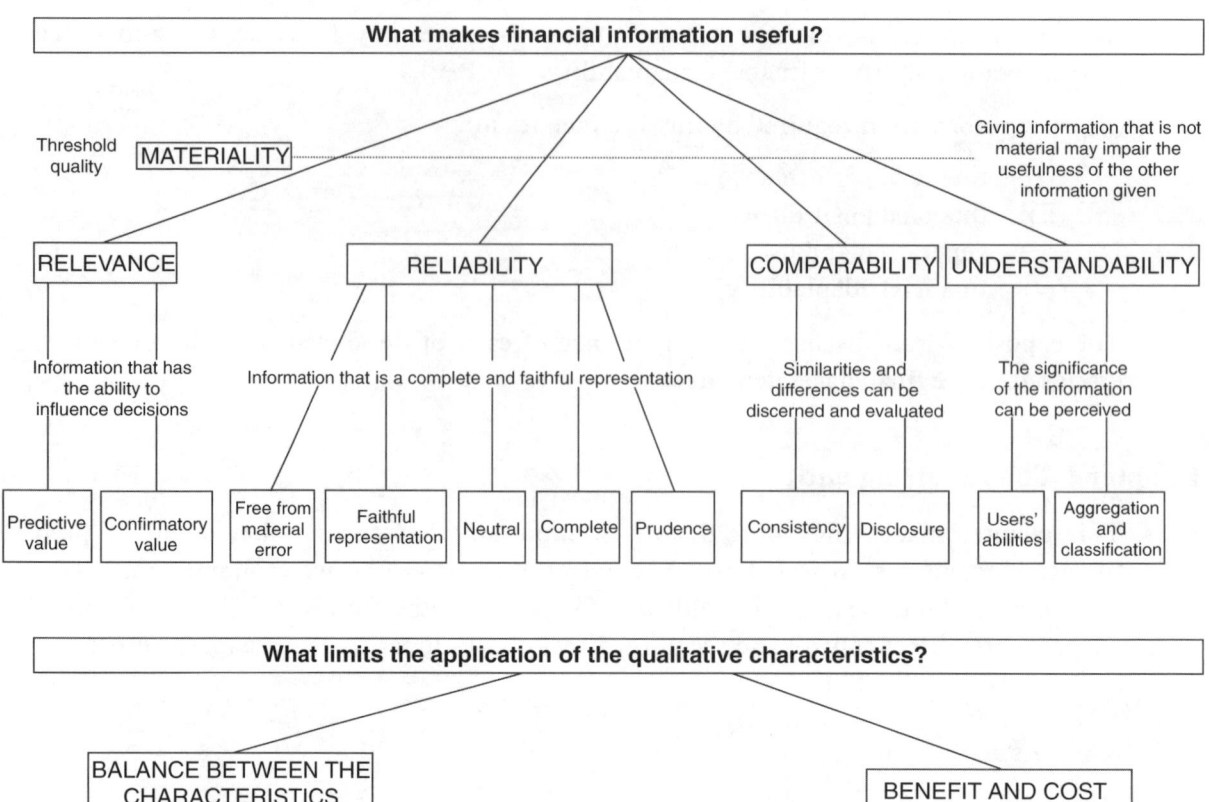

Chapter 4 Elements of financial statements

3.7 The elements of financial statements are listed. They are:

   (a) Assets
   (b) Liabilities
   (c) Ownership interest
   (d) Gains
   (e) Losses
   (f) Contributions from owners
   (g) Distributions to owners

3.8 Any item that does not fall within one of the definitions of elements should not be included in financial statements. The definitions are as follows.

   (a) **Assets** are rights or other access to future economic benefits controlled by an entity as a result of past transactions or events.

   (b) **Liabilities** are obligations of an entity to transfer economic benefits as a result of past transactions or events.

   (c) **Ownership interest** is the residual amount found by deducting all of the entity's liabilities from all of the entity's assets.

   (d) **Gains** are increases in ownership interest, other than those relating to contributions from owners.

   (e) **Losses** are decreases in ownership interest, other than those relating to distributions to owners.

   (f) **Contributions from owners** are increases in ownership interest resulting from investments made by owners in their capacity as owners.

   (g) **Distributions to owners** are decreases in ownership interest resulting from transfers made to owners in their capacity as owners.

Chapter 5 Recognition in financial statements

3.9 If a transaction or other event has created a new asset or liability or added an existing asset or liability, that effect will be recognised if:

   (a) sufficient evidence exists that the new asset or liability has been created or that there has been an addition to an existing asset or liability; and

   (b) the new asset or liability or the addition to the existing asset or liability can be measured at a monetary amount with sufficient reliability.

3.10 In a transaction involving the provision of services or goods for a net gain, the recognition criteria described above will be met on the occurrence of the critical event in the operating cycle involved.

3.11 An asset or liability will be wholly or partly derecognised if:

   (a) sufficient evidence exists that a transaction or other past event has eliminated a previously recognised asset or liability; or

   (b) although the item continues to be an asset or a liability the criteria for recognition are no longer met.

3.12 The objective of financial statements is achieved to a large extent through the recognition of elements in the primary financial statements - in other words, the depiction of elements both in words and by monetary amounts, and the inclusion of those amounts in the primary financial statement totals. Recognition is a process that has the following stages.

   (a) Initial recognition, which is where an item is depicted in the primary financial statements for the first time.

   (b) Subsequent remeasurement, which involves changing the amount at which an already recognised asset or liability is stated in the primary financial statements.

   (c) Derecognition, which is where an item that was until then recognised ceases to be recognised.

3.13 In practice, entities operate in an uncertain environment and this **uncertainty** may sometimes make it necessary to delay the recognition process. The uncertainty is twofold.

   • **Element uncertainty** - does the item exist and meet the definition of elements?
   • **Measurement uncertainty** - at what monetary amount should the item be recognised?

3.14 Even though matching is not used by the draft *Statement* to drive the recognition process, it still plays an important role in the approach described in the draft in allocating the cost of assets across reporting periods and in telling preparers where they may find assets and liabilities.

Question 3

Consider the following situations. In each case, do we have an asset or liability within the definitions given by the *Statement of Principles?* Give reasons for your answer.

(a) Pat Ltd has purchased a patent for £20,000. The patent gives the company sole use of a particular manufacturing process which will save £3,000 a year for the next five years.

(b) Baldwin Ltd paid Don Brennan £10,000 to set up a car repair shop, on condition that priority treatment is given to cars from the company's fleet.

(c) Deals on Wheels Ltd provides a warranty with every car sold.

(d) Monty Ltd has signed a contract with a human resources consultant. The terms of the contract are that the consultant is to stay for six months and be paid £3,000 per month.

(e) Rachmann Ltd owns a building which for many years it had let out to students. The building has been declared unsafe by the local council. Not only is it unfit for human habitation, but on more than one occasion slates have fallen off the roof, nearly killing passers-by. To rectify all the damage would cost £300,000; to eliminate the danger to the public would cost £200,000. The building could then be sold for £100,000.

Answer

(a) This is an asset, albeit an intangible one. There is a past event, control and future economic benefit (through cost savings).

(b) This cannot be classified as an asset. Baldwin Ltd has no control over the car repair shop and it is difficult to argue that there are 'future economic benefits'.

(c) This is a liability; the business has taken on an obligation. It would be recognised when the warranty is issued rather than when a claim is made.

(d) As a firm financial commitment, this has all the appearance of a liability. However, as the consultant has not done any work yet, there has been no past event which could give rise to a liability. Similarly, because there has been no past event there is no asset.

(e) The situation is not clear cut. It could be argued that there is a liability, depending on the whether the potential danger to the public arising from the building creates a legal obligation to do the repairs. If there is such a liability, it might be possible to set off the sale proceeds of £100,000 against the cost of essential repairs of £200,000, giving a net obligation to transfer economic benefits of £100,000.

The building is clearly not an asset, because although there is control and there has been a past event, there is no expected access to economic benefit.

Chapter 6 Measurement in financial statements

3.15 A monetary carrying amount needs to be assigned so an asset or liability can be recognised. There are two measuring tasks that can be used: **historical cost** or **current value**.

(a) Initially, when an asset is purchased or a liability incurred, the asset/liability is recorded at the transaction cost, that is historical cost, which at that time is equal to current replacement cost.

(b) An asset/liability may subsequently be 'remeasured'. In a historical cost system, this can involve writing down an asset to its recoverable amount. For a liability, the corresponding treatment would be amendment of the monetary amount to the amount ultimately expected to be paid.

(c) Such re-measurements will, however, only be recognised if there is sufficient evidence that the monetary amount of the asset/liability has changed and the new amount can be reliably measured.

Chapter 7 Presentation of financial information

3.16 Aspects of this chapter have also given rise to some controversy. The chapter begins by making the general point that financial statements need to be as simple, straightforward and brief as possible while retaining their relevance and reliability.

Components of financial statements

3.17 The primary financial statements are as follows.

Statement	Measure of
Profit and loss account	Financial performance
Statement of total recognised gains and losses	Financial performance
Balance sheet	Financial position
Cash flow statement	Cash inflows and outflows

3.18 The notes to the financial statements 'amplify and explore' the primary statements; together they form an 'integrated whole'. Disclosure in the notes does not correct or justify non-disclosure or misrepresentation in the primary financial statements.

3.19 'Supplementary information' embraces voluntary disclosures and information which is too subjective for disclosure in the primary financial statement and the notes.

Chapter 8 Accounting for interests in other entities

3.20 Financial statements need to reflect the effect on the reporting entity's financial performance and financial position of its interests in other entities. This involves various measurement, presentation and consolidation issues which are dealt with in this chapter of the *Statement*.

Different kinds of investments

3.21 The **classification** of investments should reflect the way in which they are used to further the business of the investor and their effect on the investor's financial position, performance and financial adaptability. The two key factors here are:

   (a)   the **degree of influence** of the investor; and
   (b)   the nature of the **investor's interest** in the results, assets and liabilities of its investee.

3.22 The different types of investment are summarised in the following table.

Degree of influence	Nature of interest	Resulting categorisation
Control	The investor controls the investee	Subsidiary
Joint control	The investor does not itself control the investee but shares control through some form of arrangement jointly with others	Joint venture
Significant influence	The investor has neither control nor joint control, but exerts a degree of influence over the investee's operating and financial policies that is at the least a significant influence and at the most just short of joint control	Associate
Lesser or no influence	Any influence that the investor has over the investee's operating and financial policies is less than a significant influence	Simple investment

Parent and subsidiary

3.23 Parent entities prepare **consolidated financial statements** to provide financial information about the group as a single reporting entity. Consolidation is a process that aggregates the total assets, liabilities and results of the parent and its subsidiaries.

3.24 In determining which investments should be consolidated, the principle of control should predominate. However, consolidated financial statements should also reflect the extent of **outside ownership interests** because they are important factors in considering the parent's access and exposure to the results of its subsidiaries.

Associates and joint ventures

3.25 There are interests involving significant influence and joint control respectively. The method used should recognise the reporting entity's share of the results and the changes in net assets of the investee and should not misrepresent the extent of its influence. The **equity method** is therefore used.

Business combinations

3.26 Two types are recognised.

- **Purchases/acquisitions**. The assets and liabilities of the entity acquired are treated as if the transaction was the purchase of a bundle of assets and liabilities on the open market.

- **Uniting of interests/mergers**. The assets and liabilities of one party to the transaction are treated in the same way as the assets and liabilities of all the other parties; none of the assets or liabilities are treated as being purchased as a bundle of assets and liabilities on the open market.

Questions and answers

3.27 The original November 1995 exposure draft of the *Statement of Principles* attracted a great deal of criticism, not least from the firm Ernst & Young. In an attempt to address the criticisms raised, the ASB produced a booklet to go with the *Statement*, called '*Some questions answered*'. Below is an outline of the topics covered.

Status and purpose

3.28 The points made here are as follows.

(a) The *Statement* is a description of the fundamental approach that should underpin the financial statements. It is intended to be:

- Comprehensive
- Internally consistent
- Consistent with international approaches

(b) The final version will **not** be an accounting standard.

(c) Its main influence on accounting practice will be through its influence on the standard-setting process. It is only one of the factors that will be taken into account.

Approach

3.29 The approach encompasses the following.

(a) There are similarities to existing practice and differences.

(b) The draft *Statement* is based on the International Accounting Standard Committee's framework statement and is largely consistent with the framework statements issued in Australia, Canada, New Zealand, the USA and elsewhere. This reflects the view that it will be easier to achieve harmonisation of accounting practice if standard-setters work with a common set of principles.

(c) The 'true and fair' requirement and SSAP 2's fundamental accounting concepts play a central role in the revised draft.

(d) The *Statement's* development has not been constrained by the requirements of companies legislation because:

- It does not just apply to companies
- Legal frameworks change in response to developments in accounting thought

The use of current costs and values and current cost accounting

3.30 These points are made.

(a) The previous version of the *Statement* was criticised as heralding a move towards **current cost accounting**. However, the revised draft makes it clear that this is **not on the ASB's agenda**.

(b) The draft *Statement* explains that historical cost and current value are **alternative measures**. It also explains that it is envisaged that the approach now adopted by the majority of the larger UK listed companies will continue to be used. This approach involves carrying some categories of balance sheet items at historical cost and others at current value. The draft *Statement* then goes on to describe a framework that would guide the choice of an appropriate measurement basis for each balance sheet category.

The focus on assets and liabilities and the role of transactions

3.31 These points are made.

(a) The previous draft placed great emphasis on assets and liabilities and even defined the items that are to be included in the profit and loss account in terms of assets and liabilities. This approach has been retained.

(b) The approach does not mean that the P&L is unimportant. The primary source of information provided in financial statements is the transactions undertaken by the reporting entity. The primary focus of the accounting process is to allocate these transactions to accounting periods.

(c) The *Statement* regards the profit or loss for the period as the difference between the opening and closing balance sheets adjusted for capital constructions and distributions.

Accounting standards based on the Statement

3.32 The question was raised as to whether accounting standards published in the future and therefore based on the *Statement of Principles* will be very different from past accounting standards. The ASB's view is that they won't. Some of the principles have already played very significant roles in accounting standards and have found general acceptance. The standards include:

- FRS 2 *Accounting for subsidiary undertakings*, which uses the reporting entity concept described in Chapter 2 of the draft Statement.

- FRS 4 *Capital instruments* and FRS 5 *Reporting the substance of transactions*, which use the definitions of assets and liabilities set out in Chapter 4.

- FRS 11 *Impairment of fixed assets and goodwill*, which uses the recoverable amount notion described in Chapter 6.

The way forward

3.33 At the time of writing (June 1999) the revised *Statement of Principles* has not yet had to face the barrage of criticism heaped upon the 1995 version. Possibly, the *Question and Answer* booklet has pre-empted some of the possible criticisms. Watch this space!

Question 4

What is the purpose of the ASB's *Statement of Principles?*

Answer

The following are the main reasons why the ASB developed the *Statement of Principles.*

(a) To assist the ASB by providing a basis for reducing the number of alternative accounting treatments permitted by accounting standards and company law

(b) To provide a framework for the future development of accounting standards

(c) To assist auditors in forming an opinion as to whether financial statements conform with accounting standards

(d) To assist users of accounts in interpreting the information contained in them

(e) To provide guidance in applying accounting standards

(f) To give guidance on areas which are not yet covered by accounting standards

(g) To inform interested parties of the approach taken by the ASB in formulating accounting standards

The role of the *Statement* can thus be summed up as being to provide consistency, clarity and information.

Exam focus point

As a topical issue, the *Statement* could be the subject of a question, or part of a question, soon.

4   FRS 3 REPORTING FINANCIAL PERFORMANCE   11/97

4.1 Before we look at certain provisions of FRS 3 in detail, we need to examine its partial forerunner, SSAP 6 *Extraordinary items and prior year adjustments*. This will help you to put in to context the changes introduced by FRS 3. The examiner has said that candidates still need to be aware of the contents of SSAP 6.

SSAP 6 *Extraordinary items and prior year adjustments*

4.2 The profit and loss account is arguably the most significant single indicator of a company's success or failure. It is very important to ensure that it is not presented in such a way as to be misleading. This could happen either through an inadvertent lack of consistency within a company or between different companies; or it could arise as a result of **deliberate manipulation** of accounting figures by unscrupulous directors.

4.3 One particular area where this might happen is the practice known as **reserve accounting**. This involves deducting items of expenditure not from the profits for the *current* year, but from the balance of accumulated profits brought forward. By eliminating such items from the current year's profit and loss account a more favourable presentation of the year's results may be achieved; only a close inspection of the previous year's balance sheet will disclose that the figure for reserves brought forward has been manipulated.

4.4 Possible justifications for excluding items in this way from the current year's profit and loss account include the following.

(a) The item might have arisen in a previous year without becoming apparent until the current year. It is really a charge against previous year's profits and would have appeared in an earlier year's profit and loss account if the directors had been aware of it.

(b) The item is unique in nature and unlikely to recur. It would be a misleading distortion of the trend of reported profits if such an item were charged against the current year's profits.

4.5 Each of these arguments may be valid in certain circumstances, but it is clear that scope is available for unscrupulous manipulation of the profit and loss account unless those circumstances are very clearly defined. SSAP 6 attempted to standardise the treatment of prior year adjustments and extraordinary items, which are respectively the two categories of items referred to in Paragraph 4.4 above.

Prior year adjustments

4.6 Prior year adjustments were defined in SSAP 6.

KEY TERM

Prior year adjustment: 'those material adjustments applicable to prior years arising from changes in accounting policies or from the correction of fundamental errors. They do not include normal recurring corrections or adjustments of accounting estimates made in prior years.'

4.7 Items falling within this (restricted) definition were the only ones which should be dealt with by adjusting the balance of reserves brought forward; other prior year items would be dealt with in the profit and loss account of the year in which they were recognised.

4.8 Prior year adjustments were rare, and were limited to occasions where:

(a) there had been a change in accounting policy, perhaps as a result of the issue of a new FRS; or

(b) there had been a fundamental error in the past which must now be corrected.

Any other adjustment had to be charged or credited to the current year's profit and loss account. For example, if the tax liability for 19X3 was estimated as £70,000 and was eventually agreed as £80,000 it would not be correct to treat the adjustment as a prior year adjustment. Instead, the additional £10,000 of tax payable should be disclosed as one component of the 19X4 tax charge in the profit and loss account for that year.

BPP PUBLISHING

4.9 In the accounts, prior year adjustments appeared in the statement of movements on reserves which appeared either at the foot of the profit and loss account or in the notes to the accounts. It might have been necessary to adjust not only the figures for reserves brought forward at the beginning of the current year, but also the comparative figure (the balance of reserves brought forward at the beginning of the previous year).

4.10 EXAMPLE: PRIOR YEAR ADJUSTMENTS

Wick Ltd was established on 1 January 19X0. In the first three years accounts deferred development expenditure was carried forward as an asset in the balance sheet. During 19X3 the directors decided that for the current and future years, all development expenditure should be written off as it is incurred. This decision has not resulted from any change in the expected outcome of development projects on hand, but rather from a desire to favour the prudence concept. The following information is available.

(a) Movements on the deferred development account.

Year	*Deferred development expenditure incurred during year* £'000	*Transfer from deferred development expenditure account to P & L account* £'000
19X0	525	-
19X1	780	215
19X2	995	360

(b) The 19X2 accounts showed the following.

	£'000
Retained reserves b/f	2,955
Retained profit for the year	1,825
Retained profits carried forward	4,780

(c) The retained profit for 19X3 after charging the actual development expenditure for the year was £2,030,000.

Required

Show how the change in accounting policy should be reflected in the statement of reserves in the company's 19X3 accounts.

Ignore taxation.

4.11 SOLUTION

If the new accounting policy had been adopted since the company was incorporated, the additional profit and loss account charges for development expenditure would have been:

	£'000
19X0	525
19X1 £(780 – 215)	565
	1,090
19X2 £(995 – 360)	635
	1,725

This means that the reserves brought forward at 1 January 19X3 would have been £1,725,000 less than the reported figure of £4,780,000; while the reserves brought forward at 1 January 19X2 would have been £1,090,000 less than the reported figure of £2,955,000.

The statement of reserves in Wick Ltd's 19X3 accounts should, therefore, appear as follows.

STATEMENT OF RESERVES (EXTRACT)

	19X3	Comparative (previous year) figures 19X2
	£'000	£'000
Retained profits at the beginning of year		
Previously reported	4,780	2,955
Prior year adjustment (note 1)	1,725	1,090
Restated	3,055	1,865
Retained profits for the year	2,030	1,190 (note 2)
Retained profits at the end of the year	5,085	3,055

Notes

1   The accounts should include a note explaining the reasons for and consequences of the changes in accounting policy. (See above workings for 19X3 and 19X2.)

2   The retained profit shown for 19X2 is after charging the additional development expenditure of £635,000. (SSAP 6 required that 'the effect of the prior year adjustment on the results for the preceding year should be disclosed where practicable'.)

UITF Abstract 14 *Disclosure of changes in accounting policy*

4.12   This Abstract clarifies an aspect of the statutory disclosure requirements that has caused some uncertainty as to its meaning. When there is a change of accounting policy companies legislation requires disclosure of particulars, reasons and effect. The issue concerns the extent of the disclosure necessary to give the 'effect' of the change. The UITF has received legal advice that an indication of the effect on the *current* year's figures is required. This is in addition to the effect on the results for the *preceding* period, which is a disclosure requirement of FRS 3 *Reporting financial performance*. As this is a clarification of the law this consensus should be adopted as soon as practicable.

4.13   There has also been some debate about the extent of the disclosure necessary to cover the 'reasons' for the change. In this connection FRS 3 states that 'a change in accounting may ... be made only if it can be justified on the grounds that the new policy is preferable to the one it replaces because it will give a fairer presentation of the result and of the financial position of a reporting entity'. This, together with the requirements in companies legislation for 'special reasons', is a stringent test and directors of companies contemplating a possible change of policy should ensure that the reasons for any change are compelling.

4.14   The issue of a new accounting standard requiring a change would constitute sufficient reason, since accounts prepared adopting a policy no longer permitted by a new standard would normally not give a true and fair view. On the other hand, where the existing policy continues to be acceptable, either because the relevant standard permits a choice or because, in the absence of a relevant standard, both policies are generally accepted, it would not be in accordance with the legislation or FRS 3 if a change was made from one such alternative policy to another unless the reasons for the change were compelling, in that the new policy provided better information for users of the accounts.

4.15   UITF 7 (see Chapter 2) elaborates on the requirement to state 'reasons' and in the context of a change of accounting policy this would imply a statement as to why the continuation of the previous accounting policy would not be appropriate. Where the change of accounting policy was imposed on the company, for example by a new accounting standard, a simple statement to this effect will normally suffice. However, where a change has been made from one generally accepted policy to another, in the absence of a new accounting standard or other similar requirement, the reasons justifying the change need to be clearly and fully disclosed.

Extraordinary items and exceptional items

4.16 In general, SSAP 6 prescribed that all expenditure and income should be reported in the profit and loss account.

> 'All profits and losses recognised in the financial statements for the year should be included in the profit and loss account, except for those items which are specifically permitted or required by this or other accounting standards to be taken directly to reserves or, in the absence of a relevant accounting standard, specifically permitted or required by law to be taken directly to reserves.'

This is often referred to as the *all-inclusive approach* to income and expenditure reporting.

4.17 Despite this general rule, however, it was recognised that distortion would occur if certain unusual events were hidden away in the profit and loss account without additional disclosure. SSAP 6 recognised two categories of such events.

(a) **Exceptional items**. These were items which, although they form part of a company's normal activities, are exceptional because of their size. Examples might include:

    (i)   abnormal charges for bad debts;
    (ii)   abnormal write-offs of stock or work in progress;
    (iii) abnormal provisions for losses on long-term contracts.

(b) **Extraordinary items**. These were defined by SSAP 6 as being 'material items which derive from events or transactions that fall outside the ordinary activities of the company and which are therefore expected not to recur frequently or regularly'. The difference between exceptional items and extraordinary items was that the latter arose from events 'outside the ordinary activities of the business', such as:

    (i)   the profit or loss on selling an investment not acquired with the intention of resale;

    (ii)   the expropriation of overseas assets by a foreign government.

4.18 It was important to be clear as to whether an item was exceptional or extraordinary, because SSAP 6 prescribed different accounting treatments for the two categories.

(a) Exceptional items, since they derive from the company's normal activities, should be reported as part of the current year's profit before taxation. If the amount involved is very large it may be necessary, in the notes to the accounts, to give enough detail for users of the accounts to understand the item's significance.

(b) Extraordinary items are not part of the company's normal activities and cannot be shown as part of the profit or loss on ordinary activities. Instead, after arriving at the figure of profit after taxation without taking account of extraordinary items, the next caption in the profit and loss account will show the gross amount of any extraordinary charges or income. Any tax charge or credit arising from the extraordinary item is shown as a deduction from the gross amount.

FRS 3 *Reporting financial performance*

4.19 We will look at only certain aspects of FRS 3 in this chapter, in particular:

(a) prior period adjustments;
(b) extraordinary items; and
(c) exceptional items.

4.20 Remember the definitions given to these items by FRS 3.

> **KEY TERMS**
>
> - **Prior period adjustments**. Material adjustments applicable to prior periods arising from changes in accounting policies or from the correction of fundamental errors. They do not include normal recurring adjustments or corrections of accounting estimates made in prior periods.
>
> - **Extraordinary items**. Material items possessing a high degree of abnormality which arise from events or transactions that fall outside the ordinary activities of the reporting entity and which are not expected to recur. They do not include exceptional items nor do they include prior period items merely because they relate to a prior period.
>
> - **Exceptional items**. Material items which derive from events or transactions that fall within the ordinary activities of the reporting entity and which individually or, if of a similar type, in aggregate, need to be disclosed by virtue of their size or incidence if the financial statements are to give a true and fair view.
>
> *(FRS 3)*

Prior period adjustments

4.21 Prior period adjustments should be accounted for by restating the comparative figures for the preceding period in the primary statements and notes and adjusting the opening balance of reserves for the cumulative effect. The cumulative effect of the adjustments should also be noted at the foot of the statement of total recognised gains and losses of the current period. The effect of prior period adjustments on the results for the preceding period should be disclosed where practicable.

4.22 You can see that the treatment of prior year adjustments is the same as that given in SSAP 6, but with the additional disclosure required in the statement of total recognised gains and losses.

Extraordinary items

4.23 The above definition of extraordinary items is one of the most radical changes introduced by FRS 3. It has, in effect, outlawed extraordinary items, by changing the requirement of such events being outside the normal activities of the company to those possessing a high degree of abnormality. The disposal or purchase of a large asset or the disposal or acquisition of a subsidiary business can hardly be said to possess a high degree of abnormality. This definition is now probably confined to a large meteorite dropping on to your uninsured factory.

Exceptional items

4.24 Most of those items which used to be classified as extraordinary will now usually be treated as exceptional. Note that the disclosure of exceptional items has been defined in more detail by FRS 3.

(a) All exceptional items (except those in (b) below) should be included under the statutory format heading to which they relate and disclosed by way of a note. Only disclose such items on the face of the profit and loss account if required to do so to show a true and fair view.

(b)   The following items must be shown separately on the face of the profit and loss account *after* operating profit and *before* interest:

    (i)   profits or losses on the sale or termination of an operation;

    (ii)   costs of a fundamental reorganisation or reconstruction; and

    (iii) profits or losses on the disposal of fixed assets.

4.25   The requirements in (b) above means that those events which are likely to have a significant impact on the organisation will be disclosed in a prominent place in the accounts.

Effect of FRS 3

4.26   Now we have looked at the contents of FRS 3 we can assess the **impact** it has had and the way it tackles the problems inherent in SSAP 6.

4.27   First of all, FRS 3 makes extraordinary items *much* rarer. This means that some of the manipulation of results which went on under SSAP 6 will be avoided. All exceptional items, apart from a few important exceptions, will be included under the relevant profit and loss account heading. Those exceptional items requiring disclosure on the face of the profit and loss account are indicators of important events during the accounting period and they would usually have been shown under extraordinary items under SSAP 6. There are new definitions for most of the important terms.

4.28   The effect on prior year adjustments is negligible. The effect on EPS will be studied in Chapter 25.

4.29   **A new format for the profit and loss account** has been introduced, splitting continuing and discontinued operations. The definitions of these states will again prevent manipulation. Disclosure is much fuller than under SSAP 6, where only a one line extraordinary item was given.

4.30   **A statement of total recognised gains and losses** must be provided. The ASB's aim here has been to turn attention away from particular numbers or indicators and to encourage users to make their own judgements about a company's performance based on the set of information given. This statement cannot be lost in the notes as the reserve movement note was under SSAP 6, because it must be given equal prominence with the other primary statements. (Note that one of the main reasons why this statement came into existence was the collapse of Polly Peck. The size of the exchange movements going through reserves was considerable and, although they had been disclosed, they had not been highlighted.)

4.31   The really important figure here is that of total gains and losses for the year. This will probably be of great importance to all users in the future, as much as the profit for the year.

4.32   Consideration was given to extending the statement of recognised gains and losses to provide a reconciliation of movements in shareholders' funds for the period. Instead, a separate reconciliation was suggested, which could be shown as either a note or a primary statement. This statement includes dividends and goodwill written off. Note that dividends are shown as a deduction from profit for the financial year rather than from total recognised gains and losses, because dividends cannot be paid out of unrealised profits.

4.33   The overall effect of FRS 3 can be seen as a great improvement on SSAP 6, particularly in the way it highlights reserve movements and restricts the use of extraordinary items. It has been criticised, however, and the following points show the major **criticisms**.

(a) **Restricting extraordinary items** and calculating EPS after extraordinary items will make **earnings and EPS too volatile** to obtain meaningful results over time. Analysts will probably exclude items they consider extraordinary for their purposes, thus undermining the impact of FRS 3.

(b) The old and new primary statements and the new notes are **not necessarily** easy to **relate** to each other. The formats could have been adjusted to allow the relationships to be clearer.

(c) FRS 3, by introducing new statements and notes, has made financial statements **even more confusing** for the lay user.

(d) Allowing companies to prepare **alternative EPS figures** will lead to confusion as different methods will be used in each case. Analysts also believe that the market, by its very nature, will aim for one 'across the board' earnings figure (see Section 4).

4.34 You may be able to think of other problems associated with FRS 3 but remember that it has many advantages, not the least of which is the fact that it discloses *more* information. You will be able to see this if you obtain some recent sets of company accounts. It also reflects the ASB's aim to avoid the use of just one earnings measure, such as EPS.

Discussion paper

4.35 In 1999 the ASB published a Discussion Paper entitled *Reporting Financial Performance: proposals for change*. The Discussion Paper presents a Position Paper that has been developed by the G4+1 group of accounting standard-setters.

4.36 The main proposals are as follows.

- A **single performance statement** should replace the profit and loss account and the STRGL, effectively combining them in one statement.

- All recognised gains and losses attributable to shareholders should be reported in the single statement in one of **three main components**:

  o The results of operating (or trading) activities;
  o The results of financing and other treasury activities; and
  o Other gains and losses (initially displaying those items at present shown in the STRGL).

4.37 The Paper takes the view that gains and losses should be reported only once, in the period in which they arise, and therefore they should not be reported again in another component at a later date (a practice sometimes called '**recycling**'). This reflects the view given briefly by FRS 3. However, the Paper also recognises that recycling may be permitted or required by standard-setters in certain situations, in the short term, where this represents an improvement on existing practice.

4.38 The Paper looks at the effect of the proposals for a single performance statement on the reporting of gains and losses arising from foreign currency translation adjustments and, in more detail, from the depreciation, revaluation and disposal of fixed assets.

4.39 The Paper goes on to discuss various other aspects of reporting financial performance. Many aspects of FRS 3 are retained, including the effective prohibition of extraordinary items, the treatment of changes in accounting policy and the analysis of continuing and discontinued operations. There are, however, some proposed changes.

4.40 The Board believes that **similar gains and losses** should be disclosed in the same section of the **performance statement**. The Paper's proposals would accordingly change the treatment of those items that, as required by paragraph 20 of FRS 3, are shown separately after operating profit. Most gains on asset disposals would be shown in the 'other gains and losses' section.

4.41 The Paper calls for an additional disclosure to put in context presentations of '**pre-exceptional results**', which are sometimes made on a voluntary basis.

4.42 The proposals in the Paper would express somewhat differently from UK standards the treatment of the correction of errors that are discovered after the financial statements have been issued. The view of the G4+1 is that it would not be practicable to distinguish fundamental from material errors.

4.43 **Dividends** would not be treated as items of financial performance, but rather as **appropriations of profits** and so would not be shown on the face of the performance statement.

> ### Exam focus point
> You should keep an eye on the financial press for articles about issues such as these.
>
> Although you may be faced with a question based specifically on FRS 3, you will also find that questions requiring a consolidated P&L account will involve FRS 3 disclosures.

5 ENVIRONMENTAL ACCOUNTING ISSUES

5.1 This section serves as an introduction to a topic which, in accounting, financial reporting and auditing terms, is still **very much in its infancy** in the UK. This section will look at environmental matters under the following headings:

(a) the effect of environmental matters on management information and accounting;
(b) external reporting and auditing; and
(c) possible future developments.

The section is included in this part of the syllabus because of the uncertainty surrounding valuation, measurement etc of environmental matters.

5.2 Let us consider the major areas of impact on (any) accountant's job caused by consideration of environmental matters.

(a) **Management accountant**

   (i) Investment appraisal: evaluation of environmental costs and benefits.

   (ii) Incorporating new costs, capital expenditure and so on, in to budgets and business plans.

   (iii) Undertake cost/benefit analysis of any environmental improvements.

(b) **Financial accountant**

   (i) The effect of revenue costs: site clean up costs, waste disposal or waste treatment costs and so on, which will affect the profit and loss account.

   (ii) Gauging balance sheet impacts, particularly liabilities, contingencies, provisions *and* valuation of assets.

    (iii)   The effect of environmental matters, and particularly potential liabilities, on a company's relationship with bankers, insurers and major shareholders (institutional shareholders).

    (iv)   Environmental performance evaluation in annual reports.

(c) **Project accountant**

    (i)   Environmental audit of proposed takeovers, mergers and other planning matters.
    (ii)   Investment appraisal.

(d) **Internal auditor**: environmental audit.

(e) **Systems accountant**: effect on, and required changes to management and financial information systems.

What is environmental accounting?

5.3   The following list encompasses the major aspects of environmental accounting.

    '(a)   Recognising and seeking to mitigate the negative environmental effects of conventional accounting practice.

    (b)   Separately identifying environmentally related costs and revenues within the conventional accounting systems.

    (c)   Taking active steps to set up initiatives in order to ameliorate existing environmental effects of conventional accounting practice.

    (d)   Devising new forms of financial and non-financial accounting systems, information systems and control systems to encourage more environmentally benign management decisions.

    (e)   Developing new forms of performance measurement, reporting and appraisal for both internal and external purposes.

    (f)   Identifying, examining and seeking to rectify areas in which conventional (financial) criteria and environmental criteria are in conflict.

    (g)   Experimenting with ways in which, sustainability may be assessed and incorporated into organisational orthodoxy.'
        Accounting for the Environment Bob Gary (with Jan Bebbington and Diane Walters)

5.4   'Environmental issues' covers a wide range of topics, many of which are in the news fairly constantly. Public opinion on such matters varies considerably over time and over the range of topics. There have been various measures, in different countries, industries and organisations, to pressure business into environmental change. What is certain is that the whole environmental agenda is constantly changing and businesses therefore need to monitor the situation closely. Most businesses, certainly those in the UK, have generally ignored environmental matters in the past. How long will they be able to do so?

Management information and accounting

5.5   The means of codifying a company's attitude towards the environment is often the creation of a published environmental policy document or charter. This may be internally generated or it may be adopted from a standard environmental charter, such as the **Valdez Principles**. There are relative advantages and disadvantages to each of these approaches. In-house policies can be properly tailored to the organisation, refined over time and more private. On the other hand, they are not comparable with other businesses and they may avoid the real issues. The *Valdez Principles* are summarised here.

The Valdez Principles

We adopt, support and will implement the principles of:

1   Protection of the biosphere
2   Sustainable use of natural resources
3   Reduction and disposal of waste
4   Wise use of energy
5   Risk reduction
6   Marketing of safe products and services
7   Damage compensation
8   Disclosure
9   Environmental directors and managers
10 Assessment and annual audit

5.6   The problem here, as with other similar principles or charters, is that the commitment required from companies is generally too high and the fear exists that the principles may have legal status which could have a severe effect on a company's liability. Other documents available which are similar to the *Valdez Principles* are:

(a)   the International Chamber of Commerce *Business charter for sustainable developments*;

(b)   the Chemical Industries Association *Responsible care programme*;

(c)   the Confederation of British Industry *Agenda for voluntary action*; and

(d)   Friends of the Earth *Environmental charter for local government*.

5.7   Adopting such a charter is one thing; implementing and monitoring it are more important and generally more difficult to achieve.

Environmental audit

5.8   Environmental auditing is exactly what is says: auditing a business to assess its impact on the environment, or as the CBI expressed it 'the systematic examination of the interactions between any business operation and its surroundings'.

5.9   The audit will cover a range of areas and will involve the performance of different types of testing. The scope of the audit must be determined and this will depend on each individual organisation. There are, however, some aspects of the approach to environmental auditing which are worth mentioning.

(a)   **Environmental Impact Assessments (EIAs)** are required, under EC directive, for all major projects which require planning permission and have a material effect on the environment. The EIA process can be incorporated into any environmental auditing strategy.

(b)   **Environmental surveys** are a good way of starting the audit process, by looking at the organisation as a whole in environmental terms. This helps to identify areas for further development, problems, potential hazards and so forth.

(c)   **Environmental SWOT analysis**. A 'strengths, weaknesses, opportunities, threats' analysis is useful as the environmental audit strategy is being developed. This can only be done later in the process, when the organisation has been examined in much more detail.

(d)   **Environmental Quality Management (EQM)**. This is seen as part of TQM (Total Quality Management) and it should be built in to an environmental management system. Such a strategy has been adopted by companies such as IBM, Dow Chemicals and by the Rhone-Poulenc Environmental Index which has indices for levels of water, air and other waste products.

(e) **Eco-audit**. The European Commission has adopted a proposal for a regulation for a voluntary community environmental auditing scheme, known as the eco-audit scheme. The scheme aims to promote improvements in company environmental performance and to provide the public with information about these improvements. Once registered, a company will have to comply with certain on-going obligations involving disclosure and audit.

(f) **Eco-labelling**. Developed in Germany, this voluntary scheme will indicate those EC products which meet the highest environmental standards, probably as the result of an EQM system. It is suggested that eco-audit *must* come before an eco-label can be given.

(g) **BS 7750 Environmental Management Systems**. BS 7750 also ties in with eco-audits and eco-labelling and with the quality BSI standard BS 5750. Achieving BS 7750 is likely to be a first step in the eco-audit process.

(h) **Supplier audits,** to ensure that goods and services bought in by an organisation meet the standards applied by that organisation.

Case example

In June 1999 BP Amoco commissioned KPMG to conduct an independent audit of its greenhouse gas emissions in the first ever environmental audit.

Energy costs

5.10 Energy costs and accounting for energy costs are central to environmental accounting and the issues involved are complex and wide-ranging. Energy production is generally inefficient and non-renewable sources are used far more than renewable sources in most countries. (An exception is Norway, which is 100% reliant on renewable, mainly hydro-electric sources.)

5.11 Some of the major proposals currently under debate which would have a direct impact are as follows.

(a) **Carbon and energy taxes**. EC proposals for an energy tax are gaining acceptance but the USA is against such taxes.

(b) **Tradable pollution licences**. These appeared first in the USA, but they are currently under discussion in the UK and the EC. Companies are issued licences to produce specific amounts of pollutants. Those clean companies which under use their licences can sell the excess to dirty companies, thus penalising heavy polluters. In the USA an initial stage is being undertaken whereby all companies must meet common baseline requirements.

(c) **Company initiatives in energy efficiency**. Many companies have started to monitor every costs, usually 'per output unit', leading to changes in energy management resulting in savings. Many of the basic energy saving methods are those you might use in your own home and you should be able to list some of them.

5.12 In accounting for energy costs, the accountant must separate out energy costs in the accounting and costing systems. In other words, identify the costs which must be controlled. As well as accounting for energy costs, energy *units* must be monitored, because energy efficiency can only be measured properly in units. In the energy scares of the 1970s it was even suggested that energy units should be used as bookkeeping units, rather than £ or $.

Accounting for waste

5.13   Waste in this case means all types of waste products, down to packaging, and the relevant methods of recycling. There is no doubt that we produce massive amounts of waste of every kind (nuclear, fuel emissions, packaging, refuse and sewage, abandoned buildings etc etc). Waste reduction appears to be one of the most important areas here, and many companies have policies to reduce waste.

5.14   As far as accounting for waste is concerned, many companies merely write off the total amount of waste costs. A minority of companies, however, have very sophisticated waste accounting systems, which identify all waste management and charge them to the departments responsible, thus including the cost of waste in the appraisal system.

5.15   As far as **recycling** or **re-use** is concerned, these will involve further energy and resource use and their value must be judged accordingly. Recycling costs should be identified separately so as to assess the feasibility of the activity, but then the costs should be incorporated into the product cost. This incorporation into product cost is important where recycling is compulsory and it allows the costs to be allocated to the relevant process. (It may be helpful here to look again at your cost accounting studies in the area of accounting for waste and by-products.)

5.16   The **Environmental Protection Act 1990** introduced *recycling credits*. Anyone removing material from the waste stream should receive the money which the local authority would have paid to dispose of that waste material.

Investment and budgeting

5.17   It is estimated that environmental considerations will force up investment spending by 50% by the turn of the century. It is in a company's best interest to begin that process of environmental investment as soon as possible - it will be more expensive to catch up. **The difficulty seems to be in how to incorporate environmental considerations into investment opportunity evaluation and investment appraisal.**

5.18   Traditional budgeting techniques such as discounted cashflow (DCF), payback, EPS contribution and so on are restricting in their short-term approach. Appraisal methods which place more emphasis on events in the short term and less on events in the long term conflict directly with the important environmental costs as these are likely to be long term (decommissioning costs, risks of older equipment, site clean up costs etc).

5.19   The difficulty of looking at a longer term view is that the current environmental agenda may change rapidly and significantly in the short term (new legislation, technology etc). A flexible (and therefore short term approach) is required to prevent projects becoming unfeasible and to avoid early obsolescence.

5.20   If traditional techniques are used to fix financial targets, then managers will ignore any other targets, such as environmental ones, because they are judged by their performance related to the financial targets. Environmental matters must be recognised in the performance appraisal and reward criteria.

Life cycle analysis and assessment

5.21 Life cycle analysis (LCA) is described as 'an objective process used to evaluate the environmental burdens associated with a product, process or activity'. To carry out a LCA, the following procedures must be followed.

    (a) Trace all raw material inputs from extraction from the biosphere to all earlier processes, capturing all ecological effects, energy costs etc.

    (b) Undertake the same process for all the intermediate production processes.

    (c) Trace the product in question forwards to its packaging (its manufacture and disposal), transport and final use.

    (d) The use and disposal effects of the product must be measured in ecological terms.

    (e) *All* inputs and outputs must be measured for the entire life cycle.

5.22 There is a great deal of overlap between different LCAs and the regression into the effect on the biosphere is infinite (think of the food chain). Consequently, no LCA can be absolutely complete; each one must be **bounded**.

5.23 There are limitations in the use of LCAs, because of bounding the system; uncertainty over effects; and difficulties obtaining information. LCAs are useful, however, particularly in terms of overall product assessment, BS 7750 and supplier audits and a basis for advertising claims.

External relationships

5.24 Before we look at financial reports, we will consider some other external relationships affected by environmental matters.

Bank lending

5.25 Environmental considerations are likely to affect bank lending in three ways.

    (a) Is the recipient of the loan in a business with a high risk of severe environmental problems causing unforeseen costs which might put the loan repayment in jeopardy?

    (b) If the bank repossesses the secured assets will it become liable for any associated environmental costs?

    (c) Even without repossession could the bank be held liable as a business partner?

5.26 This problem first arose in the US. The 'superfund' legislation there allowed the government to claim clean up costs of land from the owner - which in the current recessionary climate is frequently the bank. EC legislation is now developing in this area and UK banks are starting to respond to the problem. If it is not addressed, some significant sectors of industry are going to have a lot of difficulty obtaining finance.

Insurance

5.27 If your company thinks it may face environmental liabilities at some time in the future, can you insure against the risk? Since the future liability in this area is such an unknown quantity, the answer is probably no. Even if such insurance could be obtained, the premiums would be high, the conditions stringent (environmental audits etc) and the type of risks insured would be only very specific. Since insurance may not be the answer, companies may be forced to improve their environmental performance.

Ethical/environmental investment

5.28 Banks and insurance companies are concerned with business motives, not the environment. What about shareholders and investors? It seems to be generally the case that investors are not environmentally-minded; the foremost duty of an investor is to make as large a profit as possible.

5.29 Against this background, however, there are now ethical and environmentally sound investment funds which target investment opportunities based on both positive and negative criteria. The negative criteria can encompass anything from a poor environmental record to political donations; the positive criteria range from high standards of environmental awareness to charitable donations. There is some evidence that such funds are beginning to wield a direct impact on the companies in which they invest.

Financial reporting

5.30 There are **no disclosure requirements relating to environmental matters in the UK**, so any disclosures tend to be voluntary unless environmental matters happen to fall under standard accounting principles (eg recognising liabilities). In most cases disclosure is descriptive and unquantified. There is little motivation to produce environmental information and many reasons for not doing so, including secrecy. The main factor seems to be apathy on the part of businesses but more particularly on the part of shareholders and investors. The information is not demanded, so it is not provided.

5.31 Environmental matters may be reported in the accounts of companies in the following areas:

(a) contingent liabilities;
(b) exceptional charges;
(c) operating and financial review comments;
(d) profit and capital expenditure forecasts.

Summary and example

5.32 A report was produced in early 1996 called *Environmental Accounting - a practical review* (Tuppen, Bennett, James and Lane). It is based on two reports examining the practical application of environmental accounting in business. Some of the points made by the report are discussed below and an example given by the report is also reproduced.

Financial environmental information

5.33 The report points out that very few companies have attempted to produce a comprehensive assessment of the economic costs and benefits of good environmental management. Environmental performance has rather been expressed in terms of physical impacts or outputs and a few companies have disclosed their expenditure relevant to managing environmental performance.

5.34 The report then goes on to state:

'Readers and other commentators of environmental performance reports have encouraged the inclusion of more financial information. Although the justification for inclusion of such data has yet to be fully explored, it is frequently cited that this data could be used, for example to:

- support the business case for environmental improvement by demonstrating net savings, for example, through reduction in energy costs or waste disposal costs;

- demonstrate commitment to environmental improvement by identifying net voluntary expenditure, for example, on landscaping or conservation projects; and

- demonstrate the true cost of compliance with environmental legislation, for example, in relation to reduction of air emissions or disposal of hazardous wastes.

It has also been suggested that it might be possible to produce financial data to demonstrate:

- good management of environmental risk, for example either at group level, through management of insurance or property, or at a local level, through management of the environmental impacts associated with operational activities; and

- the external environmental costs and benefits of a company's activities.'

5.35 Current practice was highlighted in a 1994 review *Financial Aspects of Environmental Reporting* (ACCA).

'This summary indicated that to date only a very limited number of companies have sought to produce comprehensive "Green Accounts", although a range of businesses (mainly in sectors of industry with a high associated risk of environmental impact) now report financial data relevant to environmental performance. This information includes contingent liabilities or "clean up" provisions or comments on the capital or revenue expenditure relevant to environmental performance.

Only a handful of companies including, for example Baxter International have, to date, produced "full" environmental accounts (see below).'

Future developments

5.36 The report goes on to consider the issues which must be tackled by any organisation wishing to report financial data relevant to environmental performance.

(a) A definition of 'environmental expenditure', in particular the costs or savings which are to be attributed, directly or indirectly, to environmental performance must be determined.

(b) Interpretation of the data must be carried out carefully, in particular the aggregation or normalisation of the data to ensure that it provides an accurate picture of current environmental performance, taking account of broader developments within the business. For example, reporting total costs of energy on an annual basis may present a misleading picture of performance. To get an accurate picture of performance it will be necessary, for example, to take account of changes in business size, structure and functions.

(c) The resources required to generate the data must be considered, taking account of the current framework for environmental reporting.

(d) The value of the information provided to both internal and external audiences must be assessed.

5.37 An example of a financial environmental report is given in an appendix to the report. It is that of Baxter International, a leading producer, developer and distributor of healthcare products and services worldwide. Note that all the figures are *estimates*.

Part B: Income and value measurement

Estimated environmental costs and savings worldwide ($ in millions)

Environmental costs

Costs of proactive program	1994	1993*	1992*
Corporate environmental affairs	1.4	1.6	1.5
Auditors' and attorneys' fees	0.6	0.3	0.9
Corporate environmental engineering/facilities engineering	0.8	0.9	0.8
Division/facility environmental professionals and programs	7.0	6.5	5.0
Packaging professionals and programs for packaging reduction	2.1	2.0	1.8
Pollution controls, operations and maintenance	7.8	7.5	7.0
Pollution controls, depreciation	2.5	2.7	2.0
Total costs of proactive program	22.2	21.5	19.0
Remediation and waste disposal costs			
Attorneys' fees for clean-up claims, NOVs	0.3	0.2	0.2
Waste disposal	2.8	3.4	3.8
Remediation/clean-up - on site	1.2	0.8	5.0
Remediation/clean-up - off site	1.1	0.3	0.0
Total remediation and waste disposal costs	5.4	4.7	9.0
Total environmental costs	27.6	26.2	28.0

Environmental income, savings and cost avoidance associated with environmental initiatives in report year

	1994	1993*	1992*
Ozone-depleting substances cost reductions	1.8	1.2	1.4
Hazardous waste - disposal cost reductions	0.9	0.6	0.6
Hazardous waste - material cost reductions	0.5	0.5	0.5
Non-hazardous waste - disposal cost reductions	0.5	0.5	0.5
Non-hazardous waste - material cost reductions	5.4	1.3	3.7
Recycling income	3.5	2.7	2.2
Green lights energy conservation - cost savings	0.3	1.1	0.4
Packaging cost reductions	10.5	6.3	5.4
Total income, savings and cost avoidance for report year's initiatives ***	23.4	14.2	14.7
As a percentage of the costs of proactive programs	105%	66%	77%

	1994	1993*	1992*
Total income, savings and cost avoidance from report year's initiatives	23.4	14.2	14.7
Cost avoidance in report year from efforts initiated in prior years back to 1989	51.2	38.4	16.3
Total income, savings and cost avoidance	74.6	52.6	31.0

* 1992 and 1993 data were restated to reflect deletion of Diagnostics Division, which was sold, and to assure consistent methodology in calculating costs and savings.

** Cost avoidance from prior years included in this line item of previous reports, is listed as a separate line item in this report.

*** See separate detail in Table 1.

TABLE 1

Detail on income, saving and cost avoidance from 1994 activities ($ in millions)	Savings & income	Cost avoid-ance	Total financial benefit
Ozone-depleting substances cost savings	1.6	0.2	1.8
Hazardous waste - disposal costs reduction	0.4	0.5	0.9
Hazardous waste - material cost reductions	0.3	0.2	0.5
Non-hazardous waste - disposal costs reduction	0.2	0.3	0.5
Non-hazardous waste - material cost reductions	0.9	4.5	5.4
Recycling income	3.5	****	3.5
Green lights energy conservation - cost savings	0.3	****	0.3
Packaging cost reductions	10.5	****	10.5
Total savings	17.7	5.7	23.4

**** not applicable

Examples of undetermined costs

- Environmentally driven materials research and other research and development (this is typically offset by non-environmental benefits)

- Capital costs of modifying processes other than adding pollution controls (this is typically offset by non-environmental benefits)

- Costs of substitutes for ozone-depleting substances and other hazardous materials (this is estimated to be relatively minor)

- Lost sales from environmental issues

- Extra capital cost for environmentally superior lighting and other equipment that is more expensive than alternatives

Examples of undetermined savings

- Reduction in liability exposure resulting from tank removals, waste site evaluations and other risk-management programs

- Record-keeping and administrative costs

- Increased goodwill, sales and employee morale

- Capital cost savings for environmentally superior lighting and other equipment that is less expensive than alternatives

Definitions of terms

Income: Actual moneys received in report year.

Savings: Reduction in actual cost between report year and prior year.

Cost avoidance: Additional costs other than the report year's savings that were not incurred but would have been incurred if the waste reduction activity had not taken place in calculating cost avoidance for waste reduction activities, it is assumed that production and distribution activity grew four per cent domestically and six per cent internationally per year, and that waste quantities would have risen at those same rates in the absence of waste reduction initiatives. Waste reduction initiatives not only produce cost avoidance in the year initiated, but also in future years in which the waste remains eliminated from processes or packaging.

Packaging cost reductions: Twelve-month cost savings resulting from packaging modifications made during the year. This is calculated by summing the savings achieved from individual reaction projects completed in that year, assuming volumes at full production levels.

Question 5

Outline the Valdez Principles.

Answer

See Paragraph 5.9.

---

6 DISCOUNTING

6.1 In April 1997 the ASB produced a working paper on *Discounting in financial reporting*, which is closely related to asset valuation and profit measurement. The paper is considered below, but remember that such papers only have an ability level of 2, *Knowledge* and are unlikely to arise in any detail in the exam.

6.2 Discounting future cash flows is a technique for reflecting in the valuation of an asset or liability two factors that are taken into account in all rational economic decisions: the **time value of money** and the **risk** associated with the cash flows. Discounting is widely used in financial management and is part of most modern asset-pricing models and most option-pricing models.

6.3   In financial statements, discounting is used in the financial reporting of leases and pension costs. It has also been considered in a number of the ASB's projects, in particular goodwill, impairment of tangible fixed assets, provision and deferred tax.

6.4   In these projects the ASB is concerned that, if items are recorded in financial statements at an amount based on undiscounted future cash flows, unlike items will appear alike. For example, a riskless cash inflow of £1 million due tomorrow, a riskless cash inflow of £1 million due in ten years and a risky cash inflow of £1 million due in ten years would all be recorded at £1 million. However, no entity would regard these assets as equal nor would they cost the same to acquire. In fact, £1 million is an economically meaningless value to attribute to the two assets that generate cash flows in ten years' time. If they are recorded at £1 million, relevant information is lost to the user of the financial statements and misleading information given instead.

6.5   Notwithstanding the fundamental economic truths that discounting can reflect, the ASB believes that it is not necessary or desirable to apply discounting to every item in the balance sheet that is measured by reference to future cash flows, as the period over which the cash flows arise is often too short for the effect to be material. In particular, the ASB does not envisage any need to apply discounting to the vast majority of current assets and current liabilities. However, in certain circumstances the effect of discounting on long-term assets and liabilities may be very significant and needs to be considered.

6.6   The working paper is **not a prelude to a future FRS** on this topic and the decision on whether discounting will be prescribed in any particular circumstance will form part of the development of the relevant standard. However, some respondents to Discussion Papers have asked for a general approach to discounting to be developed. The working paper is published in response to that request. It seeks to establish principles on how discounting should be applied so that any future FRSs involving discounting will be prepared on a consistent basis. It is a working paper for the ASB's own reference as the ASB considers discounting with various projects. The ASB is particularly interested in views on the proposed application of the principles in the paper to:

- Impaired fixed assets
- Pensions
- Provisions for environmental liabilities

6.7   The working paper goes on to discuss the **different aspects of discounting** under the following headings.

- Time value of money
- Risk
- Measurement of assets
- Measurement of liabilities
- Inflation
- Tax
- Presentation in financial statements
- Change of rate

We will not go into any detail about these here, but you should be familiar with these issues or terms either within this text or in your management accounting studies.

Chapter roundup

- **Profit** can be viewed as a measure of the increase in a company's capital over the duration of an accounting period. In other words, opening capital must first be maintained and anything achieved in excess of that represents profit.

- As a result, the **measurement of profit** depends on the concept of capital maintenance adopted, as we will see in the next chapter.

- More fundamentally, profit measurement and asset valuation can only be carried out if there is an agreed underlying **conceptual framework**. This would ensure that assets and liabilities could be defined and thus would restrict the scope for manipulation of profit and balance sheet by the use of off-balance sheet finance.

- Remember the differences in the restrictions on **distributable profits** between private, public and investment and insurance companies.

Private	Accumulated realised profits
	LESS
	Accumulated realised losses
Public	AND
	Net assets ≥ called-up share
	capital *plus* undistributable reserves
Investment	Realised revenue profits
	LESS
	Realised and unrealised revenue losses
	AND
	Net assets ≥ 1.5 × aggregate liabilities

- FRS 3 changed the definition of **extraordinary** and **exceptional items** and **prior year adjustments** from those given in SSAP 6. Extraordinary items are now extremely rare.

- A revised **Statement of Principles** has been issued. The revision takes account of some of the criticisms made of the original Statement.

- **Environmental accounting matters** are very topical but undeveloped in accounting terms. Look out for them in the press.

- The ASB has produced a working paper on **discounting in financial reporting** which could affect various proposed FRSs

Quick quiz

1   What is Hicks' definition of income? (see para 1.2)

2   Explain with reasons two views of profit, each depending on a different view of which financial statement is considered to be primary. (1.3, 1.4)

3   How does the CA 1985 define realised profits? (2.4)

4   How does CA 1985 define a distribution? (2.9)

5   What are the profits statutorily available for distribution? (2.10)

6   What additional restriction is placed on the distributions of public companies? (2.13)

7   What are the undistributable reserves? (2.14)

8   What are the eight chapters of the *Statement of Principles?* (3.2)

9   What are the elements of financial statements? (3.6)

10 What are the 'degrees of influence' which an investor may have in its investee? (3.22)

11 The *Statement* favours current cost accounting. True or false? (3.30)

12 What is 'reserve accounting'? (4.3)

13 Describe the 'all inclusive approach' to income and expenditure reporting. (4.10)

14 What is the accounting treatment of prior year adjustments? (4.17)

15 What accounting treatments are prescribed by FRS 3 for exceptional items? (4.20)

16 Which matters constitute the main aspects of environmental accounting? (5.3)

17 Which items could be most affected by discounting? (6.6)

Question to try	Level	Marks	Time
24	Exam	20	36 mins

Chapter 23

CURRENT PURCHASING POWER AND CURRENT COST ACCOUNTING

Chapter topic		Syllabus reference	Ability required
1	Historical cost accounting	9(b)	Knowledge
2	Specific and general price changes	9(b)	Knowledge
3	The principles and procedures of CPP accounting	9(b)	Knowledge
4	Current cost accounting and deprival value	9(b)	Knowledge
5	Current cost adjustments to historical cost profit	9(b)	Knowledge
6	The current cost profit and loss account and balance sheet	9(b)	Knowledge
7	Accounting for the effects of changing prices: a handbook	9(b)	Knowledge

Introduction

We have already mentioned some of the problems with **historical cost accounting**. In Section 1 of this chapter we go into more detail, before going on to look at the two main alternatives proposed to historical cost accounting: **current purchasing power accounting** (CPP) and **current cost accounting** (CCA).

The examiner has said in the Syllabus Guidance Notes that:

'candidates may be required to demonstrate an ability to discuss the extent to which financial reports prepared under the historical cost convention are distorted in conditions of changing prices and evaluate the various attempts which have been made to adapt the regulatory framework to make allowances for price changes.'

However, the examiner also states that 'preparing detailed statements which are adjusted to take account of price changes, whether these be general or specific' is not examinable.

The Paper 9 syllabus only gives this topic an ability level of 2, *Knowledge*, but it is not really possible to consider the 'principles of current cost and current purchasing power methods' without actually looking at how they are applied in practice, ie by looking at the numbers.

In spite of the **low inflation** we are currently experiencing, this may not continue in the future, nor is it the case at present in other countries. Hence this topic is still of importance.

1   HISTORICAL COST ACCOUNTING   5/96

1.1   Historical cost accounting (HCA) is the term used to denote the range of accounting practices and techniques currently operating which has been built up over the years as company law has developed and accounting practice codified. There is **no strict definition of HCA**.

1.2   The **main characteristics** of HCA are generally reflected as concepts or conventions, such as those in SSAP 2. The two main characteristics are as follows.

(a) All transactions are recorded at their **historical cost**. When money is paid over, this money value will be recorded in the books of the business. The final accounts (balance sheet, profit and loss account and cash flow statement) will reflect the transactions at historical cost.

(b) The transactions thus recorded are *matched*, so that the income generated by the company is 'matched' against the costs involved in getting that income.

1.3 There has been a **modification of HCA** in that some fixed assets can be revalued to a current cost figure. Any excess on revaluation over the historical cost must be taken to a revaluation reserve, otherwise the realisation concept will be breached. Once the asset is disposed of, this unrealised holding gain can be released.

1.4 We can now look at HCA in terms of **capital maintenance**, which allows us to breakdown HCA profits into different types of gains and losses.

1.5 Profit can be measured as the difference between how wealthy a company is at the beginning and at the end of an accounting period. This wealth can be expressed in terms of the capital of a company as shown in its opening and closing balance sheets. A business which maintains its capital unchanged during an accounting period can be said to have 'broken even'. Once capital has been maintained, anything achieved in excess represents profit. This is known as **financial capital maintenance**.

1.6 For this analysis to be of any use, we must be able to draw up a company's balance sheet at the beginning and at the end of a period, so as to place a value on the opening and closing capital. There are particular difficulties in doing this during a period of rising prices.

1.7 In conventional historical cost accounts, assets are stated in the balance sheet at the amount it cost to acquire them (less any amounts written off in respect of depreciation or diminution in value). Capital is simply the difference between assets and liabilities. If prices are rising, it is possible for a company to show a profit in its historical cost accounts despite having identical physical assets and owing identical liabilities at the beginning and end of its accounting period.

1.8 For example, consider the following opening and closing balance sheets of a company.

	Opening £	Closing £
Stock (100 items at cost)	500	600
Other net assets	1,000	1,000
Capital	1,500	1,600

Assuming that no new capital has been introduced during the year, and no capital has been distributed as dividends, the profit shown in historical cost accounts would be £100, being the excess of closing capital over opening capital. And yet in physical terms the company is no better off: it still has 100 units of stock (which cost £5 each at the beginning of the period, but £6 each at the end) and its other net assets are identical. The 'profit' earned has merely enabled the company to **keep pace with inflation**.

1.9 An alternative to the concept of capital maintenance based on historical costs is to express capital in **physical terms**. On this basis, no profit would be recognised in the example above because the physical substance of the company is unchanged over the accounting period. In the UK, a system of accounting (called *current cost accounting* or CCA) was introduced in 1980 by SSAP 16 and had as its conceptual basis a concept of capital maintenance based on 'operating capability'. Capital is maintained if at the end of the period the company is in a position to achieve the **same physical output** as it was at the beginning of the period.

1.10 In practice, CCA aroused little enthusiasm and SSAP 16 was finally withdrawn in April 1988. We will be looking at the system in detail and examining why it failed to catch on. For the time being, you should just bear in mind that **financial** definitions of capital maintenance are not the only ones possible; in theory at least, there is no reason why profit should not be measured as the increase in a company's **physical** capital over an accounting period.

The inflation accounting debate

1.11 Traditionally, there have been two main reasons for the **preparation of accounts**. The first is to fulfil the needs of the owners of a business. Today it is normal that the control of a business is divorced from its ownership. The directors of a company, who manage its day-to-day affairs, are required by law to provide the shareholders with stewardship accounts. These are intended to help the shareholders assess the effectiveness with which their investment is being managed. They should give a true and fair view of the profit or loss for the accounting period and the state of affairs of the company at the balance sheet date. Published accounts are of course used by several other groups of people, potential investors, employees and creditors, and so on.

1.12 Secondly, accounts are prepared for **management**. They are intended to assist the managers of a business in controlling that business and in making decisions about its future.

1.13 Although the information needs of internal and external users may differ considerably, it has become increasingly clear that accounts prepared on a traditional historical cost basis can present financial information in a misleading manner. The greatest criticisms of traditional accounting concepts have stemmed from their inability to reflect the effects of changing price levels. The level of criticism has varied according to the level of inflation at the time.

Criticisms of historical cost accounting

1.14 Before looking at the various alternatives, we should first consider the criticisms of historical cost accounting in more detail.

Fixed asset values are unrealistic

1.15 The most striking example here is property. If fixed assets are retained in the books at their historical cost, **unrealised holding gains** are not recognised. This means that the total holding gain, if any, will be brought into account during the year in which the asset is realised, rather than spread over the period during which it was owned. Property revelations and disclosure of market values have been inconsistent and lacking in clarity. Two points should be considered.

(a) Although it has long been accepted that a balance sheet prepared under the historical cost concept is an historical record and not a statement of current worth, many people now argue that the balance sheet should at least give an indication of the **current value** of the company's tangible assets.

(b) The **prudence concept** requires that profits should only be recognised when realised in the form either of cash or of other assets the ultimate cash realisation of which can

BPP PUBLISHING

be assessed with reasonable certainty. It may be argued that recognising unrealised holding gains on fixed assets is contrary to this concept.

1.16 Those in favour of restating asset values feels that the criticism based on prudence can be met by ensuring that valuations are made as **objectively** as possible (for example, in the case of property, by having independent expert valuations) and by not taking unrealised gains through the profit and loss account.

Depreciation is inadequate to finance the replacement of fixed assets

1.17 This criticism is generally well understood and you will appreciate that what is important is not the replacement of one asset by an identical new one (something that rarely happens), but the replacement of the **operating capability** represented by the old asset.

Another criticism of historical cost depreciation is that it does not fully reflect the **value of the asset consumed** during the accounting year. Whilst this point is obviously closely related to the first, it can, as we will see, be overcome whilst still retaining sufficient profits to finance replacement.

Holding gains on stocks are included in profit

1.18 During a period of high inflation the monetary value of stocks held may increase significantly while they are being processed. The conventions of historical cost accounting lead to the realised part of this holding gain (known as *stock appreciation*) being included in profit for the year. It is estimated that in the late 1970s nearly half the declared profits of companies were due to stock appreciation.

1.19 This problem can be illustrated using a simple example. At the beginning of the year a company has 100 units of stock and no other assets. Its trading account for the year is shown below.

TRADING ACCOUNT

	Units	£		Units	£
Opening stock	100	200	Sales (made 31		
Purchases (made 31			December)	100	500
December)	100	400			
	200	600			
Closing stock (FIFO					
basis)	100	400			
	100	200			
Gross profit	-	300			
	100	500		100	500

Apparently the company has made a gross profit of £300. But, at the beginning of the year the company owned 100 units of stock and at the end of the year it owned 100 units of stock and £100 (sales £500, purchases £400). From this it would seem that a profit of £100 is more reasonable. The remaining £200 is stock appreciation arising as the purchase price increased from £2 to £4.

You will appreciate that this criticism can be overcome by using a **capital maintenance** concept based on **physical units** rather than monetary values.

Profits (or losses) on holdings of net monetary items are not shown

1.20 In periods of inflation the **purchasing power**, and thus the value, of money falls. It follows that an investment in money will have a lower real value at the end of a period of time than

it did at the beginning. A loss has been made. Similarly, the real value of a monetary liability will reduce over a period of time and a gain will be made.

The true effect of inflation on capital maintenance is not shown

1.21 To a large extent this follows from the points already mentioned. It is a widely held principle that **distributable profits** should only be recognised after full allowance has been made for any erosion in the capital value of a business. In historical cost accounts, although capital is maintained in nominal money terms, it may not be in real terms. In other words, profits may be distributed to the detriment of the long-term viability of the business. This criticism may be made by those who advocate capital maintenance in physical terms and those who prefer money capital maintenance as measured by pounds of current purchasing power.

Comparisons over time are unrealistic

1.22 This will tend to an **exaggeration of growth**. For example, if a company's profit in 1961 was £100,000 and in 1986 £500,000, a shareholder's initial reaction might be that the company had done rather well. If, however, it was then realised that with £100,000 in 1961 he could buy exactly the same goods as with £590,000 in 1986, the apparent growth would seem less impressive.

1.23 The points mentioned above have demonstrated some of the accounting problems which arise in times of severe and prolonged inflation. Of the various possible systems of accounting for price changes most fall into one of three categories as follows.

(a) General price changes bases and in particular, **current purchasing power** (CPP).

(b) **Current value bases**. The basic principles of all these are:

(i) to show balance sheet items at some form of current value rather than historical cost;

(ii) to compute profits by matching the current value of costs at the date of consumption against revenue.

The current value of an item will normally be based on replacement cost, net realisable value or economic value.

(c) A **combination** of these two systems: suggestions of this type have been put forward by many writers. Their advantages are considered in Section 9 on the ASC *Handbook*.

1.24 The most important (of many) **developments** in the search for an alternative to HCA were as follows.

(a) PSSAP 7 (a provisional SSAP) on CPP accounting was introduced in May 1974. Listed companies were recommended to follow it, but it was not mandatory.

(b) SSAP 16 *Current cost accounting* was introduced in March 1980 for a three year trial period. The popularity of the standard was never great and it flagged until the ASC withdrew its mandatory status in June 1985. It was withdrawn in full in 1988.

(c) In October 1986 the ASC published *Accounting for the effects of changing prices: a handbook*. It lays out the methods which may be adopted, but it is not mandatory.

Why modified historical cost accounting is still used

1.25 It must seem strange, given the criticisms levelled at it, that modified HCA is still in such widespread use. There are various reasons for this, not the least of which is **resistance to change** in the conservative accounting profession.

1.26 Modified historical cost accounts are **easy** to prepare, easy to read and easy to understand. While they do not reflect current values, the revaluation of fixed assets is seen as one of the most important items requiring such an adjustment, and therefore the value of the accounts is improved enormously by such revaluations taking place.

1.27 In periods of **low inflation**, historical cost accounts are seen as a reasonable reflection on the reality of the given situation.

1.28 FRS 15, which deals with valuation, carries on with modified HCA, but clears up some of the anomalies in the current system. You should refer back to the section in Chapter 22 on the *Statement of Principles* and look at how the issues of asset values and profit reporting are considered there.

UITF Abstract 9 *Accounting for operations in hyperinflationary economies*

1.29 This abstract concerns the consolidation of foreign subsidiaries in high inflation countries. The translation of the accounts of such subsidiaries using the closing rate method is likely to give distorted results, and the abstract broadly says that the local accounts should *either* be **adjusted for inflation first** *or* be prepared using a **strong currency** (rather than the local currency) as the functional currency.

2 SPECIFIC AND GENERAL PRICE CHANGES

2.1 When prices are rising, it is likely that the current value of assets will also rise, but not necessarily by the general rate of inflation. For example, if the replacement cost of a machine on 1 January 19X2 was £5,000, and the general rate of inflation in 19X2 was 8%, we would not necessarily expect the replacement cost of the machine at 31 December 19X2 to be £5,000 plus 8% = £5,400. The rate of price increase on the machinery might have been less than 8% or more than 8%. (Conceivably, in spite of general inflation, the replacement cost of the machinery might have gone down).

2.2 We can identify two different types of price inflation.

(a) **Specific price inflation** measures price changes over time for a specific asset or group of assets.

(b) **General price inflation** is the average rate of inflation, which reduces the general purchasing power of money.

2.3 To counter the problems of specific price inflation some system of current value accounting may be used (for example, the system of current cost accounting described in the following chapter). The capital maintenance concepts underlying current value systems do not attempt to allow for the maintenance of real value in money terms.

2.4 Current Purchasing Power (CPP) accounting is based on a different concept of capital maintenance. CPP measures profits as the increase in the current purchasing power of equity. Profits are therefore stated after allowing for the declining purchasing power of money due to price inflation.

2.5 In Britain attempts to introduce CPP accounting have been in a combination with historical cost accounting. When applied to historical cost accounting, CPP is a system of accounting which makes adjustments to income and capital values to **allow for the general rate of price inflation**.

3 THE PRINCIPLES AND PROCEDURES OF CPP ACCOUNTING

3.1 In CPP accounting, profit is measured after allowing for general price changes. It is a fundamental idea of CPP that capital should be maintained in terms of the same monetary purchasing power, so that:

$$P_{CPP} = D_{CPP} + \left(E_{t(CPP)} - E_{(t-1)CPP}\right)$$

where P_{CPP} is the CPP accounting profit

           D_{CPP} is distributions to shareholders, re-stated in current purchasing power terms

           $E_{t(CPP)}$ is the total value of assets attributable to the owners of the business entity at the end of the accounting period, restated in current purchasing power terms

           $E_{(t-1)CPP}$ is the total value of the owners' equity at the beginning of the year re-stated in terms of current purchasing power at the end of the year.

(A current purchasing power £ relates to the value of money on the last day of the accounting period.)

3.2 Profit in CPP accounting is therefore measured after allowing for maintenance of equity capital. To the extent that a company is financed by loans, there is no requirement to allow for the maintenance of the purchasing power of the loan creditors' capital. Indeed, as we shall see, the equity of a business can profit from the loss in the purchasing power value of loans.

Monetary and non-monetary items

> ### KEY TERMS
>
> A **monetary item** is an asset or liability whose amount is fixed by contract or statute in terms of £s, regardless of changes in general price levels and the purchasing power of the pound. The main examples of monetary items are cash, debtors, creditors and loan capital.
>
> A **non-monetary item** is an asset or liability whose value is not fixed by contract or statute. These include land and buildings, plant and machinery and stock.

3.3 In CPP accounting, there is an important **difference** between the two items.

(a) If a company borrows money in a period of inflation, the amount of the debt will remain fixed (by law) so that when the debt is eventually paid, it will be paid in £s of a lower purchasing power.

For example, if a company borrows £2,000 on 1 January 19X5 and repays the loan on 1 January 19X9, the purchasing power of the £2,000 repaid in 19X9 will be much less than the value of £2,000 in 19X5, because of inflation. Since the company by law must

repay only £2,000 of principal, it has gained by having the use of the money from the loan for 4 years. (The lender of the £2,000 will try to protect the value of his loan in a period of inflation by charging a higher rate of interest; however, this does not alter the fact that the loan remains fixed at £2,000 in money value).

(b) If a company holds cash in a period of inflation, its value in terms of current purchasing power will decline. The company will 'lose' by holding the cash instead of converting it into a non-monetary asset. Similarly, if goods are sold on credit, the amount of the debt is fixed by contract; and in a period of inflation, the current purchasing power of the money from the sale, when it is eventually received, will be less than the purchasing power of the debt, when it was first incurred.

3.4 In CPP accounting, it is therefore argued that there are **gains from having monetary liabilities and losses from having monetary assets.**

(a) In the case of monetary assets, there is a need to make a provision against profit for the loss in purchasing power, because there will be a need for extra finance when the monetary asset is eventually used for operational activities. For example, if a company has a cash balance of £200, which is just sufficient to buy 100 new items of raw material stock on 1 January 19X5, and if the rate of inflation during 19X5 is 10%, the company would need £220 to buy the same 100 items on 1 January 19X6 (assuming the items increase in value by the general rate of inflation). By holding the £200 as a monetary asset throughout 19X5, the company would need £20 more to buy the same goods and services on 1 January 19X6 that it could have obtained on 1 January 19X5. £20 would be a CPP loss on holding the monetary asset (cash) for a whole year.

(b) In the case of monetary liabilities, the argument in favour of including a 'profit' in CPP accounting is not as strong. By incurring a debt, say, on 1 January 19X5, there will not be any eventual cash input to the business. The 'profit' from the monetary liabilities is a 'paper' profit, and T A Lee has argued against including it in the CPP profit and loss account. PSSAP 7, however, noted that 'It has been argued that the gain on long-term borrowing should not be shown as profit in the CPP accounts because it might not be possible to distribute it without raising additional finance. This argument, however, confuses the measurement of profitability with the measurement of liquidity. Even in the absence of inflation, the whole of a company's profit may not be distributable without raising additional finance, for example, because it has been invested in, or earmarked for investment in, non-liquid assets'.

PSSAP 7 therefore concluded that all gains and losses from having monetary liabilities or assets should be included. As we shall see in the following examples, however, monetary assets and liabilities are not revalued for balance sheet purposes but an adjustment is made to CPP profit to reflect the net gain or loss on monetary items for the year. The concept of monetary gains and losses is an important one, and it has been introduced into current cost accounting practice in Britain.

3.5 FIRST EXAMPLE: CPP ACCOUNTING

Seep Ltd had the following assets and liabilities at 31 December 19X4.

(a) All fixed assets were purchased on 1 January 19X1 at a cost of £60,000, and they had an estimated life of six years. Straight line depreciation is used.

(b) Closing stocks have a historical cost value of £7,900. They were bought in the period November-December 19X4.

(c) Debtors amounted to £8,000, cash to £2,000 and short-term creditors to £6,000.

(d) There is long-term debt capital of £15,000.

(e) The general price index includes the following information.

Year	Date	Price index
19X1	1 January	100
19X4	30 November	158
19X4	31 December	160
19X5	31 December	180

The historical cost balance sheet of Seep Limited at 31 December 19X4 was as follows.

	£	£
Fixed assets at cost		60,000
Less depreciation		40,000
		20,000
Stocks	7,900	
Debtors	8,000	
Cash	2,000	
	17,900	
Creditors	6,000	
		11,900
		31,900
Financed by		
Equity		16,900
Loan capital		15,000
		31,900

Required

(a) Prepare a CPP balance sheet as at 31 December 19X4.

(b) What was the depreciation charge against CPP profits in 19X4?

(c) What must be the value of equity at 31 December 19X5 if Seep Ltd is to 'break even' and make neither a profit nor a loss in 19X5?

3.6 SOLUTION

		£c	£c
(a)			
Fixed assets, at cost £60,000 × 160/100			96,000
Less depreciation £40,000 × 160/100			64,000
			32,000
Stock* £7,900 × 160/158		8,000	
Debtors**		8,000	
Cash**		2,000	
		18,000	
Creditors**		6,000	
			12,000
			44,000
Loan stock**			15,000
Equity ***			29,000
			44,000

Notes

* Stocks purchased between 1 November and 31 December are assumed to have an average index value relating to the mid-point of their purchase period, 30 November.

** Monetary assets and liabilities are not re-valued, because their CPP value is the face value of the debt or cash amount.

*** Equity is a mixture of monetary and non-monetary asset values, and is the balancing figure in this example.

(b) Depreciation in 19X4 would be one sixth of the CPP value of the assets at the end of the year, $^1/_6$ of £96,000 = £16,000. Alternatively, it is ($^1/_6 \times$ £60,000) $\times$ 160/100 = £16,000.

(c) To maintain the capital value of equity in CPP terms during 19X5, the CPP value of equity on 31 December 19X5 will need to be £29,000 $\times$ 180/160 = £32,625.

3.7 SECOND EXAMPLE: CPP ACCOUNTING

Rice and Price set up in business on 1 January 19X5 with no fixed assets, and cash of £5,000. On 1 January they acquired some stocks for the full £5,000 which they sold on 30 June 19X5 for £6,000. On 30 November they obtained a further £2,100 of stock on credit. The index of the general price level gives the following index figures.

Date	Index
1 January 19X5	300
30 June 19X5	330
30 November 19X5	350
31 December 19X5	360

Required

Calculate the CPP profits (or losses) of Rice and Price for the year to 31 December 19X5.

3.8 SOLUTION

The approach is to prepare a CPP profit and loss account.

	£c	£c
Sales (£6,000 $\times$ 360/330)		6,545
Less cost of goods sold (£5,000 $\times$ 360/300)		6,000
		545
Loss on holding cash for 6 months*	(545)	
Gain by having creditor for 1 month**	60	
		485
CPP profit		60

* (£6,000 $\times$ 360/330) – £6,000 = £c 545
**(£2,100 $\times$ 360/350) – £2,100 = £c 60

3.9 Here is an exercise which you should work through to confirm your understanding of CPP accounting.

Exam focus point

Remember that, in the exam, you will not have to prepare any CPP (or CCA) accounts.

Question

Mushroom Ltd was established on 1 January 19X5. Its opening balance sheet was as follows.

	£
Land	6,000
Equipment	3,500
Stock	2,000
Cash	500
	12,000
Share capital	12,000

The following transactions took place in 19X5.

(a) Purchased extra stock for £10,000 in cash.

(b) Made cash sales of £13,000. The historical cost of goods sold was £9,000.

(c) A long-term loan of £2,000 was raised on 30 June and immediately used to purchase equipment. Interest for six months, amounting to £100, was paid on 31 December.

(d) Sundry expenses of £1,800 were paid in cash during the year.

(e) All equipment has an expected life of four years and nil residual value. Mushroom Ltd uses the straight line method of depreciation and makes a full year's charge in the year of acquisition.

(f) Closing stock on 31 December 19X5 had an historical cost of £3,000 and was bought (on average) when the RPI was 115.

(g) Movements in the RPI are as follows.

   100 on 1 January 19X5
   110 on 30 June 19X5
   120 on 31 December 19X5

You should assume that all transactions occurred evenly over the year and that the RPI increased evenly over the year.

Required

Prepare the CPP profit and loss account for the year ended 31 December 19X5 and the CPP balance sheet as at that date.

Answer

It is easier to start with the CPP balance sheet.

	£c	£c
Land (£6,000 × 120/100)		7,200
Equipment (£3,500 × 120/100) + (£2,000 × 120/110)	6,382	
Less depreciation: (£875 × 120/100) + (£500 × 120/110)	1,595	
		4,787
		11,987
Stocks (£3,000 × 120/115)	3,130	
Cash £(500 − 10,000 + 13,000 − 100 − 1,800)	1,600	
		4,730
		16,717
Loan		2,000
		14,717
Share capital (£12,000 × 120/100)		14,400
Profit (balancing figure)		317
		14,717

The profit and loss account can now be constructed. A loss on holding net monetary assets will emerge as a balancing figure.

	£c	£c
Sales (£13,000 × 120/110)		14,182
Opening stock (£2,000 × 120/100)	2,400	
Purchases (£10,000 × 120/110)	10,909	
	13,309	
Less closing stock (£3,000 × 120/115)	3,130	
Cost of sales		10,179
Gross profit		4,003
Monetary expenses		
Interest (£100 × 120/120)	100	
Sundry expenses (£1,800 × 120/110)	1,964	
		2,064
Profit after monetary expenses		1,939
Non-monetary expenses		
Depreciation (see balance sheet)		1,595
		344
Loss on holding net monetary assets (balancing figure)		27
Retained profit (per balance sheet)		317

Although the loss on holding net monetary assets can be entered as a balancing figure, a proof of the figure may assist your understanding of CPP accounting.

	£c	£c
Initial holding of net monetary assets (NMA)	500	
As expressed in £c at 31 December 19X5 (£500 × 120/100)	600	
Loss on initial holding of NMA		100
Increase in NMA per HC accounts		
(= profit after monetary expenses less increase in stock,		
£(13,000 − 2,000 − 10,000 + 3,000 − 100 − 1,800 − 1,000))	1,100	
Increase in NMA per CPP accounts £(1,939 − 730)	1,209	
Loss on increase in net monetary assets		109
Gain on long-term loan ((£2,000 × 120/110) − £2,000)		(182)
		27

Notes

(a)   The initial holding of NMA was £500. When measured in £c as at 31 December 19X5 this is equivalent to £500 × 120/100 = £600. In other words, the original NMA have fallen in purchasing power by £100.

(b)   But apart from the initial holding of NMA there is an increase in NMA during the year and a loss arises on this increase too. The loss can be calculated by comparing the increase in NMA shown by the HC accounts and the increase in NMA shown by the CPP accounts. In each case, the increase is represented by the monetary profit, ie the profit after monetary expenses (but before non-monetary expenses such as depreciation) with an adjustment for the change in stock levels (which affects gross profit but is not a monetary item).

(c)   Finally, because the new loan was raised part-way through the year, it is convenient to treat it separately from other NMA. A gain arises on this loan because the amount to be repaid remains fixed at £2,000, while the purchasing power of the £2,000 to be repaid declines.

Advantages of CPP accounting

3.10   (a)   The restatement of asset values in terms of a stable money value provides a **more meaningful basis of comparison** with other companies. Similarly, provided that previous years' profits are re-valued into CPP terms, it is also possible to compare the current year's results with past performance.

(b)   **Profit is measured in 'real' terms** and excludes 'inflationary value increments'. This enables better forecasts of future prospects to be made.

(c)   **CPP avoids the subjective valuations** of current value accounting, because a single price index is applied to all non-monetary assets.

(d) CPP provides a stable monetary unit with which to value profit and capital, £c.

(e) Since it is based on historical cost accounting, raw data is easily verified, and measurements of value can be readily audited.

Disadvantages of CPP accounting

3.11 (a) It is **not clear what £c means**. 'Generalised purchasing power' as measured by the Retail Price Index, or indeed any other general price index, has no obvious practical significance.

> 'Generalised purchasing power has no relevance to any person or entity because no such thing exists in reality, except as a statistician's computation.' (T A Lee)

(b) The use of indices inevitably involves **approximations** in the measurements of value.

(c) The **value of assets** in a CPP balance sheet has **less meaning** than a current value balance sheet. It cannot be supposed that the CPP value of net assets reflects:

(i) the general goods and services that could be bought if the assets were released; nor

(ii) the consumption of general goods and services that would have to be forgone to replace those assets.

In this respect, a CPP balance sheet has similar drawbacks to an historical cost balance sheet.

4 CURRENT COST ACCOUNTING AND DEPRIVAL VALUE

4.1 Current cost accounting (CCA) reflects an approach to capital maintenance based on maintaining the **operating capability** of a business. The conceptual basis of CCA is that the value of assets consumed or sold, and the value of assets in the balance sheet, should be stated at their **value to the business** (also known as 'deprival value').

4.2 A system of current cost accounting was introduced into the UK by SSAP 16 *Current cost accounting* in March 1980. This was the culmination of a long process of research into the problems of accounting in times of inflation. One result of this process had been the publication of PSSAP 7 on current purchasing power accounting, which was described earlier. SSAP 16 itself encountered heavy criticism and was finally withdrawn in April 1988. Students are recommended to read this chapter with an eye to the general principles of CCA as you do not need to know the detailed provisions of SSAP 16.

4.3 *Deprival value* is an important concept, which you may find rather difficult to understand at first, and you should read the following explanation carefully.

> **KEY TERMS**
>
> - The **deprival value** of an asset is the loss which a business entity would suffer if it were deprived of the use of the asset.
>
> - A basic assumption in CCA is that 'capital maintenance' should mean maintenance of the 'business substance' or 'operating capability' of the business entity. As we have seen already, it is generally accepted that profit is earned only after a sufficient amount has been charged against sales to ensure that the capital of the business is maintained. In CCA, a *physical* rather than financial definition of capital is used: capital maintenance is measured by the ability of the business entity to keep up the same level of operating capability.
>
> - **'Value to the business'** is the required method of valuation in current cost accounting, because it reflects the extra funds which would be required to maintain the operating capability of the business entity if it suddenly lost the use of an asset.

4.4 Value to the business, or deprival value, can be any of the following values.

(a) **Replacement cost**. In the case of fixed assets, it is assumed that the replacement cost of an asset would be its net replacement cost (NRC), its gross replacement cost minus an appropriate provision for depreciation to reflect the amount of its life already 'used up'.

(b) **Net realisable value** (NRV), which is what the asset could be sold for, net of any disposal costs.

(c) **Economic value** (EV), or utility, which is what the existing asset will be worth to the company over the rest of its useful life.

4.5 The choice of deprival value from one of the three values listed will depend on circumstances. The decision tree below illustrates the principles involved in the choice, but in simple terms you should remember that in CCA deprival value is nearly always replacement cost.

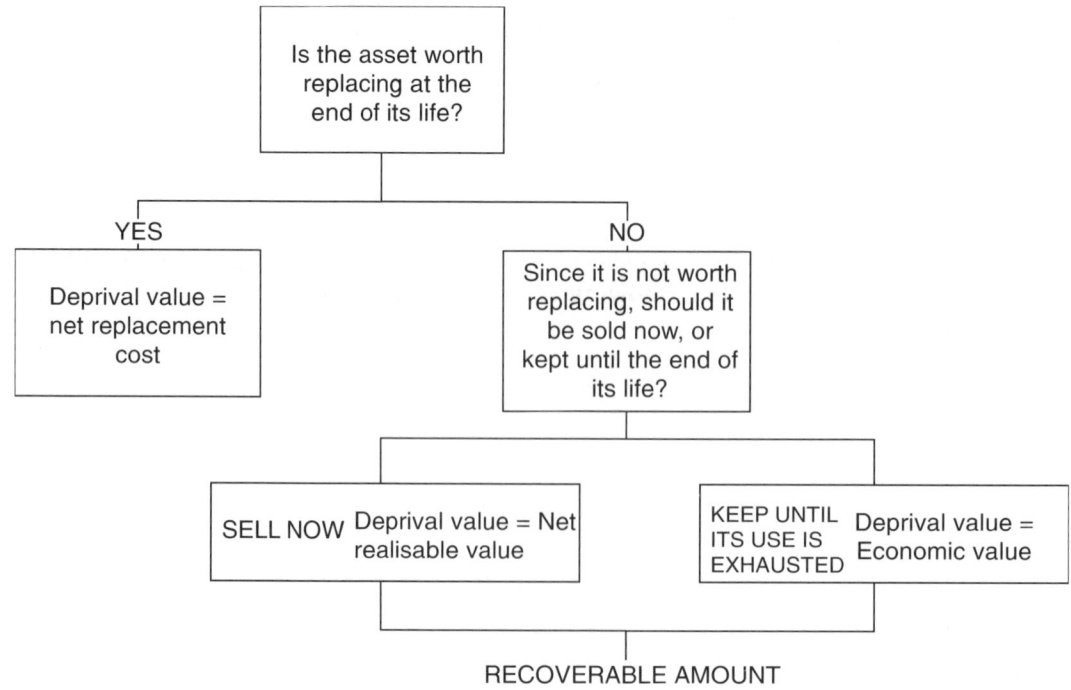

4.6 If the asset is worth replacing, its deprival value will always be net replacement cost. If the asset is not worth replacing, it might be disposed of straight away, or else it might be kept in operation until the end of its useful life.

4.7 You may therefore come across a statement that deprival value is the **lower** of:

(a) **net replacement cost**; and

(b) the **higher of net realisable value and economic value**.

4.8 We have already seen that if an asset is not worth replacing at the end of its life, the deprival value will be NRV or EV. However, there are many assets which will not be replaced either:

(a) because the asset is technologically obsolete, and has been (or will be) superseded by more modern equipment; or

(b) because the business is changing the nature of its operations and will not want to continue in the same line of business once the asset has been used up.

4.9 Such assets, even though there are reasons not to replace them, would still be valued (usually) at net replacement cost, because this 'deprival value' still provides an estimate of the operating capability of the company.

CCA profits and deprival value

4.10 The deprival value of assets is **reflected in the CCA** profit and loss account by the following means.

(a) **Depreciation** is charged on fixed assets on the basis of **gross replacement cost** of the asset (where NRC is the deprival value).

(b) Where **NRV or EV is the deprival value**, the **charge** against CCA profits will be the **loss in value of the asset** during the accounting period, from its previous balance sheet value to its current NRV or EV.

(c) **Goods sold are charged at their replacement cost**. Thus if an item of stock cost £15 to produce, and sells for £20, by which time its replacement cost has risen to £17, the CCA profit would be £3.

	£
Sales	20
Less replacement cost of goods sold	17
Current cost profit	3

4.11 It is useful to explain the distinction here between CCA and accounting for inflation, and a simple example may help to describe the difference. Suppose that Arthur Smith Ltd buys an asset on 1 January for £10,000. The estimated life of the asset is 5 years, and straight line depreciation is charged. At 31 December the gross replacement cost of the asset is £10,500 (5% higher than on 1 January) but general inflation during the year, as measured by the retail price index, has risen 20%.

(a) To maintain the value of the business against inflation, the asset should be revalued as follows.

	£
Gross (£10,000 × 120%)	12,000
Depreciation charge for the year (@ 20%)	2,400
Net value in the balance sheet	9,600

(b) In CCA, the business maintains its operating capability if we revalue the asset as follows.

	£
Gross replacement cost	10,500
Depreciation charge for the year (note 1)	2,100
NRC: balance sheet value	8,400

Note	£
Historical cost depreciation	2,000
CCA depreciation adjustment (5%)	100
Total CCA depreciation cost	2,100

4.12 CCA preserves the operating capability of the company but does not necessarily preserve it against the declining value in the purchasing power of money (against inflation). As mentioned in the previous chapter, CCA is a system which takes account of specific price inflation (changes in the prices of specific assets or groups of assets) but not of general price inflation.

4.13 Our next step will be to look at some of the practical procedures involved in preparing current cost accounts. A strict view of current cost accounting might suggest that a set of CCA accounts should be prepared from the outset on the basis of deprival values. In practice that has not been the procedure adopted in the UK. Instead, current cost accounts have been prepared by starting from historical cost accounts and making appropriate adjustments.

5 CURRENT COST ADJUSTMENTS TO HISTORICAL COST PROFIT

5.1 In current cost accounting profit is calculated as follows.

	£	£
Historical cost profit		X
Less: cost of sales adjustment (COSA)	X	
depreciation adjustment	X	
		(X)
Current cost profit		X

The holding gains, both realised and unrealised, are therefore excluded from current cost profit. The double entry for the debits in the current cost profit and loss account is to credit both COSA and depreciation adjustment to a non-distributable revaluation reserve.

Cost of sales adjustment (COSA)

5.2 Suppose that an item of stock is bought at a cost of £45 and is sold some months later for £80. By that time, its replacement cost had risen to £56.

(a) The strict method of calculating the CC profit on sale would be as illustrated earlier.

	£
Sales	80
Less replacement cost of goods sold	56
CC profit	24

(b) In practice the position would be disclosed as follows.

	£
Sales	80
Less historical cost of sales	45
HC profit	35
Less cost of sales adjustment (COSA)*	11
CC profit	24

* This is the difference between the historical cost and the deprival value of goods sold.

5.3 The CC profit is £11 less than the HC profit. This is because the £11 represents a realised holding gain and in CCA all holding gains (realised or unrealised) are **excluded** from profit. We say that a holding gain arises on an asset when the deprival value of the asset increases between the date of its purchase and the date of its sale (or the date of the balance sheet in the case of an asset still unsold). Here the deprival value (replacement cost) of the stock item rose by £11 from £45 to £56 before it was sold.

5.4 The exclusion of holding gains from CC profit is a necessary consequence of the need to maintain operating capability. The historical cost accounts show a profit of £35, but the company is not £35 better off if it intends to continue in business. £11 of the £35 HC profit must be consumed in replacing the stock item sold so that trading can continue. The CC profit of £24 is a measure of how much better off the company is after maintaining its operating capability, which in this case is its ability to supply one stock item to a customer.

5.5 It is worth mentioning that SSAP 16 did not use the term 'holding gain'. The £11 in the above example would be called a **realised revaluation surplus**. The double entry would be to debit profit and loss account (as shown above) and to credit a revaluation reserve (called the **current cost reserve** in SSAP 16).

Depreciation adjustment

5.6 In the same way as a COSA is applied to the cost of goods sold to derive CCA profit from historical cost profit, so too can a **depreciation adjustment** be applied for the cost of fixed assets to **reconcile HCA and CCA profits**.

5.7 Suppose that a fixed asset was bought on 1 January 19X5 at a cost of £16,000. Its expected life is 4 years and residual value nil. The straight line method of depreciation is used. The financial year ends on 31 December 19X5. The gross replacement cost of the asset was:

(a) £16,800 at 30 June 19X5;
(b) £18,000 at 31 December 19X5.

5.8 The depreciation charge for the year should ideally be based on the gross replacement cost at 30 June, but in practice it may be based on the GRC at 31 December.

5.9 Depreciation based on the mid-year gross replacement cost.

(a) One method of calculating the CCA cost of depreciation for the year is as follows.

Gross replacement cost at 30 June	£16,800
Depreciation for the year (one-quarter)	£4,200

(b) An alternative method of calculation is shown here.

	£
Historical cost depreciation (one quarter of £16,000)	4,000
Depreciation adjustment	200
CCA depreciation	4,200

5.10 This alternative form of statement, using a depreciation adjustment to historical cost figures, is the method of presentation preferred in practice (because, as with COSA, it enables CCA profit to be calculated as an adjustment to the historical cost profit).

The depreciation adjustment is a realised holding gain which is excluded from profit in current cost accounting.

5.11 If depreciation had been based on the 31 December value of the asset (£18,000), the annual charge in the CCA profit and loss account would have been (¼) £4,500.

	£
Historical cost depreciation	4,000
Depreciation adjustment	500
CCA depreciation	4,500

The modern equivalent asset concept

5.12 It is recognised that in some cases it would be impossible for companies to replace their existing plant and machinery with anything comparable owing to obsolescence of the old equipment. To find the current value of the old equipment comparison may have to be made with a quite different machine, in which case allowance must be made for different useful lives and different production capacities. For example, Kagan Ltd currently owns four old button machines. Each machine produces one million buttons per annum, and the machines were all bought on 1 January 19X2 for £10,000 each, with a total estimated life of ten years. It is now 31 December 19X4 and the only machine now available costs £100,000 and produces five million buttons a year for seven years.

5.13 The value to the business of the four old machines must be found by reference to the current cost of replacing their service potential. At present the historical cost of producing four million buttons a year is:

$$£10,000 \times 4 \times 1/10 = £4,000$$

This would be the HC depreciation charge. The current cost of producing the same number of buttons for one year would be:

$$£100,000 \times 4/5 \times 1/7 = 11,429$$

This would be the CC depreciation charge. The HC balance sheet value of the machines represents the historical cost of the ability to produce four million buttons a year for the next seven years.

$$7 \times £4,000 = £28,000$$

Alternatively:

	£
Cost	40,000
Less depreciation	12,000
Net book value	28,000

Similarly, the net replacement cost of the same service potential can be found as:

$$7 \times £11,429 = £80,003$$

(*Note.* The same figures can be arrived at using a variety of different calculations.)

Indexing

5.14 There are **serious practical difficulties** in the estimation of replacement costs. SSAP 16 recommended the use of external indices (such as those prepared by the government) which can be applied to historical costs so as to arrive at replacement costs.

5.15 Where companies are content to use an historical cost accounting system, a simple indexing technique may be used to estimate the COSA. This technique works as follows.

(a) Sales for the period are taken at actual value.

(b) The cost of sales at replacement cost is calculated as:

(i) opening stock, revalued from HC value to an estimated mid-period value;

(ii) plus purchases (or costs of production);

(iii) less closing stock, reduced from HC value to an estimated mid-period value.

(It is assumed here that costs are rising with inflation, so that opening stock will be revalued upwards and closing stock downwards to average or mid-year figures.)

Mid-period figures are taken because sales and purchases are assumed to occur evenly throughout the period, so that in total the figures for sales and purchases must represent average values for the period.

5.16 EXAMPLE: INDEXING

Arthur Smith Ltd makes and sells 100 units of output each month. Finished goods stocks are kept at 3 months' sales, ie at 300 units. Sales are £250 per month.

		Production of finished goods at cost	*Historical cost of sales*	*Current cost (replacement cost)*	*COSA*
		£	£	£	£
19X1	Month 10	200			
	Month 11	202			
	Month 12	204			
19X2	Month 1	206	200	206	6
	Month 2	208	202	208	6
	Month 3	210	204	210	6
	Month 4	212	206	212	6
	Month 5	214	208	214	6
	Month 6	216	210	216	6
	6 month total		1,230	1,266	36

The index for stock prices was as follows.

		Index (middle of each month)	
Year 19X1	Month 10	100	
	Month 11	101	Opening stocks of 3 months;
	Month 12	102	average index value 101
Year 19X2	Month 1	103	
	Month 2	104	
	Month 3	105	
	Month 4	106	Closing stocks of 3 months
	Month 5	107	production; average index
	Month 6	108	value 107

What is the current cost profit for the first 6 months of 19X2:

(a) using actual replacement costs to calculate COSA;

(b) using the indexing technique to calculate COSA?

5.17 SOLUTION

(a)

	£
Sales (6 × £250)	1,500
Less historical cost of sales (here FIFO)	1,230
Historical cost profit	270
COSA	(36)
CCA profit	234

This can also be calculated as follows.

	£
Sales	1,500
Less replacement costs	1,266
CCA profit	234

(b) The mid-period index value is the 'average' index value for the accounting period in question, months 1 to 6 of 19X2. An average of 105.5 would represent 31 March price levels (mid-way between mid-month 3 and mid-month 4 index levels).

Opening stocks, valued at £(200+202+204) = £606, have an index value of 101, being the average price of stocks built up between month 10 and month 12 of 19X1. These are revalued to mid-period figures by applying the factor:

$$\frac{\text{Mid period price index}}{\text{Opening price index}} \qquad \therefore £606 \times \frac{105.5}{101} = £633$$

Closing stocks, valued at £(212+214+216) = £642 have an index value of 107, being the average price of stocks built up between months 4 and 6 of 19X2. These are revalued to mid-period figures by applying the factor:

$$\frac{\text{Mid period price index}}{\text{Closing stock price index}} \qquad \therefore £642 \times \frac{105.5}{107} = £633$$

The current cost profit would be calculated as follows.

	£	£
Sales		1,500
Opening stock	633	
Add cost of production (months 1-6)	1,266	
	1,899	
Less closing stock	633	
Cost of sales		1,266
Current cost profit		234

5.18 In this example, because figures have been 'conveniently' selected, the cost of sales figure derived by indexing is exactly the same as the replacement costs calculated previously. In practice, there will inevitably be some (small) discrepancies.

5.19 The COSA is calculated as follows.

	£
Historical cost of sales (FIFO)	1,230
Cost of sales just calculated	1,266
COSA	(36)

Since the historical cost of sales is below the 'replacement cost' of sales, the COSA reduces the profit.

	£
Sales	1,500
Less historical cost of sales	1,230
Historical cost profit	270
COSA	(36)
Current cost profit	234

Price and volume changes of stocks

5.20 You may have noticed in the previous example of indexing that the adjusted costs of opening and closing stocks to mid-period values were the same figure, £633.

5.21 This should be expected, because both opening and closing stocks were the same in quantity, or volume, so that their mid-year values ought to be the same. The difference between the opening stock and closing stock values in the historical cost accounts is entirely the result of price changes on the same volume of goods.

	At HC £	Revalued £		Price changes £
Opening stock (300 units)	606	633	(up)	27
Closing stock (300 units)	642	633	(down)	9
Volume change		nil		36

5.22 The COSA represents changes in *prices* of stocks, not volume: it represents the extra costs of maintaining the same volume of stocks. These costs must therefore be charged against revenue to ensure that the operating capacity of the business is maintained before (current cost) profits can be earned.

5.23 EXAMPLE: PRICE AND VOLUME CHANGES OF STOCKS

The historical cost profit and loss account of Hope and Downs Ltd for the year 19X3 is as follows.

	£	£
Sales		2,520
Opening stock	320	
Cost of production	2,160	
	2,480	
Less closing stock	192	
Cost of sales		2,288
HC profit		232

Opening stocks represent production in November and December 19X2 and closing stocks represent production in December 19X3. Sales and production occurred evenly throughout the year, so that the diminution in stocks was gradual.

The stock index levels are as follows.

		Index
19X2	30 November	100
	31 December	102
19X3	30 June	112.5
	30 November	119
	31 December	121

What is the current cost profit for 19X3?

5.24 SOLUTION

The appropriate indices are as follows.

Mid year prices	112.5
Opening stock (mid Nov-Dec = 30 November)	100
Closing stock (mid Dec = (119+121) ÷ 2)	120

	Historical cost		Current cost		Price change
	£		£		£
Opening stock	$320 \times \dfrac{112.5}{100} =$		360	(plus)	40
Closing stock	$192 \times \dfrac{112.5}{120} =$		180	(minus)	12
Volume change			(180)	Price change	52

Stock holding has been halved, and the COSA (the price change) is £52 adverse.

	£
Historical cost profit	232
COSA	(52)
Current cost profit	180

Monetary working capital adjustment

5.25   In a period of rising prices, money loses value. If a company, A, buys a regular monthly supply of goods from company B, and takes 2 months credit, the supplier B is effectively providing funds to sustain the business operations of A. This funding of A by B is shown in the balance sheet of A as creditors and in the balance sheet of B as debtors.

5.26   In a period of rising prices, if A continues to take 2 months' credit from B, A will be:

(a)   receiving goods each month from B; and
(b)   paying B for goods bought at 2 month old prices.

A only needs to pay the replacement cost of 2 months ago and not the current replacement cost. The price increase is borne by B.

On the other hand, B must pay for stocks at current prices, but will not receive revenue for 2 months. In a period of rising prices, B is 'losing out' because when the revenue is eventually received, it will cost more for replacement than it would if the sales to A had been for cash.

5.27   There are therefore **monetary gains and losses**. If a company measures profit as the excess of revenue over replacement cost:

(a)   creditors protect the company to some extent from price changes because the company lags behind current prices in its payments; but

(b)   debtors would be a burden on profits in a period of rising prices because sales receipts will always relate to previous months' sales at a lower price/cost/profit level.

5.28   In CCA, there is an attempt to identify these effects as a monetary working capital adjustment (MWCA). Some examples may help to illustrate the principles more clearly.

5.29   EXAMPLE: CREDITORS AND MWCA

Hank Reddit Ltd sells 100 units of a product each month. All sales are for cash. The units are bought one month before the month of sale, and paid for in the month following the sale. The results for a 3 month period (January-March) were as follows.

Month	Purchase/replacement cost of 100 units £		Payments to creditors £		Sales (for cash) in the month £
November	180	(sold in Dec)			
December	190	(sold in Jan)			
January	195	(sold in Feb)	180	(for Dec sales)	210
February	205	(sold in March)	190	(for Jan sales)	215
March	215	(sold in April)	195	(for Feb sales)	218
	615		565		643

What is the current cost profit?

5.30 SOLUTION

At the beginning of the period, creditors are financing the business to the value of 200 units of stocks. The total price of the debt for the units, £370, represents a mid-period price for November and December.

At the end of the period, creditors are similarly financing the business to the value of 200 units of stock. There is no 'volume' change in creditors, but there is a price change, because the total price of the debt is now £420 (£205+£215) which represents a mid-period price for February and March.

The total price change in the value of creditors is £420 less £370; ie £50. This is a favourable MWCA. (*Note.* The MWCA is also calculated in this example as the difference between the replacement cost of 300 units in January-March £615, and the payments to creditors for the same volume of units in the period £565.)

	£	£
Sales		643
Less historical cost of sales £(190+195+205)		590
Historical cost profit		53
CCA adjustments		
COSA	(25)	
MWCA	50	
		25
CCA profit		78

5.31 EXAMPLE: DEBTORS AND MWCA

Mothpurse Ltd buys and sells 100 units of stock each month, keeping a permanent stock to meet 2 months' demand (stocks are bought in advance of sales). Purchases are paid for on receipt. The goods are sold on 2 months' credit. Results for the 3 month period January to March were as follows.

Month	Purchases & payments (100 units per month) £		Sales £		Receipts from debtors £
November	400	(sold in Jan)	500	(paid for in Jan)	
December	450	(sold in Feb)	530	(paid for in Feb)	
January	480	(sold in March)	560	(paid for in March)	500
February	520		600		530
March	550		620		560
3 month total	1,550		1,780		1,590

What is the CCA profit for the period January to March?

5.32 SOLUTION

The company begins and ends the period with debtors for 200 units of stock. Opening debtors are £1,030 (representing November-December price levels) and closing debtors are £1,220 (representing February-March price levels), so that an extra £190 has been tied up in financing the same volume of debtors. Since the cost of stocks is rising, the company is effectively losing profit by giving credit, because when the money is eventually received, the stocks will be more expensive to replace than if sales had been for cash.

	£	£
Sales		1,780
Less historical cost of sales £(400+450+480)		1,330
Historical cost profit		450
CCA adjustments		
COSA (replacement cost £(480+520+550) = £1,550)	(220)	
MWCA (see above)	(190)	
		(410)
CCA profit		40

Volume changes and price changes in MWC

5.33 In the previous examples of MWCA, you may have noticed that the volume of debtors or creditors at the beginning and end of each period was unchanged in terms of units, and that increases (or decreases) in either were entirely the result of price changes in stocks purchased (for creditors) or goods sold (for debtors). In practice, of course, changes in the money value of debtors and creditors between the beginning and end of a period will be a combination of both volume changes and price changes. Only the price changes, however, should be the MWCA, because this allows for:

(a) the extra money required to finance the same volume of debtors and thus maintain the operating capability of the company; and

(b) the extra funds provided by creditors to finance the same volume of stocks, thereby maintaining the operating capability of the company at no cost to the company itself.

5.34 As with the calculation of the COSA, a simple averaging method may be used to segregate the effects of volume changes from those of price changes. All opening monetary working capital and closing monetary working capital should be expressed at a mid-period value. The difference between these mid-period values must represent (an estimate of) the volume change in MWC during the period.

	£
Total change in the value of monetary working capital	X
Minus volume change in the MWC	X
Equals the price change in the MWC: the MWCA	X

5.35 EXAMPLE: VOLUME CHANGES AND PRICE CHANGES IN MWC

Hopper, Hope and Heighway Ltd had the following results for the year to 31 December 19X2 (in historical cost terms).

	£	£
Sales		1,290
Opening stock (bought in Nov and Dec 19X1)	206	
Purchases	1,170	
	1,376	
Less closing stock (bought in Sept and Dec 19X2)	504	
		872
Profit		418

The increase in stock volume was a steady build up through the year (therefore simple averaging for the year may be used).

Opening creditors were £104 and opening debtors were £143, both representing December 19X1 transactions (purchases and sales). Closing debtors were £352 and closing creditors were £257, both representing November and December 19X2 transactions. All debtors and creditors arise from trading. Purchases and sales were fairly even throughout the year. An index of prices for stocks and related monetary working capital is given below.

What is the CCA profit?

		Index
19X1	mid-November	102
	mid-December	104
19X2	30 June	117
	31 October	126
	30 November	128

5.36 SOLUTION

The appropriate indexes are as follows.

	Index
Opening stock (mid-way between November and December)	103
Closing stock (mid-way between September and December = 31 October)	126
Opening monetary working capital	104
Closing monetary working capital (mid-way between November & December = 30 November)	128

Monetary working capital may be aggregated, to avoid unnecessary separate calculations for trade debtors and trade creditors.

	£
Opening MWC £(143 – 104)	39
Closing MWC £(352 – 257)	95
Total change (positive MWC, therefore adverse MWCA)	56

	£
Adjust to mid-year values (index 117)	
Opening MWC (£39 × 117/104)	43.90
Closing MWC (£95 × 117/128)	86.80
Volume change in MWC (increase)	42.90

	£
Total change in MWC	56
Volume change in MWC (rounded up)	43
Price change = MWCA =	13

The COSA is similarly calculated.

	Historic value		Mid year value
	£		£
Opening stocks	206 × 117/103		234
Closing stocks	504 × 117/126		468
Total increase	298	Volume change (increase)	234
Less volume change	234		
Price change (COSA)	64		

	£	£
Historical cost profit		418
CCA adjustments		
COSA	(64)	
MWCA	(13)	
		(77)
CCA profit		341

Gearing adjustment

5.37 If a company has external creditors who are financing some part of the net assets of the business (stocks, fixed assets and monetary working capital), since the amount owed to these creditors is fixed in monetary terms, and does not rise with inflation, it follows that they are financing some part of the holding gains represented by COSA, depreciation adjustment and MWCA. In calculating the amount of current cost profit earned by the

shareholders it is therefore inappropriate to deduct the whole of these adjustments from historical cost profit. The **deduction must be abated by the amount of the adjustments which is financed by external creditors.**

This is an important point and we shall consider a numerical example as a means of illustrating the principle.

5.38 If a company borrows £5,000 to buy a widget, which subsequently increases in value to the business to, say £5,400, the amount owing on the loan (excluding interest) remains at £5,000 and the difference of £400 is a gain to the shareholder. Suppose now that the widget is sold for £5,600 when its replacement cost is £5,400. The current cost operating profit would be £200.

	£
Historical cost profit £(5,600 – 5,000)	600
COSA	400
Current cost operating profit	200

The profit attributable to equity shareholders, however, is £600. Although £5,400 would be required to replace the asset, only £5,000 would be required for the company to settle the debt, leaving £600 for the shareholders.

5.39 This is perhaps most easily understood by looking at the company's balance sheet at each point in the transaction.

	Purchase	*Revaluation*	*Sale*	*Replacement*
	£	£	£	£
Widget	5,000	5,400	-	5,400
Cash	-	-	5,600	200
	5,000	5,400	5,600	5,600
Financed by				
Loan	5,000	5,000	5,000	5,000
Equity	-	400	600	600
	5,000	5,400	5,600	5,600

5.40 A *gearing adjustment* may be calculated, showing the benefit (or perhaps cost) to shareholders which is realised in the period, measured by the extent to which a proportion of the net operating assets are financed by borrowing. In our simple example, all the assets are financed by borrowing, therefore:

	£
Historical cost profit	600
COSA	(400)
Current cost operating profit (interest and taxation ignored)	200
Gearing adjustment	400
Current cost profit attributable to shareholders	600

5.41 We shall now consider a slightly more complex example, which will re-introduce other principles of CCA which have already been described.

5.42 EXAMPLE: CURRENT COST ACCOUNTS

At the beginning of a period, Arthur Smith Ltd has the following balance sheet.

	£
Fixed assets (newly acquired)	10,000
Stocks (newly acquired)	2,000
	12,000

Financed by

Equity	8,000
Loan stock (10% interest)	4,000
	12,000

5.43 The company gearing is 332%, in terms of both HC and CCA. During the period, sales of stocks amounted to £15,000, the replacement cost of sales was £13,200 and the historical cost of sales was £12,000. Closing stocks, at replacement cost, were £4,600 and at HC were £4,400. Depreciation is provided for at 10% straight line, and at the end of the period the fixed asset had a gross replacement cost of £11,000. The HC accounts were as follows.

PROFIT AND LOSS ACCOUNT

	£
Sales	15,000
Less cost of sales	12,000
	3,000
Depreciation	1,000
Profit before interest	2,000
Interest	400
Profit	1,600

CLOSING BALANCE SHEET

	£
Fixed asset at cost less depreciation	9,000
Stocks	4,400
Cash	200
	13,600
Equity	9,600
Loan stock	4,000
	13,600

Taxation is ignored.

Required

Prepare CCA accounts. (Depreciation for the period will be based on the end of year value of the fixed asset).

5.44 SOLUTION

The COSA is (£13,200 − £12,000)	£1,200
The depreciation adjustment is	£100

The MWCA is nil (there are no purchases or sales on credit).

(*Note.* The small cash balance in the closing balance sheet would probably be regarded as necessary for business purposes and therefore taken up in the MWCA as monetary working capital. In this example, we will treat the £200 as a cash surplus.)

	£	£
Historical cost profit (before interest)		2,000
Current cost adjustments		
COSA	1,200	
MWCA	0	
Depreciation	100	
		1,300
Current cost operating profit		700

The gearing adjustment is calculated by multiplying the three current cost adjustments (here £1,300) by the gearing proportion (that is, by the proportion of the gains which is financed by borrowing and which therefore provides additional profits for equity, since the real value of the borrowing is declining in a period of rising prices).

The gearing proportion is the ratio:

$$\frac{\text{Net borrowing}}{\text{Average net operating assets in the year}}$$

Net operating assets consist of fixed assets, stocks and monetary working capital. They are financed partly by net borrowings and partly by equity. The gearing proportion can therefore equally well be expressed as:

$$\frac{\text{Average net borrowing in the period}}{\text{Average equity interests plus average net borrowing in the period}}$$

Equity interests include the current cost reserve, and also any proposed dividends. Average figures are taken as being more representative than end of year figures.

	£
Opening figures	
Net borrowing	4,000
Equity interests	8,000
Equity plus net borrowing	12,000

Closing figures: since cash is here regarded as a surplus amount, the company is losing value during a period of inflation by holding cash, just as it is gaining by having fixed loans. If cash is not included in MWC, it is:

(a) deducted from net borrowings; and

(b) excluded from net operating assets.

(Net operating assets consist of fixed assets, long term trade investments, stocks and monetary working capital.)

The closing figures are therefore as follows.

	£	£
Fixed assets (at net replacement cost		
£11,000 – £1,100)		9,900
Stocks (at replacement cost)		4,600
Monetary working capital		0
Net operating assets (equals equity interest		
plus net borrowings)		14,500
Less: net borrowings	4,000	
cash in hand	(200)	
		3,800
Therefore equity interest		10,700

Average figures	*Opening*	*Closing*	*Average*
Net borrowing	£4,000	£3,800	£3,900
Net operating assets	£12,000	£14,500	£13,250

The gearing proportion is $\dfrac{3,900}{13,250} \times 100\% = 29.43\%$

The CCA accounts will therefore appear as follows.

CCA PROFIT AND LOSS ACCOUNT

	£	£
Historical cost profit before interest		2,000
Current cost adjustments		
COSA	1,200	
MWCA	0	
Depreciation	100	
		(1,300)
Current cost operating profit		700
Interest	(400)	
Gearing adjustment (£1,300 × 29.43%)	383	
		(17)
Current cost profit attributable to shareholders		683

CCA BALANCE SHEET (end of year)

	£
Fixed assets (net replacement cost)	9,900
Stocks (replacement cost)	4,600
Cash	200
	14,700

	£	£
Financed by		
Equity at start of year		8,000
Addition to P & L reserve during year		683
Current cost reserve		
Excess of net replacement cost over net book value		
(9,900 – 9,000)	900	
Depreciation adjustment	100	
COSA	1,200	
MWCA	0	
	2,200	
Less gearing adjustment	(383)	
	1,817	
Add revaluation of year-end stocks	200	
		2,017
		10,700
Loan stock		4,000
		14,700

6 THE CURRENT COST PROFIT AND LOSS ACCOUNT AND BALANCE SHEET

6.1 The format of the **current cost profit and loss account** would show the following information, although not necessarily in the order given.

	£	£
Historical cost profit (before interest & taxation)		X
Current cost operating adjustments		
Cost of sales adjustment	(X)	
Monetary working capital adjustment (loss or gain)	(X) or X	
Depreciation adjustment	(X)	
		(X)
Current cost operating profit (before interest and taxation)		X
Less interest payable and receivable		(X)
Add gearing adjustment		X
Current cost profit attributable to shareholders		X
Less taxation		(X)
Current cost profit after tax		X
Extraordinary items (loss or gain)	(X) or	X
Current cost profit or loss for the financial year		X

6.2 In the current cost balance sheet assets will be valued at their 'value to the business' and liabilities at their monetary amount. There will be a current cost reserve to reflect the revaluation surpluses. This has already been described in some detail.

6.3 It may be useful to summarise the double-entry system in CCA, in which the current cost reserve has a central role.

(a) For fixed assets, there will be an excess of net replacement cost over (historical cost) net book value. The increase in this excess amount each accounting period will be recorded as:

DEBIT   Net assets (asset account and provision for depreciation account)
CREDIT   Current cost reserve account

with the increase in the gross replacement cost minus total extra provision for depreciation.

(b) The various adjustments will be as follows:

DEBIT   Current cost profit and loss account
CREDIT   Current cost reserve account

with the amount of the COSA, the depreciation adjustment and the MWCA, if this reduces the current cost profit. If the MWCA increases the current cost profit, the entries would be 'credit P & L account' 'debit current cost reserve'.

(c) The gearing adjustment is shown as:

CREDIT   Current cost profit and loss account
DEBIT   Current cost reserve.

(d) At the end of an accounting period, there may be some revaluations of closing stocks:

DEBIT   Stocks
CREDIT   Current cost reserve account

with the amount of the revaluation.

On the first day of the next accounting period, this entry is reversed:

CREDIT   Stocks (to reduce them to historical cost)
DEBIT   Current cost reserve account.

Advantages of CCA

6.4 (a) By **excluding holding gains** from profit, CCA can be used to **indicate** whether the **dividends paid to shareholders** (which by UK law can exceed the size of the CCA profit) will **reduce the operating capability** of the business.

(b) Assets are valued after management has considered the opportunity cost of holding them, and the expected benefits from their future use. CCA is therefore a useful guide for management in deciding whether to hold or sell assets.

(c) It is **relevant to the needs of information users** in:

(i) assessing the stability of the business entity;

(ii) assessing the vulnerability of the business (perhaps to a takeover), or the liquidity of the business, although it is not as accurate in this respect as **current exit value accounting**;

(iii) evaluating the performance of management in maintaining and increasing the business substance;

(iv) judging future prospects.

(d) It can be **implemented fairly easily in practice**, by making simple adjustments to the historical cost accounting profits. A current cost balance sheet can also be prepared with reasonable simplicity.

Disadvantages of CCA

6.5 (a) It is impossible to make valuations of EV or NRV without **subjective judgements**. The measurements used are therefore not objective.

(b) There are several **problems** to be overcome in deciding how to provide an estimate of replacement costs for fixed assets.

(i) It must be understood from the outset that whereas depreciation based on the historical cost of an asset can be viewed as a means of spreading the cost of the asset over its estimated life, depreciation based on replacement costs does not conform to this traditional accounting view.

(ii) Depreciation based on replacement costs would appear to be a means of providing that sufficient funds are set aside in the business to ensure that the asset can be replaced at the end of its life. But if it is not certain what technological advances might be in the next few years and how the type of assets required might change between the current time and the estimated time of replacement, it is difficult to argue that depreciation based on today's costs is a valid way of providing for the eventual physical replacement of the asset.

(iii) It is correct, however, that depreciation in CCA does not set aside funds for the physical replacement of fixed assets.

'CCA aims to maintain no more and no less than the facilities that are available at the accounting date.... despite the fact that the fixed assets which provide those facilities might never be replaced in their existing or currently available form.... In simple language, this means charging depreciation on the basis of the current replacement cost of the assets at the time the facilities are used.'

(Mallinson)

(iv) It may be argued that depreciation based on historical cost is more accurate than replacement cost depreciation, because the historical cost is known, whereas replacement cost is simply an estimate. However, replacement costs are re-assessed each year, so that inaccuracies in the estimates in one year can be rectified in the next year.

(c) The **mixed value approach** to valuation means that some assets will be valued at replacement cost, but others will be valued at net realisable value or economic value. It is arguable that the total assets will, therefore, have an aggregate value which is not **particularly meaningful** because of this mixture of different concepts.

(d) It can be argued that **'deprival value'** is an **unrealistic concept**, because the business entity has not been deprived of the use of the asset. This argument is one which would seem to reject the fundamental approach to 'capital maintenance' on which CCA is based.

7 ACCOUNTING FOR THE EFFECTS OF CHANGING PRICES: A HANDBOOK

7.1 Now that we have studied in detail the different systems of inflation accounting, it is appropriate to consider the most recent publication on the subject by the ASC, the *Handbook*. It is **not a prescriptive document** but is intended as a reference work to provide useful guidance. The *Handbook* and its appendices describe in detail the concepts and principles of both CCA and CPP.

7.2 After a brief introduction which summarises the limitations of historical cost accounting in times of changing prices, the Handbook identifies three choices that need to be made in deciding on an appropriate system of accounting (at this stage, you may wish to refer back to Chapter 22 which discussed these issues in broader terms than the Handbook). According to the Handbook:

> 'Although the debate has often been expressed in terms of a straight choice between CCA and CPP, it is in fact necessary, when establishing a method of determining profit, to specify:
>
> (a) the basis that is to be adopted for valuing assets (the two most generally recognised being *historical* or *current* cost);
>
> (b) the capital maintenance concept that is to be used (the *operating* or *financial* capital maintenance concept); and
>
> (c) the unit of measurement that is to be used (the *nominal* pound or the unit of *constant purchasing power*).'

7.3 Chapter 2 of the *Handbook* discusses ways in which these three choices may be combined to produce different systems of accounting. The following table illustrates the possible approaches.

	Asset valuation +	Capital maintenance + concept	Unit of measurement =	System of accounting
1	HC	FCM	£	HCA
2	HC	FCM	UCPP	CPP
3	HC	OCM	£	★
4	HC	OCM	UCPP	★
5	CC	FCM	£	Real terms version of CCA
6	CC	FCM	UCPP	★
7	CC	OCM	£	OCM version of CCA
8	CC	OCM	UCPP	★

Combining the three factors into systems of accounting

★ See below

Key

CC	Current cost
CCA	Current cost accounting
CPP	Constant (or current) purchasing power accounting
FCM	Financial capital maintenance
HC	Historical cost
HCA	Historical cost accounting
UCPP	Unit of constant (or current) purchasing power (the 'stabilised unit')
OCM	Operating capital maintenance
£	The 'nominal pound'

7.4 If each of the capital maintenance concepts and each of the units of measurement is combined with each of the valuation bases, eight methods of accounting result. The Handbook rejects lines 3, 4, 6 and 8 for various reasons, but the other combinations (1, 2, 5 and 7) are discussed further.

Methods based on historical cost

7.5 As line 1 of the table shows, historical cost accounting is based on the financial capital maintenance concept, uses the nominal pound as the unit of measurement and states assets at historical cost. The limitations of historical cost accounting in times of changing prices have already been described.

7.6 Most variations of the method of accounting known as constant (or current) purchasing power accounting are also based on historical cost (although the CPP unit can also be used in connection with methods of accounting based on current costs). CCP accounting (as discussed above) can be regarded as a type of historical cost accounting that adjusts for general inflation. Whilst the calculations under CPP are relatively straightforward, it has the disadvantage that, as input prices specific to a company may fluctuate independently of general price indices, the resultant CPP asset amounts may bear no relationship to the underlying current values.

Methods based on current cost

7.7 The remaining combinations of factors all involve the current cost basis of valuation but are based on different capital maintenance concepts and (although it is arguably less important with CC than with HC asset valuation) on different units of measurement. Because of the divergence between general indices and the movements of prices specific to a particular business, industry and users of accounts have generally preferred CCA to CPP accounting data. The ASC considered that, despite its inherent judgemental difficulties, CCA generally yields more relevant information than CPP accounting and is therefore the preferable basis for external reporting purposes. Specifically, the ASC believed that the usefulness of financial statements is substantially enhanced by the inclusion of information on the operating or real financial capital maintenance concepts, with current cost as the method of valuing assets.

Real terms version of CCA 5/96

7.8 Of the systems above considered feasible by the ASC, the one that perhaps needs further explanation is the **real terms version of CCA**. The real terms version of CCA is almost a hybrid of CPP and CCA. However, in the watered down form proposed by the *Handbook*, it is actually quite straightforward to implement.

7.9 The simplest way to convert from CCA to a real terms version can be summarised by the following steps.

(a) Start with the current cost profit after charging the depreciation adjustment and cost of sales adjustment only (the monetary working capital and gearing adjustments are inconsistent with the approach taken to monetary items by the financial capital maintenance concept).

(b) Add back holding gains arising during the year (these will comprise the realised holding gains being the CC operating adjustments and the unrealised holding gains reflected in the current cost reserve).

(c) Deduct an inflation adjustment to shareholders' funds, which is simply calculated by applying the general inflation rate (measured by the movement in the RPI) to the opening **current cost** shareholders' funds.

(d) This will arrive at a total that may be described as 'total real gains'.

The ASC's suggested solution

7.10 Although not a prescriptive document, the *Handbook* does contain a recommendation by the ASC as to the most appropriate approach. Of the methods available, the ASC considered it most appropriate for companies to disclose information about the current year's result and financial position on the basis of:

(a) current cost asset valuation; *using*

(b) either the operating or financial capital maintenance concept; *and*

(c) the nominal pound as the unit of measurement.

In addition, the ASC said companies that publish five or ten year historical summaries should restate, in units of current purchasing power, certain figures which are either adjusted for the effects of specific changing prices (such as adjusted earnings) or require no adjustment (such as turnover and dividends).

7.11 Information on the basis described in Paragraph 7.2 can be incorporated into a company's main accounts, but that approach is rarely seen in practice amongst British and Irish companies. More commonly, a company's main accounts will be on an historical cost (or modified historical cost) basis. In these circumstances, information on the effects of changing prices along the lines described above can most readily be disclosed in the notes to the accounts.

7.12 Firstly, the ASC suggested that the notes to the accounts should include an 'adjusted earnings statement'. This would show:

(a) the difference between the earnings attributable to ordinary shareholders on the basis used in the profit and loss account and those earnings stated after maintaining the operating or real financial capital of the company;

(b) the adjustments for additional depreciation and additional costs of sales;

(c) any further adjustments consistent with the capital maintenance concept adopted.

A company that reports information of the type just described will have to select one of the two capital maintenance concepts. Briefly, the selection depends on the nature of the company's business and on its perception of the users of its accounts.

7.13 Secondly, the ASC considered it helpful for companies to disclose certain key pieces of information from the current cost balance sheet such as:

(a) the gross and net current cost of fixed assets;

(b) the accumulated current cost depreciation;

(c) the current cost of stocks.

Alternatively, an abridged balance sheet prepared on a current cost basis could be disclosed.

Chapter roundup

- **CPP accounting** is a method of accounting for **general** (not specific) inflation. It does so by expressing asset values in a stable monetary unit, the **£c** or £ of current purchasing power. Under this method, capital is maintained if the current purchasing power of equity is at least as great at the end of the period as it was at the beginning. As always, any excess over this is regarded as profit. In the CPP balance sheet, monetary items are stated at their face value. Non-monetary items are stated at their current purchasing power as at the balance sheet date.

- **CCA** is an alternative to the historical cost convention which attempts to overcome the problems of accounting for **specific price inflation**. Unlike CPP accounting, it does not attempt to cope with **general** inflation.

- CCA is based on a **physical concept of capital maintenance**. Profit is recognised after the operating capability of the business has been maintained.

- This capital maintenance concept is applied by stating assets in the current cost balance sheet at their **deprival value**, which in most cases is their net replacement cost. Adjustments are made to the historical cost profit and loss account so as to remove any holding gains on stock or fixed assets. To recognise holding gains as part of current cost profit would conflict with the principle of maintaining operating capability.

- The **current cost profit and loss account** is constructed by taking historical cost profit before interest and taxation as a starting point. Current cost operating adjustments in respect of cost of sales, monetary working capital and depreciation are made so as to arrive at current cost operating profit. A gearing adjustment is then necessary to arrive at a figure of current cost profit attributable to shareholders.

Quick quiz

1 Define modified historical cost accounting (see paras 1.1, 1.3)

2 Define a company's profit for the year in capital maintenance terms. (1.5)

3 What are the major criticisms of historical cost accounting? (1.15 - 1.22)

4 Distinguish between specific price inflation and general price inflation. (2.2)

5 What is the concept of capital maintenance which underlies the system of CPP accounting? (2.4)

6 In CPP accounting, it is argued that there are gains from having monetary assets and losses from having monetary liabilities. True or false? (3.4)

7 List four advantages and three disadvantages of CPP accounting. (3.10, 3.11)

8 What is meant by 'deprival value'? (4.3)

9 What is an asset's deprival value if it is not worth replacing? (4.6)

10 Why would it be incorrect to describe current cost accounting as a system of inflation accounting? (4.12)

11 In CCA, only realised holding gains are included in profit. True or false? (5.3)

12 What is the monetary working capital adjustment? (5.27, 5.28)

13 What is the purpose of the gearing adjustment? (5.37, 5.40)

14 List four advantages and four disadvantages of CCA. (6.4, 6.5)

15 What are the three choices identified by the ASC *Handbook* when selecting a method of price level accounting? (7.2) Which selection of choices is used in (a) CPP (b) CCA (c) real terms version of CCA? (7.3)

Question to try	Level	Marks	Time
25	Exam	20	36 mins

Part C
Interpretation of accounts

Chapter 24

ADDITIONAL STATEMENTS

Chapter topic		Syllabus reference	Ability required
1	FRS 1 (Revised) *Cash flow statements:* single company	9(c)	Application
2	Consolidated cash flow statements	9(c)	Application
3	Foreign exchange and cash flow statements	9(c)	Application
4	Analysis of cash flow statements	9(c)	Application
5	Other statements	9(c)	Application
6	Year 2000 and the Euro	9(c)	Application

Introduction

You should be familiar with the basic principles, techniques and definitions relating to cash flow statements from your earlier studies. This chapter develops the principles and preparation techniques to include **consolidated statements** and foreign currency problems.

You may wish to revise consolidation in Chapters 12 to 19 and foreign currency translation in Chapter 20 before reading this chapter. This will help you to understand some of the problems associated with consolidated cash flow statements.

The **analysis of cash flow statements** is considered in Section 4 and Section 5 briefly considers other reports which companies may produce.

1 FRS 1 (REVISED) CASH FLOW STATEMENTS: SINGLE COMPANY   11/97

1.1   We have covered this in Paper 5, so only a summary is given here. However, if you have any problems with the question at the end of this section, look back to your earlier study material.

Knowledge brought forward from Paper 5

FRS 1 (Revised) Cash flow statements

- Information on cash flows assists the user in assessing company's viability.

    - Shows enterprise's cash generation ability
    - Shows enterprise's cash utilisation needs

- *Format of statement*

    Inflows and outflows of cash of an enterprise are classified between the major economic activities.

    - Operating activities
    - Dividends from associates and joint ventures
    - Returns on investments and servicing of finance

Knowledge brought forward from Paper 5 (cont)
- ○ Taxation
- ○ Capital expenditure and financial investment
- ○ Acquisitions and disposals
- ○ Equity dividends paid
- ○ Management of liquid resources
- ○ Financing

The last two headings can be shown in a single section provided a subtotal is given for each heading.

- *Notes*

  FRS 1 requires two reconciliations.

  - ○ Operating profit to net cash flow from operating activities
  - ○ Movement in cash in the period to movement in net debt

  Give either adjoining the statement or in a separate note.

- *Definitions*

  - ○ Cash: cash in hand and deposits repayable on demand ... less overdrafts ... repayable on demand. Deposits are repayable on demand if they can be withdrawn at any time without notice and without penalty or if a maturity/period of notice of ≤ 24 hours or one working day has been agreed. Includes cash in hand and deposits in foreign currencies.

  - ○ Liquid resources: current asset investments held as readily disposable stores of value. A readily disposable investment is one that:

    - - Is disposable by the reporting entity without curtailing or disrupting its business, and is either:
    - - Readily convertible into known amounts of cash at or close to its carrying amount, or
    - - Traded in an active market

  - ○ Net debt: the borrowings of the reporting entity less cash and liquid resources; may be 'net funds' rather than 'net debt'.

- *Direct and indirect methods*

  The cash flow statement may be presented using either the direct or indirect method.

  - ○ Direct method: the components of operating cash flows (cash from customers, payments to suppliers, other cash payments) are reported under this method; encouraged because of the value of the extra information given but not required because of the recognised extra costs involved in extracting the operating cash flows

  - ○ Indirect method: the net cash flow from operating activities is arrived at by starting with the operating profit and adjusting it for non-cash charges and credits

---

1.2 Summary of techniques

Remember the steps involved in preparation of a cash flow statement.

Step 1 Set out the proforma leaving plenty of space.

Step 2 Complete the reconciliation of operating profit to net cash inflow, as far as possible.

Step 3 Calculate the following where appropriate.

- Tax paid
- Dividends paid
- Purchase and sale of fixed assets
- Issues of shares
- Repayment of loans

Step 4 Work out the profit if not already given using: opening and closing balances, tax charge and dividends.

Step 5 Complete the note of gross cash flows. Alternatively the information may go straight into the statement.

Step 6 Slot the figures into the statement.

Step 7 Complete the note of the analysis of changes in net debt.

Step 8 Complete the reconciliation of net cash flow to movement in net debt.

Question 1

The summarised accounts of Ashley plc for the year ended 31 December 19X8 are as follows.

ASHLEY PLC
BALANCE SHEET AS AT 31 DECEMBER 19X8

	19X8		19X7	
	£'000	£'000	£'000	£'000
Fixed assets				
Tangible assets		628		514
Current assets				
Stocks	214		210	
Debtors	168		147	
Cash	7		-	
	389		357	
Creditors: amounts falling due within one year				
Trade creditors	136		121	
Tax payable	39		28	
Dividends payable	18		16	
Overdraft	-		14	
	193		179	
Net current assets		196		178
Total assets less current liabilities		824		692
Creditors: amounts falling due after more than one year				
10% debentures		(80)		(50)
		744		642
Capital and reserves				
Share capital (£1 ords)		250		200
Share premium account		70		60
Revaluation reserve		110		100
Profit and loss account		314		282
		744		642

ASHLEY PLC
PROFIT AND LOSS ACCOUNT
FOR THE YEAR ENDED 31 DECEMBER 19X8

	£'000
Sales	600
Cost of sales	(319)
Gross profit	281
Other expenses (including depreciation of £42,000)	(194)
Profit before tax	87
Tax	(31)
Profit after tax	56
Dividends	(24)
Retained profit for the year	32

You are additionally informed that there have been no disposals of fixed assets during the year. New debentures were issued on 1 January 19X8. Wages for the year amounted to £86,000.

Required

Produce a cash flow statement using the direct method suitable for inclusion in the financial statements, as per FRS 1 (revised 1996).

Answer

ASHLEY PLC
CASH FLOW STATEMENT FOR THE YEAR ENDED 31 DECEMBER 19X8

	£'000	£'000
Operating activities		
Cash received from customers (147 + 600 − 168)	579	
Cash payments to suppliers (121 + 381 (W1) − 136)	(366)	
Cash payments to and on behalf of employees	(86)	
		127
Returns on investments and servicing of finance		
Interest paid		(8)
Taxation		
UK corporation tax paid (W2)		(20)
Capital expenditure		
Purchase of tangible fixed assets (W3)		(146)
		(47)
Equity dividends paid (16 + 24 − 18)	-	(22)
Financing		
Issue of share capital	60	
Issue of debentures	30	
Net cash inflow from financing		90
Increase in cash		21

NOTES TO THE CASH FLOW STATEMENT

1   *Reconciliation of operating profit to net cash inflow from operating activities*

	£'000
Operating profit (87 + 8)	95
Depreciation	42
Increase in stock	(4)
Increase in debtors	(21)
Increase in creditors	15
	127

2   *Reconciliation of net cash flow to movement in net debt*

	£'000
Net cash inflow for the period	21
Cash received from debenture issue	(30)
Change in net debt	(9)
Net debt at 1 January 19X8	(64)
Net debt at 31 December 19X8	(73)

3   *Analysis of changes in net debt*

	At 1 January 19X8 £'000	Cash flows £'000	At 31 December 19X8 £'000
Cash at bank	-	7	7
Overdrafts	(14)	14	-
		21	
Debt due after 1 year	(50)	(30)	(80)
Total	(64)	(9)	(73)

Workings

1   *Purchases*

	£'000
Cost of sales	319
Opening stock	(210)
Closing stock	214
Expenses (194 – 42 – 86 – 8 debenture interest)	58
	381

2   *Taxation*

TAXATION

	£'000		£'000
∴ Tax paid	20	Balance b/f	28
Balance c/f	39	Charge for year	31
	59		59

3   *Purchase of fixed assets*

	£'000
Opening fixed assets	514
Less depreciation	(42)
Add revaluation (110 – 100)	10
	482
Closing fixed assets	628
Difference = additions	146

2   CONSOLIDATED CASH FLOW STATEMENTS   5/97

2.1   The following format is given in the standard for a group cash flow statement.

XYZ GROUP PLC
CASH FLOW STATEMENT FOR THE YEAR ENDED 31 DECEMBER 1996

	£'000	£'000
Cash flow from operating activities (note 1)		15,672
Dividends received from associates		350
Returns on investments and servicing of finance* (note 2)		(2,239)
Taxation		(2,887)
Capital expenditure and financial investment (note 2)		(865)
Acquisitions and disposals (note 2)		(17,824)
Equity dividends paid		(2,606)
Cash outflow before use of liquid resources and financing		(10,399)
Management of liquid resources (note 2)		700
Financing (note 2) Issue of shares	600	
Increase in debt	2,347	
		2,947
Decrease in cash in the period		(6,752)
Reconciliation of net cash flow to movement in net debt (note 3)		
Decrease in cash in the period	(6,752)	
Cash inflow from increase in debt and lease financing	(2,347)	
Cash inflow from decrease in liquid resources	(700)	
Change in net debt resulting from cash flows		(9,799)
Loans and finance leases acquired with subsidiary		(3,817)
New finance leases		(2,845)
Translation difference		643
Movement in net debt in the period		(15,818)
Net debt at 1.1.96		(15,215)
Net debt at 31.12.96		(31,033)

* This heading would include any dividends received *other than* those from equity accounted entities included in operating activities.

NOTES TO THE CASH FLOW STATEMENT

1   *Reconciliation of operating profit to operating cash flows*

		Continuing	Dis-continued	Total
	£'000	£'000	£'000	£'000
Operating profit		18,829	(1,616)	17,213
Depreciation charges		3,108	380	3,488
Cash flow relating to previous year restructuring provision (note 4)			(560)	(560)
Increase in stocks		(11,193)	(87)	(11,280)
Increase in debtors		(3,754)	(20)	(3,774)
Increase in creditors		9,672	913	10,585
Net cash inflow from continuing operating activities		16,662		
Net cash outflow in respect of discontinued activities			(990)	
Net cash inflow from operating activities				15,672

2   *Analysis of cash flows for headings netted in the cash flow statement*

	£'000	£'000
Returns on investments and servicing of finance		
Interest received	508	
Interest paid	(1,939)	
Preference dividend paid	(450)	
Interest element of finance lease rental payments	(358)	
Net cash outflow for returns on investments and servicing of finance		(2,239)
Capital expenditure and financial investment		
Purchase of tangible fixed assets	(3,512)	
Sale of trade investment	1,595	
Sale of plant and machinery	1,052	
Net cash outflow for capital expenditure and financial investment		(865)
Acquisitions and disposals		
Purchase of subsidiary undertaking	(12,705)	
Net overdrafts acquired with subsidiary	(5,516)	
Sale of business	4,208	
Purchase of interest in a joint venture	(3,811)	
Net cash outflow for acquisitions and disposals		(17,824)
Management of liquid resources ★		
Cash withdrawn from 7 day deposit	200	
Purchase of government securities	(5,000)	
Sale of government securities	4,300	
Sale of corporate bonds	1,200	
Net cash inflow from management of liquid resources		700
Financing		
Issue of ordinary share capital		600
Debt due within a year		
Increase in short-term borrowings	2,006	
Repayment of secured loan	(850)	
Debt due beyond a year		
New secured loan repayable in 2000	1,091	
New unsecured loan repayable in 1998	1,442	
Capital element of finance lease rental payments	(1,342)	
		2,347
Net cash inflow from financing		2,947

★ XYZ Group plc includes as liquid resources term deposits of less than a year, government securities and AA rated corporate bonds.

BPP PUBLISHING

3   *Analysis of net debt*

	At 1 Jan 1996 £'000	Cash flow £'000	Acquisition* (excl. cash and overdrafts) £'000	Other non-cash changes £'000	Exchange movement £'000	At 31 Dec 1996 £'000
Cash in hand, at bank	235	(1,250)			1,392	377
Overdrafts	(2,528)	(5,502)			(1,422)	(9,452)
		(6,752)				
Debt due after 1 year	(9,640)	(2,533)	(1,749)	2,560	(792)	(12,154)
Debt due within 1 year	(352)	(1,156)	(837)	(2,560)	1,465	(3,440)
Finance leases	(4,170)	1,342	(1,231)	(2,845)		(6,904)
		(2,347)				
Current asset investments	1,240	(700)				540
Total	(15,215)	(9,799)	(3,817)	(2,845)	643	(31,033)

4   *Cash flows relating to exceptional items*

The operating cash outflows include under discontinued activities an outflow of £560,000, which relates to the £1,600,000 exceptional provision for a fundamental restructuring made in the 1995 accounts.

5   *Major non-cash transactions*

(a)   During the year the group entered into finance lease arrangements in respect of assets with a total capital value at the inception of the leases of £2,845,000.

(b)   Part of the consideration for the purchases of subsidiary undertakings and the sale of a business that occurred during the year comprised shares and loan notes respectively. Further details of the acquisitions and the disposal are set out below.

6   *Purchase of subsidiary undertakings*

	£'000
Net assets acquired	
Tangible fixed assets	12,194
Investments	1
Stocks	9,384
Debtors	13,856
Taxation recoverable	1,309
Cash at bank and in hand	1,439
Creditors	(21,715)
Bank overdrafts	(6,955)
Loans and finance leases	(3,817)
Deferred taxation	(165)
Minority shareholders' interests	(9)
	5,522
Goodwill	16,702
	22,224
Satisfied by	
Shares allotted	9,519
Cash	12,705
	22,224

The subsidiary undertakings acquired during the year contributed £1,502,000 to the group's net operating cash flows, paid £1,308,000 in respect of net returns on investments and servicing of finance, paid £522,000 in respect of taxation and utilised £2,208,000 for capital expenditure.

7   *Sale of business*

	£'000
Net assets disposed of	
Fixed assets	775
Stocks	5,386
Debtors	474
	6,635
Loss on disposal	(1,227)
	5,408
Satisfied by	
Loan notes	1,200
Cash	4,208
	5,408

The business sold during the year contributed £200,000 to the group's net operating cash flows, paid £252,000 in respect of net returns on investments and servicing of finance, paid £145,000 in respect of taxation and utilised £209,000 for capital expenditure.

2.2   Cash flows that are **internal to the group** should be eliminated in the preparation of a consolidated cash flow statement. Where a subsidiary undertaking **joins or leaves** a group during a financial year the cash flows of the group should include the cash flows of the subsidiary undertaking concerned for the same period as that for which the group's P&L account includes the results of the subsidiary undertaking.

Acquisitions and disposals of subsidiary undertakings   5/97

2.3   A note to the cash flow statement should show a summary of the effects of acquisitions and disposals of subsidiary undertakings indicating how much of the **consideration comprised cash**. Material effects on amounts reported under each of the standard headings reflecting the cash flows of a subsidiary undertaking acquired or disposed of in the period should be disclosed, as far as practicable. This information could be given by dividing cash flows between continuing and discontinued operations and acquisitions.

Consolidation adjustments and minority interests

2.4   The group cash flow statement should only deal with flows of cash and cash equivalents external to the group, so all intra-group cash flows should be eliminated. **Dividends paid to minority interests** should be included under the heading 'returns on investments and servicing of finance' and disclosed separately.

2.5   EXAMPLE: MINORITY INTERESTS

The following are extracts of the consolidated results for Jarvis plc for the year ended 31 December 19X2.

CONSOLIDATED PROFIT AND LOSS ACCOUNT (EXTRACT)

	£'000
Group profit before tax	90
Taxation	(30)
Profit after tax	60
Minority interest	(15)
Retained profit	45

CONSOLIDATED BALANCE SHEET (EXTRACT)

	19X1	*19X2*
	£'000	£'000
Minority interest	300	306

Calculate the dividends paid to the minority interest during the year.

2.6 SOLUTION

The minority interest share of profit after tax represents retained profit plus dividends paid.

	£'000
Minority interest brought forward	300
Minority interest carried forward	306
	(6)
Profit and loss account	15
Dividend paid	9

Associated undertakings

2.7 Only the actual cash flows from sales or purchases between the group and the associate, and investments in and dividends from the entity should be included. Dividends should be included as a separate item between operating activities and **returns on investments and servicing of finance**. Any other cash flows between the investment its associates should be included under the appropriate cash flow heading for the activity giving rise to the cash flow. (Note that this is the treatment prescribed by FRS 9 *Associates and joint ventures*, covered in Chapter 17.)

2.8 EXAMPLE: ASSOCIATED COMPANY

The following are extracts of the consolidated results of Pripon plc for the year ended 31 December 19X2.

CONSOLIDATED PROFIT AND LOSS ACCOUNT (EXTRACT)

	£'000	£'000
Operating profit of group		150
Share of associated undertaking profit		60
		210
Tax: group	75	
share of associate	30	
		105
Profit after tax		105

CONSOLIDATED BALANCE SHEET (EXTRACTS)

	19X1	*19X2*
	£'000	£'000
Investment in associated undertaking	264	276

Calculate the dividend received from the associated company.

2.9 SOLUTION

The associated undertaking profit before tax represents retained profit plus dividend plus tax.

	£'000	£'000
Investment brought forward		264
Investment carried forward		276
		(12)
Profit before tax	60	
Tax	(30)	
		30
Dividend from associate		18

Finance lease transactions

2.10 When rentals under a finance lease are paid the **capital and interest elements are split out** and included under the 'financing' and 'servicing of finance' headings respectively.

> **Exam focus point**
> Various complications may arise in a consolidated cash flow statement in the exam, the most important of which are covered above. The December 1997 exam contained a particularly long, complicated consolidated cash flow statement. Question 2, given below, is comprehensive.

2.11 Section summary

The preparation of consolidated cash flow statements will, in many respects, be the same as those for single companies, with the following **additional complications.**

- Acquisitions and disposals of subsidiary undertaking
- Cancellation of intra-group transactions
- Minority interests
- Associated undertakings
- Finance leases
- Foreign currency (see Section 4)

Question 2

Topiary plc is a 40 year old company producing garden statues carved from marble. In 19V5 it acquired a 100% interest in a marble importing company, Hardstuff Ltd; in 19W9 it acquired a 40% interest in a competitor, Landscapes Ltd; and on 1 January 19X7 it acquired a 75% interest in Garden Furniture Designs. The draft consolidated accounts for the Topiary Group are as follows.

Part C: Interpretation of accounts

DRAFT CONSOLIDATED PROFIT AND LOSS ACCOUNT
FOR THE YEAR ENDED 31 DECEMBER 19X7

	£'000	£'000
Group operating profit		4,455
Share of operating profit in associates		1,485
Income from fixed asset investment		600
Interest payable (group)		(450)
Profit on ordinary activities before taxation		6,090
Tax on profit on ordinary activities		
Corporation tax	1,173	
Deferred taxation	312	
Tax attributable to income of associated undertakings	435	
Tax attributable to franked investment income	135	
		(2,055)
Profit on ordinary activities after taxation		4,035
Minority interests		(300)
Profit for the financial year		3,735
Dividends paid and proposed		(1,200)
Retained profit for the year		2,535

DRAFT CONSOLIDATED BALANCE SHEET
AS AT 31 DECEMBER

	19X6		19X7	
	£'000	£'000	£'000	£'000
Fixed assets				
Tangible assets				
Buildings at net book value		6,600		6,225
Machinery: cost	4,200		9,000	
aggregate depreciation	(3,300)		(3,600)	
net book value		900		5,400
		7,500		11,625
Investments in associated undertaking		3,000		3,300
Fixed asset investments		1,230		1,230
		11,730		16,155
Current assets				
Stocks		3,000		5,925
Trade debtors		3,825		5,550
Cash		5,460		13,545
		12,285		25,020
Creditors: amounts falling due within one year				
Trade creditors		840		1,500
Obligations under finance leases		600		720
Corporation tax		450		1,125
Dividends		801		1,161
Accrued interest and finance charges		90		120
		2,781		4,626
Net current assets				
Total assets less current liabilities		9,504		20,394
Creditors: amounts falling due after more than one year		21,234		36,549
Obligations under finance leases		510		2,130
Loans		1,500		4,380
Provisions for liabilities				
Deferred taxation		39		90
Net assets		19,185		29,949

	19X6		19X7	
	£'000	£'000	£'000	£'000
Capital and reserves				
Called up share capital in 25p shares		6,000		11,820
Share premium account		6,285		8,649
Profit and loss account		6,900		9,135
Total shareholders' equity		19,185		29,604
Minority interest		-		345
		19,185		29,949

Notes

1 There had been no acquisitions or disposals of buildings during the year.

Machinery costing £1.5m was sold for £1.5m resulting in a profit of £300,000. New machinery was acquired in 19X7 including additions of £2.55m acquired under finance leases.

2 *Information relating to the acquisition of Garden Furniture Designs*

	£'000
Machinery	495
Stocks	96
Trade debtors	84
Cash	336
Trade creditors	(204)
Corporation tax	(51)
	756
Minority interest	(189)
	567
Goodwill	300
	867
2,640,000 shares issued as part consideration	825
Balance of consideration paid in cash	42
	867

Goodwill has been fully amortised.

3 Loans were issued at a discount in 19X7 and the carrying amount of the loans at 31 December 19X7 included £120,000 representing the finance cost attributable to the discount and allocated in respect of the current reporting period.

Required

Prepare a consolidated cash flow statement for the Topiary Group for the year ended 31 December 19X7 as required by FRS 1 (revised) with supporting notes for the following.

(a) Reconciliation of operating profit to net cash flow from operating activities
(b) Analysis of cash flows netted in the cash flow statement
(c) Analysis of changes in net debt

Answer

(a) TOPIARY PLC
CONSOLIDATED CASH FLOW STATEMENT
FOR THE YEAR ENDED 31 DECEMBER 19X7

	Note	£'000	£'000
Cash flows from operating activities	1		1,116
Dividend received from associate (W2)	1		750
Returns on investments and servicing of finance	2		21
Taxation (W10)			(810)
Capital expenditure and financial investment	2		(1,755)
Acquisitions and disposals	2		294
Equity dividends paid (801 + 1,200 – 1,161)			(840)
Cash outflow before financing			(1,224)
Financing	2		
Issue of shares		7,359	
Increase in debt		1,950	
			9,309
Increase in cash in the period			8,085
Reconciliation of net cash flow to movement in net funds	3		
Increase in cash in the period			8,085
Cash inflow from loan issue			(2,760)
Capital element of finance lease instalments			810
Movement resulting from cash flows			6,135
Non-cash movements			
Accretion of finance costs			(120)
Additions to fixed assets under finance leases			(2,550)
Movement in net funds in period			3,465
Net funds at 1.1.X7			2,850
Net funds at 31.12.X7			6,315

NOTES TO THE CASH FLOW STATEMENT

1 *Reconciliation of operating profit to operating cash flows*

	£'000	£'000
Operating profit		4,455
Depreciation charges (W1)		975
Profit on sale of machinery		(300)
Increase in stocks (5,925 – 3,000 – 96)		(2,829)
Increase in debtors (5,500 – 3,825 – 84)		(1,641)
Increase in creditors (1,500 – 840 – 204)		456
Net cash inflow from operating activities		1,116

2 *Analysis of cash flows for headings netted in the cash flow statement*

	£'000	£'000
Returns on investments and servicing of finance		
Interest paid (W3)*	(300)	
Dividends from fixed asset investment (600 – 135)	465	
Dividends paid to minority interest (W4)	(144)	
		21
Capital expenditure and financial investment		
Purchase of tangible fixed assets (W5)	(3,255)	
Sale of tangible fixed assets	1,500	
		(1,755)
Acquisitions and disposals		
Purchase of subsidiary undertaking (W6)		(294)

	£'000	£'000
Financing		
Issue of ordinary share capital (W7)		7,359
Debt due beyond a year (W8)	2,760	
Capital element of finance lease rental payments (W9)	(810)	
		1,950
		9,309

* There is not sufficient information in the question to identify separately interest on finance leases.

3   *Analysis of changes in net funds*

	At 1 Jan 19X7	*Cash flow*	*Other changes*	*At 31 Dec 19X7*
	£'000	£'000	£'000	£'000
Cash at bank	5,460	8,085	-	13,545
Debt due > 1yr	(1,500)	(2,760)	(120)	(4,380)
Finance leases	(1,110)	810	(2,550)	(2,850)
	-	(1,950)		-
	2,850	6,135	(2,670)	6,315

Workings

1   *Depreciation charges*

	£'000	£'000
Freehold buildings (6,600 – 6,225)		375
Plant		
Closing balance	3,600	
Opening balance	3,300	
	300	
Depreciation on disposal	300	
		600
		975

2   *Dividends from associates*

	£'000	£'000
Opening balance		3,000
Share of profit	1,485	
Taxation	(435)	
		1,050
		4,050
Closing balance		3,300
		750

3   *Interest*

	£'000
Accrued interest b/f	90
P & L account	450
Discount	(120)
Less accrued interest c/f	(120)
	300

4   *Minority interests*

	£'000
Opening balance	-
Profit for year	300
On acquisition	189
	489
Closing balance	(345)
Cash outflow	144

Part C: Interpretation of accounts

5   *Purchase of tangible fixed assets: machinery*

	£'000	£'000
Cost at 31 December 19X7		9,000
Cost at 1 January 19X7		4,200
		4,800
Disposal		1,500
		6,300
On acquisition	495	
Leased	2,550	
		(3,045)
Cash outflow		3,255

6   *Purchase of subsidiary undertaking*

	£'000
Cash received on acquisition	336
Less cash consideration	(42)
Cash inflow	294

7   *Issue of ordinary share capital*

	£'000	£'000
Closing balance		
Shares	11,820	
Premium	8,649	
		20,469
Non-cash consideration		
Shares	660	
Premium	165	
		(825)
Opening balance		
Shares	6,000	
Premium	6,285	
		(12,285)
Cash inflow		7,359

8   *Issue of loan stock*

	£'000
Closing balance	4,380
Opening balance	1,500
	2,880
Finance cost	120
Cash inflow	2,760

9   *Capital payments under leases*

	£'000	£'000
Opening balances		
Current		600
Long-term		510
		1,110
New lease commitment		2,550
Closing balances		
Current	720	
Long-term	2,130	
		(2,850)
Cash outflow		810

10   *Taxation*

	£'000	£'000
Opening balance		
Corporation tax	450	
Deferred tax	39	
		489
Profit and loss account transfer (1,173 + 312)		1,485
Closing balances		
Corporation tax	1,125	
ACT	261	
Deferred tax	90	
		(1,215)
		759
On acquisition		51
Cash outflow		810

3   FOREIGN EXCHANGE AND CASH FLOW STATEMENTS

Individual companies

3.1   Receipts and payments should be translated into the reporting currency at the **rate ruling** at the date on which the receipt or payment is made.

Exchange differences **do not give rise to cash flows** and therefore they would not be reflected in the cash flow statement.

Group companies

3.2   The main problems relating to foreign exchange differences are when dealing with the cash flows of an overseas subsidiary. FRS 1 requires that all cash flows relating to an overseas subsidiary be translated into sterling using the **same exchange rate** as is used for the translation of the subsidiary's P&L account. Where the net investment method has been used to consolidate the subsidiary's results (as will be the case most of the time) then the subsidiary's cash flows will be translated using either the average or the closing rate.

3.3   If the **closing rate** is used, then the group cash flow statement can be prepared by using only the opening and closing group balance sheets. If the **average rate** is used, then merely using the balance sheets would not be appropriate as the resulting cash flow statement would not comply with FRS 1, some items being translated at the closing rate. The practical answer to this problem is to use the following method (which would be time consuming in practice).

Step 1   Produce a cash flow statement for each subsidiary.

Step 2   Translate each into sterling using the average rate.

Step 3   Consolidate them into the group cash flow statement (after eliminating inter-company items).

3.4   The other main point to note is that the exchange differences on translation must be **analysed into their constituent parts**, namely fixed assets, debtors, cash, creditors and minority interests and so forth. You may be asked to perform this exercise in the examination although, in the example shown below, the split is given.

BPP
PUBLISHING

Hedging transactions

3.5 Cash flows that result from a transaction undertaken to hedge another should be reported under the **same standard heading** as the transaction which is the subject of that hedge. This does *not* apply to hedging investments in foreign subsidiaries.

3.6 EXAMPLE: FOREIGN CURRENCY TRANSLATION

The draft balance sheets and P&L account of Guinevere plc are as follows.

CONSOLIDATED BALANCE SHEETS
AS AT 31 DECEMBER

	19X2 £'000	19X1 £'000
Fixed assets		
Tangible assets	32,907	22,926
Investments	6,300	6,300
	39,207	29,226
Current assets		
Stock	21,735	18,300
Debtors	19,230	21,633
Cash in bank and in hand	2,859	495
	43,824	40,428
Creditors: amounts falling due within one year		
Trade creditors	5,760	5,070
Dividend payable by Guinevere plc	801	720
Dividend payable to minority	225	180
Corporation tax	8,232	8,454
	15,018	14,424
Net current assets	28,806	26,004
Creditors: amounts falling due after more than one year		
Loans	7,557	5,991
Minority interest	3,006	4,230
	57,450	45,009

	19X2 £'000	19X1 £'000
Capital and reserves		
Called up share capital	15,000	15,000
Share premium	9,000	9,000
Profit and loss account	33,450	21,009
	57,450	45,009

There were no fixed asset disposals during the year. The depreciation charge for the year was £5,931,000. There were no fixed asset creditors at either year end.

Debtors as at 31 December 19X2 include called up share capital not paid of £3,805,000 (19X1: £8,238,000).

DRAFT CONSOLIDATED PROFIT AND LOSS ACCOUNT
FOR THE YEAR ENDED 31 DECEMBER 19X2

	£'000
Group operating profit	20,865
Income from fixed asset investments	192
Interest payable	522
Group profit before tax	20,535
Tax: corporation tax	8,490
tax credits on dividends	48
Group profit after tax	11,997
Minority interest	678
Profit attributable to members of Guinevere plc	11,319
Dividends	1,800
Retained profit	9,519
Reserves as at 1 January 19X1	21,009
Exchange gain on translation (note 1)	4,068
Exchange loss on loan	(1,146)
Reserves as at 31 December 19X2	33,450

Note: exchange gain

The exchange gain on translation is made up as follows.

	£'000
Fixed assets	3,684
Stocks	1,179
Debtors	633
Cash	117
Creditors	(189)
Minority interest	(1,356)
	4,068

Required

Prepare the group cash flow statement for Guinevere plc for the year ended 31 December 19X2, in accordance with FRS 1 (revised).

3.7   SOLUTION

CASH FLOW STATEMENT FOR THE YEAR ENDED 31 DECEMBER 19X2

	Note	£'000	£'000
Operating activities	1		23,544
Returns on investments and servicing of finance			
Interest paid		(522)	
Dividends received		144	
Dividends paid to minority interest			
(5,991 + 180 + 678 + 1,356 – 7,557 – 225)		(423)	
Taxation			
Corporation tax paid (8,454 + 8,490 – 8,232)			(8,712)
Capital expenditure			
Payments to acquire tangible fixed assets			
(5,931 + 32,907 – 22,926 – 3,684)			(12,228)
Equity dividends paid (720 + 1,800 – 801)			(1,719)
Financing			
Proceeds of share issue		4,533	
Repayment of loans		(2,370)	
			2,163
Increase in cash			2,247

Reconciliation of net cash flows to movements in net debt (note 2)

	£'000
Increase in cash in the period	2,247
Cash inflow from increase in debt	(420)
Change in net debt resulting from cash flows	1,827
Translation difference	(1,029)
Movement in net debt in period	798
Net debt at 1.1.X2	(5,496)
Net debt at 31.12.X2	(4,698)

NOTES TO THE CASH FLOW STATEMENT

1 *Reconciliation of operating profit to net cash inflow from operating activities*

	£'000
Operating profit	20,865
Depreciation	5,931
Increase in stocks (21,735 – 18,300 – 1,179)	(2,256)
Increase in debtors (19,230 – 3,705 – 21,633 + 8,238 – 633)	(1,497)
Increase in creditors (5,760 – 5,070 – 189)	501
	23,544

2 *Analysis of net debt*

	At 1.1.X2 £'000	Cash flows £'000	Exchange movement £'000	At 31.12.X2 £'000
Cash in hand	495	2,247	117	2,859
Debt due > 1 year	(5,991)	(420)	(1,146)	(7,557)
Net debt	(5,496)	1,827	(1,029)	(4,698)

An analysis of the cash flow statement above shows that a major inflow of cash relates to the proceeds of a share issue even though the called up share capital has not altered, because it was called up but not paid at the beginning of the year and therefore included in debtors.

4 ANALYSIS OF CASH FLOW STATEMENTS

4.1 FRS 1 *Cash flow statements* was introduced on the basis that it would provide better, more comprehensive and more useful information than its predecessor standard. So **what kind of information does the cash flow statement,** along with its notes, **provide?**

4.2 Some of the main areas where FRS 1 should provide information not found elsewhere in the accounts are as follows.

(a) The **relationships between profit and cash** can be seen clearly and analysed accordingly.

(b) **Management of liquid resources** is shown separately, giving a better picture of the liquidity of the company.

(c) A full breakdown is given of the value of **assets and liabilities in purchased subsidiaries,** highlighting the value of goodwill.

(d) **Financing inflows and outflows must be shown,** rather than simply passed through reserves.

4.3 One of the most important things to realise at this point is that, as the ASB is always keen to emphasise, it is wrong to try to assess the health or predict the death of a reporting entity solely on the basis of a single indicator. When analysing cash flow data, the **comparison** should not just be **between cash flows and profit,** but also **between cash flows over a period of time** (say three to five years).

4.4 Cash is not synonymous with profit on an annual basis, but you should also remember that the 'behaviour' of profit and cash flows will be very different. Profit is smoothed out through accruals, prepayments, provisions and other accounting conventions. This does not apply to cash, so the **cash flow figures are likely to be 'lumpy' in comparison.** You must distinguish between this 'lumpiness' and the trends which will appear over time.

4.5 The **relationship between profit and cash flows** will **vary constantly.** Note that healthy companies do not always have reported profits exceeding operating cash flows. Similarly, unhealthy companies can have operating cash flows well in excess of reported profit. The value of comparing them is in determining the extent to which earned profits are being converted into the necessary cash flows.

4.6 Profit is not as important as the extent to which a company can convert its profits into cash on a continuing basis. **This process should be judged over a period longer than one year.** The cash flows should be compared with profits over the same periods to decide how successfully the reporting entity has converted earnings into cash.

4.7 Cash flow figures should also be considered in terms of their **specific relationships** with each other over time. A form of 'cash flow gearing' can be determined by comparing operating cash flows and financing flows, particularly borrowing, to establish the extent of dependence of the reporting entity on external funding.

4.8 Other relationships can be examined.

 (a) Operating cash flows and investment flows can be related to match cash recovery from investment to investment.

 (b) Investment can be compared to distribution to indicate the proportion of total cash outflow designated specifically to investor return and reinstatement.

 (c) A comparison of tax outflow to operating cash flow minus investment flow will establish a 'cash basis tax rate'.

4.9 The 'ratios' mentioned above can be monitored inter- and intra-firm and the analyses can be undertaken in monetary, general price-level adjusted, or percentage terms.

5 OTHER STATEMENTS

5.1 A number of other reports may be produced by a company, usually internally, which often provide valuable information. Some of these reports are derived from normal accounting information, rearranged or simplified for a specific purpose. They are still useful as they give a different viewpoint on the same information.

Value added statements

5.2 In 1975 an ASC discussion paper *The Corporate Report* suggested the inclusion of a 'statement of value added' with the conventional annual report. Some interest was shown, but this has died off and the ASB has shown no interest in the statement.

5.3 Suppose for example that a company buys raw materials and components which cost £2,000. By committing resources (labour time, machine time, capital funds) to production and sales, the raw materials and components are transformed into finished goods which are sold for £11,000. The business entity, as a unit or 'team' will have created extra wealth of £11,000 –

£2,000 = £9,000. In other words, £9,000 will have been added to the value of bought-in materials and components.

> ## KEY TERM
>
> 'Value added' or 'added value' is the **extra 'wealth' created** by a business entity.

5.4 Another way of expressing the same idea is that the £2,000 of bought-in materials and components represent the value of the output of other business entities, the supplier firms. The company itself creates output which has a value of £11,000. As a result of its own efforts, it has added £9,000 to value.

5.5 The business entity is a 'team' consisting of:

(a) employees;
(b) fixed assets and machinery;
(c) providers of capital (shareholders and long-term creditors).

5.6 Value added is the wealth created by the 'team' and it should be used to reward the members of the 'team'. However, some of the value added may have to be paid out in taxation, and the company might also wish to reinvest some money. Value added can therefore be thought of as a 'cake', with slices being cut for:

- Employees
- Depreciation (which is a form of reinvestment)
- Dividends
- Interest payments
- Taxation
- Retained profits

5.7 A value added statement is **particularly informative for employees**, because it presents accounting data in a relatively simple manner which is more easily understood than a profit and loss account. Some companies have actually negotiated wage bonus schemes for productivity on the basis of improvements in added value.

5.8 *The Corporate Report* did not give a prescriptive format for value added statements, but included a simple illustrative example of a statement for a manufacturing company. Such a statement might be shown as follows.

	Current year			*Previous year*		
	£'000	£'000	%	£'000	£'000	%
Turnover		1,120			1,006	
Bought-in materials and services		784			710	
Value added		336			296	

	Current year			Previous year		
	£'000	£'000	%	£'000	£'000	%
Applied the following way:						
(a) To pay employees (wages, pensions and fringe benefits)		232	69		202	68
(b) To pay providers of capital:						
(i) Interest on loans	23		7	17		6
(ii) Dividends to shareholders	23		7	22		7
		46			39	
(c) To pay government:						
Corporation tax payable		8	2		12	4
(d) To provide for maintenance and expansion of assets:						
(i) Depreciation	24		7	20		7
(ii) Retained profits	26		8	23		8
		50			43	
Value added		336	100%		296	100%

Notes

1   The cost of bought-in materials and services includes raw materials, energy costs, payments of fees (including audit fees). They are payments to individuals or business entities, who are not a part of the business entity itself. (Exceptions are the government and payments for capital assets).

Strictly, these costs ought to consist only of those bought-in materials and services which are included in the cost of sales, so that increases or decreases in stock levels should be allowed for.

2   Payments to employees will probably include gross pay, pension contributions and related costs (for example employer's national insurance contributions) and fringe benefits.

3   Providers of capital might also include payments on leases.

4   Payments to the government might include local rates as well as corporation tax; otherwise rates would be shown as a bought-in service. VAT, if excluded from the turnover figure, would not be shown. Similarly, Customs and Excise duties might be included; alternatively, they would be deducted in arriving at the figure for turnover.

Employment reports

5.9   Employees' information needs are not given high priority in the UK. The CA 1985 requires the following disclosures.

(a)   The average number of employees in the UK and their aggregate remuneration during the year should be shown.

(b)   An analysis should be given of aggregate employee remuneration between:

   (i)   wages and salaries paid to employees;
   (ii)   social security costs incurred by the company on the employees' behalf; and
   (iii)   other pension costs incurred by the company on the employees' behalf.

(c)   The average number of employees within each category of employees must be shown, the categories being selected by the directors in the light of the company's business.

5.10 Finally, a requirement relating to companies employing more than 250 people was introduced by the Employment Act 1982. This calls for disclosure in the directors' report of

any measures taken to involve employees in the company's performance or to provide them with means of information and consultation.

5.11 *The Corporate Report* recommended that an **employment report** be provided to supplement the statutory information described above and it should contain the following information:

(a) numbers employed (average for the year, and actual figures on the first and last days of the year);

(b) broad reasons for changes in the numbers employed;

(c) the age distribution and sex of employees;

(d) the functions of employees;

(e) the geographical location of major employment centres;

(f) major plant and site closures, disposals and acquisitions during the year;

(g) the hours scheduled and worked by different groups of employees during the year;

(h) employment costs, including fringe benefits;

(i) the costs and benefits of pension schemes;

(j) the costs and time spent on training;

(k) the names of unions recognised by the business entity for the purpose of collective bargaining, and membership figures where available;

(l) information concerning health and safety at work;

(m) selected ratios relating to employment (such as average sales per employee, employment costs as a percentage of sales, labour turnover ratio and so on).

Employee reports

5.12 Many large companies publish employee reports, usually annually. Sometimes, these take the form of **simplified financial statements** but often considerable use is made of graphs, pie charts, photographs and so on to make the report attractive. The financial information included will usually be **much less comprehensive** than that in the statutory **financial statements**, so that employees are given the important figures without being swamped by unnecessary detail. Although this can lead to oversimplification, there is often extra information in employee reports, such as segmental results analysed by product line or division.

5.13 **Employees**, it would seem, generally **appreciate receiving this financial information** and may consequently feel more involved with the employing company, but companies need to make sure the report is not just a cheap 'PR' exercise.

5.14 Other reports suggested by *The Corporate Report*, but which have failed to catch on, included:

(a) Money exchanges with government
(b) Transactions in foreign currency
(c) Statement of future prospects
(d) Statement of corporate objectives

5.15 Most recently, large companies are now required to produce an **operating and financial review** (OFR): see Chapter 26.

6 YEAR 2000 AND THE EURO

Year 2000: accounting

6.1 In March 1998 the ASB issued UITF Abstract 20 *Year 2000 issues: accounting and disclosures.* The Abstract deals with accounting and disclosure implications of the year 2000 problem, which has been receiving increasing attention as the time shortens before the start of the new millennium. As is now becoming well recognised, the potential impact may be pervasive throughout an entity, extending beyond software to many other aspects, such as chips embedded in control equipment. The high level of dependence by businesses, both large and small, on sophisticated computer systems and the interdependence of such systems among businesses, their suppliers and their customers, are such that even seemingly minor failures in addressing the issue may result in significant consequences for any particular entity in its ability to run its business.

6.2 The **Abstract requires that costs incurred in rendering existing software year 2000 compliant should be written off to the P&L account** except in those cases where:

(a) an entity already has an accounting policy for capitalising software costs; and

(b) to the extent that the expenditure clearly represents an enhancement of an asset beyond that originally assessed, rather than merely maintaining its service potential.

6.3 Where relevant costs qualify as an **exceptional** item, they should be *disclosed* as such.

6.4 Where relevant commitments at the balance sheet date qualify as disclosable financial commitments under company law, they should be disclosed.

6.5 The following should also be disclosed.

(a) The **risks and uncertainties** associated with the year 2000 problem.

(b) The entity's general plans to address year 2000 issues.

(c) **Whether the total estimated costs** of these plans, including amounts to be spent in future periods, have been **quantified** and, where applicable, an indication of the total costs likely to be incurred.

6.6 The Abstract is effective for accounting periods ending on or after 23 March 1998.

Year 2000: auditing

6.7 The ICAEW's Audit Faculty has issued guidance for auditors who are asked for a certificate stating that their clients are year 2000 compliant and that their accounts will not be qualified.

6.8 It is concerned that the approach appears to misunderstand the auditors' role and responsibilities. They are not responsible for ensuring that their clients are prepared for the date change. The Faculty therefore strongly advises auditors not to issue reports or certificates giving assurance on year 2000 compliance, whether to their audit client companies or third parties.

6.9 It also stresses that no auditor is capable of giving comment in advance on whether future accounts will be unqualified.

The euro

6.10 In March 1998 the ASB also issued UITF Abstract 21 *Accounting issues arising from the proposed introduction of the euro*.

6.11 Although the overall impact of the proposed introduction of the euro will probably be less stark, at least in the short term, than for year 2000 compliance, it will affect many business entities, even though they may not be located in a participating Member State, by requiring operations and information systems to be adapted. The UITF considered three issues.

(a) The treatment of costs incurred in connection with the introduction of the euro, together with the appropriate disclosure.

(b) The impact on cumulative foreign exchange differences that become permanent.

(c) The impact on anticipatory hedging instruments existing at the date of introduction of the euro in respect of future transactions.

6.12 The issues arising in respect of the treatment of costs incurred in connection with the introduction of the euro are **very similar to those arising in respect of year 2000 costs** and consequently **Abstract 21 requires treatment similar to that outlined above**. Where the potential impact is likely to be significant to the entity the Abstract indicates that **information on likely total costs and some discussion of the impact should be given**.

6.13 For cumulative foreign exchange differences, the Abstract follows the principle set out in FRS 3 that the same gains and losses should not be recognised twice. Consequently, the exchange differences should remain in reserves and not be recycled through the profit and loss account.

6.14 Where gains and losses on financial instruments used as anticipatory hedges are at present deferred and matched with the related income or expense in a future period, the Abstract states that the introduction of the euro should not alter this deferral and matching treatment.

Chapter roundup

- You must be able to produce a **single company cash flow statement**. You should also know the scope, formats and definitions given in FRS 1 (revised). Your earlier study material may only cover the old version of the standard.

- **Consolidated cash flows** should not present a great problem if you understand how to deal with **acquisitions and disposals of subsidiaries**, minority interests and dividends.

- A **foreign exchange difference** in a group cash flow statement must be **analysed** into its constituent parts.

- **Other statements** which might be included in financial reports are even less likely to be encountered in practice but are of interest in helping to focus the thoughts of preparers of accounts on what will be of most use to readers of accounts.

Quick quiz

1   Why might a historical cost profit figure be misleading? (see para 1.1)

2   State the advantages of cash flow accounting (1.2)

3   Which subsidiary undertakings are excluded from the requirement to produce cash flow statements under FRS 1 (revised)? (2.3(a))

4   List the standard headings of a cash flow statement under the revised FRS 1 (2.5)

5   Define cash (per FRS 1) (2.10(b))

6   Distinguish between the direct and indirect methods. (2.41, 2.42)

7   How should an acquisition or disposal of a subsidiary be shown in the cash flow statement? (3.3)

8   How should an associated undertaking be reported in the cash flow statement? (3.7)

9   State the FRS 1 requirements for translation of cash flows relating to an overseas subsidiary. (4.2, 4.5)

10 What is meant by value added? (5.3)

11 Distinguish between an employment report and an employee report. (5.11, 5.12)

Question to try	Level	Marks	Time
26	Exam	20	36 mins

Chapter 25

EARNINGS PER SHARE

Chapter topic	Syllabus reference	Ability required
1 What is earnings per share?	9(c)	Application
2 Basic EPS	9(c)	Application
3 'Headline' EPS	9(c)	Application
4 Diluted EPS	9(c)	Application
5 Disclosure	9(c)	Application

Introduction

We have mentioned EPS in various parts of this Study Text, particularly in relation to FRS 3 *Reporting financial performance*. EPS is also important in the context of the price/earnings ratio (and performance in general) which we will look at in the next chapter.

EPS is an important indicator of a company's performance. It is also the subject of a very recent standard: FRS 14.

1 WHAT IS EARNINGS PER SHARE?

1.1 Earnings per share (EPS) is widely used by investors as a **measure of a company's performance** and is of particular importance in:

(a) comparing the results of a company over a period of time;

(b) comparing the performance of one company's equity shares against the performance of another company's equity, and also against the returns obtainable from loan stock and other forms of investment.

The purpose of any earnings yardstick is to achieve as far as possible clarity of meaning, comparability between one company and another, one year and another, and attributablity of profits to the equity shares. FRS 14 *Earnings per share* goes some way to ensuring that all these aims are achieved.

1.2 FRS 14 supersedes **SSAP 3** *Earnings per share*. It applies to all accounting periods ending on or after **23 December 1998.** The standard applies to all companies who have publicly traded shares or who are in the process of issuing shares publicly. However, where companies present EPS on a voluntary basis, FRS 14 **must** be adopted.

1.3 The ASB stated that earnings per share (EPS) was not a priority, but the development of new **international standards** on the area led to efforts to adopt a similar approach.

1.4 The following key terms may be useful for the remainder of this chapter.

KEY TERMS

- **Equity instrument**: any contract that evidences a residual interest in the assets of an entity after deducting all of its liabilities.

- **Fair value**: the amount for which an asset could be exchanged, or a liability settled, between knowledgeable, willing parties in an arm's length transaction.

- **Financial instrument**: any contract that gives rise to both a financial asset of one entity and a financial liability or equity instrument of another entity.

- **Ordinary shares**: any equity instrument that is subordinate to all other classes of equity instruments.

- **Potential ordinary share**: a financial instrument or other contract that may entitle its holder to ordinary shares.

- **Warrants or options**: financial instruments that give the holder the right to purchase ordinary shares. *(FRS 14)*

2   BASIC EPS

2.1   The standard has been developed with the user of the accounts in mind. EPS is a popular measure of profitability. The ASB have actively discouraged reliance on EPS, preferring a more rounded approach. The aim of the standard is to provide a consistent approach to EPS which will allow:

(a)   comparisons between entities' results;
(b)   and comparison of an entity's results over the years.

KEY TERM

EPS is profit in pence attributable to each equity share.

The basic EPS calculation is:

$$\frac{\text{Earnings}}{\text{Issued ordinary shares}}$$

KEY TERMS

Earnings are the net profits after tax, interest, minority earnings and dividends on other classes of shares (also after extraordinary items, but in practice, these are rare).

Issued ordinary shares are all ordinary shares in circulation during the year. The weighted average approach is taken to calculate this amount.

Changes to ordinary share numbers

Share issues at market value

2.2   The following example will show how this issue is treated. Note that:

(a) the weighted average number for the period is used;

(b) there is no retrospective effect.

2.3 EXAMPLE: WEIGHTED AVERAGE NUMBER OF SHARES

Consider the following issues and buy-backs of shares. What is the weighted average number of shares?

	Issued shares	Shares bought back	Balance
1 January 19X9	10,000	-	10,000
31 March 19X9 Issue of new shares for cash	2,000	-	12,000
1 July 19X9 Purchase of shares for cash	-	4,000	8,000
31 December 19X9 Year end balance	12,000	4,000	8,000

2.4 SOLUTION

Weighted average

$(10,000 \times 3/12) + (12,000 \times 3/12) + (8,000 \times 6/12) = 9,500$

or

$10,000 + (2,000 \times 9/12) - (4,000 \times 6/12) = 9,500$

2.5 There are a number of events which will alter the number of ordinary shares issued by a company. These include:

- Bonus issues
- Bonus elements (ie rights issues)
- Share splits
- Share consolidation

2.6 These events must be reflected in the EPS calculations. The basic EPS should reflect issues of ordinary shares from the date consideration is receivable. An event should be included in the diluted EPS calculation even if it occurs after the balance sheet date. All events must be allowed for up to the date of approval of the accounts.

Bonus issues

2.7 A bonus issue involves an increase in the issued shares without a corresponding increase in capital. The adjustment for bonus issues should be made back to the earliest possible period. This means that

(a) The issue is included for the full year.

(b) The issue applies to the prior year.

2.8 The following example shows how a bonus issue should be treated.

2.9 EXAMPLE: BONUS ISSUE

	19X8	19X9
Net profit 31 December	£1,000	£1,500
Ordinary shares until 30 June 19X9	500	

Bonus issue 1 July 19X9: one share for every two ordinary shares held at 30 June 19X9

2.10 SOLUTION

Bonus issue $\qquad$ $500 \times 1/2 = 250$

EPS for 19X9 $\qquad$ $\dfrac{£1,500}{(500 + 250)} = 200\text{p}$

Adjusted EPS for 19X8 $\qquad$ $\dfrac{£1,000}{(500 + 250)} = 133.3\text{p}$

Note that, as the bonus issue involved no consideration, it is treated as though it had occurred at the **earliest period reported**.

Rights issues

2.11 A rights issue usually involves shares issued for an exercise price, that is, less than the fair value of the currently issued shares. The current year's ordinary shares are multiplied by an adjustment factor:

$$\frac{\text{Fair value of current shares}}{\text{Theoretical ex - rights value per share}}$$

2.12 The following example shows how a rights issue should be calculated. Note that fair value is the average price of the ordinary shares during the period.

2.13 EXAMPLE: RIGHTS ISSUE

	19X7	19X8	19X9
	£	£	£
Net profit as at 31 December	6,000	7,600	9,000
Shares before the rights issue	100,000		

The rights issue is to be one share for every five currently held (giving 20,000 new shares). Exercise price £1.00. The last date to exercise rights is 1 April 19X8.

The fair value of an ordinary share before the issue is £2.20.

2.14 SOLUTION

Theoretical ex-rights value per share is

$$\frac{\text{Fair value of current shares} + \text{Amount received from exercise of rights}}{\text{Number of current shares} + \text{Number of shares issued}}$$

$$\frac{(£2.20 \times 100,000 \text{ shares}) + (£1.00 \times 20,000)}{100,000 \text{ shares} + 20,000 \text{ shares}}$$

Theoretical ex-rights value per share = £2

Adjustment factor

$$\frac{\text{Fair value of current shares}}{\text{Theoretical ex - rights value per share}} = \frac{£2.20}{£2.00} = 1.1$$

Earnings per share

	19X7	*19X8*	*19X9*
19X7 EPS as originally stated: £6,000/100,000 shares	6p		
19X7 EPS restated for rights issue: £6,000/(100,000 shares × 1.1)	5.5p		
19X8 EPS allowing for rights issue: $\dfrac{7,600}{(100,000 \times 1.1 \times 3/12) + (120,000 \times 9/12)}$		6.5p	
19X9 EPS 9,000/120,000			7.5p

Note that the adjustment factor is used on the original number of shares. Once the rights issue has taken place, the new number of shares (in this case 120,000) is included. For 19X8 the weighted average principle is applied.

Contingently issuable shares

2.15 Contingently issuable shares are issued after certain conditions have been fulfilled. They are not included in the basic EPS calculation until all the criteria have been met fully.

Part paid shares

2.16 If shares are part paid, then only the element which has been paid up is included in the calculation.

Alternative EPS

2.17 It should be noted that the adjustments covered so far affect the number of shares in the EPS calculation. This figure is the **denominator.**

> **KEY TERM**
>
> The **denominator** is the number of shares which are deemed to be entitled to the earnings of the entity.

2.18 The standard's emphasis is strongly upon the weighted average number of ordinary shares as opposed to the earnings figure. Many companies provide alternative EPS figures. The standard is very clear on this.

(a) The basic EPS and the diluted EPS must have the same prominence as any other EPS figure disclosed.

(b) The weighted average ordinary shares may only be calculated on the basis prescribed by the standard.

(c) The reason for the alternative calculation should be disclosed.

(d) The alternative calculation must be calculated on a consistent basis, year on year.

2.19 Alternative EPS calculations will therefore only have an alternative earnings figure; the **numerator.**

KEY TERM

The **numerator** is the earnings figure used in the EPS calculation.

2.20   If this amount is different from the reported net profit of the entity then a reconciliation must be provided to show how the numerator has been derived.

2.21   The EPS calculation in simple terms is therefore:

$$\frac{\text{Numerator}}{\text{Denominator}}$$

2.22   A favoured alternative EPS is the **headline EPS.**

3   'HEADLINE' EPS

3.1   The ASB effectively destroyed the analysts' favourite EPS figure with the publication of FRS 3 and the subsequent publication of FRS 14, making clear that it did not believe anyone should rely on a single earnings figure. FRS 3 did allow for an EPS, but the figure was calculated after every conceivable expense, including extraordinary items if companies are able to identify any in future. The publication of FRS 3 drew loud protests from some investment houses, which felt that the new EPS figure would prove **volatile and confusing** to users. This is the EPS taken up by FRS 14.

3.2   The Institute of Investment Management and Research (IIMR) set up a sub-committee to investigate whether a definition for some kind of maintainable earnings could be developed. The sub-committee concluded that a standard measure for maintainable earnings, which could be used as a basis for forecasts, was not feasible, as too much **conjecture and subjectivity** are involved. This view falls in line with the ASB's.

3.3   Instead, the IIMR defines a **'headline' figure for earnings** which, it acknowledges, 'is inferior to maintainable earnings as a basis for forecasts', but is nevertheless robust and factual. 'The number is justified by its practical usefulness, even if it cannot encapsulate the company's performance in itself.'

3.4   The headline earnings figure **includes** all the trading profits and losses for the year, including interest, and profits and losses arising from operations discontinued or acquired at any point during the year. **Excluded** from the figure are profits or losses from the sale or termination of a discontinued operation, from the sale of fixed assets or businesses or from any permanent diminution in their value or write-off (except for assets acquired for resale). Abnormal trading items (any defined by FRS 3 as extraordinary or exceptional), says the IIMR, should be included in the figure but prominently displayed in a note if they are significant.

3.5   When the IIMR's original ED was published, the *Financial Times* announced that it would use the method to calculate **price/earnings ratios**, and Extel also announced that it would use the figure. The statement was specifically not directed at companies, but many are expected to take up the definition. A large number of listed companies already disclose an EPS figure in addition to the one required by FRS 3 (and 14).

3.6 As with all EPS figures which are offered as an alternative to the FRS 3 and 14 figure, a **reconciliation** of the two EPS figures must be shown. Also, the alternative method must be applied consistently from year to year. No companies are *required* to produce the IIMR figure.

Example of 'headline' EPS

3.7 An **example** of the reconciliation between EPS as calculated under FRS 3 and 14 and 'headline' EPS might be as follows.

	19X6 pence	*19X5* pence
EPS as required by FRS 14	63.9	58.6
Exceptional items		
Classification of restructuring costs	-	6.3
Sale of property adjustments	13.8	2.6
'Headline' EPS	77.7	67.5

4 DILUTED EPS 5/99

Exam focus point

You should pay particular attention to this area as it may cause problems in the exam.

4.1 At the end of an accounting period a company may have securities which do not have a claim to equity earnings, but they may do **in the future**. These include:

(a) **Separate classes of equity share** not yet entitled to a share of equity earnings, but becoming so at a future date

(b) **Convertible loan stock** or **convertible preference shares** which enable their holders to exchange their securities at a later date for ordinary shares at a predetermined rate

(c) **Options** or **warrants**

4.2 These securities have the potential effect of increasing the number of equity shares ranking for dividend and so diluting or 'watering down' the EPS. These securities may be **dilutive potential ordinary shares.**

KEY TERM

A **dilutive** potential ordinary share is one which decreases the share of net profit, or increases the loss shared.

4.3 The diluted EPS gives users of the accounts a view on the potential ordinary shares of the entity. There is the potential to forecast the future EPS from the amounts given. Again, the ASB is careful to point out that a number of measures should be used in order to assess the returns from an entity, stating that no one measure is accurate enough to rely on.

Pro forma calculations

4.4 The following are the simple pro forma calculations for the three main sets of securities.

(a) **Shares not yet ranking for dividend**

    (i) *Earnings*

	£
Earnings	X

    (ii) *Number of shares*

	No
Basic weighted average	X
Add shares that will rank in future periods	X
Diluted number	X

(b) **Convertible loan stock or preference shares**

    (i) *Earnings*

	£
Earnings	X
Add back loan stock interest net of CT (or preference dividends) 'saved'	X
	X

    (ii) *Number of shares*

	No
Basic weighted average	X
Add additional shares on conversion (using terms giving maximum dilution available after the year end)	X
Diluted number	X

(c) **Options or warrants**

    (i) *Earnings*

	£
Earnings	X

    (ii) *Number of shares*

	No
Basic weighted average	X
Add additional shares issued at nil consideration	X
Diluted number	X

Share options

4.5 A share option allows the purchase of shares at a favourable amount which is less than the fair value of existing shares. The calculation of diluted EPS includes those shares deemed as issued for no consideration. For this purpose, the following calculation is used.

$$\frac{\text{Shares under option X exercise price}}{\text{Fair value of ordinary shares}}$$

4.6 This gives the number of shares that are to be excluded from the EPS calculation. This will become more clear in the following example

4.7 EXAMPLE: EFFECTS OF SHARE OPTIONS ON DILUTED EARNINGS PER SHARE

Net profit for 19X9	£1,000,000
Weighted average number of ordinary shares for 19X9	10 million
Average fair value of one ordinary share	£2.50
Weighted average number of shares under option during 19X9	3 million
Exercise price for shares under option in 19X9	£2.00

4.8 SOLUTION

	Shares	*Net profit*	*EPS*
Net profit for 19X9		£1,000,000	
Weighted average shares for 19X9	10m		
Basic EPS			10p
Number of shares on option			
Number of shares that would have been issued at fair value: (3m × £2)/£2.50	(2.4m)		
Diluted EPS	10.6m	£1,000,000	9.4p

Note that the net profit has not been increased. This is because the calculation only includes shares deemed to be issued for no consideration.

Employee share option schemes

4.9 Employee share option schemes are becoming increasingly popular as an incentive scheme in organisations. Many schemes relate to performance criteria which mean that they are contingent on certain conditions being met. The section on contingently issuable shares further on in this chapter explains how these schemes should be treated when calculating diluted EPS.

4.10 Certain schemes do not have performance measures. As with the share option approach, only those shares deemed as issued for no consideration are included. UITF 17 also affects the calculation as the cost of the scheme is written off to the profit and loss account over its life and these costs are effectively included in the option proceeds. The following example shows how these schemes should be treated.

4.11 EXAMPLE: SHARE OPTION SCHEME (NOT PERFORMANCE RELATED)

A company runs a share option scheme based on the employee's period of service with the company.

As at 31 December 19X7 the provisions of the scheme were:

Date of grant	1 January 19X7
Market price at grant date	£2.00
Exercise price of option	£1.25
Date of vesting	31 December 19X9
Number of shares under option	3 million

Under UITF 17, 25p per option (£2.00 – £1.25/3 years) is charged to the profit and loss in each of the three years 19X7-19X9.

Net profit for the year 19X7	£1,000,000
Weighted average number of ordinary shares	10 million
Average fair value of an ordinary share	£2.50
Assumed proceeds from each option	£1.75 (Exercise price of £1.25 plus the cost relating to future service not recognised of two years at 25p:50p). The following year would be £1.50 (ie £1.25 plus 25p).

4.12 SOLUTION

	Shares	Net profit	EPS
Net profit for 19X7		£1,000,000	
Weighted average shares for 19X7	10m		
Basic EPS			10p
Number of shares on option	3m		
Number of shares that would have been issued			
at fair value: (3m × £1.75)/£2.50	(2.1m)		
Diluted EPS	10.9m	£1,000,000	9.2p

Contingently issuable shares

4.13 These are shares issued after certain criteria have been met. For the purposes of the diluted EPS calculation these shares are included in full.

4.14 The following example gives two contingent events arising after the acquisition of a business. Most contingent events will be based on target sales or profit. The example includes the opening of new branches. This is also a measure of the entity's successful expansion. Note that many employee share option schemes operate in this manner.

4.15 EXAMPLE: CONTINGENTLY ISSUABLE SHARES

A company has 500,000 ordinary shares in issue at 1 January 19X7. A recent business acquisition has given rise to the following contingently issuable shares.

- 10,000 ordinary shares for every new branch opened in the three years 19X7-19X9

- 1,000 ordinary shares for every £2,000 of net profit in excess of £900,000 over the three years ended 31 December 19X9

(Shares will be issued on 1 January following the period in which a condition is met.)

A new branch was opened on 1 July 19X7, another on 31 March 19X8 and another on 1 October 19X9.

Reported net profits over the three years were £350,000, £400,000 and £600,000 respectively.

4.16 SOLUTION

Basic EPS

	19X7 £		19X8 £		19X9 £	
Numerator	350,000		400,000		600,000	
Denominator						
Ordinary shares	500,000		510,000		520,000	
Branch contingency	5,000	(i)	7,500	(i)	2,500	(i)
Earnings contingency	-	(ii)	-	(ii)	-	(ii)
Total shares	505,000		517,500		522,500	
Basic EPS	69.3p		77.3p		114.8p	

BPP PUBLISHING

Diluted EPS

	19X7		*19X8*		*19X9*	
	£		£		£	
Numerator	350,000		400,000		600,000	
Denominator						
Ordinary shares in basic EPS	505,000		517,500		522,500	
Additional shares:						
Branch contingency	5,000	(iii)	2,500	(iii)	7,500	(iii)
Earnings contingency	-		-		225,000	(iv)
Total shares	510,000		520,000		755,000	
Diluted EPS	68.6p		76.9p		79.5p	

(i)   This figure is simply the shares due for opening a branch pro-rated over the year.

(ii) It is not certain the net profit condition has been satisfied until after the three year period.

(iii) The contingently issuable shares are included from the start of the period they arise so these figures are increasing the denominator by the full 10,000 shares.

(iv) This is (£1,350,000 – £900,000)/£2,000 × 1,000. This figure will be included in the basic EPS figure in the following year 20X0. Note that the £900,000 criteria was not exceeded in the prior year.

4.17   The example highlights FRS 14's emphasis on the denominator as opposed to the numerator. All of the adjustments in this case were to the number of shares.

Convertible bonds

4.18   In cases where the issue of shares will affect earnings, the numerator should be adjusted accordingly. This occurs when bonds are converted. Interest is paid out on the bond. When conversion takes place this interest is no longer payable.

4.19 EXAMPLE: CONVERTIBLE BONDS

Net profit	£500
Ordinary shares in issue	1,000
Basic EPS	50p
Convertible 15% bonds	200

Each block of 5 bonds is convertible to 8 ordinary shares. The tax rate (including any deferred tax) is 40%.

4.20 SOLUTION

Interest expense relating to the bonds 200 @ 15% =	£30
Tax @ 40%	£12
Adjusted net profit £500 + £30 – £12 =	£518
Number of ordinary shares resulting from the bond conversion	320
Number of ordinary shares used for the diluted EPS calculation 1,000 + 320 =	1,320

Diluted EPS $\frac{£518}{1,320}$ = 39.2p

4.21   Earnings should be adjusted for savings or expenses occurring as a result of conversion. Other examples of this are:

(a)   preference dividends saved when preference shares are converted;

(b) additional liability on a profit sharing scheme as a result of higher profits (ie if conversion of bonds increases profit, a higher amount will be payable to members of a profit related pay scheme).

Ranking dilutive securities

4.22 The approach prescribed by FRS 14 involves including only dilutive potential ordinary shares. Antidilutive shares are not to be included. This is a prudent approach which recognises potential reduction of earnings but not increases.

4.23 The following examples show how dilutive potential ordinary shares are identified and included in the calculation of EPS. The standard also states that the dilutive shares should be ranked and taken into account from the most dilutive down to the least dilutive. Potential ordinary shares likely to have a dilutive effect on EPS include options, convertible bonds and convertible preference shares.

4.24 EXAMPLE: RANKING DILUTIVE SECURITIES FOR THE CALCULATION OF WEIGHTED AVERAGE NUMBER OF SHARES

Net profit attributable to ordinary shareholders	£20 million
Net profit from discontinued activities	£5 million
Ordinary shares outstanding	50 million
Average fair value of one ordinary share	£5.00

Potential ordinary shares

Convertible preference shares 500,000	entitled to a cumulative dividend of £5. Each is convertible to 3 shares
3% convertible bond	Nominal amount £50 million. Each £1,000 bond is convertible to 50 shares. There is no amortisation of premium or discounting affecting the interest expense
Options	10 million with exercise price of £4
Tax rate	30%

4.25 SOLUTION

The effect on earnings on conversion of potential ordinary shares

	Increase in earnings £	Increase in ordinary shares Number	Earnings per share £
Convertible preference shares			
Increase in net profit (£5 × 500,000)	2,500,000 (i)		
Incremental shares (3 × 500,000)		1,500,000	1.67
3% convertible bonds			
Increase in net profit			
50,000,000 × 0.03 × (1 − 0.3) (ii)	1,050,000		
Incremental shares (50,000 × 50)		2,500,000	0.42
Options			
Increase in earnings:	Nil		
Incremental shares 10 million × (£5 − £4)/£5		2,000,000	Nil

Identifying the dilutive shares to include in the diluted EPS

	Net profit from continuing operations £	Ordinary shares Number	Per share £	
Reported	15,000,000	50,000,000	0.30	
Options	-	2,000,000		
	15,000,000	52,000,000	0.29	Dilutive
3% convertible bonds	1,050,000	2,500,000		
	16,050,000	54,500,000	0.29	Antidilutive
Convertible preference shares	2,500,000	1,500,000		
	18,550,000	56,000,000	0.33	Antidilutive

Note that:

- The potential share issues are considered from the most dilutive to the least dilutive.

- The diluted EPS is increased by both the bonds and the preference shares. These are therefore ignored in the diluted EPS calculation.

Basic EPS

Net profit	£20 million
Weighted average number of shares	50 million
Basic EPS	40p

Diluted EPS

Net profit (remains at)	£20 million
Weighted average number of shares	52 million
	38.5p

(i) The cumulative dividend on the preference shares is not taken into consideration. Only the dividend for the year is included in the increase in earnings.

(ii) It is important to remember the tax element in the bond interest.

4.26 It should be noted that the **numerator,** for the purposes of ranking the dilutive shares, is nct profit from continuing operations only. This is net profit after preference share dividends but excluding discontinued operations and extraordinary items. The EPS calculation includes the full amount of net profit attributable to ordinary shareholders.

4.27 The following question is based on the previous example but with dilutive convertible bonds

Question

Details as above except that the convertible bonds are 1.5% bonds.

Answer

Effect on earnings on conversion of potential ordinary shares

	Increase in earnings £	Increase in ordinary shares Number	Earnings per share £
1.5% Convertible bonds			
Increase in net profit (50,000 × 0.015 × (1 − 0.3)	525,000		
Incremental shares (50,000 × 50)		2,500,000	0.21

Identifying the dilutive shares to include in the diluted EPS

	Net profit from continuing operations £	Ordinary shares Number	Per share £	
Reported	15,000,000	50,000,000	0.30	
Options	-	2,000,000		
	15,000,000	52,000,000	0.29	Dilutive
1.5% convertible bonds	525,000	2,500,000		
	15,525,000	54,500,000	0.28	Dilutive

The convertible preference shares will remain antidilutive and basic EPS will remain at 40p.

Diluted EPS

Net profit (20,000,000 + 525,000 bond interest)	£20,525,000
Weighted average number of shares	54.5 million
Diluted EPS	37.7p

4.28 The example in the above question emphasises the adjustments made to earnings and the use of net profit from continuing operations as the numerator.

5 DISCLOSURE

5.1 Note the following.

(a) FRS 14 requires that **basic EPS** and **diluted EPS** are disclosed on the face of the profit and loss account, even if the amounts are negative. Comparative figures are also required.

(b) A basic and diluted EPS figure is required for every set of ordinary shares with different rights.

(c) The standard requires inclusion of all potential ordinary shares which will have a dilutive effect on the diluted EPS, regardless of materiality.

(d) The nil basis EPS is no longer required as this information can be derived from other disclosures in the financial statements.

(e) EPS need only be presented in the consolidated results of a group where the parent's results are shown as well.

BPP PUBLISHING

Chapter roundup

- FRS 14 has superseded SSAP 3. This has brought the UK's treatment of the EPS calculation in line with international standards.

- Disclosure of the basic EPS and diluted EPS on the face of the profit and loss is required, along with comparatives for both figures. This is the case even if the figures are negative.

- Other EPS figures can be disclosed in the accounts.
    - These must use the same basis for calculating the denominator.
    - The reason for the method used must be disclosed.
    - They must be consistent year on year.
    - The required EPS figures should have the same prominence within the accounts.

- The denominator is calculated by finding the weighted average number of ordinary shares in issue in the year.

- Any effect that conversion to ordinary shares has on the earnings figure must be reflected in the calculation of the diluted EPS.

- Only dilutive shares are included in the diluted EPS. Anti-dilutive shares are ignored.

Quick quiz

1   To which companies does FRS 14 apply? (1.2)

2   For the purposes of EPS what are 'earnings'? (2.1)

3   At what point should issues of ordinary shares be included in the basic EPS? (2.6)

4   What is diluted EPS? (4.1)

5   List the possible adjustments to earnings for the diluted EPS calculation. (4.1)

6   Define 'dilutive potential ordinary share'. (4.2)

7   Which numerator is used to rank dilutive shares? (4.26)

8   List the basic disclosure requirements of FRS 14. (5.1)

Questions to try	Level	Marks	Time
27	Introductory	n/a	n/a

Chapter 26

RATIO ANALYSIS

Chapter topic	Syllabus reference	Ability required
1 The broad categories of ratios	9(c)	Application
2 Profitability and return on capital	9(c)	Application
3 Liquidity and working capital	9(c)	Application
4 Long-term solvency: debt and gearing	9(c)	Application
5 Shareholders' investment ratios	9(c)	Application
6 Other matters	9(c)	Application
7 Presentation of reports	9(c)	Application

Introduction

Some of this material should be familiar from your Stage 2 Financial Accounting studies. As far as the Stage 3 topic is concerned, you should bear in mind what the Syllabus Guidance Notes for Paper 9 say on the subject.

'As well as preparing financial statements, the Chartered Management Accountant needs to be able to interpret them and draw sensible conclusions which he or she can express in the form of a report to non-financial managers. Such a task often involves, as a first step, the calculation of relevant accounting ratios.

However at Stage 3 the emphasis of assessment will be shifted to the conclusions which candidates draw from the ratios and the way those conclusions are expressed in the form of a report. In questions of this nature a pass mark will not be gained by candidates who produce a large number of ratios unaccompanied by analysis. In addition to asking candidates to evaluate the financial performance of an undertaking (which could be a not-for-profit undertaking), a typical question might also ask candidates to reflect on the non-financial criteria which should be borne in mind to make a more rounded evaluation of the undertaking's performance.'

Pay close attention to Section 7 on report writing, as this will help to set (or improve) your exam technique.

It cannot be over-emphasised that it is not sufficient for you to demonstrate that you can calculate ratios. You must also be able to **comment** on the ratios and give suggested reasons for trends and differences.

1 THE BROAD CATEGORIES OF RATIOS   5/95–5/99

1.1 Ratio analysis involves comparing **one figure against another** to produce a ratio, and assessing whether the ratio indicates a weakness or strength in the company's affairs.

The broad categories of ratios

1.2   Broadly speaking, basic ratios can be grouped into five categories.

- Profitability and return
- Short-term solvency and liquidity
- Long-term solvency and stability
- Efficiency (turnover ratios)
- Shareholders' investment ratios

1.3   Ratio analysis on its own is **not sufficient** for interpreting company accounts, and that there are other items of information which should be looked at, for example:

(a) **comments** in the chairman's report, the directors' report and the operating and financial review.

(b) the age and nature of the **company's assets**

(c) current and future **developments** in the company's markets, at home and overseas, recent acquisitions or disposals of a subsidiary by the company;

(d) any other **noticeable features** of the report and accounts, such as post balance sheet events, contingent liabilities, a qualified auditors' report, the company's taxation position, and so on.

1.4   The following sections summarise what you already know about ratio analysis from your studies for Stages 1 and 2. You should then perform the comprehensive questions given in this chapter. The following three chapters look at more complex areas of analysis and interpretation, which build on the knowledge in this chapter.

2   PROFITABILITY AND RETURN ON CAPITAL

2.1   One profit figure that should be calculated and compared over time is **PBIT, profit before interest and tax**, the amount of profit which the company earned before having to pay interest to the providers of loan capital. By providers of loan capital, we usually mean longer-term loan capital, such as debentures and medium-term bank loans, which will be shown in the balance sheet as 'creditors: amounts falling due after more than one year'. Also, tax is affected by unusual variations which have a distorting effect.

2.2   Profit before interest and tax is therefore:

(a) the profit on ordinary activities before taxation; plus

548

(b)   interest charges on long-term loan capital.

Published accounts do not always give sufficient detail on interest payable to determine how much is interest on long-term finance.

Knowledge brought forward from Papers 1 and 5

Profitability

Return on capital employed

$$\text{ROCE} = \frac{\text{PBIT}}{\text{Capital employed}} = \frac{\text{PBIT}}{\text{Total assets less current liabilities}}$$

When **interpreting** ROCE look for the following.

- How risky is the business?
- How capital intensive is it?
- What ROCE do similar businesses have?

Problems: which items to consider to achieve comparability:

- Revaluation reserves
- Policies, eg goodwill, R & D
- Bank overdraft: short/long-term liability
- Investments and related income: exclude

The following **considerations** are important.

- Change year to year
- Comparison to similar companies
- Comparison with current market borrowing rates

Return on equity

$$\text{ROE} = \frac{\text{Profit after tax and pref div}}{\text{Ordinary share capital + reserves}}\%$$

This gives a more **restricted view** of capital than ROCE, but the same principles apply.

Secondary ratios

Profit margin × Asset turnover = ROCE

Profit margin

$$\text{Profit margin} = \frac{\text{PBIT}}{\text{Turnover}}\% \quad \text{Gross profit margin} = \frac{\text{Gross profit}}{\text{Turnover}}\%$$

It is useful to compare profit margin to gross profit % to investigate movements which do not match. Take into account:

- **Gross profit margin**
    - Sales prices, sales volume and sales mix
    - Purchase prices and related costs (discount, carriage etc)
    - Production costs, both direct (materials, labour) and indirect (overheads both fixed and variable)
    - Stock levels and stock valuation, including errors, cut-off and stock-out costs
- **Net profit margin**
    - Sales expenses in relation to sales levels
    - Administrative expenses, including salary levels
    - Distribution expenses in relation to sales levels

Depreciation should be considered as a separate item for each expense category.

Asset turnover

$$\text{Asset turnover} = \frac{\text{Turnover}}{\text{Total assets less current liabilities}}$$

This measures the **efficiency** of the use of assets. Amend to just fixed assets for capital intensive businesses.

A warning about comments on profit margin and asset turnover

2.3   It might be tempting to think that a high profit margin is good, and a low asset turnover means sluggish trading. In broad terms, this is so. But there is **a trade-off** between profit margin and asset turnover, and you cannot look at one without allowing for the other.

(a)   A high profit margin means a high profit per £1 of sales, but if this also means that sales prices are high, there is a strong possibility that sales turnover will be depressed, and so asset turnover lower.

(b)   A high asset turnover means that the company is generating a lot of sales, but to do this it might have to keep its prices down and so accept a low profit margin per £1 of sales.

3   LIQUIDITY AND WORKING CAPITAL

3.1   Profitability is of course an important aspect of a company's performance and debt or gearing is another. Neither, however, addresses directly the key issue of liquidity in the **short term**.

3.2   **Liquidity** is the amount of cash a company can put its hands on quickly to settle its debts (and possibly to meet other unforeseen demands for cash payments too). Liquid funds consist of:

(a)   cash;

(b)   short-term investments for which there is a ready market (short-term investments are distinct from investments in shares in subsidiaries or associated companies);

(c)   fixed-term deposits with a bank or building society, for example, a six month high-interest deposit with a bank;

(d)   trade debtors (because they will pay what they owe within a reasonably short period of time);

(e)   bills of exchange receivable (because like ordinary trade debtors, these represent amounts of cash due to be received within a relatively short period of time).

3.3   A company can obtain liquid assets from sources other than sales, such as the issue of shares for cash, a new loan or the sale of fixed assets. But a company cannot rely on these at all times, and in general obtaining liquid funds depends on making sales and profits. Even so, **profits do not always lead to increases in liquidity**. This is mainly because funds generated from trading may be immediately invested in fixed assets or paid out as dividends.

3.4   **Efficiency ratios** indicate how well a business is controlling aspects of its working capital.

Knowledge brought forward from Papers 1 and 5

Liquidity and working capital

This was very topical in the late 1980s as interest rates were high, and there was a recession Can a company meet its short-term debts.

Current ratio

$$\text{Current ratio} = \frac{\text{Current assets}}{\text{Current liabilities}}$$

Assume assets realised at book level ∴ theoretical. 2:1 acceptable? 1.5:1? It depends on the industry.

Quick ratio

$$\text{Quick ratio (acid test)} = \frac{\text{Current assets - Stock}}{\text{Current liabilities}}$$

Eliminates illiquid and subjectively valued stock. Care is needed: it could be high if **overtrading** with debtors, but no cash. Is 1:1 OK? Many supermarkets operate on 0.3.

Collection period

$$\text{Average collection period} = \frac{\text{Trade debtors}}{\text{Credit turnover}} \times 365$$

Is it **consistent** with quick/current ratio? If not, investigate.

Stock turnover

$$\text{Stock turnover} = \frac{\text{Cost of sales}}{\text{Stock}} \qquad \text{Stock days} = \frac{\text{Stock}}{\text{Cost of sales}} \times 365$$

Higher the better? But remember:

- Lead times
- Seasonal fluctuations in orders
- Alternative uses of warehouse space
- Bulk buying discounts
- Likelihood of stock perishing or becoming obsolete

Creditors' payment period

$$\text{Creditors' payment period} = \frac{\text{Trade creditors}}{\text{Purchases}} \times 365$$

Use **cost of sales** if purchases are not disclosed.

Cash cycle

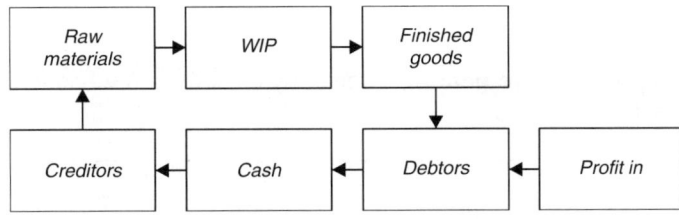

- Cash flow timing does not match sales/cost of sales timing as credit is taken
- Holding stock delays the time between payments for goods and sales receipts

Reasons for changes in liquidity

- **Credit control** efficiency altered
- Altering **payment period** of creditors as a source of funding
- Reduce **stock holdings** to maintain liquidity

4   LONG TERM SOLVENCY: DEBT AND GEARING

4.1   Debt and gearing ratios are concerned with a company's **long-term stability**: how much the company owes in relation to its size, whether it is getting into heavier debt or improving its situation, and whether its debt burden seems heavy or light.

(a)   When a company is heavily in debt, banks and other potential lenders may be unwilling to advance further funds.

(b)   When a company is earning only a modest profit before interest and tax, and has a heavy debt burden, there will be very little profit left (if any) over for shareholders after the interest charges have been paid. And so if interest rates were to go up (on bank overdrafts and so on) or the company were to borrow even more, it might soon be incurring interest charges in excess of PBIT. This might eventually lead to the liquidation of the company.

Knowledge brought forward from Papers 1 and 5

Debt and gearing

Debt/equity

$$\text{Debt/equity ratio} = \frac{\text{Interest bearing net debts}}{\text{Shareholders' funds}}\% \quad (> 100\% = \text{high})$$

$$\text{Or} \quad \frac{\text{Interest bearing net debt}}{\text{Shareholders' funds}}\% \ (> 50\% = \text{high})$$

There is **no definitive answer**; elements included are subjective. The following could have an impact.

*   Convertible loan stock
*   Preference shares
*   Deferred tax
*   Goodwill and development expenditure capitalisation
*   Revaluation reserve

Gearing ratio

$$\text{Gearing ratio} = \frac{\text{Prior charge capital}}{\text{Total capital}}$$

Interest cover

$$\text{Interest cover} = \frac{\text{PBIT(incl int receivable)}}{\text{Interest payable}}$$

Is this a better way to **measure gearing**? Company must generate enough profit to cover interest. Is a figure of 3+ safe?

The implications of high or low gearing

4.2   Gearing is, amongst other things, an attempt to quantify the **degree of risk** involved in holding equity shares in a company, both in terms of the company's ability to remain in business and in terms of expected ordinary dividends from the company. The problem with a highly geared company is that, by definition, there is a lot of debt. Debt generally carries a fixed rate of interest (or fixed rate of dividend if in the form of preference shares), hence there is a given (and large) amount to be paid out from profits to holders of debt before arriving at a residue available for distribution to the holders of equity.

4.3 The more highly geared the company, the greater the risk that little (if anything) will be available to distribute by way of dividend to the ordinary shareholders. The more highly geared the company, the greater the percentage change in profit available for ordinary shareholders for any given percentage change in profit before interest and tax. The relationship similarly holds when profits increase. This means that there will be greater **volatility** of amounts available for ordinary shareholders, and presumably therefore greater volatility in dividends paid to those shareholders, where a company is highly geared. That is the risk. You may do extremely well or extremely badly without a particularly large movement in the PBIT of the company.

4.4 The risk of a company's ability to remain in business was referred to earlier. Gearing is relevant to this. A highly geared company has a large amount of interest to pay annually. If those borrowings are 'secured' in any way (and debentures in particular are secured), then the holders of the debt are perfectly entitled to force the company to realise assets to pay their interest if funds are not available from other sources. Clearly, the more highly geared a company, the more likely this is to occur when and if profits fall. Note that problems related to **off balance sheet finance** hiding the level of gearing have gradually become rarer, due to standards such as FRS 2 and SSAP 21.

4.5 Companies will only be able to increase their gearing if they have **suitable assets** to offer for security. Companies with assets which are depreciated rapidly or which are at high risk of obsolescence will be unable to offer sufficient security, eg computer software companies. On the other hand, a property company will have plenty of assets to offer as security whose value is fairly stable (but note the effect of a property slump as in the late 1980s).

4.6 Ideally, the following **gearing profiles** would apply, so that only certain types of company could have higher gearing.

Type of company	Assets	Profits
Highly geared companies	Holding value, long-term	Stable, steady trends
Low geared companies	Rapid depreciation/change	Erratic, volatile

The effect of GAAP on gearing

4.7 **Variations in accounting policy** can have a significant impact on gearing and it will be necessary to consider the individual policies of companies. The main areas which are likely to require consideration area as follows.

(a) FRS 4 *Capital instruments* has halted the practice of classifying an instrument as equity when the true nature is that of debt and also of accounting for debt at an amount lower than its repayable amount (see Chapter 9).

(b) Revaluation of fixed assets will have an impact on equity and it will be necessary to consider the frequency of such revaluations (see Chapter 3).

(c) Assets held under leases may be excluded from a company's balance sheet if the leases are classified as operating leases (see Chapter 10).

(d) The treatment of deferred development expenditure will have an impact on gearing, ie capitalise or write off (see Chapter 4 on SSAP 13).

(e) The structure of group accounts and methods of consolidation will also have a substantial impact on gearing (use of acquisition/merger/equity accounting; exclusion of subsidiaries; FRSs 2 and 6 in Chapters 12 to 18).

5 SHAREHOLDERS' INVESTMENT RATIOS

5.1 These are the ratios which help equity shareholders and other investors to assess the value and quality of an investment in the **ordinary shares** of a company.

5.2 The value of an investment in ordinary shares in a **listed company** is its market value, and so investment ratios must have regard not only to information in the company's published accounts, but also to the current price.

5.3 Earnings per share is a valuable indicator of an ordinary share's performance and you should refer back to Chapter 25 to study its calculation.

Knowledge brought forward from Papers 1 and 5

Investors' ratios

Dividend yield

$$\text{Dividend yield} = \frac{\text{Div per share}}{\text{Mid-market price}}\%$$

- **Low yield**: the company retains a large proportion of profits to reinvest
- **High yield**: this is a risky company or slow-growing

Dividend cover

$$\text{Dividend cover} = \frac{\text{EPS}}{\text{Div per share}}$$

$$\text{Or} \quad \frac{\text{Profit after tax and pref div}}{\text{Div on ordinary shares}}$$

This shows **how safe the dividend is**, or the extent of profit retention. Variations are due to maintaining dividend when profits are declining.

P/E ratio

$$\text{P/E ratio} = \frac{\text{Mid - market price}}{\text{EPS}}$$

The **higher the better** here: it reflects the confidence of the market. A rise in EPS will cause an increase in P/E ratio, but maybe not to same extent: Look at the context of the market and industry norms.

Earnings yield

$$\text{Earnings yield} = \frac{\text{EPS}}{\text{Mid - market price}}$$

This shows the dividend yield if there is no retention of profit. It allows you to compare companies with **different dividend policies**, showing growth rather than earnings.

Net assets per share

$$\text{Net assets per share} = \frac{\text{Net assets}}{\text{No of shares}}$$

This is a **crude measure** of value of a company, liable to distortion.

See also **EPS** and **dividend per share**

Question 1

RST plc is considering purchasing an interest in its competitor XYZ Ltd. The managing director of RST plc has obtained the three most recent P&L accounts and balance sheets of XYZ Ltd as shown below.

XYZ LTD
PROFIT AND LOSS ACCOUNTS FOR YEARS ENDED 31 DECEMBER

	19X0	19X1	19X2
	£'000	£'000	£'000
Turnover	18,000	18,900	19,845
Cost of sales	10,440	10,340	11,890
Gross profit	7,560	8,560	7,955
Distribution costs	1,565	1,670	1,405
Administrative expenses	1,409	1,503	1,591
Operating profit	4,586	5,387	4,959
Interest payable on bank overdraft	104	215	450
Interest payable on 12% debentures	600	600	600
Profit on ordinary activities before taxation	3,882	4,572	3,909
Taxation on ordinary activities	1,380	2,000	1,838
Profit on ordinary activities after taxation	2,502	2,572	2,071
Proposed dividend	1,600	1,693	1,800
Retained profit	902	879	271

XYZ LTD
BALANCE SHEETS AS AT 31 DECEMBER

	19X0		19X1		19X2	
	£'000	£'000	£'000	£'000	£'000	£'000
Fixed assets						
Land and buildings	11,460		12,121		11,081	
Plant and machinery	8,896		9,020		9,130	
		20,356		21,141		20,211
Current assets						
Stock	1,775		2,663		3,995	
Trade debtors	1,440		2,260		3,164	
Cash	50		53		55	
	3,265		4,976		7,214	
Current liabilities						
Trade creditors	390		388		446	
Bank	1,300		2,300		3,400	
Taxation	897		1,420		1,195	
Proposed dividend	1,600		1,696		1,800	
	4,187		5,804		6,841	
Net current assets/(liabilities)		(922)		(828)		373
12% debentures 19X5 - 19X8		(5,000)		(5,000)		(5,000)
		14,434		15,313		15,584
Share capital		8,000		8,000		8,000
Profit and loss account		6,434		7,313		7,584
		14,434		15,313		15,584

Required

Prepare a report for the managing director of RST plc commenting on the financial position of XYZ Ltd and highlighting any areas that require further investigation.

(Marks will be awarded for ratios and other financial statistics where appropriate.)

Answer

To: MD of RST plc
From: An Accountant
Date: XX.XX.XX
Subject: *The financial position of XYZ Ltd*

Introduction

This report has been prepared on the basis of the three most recent P&L accounts and balance sheets of XYZ Ltd covering the years 19X0 to 19X2 inclusive. Ratio analysis used in this report is based on the calculations shown in the appendix attached.

Performance

Sales have increased at a steady 5% per annum over the three year period.

In contrast, the gross profit percentage has increased from 42% in 19X0 to 45% in 19X1 before dropping back to 40% in 19X2. Similarly, operating profit as a percentage of sales was 26% in 19X0, 28.5% in 19X1 and 25% in 19X2. This may indicate some misallocation of costs between 19X1 and 19X2 and should be investigated or it may be indicative of a longer downward trend in profitability.

Return on capital employed, as one would expect, has shown a similar pattern with an increase in 19X1 with a subsequent fall in 19X2 to a level below that of 19X0.

Debt and liquidity

The debt ratio measures the ratio of a company's total debt to its total assets. Although we have no information as to the norm for the industry as a whole, the debt ratios appear reasonable. However, it should be noted that it has risen steadily over the three year period.

When reviewing XYZ Ltd's liquidity the situation has improved over the period. The current ratio measures a company's ability to meet its current liabilities out of current assets. A ratio of at least 1 should therefore be expected. XYZ Ltd did not meet this expectation in 19X0 and 19X1.

This ratio can be misleading as stock is included in current assets. Because stock can take some time to convert into liquid assets a second ratio, the quick ratio, is calculated which excludes stock. As can be seen, the quick ratio, although improving, is low and this shows that current liabilities cannot be met from current assets if stock is excluded. As a major part of current liabilities is the bank overdraft, the company is obviously relying on the bank's continuing support with short-term funding. It would be useful to find out the terms of the bank funding and the projected cash flow requirements for future funding.

Efficiency ratios

The efficiency ratios, debtors ratio and stock turnover, give a useful indication of how the company is managing its current assets.

As can be seen from the appendix the debtors collection period has increased over the three years from 29 days to 58 days. This may indicate that the company is failing to follow up its debts efficiently or that it has given increased credit terms to some or all of its customers.

Looking at stock turnover, this has also risen from 62 days to 122 days. This may be an indication of over-stocking, stocking up on the expectation of a substantial sales increase or the holding of obsolete or slow-moving stock items which should be written down. More investigation needs to be done on both debtors and stock.

The financing of additional debtors and stock has been achieved in the main through the bank overdraft as the trade creditors figure has not increased significantly.

Conclusion

The review of the three year financial statements for XYZ Ltd has given rise to a number of queries which need to be resolved before a useful conclusion can be reached on the financial position of XYZ Ltd. It may also be useful to compare XYZ Ltd's ratios to those of other companies in the same industry in order to obtain some idea of the industry norms.

APPENDIX TO MEMORANDUM

	19X0	19X1	19X2
% sales increase		5%	5%
Gross profit %	42%	45%	40%
Operating profit %	25.5%	28.5%	25%

Return on capital employed

$$= \frac{\text{Profit before interest and tax}}{\text{Capital employed}} \times 100\%$$

	19X0	19X1	19X2
	$\frac{4{,}586-104}{14{,}434+5{,}000}$	$\frac{5{,}387-215}{15{,}313+5{,}000}$	$\frac{4{,}959-450}{15{,}584+5{,}000}$
	= 23%	= 25.5%	= 21.9%

Debt ratio

$$= \frac{\text{Total debt}}{\text{Total assets}} \times 100\%$$

	19X0	19X1	19X2
	$\frac{4{,}187+5{,}000}{20{,}356+3{,}265}$	$\frac{5{,}804+5{,}000}{21{,}114+4{,}976}$	$\frac{6{,}841+5{,}000}{20{,}211+7{,}214}$
	= 38.9%	= 41.4%	= 43.2%

Current ratio

$$= \frac{\text{Current assets}}{\text{Current liabilities}}$$

	19X0	19X1	19X2
	$\frac{3{,}265}{4{,}187}$	$\frac{4{,}976}{5{,}804}$	$\frac{7{,}214}{6{,}814}$
	= 0.78	= 0.86	= 1.06

Quick ratio

$$= \frac{\text{Current assets} - \text{stock}}{\text{Current liabilities}}$$

	19X0	19X1	19X2
	$\frac{3{,}265-1{,}775}{4{,}187}$	$\frac{4{,}976-2{,}663}{5{,}804}$	$\frac{7{,}214-3{,}995}{6{,}814}$
	= 0.36	= 0.40	= 0.47

Debtors ratio

$$= \frac{\text{Trade debtors}}{\text{Sales}} \times 365 \text{ days}$$

	19X0	19X1	19X2
	$\frac{1{,}440}{18{,}000}$	$\frac{2{,}260}{18{,}900}$	$\frac{3{,}164}{19{,}845}$
	= 29.2 days	= 43.6 days	= 58.2 days

	19X0	19X1	19X2

Stock turnover

$$= \frac{\text{Stock}}{\text{Cost of sales}} \times 365 \text{ days}$$

	19X0	19X1	19X2
	$\frac{1{,}775}{10{,}440}$	$\frac{2{,}663}{10{,}340}$	$\frac{3{,}995}{11{,}890}$
	= 62 days	= 94 days	= 122.6 days

Question 2

You are the management accountant of Fry plc. Laurie plc is a competitor in the same industry and it has been operating for 20 years. Summaries of Laurie plc's P&L accounts and balance sheets for the previous three years are given below.

BPP PUBLISHING

SUMMARISED PROFIT AND LOSS ACCOUNTS
FOR THE YEAR ENDED 31 DECEMBER

	19X0	19X1	19X2
	£m	£m	£m
Turnover	840	981	913
Cost of sales	554	645	590
Gross profit	286	336	323
Selling, distribution and administration expenses	186	214	219
Profit before interest	100	122	104
Interest	6	15	19
Profit on ordinary activities before taxation	94	107	85
Taxation	45	52	45
Profit on ordinary activities after taxation	49	55	40
Dividends	24	24	24
Retained profit for year	25	31	16

SUMMARISED BALANCE SHEETS AS AT 31 DECEMBER

	19X0	19X1	19X2
	£m	£m	£m
Fixed assets			
Intangible assets	36	40	48
Tangible assets at net book value	176	206	216
	212	246	264
Current assets			
Stocks	237	303	294
Debtors	105	141	160
Bank	52	58	52
	606	748	770
Creditors: amounts falling due within one year			
Trade creditors	53	75	75
Other creditors	80	105	111
	133	180	186
Creditors: amounts falling due after more than one year			
Long-term loans	74	138	138
	207	318	324
Shareholders' interest			
Ordinary share capital	100	100	100
Retained profits	299	330	346
	606	748	770

You may assume that the index of retail prices has remained constant between 19X0 and 19X2.

Required

Write a report to the finance director of Fry plc:

(a) analysing the performance of Laurie plc and showing any calculations in an appendix to this report;

(b) summarising five areas which require further investigation, including reference to other pieces of information which would complement your analysis of the performance of Laurie plc

Answer

(a) To: Finance Director
From: Management accountant
Subject: *Performance of Laurie plc 19X0 to 19X2*

An appendix is attached to this report which shows the ratios calculated as part of the performance review.

Profitability

The gross profit margin has remained relatively static over the three year period, although it has risen by approximately 1% in 19X2. ROCE, while improving very slightly in 19X1 to 21.5% has dropped dramatically in 19X2 to 17.8%. The net profit margin has also fallen in 19X2, in spite of the improvement in the gross profit margin. This marks a rise in expenses which suggests that

they are not being well controlled. The utilisation of assets compared to the turnover generated has also declined reflecting the drop in trading activity between 19X1 and 19X2.

Trading levels

It is apparent that there was a dramatic increase in trading activity between 19X0 and 19X1, but then a significant fall in 19X2. Turnover rose by 17% in 19X1 but fell by 7% in 19X2. The reasons for this fluctuation are unclear. It may be the effect of some kind of one-off event, or it may be the effect of a change in product mix. Whatever the reason, it appears that improved credit terms granted to customers (debtors payment period up from 46 to 64 days) has not stopped the drop in sales.

Working capital

Both the current ratio and quick ratio demonstrate an adequate working capital situation, although the quick ratio has shown a slight decline. There has been an increased investment over the period in stocks and debtors which has been only partly financed by longer payment periods to trade creditors and a rise in other creditors (mainly between 19X0 and 19X1).

Capital structure

The level of gearing of the company increased when a further £64m was raised in long term loans in 19X1 to add to the £74m already in the balance sheet. Although this does not seem to be a particularly high level of gearing, the debt/equity ratio did rise from 18.5% to 32.0% in 19X1. The interest charge has risen to £19m from £6m in 19X0. The 19X1 charge was £15m, suggesting that either the interest rate on the loan is flexible, or that the full interest charge was not incurred in 19X1. The new long-term loan appears to have funded the expansion in both fixed and current assets in 19X1.

APPENDIX

Ratio	Working	19X0	19X1	19X2
Gross profit margin	(1)	34.0%	34.3%	35.4%
ROCE	(2)	21.1%	21.5%	17.8%
Profit margin	(3)	11.9%	12.4%	11.4%
Assets turnover	(4)	1.78	1.73	1.56
Gearing ratio	(5)	15.6%	24.3%	23.6%
Debt/equity ratio	(6)	18.5%	32.0%	30.9%
Interest cover	(7)	16.7	8.1	5.5
Current ratio	(8)	3.0	2.8	2.7
Quick ratio	(9)	1.2	1.1	1.1
Debtor's payment period (days)	(10)	46	52	64
Stock turnover period (days)	(11)	156	171	182
Creditor's turnover period	(12)	35	42	46

Workings (all in £m)

		19X0	19X1	19X2
1	Gross profit margin	$\frac{286}{840}$	$\frac{336}{981}$	$\frac{323}{913}$
2	ROCE *	$\frac{100}{473}$	$\frac{122}{568}$	$\frac{104}{584}$
3	Profit margin	$\frac{100}{840}$	$\frac{122}{981}$	$\frac{104}{913}$
4	Assets turnover	$\frac{840}{473}$	$\frac{981}{568}$	$\frac{913}{584}$
5	Gearing ratio	$\frac{74}{74+399}$	$\frac{138}{138+430}$	$\frac{138}{138+446}$
6	Debt/equity ratio	$\frac{74}{399}$	$\frac{138}{430}$	$\frac{138}{446}$

		19X0	19X1	19X2
7	Interest cover	$\dfrac{100}{6}$	$\dfrac{122}{15}$	$\dfrac{104}{19}$
8	Current ratio	$\dfrac{394}{133}$	$\dfrac{502}{180}$	$\dfrac{506}{186}$
9	Quick ratio	$\dfrac{157}{133}$	$\dfrac{199}{180}$	$\dfrac{212}{186}$
10	Debtors' payment period	$\dfrac{105}{840} \times 365$	$\dfrac{141}{981} \times 365$	$\dfrac{160}{913} \times 365$
11	Stock turnover period	$\dfrac{237}{554} \times 365$	$\dfrac{303}{645} \times 365$	$\dfrac{294}{590} \times 365$
12	Creditors' payment period	$\dfrac{53}{554} \times 365$	$\dfrac{75}{645} \times 365$	$\dfrac{75}{590} \times 365$

* ROCE has been calculated here as:

$$\frac{\text{Profit on ordinary activities before interest and taxation (PBIT)}}{\text{Capital employed}}$$

where capital employed = shareholders' funds plus creditors falling due after one year and any long-term provision for liabilities and charges. It is possible to calculate ROCE using net profit after taxation and interest, but this admits variations and distortions into the ratio which are not affected by *trading* activity.

(b) Areas for further investigation include the following.

(i) *Long-term loan*

There is no indication as to why this loan was raised and how it was used to finance the business. Further details are needed of interest rate(s), security given and repayment dates.

(ii) *Trading activity*

The level of sales has fluctuated in quite a strange way and this requires further investigation and explanation. Factors to consider would include pricing policies, product mix, market share and any unique occurrence which would affect sales.

(iii) *Further breakdown*

It would be useful to break down some of the information in the financial statements, perhaps into a management accounting format. Examples would be:

(1) sales by segment, market or geographical area;
(2) cost of sales split, into raw materials, labour and overheads;
(3) stocks broken down into raw materials, work in progress and finished goods;
(4) expenses analysed between administrative expenses, sales and distribution costs.

(iv) *Accounting policies*

Accounting policies may have a significant effect on certain items. In particular, it would be useful to know what the accounting policies are in relation to intangible assets (and what these assets consist of), and whether there has been any change in accounting policies.

(v) *Dividend policy*

The company has maintained the level of dividend paid to shareholders (although it has not been raised during the three year period). Presumably the company would have been able to reduce the amount of long-term debt taken on if it had retained part or all of the dividend during this period. It would be interesting to examine the share price movement during the period and calculate the dividend cover.

Tutorial note. Other matters raised could have included:

(1) working capital problems, particularly stock turnover and control over debtors; and

(2) EPS (which cannot be calculated here as the number of shares is not given) and other related investor statistics, such as the P/E ratio.

6   OTHER MATTERS

6.1   We discussed the disclosure of accounting policies in our examination of SSAP 2. The choice of accounting policy and the effect of its implementation are almost as important as its disclosure in that the results of a company can be altered significantly by the choice of accounting policy.

The effect of choice of accounting policies

6.2   Where accounting standards allow alternative treatment of items in the accounts, then the accounting policy note should declare which policy has been chosen. It should then be applied consistently.

6.3   Consider, though, the **radically different effects produced by the different treatment of some items**. An example is the treatment of development expenditure under SSAP 13. Although the criteria for capitalising development expenditure are very strict, the choice of whether to capitalise and amortise or write off such costs can have a significant impact on profit. Consider the size of the R & D expenditure of the large drugs companies and you can see how important such an accounting policy could be.

6.4   You should be able to think of other examples of how the choice of accounting policy can affect the financial statements.

Changes in accounting policy

6.5   The effect of a change of accounting policy is treated as a prior year adjustment according to FRS 3 *Reporting financial performance* (see Chapter 22). This just means that the comparative figures are adjusted for the change in accounting policy for comparative purposes and an adjustment is put through reserves.

6.6   FRS 3 states that, as consistency is a fundamental accounting concept, any change in policy may:

> 'only be made if it can be justified on the grounds that the new policy is preferable to the one it replaces because it will give a fairer presentation of the result and of the financial position of a reporting entity.'

6.7   The problem with this situation is that the directors may be able to manipulate the results through change(s) of accounting policies. This would be done to avoid the effect of an old accounting policy or gain the effect of a new one. It is likely to be done in a sensitive period, perhaps when the company's profits are low or the company is about to announce a rights issue. The management would have to convince the auditors that the new policy was much better, but it is not difficult to produce reasons in such cases.

6.8   The effect of such a change is very short-term. Most analysts and sophisticated users will discount its effect immediately, except to the extent that it will affect any dividend (because of the effect on distributable profits). It may help to avoid breaches of banking covenants because of the effect on certain ratios.

6.9   Obviously, the accounting policy for any item in the accounts could only be changed once in quite a long period of time. No auditors would allow another change, even back to the old policy, unless there was a wholly exceptional reason.

BPP PUBLISHING

6.10 The managers of a company can choose accounting policies **initially** to suit the company or the type of results they want to get. Any changes in accounting policy must be justified, but some managers might try to change accounting policies just to manipulate the results.

Performance measurement of non-profit making bodies 11/96

6.11 Non-profit making bodies often have multiple objectives, unlike companies. Think, for example, of all the objectives of a local authority. The performance of such bodies must be assessed, however.

  (a) Without information about what is being achieved (outputs) and what it is costing (inputs) it is impossible to make efficient resource allocations.

  (b) Good management cannot be maintained without such information.

  (c) Government may require performance information to decide how much to invest in the public sector and where, within the sector, it should be allocated.

6.12 Performance is usually judged in terms of inputs and outputs and this ties in with the 'value for money' criteria that are often used to assess non-profit making bodies.

  (a) **Economy** (spending money frugally)
  (b) **Efficiency** (getting out as much as possible for what goes in)
  (c) **Effectiveness** (getting done, by means of (a) and (b), what was supposed to be done)

6.13 More formally, effectiveness is the relationship between an organisation's outputs and its objectives, efficiency is the relationship between inputs and outputs, and economy equates to cost control in the commercial sector.

6.14 **Outputs** can seldom be measured in a way that is generally agreed to be meaningful. One possible solution is to judge performance in terms of **inputs**. Alternatively, **subjective judgements** can be made by experts in that particular non-profit making activity.

Limitations of ratio analysis

6.15 The consideration of how accounting policies may be used to manipulate company results leads us to some of the other limitations of ratio analysis. These can be summarised as follows.

  • Availability of comparable information
  • Use of historical/out of date information
  • Ratios are not definitive - they are only a guide
  • Interpretation needs careful analysis and should not be considered in isolation
  • It is a subjective exercise
  • It can be subject to manipulation
  • Ratios are not defined in standard form

6.16 In the exam, always bear these points in mind; you may even be asked to discuss such limitations, but in any case they should have an impact on your analysis of a set of results. The limitations of ratio analysis are picked up again in Chapter 28.

Operating and Financial Review (OFR)

6.17 The ASB's statement on the *Operating and Financial Review* also contains some useful material which demonstrates some of the problems associated with the interpretation of accounting standards.

6.18 In July 1993, the ASB published a document, *Operating and Financial Review*. The statement is voluntary rather than mandatory and it applies mainly to listed companies, but also those large corporations where there is a legitimate public interest. Such companies would be called on to produce an Operating and Financial Review (OFR) in their financial statements.

6.19 The purpose of the OFR is to provide:

> 'a **framework** for the directors to **discuss and analyse** the **business's performance** and the factors underlying its results and financial position, in order to assist users to assess for themselves the future potential of the business.'

6.20 The OFR should be developed in format and content to suit each organisation, but there would be some essential features of an OFR, given by the statement as follows.

(a) It should be written in a **clear style** and as succinctly as possible, to be readily understandable by the general reader of annual reports, and should include only matters that are likely to be significant to investors.

(b) It should be **balanced and objective**, dealing even-handedly with both good and bad aspects.

(c) It should **refer to comments made in previous statements** where these have **not been borne out by events**.

(d) It should contain **analytical discussion** rather than merely numerical analysis.

(e) It should follow a '**top-down**' structure, discussing individual aspects of the business in the context of a discussion of the business as a whole.

(f) It should explain the reason for, and effect of any **changes in accounting policies**.

(g) It should make it clear how any **ratios or other numerical** information given **relate to the financial statements**.

(h) It should include discussion of:

(i) trends and factors underlying the business that have affected the results but are not expected to continue in the future; and

(ii) known events, trends and uncertainties that are expected to have an impact on the business in the future.

6.21 The detailed guideline gives the following contents of each part of the OFR.

Operating review

6.22 The main contents of this part of the OFR would be as follows.

(a) **Operating results for the period.** As well as examining the results themselves, the report should look at factors such as:

(i) changes in market conditions;

(ii) new products and services introduced or announced;

(iii) changes in market share or position;

(iv) changes in turnover and margins;

    (v)   changes in exchange rates and inflation rates;

    (vi)   new activities, discontinued activities; and

    (vii) other acquisitions and disposals.

(b) **Dynamics of the business.** The main factors and influences affecting the business during the period will be discussed, including:

    (i)   scarcity of raw materials;

    (ii)   skill shortages and expertise of uncertain supply;

    (iii)   patents, licences or franchises;

    (iv)   dependence on major suppliers or customers;

    (v)   product liability;

    (vi)   health and safety;

    (vii)   environmental protection costs and potential environmental liabilities (see Chapter 22);

    (viii) self insurance;

    (ix)   exchange rate fluctuations;

    (x)   rates of inflation differing between costs and revenues, or between different markets.

(c) **Investments for the future.** As well as covering capital expenditure and its related benefits, certain types of revenue expenditure should be mentioned which would be expected to have an impact on future profits, such as:

    (i)   marketing and advertising campaigns;

    (ii)   training programmes;

    (iii)   refurbishment and maintenance programmes;

    (iv)   pure and applied research which may lead to potential new products and services;

    (v)   development of new products and services;

    (vi)   technical support to customers.

(d) Profit for the financial year, total recognised gains and losses and shareholders' perspective, ie overall return to shareholders.

(e) Profit for the financial year compared to dividends per share and earnings per share.

(f) Accounting policies.

Financial review

6.23 The principal aim of this section of the OFR is to explain to the user of the annual report the capital structure of the business, its treasury policy and the dynamics of its financial position - its sources of liquidity and their application, including the implications of the financing requirements arising from its capital expenditure plans.

6.24 The main contents should be as follows.

(a) **Capital structure and treasury policy,** including maturity profile of debt, type of capital instruments used, currency and interest rate structure. The OFR should discuss capital funding and treasury policies and the implementation of these policies.

(b) **Taxation.** Where the overall tax charge is significantly different from that calculated using the 'normal' UK tax rate, then this should be explained.

(c) **Funds** from operating activities and other sources of cash.

(d) **Current liquidity** and the end of the period including comments on the current level of borrowing.

(e) **Going concern.** The going concern statement required by the *Cadbury Report* may be included here.

(f) **Balance sheet value.** Where values or resources are not mentioned in the balance sheet they can be mentioned here, for example brands.

6.25 A statement of compliance with the OFR statement is not required, although it might be helpful to the users of the accounts.

6.26 You can see that the OFR should be of great benefit to less sophisticated users of accounts as it should carry out the analysis of a company's performance on the user's behalf. It should thus highlight the important items in the current year annual report, as well as drawing out 'those aspects of the year under review that are relevant to an assessment of future prospects'.

7 PRESENTATION OF REPORTS

7.1 You may have experience already in writing reports within your organisation. Accountants are called upon to write reports for many different purposes. These range from very formal reports, such as those addressed to the board of directors or the audit committee, to one-off reports of a more informal nature. You should appreciate the following general points about report writing.

Checklist for report writing

7.2 The following check list for report writing indicates many of the factors that should be considered.

(a) **Purpose or terms of reference**

(i) What is the report being written about?

(ii) Why is it needed?

(iii) What effect might the report have if its findings or recommendations are acted upon?

(iv) Who are the report users? How much do they know already?

(v) What is wanted - a definite recommendation or less specific advice?

(vi) What previous reports have there been on the subject, what did they find or recommend, and what action was taken on these findings, or recommendations?

(b) **Information in the report**

(i) What is the source of each item of information in the report?

(ii) How old is the information?

(iii) What period does the report cover - a month, a year?

(iv) How can the accuracy of the information be checked and verified? To what extent might it be subject to error?

(c) **Preparing the report**

    (i)   Who is responsible for preparing the report?

    (ii)   How long will it take to prepare?

    (iii)   How is the information in the report put together (for numerical information, what computations are carried out on the source data to arrive at the figures in the report?)

    (iv)   How many copies of the report should be prepared and to whom should they be sent?

(d) **Usefulness of the report**

    (i)   What use will the report be in its present form? What action is it intended to trigger?

    (ii)   How will each recipient of the report use it for his or her own purposes?

    (iii)   Does the report meet the requirements of the terms of reference?

Format of reports in the examination

7.3   In an examination your time is limited and you are under pressure. To make life a little easier, we suggest that you adopt the following format for any report you are requested to write.

REPORT [OR MEMORANDUM]

To: Board of Directors [or Chief Accountant, etc]

From: Management Accountant   **Date:**

Subject: Report Format

Body of report

Signed: Management Accountant

7.4   If you adopt this style in your practice questions, you should end up producing it automatically. This should ensure that you do not lose any presentation marks.

7.5   Note that the date is always set to the right in CIMA solutions and is always left blank. The word 'Re' is sometimes used in place of 'Subject'. CIMA model solutions *always* include 'Signed' at the bottom, and although you might think this is superfluous (you have already said who the report is from) we recommend that you follow this style. Do not sign your own name, however! Do not draw a box round your report: we have only done this to make our example stand out. You may like to use underlining to distinguish headings. If so, use a ruler and stick to your normal colour ink (*not* a colour that the marker of your script might be using).

Chapter roundup

- Keep the various **sources of financial information** in mind and the effects of insider dealing, the efficient market hypothesis and Stock Exchange regulations.

- Much of the material here on **basic ratios** should have been revision for you. The next few chapters will cover much more complicated aspects of financial analysis.

- Make sure that you can **define** all the ratios. Look out for variations in definitions of ratios which might appear in questions.

- Always remember that 'profit' and 'net assets' are fairly **arbitrary figures**, affected by different accounting policies and manipulation.

Quick quiz

1 Apart from ratio analysis, what other information might be helpful in interpreting a company's accounts? (1.3)

2 In a period when profits are fluctuating, what effect does a company's level of gearing have on the profits available for ordinary shareholders? (4.3)

3 How does the type of assets held by a company affect its gearing ratio? (4.5, 4.6)

4 How might ratio analysis be useful when reporting on a profit forecast? (7.2 (d))

5 What are the main limitations of ratio analysis? (6.15)

6 What are the suggested contents for each part of an operating and financial review? (6.22, 6.24)

Question to try	Level	Marks	Time
28	Exam	20	36 mins

Chapter 27

BUSINESS AND SHARE VALUATION

Chapter topic	Syllabus reference	Ability required
1 Reasons for share valuations	9(c)	Skill
2 Methods of valuing shares	9(c)	Skill

Introduction

The Syllabus Guidance Notes state:

'The Examiner does not intend to set questions on the use of published financial data to suggest a valuation of a business or of shares in a business.'

As the subject is definitely still in the syllabus, however, it is covered here in full pending further clarification from the examiner.

The two main methods of share valuation are the earnings basis and the asset value basis. We have given fairly equal weighting to a variety of methods of valuation in this chapter, although the earnings and asset methods are given some prominence. This is because there are situations where one method may be easier to use or more appropriate than the others.

This chapter draws on some financial management knowledge, but some areas are too complex for discussion at Stage 3 and these (such as the CAPM) will be covered in your Stage 4 studies.

1   REASONS FOR SHARE VALUATIONS

1.1   It may be wondered why, given quoted share prices on the Stock Exchange, there is any need to devise techniques for estimating the value of a share. A share valuation will be necessary:

(a) **for quoted companies,** when there is a takeover bid and the offer price is an estimated 'fair value' in excess of the current market price of the shares;

(b) **for unquoted companies,** when:

　　(i)　　the company wishes to 'go public' and must fix an issue price for its shares;
　　(ii)　　there is a scheme of merger, and each company's shares must be assessed;
　　(iii)　　shares are sold;
　　(iv)　　shares need to be valued for the purposes of taxation;
　　(v)　　shares are pledged as collateral for a loan;

(c) **for subsidiary companies,** when the group's holding company is negotiating the sale of the subsidiary to a management buyout team or to an external buyer.

1.2   Valuing **unquoted companies** presents some special considerations.

(a) It may not be sensible to use P/E ratios of a quoted company for comparative purposes because the market value of a quoted company is likely to include a premium to reflect the marketability of its shares.

(b)   A small unquoted company may be highly sensitive to the loss of key employees which may follow a merger or buyout. An arrangement of tie key employees in to the enterprise could be very costly.

1.3   Our main interest is with methods of valuing the **entire equity** in a company, perhaps for the purpose of making a takeover bid, rather than with the value of small blocks of shares which an investor might choose to buy or sell on the stock market or, in the case of unquoted companies, privately.

2   METHODS OF VALUING SHARES

2.1   The most common methods of valuing shares are as follows.

(a)   Earnings (P/E ratio)
(b)   Accounting rate of return
(c)   Net assets
(d)   Dividend yield
(e)   Use of the CAPM
(f)   Super-profits
(g)   DCF-based valuations

Each method will give a different share valuation.

2.2   It is unlikely that one method would be used in isolation. **Several valuations** are made using different techniques or assumptions. The valuations can then be compared, and a final price reached as a compromise between the different values.

Issues in share valuation

2.3   The method(s) of valuation chosen will depend on a variety of issues.

(a)   Is the company a **going-concern**? If not, only a break-up valuation is required, future earnings are irrelevant; the value of net assets is important.

(b)   From which **perspective** are you viewing the valuation (buyer's or seller's)? If it is the buyer the lowest possible value should be used as a starting point, if the seller then **vice versa**.

(c)   What **percentage of share capital** is to be bought or sold? A premium will usually be required for a participating interest (>20%) and a greater premium for a controlling interest (>50%). For a controlling interest the ability to sell the assets of the company means both net assets and earnings will be of great interest. But bear in mind that a small holding can be key when its sale could give another shareholder control or more power.

(d)   Is the company **quoted**? A private company will usually be valued at a discount against a similar quoted company due to the lack of marketability of its shares.

(e)   How **marketable** is the share? This can have an impact on the method applied and the solution.

The P/E ratio (earnings) method of valuation

2.4   This is a common method of **valuing a controlling interest** in a company, where the owner can decide on dividend and retentions policy. The P/E ratio relates earnings per share to a share's value.

$$\text{Since P/E ratio} = \frac{\text{Market value}}{\text{EPS}}$$

$$\text{Market value} = \text{EPS} \times \text{P/E ratio}$$

2.5 The concept of the P/E ratio can be used to make an earnings-based valuation of shares. This is done by deciding a **suitable P/E ratio** and multiplying this by the EPS for the shares which are being valued. The EPS could be historical or prospective.

2.6 For a given EPS figure, a higher P/E ratio will result in a higher price. A **high P/E ratio** may indicate various factors.

 (a) **Expectations** that the EPS will grow rapidly in the years to come, so that a high price is being paid for future profit prospects. Many small, but successful and fast-growing companies are valued on the stock market on a high P/E ratio.

 (b) **Security of earnings**: a well-established low-risk company would be valued on a higher P/E ratio than a similar company whose earnings are subject to greater uncertainty.

 (c) **Status**: if a quoted company made a share-for-share takeover bid for an unquoted company, it would normally expect its own shares to be valued on a higher P/E ratio than the target company's shares. This is because a quoted company ought to be a lower-risk company; but in addition, there is a clear advantage in having shares which are quoted on a stock market: the shares can be readily sold. As a general guideline, the P/E ratio of an unquoted company's shares might be around 50% to 60% of the P/E ratio of a similar public company with a full Stock Exchange listing (and perhaps 70% of that of a company whose shares are traded on the AIM).

2.7 EXAMPLE: P/E RATIO OF VALUATION

Spider plc is considering the takeover of an unquoted company, Fly Ltd. Spider's shares are quoted on the Stock Exchange at a price of £3.20 and since the most recent published EPS of the company is 20p, the company's P/E ratio is 16. Fly Ltd is a company with 100,000 shares and current earnings of £50,000, 50p per share. How might Spider plc decide on an offer price?

2.8 SOLUTION

The decision about the offer price is likely to be based on deciding first of all what a reasonable P/E ratio would be.

 (a) If Fly Ltd is in the same industry as Spider plc, its P/E ratio ought to be lower, because of its lower status as an unquoted company.

 (b) If Fly Ltd is in a different industry, a suitable P/E ratio might be based on the P/E ratio that is typical for quoted companies in that industry.

 (c) If Fly Ltd is thought to be growing fast, so that its EPS will rise rapidly in the years to come, the P/E ratio that should be used for the share valuation will be higher than if only small EPS growth is expected.

 (d) If the acquisition of Fly Ltd would contribute substantially to Spider's own profitability and growth, or to any other strategic objective that Spider has, then Spider should be willing to offer a higher P/E ratio valuation, in order to secure acceptance of the offer by Fly's shareholders.

Of course, the P/E ratio on which Spider bases its offer will probably be lower than the P/E ratio that Fly's shareholders think their shares ought to be valued on. Some haggling over the price might be necessary.

(a) Spider might decide that Fly's shares ought to be valued on a P/E ratio of 60% × 16 = 9.6, that is, at 9.6 × 50p = £4.80 each.

(b) Fly's shareholders might reject this offer, and suggest a valuation based on a P/E ratio of, say, 12.5, that is, 12.5 × 50p = £6.25.

(c) Spider's management might then come back with a revised offer, say valuation on a P/E ratio of 10.5, that is, 10.5 × 50p = £5.25.

The haggling will go on until the negotiations either break down, or succeed in arriving at an agreed price.

2.9 When a company is thinking of acquiring an **unquoted company** in a takeover, the final offer price will be agreed by negotiation, but a list of some of the factors affecting the valuer's choice of P/E ratio is given below.

(a) General economic and financial **conditions**.

(b) The type of **industry** and the prospects of that industry.

(c) The **size** of the undertaking and its status within its industry. If an unquoted company's earnings are growing annually and are currently around £300,000 or so, then it could probably get a quote in its own right on the AIM and a higher P/E ratio should therefore be used when valuing its shares.

(d) **Marketability**: the market in shares which do not have a Stock Exchange quotation is always a restricted one and a higher yield is therefore required. As noted above, for examination purposes you should normally take a figure around one half to two thirds of the industry average when valuing an unquoted company.

(e) The **diversity of shareholdings** and the financial status of any principal shareholders.

(f) The **reliability** of profit estimates and the past profit record.

(g) **Asset backing** and liquidity.

(h) The **nature of the assets**, eg whether some of the fixed assets are of a highly specialised nature, and so have only a small break-up value.

(i) **Gearing**: a relatively high gearing ratio will generally mean greater financial risk for ordinary shareholders and call for a higher rate of return on equity.

(j) The extent to which the business is dependent on the technical skills of one or more **individuals**.

Exam focus point

In an exam question you might be asked to adjust earnings to reflect expected results post-acquisition and then apply a P/E ratio.

Question 1

Flycatcher Ltd wishes to make a takeover bid for the shares of an unquoted company, Mayfly Ltd. The earnings of Mayfly Ltd over the past five years have been as follows.

19X0	£50,000	19X3	£71,000
19X1	£72,000	19X4	£75,000
19X2	£68,000		

The average P/E ratio of quoted companies in the industry in which Mayfly Ltd operates is 10. Quoted companies which are similar in many respects to Mayfly Ltd are:

(a)   Bumblebee plc, which has a P/E ratio of 15, but is a company with very good growth prospects;

(b)   Wasp plc, which has had a poor profit record for several years, and has a P/E ratio of 7.

What would be a suitable range of valuations for the shares of Mayfly Ltd?

Answer

(a)   *Earnings.* Average earnings over the last five years have been £67,200, and over the last four years £71,500. There might appear to be some growth prospects, but estimates of future earnings are uncertain.

   A low estimate of earnings in 19X5 would be, perhaps, £71,500.

   A high estimate of earnings might be £75,000 or more. This solution will use the most recent earnings figure of £75,000 as the high estimate.

(b)   *P/E ratio.* A P/E ratio of 15 (Bumblebee's) would be much too high for Mayfly Ltd, because the growth of Mayfly Ltd earnings is not as certain, and Mayfly Ltd is an unquoted company.

   On the other hand, Mayfly Ltd's expectations of earnings are probably better than those of Wasp plc. A suitable P/E ratio might be based on the industry's average, 10; but since Mayfly is an unquoted company and therefore more risky, a lower P/E ratio might be more appropriate: perhaps 60% to 70% of 10 = 6 or 7, or conceivably even as low as 50% of 10 = 5.

   The valuation of Mayfly Ltd's shares might therefore range between:

   (i)   high P/E ratio and high earnings: 7 × £75,000 = £525,000; and
   (ii)   low P/E ratio and low earnings: 5 × £71,500 = £357,500.

2.10   When one company is thinking about taking over another, it should look at the target company's **forecast earnings,** not just its historical results. Forecasts of the future earnings of a target company might be attempted by managers in the company which is planning to make the takeover bid. Quite commonly, however, the management of the predator company will make an initial approach to the board of directors of the target company, to sound them out about a possible takeover bid. If the target company's directors are amenable to a bid, they might agree to produce forecasts of their company's future earnings and growth. These forecasts (for the next year and possibly even further ahead) might then be used by the predator company in choosing an offer price.

2.11   Forecasts of earnings growth should **only be used** if:

(a)   there are good reasons to believe that earnings growth will be achieved;

(b)   a reasonable estimate of growth can be made;

(c)   any forecasts supplied by the target company's board of directors are made in good faith.

2.12   There are **problems** with using price earnings multiples.

(a)   The calculation of the earnings figure is arbitrary.
(b)   Selecting a suitable P/E ratio is difficult.
(c)   Any discounting of the selected P/E ratio of a quoted company is to an extent arbitrary.

The accounting rate of return (ARR) method of share valuation

2.13 This method considers the accounting rate of return which will be **required from the company** whose shares are to be valued. It is therefore distinct from the P/E ratio method, which is concerned with the market rate of return required. The following formula should be used.

$$\text{Value} = \frac{\text{Estimated future profits}}{\text{Required return on capital employed}}$$

2.14 For a takeover bid valuation, it will often be necessary to **adjust the profits figure** to allow for expected changes after the takeover. Those arising in an examination question might include:

(a) new levels of **directors' remuneration**;

(b) new levels of **interest charges** (perhaps because the predator company will be able to replace existing loans with new loans at a lower rate of interest, or because the previous owners had lent the company money at non-commercial rates);

(c) a charge for **notional rent** where it is intended to sell existing properties or where the rate of return used is based on the results of similar companies that do not own their own properties;

(d) the effects of **product rationalisation** and **improved management**.

2.15 EXAMPLE: ARR METHOD OF SHARE VALUATION

Chambers Ltd is considering acquiring Hall Ltd. At present Hall Ltd is earning, on average, £480,000 after tax. The directors of Chambers Ltd feel that after reorganisation, this figure could be increased to £600,000. All the companies in the Chambers group are expected to yield a post-tax accounting return of 15% on capital employed. What should Hall Ltd be valued at?

2.16 SOLUTION

$$\text{Valuation} = \frac{£600,000}{15\%} = £4,000,000$$

This figure is the maximum that Chambers should be prepared to pay. The first offer would probably be much lower.

2.17 An ARR valuation might be used in a takeover when the acquiring company is trying to assess the **maximum amount** it can afford to pay. This is because it is a measure of management efficiency and the rate used can be selected to reflect (among other things) the return which the acquiring company thinks should be obtainable after any post-acquisition reorganisation has been completed. A valuation on this basis should then be compared with the stock market price (for quoted companies) or a price arrived at using the P/E ratio of similar quoted companies.

2.18 There are **problems** associated with this method of valuation.

(a) It is difficult to calculate an accurate figure for post-acquisition profits, having taken into account the changing cost profile following the takeover.

(b) The method does not take account of future growth in profits.

The net assets method of share valuation

2.19 Using this method of valuation, the value of a share in a particular class is equal to the **net tangible assets** attributable to that class, divided by the number of shares in the class. Intangible assets (including goodwill) should be excluded, unless they have a market value (for example patents and copyrights, which could be sold).

(a) Goodwill, if shown in the accounts, is unlikely to be shown at a true figure for purposes of valuation, and the value of goodwill should be reflected in another method of valuation (for example the earnings basis, the dividend yield basis or the super-profits method).

(b) Development expenditure, if shown in the accounts, would also have a value which is related to future profits rather than to the worth of the company's physical assets.

2.20 EXAMPLE: NET ASSETS METHOD OF SHARE VALUATION

The balance sheet of Cactus Ltd is as follows.

	£	£
Fixed assets		
Land and buildings		160,000
Plant and machinery		80,000
Motor vehicles		20,000
		260,000
Goodwill		20,000
		280,000
Current assets		
Stocks	80,000	
Debtors	60,000	
Short-term investments	15,000	
Cash	5,000	
	160,000	
Current liabilities		
Creditors	60,000	
Taxation	20,000	
Proposed ordinary dividend	20,000	
	100,000	
Net current assets		60,000
		340,000
12% debentures		60,000
Deferred taxation		10,000
		270,000
Capital and reserves		
Ordinary shares of £1		80,000
Reserves		140,000
		220,000
4.9% preference shares of £1		50,000
		270,000

What is the value of an ordinary share using the net assets basis of valuation?

2.21 SOLUTION

If the figures given for asset values are not questioned, the valuation would be as follows.

	£	£
Total value of net assets		340,000
Less intangible asset (goodwill)		20,000
Total value of tangible assets (net)		320,000
Less: preference shares	50,000	
debentures	60,000	
deferred taxation	10,000	
		120,000
Net asset value of equity		200,000
Number of ordinary shares		80,000
Value per share		£2.50

2.22 The difficulty in an asset valuation method is establishing the **asset values to use**. Values ought to be realistic. The figure attached to an individual asset may vary considerably depending on whether it is valued on a going concern or a break-up basis.

2.23 The following list should give you some idea of the **factors** that must be considered.

(a) Do the assets need **professional valuation**? If so, how much will this cost?

(b) Have the **liabilities** been accurately quantified, eg deferred taxation? Are there any contingent liabilities? Will any balancing tax charges arise on disposal?

(c) How have the **current assets** been valued? Are all debtors collectable? Is all stock realisable? Can all the assets be physically located and brought into a saleable condition? This may be difficult in certain circumstances where the assets are situated abroad.

(d) Can any **hidden liabilities** be accurately assessed? Would there be redundancy payments and closure costs?

(e) Is there an **available market** in which the assets can be realised (on a break-up basis)? If so, do the balance sheet values truly reflect these break-up values?

(f) Are there any **prior charges** on the assets?

2.24 The net assets basis of valuation should be used in the following circumstances.

(a) **As a measure of the 'security' in a share value**. A share might be valued using the earnings basis, and this valuation might be:

(i) higher than the net asset value per share. If the company went into liquidation, the investor could not expect to receive the full value of his shares when the underlying assets were realised;

(ii) lower than the net asset value per share. If the company went into liquidation, the investor might expect to receive the full value of his shares (perhaps much more) when the underlying assets were realised.

The asset backing for shares thus provides a measure of the possible loss if the company fails to make the expected earnings or dividend payments. It is often thought to be a good thing to acquire a company with valuable tangible assets, especially freehold property which might be expected to increase in value over time.

(b) **As a measure of comparison in a scheme of merger**. For example, if company A, which has a low asset backing, is planning a merger with company B, which has a high asset backing, the shareholders of B might consider that their shares' value ought to reflect this. It might therefore be agreed that something should be added to the value of the company B shares to allow for this difference in asset backing.

For these reasons, it is always advisable to calculate the net assets per share.

The dividend yield method of share valuation

2.25 The dividend yield method of share valuation is suitable for the valuation of **small shareholdings in unquoted companies.** It is based on the principle that small shareholders are mainly interested in dividends, since they cannot control decisions affecting the company's profits and earnings. A suitable offer price would therefore be one which compensates them for the future dividends they will be giving up if they sell their shares. You might be expected to value shares using gross dividend yield rather than net dividend yield. Read any examination question carefully.

2.26 The simplest dividend capitalisation technique is based on the assumption that the level of dividends in the future will be **constant.** A dividend yield valuation would be:

$$\text{Value} = \frac{\text{Dividend in pence}}{\text{Expected dividend yield \%}}$$

2.27 It may be possible to use expected future dividends for a share valuation and to predict **dividend growth.** For this purpose, it is first necessary to predict future earnings and then to decide how changes in earnings will be reflected in the company's dividend policy.

2.28 The **dividend growth model** for share valuation, you may recall from your other studies, is as follows.

$$MV = \frac{d_0(1+g)}{(r-g)}$$

where

	MV	is the current market value ex-dividend
	d_0	is the current dividend
	g	is the expected annual growth in dividend, so
	d_0	$(1 + g)$ is the expected dividend next year
	r	is the return required

2.29 There are **problems** with these methods of share valuation.

(a) Predicting future earnings and hence dividends.

(b) Calculating an appropriate discount rate. An investor may be prepared to accept a lower rate of return where he achieves significant influence ($>20\%$), or where he can block the company on special resolutions ($>25\%$).

The super-profits method of share valuation

2.30 This method starts by applying a 'fair return' to the net tangible assets and comparing the result with the expected profits. Any **excess of profits** (the super-profits) is used to calculate goodwill.

The goodwill is normally taken as a fixed number of years super-profits. The goodwill is then added to the value of the target company's tangible assets to arrive at a value for the business. Profits should be adjusted for any directors' rewards beyond their value to the business.

2.31 EXAMPLE: SUPER-PROFITS METHOD OF SHARE VALUATION

Light Ltd has net tangible assets of £120,000 and present earnings of £20,000. Doppler Ltd wants to take over Light Ltd and considers that a fair return for this type of industry is 12%, and decides to value Light Ltd taking goodwill at three years super-profits.

2.32 SOLUTION

	£
Actual profits	20,000
Less fair return on net tangible assets: 12% × £120,000	14,400
Super-profits	5,600
Goodwill: 3 × £5,600	£16,800
Value of Light Ltd: £120,000 + £16,800	£136,800

2.33 The principal **drawbacks** to this valuation method are as follows.

(a) The rate of return required is chosen subjectively.

(b) The number of years purchase of super-profits is arbitrary. In the example above, goodwill was valued at three years of super-profits, but it could have been, for example, two years or four years of super-profits.

While this method is unscientific, it is widely used, particularly in the sale of smaller businesses for which there are very often yardsticks set within in a trade.

The discounted future profits method of share valuation

2.34 This method of share valuation may be appropriate when one company intends to **buy the assets** of another company and to make further investments in order to improve profits in the future.

2.35 EXAMPLE: DISCOUNTED FUTURE PROFITS METHOD OF SHARE VALUATION

Diversification Ltd wishes to make a bid for Tadpole Ltd. Tadpole Ltd makes after-tax profits of £40,000 a year. Diversification Ltd believes that if further money is spent on additional investments, the after-tax cash flows (ignoring the purchase consideration) could be as follows.

Year	Cash flow (net of tax)
	£
0	(100,000)
1	(80,000)
2	60,000
3	100,000
4	150,000
5	150,000

The after-tax cost of capital of Diversification Ltd is 15% and the company expects all its investments to pay back, in discounted terms, within five years.

What is the maximum price that the company should be willing to pay for the shares of Tadpole Ltd?

2.36 SOLUTION

The maximum price is one which would make the return from the total investment exactly 15% over five years, so that the NPV at 15% would be 0.

Year	Cash flows ignoring purchase consideration £	Discount factor @ @ 15%	Present value £
0	(100,000)	1.000	(100,000)
1	(80,000)	0.870	(69,600)
2	60,000	0.756	45,360
3	100,000	0.658	65,800
4	150,000	0.572	85,800
5	150,000	0.497	74,550
Maximum purchase price			101,910

2.37 This method is unusually **unworkable in practice** because of:

(a) the difficulty of predicting future cash flows; and

(b) the problem of choosing an appropriate discount rate.

2.38 Section summary

Which of the above methods you use in an exam depends on the **requirements of the question** and the **circumstances given**. Remember the following points.

- Adjustments to earnings for post-acquisition changes
- Quoted vs unquoted companies
- Availability of information
- Size of shareholding to be acquired (<20%, 20-50%, 50% +)

Question 2

Black Raven Ltd is a prosperous private company, whose owners are also the directors. The directors have decided to sell their business, and have begun a search for organisations interested in its purchase. They have asked for your assessment of the price per ordinary share a purchaser might be expected to offer.

Relevant information is as follows.

BALANCE SHEET (MOST RELEVANT)

	£'000	£'000
Fixed assets (net book value)		
Land and buildings		800
Plant and equipment		450
Motor vehicles		55
Patents		2
		1,307
Current assets		
Stock	250	
Debtors	125	
Cash	8	
	383	
Current liabilities		
Creditors	180	
Taxation	50	
	230	
Net current assets		153
Long-term liability		1,460
Loan secured on property		400
		1,060

	£'000	£'000
Capital and reserves		
Share capital (300,000 ordinary shares of £1)		300
Reserves		760
		1,060

The profits after tax and interest but before dividends over the last five years have been as follows.

		£
Year	1	90,000
	2	80,000
	3	105,000
	4	90,000
	5 (most recent)	100,000

The annual dividend has been £45,000 (gross) for the last six years.

The company's five year plan forecasts an after-tax profit of £100,000 for the next 12 months, with an increase of 4% a year over each of the next four years.

As part of their preparations to sell the company, the directors of Black Raven Ltd have had the fixed assets revalued by an independent expert, with the following results.

	£
Land and buildings	1,075,000
Plant and equipment	480,000
Motor vehicles	45,000

The dividend yields and P/E ratios of three quoted companies in the same industry as Black Raven Ltd over the last three years have been as follows.

	Aardvark plc		Bullfinch plc		Crow plc	
	Div. yield %	P/E ratio	Div. yield %	P/E ratio	Div. yield %	P/E ratio
Recent year	12	8.50	11.0	9.0	13.0	10.0
Previous year	12	8.00	10.6	8.5	12.6	9.5
Three years ago	12	8.50	9.3	8.0	12.4	9.0
Average	12	8.33	10.3	8.5	12.7	9.5

Large companies in the industry apply an after-tax cost of capital of about 18% to acquisition proposals when the investment is not backed by tangible assets, as opposed to a rate of only 14% on the net tangible assets.

Your assessment of the net cash flows which would accrue to a purchasing company, allowing for taxation and the capital expenditure required after the acquisition to achieve the company's target five year plan, is as follows.

	£
Year 1	120,000
Year 2	120,000
Year 3	140,000
Year 4	70,000
Year 5	120,000

Required

Use the information provided to suggest seven valuations which prospective purchasers might make.

Answer

(a) *An assets basis valuation*

If we assume that a purchaser would accept the revaluation of assets by the independent valuer, an assets valuation of equity would be as follows.

Part C: Interpretation of accounts

Fixed assets	£	£
(ignore patents, assumed to have no market value)		
Land and buildings		1,075,000
Plant and equipment		480,000
Motor vehicles		45,000
		1,600,000
Current assets		383,000
		1,983,000
Less: current liabilities	230,000	
loan	400,000	
		630,000
Asset value of equity (300,000 shares)		1,353,000
Value per share = £4.51		

Unless the purchasing company intends to sell the assets acquired, it is more likely that a valuation would be based on earnings.

(b) *Earnings basis valuations*

If the purchaser believes that earnings over the last five years are an appropriate measure for valuation, we could take average earnings in these years, which were

$$\frac{£465,000}{5} = £93,000$$

An appropriate P/E ratio for an earnings basis valuation might be the average of the three publicly quoted companies for the recent year. (A trend towards an increase in the P/E ratio over three years is assumed, and even though average earnings have been taken, the most recent year's P/E ratios are considered to be the only figures which are appropriate.)

	P/E ratio	
Aardvark plc	8.5	
Bullfinch plc	9.0	
Crow plc	10.0	
Average	9.167	(i)
Reduce by about 40% to allow for unquoted status	5.5	(ii)

Share valuations on a past earnings basis are as follows.

	P/E ratio	Earnings £'000	Valuation £'000	Number of shares	Value per share
(i)	9.167	93	852.5	300,000	£2.84
(ii)	5.5	93	511.5	300,000	£1.71

Because of the unquoted status of Black Raven Ltd, purchasers would probably apply a lower P/E ratio, and an offer of about £1.71 per share would be more likely than one of £2.84.

Future earnings might be used. Forecast earnings based on the company's five year plan will be used.

		£	
Expected earnings:	Year 1	100,000	
	Year 2	104,000	
	Year 3	108,160	
	Year 4	112,486	
	Year 5	116,986	
	Average	108,326.4	(say £108,000)

A share valuations on an expected earnings basis would be as follows.

P/E ratio	Average future earnings	Valuation	Value per share
5.5	£108,000	£594,000	£1.98

It is not clear whether the purchasing company would accept Black Raven's own estimates of earnings.

(c) *A dividend yield basis of valuation with no growth*

There seems to have been a general pattern of increase in dividend yields to shareholders in quoted companies, and it is reasonable to suppose that investors in Black Raven would require at least the same yield.

An average yield for the recent year for the three quoted companies will be used. This is 12%. The only reliable dividend figure for Black Raven Ltd is £45,000 a year gross, in spite of the expected increase in future earnings. A yield basis valuation would therefore be:

$$\frac{£45,000}{12\%} = £375,000 \text{ or £1.25 per share.}$$

A purchasing company would, however, be more concerned with earnings than with dividends if it intended to buy the entire company, and an offer price of £1.25 should be considered too low. On the other hand, since Black Raven Ltd is an unquoted company, a higher yield than 12% might be expected.

(d) *A dividend yield basis of valuation, with growth*

Since earnings are expected to increase by 4% a year, it could be argued that a similar growth rate in dividends would be expected. We shall assume that the required yield is 17%, rather more than the 12% for quoted companies because Black Raven Ltd is unquoted. However, in the absence of information about the expected growth of dividends in the quoted companies, the choice of 12%, 17% or whatever, is not much better than a guess.

$$MV = \frac{d_0\,(1+g)}{(r-g)} = \frac{45,000(1.04)}{(0.17-0.04)} = £360,000 \text{ or £1.20 per share}$$

(e) *The discounted value of future cash flows*

The present value of cash inflows from an investment by a purchaser of Black Raven Ltd's shares would be discounted at either 18% or 14%, depending on the view taken of Black Raven Ltd's assets. Although the loan of £400,000 is secured on some of the company's property, there are enough assets against which there is no charge to assume that a purchaser would consider the investment to be backed by tangible assets.

The present value of the benefits from the investment would be as follows.

Year	Cash flow £'000	Discount factor 14%*	PV of cash flow £'000
1	120	0.877	105.24
2	120	0.769	92.28
3	140	0.675	94.50
4	70	0.592	41.44
5	120	0.519	62.28
			395.74

$$* \ \frac{1}{1.14},\ \frac{1}{(1.14)^2} \ \text{etc}$$

A valuation per share of £1.32 might therefore be made. This basis of valuation is one which a purchasing company ought to consider. It might be argued that cash flows beyond year 5 should be considered and a higher valuation could be appropriate, but a figure of less than £2 per share would be offered on a DCF valuation basis.

(f) *The accounting rate of return method*

If a company wishing to take over Black Raven Ltd expects to make an accounting rate of return of, say, 20%, and assuming that a return of £100,000 is assumed for this purpose the valuation of Black Raven Ltd might be

$$\frac{£100,000}{20\%} = £500,000, \text{ or £1.67 per share.}$$

(g)   *The super-profits method*

If we assume that the normal rate of profit is 5% on net assets, the normal profits might be as follows (although 'net assets' could be defined in other ways).

	£
Asset value of equity (see (a))	1,353,000
Add asset value of loan stock	400,000
Net assets	1,753,000
Actual (current) profit	100,000
Less normal profit after taxation (5%)	87,650
Super-profits	12,350
Goodwill (say two years purchase of super-profits)	£24,700

The total purchase consideration for equity would be £1,353,000 + £24,700 = £1,377,700 or £4.59 per share.

(h)   *Summary*

Any of the preceding valuations might be made, but since share valuation is largely a subjective matter, many other prices might be offered. In view of the high asset values of the company an asset stripping purchaser might come forward.

Case examples: share valuations

Share valuations can take place on the occasion of a *demerger*. Hanson, the conglomerate built up and run by Lord Hanson and the late Lord White, has demerged and you will find it useful to investigate how the individual demerged parts of the group have been valued. In particular, articles in the *Financial Times* on 1 February 1996 will be of great interest.

Takeover battles are also of interest from the point of view of share valuation. The takeover battle which led up to Granada's takeover of Forte is a good example and an article in the *Financial Times* on 23 November 1995 looks at the value placed on Forte.

Chapter roundup

- There are a number of different ways of putting a value on a business, or on shares in an unquoted company. It makes sense to use **several methods of valuation**, and to compare the values they produce.

- At the end of the day, however, what really matters is the final price that the **buyer and the seller agree.** The purchase price for a company will usually be discussed mainly in terms of:

  o   P/E ratios, when a large block of shares, or a whole business is being valued;
  o   alternatively, a DCF valuation;
  o   to a lesser extent, the net assets per share.

- When advising on the price of a block of shares you must always take into account the **size of the holding** under consideration ie is it 5-10%? >20% or >50%?

- The dividend yield method is more relevant to **small shareholdings**.

Quick quiz

1   Why are valuations of companies sometimes necessary? (see para 1.1)

2   What guidelines should help to determine the P/E ratio on which to base an offer price for shares in a target company? (2.10)

3   What is a dividend growth model? (2.28)

4   How should the net assets of a company be valued, for a net assets method valuation? (2.19 - 2.23) Why is the net assets method of valuation used as a reference value? (2.24)

Question to try	Level	Marks	Time
29	Introductory	n/a	n/a

BPP PUBLISHING

Chapter 28

SEGMENTAL REPORTING AND TREND ANALYSIS

Chapter topic	Syllabus reference	Ability required
1 SSAP 25 *Segmental reporting*	9(c)	Application
2 The nature of profit	9(c)	Application
3 Other problems with financial analysis	9(c)	Application

Introduction

This chapter looks at segmental reporting and trend analysis as well as some of the problems with financial analysis in general.

You covered segmental reporting in your earlier studies, so it is summarised here. A new discussion draft on segmental reporting has been produced by the ASB, in response to international developments.

Issues around the nature of profit are very topical.

1 SSAP 25 SEGMENTAL REPORTING 5/97

1.1 The Companies Act 1985 and the Stock Exchange both require the disclosure of segmental information. The purpose of SSAP 25 *Segmental reporting* is twofold:

(a) it provides guidance to all companies on how best to comply with Companies Act requirements on segmental information; and

(b) it requires plcs and large private companies to disclose more segmental information than CA 1985 requires.

Exam focus point
Read the discussion carefully as you may be asked for these arguments in an exam. If you are asked for number crunching the numbers should be fairly straightforward.

Reasons for segmental information

1.2 Segmental information is considered useful for the following reasons.

(a) Segmental information can **explain** factors which have **contributed to company results**.
(b) Users can **compare the results of different products from year to year**.
(c) Users can **compare performance** with companies **within the same market**.
(d) Users can **assess the future risks and rewards** associated with the business.

Arguments against reporting by segment

1.3   Those who argue against this form of disclosure generally emphasise the practical problems, which include:

- **Identifying segments** for reporting purposes

- **Allocating common income and costs** among the different segments

- Reporting **inter-segment** transactions

- Providing information in such a way as to **eliminate misunderstanding** by investors

- **Avoiding any potential damage** that may be done to the reporting entity by disclosing information about individual segments

---

Knowledge brought forward from Paper 5

SSAP 25 and CA 1985 on segmental reporting

Reportable segment: definition

- SSAP 25

  - A class of business is a distinguishable component of an enterprise that provides a separate product or a separate group of related products or services.

  - A geographical segment is an area comprising an individual country or group of countries in which a company operates or to which it supplies products or services.

- CA 1995 (directors' opinion)

  - A class of business is a component of an enterprise that differs substantially from other elements of the business.

  - A geographical segment is a market supplied by a business which differs substantially from other geographical markets supplied.

- $\geq$ 10% of third party turnover/net assets/profit should be used to identify a segment.

Scope

- SSAP 25 applies only to plcs, banks/insurance companies, and companies exceeding medium-sized company criteria $\times$ 10.

- Companies can dispense with the disclosure of segmental information if, in the opinion of the directors, it would be seriously prejudicial to the interests of the company: a statement to that effect is required.

Disclosure

An example of disclosure is shown on the next two pages.

BPP PUBLISHING

CLASSES OF BUSINESS

	Industry A 19X2 £'000	Industry A 19X1 £'000	Industry B 19X2 £'000	Industry B 19X1 £'000	Other Industries 19X2 £'000	Other Industries 19X1 £'000	Group 19X2 £'000	Group 19X1 £'000
Turnover								
Total sales	33,000	30,000	42,000	38,000	26,000	23,000	101,000	91,000
Inter-segment sales	(4,000)	-	-	-	(12,000)	(14,000)	(16,000)	(14,000)
Sales to third parties	29,000	30,000	42,000	38,000	14,000	9,000	85,000	77,000
Profit before taxation								
Segment profit	3,000	2,500	4,500	4,000	1,800	1,500	9,300	8,000
Common costs							(300)	(300)
Operating profit							9,000	7,700
Net interest							(400)	(500)
							8,600	7,200
Group share of the profit before taxation of associated undertakings	1,000	1,000	1,400	1,200	-	-	2,400	2,200
Group profit before taxation							11,000	9,400
Net assets								
Segment net assets	17,600	15,000	24,000	25,000	19,400	19,000	61,000	59,000
Unallocated assets*							3,000	3,000
							64,000	62,000
Group share of the net assets of associated undertakings	10,200	8,000	8,800	9,000	-	-	19,000	17,000
Total net assets							83,000	79,000

* Unallocated assets consist of assets at the group's head office in London amounting to £2.4 million (19X1: £2.5 million) and at the group's regional office in Hong Kong amounting to £0.6 million (19X1: £0.5 million).

GEOGRAPHICAL SEGMENTS

	United Kingdom		North America		Far East		Other		Group	
	19X2 £'000	19X1 £'000	19X2 £'000	19X1 £'000	19X2 £'000	19X1 £'000	19X2 £'000	19X1 £'000	19X2 £'000	19X1 £'000
Turnover										
Turnover by destination										
Sales to third parties	34,000	31,000	16,000	14,500	25,000	23,000	10,000	8,500	85,000	77,000
Turnover by origin										
Total sales	38,000	34,000	29,000	27,500	23,000	23,000	12,000	10,500	102,000	95,000
Inter-segment sales	-	-	(8,000)	(9,000)	(9,000)	(9,000)	-	-	(17,000)	(18,000)
Sales to third parties	38,000	34,000	21,000	18,500	14,000	14,000	12,000	10,500	85,000	77,000
Profit before taxation										
Segment profit	4,000	2,900	2,500	2,300	1,800	1,900	1,000	900	9,300	8,000
Common costs									(300)	(300)
Operating profit									9,000	7,700
Net interest									(400)	(500)
									8,600	7,200
Group share of the profit before taxation of associated undertakings	950	1,000	1,450	1,200	-	-	-	-	2,400	2,200
Group profit before taxation									11,000	9,400
Net assets										
Segment net assets	16,000	15,000	25,000	26,000	16,000	15,000	4,000	3,000	61,000	59,000
Unallocated assets*									3,000	3,000
									64,000	62,000
Group share of the net assets of associated undertakings	8,500	7,000	10,500	10,000	-	-	-	-	19,000	17,000
Total net assets									83,000	79,000

* Unallocated assets consist of assets at the group's head office in London amounting to £2.4 million (19X1: £2.5 million) and at the group's regional office in Hong Kong amounting to £0.6 million (19X1: £0.5 million).

BPP PUBLISHING

ASB *Segmental reporting* (discussion paper)

1.4   In May 1996, the ASB issued a discussion paper on segmental reporting. The paper seeks comments on two **international proposals**;

(a)   E 51 *Reporting financial information by segment* (IASC); and

(b)   *Reporting disaggregated information about a business* (US FASB).

1.5   The **key issues** in this area are:

(a)   the division of operations into segments;

(b)   the information to be given for each segment; and

(c)   whether the information given is verifiable and easy to understand.

1.6   The **IASC proposals** develop the risks and returns approach used in the current UK SSAP 25. The IASC envisages that segments should be identified by the different **risks and returns** an entity faces, either through providing different products or services or through providing products or services in different geographical locations.

1.7   The IASC proposes that **more information** should be given for each primary segment (the dominant source of risk for the entity) than is currently required for a segment under SSAP 25. The information should be prepared on the same basis as that given in the external financial statements.

1.8   The **FASB proposals** reflect a **managerial approach** under which segments reflect the way management disaggregates the entity for making operating decisions. Amounts reported by segment would be based on the information used internally by the chief executive or equivalent management committee to manage the business.

1.9   Although the IASC and the FASB approaches differ, the effect in practice, at least in the identification of segments, may be similar in that the IASC notes that the **dominant source** of risk affects how most enterprises are organised and managed. An enterprise's organisational structure and its internal financial reporting system should thus normally be the basis for identifying its segments under the IASC proposals.

2   THE NATURE OF PROFIT

2.1   We have seen throughout this text that accounting 'profit' is an arbitrary figure, subject to the whims and biases of accountants and the variety of treatments in accounting standards. Go back to the contents page and pick out all the topics which demonstrate or indicate how company results are manipulated. Isn't it nearly all of them? Let us briefly mention some of them again.

SSAP 4 *Accounting for government grants*

2.2   SSAP 4 allows capital grants to be credited to revenue over the expected life of the asset in two ways:

(a)   by reducing the acquisition cost of the fixed asset by the amount of the grant and providing depreciation on the reduced amount; or

(b)   by treating the amount of the grant as a deferred credit and transferring a portion of it to revenue annually.

The final profit figure is the same under both methods but the depreciation charge disclosed will be different, as will the carrying value of the asset.

SSAP 9 *Stocks and long-term contracts*

2.3 Companies are allowed to use different methods of valuing stock under SSAP 9, which means that the final stock figure in the balance sheet will be different under each method. Profit will be affected by the closing stock valuation, particularly where the level of stock fluctuates to a great extent.

FRS 15 *Tangible fixed assets*

2.4 As with SSAP 9, FRS 15 allows different accounting bases for depreciation. Choosing to use the reducing balance method rather than the straight line method can front-load the depreciation charge for assets. It is also the case that the subjectivity surrounding the estimated economic lives of assets can lead to manipulation of profits. (*Note.* Remember that some companies refuse to depreciate some assets at all - mainly freehold property.)

SSAP 13 *Accounting for research and development*

2.5 Development costs can be capitalised under SSAP 13, whereas all research costs should be written off. Although the criteria for capitalisation are quite strict, there is room for manipulation.

2.6 You should note that the ASB is trying to stop abuses such as those described here by forcing companies to follow general tenets (FRS 5, *Statement of Principles*) and also by restricting abusive practice, eg merger accounting and FRS 6.

3 OTHER PROBLEMS WITH FINANCIAL ANALYSIS

3.1 Two frequent problems affecting financial analysis are discussed here:

(a) **seasonal fluctuations**; and
(b) **window dressing**.

Seasonal fluctuations

3.2 Many companies are located in industries where trade is **seasonal**. For example:

(a) firework manufacturers;
(b) swimwear manufacturers;
(c) ice cream makers;
(d) umbrella manufacturers;
(e) gas companies;
(f) travel agents;
(g) flower suppliers and deliverers;
(h) football clubs.

3.3 Year on year the seasonal fluctuations affecting such companies does not matter; a year end has to be chosen and as long as the fluctuations are at roughly the same time every year, then there should be no problem. Occasionally a perverse sense of humour will cause a company to choose an accounting period ending in the middle of the busy season: this may affect the cut off because the busy season might be slightly early or late.

3.4 A major difficulty can arise if companies affected by seasonal fluctuations change their accounting date. A shorter period (normally) may encompass part, all or none of the busy season. Whatever happens, the figures will be distorted and the comparatives will be

meaningless. Analysts would not know how to extrapolate the figures from the shorter period to produce a comparison for the previous year. Weightings could be used, but these are likely to be inaccurate.

3.5   An example of the problems this can cause occurred when. British Gas plc changed its accounting period to 31 December from 31 March. The company published two reports and accounts for:

(a)   the year to 31 March 1991; and

(b)   the year to 31 December 1991;

thus including the first three months of the calendar year in both reports. As a note to the later accounts, the company produced a profit and loss account for the last nine months of the calendar year.

3.6   Although the British Gas auditors did not qualify the audit report, the Review Panel was not very happy about this double counting of results. The nine month profit and loss account did not meet the provisions of CA 1985 'either as to its location or its contents, nor did it contain the relevant earnings per share figure'. British Gas had to promise that, in their 1992 results, the 1991 comparative would be for the nine months period only.

3.7   The effect here is obvious. The first three months of the calendar year are when British Gas earns a high proportion of its profits (winter!). If the 1991 results had covered the period from 1 April only, then the profits would have been reduced by more than an average loss of three months' profit. By using a 12 month period, British Gas avoided the risk of the period's results looking too bad.

Window dressing

3.8   Window dressing transactions were made largely redundant by SSAP 17 *Accounting for post balance sheet events*. SSAP 17 stated that non-adjusting events requiring disclosure include the reversal or maturity after the balance sheet date of transactions, the substance of which was primarily to alter the appearance of the balance sheet. This gives a good description of window dressing transactions. Note that window dressing transactions were not outlawed, but full disclosure would render such transactions useless.

3.9   One example of window dressing is a situation where a large cheque is written against one group company's positive bank balance in favour of another group company with a large overdraft. The cheque is put through at the year end and then cancelled at the beginning of the next year, thus concealing the overdraft in the consolidated balance sheet (where positive and negative bank balances cannot be netted off).

3.10   CA 1985 requires coterminous accounting periods for all group companies. This is to avoid window dressing, for example where a subsidiary with a period end three months later than that of the group makes a profit in one part of its year and a loss in the other. By choosing whatever method will produce the best results, the company could book a result which will be wholly or partly reversed in the next period.

3.11   You may be able to think of other examples of window dressing and you should look for any potential examples which come up in examination questions.

Summary of limitations of financial analysis

3.12 (a) **Information problems**

   (i) The base information is often out of date, so timeliness of information leads to problems of interpretation.

   (ii) Historic cost information may not be the most appropriate information for the decision for which the analysis is being undertaken.

   (iii) Information in published accounts is generally summarised information and detailed information may be needed.

   (iv) Analysis of accounting information only identifies symptoms not causes and thus is of limited use.

(b) **Comparison problems: inter-temporal**

   (i) Effects of price changes make comparisons difficult unless adjustments are made.

   (ii) Impacts of changes in technology on the price of assets, the likely return and the future markets.

   (iii) Impacts of a changing environment on the results reflected in the accounting information.

   (iv) Potential effects of changes in accounting policies on the reported results.

   (v) Problems associated with establishing a normal base year to compare other years with.

(c) **Comparison problems: inter-firm**

   (i) Selection of industry norms and the usefulness of norms based on averages.

   (ii) Different firms having different financial and business risk profiles and the impact on analysis.

   (iii) Different firms using different accounting policies.

   (iv) Impacts of the size of the business and its comparators on risk, structure and returns.

   (v) Impacts of different environments on results, for example different countries or home-based versus multinational firms.

You should use this summary as a type of checklist.

Chapter roundup

- SSAP 25 Segmental reporting requires listed companies to provide a breakdown of their operations in different geographical and business areas.

- Ratios based on current cost and current purchasing power accounts are more useful for trend analysis over time than ratios based on historical cost accounts.

- *Financial analysis* is not a precise science. The nature of accounting information means that distortions and differences will always exist between sets of accounts, not only from company to company, but also over time.

- *Seasonal fluctuations* and *window dressing* arise quite often in practice. You must be on your guard to spot them.

Quick quiz

1   Why is segmental reporting considered useful? (see para 1.2)

2   What are the arguments against segmental reporting? (1.3)

3   What are the key issues in segmental reporting identified by the ASB's discussion draft? (1.5)

6   Name some accounting standards which currently allow choice of accounting policy. (2.2 - 2.9)

7   What kinds of businesses are affected by seasonal fluctuations? (3.2)

8   When can seasonal fluctuations have a strong impact? (3.4)

9   Which accounting standard largely outlawed window dressing? (3.8)

Question to try	Level	Marks	Time
30	Exam	20	36 mins

Part D
International regulation

Chapter 29

INTERNATIONAL ISSUES AND COMPARATIVE ACCOUNTING

Chapter topic	Syllabus reference	Ability required
1 International harmonisation	9(d)	Knowledge
2 Accounting overseas	9(d)	Knowledge
3 Financial reporting in the USA	9(d)	Knowledge
4 Restating overseas and UK accounts	9(d)	Knowledge

Introduction

The examiner has stated the following in the Syllabus Guidance Notes.

'Chartered Management Accountants needs to be aware of international accounting regulation and how it affects their own organisations. In particular, they should be aware of the fact that the nature and extent of the regulatory framework differs from country to country. Candidates should be aware of the major financial reporting issues on which opinion differs from country to country.

The following items are *not* examinable.

- Detailed knowledge of individual regulatory frameworks, other than the UK frameworks.
- Details of any IASs.'

In this chapter we will concentrate on some of the major European systems and the US system of financial accounting and reporting as these are still the major accounting models.

As business expands on an international scale so financial reporting must be viewed as it operates on an international rather than a national level. In studying the impact of the international environment we will look at the influences on accounting in a number of countries. These influences vary from country to country and include legal, political, socio-cultural and economic conditions prevailing at any time.

1   INTERNATIONAL HARMONISATION   5/95, 5/96, 5/97, 5/98

1.1   As an introduction to this topic, it is useful to consider what the examiner has said about it, in response to questions about this part of the syllabus. This expands on the part of the Syllabus Guidance Notes quoted in the introduction above.

'Candidates will not be required to be conversant with the detail of international accounting and auditing standards. They will need to be familiar with the workings of the International Accounting Standards Committee (IASC) and how it aims to achieve harmonisation. They should know that international regulation is undertaken by the IASC and, within Europe, by the European Commission; that individual countries are expected to incorporate IASC and EC provisions in their own regulations. As companies become more and more international, it is important for the management accountant to be familiar with international regulation.

BPP PUBLISHING

> Accounting has developed along two main streams, which can be referred to as the UK model and the Continental model. The UK model is followed by such countries as the USA, Australia and New Zealand and the Continental model by countries such as France, Germany and Spain. The models differ because of the differing purposes behind preparing accounts. The main purpose of the UK model is to provide information to the shareholders who need published information regarding their investment and need to ensure that it is managed well. The main purpose of the Continental model is to provide information to the taxation authorities. The UK model aims to give the highest profit possible and the Continental model the lowest. The management accountant needs to be aware of these differences when looking at financial statements from different countries.'

1.2   Before we look at any other countries in particular, we must consider what barriers there are to international harmonisation and why harmonisation is considered so desirable, before looking at comparative accounting systems.

Barriers to harmonisation

1.3   There are undoubtedly many barriers to international harmonisation: if there were not then greater progress would probably have been made by now. The main problems are as follows.

(a)   **Different purposes of financial reporting.** In some countries the purpose is solely for tax assessment, while in others it is for investor decision-making.

(b)   **Different legal systems.** These prevent the development of certain accounting practices and restrict the options available.

(c)   **Different user groups.** Countries have different ideas about who the relevant user groups are and their respective importance. In the USA investor and creditor groups are given prominence, while in Europe employees enjoy a higher profile.

(d)   **Needs of developing countries.** Developing countries are obviously behind in the standard setting process and they need to develop the basic standards and principles already in place in most developed countries.

(e)   **Nationalism** is demonstrated in an unwillingness to accept another country's standard.

(f)   **Cultural differences** result in objectives for accounting systems differing from country to country.

(g)   **Unique circumstances.** Some countries may be experiencing unusual circumstances which affect all aspects of everyday life and impinge on the ability of companies to produce proper reports, for example hyperinflation, civil war, currency restriction and so on.

(h)   **The lack of strong accountancy bodies.** Many countries do not have strong independent accountancy or business bodies which would press for better standards and greater harmonisation.

1.4   These are difficult problems to overcome, and yet attempts are being made continually to do so. We must therefore consider what the perceived advantages of harmonisation are, which justify so much effort.

Advantages of global harmonisation

1.5   The advantages of harmonisation will be based on the benefits to users and preparers of accounts, as follows.

(a)   **Investors,** both individual and corporate, would like to be able to compare the financial results of different companies internationally as well as nationally in making

investment decisions. Differences in accounting practice and reporting can prove to be a barrier to such cross-border analysis. There is a growing amount of investment across borders and there are few financial analysts able to follow shares in international markets. For example, it is not easy for an analyst familiar with UK accounting principles to analyse the financial statements of a Dutch or German company. Harmonisation would therefore be of benefit to such analysts.

(b) **Multinational companies** would benefit from harmonisation for many reasons including the following.

    (i)   Better access would be gained to foreign investor funds.

    (ii)   Management control would be improved, because harmonisation would aid internal communication of financial information.

    (iii)   Appraisal of foreign enterprises for take-overs and mergers would be more straightforward.

    (iv)   It would be easier to comply with the reporting requirements of overseas stock exchanges.

    (v)   Consolidation of foreign subsidiaries and associated companies would be easier.

    (vi)   A reduction in audit costs might be achieved.

    (vii)   Transfer of accounting staff across national borders would be easier.

(c) **Governments of developing countries** would save time and money if they could adopt international standards and, if these were used internally, governments of developing countries could attempt to control the activities of foreign multinational companies in their own country. These companies could not 'hide' behind foreign accounting practices which are difficult to understand.

(d) **Tax authorities**. It will be easier to calculate the tax liability of investors, including multinationals who receive income from overseas sources.

(e) **Regional economic groups** usually promote trade within a specific geographical region. This would be aided by common accounting practices within the region.

(f) **Large international accounting firms** would benefit as accounting and auditing would be much easier if similar accounting practices existed throughout the world.

Progress with harmonisation to date

1.6   The barriers to harmonisation may be daunting but some progress has been made. There are various bodies which are working on different aspects of harmonisation and these are discussed below. The most important of these bodies, in the light of recent developments, is the IASC.

International Accounting Standards Committee (IASC)

1.7   The function and role of the IASC was discussed briefly in Chapter 1. In particular, the effect of the IASC's *Framework for the Preparation and Presentation of Financial Statements* on the UK standard setting regime has been profound.

1.8   The IASC is tackling the issue of harmonisation through a review of its International Accounting Standards (IASs). This review was embodied in a Statement of Intent *Comparability of Financial Statements*, published in mid-1990. This statement laid out proposed revisions of certain IASs and the programme of amendment should be completed soon.

Comparability of financial statements

1.9 The Statement proposes that IASs restrict where possible the permissible accounting treatment to just one, but it does not preclude the use of others. Where countries adopt methods other than the IASC preferred method, businesses following the alternative should reconcile their net income and shareholders' interests as reported to the amounts that would be determined using the (benchmark) preferred treatment.

1.10 It is interesting to examine the criteria used by the board of the IASC to decide whether alternative treatments should be required, preferred or eliminated. The criteria are:

(a) current world-wide practice and trends in national accounting standards, law and generally accepted accounting principles;

(b) conformity with the *Framework*;

(c) the views of regulators and their representative organisation, such as the International Organisation of Securities Commissions (IOSCO); and

(d) consistency within an IAS and with other IASs.

1.11 As well as these revisions to IASs the IASC stated that it would carry out an improvements project 'to ensure that International Accounting Standards are sufficiently detailed and complete and contain adequate disclosure requirements'.

1.12 The current list of IASs is as follows.

International Accounting Standards

IAS 1 (revised)	Presentation of financial statements
IAS 2	Inventories
IAS 4	Depreciation accounting
IAS 5	Information to be disclosed in financial statements
IAS 7	Cash flow statements
IAS 8	Net profit or loss for the period, fundamental errors and changes in accounting policies
IAS 9	Research and development costs
IAS 10 (revised)	Events occurring after the balance sheet date
IAS 11	Construction contracts
IAS 12 (revised)	Income taxes
IAS 13	Presentation of current assets and current liabilities
IAS 14 (revised)	Segment reporting
IAS 15	Information reflecting the effects of changing prices
IAS 16	Property, plant and equipment
IAS 17 (revised)	Leases
IAS 18	Revenue
IAS 19 (revised)	Employee benefits
IAS 20	Accounting for government grants and disclosure of government assistance
IAS 21	The effects of changes in foreign exchange rates
IAS 22 (revised)	Business combinations
IAS 23	Borrowing costs
IAS 24	Related party disclosures
IAS 25	Accounting for investments
IAS 26	Accounting and reporting by retirement benefit plans
IAS 27	Consolidated financial statements and accounting for investments in subsidiaries
IAS 28	Accounting for investment in associates

IAS 29	Financial reporting in hyperinflationary economies
IAS 30	Disclosure in the financial statements of banks and similar financial institutions
IAS 31	Financial reporting of interests in joint ventures
IAS 32	Financial instruments: disclosure and presentation
IAS 33	Earnings per share
IAS 34	Interim financial reporting
IAS 35	Discontinuing operations
IAS 36	Impairment of assets
IAS 37	Provisions, contingent liabilities and contingent assets
IAS 38	Intangible assets
IAS 39	Financial instruments: recognition and measurement

Worldwide effect of IASs and the IASC

1.13 The IASC has now been in existence for 26 years, and it is worth looking at the effect it has had in that time.

1.14 As far as Europe is concerned, the consolidated financial statements of **many of Europe's top multinationals are prepared in conformity with national requirements**, EC directives and IASs. Furthermore, IASs are having a growing influence on national accounting requirements and practices. Many of these developments have been given added impetus by the internationalisation of capital markets.

1.15 IASs have had a particularly significant impact on the presentation of consolidated financial statements in Europe. The IASC approved IAS 3 *Consolidated financial statements* before many European IASC Board countries required the publication of consolidated financial statements. IAS 3 formed the basis of the EC's 7th Directive on consolidated accounts and has influenced the implementation of the Directive by EC member states.

1.16 Europe continues to make extensive use of IASs. The Italian securities regulator, CONSOB, requires listed companies to comply with IASs when there are no equivalent Italian requirements. French law allows French companies to adopt IASs, rather than tax accounting principles, in their consolidated financial statements. IASs influenced the guidelines issued by the Dutch Council for Annual Reporting and are being used in current work in Denmark, Norway and Sweden. The UK's Accounting Standards Board has argued that there has to be good reason to depart from IASs and it has based its conceptual framework on the IASC's *Framework*.

1.17 The European accountancy profession is well represented on the IASC Board and the IASC has close links with the Fédération des Experts Comptables Européens. It has also developed its relationship with the European Commission.

1.18 The IASC also has **growing influence outside Europe**. In North America, for example, Canada used an IAS to develop its recommendation on revenue recognition and the Toronto Stock Exchange has encouraged Canadian companies to disclose that their financial statements conform with IASs. The FASB in the US sends a Board member to IASC meetings, provides a staff response to all IASC exposure drafts, and co-operates with the IASC on a number of projects.

1.19 In Japan, the influence of the IASC had, until recently, been negligible. This was mainly because of links in Japan between tax rules and financial reporting. The Japanese Ministry of Finance set up a working committee to consider whether to bring national requirements into line with IASs. The Tokyo Stock Exchange has now announced that it will accept financial statements from foreign issue that conform with home country standards. This

BPP PUBLISHING

was widely seen as an attempt to attract foreign issuers, in particular companies from Hong Kong and Singapore. As these countries base their accounting on international standards, this action is therefore implicit acknowledgement by the Japanese Ministry of Finance of IAS requirements.

IASC and IOSCO

1.20 At the international level, the International Organisation of Securities Commissions (IOSCO) is looking to the IASC to provide a set of mutually acceptable international standards of accounting and disclosure that can be used in the financial statements of any company looking to list its securities, on any stock exchange. This effort is directed primarily at companies that are involved in multinational securities offerings and which have multiple listings of their securities.

1.21 The major breakthrough in the recognition of worldwide standards came in July 1995 when an agreement was made between the IASC and IOSCO (which is the international organisation representing securities market regulators). IOSCO agreed a four year timetable for the IASC to revise its '**core standards**', after which IOSCO members will be recommended to recognise these rules for cross-border capital raisings and listings.

1.22 The IASC has now completed its set of core IASs. However, IAS 39, the controversial standard on recognition and measurement of financial instruments scraped through with the minimum number of votes at the 'eleventh hour'. This means that IOSCO can begin its task of assessing the core set for use in the world's capital markets. (Two other standards - on events after the balance sheet date and investment properties - have yet to be completed, but IOSCO has said that it will go ahead without them.)

1.23 At the time of writing (July 1999) IOSCO has yet to complete its evaluation. However, there is growing acceptance that IOSCO, and particularly the US Securities and Exchange Commission, will not grant an unconditional endorsement of the core standards at the first attempt. Moreover, one FASB member, Jim Leisenring has stated at a recent conference that the FASB does not support IASs for either cross-border listings or for domestic use.

Exam focus point
Watch this space! IOSCO may make a decision at any moment.

IASC and current developments

1.24 America and Japan have been two of the developed countries which have been most reluctant to accept accounts prepared under IASs, but recent developments suggest that such financial statements may soon be acceptable on these important stock exchanges. The Japanese situation was discussed above.

1.25 In **America**, the Securities and Exchange Commission (SEC) agreed in 1993 to allow foreign issuers (of shares, etc) to follow IASC treatments on business combinations, goodwill and subsidiaries in hyper-inflationary economies, and to file cash flow statements under IAS 7. The SEC also allowed foreign issuers to use proportional consolidations (favoured by the IASC) to report interests in joint ventures. The overall effect is that, where IASC treatments differ from US GAAP, these treatments will now be acceptable. The SEC is now supporting the IASC because it wants to attract foreign listings.

1.26 This SEC decision was supported by the findings of a report by Professor Trevor Harris of the University of Columbia on the reporting practices of several large multi-national companies. His report concludes that on both measurement issues and disclosure, the revised IASs had reduced differences between IASs and US GAAP where differences still existed. IAS treatments or disclosures were often as good as or even better than US GAAP. In addition, in early 1996, the FASB and IASC approved similar draft codes on the disclosure of EPS.

1.27 This **close conformity between IASs and US GAAP** could, however, **cause problems for the IASC**. Some countries will see these moves as an attempt to force an international version of US GAAP on the rest of the world. It is not only developing countries which have reservations; the IOSCO review of IASs highlighted a number of European and Japanese issues which are outstanding. The IASC agreement with IOSCO has added substance to the perception that the IASC attaches more importance to American issues than to those of Europe or Japan.

1.28 The IASC therefore runs a fine balancing act between various strong interests. It must maintain support from all areas in order to ensure that pronouncements are accepted worldwide and this is a difficult political talk. The main methods of achieving this will be by:

(a) ensuring the quality of the IASC's technical work; and

(b) involving national standard-setting bodies (and multi-national companies) in the IASC's work.

1.29 This will also help to ensure that IASs are 'marketed' as the best approach based on accepted principles, rather than 'lowest-common denominator' standards.

ASB and international standards

1.30 The ASB considers the development of international standards of **fundamental importance**. In addition, the ASB meets on a formal, and regular basis with standard-setters around the world. Three times a year it meets with Australia, Canada and the US with the IASC in attendance, in the so-called 'G4 plus One' meetings. Once a year it meets with Australian, New Zealand and South African standard setters, twice a year with other European bodies.

Exam focus point

FRS 12 *Provisions, contingent liabilities and contingent assets* is almost identical to IAS 37 of the same name.

European Commission (EC)

1.31 As we have already seen, the EC regulations form one part of a broader programme for the harmonisation of company law in member states. The commission is uniquely the only organisation to produce **international** standards of accounting practice which are legally enforceable, in the form of directives which must be included in the national legislation of member states. The directives have been criticised as they might become constraints on the application of world-wide standards and bring accounting standardisation and harmonisation into the political arena.

1.32 The EC, however, acknowledged the role of the IASC in harmonising world-wide accounting rules and EC representatives will in future attend IASC board meetings and join steering committees involved in setting IASs. This move should bring to an end the idea of a separate layer of European reporting rules. The commission has therefore recognised that it needs to operate within a world-wide context. The EC has also set up a committee to investigate where there are conflicts between EU norms and international standards so that compatibility can be achieved.

1.33 In 1999 the European Commission proposed that all Stock Exchange listed companies should adopt IASs. This blanket proposal has been criticised on the grounds that it would mean a backward step for some countries in some cases, eg the UK with off balance sheet finance.

United Nations (UN)

1.34 The UN has a Commission and Centre on Transnational Reporting Corporations through which it gathers information concerning the activities and reporting of multinational companies. The UN processes are **highly political** and probably reflect the attitudes of the governments of developing countries to multinationals. For example, there is an inter-governmental working group of 'experts' on international standards of accounting and reporting which is dominated by the non-developed countries.

International Federation of Accountants (IFAC)

1.35 The IFAC is a private sector body established in 1977 and which now consists of over 100 professional accounting bodies from around 80 different countries. The IFAC's main objective is to co-ordinate the accounting profession on a global scale by issuing and establishing international standards on auditing, management accounting, ethics, education and training. The IFAC has separate committees working on these topics and also organises the World Congress of Accountants, which is held every five years.

Organisation for Economic Co-operation and Development (OECD)

1.36 The OECD was established in 1960 by the governments of 21 countries to 'achieve the highest sustainable economic growth and employment and a rising standard of living in member countries while maintaining financial stability and, thus, to contribute to the world economy'. The OECD supports the work of the IASC but also undertakes its own research into accounting standards via *ad hoc* working groups. For example, in 1976 the OECD issued guidelines for multinational companies on financial reporting and non-financial disclosures. The OECD appears to work on behalf of developed countries to protect them from the extreme proposals of the UN.

The situation today and in the future

1.37 Many organisations committed to global harmonisation have done a great deal of work towards this goal. It is the case at present, however, that fundamental disagreements exist between countries and organisations about the way forward. One of the major gulfs is between the reporting requirements in developed countries and those in non-developed countries. It will be some time before these difficulties can be overcome. The IASC is likely to be the lead body in attempting to do so, as discussed above.

2 ACCOUNTING OVERSEAS 5/95

2.1 We have looked at the barriers to harmonisation and the efforts made to date to overcome them, but what are the differences between UK accounts and accounts from other countries? One of the leading bodies in the field of standard setting is the Financial Accounting Standards Board (FASB) in the USA. As a standard setting body in a developed country, FASB offers interesting parallels with the ASB (and the IASC). We will discuss the FASB in the next section, but first let us consider accounting in other areas of the world.

Europe

2.2 You would expect that countries which are members of the EU, and which are therefore bound by European Commission directives (particularly the 4th and 7th), would have very similar reporting and accounting requirements. This is not necessarily the case, however, and many influences have shaped financial reporting practices, even events as far back as the Second World War. In an effort to understand what differences exist between European countries, we will examine four areas and their impact on financial reporting:

   (a)   the legal system;
   (b)   the taxation system;
   (c)   the forms of organisations; and
   (d)   the accounting profession.

We have limited the scope of our comparison to France and Germany, which will give you a good idea of the differences which can exist across Europe.

Exam focus point

The discussion that follows on the differences in these four areas is useful background reading, so that you can understand why international differences exist. You are unlikely to be asked about such matters in the exam. The main area of importance is the differences in accounting practice, which are considered towards the end of this section.

Legal system

2.3 European countries have historically had either a **common law system,** such as in the UK, or a **Roman codified system,** such as in France and Germany. These different systems have had a direct effect on the development of the variety of accounting practices found in Europe.

2.4 In **France** the Roman codified system is made up of commercial codes and related decrees and amendments. The significant influence of legislation on French financial accounting reflects the national planning policy of the government, which requires a high level of standardised accounting practice and reporting. This process is aided by the use of a national plan. The plan has been adopted by almost all enterprises in the country, and provides:

   (a)   a national uniform chart of accounts;
   (b)   definitions and explanations of terminology;
   (c)   details of bookkeeping entries;
   (d)   principles of accounting measurement (valuation);
   (e)   standard forms of financial statements;
   (f)   details of permitted cost accounting methods.

BPP PUBLISHING

2.5   The main principles of the French plan reflect **conservatism** and adherence to legal form rather than economic substance. This is similar to the situation in Germany, whose system influenced the French during the 1930s and 1940s.

2.6   In **Germany** the provision of detailed accounting requirements by law has a long history, during which period these legal regulations have remained dominant in the field of prescribing basic accounting practices. The majority of the current legislation is laid down in the Commercial Code (first established in 1897), the Corporation Act 1965 and tax laws. The Commercial Code regulates the maintenance of accounting records in accordance with 'principles of proper bookkeeping' and the preparation of periodic financial statements. The Corporation Act 1965 regulates the accounting standards and practices that should be adopted in preparing financial statements.

2.7   A feature of German financial accounting which is important is the legal and revenue reserves that are required, plus the '**secret reserves**', which exist because revaluation of appreciating assets is not allowed and depreciation in line with the tax rules is often in excess of that which is required to measure the periodic cost of depreciating assets. Such reserves have no exact UK equivalent.

Taxation system

2.8   In some European countries the tax system, in line with the legal system, has a **considerable effect** on financial accounting practices while in others, including the UK, it has only a minor indirect influence.

2.9   The **French** tax system is an imputation system (as is the UK tax system) and has a very strong influence on French accounting practices including the values incorporated in financial statements. Accounting profit measurement rules are the same as those for tax profit measurement, mainly because for an item to be allowed as a tax deduction it must be included in the financial accounts. Depreciation rules, for example, are based on tax rules and assets are only revalued in line with tax regulations. Voluntary revaluations are permitted but are unlikely to occur as income tax is payable on the unrealised profit on revaluation. A French company's tax return will therefore look like a detailed copy of the financial statements.

2.10   In **Germany** the tax system is an integral part of the legal system. For example, there is a fundamental legal principle that values of profit/assets and liabilities in financial accounts may be no higher or lower, respectively, than their counterparts allowed for tax purposes. The financial accounts should agree with the tax requirements, and so changes in accounting practice are often made in the name of changes in the accounting requirements of the tax system.

2.11   The **emphasis on compliance** with the tax rules and regulations limits the usefulness of German financial statements for decision making by readers. The reported profit and the valuations contained in the statements will reflect the most favourable tax position. This may not reflect the economic profitability and position of the company, making them too conservative for readers to (say) estimate the future net cash flows due to the company. This is obviously not the objective of German financial reporting.

Forms of organisation

2.12   The types of organisation and their ownership will also have varying effects on a nation's accounting practices. In some countries ownership is mainly in the **hands of a family** and

finance is provided by the banks. Both these parties have access to internal financial information concerning the business and therefore there is little demand for the development of forms of external financial reporting. In other countries the ownership of the business organisation is in the hands of **external widely dispersed shareholders** (as in the UK and US). Such providers of finance will probably not have direct access to internal financial information and will therefore demand some form of external reporting to provide them with the information they require to make investment decisions. The existence and importance of shareholders will determine the influence of the national stock exchange.

2.13 A wide spectrum of organisations exist in **France** including:

(a) partnerships (Société en nom Collectif);
(b) companies (Société Anonyme (SA) and Société à Responsibilité Limitée (SARL));
(c) family holdings.

The accounts produced by all these organisations are governed by the National Plan; the stock exchange (Bourse) has not had a particularly strong influence over financial reporting practices.

2.14 There are various forms of organisations in **Germany** and the distinction is important because financial reporting and disclosure requirements are dependent on the organisational form of business. Public companies consist of the following.

(a) 'Aktiengesellschaft' (AG). This is similar to a large UK public company, although the shares are usually 'bearer'. These companies have a supervisory body; 50% is appointed by shareholders and 50% by employees. This board appoints a management board and approves the annual accounts.

(b) 'Kommanditgesellschaft auf Aktien' (KGaA). This is a form of limited partnership and company combined. One shareholder is liable to the creditors in full, while the others enjoy limited liability. It is not a particularly popular form of company.

2.15 Another form of company is a 'Gesellschaft mit beschränkter Haftung' (GmbH). It is not quoted on the stock exchange and is subject to different legal reporting requirements. It is similar to, but not the same as, a UK private company. There are numerous organisations operating as partnerships or sole traders. Banks and other lenders are an important source of finance in Germany, and therefore the German stock exchange, while being an efficient medium for raising new finance, does not appear to have a great influence on financial reporting.

Accounting profession

2.16 The accounting profession in a country has **varying levels of influence** on national accounting practices. For example, until recently the accounting profession in the UK was very influential because of its control of the old Accounting Standards Committee, while in Germany the accounting profession does not directly influence German accounting practices. However, care must be taken in interpreting the influence of the accounting profession because in some countries an 'accountant' may not be considered to be part of the 'profession'.

2.17 In **France**, the accounting profession is split into two distinct organisations:

(a) accountants (Ordre des Experts Comptables et des Comptables Agrées); and
(b) auditors (Compaigne Nationale des Commissaires aux Agrées).

2.18 Most members of the auditors' organisation are also members of the more important accountants' organisation. Examinations, work experience and articles are similar to those of the UK accountancy bodies, but there are only an estimated 11,000 qualified accountants in France. The profession's main influence is through the issue of non-mandatory opinions and recommendations of accounting principles relevant to the implementation of the National Plan.

2.19 The main professional body in **Germany** is the Institute of Certified Public Accountants (Institut der Wirtschafstprüfer). Members of this institute carry out all the statutory audits, and are required to have very high educational and experience qualifications. The Institute issues a form of auditing standard but this is tied very closely to legislation. As well as auditing, members are mainly involved in tax and business management, with no obvious significant role in establishing financial accounting principles and practices. There is no independent accounting standard-setting body.

Former communist and developing countries

2.20 The sophisticated regulatory frameworks discussed above, along with those in the UK and the USA, contrast sharply with the situation in former communist and developing countries. The problems in these countries are covered briefly here.

2.21 In socialist countries the economic system has usually been **resource constrained** and enterprise management operating within such an environment required quantity data on resource availability and resource utilisation. The accounting function was *passive*. Price signals were not influential and enterprises did not need to be 'profitable'. There was not the same call for accounting development and innovation that exists where accounting is *active* (as in capitalist countries). For the country trying to recover from events such as revolution or war, such a system is appropriate but after the short-term resource problems have been solved the economy needs to develop along the lines of the demand constrained economy. Many socialist and former socialist countries are currently attempting to move to such a system which includes enterprise independence and market conditions of supply and demand. Accounting will therefore (hopefully) develop in these socialist countries into a more active information source.

2.22 Developing countries are often defined as such by using *per capita* **gross national product**, relating development to economic growth and social improvements. The general characteristics of such countries include unbalanced distribution of wealth, few exports (agricultural/mineral), basic but developing domestic industries, long-term balance of payments deficits, authoritarian political systems and inadequate education.

2.23 Both developing and former socialist countries have the same problems in relation to financial accounting and many will be overcome in the same way. In general, most of these countries are **adopting financial reporting systems** from developed countries and adjusting them to suit the individual needs of the country concerned. This is a long and slow process as such sophisticated reporting systems are rarely suitable and require a great deal of modification. The local workers do not have the requisite skills, which have to be imported from abroad. More sophisticated financial reporting may be required by multinational companies who have subsidiaries or investments in such countries.

Other countries

2.24 Of the other **main developed countries,** such as Canada, Australia and New Zealand, some have developed framework projects like the IASC and some have detailed standards, often with the force of law. The country which has had most impact on world financial reporting, however, is the USA (as we shall see in the next section).

2.25 The table below shows some examples of the way the formats, treatments and policies change from country to country, although once again our comparison is restricted to the UK, Germany and France. (*Note.* HC = historical cost, MV = market value, NRV = net realisable value.)

Subject	UK	Germany	France
Valuation: tangible fixed assets	Majority use of HC, except that many large companies re-value assets from time to time to MVs, particularly for land and buildings. Possible to revalue every year, and to use replacement costs for some or all assets. Investment properties must be revalued annually. Finance leases are capitalised. (These rules have been extended and modified in FRS 15.)	Strict HC except for depreciation and other write offs. Finance leases must be capitalised but this is avoided as definition related to tax rules.	HC, except that assets had to be revalued in 1978 by using government-published indices based on 31 December 1976 prices. This 'fiscal revaluation' may still affect balance sheets. Depreciation charges are initially calculated on these book values, then adjusted downwards to HC. For group accounts, HC is generally used and finance leases may be capitalised. Property companies may annually revalue tax free (postponed until realisat-ion).

BPP PUBLISHING

Subject	UK	Germany	France
Valuation: stock	FIFO is the usual basis. SSAP 9 states that use of LIFO would not usually be 'fair' (and case law prohibits its use for tax purposes). Consequently, LIFO is very rare. 'Market' is taken to mean NRV. Production overheads are included in costs, but administrative and selling overheads are not to be included. Long-term contracts are valued on the percentage-of-completion basis, with profit capable of being included before completion. The asset thereby recorded is shown as a debtor (amount recoverable on contracts) rather than as an addition to stock.	Conservatism and tax rules are evident. Stocks are to be stated at the lowest of HC, replacement cost, NRV or other value permitted by tax rules. Average cost is the most usual method for determining cost, but FIFO is allowed, as is LIFO where it corresponds to physical usage. Despite general conservatism an appropriate proportion of administrative overheads may be included in cost. Long-term contract WIP is valued at cost, and not by the percentage-of-completion method.	The lower of cost or MVR is used in France, 'cost' must be calculated using FIFO or weighted average; LIFO is not permitted. For tax accounts and individual company accounts, there are often tax-deductible provisions recorded in the accounts for rises in the price of stocks. Such provisions can be excluded from group accounts. Long-term contracts are usually accounted for by the completion method.
Use of merger accounting	Companies Act 1989. The subsidiary must be at least 90% owned by the group; the fair value of any non-share consideration must not exceed 10% of the nominal value of shares issued. FRS 6. Restricts merger accounting to true merger situations which are very rare.	The subsidiary must be at least 90% owned. Cash consideration must not exceed 10% of the nominal value of shares issued. The method is very rare.	Allowed, but rare.

Subject	UK	Germany	France
Goodwill	Goodwill should be amortised to the P&L over its expected life (FRS10), but if its life is indefinite it need only be written down if its value drops below that in the balance sheet. There is a rebuttable presumption that the life of goodwill will be no more than 20 years. Impairment reviews must be performed annually where lives of more than 20 years are chosen.	Goodwill may be written off against reserves or be amortised over four years or over years that are likely to benefit.	Goodwill should be amortised over its useful life, but in exceptional cases may be written off against reserves. 20-40 year amortisation periods normal.
Proportional consolidation	Proportional consolidation may be used for unincorporated joint ventures. FRS 9 does not permit proportional consolidation for incorporated joint ventures.	Proportional consolidation may be used where enterprises are jointly managed.	Proportional consolidation must be used for enterprises controlled jointly by a limited number of others.

	UK	Germany/France
Depreciation	*Source of rules* Calculation of depreciation charges is based on professionally-set accounting standards. Involves estimation of asset lives and residual values. In theory, the manner of wearing out of the asset should also be considered, but in practice the straight-line method is dominant because it is simple. Depreciation for tax purposes is a different matter in the UK, as capital allowances are a separate scheme. Depreciation is therefore a source of the timing differences which create deferred tax.	*Source of rules* Depreciation for accounting purposes is connected to tax rules. So, for example, in Germany accounting depreciation is based on the tax tables for the particular asset in its particular location. Often the asset lives implied by the tax depreciation rates are broadly in line with commercial reality. However, accelerated tax depreciation is fairly common for certain assets or certain areas.

BPP
PUBLISHING

Subject	UK	Germany/France
	Revaluation Where fixed assets have been revalued upwards, depreciation charges will subsequently rise. *Investment and commercial properties* One peculiar feature of UK practice is the lack of depreciation of investment properties, which is the required treatment under SSAP 19 in order to give a true and fair view. This runs counter to the Directive's detailed instructions and is not found in other EU countries. Furthermore, the fairly widespread UK practice of not depreciating some commercial properties because they have been fully maintained is not followed elsewhere.	*Revaluation* Revaluation is not allowed in Germany, so this is not relevant for depreciation. In France, revaluation mainly occurs as a result of the 1978 fiscal laws. Depreciation charges are 'equalised' so that they fall to what they would have been before revaluation. This may be eliminated in group accounts.
Provisions	Provisions must be made for probable future losses or expenses, but only for specifically identified likely future events. Whether or not a provision is made should not depend upon the level of profit; either a provision is needed or it is not. FRS 3 and FRS 7 have restricted the use of provisions. Further rules have been introduced under FRS 12.	In France and Germany the concept of prudence requires that accruals be set up for uncertain liabilities. For example, in Germany these would include impending losses from uncompleted business transactions, repairs and maintenance expenses to be incurred in the first quarter of the next year (or optionally, within the whole year), and certain warranties. In Germany, provision amounts may be found, in translation, under 'other accruals' or some similar title. In France, there are also elements of shareholders' funds called *provisions réglementées* which are the double entry for tax-induced accelerated depreciation. There are several other provisions which are tax-deductible but may have little to do with commercial reality. In French consolidated accounts, the tax-based provisions are corrected for.

Question 1

In recent years, only two German companies, Daimler Benz and Veba, have filed accounts prepared under US GAAP, although other German companies are likely to follow suit. Why should German companies take the trouble to produce such accounts, and what do you think was the impact on reported results?

Answer

The reasons given by Veba for producing US GAAP accounts were based on the fact that, although Veba still earns 70% of its revenues within Germany, only about 44% of its equity is held in Germany, with 15% held in the US. The company saw the need to become 'more international' and US GAAP accounts would increase transparency and shareholder value. An article in the *Financial Times* on 28 March 1996 stated the following.

> 'Converting accounts to US accounting standards has been problematic for German companies, many of whom prefer the inscrutability of the German accounting system. It enables them to build up reserves which might otherwise be paid out to shareholders.

> Mr Kurt Lauk, Veba's finance director, said he had conducted 'difficult' negotiations with the Securities and Exchange Commission, the agency supervising the New York Stock Exchange, for two years before all differences were resolved.

> Mr Lauk said Veba had chosen GAAP over the rival IAS accounting standard, widely used by large European companies, because the latter did not permit a listing in New York.'

The likely effect and reported results can be difficult to judge. One might expect that German accounting rules, generally perceived as more conservative than UK/US GAAP, would produce lower profits and shareholder funds. This was the case recently when BMW reported its results, including Rover, a British subsidiary.

'BMW, the German carmaker, yesterday reported that Rover, its UK subsidiary, lost DM355m (£157m) last year, in spite of having earlier reported a 9 per cent rise in profits before interest and tax to £91m for the same period.

The discrepancy came from the 'stricter valuation criteria' applied by BMW compared with its UK subsidiary, according to the German company.'   (*Financial Times,* 3 April 1996)

This is not always the case, however, as was demonstrated when Daimler Benz first produced US GAAP accounts. Analysts were shocked when a substantial loss was reported under US GAAP rather than the modest profit under German rules. (DM 949m loss vs DM 168m profit, 1991 half year results). This was partly because the company was caught during a slump, but it demonstrates how dramatic the differences can be under the different accounting regimes.

---

3   FINANCIAL REPORTING IN THE USA   5/96

3.1   Standard setting in the USA is characterised by a **plethora of highly detailed legislative rules**. These have largely obscured the concept of 'fair presentation', despite the development of a conceptual framework as discussed below. The Financial Accounting Standards Board (FASB) has produced well over 100 Statements of Financial Accounting Standards (SFASs).

A conceptual framework in the USA

3.2   The FASB has been developing a conceptual framework since 1973. According to the FASB, the conceptual framework was expected:

(a)   to **guide the body** responsible for establishing standards;

(b)   to provide a **frame of reference** for resolving accounting questions in the absence of a specific promulgated standard;

(c)   to determine **bounds for judgement** in preparing financial statements;

(d)   to increase financial statement **users' understanding** of and confidence in financial statements; and

(e)   to enhance **comparability**.

3.3   To date, the FASB has issued six **Statements of Financial Accounting Concepts (SFACs)**, of which one (SFAC 4) deals with the objectives of financial reporting by non-business organisations and is therefore not comparable with UK accounting, whilst another (SFAC 3) dealt with elements of financial statements by business enterprises, and was superseded by SFAC 6, which expanded the scope of SFAC 3 to encompass not-for-profit organisations.

SFAC 1   Objectives of financial reporting by business enterprises
SFAC 2   Qualitative characteristics of accounting information
SFAC 5   Recognition and measurement in financial statements of business enterprises
SFAC 6   Elements of financial statements

Success/failure of the FASB work

3.4   In order to be able to assess the success or failure of the FASB's conceptual framework project, one must refer back to the originally perceived benefits of the project and evaluate whether or not any of them has been achieved. Perhaps the acid test may be found in analysing the extent to which the FASB has used the framework in the **development of accounting standards**. Possibly the best example of where the framework has been used as the basis for an accounting standard is in the development of SFAS 95 *Statement of cash flows*; however, this is clearly the exception and where reference is made to the concepts statements it is generally to broad objectives or qualitative characteristics. On the other hand, it might be argued that the concepts statements have guided the thinking of FASB members without it being expressly stated.

3.5   The weakness of the FASB's conceptual framework project may be attributed to a number of factors; however, the most significant reason will probably be shown to be the Board's failure to deal with the fundamental issues of **recognition** and **measurement**. A statement of accounting concepts should provide a frame of reference for the formulation of financial reporting practice, and not be a description of what current reporting practices are. This is not to say that the FASB's project should be rejected out of hand; it contains some outstanding work, particularly in the area of qualitative characteristics.

Comparison with UK/IASC view

3.6   The ASB has acknowledged that, in drafting the *Statement of Principles*, it drew heavily on the **work done in previous projects** in other countries, mainly the FASB concept statements *and* the IASC *Framework*. This is particularly true of the early chapters, and indeed Chapter 1 opens with the statement that 'the objective of financial statements is to provide information ... that is useful to a wide range of users in making economic decisions', almost a repetition of the FASB wording. The ASB has, however, extended this function to include showing the results of the stewardship of management.

3.7   The ASB has also identified various users, but it has also **narrowed down the focus** by stating that, in essence, the investor's perspective is chosen as the one most useful in the preparation of financial statement as such statements will tend to meet the needs of most other users.

3.8   Some aspects of the FASB's concept statements are **fundamentally flawed**. It is the case, however, that the ASB and IASC work follows roughly the same structure, and that the

Statement of Principles draws on the best aspects of the FASB's work, including some definitions. As the *Statement of Principles* has yet to be completed, a full comparison is difficult. In Chapter 3 of the *Statement of Principles*, the definitions of assets, liabilities and so on are based on those in SFAC 6, although there are variations.

3.9   The IASC's *Framework* was **based very closely** on the FASB's concept statements, and it is perceived as an attempt by the IASC to justify the *status quo*; the IASC tried to make the proposed framework consistent with current external financial reporting practice. The ASB stated that it would use the IASC *Framework* as much as possible in its own work on the conceptual framework. It remains to be seen whether the flaws in both the FASB's concept statements and the IASC's *Framework* will be tackled adequately by the ASB.

4   RESTATING OVERSEAS AND UK ACCOUNTS   5/97

4.1   In your examination, as well as written questions on this topic, you may be asked to reproduce a sets of overseas accounts using **UK accounting principles**. Multi-national companies already provide this type of information if they have a large number of investors in another country, say the USA. Here is an example of such a reconciliation. (*Note.* GAAP stands for generally accepted accounting principles.)

UK vs US GAAP

4.2   The following is a summary of the differences between UK and US GAAP which you might expect to find in the notes to the accounts of a **multinational company**. It is not comprehensive, but gives you a good idea of the type of reconciling items you will find.

SUMMARY OF DIFFERENCES BETWEEN UK AND US GAAP

Deferred taxation

There are two principal differences between UK GAAP and US GAAP in respect of deferred taxation. First, under UK GAAP, deferred taxation is only accounted for to the extent that it is probable that taxation liabilities or benefits will crystallise; US GAAP requires that full provision is made for all deferred taxation liabilities. Second, UK GAAP requires that deferred taxation is provided using the liability method whereby taxation is provided at the same rates at which timing differences are expected to reverse; under US GAAP, the deferred method is currently used whereby deferred taxation is provided at the rates applicable to the year when provision is made.

Pension costs

The methods used to determine the annual pensions costs for defined benefit schemes under both UK GAAP and US GAAP are similar in that they required pension costs to be spread over the expected service lives of employees. However, the use of different actuarial methodologies and assumptions gives rise to a difference in reported pension costs.

Ordinary dividends

Under UK GAAP, ordinary dividends proposed are provided for in the year in respect of which they are recommended by the Board of Directors for approval by the shareholders. Under US GAAP, such dividends are not provided for until declared by the Board of Directors.

The following is a summary of the estimated material adjustments to profit and ordinary shareholders' equity which would be required if US GAAP had been applied instead of UK GAAP.

BPP PUBLISHING

PROFIT FOR THE YEAR ENDED 31 DECEMBER

	19X2 £m	19X1 £m
Profit under UK GAAP	1,033	912
US GAAP adjustments		
Deferred taxation	(18)	(35)
Pension costs	(4)	-
Net income under US GAAP	1,011	877
Income per ordinary share of 25p under US GAAP	33.5p	28.0p

ORDINARY SHAREHOLDERS' EQUITY
AS AT 31 DECEMBER

	19X2 £m	19X1 £m
Ordinary shareholders' equity under UK GAAP	3,572	3,208
US GAAP adjustments		
Deferred taxation	(218)	(199)
Pension costs	(1)	-
Dividend proposed	331	292
Ordinary shareholders' equity under US GAAP	3,684	3,307

Question 2

The following are the main US accounting principles which differ from those generally accepted in the United Kingdom as applied by XYZ plc in its financial statements.

Taxation

Deferred taxation is not provided where, in the opinion of the directors, no liability is likely to arise in the foreseeable future. However, under US GAAP, deferred taxation would be provided on a full deferral basis (net effect profit and loss account £96m; balance sheet £102m).

Revaluation of land and buildings

Periodically land and buildings are revalued on an existing use basis by professionally qualified external valuers and such assets are written up to the appraised value. Depreciation is, where applicable, calculated on these revalued amounts. When revalued properties are sold, the gain or loss on sale is calculated based on revalued carrying amounts and reflected in income and any revaluation surplus thus realised is reclassified directly to retained earnings. Under US GAAP such revaluations would not be reflected in financial statements and the gain or loss on sale would be calculated based on original cost and reflected in income. The amount of additional depreciation charged in respect of the revalued properties is not material (net effect: profit and loss account nil; balance sheet £166m).

Timberlands

Reforestation costs are charged to the profit and loss account when incurred and depletion of timberlands is only provided to the extent that the amount of timber harvested exceeds the estimated growth of standing timber. Under US GAAP depletion on a unit of production basis is charged to the profit and loss account and reforestation costs are capitalised as part of the carrying cost of timberlands (net effect: profit and loss account £36m; balance sheet £60m).

Foreign currencies

Revenues, expenses, assets and liabilities relating to overseas subsidiaries are translated at the year end rate. Under US GAAP assets and liabilities are translated as under UK GAAP; however, revenues and expenses are translated at average rates for the year (net effect: profit and loss account £11m; balance sheet nil).

Revisions

The accounting policy of the group has not been to account for exceptional past pension surpluses. Under US GAAP, such surpluses are recognised and credited over an appropriate future period (net effect: profit and loss account £52m; balance sheet £189m).

Other information

Profit available for appropriation under UK GAAP = £1,089m.

Ordinary shareholders' equity under UK GAAP = £4,224m

Required

Provide the reconciliation to US GAAP for:

(a) profit available for appropriation; and
(b) ordinary shareholders' equity.

Answer

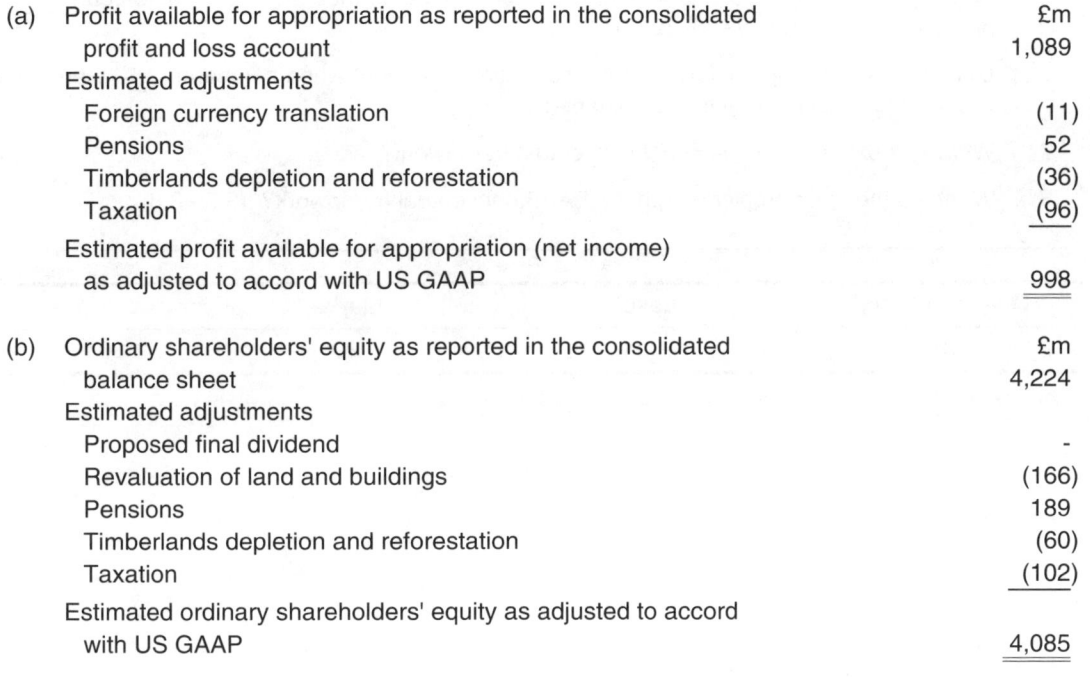

		£m
(a)	Profit available for appropriation as reported in the consolidated profit and loss account	1,089
	Estimated adjustments	
	Foreign currency translation	(11)
	Pensions	52
	Timberlands depletion and reforestation	(36)
	Taxation	(96)
	Estimated profit available for appropriation (net income) as adjusted to accord with US GAAP	998
		£m
(b)	Ordinary shareholders' equity as reported in the consolidated balance sheet	4,224
	Estimated adjustments	
	Proposed final dividend	-
	Revaluation of land and buildings	(166)
	Pensions	189
	Timberlands depletion and reforestation	(60)
	Taxation	(102)
	Estimated ordinary shareholders' equity as adjusted to accord with US GAAP	4,085

Chapter roundup

- **Harmonisation** in accounting is likely to come from international accounting standards, but not in the near future. There are enormous difficulties to overcome, both technical and political.

- You should be able to discuss the **barriers to harmonisation** and the advantages of and **progress towards harmonisation**.

- We have concentrated on certain countries in our **comparison** between UK and overseas accounts, but you should be able to highlight the differences to UK accounting if you are presented with a set of accounts from any other country.

- You should be able to discuss the role and impact of:

  - the **IASC** and **IASs**;
  - the **FASB** and **concept statements**;
  - the **ASB** and the **Statement of Principles**.

- You may be given a **set of accounts from another country**, with their accounting policies, and asked to discuss how the statements would appear **under UK accounting conventions** and disclosure rules.

Quick quiz

1   What are the main barriers to harmonisation? (see para 1.3)

2   What are the main advantages of global harmonisation? (1.5)

3   What impact has IOSCO had on the development of IASs? (1.20-1.23)

4   What are the main characteristics of the Roman codified system of law? (2.4, 2.5)

5   What are the main problems facing former socialist countries and developing countries from an accounting point of view? (2.20 - 2.23)

6   List some of the major differences in accounting treatment when comparing UK, German and French financial statements. (2.25, table)

7   What was expected of the FASB conceptual framework? (3.2)

8   What are the main problems with the FASB conceptual framework? (3.5 - 3.8)

Question to try	Level	Marks	Time
31	Exam	20	36 mins

Exam question and answer bank

Examination standard questions are indicated by mark and time allocations.

1   CHARACTERISTICS

The following characteristics have been suggested as being essential in the preparation of financial accounting reports:

(a)   understandable;
(b)   objective;
(c)   comparable;
(d)   realistic (ie complete in form and substance);
(e)   relevant;
(f)   reliable;
(g)   consistent;
(h)   timely;
(i)   prudent;
(j)   economy of presentation.

REQUIREMENT:

Comment on the suggested characteristics saying whether in your view year end accounts and statements prepared in accordance with normally accepted accounting rules and practices meet these criteria and whether the needs of the various users groups are being met. Give your reasons and if necessary suggest other criteria that you may consider important.

2   STATEMENT OF PRINCIPLES   *36 mins*

'A major achievement of the ASB was the development of its *Statement of Principles*. However, it is too theoretical to be applied to accounting standards.'

What are the merits of the *Statement of Principles* and do you agree with the criticism that it is too theoretical.

20 Marks

3   RYMACHINES   *45 mins*

Rymachines plc is a manufacturing company with a number of separate factories scattered around England, and its head office in York. The chief accountant, Arthur Isation, is concerned about the effect on their figures for the year ending 31 December 19X7 of various transactions involving fixed assets. He has come to you with the following information.

(a)   A revaluation exercise took place on 1 July 19X7. Items of plant that originally cost £80,000 on 1 January 19X5 were revalued to £97,500. The plant was, and still is, being depreciated down to zero over a ten year period from new.

(b)   They are rather concerned regarding their ability to replace a specific type of machine because the price has risen so dramatically. With this in mind, Arthur would like to charge extra depreciation of £25,000 to 'retain more in the business to enable them to replace assets at the higher prices'.

(c)   The use lives of two groups of plant have been revised downwards following an impairment review.

   (i)   Plant costing £140,000 is 3 years old at the balance sheet date, and was originally to be depreciated over 7 years. The machinery is not surviving as well as hoped and it is now envisaged that it will be worthless in two years' time.

   (ii)   Plant originally costing £400,000 is 4 years old at the balance sheet date, and originally had an estimated useful life of 10 years and residual value of £10,000. The factory in which the plant is used is to be closed next May and the plant will have to be sold then for scrap of £10,000.

(d)   The company has a freehold warehouse in Toxteth which it bought in July 19X5 for £160,000. One half of this is for the land, the other half for the building. Freehold buildings are depreciated over 50 years. A valuation on 1 July 19X7 valued the property at £115,000 with the land element still being £80,000.

Required

Draft notes in preparation for a meeting with Mr Isation explaining the accounting required in respect of each of the points raised.

25 Marks

4   **FRS 11**   *15 mins*

A new FRS has been produced, FRS 11 *Impairment of fixed assets and goodwill,* under which it may be necessary to calculate an asset's value in use to compare with its carrying value. Where the income stream of an asset cannot be identified separately, it can be grouped with other assets in an 'income-generating unit'. In relation to the allocation of assets to such units, consider the following two scenarios, and answer the related questions.

(a)   Suppose an entity has three independent streams, A, B and C, with net asset directly involved in the income streams with carrying amounts of £100m, £150m and £200m respectively. In addition there are head office net assets with a carrying amount totalling £150m. The relative amounts of the net assets are a reasonable indication of the proportion of head office resources devoted to each income stream. The income-generating units are defined as follows.

Income-generating unit	A	B	C	Total
	£m	£m	£m	£m
Net assets directly involved in income-generating unit	100	150	200	450
Head office net assets	33	50	67	150
Total	133	200	267	600

Required

Suppose that there is an indication that a fixed asset in Unit B is impaired, what figure would be used as the value in use of B?

(b)   Suppose an entity acquires a business comprising three income-generating units, X, Y and Z. After five years, the carrying amount of the net assets in the income-generating units and the purchased goodwill compares with the value in use as follows.

Income-generating unit	X	Y	Z	Goodwill	Total
	£m	£m	£m	£m	£m
Carrying amount	80	120	140	50	390
Value in use	100	140	120		360

Required

What should be recognised by way of an impairment loss?

5   **MILLER**   *54 mins*

Miller Ltd is a manufacturing company which has always valued its stock on the basis of direct cost. However, in order to avoid further audit qualifications, the directors of Miller Limited have decided to comply with the requirements of SSAP 9 *Stocks and long-term contracts* in the year ended 31 December 19X2.

From the information given below you are required to prepare:

(a)   two summarised profit and loss accounts for the year ended 31 December 19X2 on the direct cost and SSAP 9 bases of valuation;

(b)   two summarised balance sheets as at 31 December 19X2 on the direct cost and SSAP 9 bases of valuation;

(c)   a report for the directors of Miller Ltd summarising the effects on Miller Ltd's financial statements of this change in stock valuation.

Workings should be shown and taxation is to be ignored.

(1)   The stock valuation on the balance sheet as at 31 December 19X1 was £54,000.

(2)   During the year ended 31 December 19X2, the first year in which SSAP 9 is to be applied, Miller Ltd incurred production overhead of £324,000 (leaving the productive overhead applicable to each unit unchanged from the previous year at £6.00) and other overhead of £210,000.

(3)   On 1 December 19X2 the direct cost per unit increased, for the first time in two years, from £9.00 to £10.00.

(4)   Production was constant throughout 19X2 and a FIFO stock issue price basis was used.

(5)   55,000 units were sold for £25.00 each during the year ended 31 December 19X2.

(6)   Other balance sheet data at 31 December 19X2 were as follows.

	£
Fixed assets	600,000
Debtors	252,000
Cash at bank	44,100
Trade creditors	119,400
Authorised and issued share capital	180,000
12% Debenture stock	60,000

(7)   Retained profits at 1 January 19X2 were £247,400.

(8)   No dividend was to be paid for the year ended 31 December 19X2.

30 Marks

6   SOAP

Soap plc is working on a number of short-term and long-term contracts. Its policy with regard to attributable profit on the long term contracts is to calculate it as follows.

Degree of completion (%) × total estimated profit (adjusted for known variations in costs accruing in the period)

The directors are sure that their cost calculations for the contracts are accurate. It is 31 December 19X7, the company's accounting year end. Further details of the contracts are as follows.

(a)   The short term contracts are 7 to 9 months in duration. Some of them will not be completed until 31 March 19X8. It is the directors' policy to accrue profit earned to date on these contracts in the accounts as at 31 December 19X7.

(b)   On 1 April 19X7 Soap plc commenced work on a contract with Emmerdale plc. The total contract price was £9 million and the total contract costs were expected to be £7.5 million. The contract is expected to run for two years.

During the year to 31 December 19X7, Soap plc incurred unforeseen additional costs of £500,000 on the contract in the light of which it revised its estimate of the total expected costs to £8 million. The following details are relevant to the position as at 31 December 19X7.

(i)   Costs incurred to date: £4m
(ii)   Payments on account: £3m
(iii)   Percentage complete per independent surveyor: 45%.

(c)   On 1 July 19X7 Soap plc entered into a contract with Archers plc. The details of the contract were as follows.

(i)   Duration of contract: 2 years

(ii)   Total contract price: £150,000

(iii)   Estimated total cost: £120,000

(iv)   Percentage of completion (directors' estimate): 20%

(The terms of the contract did not require an independent valuation by a surveyor.)

(v)   Costs incurred up to 31 December 19X7: £47,500

(vi)   Payments on account received: £40,000

A special machine had been purchased for the purposes of the contract and was being depreciated over the two year period on a straight line basis. The cost of the machine was £20,000, and the depreciation charge to date had been included in the costs incurred figure (v). On 31 December 19X7 it was decided that this machine should be written off. (Assume no residual value.)

(d)   On 1 August 19X7, Soap plc entered into a contract with Neighbours Ltd. The details of the contract were as follows.

(i)   Duration: 1½ years

(ii)   Total contract price: £6.4 million

(iii)   Estimated total costs: £5 million

(iv)   Payments on account: £2.5 million

(v)   Costs incurred up to 31 December 19X7: £1.8 million

(vi)   Percentage of completion (independent surveyor's estimate): 25%

Neighbours Ltd was a new customer, so as a precaution, Soap plc had asked for a large deposit.

REQUIREMENTS:

(a)   State whether you think it is good accounting practice to accrue profit on the short term contracts. Give reasons for your view.

(b)   For the year ended 31 December 19X7, show the relevant extracts from the profit and loss account and balance sheet of Soap plc as regards the contracts with Emmerdale plc, Archers plc and Neighbours Ltd. You do not need to show the cash and bank balances.

7   QUOTED COMPANY

The following is an extract from the notes to the report and accounts for the year ended 30 December 19X4 of a quoted public company.

	19X3		19X4	
	Full potential liability £'000	Provision made £'000	Full potential liability £'000	Provision made £'000
Group				
Tax deferred by reason of				
Accelerated capital allowances	13,063	12,665	12,185	11,735
Other timing differences	(423)	(423)	(120)	(120)
	12,640	12,242	12,065	11,615

If the group's interest in freehold land and buildings was disposed of at its balance sheet value the ultimate tax liability not provided for in these accounts is estimated to be in the order of £3m. (In 19X3 the comparable figure was also £3m.)

REQUIREMENTS:

(a)   Explain the arguments for and against the maintenance of a deferred tax account.

(b)   Discuss the major provisions of SSAP 15 *Accounting for deferred tax* illustrating your discussion using the figures given above.

8   PENSION COSTS   *45 mins*

(a)   (i)   Curtis Ltd runs a pension scheme for its employees, who have an estimated remaining service life of 10 years. The scheme is over-funded by £4m.

      (ii)   The same situation applies as in part (i) except that the scheme is under-funded by £4m.

      Notes.

      (i)   The actuary has recommended a 4 year contribution holiday after which the company will resume paying regular contributions of £1m per annum.

      (ii)   The deficit is to be cleared by a one-off lump sum payment of £4m as well as maintaining the regular contribution of £1m per annum.

      Required

      For (i) and (ii) above calculate the necessary profit and loss account and balance sheet figures for the next 10 years for pension contributions.

(b)   SSAP 24 has been criticised for ignoring the balance sheet aspects of the pension cost problem. Discuss these criticisms and potential solutions to the problem.   **25 Marks**

9   FRS 5 SCENARIO

Shaky plc enters into an agreement with Farant Factors plc with the following principle terms.

(a)   Shaky plc will transfer (by assignment) to Farant Factors plc such trade debts as Shaky plc shall determine, subject only to credit approval by Farant Factors plc and a limit placed on the proportion of the total that may be due from any one debtor. Farant Factors plc levies a charge of 0.15 per cent of turnover, payable monthly, for this facility.

(b)   Shaky plc continues to administer the sales ledger and handle all aspects of collection of the debts.

(c)   Shaky plc may draw up to 80% of the gross amount of debts assigned at any one time, such drawings being debited in the books of Farant Factors plc to a factoring account operated by Farant Factors plc for Shaky plc.

(d)   Weekly, Shaky plc assigns and sends copy invoices to Farant Factors plc as they are raised.

(e)   Shaky plc is required to bank the gross amounts of all payments received from debts assigned to Farant Factors plc direct into an account in the name of Farant Factors plc. Credit transfers made by debtors direct into Shaky plc's own bank account must immediately be paid to Farant Factors plc.

(f)   Farant Factors plc credits such collections from debtors to the factoring account, and debits the account monthly with interest calculated on the basis of the daily balances on the account using a rate of base rate plus 2.5%. Thus this interest charge varies with the amount of finance drawn by Shaky plc under the finance facility from Farant Factors plc, the speed of payment of the debtors and base rate.

(g)   Farant Factors plc provides protection from bad debts. Any debts not recovered after 90 days are credited to the factoring account, and responsibility for their collection is passed to Farant Factors plc. A charge of 1% of the gross value of all debts factored is levied by Farant Factors plc for this service and debited to the factoring account.

(h)   Farant Factors plc pays for the debts, less any advances, interest charges and credit protection charges, 90 days after the date of purchase, and debits the payment to the factoring account.

(i)   On either party giving 90 days' notice to the other, the arrangement will be terminated. In such an event, Shaky plc will transfer no further debts to Farant Factors plc, and the balance remaining on the factoring account at the end of the notice period will be settled in cash in the normal way.

REQUIREMENT:

Consider the nature of the above agreement and resulting transactions and state how these should be reflected in the accounts of Shaky plc.

10   FRS 4 CALCULATION

A company issues a deep discount bond of £200,000 on 1.1.X1 for proceeds of £157,763. Interest of 4% is payable annually on 31 December. The bond will be redeemed on 31.12.X5 for £200,000 (ie at par).

The total cost of borrowing thus to be charged through the profit and loss account over the five year period is made up as follows.

	£
Annual interest payments (5 × £8,000)	40,000
Deep discount (£200,000 − £157,763)	42,237
	82,237

The internal rate of return is 9.5%

REQUIREMENT:

Calculate the figures for the balance sheet and the profit and loss account for each of the five years 19X1 - 19X5 in relation to the bond.

11   LEASES   *27 mins*

'There are two main types of leases with quite different characteristics. Each kind of lease therefore needs its own accounting treatment in both the lessor's and lessee's books.'

Explain fully the above statement. **15 Marks**

12 ANGUS PLC

36 mins

During the completion of the financial statements of Angus plc for the year ended 28 February 19X7, the following matters have been brought to your attention.

(a) On 1 March 19X6, the company revalued its freehold land and buildings (for the first time) to £20 million (land element £4 million) and the accounting records were adjusted to this value. The property originally cost £16 million on which annual depreciation of £280,000 had been charged. Accumulated depreciation to 29 February 19X6 was £2.8 million. Depreciation of £400,000 has been charged to the profit and loss account for the year ended 28 February 19X7.

(b) The company's accounting policy for research and development has been to capitalise the cost and amortise this over 10 years. On 1 March 19X6, when deferred development expenditure of £1.5 million was held as an intangible fixed asset, this policy was changed to immediate write off of development expenditure.

(c) The company announced the intended closure of its European operations on 31 January 19X7 when a formal closure plan was approved and adopted. On 10 March 19X7, the company contracted to terminate various operating leases and an agreed sale value of £9 million. The lessors of the assets held under operating leases agreed to terminate the contracts for a payment of £350,000. The European operations contributed 10% of turnover and profit.

(d) As a result of the closure in (c) above, the company will need to carry out a fundamental reorganisation of its other activities at a cost of £1.25 million.

(e) After accounting for the above items, the company's draft financial statements show turnover of £200 million, profit before taxation of £18 million and a tax charge of £6 million. The company has proposed a dividend of £2 million. Shareholders' funds at 1 March 19X6 were £500 million.

REQUIREMENT:

(a) Prepare the following statements, suitable for publication, for Angus plc for the year ended 28 February 19X7:

    (i)   profit and loss account;
    (ii)   statement of total recognised gains and loses;
    (iii) reconciliation of movements in shareholders' funds; and
    (iv) note of historical cost profits and losses.

(b) Explain briefly:

    (i)   the purpose of the statement of total recognised gains and losses; and

    (ii)   the extent to which a user of the accounts will be better able to make decisions by referring to a statement of total recognised gains and losses rather than the statement of movements on reserves that is produced to comply with the Companies Act 1985.

20 Marks

13 EXCLUSION

State the various circumstances given by the Companies Act 1985 where a subsidiary undertaking may (or must) be excluded from consolidation and state the alternative accounting treatments which should be adopted if a subsidiary undertaking is excluded from consolidation.

14 ZED AND TEE

Z plc acquired 80% of the share capital of T Ltd on 31 December 19X0. The balance of T Ltd's profit and loss account at that date was £350,000.

The balance sheets of the two companies at 31 December 19X5 were as follows.

	Z plc		T Ltd	
	£'000	£'000	£'000	£'000
Fixed assets				
Investment in T Ltd		500		-
Premises		300		200
Plant		250		140
		1,050		340
Current assets				
Stock	160		90	
Debtors	120		70	
Bank	60		30	
	340		190	
Current liabilities				
Creditors	90		35	
Proposed dividend	20		15	
	110		50	
Working capital		230		140
		1,280		480
Share capital		170		80
Profit and loss		1,110		400
		1,280		480

Notes

(a)   Goodwill on acquisition is capitalised and amortised over a period of four years..

(b)   At 31 December 19X5, T Ltd owed £20,000 to Z plc for some goods which had been purchased during the final month of the financial year.

This amount was shown as a creditor in T Ltd's balance sheet and as a debtor in Z plc's.

(c)   The goods referred to in (b) above had cost Z plc £15,000. Only 40% of the goods were resold by T Ltd by 31 December 19X5.

(d)   Z plc calculates depreciation on plant using the reducing balance method of calculating depreciation and T Ltd uses the straight-line method. It has been estimated that the book value of T Ltd's plant would have been reduced by £10,000 if the company had switched to Z plc's basis for the calculation of depreciation when the company was acquired.

(e)   Z plc has not yet accounted for its share of T Ltd's proposed dividend.

REQUIREMENT:

Prepare a consolidated balance sheet for the Z plc group at 31 December 19X5.

15   **AXY**

The summarised balance sheets at 30 June 19X3 of A Ltd and its subsidiaries X Ltd and Y Ltd are set out below.

	A Ltd		X Ltd		Y Ltd	
	£	£	£	£	£	£
Fixed assets						
Tangible assets		-		20,000		45,000
Investments in subsidiaries		68,000		-		-
		68,000		20,000		45,000
Current assets						
Stocks	5,000		30,000		8,000	
Debtors	2,000		12,000		18,000	
Inter-company a/cs						
With X Ltd	-		-		4,000	
With Y Ltd	8,000		-		-	
Bank	3,000		5,000		-	
	18,000		47,000		30,000	
Current liabilities						
Bank overdraft	-		-		6,000	
Creditors	3,000		14,000		9,000	
Inter-company a/cs						
With A Ltd	-		-		6,000	
With Y Ltd	-		3,000		-	
	3,000		17,000		21,000	
		15,000		30,000		9,000
		83,000		50,000		54,000
Capital and reserves						
Ordinary share capital		30,000		10,000		20,000
Revenue reserves		53,000		40,000		34,000
		83,000		50,000		54,000

You ascertain the following information.

(a) A Ltd acquired 8,000 ordinary shares in X Ltd for £20,000 in 19X1. At that time the reserves of X Ltd stood at £18,000.

(b) A Ltd acquired 15,000 ordinary shares in Y Ltd for £48,000 on 1 January 19X3. On 30 June 19X2 the reserves of Y Ltd had stood at £26,000.

(c) On 30 June 19X3 Y Ltd paid a first and final dividend of £6,000 for the year ended on that date. A Ltd has accounted for its share of the dividend by crediting it to profit and loss account.

(d) The stock of X Ltd at 30 June 19X3 included items purchased from A Ltd at £6,000. This price included A Ltd's mark-up of 20% on cost.

(e) Any differences on inter-company accounts relate to cash in transit.

(f) Goodwill arising on consolidation should be amortised evenly over five years.

REQUIREMENT:

Prepare the consolidated balance sheet of A Ltd as at 30 June 19X3.

16 **WATER** *36 mins*

Fire Ltd, Brimstone Ltd and Water Ltd are three companies which work in association within the music industry. So close is their association that they operate a current account system for transactions between themselves, and have adopted 31 December as their accounting date.

On 1 January 19X0 Fire Ltd purchased 80,000 ordinary shares of 50p each in Brimstone Ltd for £55,000. On 31 December 19X0 Water Ltd purchased 60,000 ordinary shares of 50p each in Brimstone Ltd for £48,000 and the entire share capital of Fire Ltd for £280,000.

Draft accounts in respect of the year ended 31 December 19X0 reveal balance sheets for the three companies as follows.

	Water Ltd £	Fire Ltd £	Brimstone Ltd £
Credits			
Called up share capital			
Ordinary shares of £1 each	500,000	200,000	-
Ordinary shares of 50p each	-	-	100,000
Capital reserves 1 January 19X0	80,000	35,000	24,000
Profit and loss account as at 1 January 19X0	18,000	4,900	6,000
Profit for the year ended 31 December 19X0	77,219	31,200	12,000
Provision for depreciation of plant	60,406	45,215	14,623
Overdraft	-	1,613	-
Trade creditors	42,068	37,917	32,989
Current accounts	8,300	-	-
	785,993	355,845	189,612
Debits			
Freehold land and buildings	200,000	150,000	102,000
Plant and machinery	122,415	80,690	25,081
Investments at cost			
Shares in Fire Ltd	280,000	-	-
Shares in Brimstone Ltd	48,000	55,000	-
Stocks	65,820	37,820	34,215
Debtors	58,931	31,615	18,097
Current accounts	-	720	7,800
Cash	10,827	-	2,419
	785,993	355,845	189,612

The following additional information is available.

(a) The current account balances are made up as follows.

Water Ltd	Fire Ltd - £820 Cr, and Brimstone Ltd - £7,480 Cr.
Fire Ltd	Water Ltd - £820 Dr, and Brimstone Ltd £100 Cr.
Brimstone Ltd	Water Ltd - £7,700 Dr, and Fire Ltd - £100 Dr.

(b) A cheque for £220, drawn by Water Ltd in favour of Brimstone Ltd, is in transit at 31 December 19X0.

(c) 20% of the closing stock of Fire Ltd has been sold to that company by Water Ltd at a mark-up of $33^{1}/3$ % on cost.

(d) Water Ltd proposed to pay a dividend of 2%.

(e) The estimated liability of the three companies for corporation tax for the year to 31 December 19X0 is as follows: Water Ltd - £24,300; Fire Ltd - £9,600; Brimstone Ltd - £4,800. Tax has not yet been provided for in the accounts.

(f) Any goodwill is to be capitalised as an asset in the balance sheet, subject to an annual impairment review.

You are required to prepare the consolidated balance sheet of Water Ltd and its subsidiary companies as at 31 December 19X0.

20 Marks

17   **PROJECTION**   *72 mins*

The board of ABC plc, a retail organisation, is considering the acquisition of an 80% interest in the ordinary share capital of its main wholesale supplier, DEF plc on 1 January 19X1. You are given the following information.

PROJECTED PROFIT AND LOSS ACCOUNTS
FOR THE YEAR ENDING 31 DECEMBER 19X0

	ABC plc	DEF plc
	£m	£m
Turnover	800	200
Cost of sales	500	120
Gross profit	300	80
Distribution costs	90	3
Administration expenses	50	5
Profit on ordinary activities before taxation	160	72
Taxation	60	32
Profit on ordinary activities after taxation	100	40
Dividends	30	10
Retained profit for the year	70	30

Notes

(a) The interest in DEF plc will be acquired for £100 million. This will be financed by raising a new 12% fixed interest loan. £40 million of this loan will be convertible to ordinary shares after 19X1 at the rate of one ordinary 25p share in ABC plc for every £1 of loan stock. At the date of acquisition the shareholders' interest in DEF plc will be as follows.

	£m
Ordinary share capital	20
Retained profits	35
Fair value revaluation reserve*	20
	75

*This reserve, which will be created only for purposes of consolidation, comprises the following individual revaluations:

	£m
Stock	5
Depreciable sales vehicles	
(with an average remaining life of five years)	15
	20

(b) ABC plc purchases one quarter of its supplies from DEF plc. This pattern of purchases is mirrored exactly in stockholdings. ABC plc maintains its stock level at 20% of its preceding annual cost of sales.

(c) Both companies pursue a uniform 'cost plus' pricing policy based on a standard gross margin for all their customers and consistently distribute, as dividends, 30% (ABC plc) and 25% (DEF plc) of profits available for distribution.

(d) ABC plc writes off goodwill, as an administration expense, on a straight-line basis over five years. All other assets are also depreciated on a straight line basis.

(e) ABC plc's issued share capital consists of £50 million of 25p ordinary shares.

(f) The following assumptions can be made for 19X1.

    (i) Sales of both companies will grow in volume by 5% in 19X1. Their unit selling prices will be unchanged and existing cost plus pricing policies will be maintained.

    (ii) ABC plc will continue to purchase one quarter of its supplies from DEF plc. Stockholding policies will not change.

    (iii) The expenditures for administration, selling and distribution shown in the 19X0 profit and loss accounts will be repeated in 19X1.

    (iv) Tax charges in 19X1 will be 30% of the profit before tax figure for each company.

    (v) The 19X1 dividend cover will also be maintained.

    (vi) ABC plc will acquire an 80% interest in the ordinary share capital of DEF plc on 1 January 19X1.

You are required to prepare for the board of ABC plc the projected consolidated profit and loss account for ABC plc for the year ending 31 December 19X1.

40 Marks

18   BOLD   *36 mins*

Bold plc, the holding company of the Bold Group, acquired 25% of the ordinary shares of Face plc on 1 September 19X0 for £54 million. Face plc carried on business as a property investment company. The draft accounts as at 31 August 19X1 are as follows.

PROFIT AND LOSS ACCOUNTS FOR THE YEAR ENDED 31 AUGUST 19X1

	Bold Group £m	Face plc £m
Sales	175	200
Profit before interest and tax	90	80
Exceptional profit on sale of property	20	-
Interest	(2)	(20)
	108	60
Taxation	(29)	(20)
	79	40
Proposed dividends	(61)	-
	18	40

BALANCE SHEETS AS AT 31 AUGUST 19X1

	Bold Group £m	Face plc £m
Fixed assets		
Tangible fixed assets	135	200
Investment in Face plc	54	-
Current assets		
Stock	72	210
Debtors	105	50
Current liabilities		
Creditors	(95)	(20)
Overdraft	(14)	(100)
Net current assets	68	140
	257	340
Capital and reserves		
Ordinary shares of £1 each	135	50
Reserves	122	90
10% loan	-	200
	257	340

On 1 September 19X0 Bold plc sold a property with a book value of £40 million to Face plc at its market value of £60 million. The tax suffered on this gain was £7 million. Face plc obtained the funds to pay the £60 million by raising a loan which is included in the 10% loan that appears in its balance sheet at 31 August 19X1.

Premiums on acquisition are amortised over 5 years.

REQUIREMENTS:

(a)   Prepare:

(i)   the consolidated profit and loss account of the Bold Group for the year ended 31 August 19X1 and a consolidated balance sheet as at that date; and

(ii)   relevant notes to comply with the requirements of FRS 9 *Associates and joint ventures*.

(b)   Explain *two* defects of equity accounting and how the new requirements in FRS 9 overcame these defects. Please illustrate your answer with the data from the Bold group.

(c)   If Face plc issued 30 million ordinary shares, each of £1 par value, to a third party on 1 September 19X1, for a cash consideration of £4 per share:

(i)   explain any matters to be taken into consideration in finalising the 19X1 consolidated accounts; and

(ii)   calculate the carrying value of the investment in Face plc in the consolidated balance sheet at 31 August 19X2 and comment upon any related items.)

20 Marks

19   ANGEL AND SHANE

Angel Ltd bought 70% of the share capital of Shane Ltd for £120,000 a number of years ago. At that date Shane Ltd's profit and loss account balance stood at £10,000.

The balance sheets at 31 December 19X8 and the summarised profit and loss accounts to that date are given below.

	Angel Ltd	Shane Ltd
	£'000	£'000
Fixed assets	200	80
Investment in Shane Ltd	120	-
Net current assets	580	110
	900	190
Capital and reserves		
£1 ordinary shares	500	100
Profit and loss account	400	90
	900	190
Operating profit	110	30
Tax	(40)	(12)
Retained profit	70	18
Retained profit b/f	330	72
Retained profit c/f	400	90

No entries have been made in the accounts for any of the following transactions.

Assume that profits accrue evenly throughout the year and that any goodwill is written off to reserves.

Taxation on capital gain is 33%.

REQUIREMENTS:

Prepare the consolidated balance sheet and profit and loss account at 31 December 19X8 in each of the following circumstances.

(a)   Angel Ltd sells its entire holding in Shane Ltd for £320,000 on 30 September 19X8.

(b)   Angel Ltd sells one half of its holding in Shane Ltd for £160,000 on 30 June 19X8, and the remaining holding is to be dealt with as an associate.

20   DYNASTY

On 1 January 19X5 Dynasty plc acquired 10% of the ordinary share capital of Carrington plc for £12,000 paid in cash. On 1 October 19X5 they made an offer for the remaining 180,000 ordinary shares; the offer was accepted in respect of 160,000 shares. The consideration paid comprised 13 newly issued ordinary shares in Dynasty plc for every 16 shares in Carrington plc. The fair value of Dynasty shares on 1 October 19X5 was £3 each.

The draft balance sheets of the two companies at 31 December 19X5 are set out below.

	Dynasty		Carrington	
	£'000	£'000	£'000	£'000
Fixed assets				
Tangible assets	734		236	
Investment in Carrington	141		-	
		875		236
Current assets	598		394	
Creditors: amounts falling due				
within one year	299		180	
		299		214
		1,174		450
Creditors: amounts falling due				
after more than one year				
10% debentures		100		40
		1,074		410

	Dynasty		Carrington	
	£'000	£'000	£'000	£'000
Capital and reserves				
Share capital (£1 ordinary shares)		730		200
Profit and loss account		344		210
		1,074		410

You ascertain the following information.

(a) Dynasty's investment in Carrington is made up as follows.

	£'000
Shares acquired on 1 January 19X5	12
Shares acquired on 1 October 19X5 *	130
	142
Interim dividend received 1 August 19X5	(1)
	141

* Dynasty has taken advantage of s 131 CA 1985. No share premium account has been created in respect of the shares issued on 1 October 19X5.

(b) As at 31 December 19X5 Dynasty holds stock purchased from Carrington for £20,000. Carrington sells goods at a 25% mark-up on cost.

(c) Creditors falling due within one year include the following.

	Dynasty	Carrington
	£'000	£'000
Debenture interest payable	10	4
Proposed dividends	73	10
	83	14

Dynasty has not yet accounted for its share of the dividend proposed by Carrington.

REQUIREMENT:

Prepare the consolidated balance sheet as at 31 December 19X5 using the merger method of accounting. (*Note.* Assume the FRS 6 criteria for merger accounting have been met.)

---

21 **T GROUP** *27 mins*

You are the group accountant in the T Group which has just acquired its first foreign subsidiary. The T Group has financed the acquisition of this new overseas subsidiary by foreign currency borrowing. Your managing director has asked you to explain how the financial statements of this foreign subsidiary will be translated in £ sterling.

You are required to write a memorandum to your managing director explaining:

(a) the choice of foreign currency translation methods; **3 Marks**

(b) the treatment of foreign exchange differences; **8 Marks**

(c) the disclosure required of the foreign exchange translation method and of the treatment of foreign exchange differences. **4 Marks**

Total Marks = 15

---

22 **ROWEN** *45 mins*

Rowen plc was formed 18 years ago to manufacture executive toys. The directors decided to expand their exports and on 1 January 19X4 it acquired investments in an American company, Overseas Inc, and a French company, Europe SA, which were to act as selling agencies for the company's products.

The investments consisted of 800,000 shares of US$10 each in Overseas Inc when its reserves were US$25m and of 2,250,000 shares of FF20 each in Europe SA when its reserves were FF230m. At the dates of acquisition, the book values were the same as the fair values.

The directors have instructed their accountant to prepare draft consolidated accounts as at 31

December 19X8 on the basis that Overseas Inc is a subsidiary undertaking due to the fact that they exercise a dominant influence; and that Europe SA is a participating interest but not an associated undertaking.

BALANCE SHEET
AS AT 31 DECEMBER 19X8

	Rowen £m	Overseas US$m	Europe FFm
Fixed assets			
Tangible assets	669	458	4,231
Investment in Overseas Inc	12		
Investment in Europe SA	10		
Current assets			
Stocks	675	44	404
Cash	46	113	1,038
Current liabilities			
Creditors	(490)	(31)	(288)
Creditors falling due after more than one year			
Loan	(370)	(103)	(954)
	552	481	4,431
Capital and reserves			
Share capital	185	20	180
Profit and loss account	367	461	4,251
	552	481	4,431

PROFIT AND LOSS ACCOUNTS
FOR THE YEAR ENDED 31 DECEMBER 19X8

	Rowen £m	Overseas US$m	Europe FFm
Turnover	2,784	1,150	10,615
Cost of sales	1,822	775	7,154
Gross profit	962	375	3,461
Distribution costs	392	90	831
Administrative expenses	370	30	278
Depreciation	35	24	230
Dividend from Overseas Inc	(12)		
Dividend from Europe SA	(11)		
Profit before tax	188	231	2,122
Tax	93	90	831
Profit after tax	95	141	1,291
Dividends paid 31.7.93	37	51	440
Retained profit	58	90	851

Further information

1   The fixed assets in both Overseas Inc and Europe SA were acquired on 1 January 19X0. They are stated at cost less depreciation and there have been no acquisitions or disposals during the year.

2   Stocks

	31 December 19X7		31 December 19X8	
	Stock	Exchange rate at purchase date	Stock	Exchange rate at Purchase date
Overseas US$m	57	2.0	44	1.6
Europe FFm	523	11.5	404	8.5

3   Exchange rates have been as follows.

	US$ = £1	FF = £1
1 January 19X0	2.4	12.0
1 January 19X4	2.0	12.5
31 December 19X7	1.8	11.0
Average for 19X8	1.7	10.0
31 July 19X8	1.7	10.0
31 December 19X8	1.5	8.0

4   Goodwill arising on the acquisition has been fully amortised.

5   The foreign exchange translation of the foreign subsidiary is to be on the basis that the functional currency of the American operation is sterling.

6   There has been no change in the share capital of Overseas Inc or Europe SA since the date of acquisition.

REQUIREMENTS:

(a)   Prepare a draft consolidated profit and loss account for the Rowen Group for the year ended 31 December 19X8 and a draft consolidated balance sheet as at that date.   **20 Marks**

(b)   (i)   Calculate the effect on the consolidated profit and loss account for the year ended 31 December 19X8 if the investment in Europe SA is classified as an associated interest.

(ii)   Calculate the carrying value of the investment in the consolidated balance sheet as at 31 December 19X8.   **5 Marks**

Total marks = 25

23   **SHIPCO**   *63 mins*

Shipco plc is an old-established shipbuilding company which in recent years has diversified its operations by manufacturing rigs for use in oil exploration and recovery. After initial success, the company experienced financial setbacks and for the past few years has traded at a loss. The company has therefore decided to re-organise its business, with the approval of its members and the agreement of its creditors. In future years, it will trade under the name of Shipco (19X5) plc and revert entirely to its original business of shipbuilding as from 1 January 19X5.

(a)   The balance sheet of Shipco plc as at 31 December 19X4 is expected to be as follows.

	£	£	£
Fixed assets			
Development expenditure		50,000	
Patent rights		15,000	
			65,000
Yards at cost	200,000		
Aggregate depreciation	40,000		
		160,000	
Equipment at cost	80,000		
Aggregate depreciation	20,000		
		60,000	
			220,000
			285,000
Current assets			
Stocks		20,000	
Debtors		10,000	
		30,000	
Creditors: amounts falling due within one year			
Bank		45,000	
Creditors		15,000	
		60,000	
Net current liabilities			(30,000)
Total assets less current liabilities			255,000
Creditors: amounts falling due			
after more than one year			
6% secured debenture repayable in 19X6			(65,000)
			190,000

	£	£	£
Capital and reserves			
Share capital authorised, issued and fully paid			
50,000 ordinary shares of £4 each			200,000
30,000 5% cumulative preference shares £1 each			30,000
			230,000
Reserve			
Profit and loss account: debit balance			(40,000)
			190,000

(b) (i) Shipco plc has two yards, one of which was designed specifically for the construction of rigs. This latter (with a net book value of £80,000) will be surplus to Shipco (19X5) plc's requirements. A sale has been negotiated, at a cash price of £21,000, to take place on 31 December 19X4 before the creation of Shipco (19X5) plc. This sale is not included in Shipco plc's existing financial statements.

(ii) All Shipco plc's equipment can be used for both rig construction and shipbuilding.

(iii) Development expenditure was incurred on the design and testing of prototype oil rigs. This is being written off at £10,000 per annum.

(iv) The patent rights relate to Shipco plc's unique design of an oil rig. These have a further ten years to run.

(v) £15,000 of stocks are for shipbuilding and the remainder have no value.

(vi) The debtor of £10,000 is the final payment due for the sale of an oil rig. The purchaser of this rig has recently gone into liquidation.

(vii) The creditors comprise:

	£
Trade creditors	5,000
Arrears of preference dividends	10,000
	15,000

(viii) The 6% debenture is secured over Shipco plc's assets by floating charge.

(c) The scheme of reconstruction is as follows.

(i) *Ordinary shareholders*

(1) The authorised and issued share capital of Shipco (19X5) plc will be set at £100,000.

(2) Existing ordinary shareholders will receive one partly paid £2 share in Shipco (19X5) plc for every one of their present shares in Shipco plc.

(3) Each new £2 share in Shipco (19X5) plc will be issued to shareholders in Shipco plc as £1 paid up, with the remaining £1 to be paid on 1 January 19X5.

(ii) The 6% debenture of £65,000 is to be fully discharged, as part of the purchase consideration, on 31 December 19X4.

(iii) The arrears of preference dividend are to be cancelled. Existing preference shares are to be exchanged for a new issue of 10% £1 cumulative preference shares in the ratio of two existing preference shares for one new preference share.

(iv) Unsecured trade creditors are to be discharged by cash payment of 20 pence in the £.

(v) The bank overdraft in the books of Shipco plc at 31 December 19X4, after any necessary adjustments, is to be fully discharged by a debenture issue at 5% interest, to be secured on Shipco (19X5) plc's yard.

(vi) The debit of £40,000 on profit and loss account is to be eliminated. All assets useful to the new company will be transferred at book value.

You are required to prepare:

(a) the ledger accounts of Shipco plc showing the entries necessary to effect the realisation;
(b) the opening journal entries for Shipco (19X5) plc;
(c) the balance sheet of Shipco (19X5) plc as at 1 January 19X5.

35 Marks

24 CAPITAL MAINTENANCE AND PROFIT REPORTING

36 mins

(a) State what you understand by the term 'capital maintenance' and give examples of two capital maintenance concepts. **10 Marks**

(b) Outline the practical reasons for measuring and reporting profit. **10 Marks**

Total Marks = 20

25 COCOA

36 mins

Cocoa plc is a company that manufactures flavoured drinks. The management had for a number of years attempted to produce inflation adjusted financial statements that complied with recommendations from the accountancy profession. They became disenchanted after expending considerable time and resource attempting to implement each new method and discontinued preparing inflation adjusted financial statements eight years ago.

They have recently become interested again after attending a seminar on the implication of inflation adjusted accounts for dividend policy. At the seminar they were informed that the current professional pronouncement was the *Handbook: Accounting for the effects of changing prices* issued by the ASC. They had referred briefly to the document but were confused by the reference to eight possible accounting systems based on a combination of two asset valuation bases, two units of measurement and two capital maintenance concepts.

They have requested the company accountant to prepare a brief report for them to explain the feasibility of each of the systems. They have also requested him to illustrate the report by adjusting the company's accounts for the year ended 30 June 19X3 under each of the eight systems.

An extract from the accounts of Cocoa plc for the year ended 30 June 19X3 prepared on a historical cost basis showed the following information.

	£
Capital and reserves	
Ordinary share capital in shares of 50p each	100,000
Profit and loss account balance as at 1.7.X2	75,000
Profit after tax for year ended 30.6.X3	42,000

Dividends

An interim dividend of 5p per share was paid on 15 January 19X2 and a final dividend of 10p per share was declared on 15 June 19X3.

	£
Fixed assets	
Plant and machinery (net book value)	55,000
Current assets	
Stock	39,000

The following information was obtained relating to the Retail Price Index and current costs.

The Retail Price Index was:

1.7.X2	116
1.1.X3	121
30.6.X3	128

Current cost of assets in the balance sheet as at 30 June 19X3 were as follows.

	£
Plant and machinery (net)	62,000
Stock	44,000

Current cost adjustment calculations were as follows.

	£
Cost of sales adjustment	9,000
Depreciation adjustment	1,000
Monetary working capital adjustment	4,500
Gearing adjustment	(3,625)

REQUIREMENTS:

(a) (i) Discuss the relevance of the historical cost accounting system in times of price instability in relation to the unit of measurement used, the asset valuation base and the capital maintenance concept.

(ii) Explain the purpose and feasibility of the following two accounting systems both of which value assets at current cost.

System 1 Uses constant purchasing power as the unit of measurement and operating capital as the capital to be maintained.

System 2 Uses nominal £ as the unit of measurement and financial capital as the capital to be maintained. **12 Marks**

(b) Prepare a profit and loss account for Cocoa plc for the year ended 30 June 19X3 on the assumption that the company values assets at current cost, uses nominal £ as the unit of measurement and maintains its financial capital. **8 Marks**

Total Marks = 20

26 CARVER

36 mins

Carver plc is a listed company incorporated in 19T8 to produce models carved from wood. In 19V5 it acquired a 100% interest in a wood importing company, Olio Ltd; in 19W9 it acquired a 40% interest in a competitor, Multi-products Ltd; and on 1 October 19X3 it acquired a 75% interest in Good Display Ltd. It is planning to make a number of additional acquisitions during the next three years.

The draft consolidated accounts for the Carver Group are as follows

DRAFT CONSOLIDATED PROFIT AND LOSS ACCOUNT
FOR THE YEAR ENDED 30 SEPTEMBER 19X4

	£'000	£'000
Operating profit		1,485
Share of operating profit in associate		495
Income from fixed asset investment		155
Interest payable		(150)
Profit on ordinary activities before taxation		1,985
Tax on profit on ordinary activities		
Corporation tax	391	
Deferred taxation	104	
Tax attributable to income of associated undertakings	145	
		(640)
Profit on ordinary activities after taxation		1,345
Minority interests		(100)
Profit for the financial year		1,245
Dividends paid and proposed		(400)
Retained profit for the year		845

DRAFT CONSOLIDATED BALANCE SHEET
AS AT 30 SEPTEMBER

	19X3		19X4	
	£'000	£'000	£'000	£'000
Fixed assets				
Intangible asset: goodwill		-		100
Tangible assets				
Buildings at net book value		2,200		2,075
Machinery: cost	1,400		3,000	
aggregate depreciation	(1,100)		(1,200)	
net book value		300		1,800
		2,500		3,975
Investments in associated undertaking		1,000		1,100
Fixed asset investments		410		410
Current assets				
Stocks		1,000		1,975
Trade debtors		1,275		1,850
Cash		1,820		4,515
		4,095		8,340
Creditors: amounts falling due within one year				
Trade creditors		280		500
Obligations under finance leases		200		240
Corporation tax		217		462
Dividends		200		300
Accrued interest and finance charges		30		40
		927		1,542
Net current assets		3,168		6,798
Total assets less current liabilities		7,078		12,283
Creditors: amounts falling due after more than one year				
Obligations under finance leases		170		710
Loans		500		1,460
Provisions for liabilities				
Deferred taxation		13		30
Net assets		6,395		10,083
Capital and reserves				
Called up share capital in 25p shares		2,000		3,940
Share premium account		2,095		2,883
Profit and loss account		2,300		3,145
Total shareholders' equity		6,395		9,968
Minority interest		-		115
		6,395		10,083

Notes

1   There had been no acquisitions or disposals of buildings during the year.

Machinery costing £500,000 was sold for £500,000 resulting in a profit of £100,000. New machinery was acquired in 19X4 including additions of £850,000 acquired under finance leases.

2   Information relating to the acquisition of Good Display Ltd.

	£'000
Machinery	165
Stocks	32
Trade debtors	28
Cash	112
Trade creditors	((68)
Corporation tax	(17)
	252
Minority interest	(63)
	189
Goodwill	100
	289

	£'000
880,000 shares issued as part consideration	275
Balance of consideration paid in cash	14
	289

Goodwill in Olio Ltd and Multi-products Ltd is fully amortised. However, the goodwill arising on the acquisition of Good Display Ltd is considered to have an indefinite useful life and is to remain in the balance sheet.

3   Loans were issued at a discount in 19X4 and the carrying amount of the loans at 30 September 19X4 included £40,000 representing the finance cost attributable to the discount and allocated in respect of the current reporting period.

Required

Prepare a consolidated cash flow statement for the Carver Group for the year ended 30 September 19X4 as required by FRS 1 (revised) with supporting notes for the following.

(a)   Reconciliation of operating profit to net cash flow from operating activities
(b)   Analysis of cash flows netted in the cash flow statement
(c)   Analysis of changes in net debt   **20 Marks**

27   WRIGHT SHOES

The Wright Shoes Group plc recorded the following results for their recent financial year (ended 31 December).

	£'000
Profit after taxation attributable to parent company shareholders	1,550
Expenses of rights issue	100
	1,450
Dividends paid and proposed	950
Retained profit	500

	Recent year	Previous year
	£'000	£'000
Ordinary shares of £1 each	8,200	5,500
4.2% cumulative preference shares of £1	1,000	1,000

The increases in ordinary shares were:

(a)   on 1 March, 500,000 shares were issued at a premium of £0.50 on the acquisition of Apple Blossom Ltd;

(b)   on 1 August, a rights issue of 1 for 3 was made at a price of £1.10 per share. The market price per share immediately before the rights issue was £1.42;

(c)   on 1 November, 200,000 shares were issued at a premium of £0.40 per share on the acquisition of Shoeshine Ltd.

REQUIREMENT:

Calculate the EPS. If the EPS in the previous year had been 21.2p, how should this be adjusted to obtain comparison with the recent year's EPS?

28 CONWAY

36 mins

You are the chief accountant of Conway plc, a company which produces fork lift trucks. The company has a new finance director, to whom you report. She and the rest of the board have determined that the company is in an ideal position to undertake an aggressive expansion policy through acquisition. A potential acquisition target is Uplift Ltd, a competitor. It is thought that this company is vulnerable to a takeover bid as there are management weaknesses. Any takeover target must show potential for improvements in profitability and utilisation of assets.

The financial statements of Uplift Ltd have been obtained for the last three years and your assistant has prepared a list of ratios for those years. He has also obtained averages for the ratios he has calculated for this particular industry through the trade press. The ratios are as follows.

	19X3	19X4	19X5	Industry average
Equity/Total assets (%)	21.0	40.5	34.0	30.0
Net fixed assets/Equity	3.17	1.36	1.88	0.57
Net fixed assets/Total assets (%)	66.7	55.0	63.8	17.1
Total liabilities/Total assets (%)	79.0	59.5	66.0	70.0
Long-term debt/Total assets (%)	35.0	19.5	30.0	20.0
Total liabilities/Equity	3.76	1.47	1.94	2.33
Current liabilities/Total assets (%)	44.0	40.0	36.0	50.0
Current assets/Current liabilities	0.76	1.12	1.01	1.66
(Current assets – Stock)/Current liabilities	0.41	0.62	0.67	0.78
Stock/Total assets (%)	15.2	20.0	12.0	44.0
Cash/Total assets (%)	14.3	22.0	22.0	13.0
Debtors/Total assets (%)	3.81	3.10	2.31	24.17
Cost of sales/Creditors	6.50	6.15	6.05	13.00
Cost of sales/Stock	10.67	8.58	12.56	5.01
Gross profit/Sales (%)	19.0	22.0	18.5	24.0
Sales growth (%)	20.0	30.0	8.0	7.0
Sales/Total assets	2.0	2.2	1.9	2.9
Sales/Net fixed assets	3.0	4.0	2.9	17.0
Sales/Working capital	−18.75	44.0	894.0	8.8
Sales/Debtors	52.5	71.0	80.0	12.0
Profit before tax/Sales (%)	7.0	14.0	12.0	4.0
Profit after tax/Total assets (%)	12.6	30.4	12.9	9.0
Profit after tax/Equity (%)	60.0	75.0	38.0	30.0
Profit before interest/Interest	5.5	15.0	9.0	5.0

Notes

1   Working capital = (Debtors + Stock + Cash + Other equivalent current assets) − (Creditors + Other current liabilities)

2   Total assets = Fixed assets (NBV) + Current assets

3   Net fixed assets = Fixed assets at NBV

REQUIREMENTS:

(a)   Draft a report for the finance director to present to the board, analysing the ratios provided for Uplift Ltd over the three years and compared to the averages for the industry.   **12 Marks**

(b)   Product a general memorandum to be circulated to the board outlining why it may not be appropriate to rely on a comparison between ratios from one year to the next or to those of other companies.   **4 Marks**

(c)   State how the problems discussed in (b) above might affect particular ratios in your answer to (a), and the resulting conclusions of your report.   **4 Marks**

Total Marks = 20

29 TERMS FOR A MERGER

Two companies, S plc and T plc, are engaged in the exploitation of similar mineral resources, involving highly specialised skills and considerable investment in exploration and site development costs.

Current statistics relating to the two companies are as follows.

	S plc	T plc
Number of shares in issue	1,064,000	800,000
Earnings	£165,000	£239,000
Earnings per share	15.5p	29.9p
Stock market price per share	£1.03	£2.40
Price/earnings ratio	6.6	8.0

Over recent years, S plc has provided its shareholders with high rates of growth in both dividends and share prices. Its plans for the next three years, however, show the company will not have the financial strength to cope with the needs of expansion within an increasingly competitive market. This is believed to be a problem only in the medium term, beyond which the prospects could be very good.

T plc has not been so aggressive in exploration, but by prudent exploitation of its resources it has managed to maintain relatively stable earnings and dividends per share. Its P/E ratio is higher than that of S plc and is also in the upper quartile for the industry as a whole. The board of T plc now realises, however, that unless it undertakes major new exploration its profits are likely to peak during the next three years and then decline significantly. Unfortunately, its past policy has left the company short of certain necessary skills which are possessed in abundance by S plc.

The boards of the two companies have therefore been exploring the possibility of a merger based, so far, on the assumption that shares in T plc will be issued in exchange for the existing shares in S plc.

They are uncertain at this stage whether the number of T plc shares to be issued to the existing shareholders in S plc should be calculated by reference to the current stock market prices of shares in the two companies or whether S plc should be valued for the purpose of the merger at a P/E ratio of 8.0.

REQUIREMENTS:

(a) Calculate and comment on the effects of these two alternative methods on the earnings and share values attributable to the shareholders in each company.

(b) Indicate what factors might influence the choice of P/E ratio to be used.

30 SEGMENTAL REPORTING   36 mins

Tickers plc is preparing a segmental report for inclusion in its financial accounts for the year ended 31 December 19X5. The figures given relate to Tickers Ltd and its subsidiaries but information in relation to associated companies is not shown.

	19X6	19X5
	£'000	£'000
Sales to customers outside the group by the Stationery Division	11,759	10,479
Sales to customers outside the group by the UK companies	28,200	26,912
Sales not derived from Stationery, Tissue or Packaging activities	3,290	1,992
Sales made to customers outside the group by the Tissue Division	18,390	14,608
Assets used by the US companies	30,600	21,788
Assets not available to be allocated to Stationery Tissue Packaging activities	14,856	12,007
Assets used by the Stationery Division	31,750	29,480
Sales by the Tissue Division to other group members	3,658	3,211
Assets used by the Packaging Division	17,775	16,440
Assets used by the UK companies	41,820	39,042
Sales by the Stationery Division to other group members	1,227	1,398
Sales not allocated to the UK, US or other areas	3,290	1,992
Sales made by group to other areas of the world	1,481	1,117
Expenses not allocated to UK, US or other areas	4,073	3,560
Sales to customers outside the group by US companies	7,227	5,920
Expenses not allocated to Stationery, Tissue or Packaging Service	5,004	4,833
Sales by US companies to group members	2,117	1,180

	19X6	19X5
	£'000	£'000
Sales to customers outside the group for Bureau service	5,200	3,955
Sales made by UK companies to other group members	2,430	1,270
Assets used by Tissue Division	44,620	37,254
Assets used by group in other areas	21,660	21,792
Assets not allocated to UK, US or other areas	14,921	12,559
Segmental net operating profit by industry		
Stationery	2,442	3,627
Tissue	5,916	4,599
Packaging	821	915
Consolidated segmental net operating profit	8,978	8,820
Segmental net operating profit by geographical area		
UK	4,873	4,230
US	3,127	2,249
Other areas	487	594
Consolidated segmental net operating profit by geographical area	8,047	7,547

REQUIREMENTS:

(a) Draft an industry and geographical segmental report for inclusion in the annual report to give the maximum information to the shareholders. **15 Marks**

(b) Discuss items, using the Tickers plc figures as illustrations, where you consider there is a need for further information to assist the reader to interpret the segmental data. **5 Marks**

Total Marks = 20

31 WORLD PROBLEMS
36 mins

You are the finance director of a subsidiary company of a large multinational group. A new managing director has been appointed to your subsidiary. She has been studying both the subsidiary's accounts and the annual report of the group and there she has found one or two things that have puzzled her.

(a) In the company's accounts, a major fixed asset was sold on 31 December 19X6 for £5.5m. On 1 January 19X4 the asset, which had a remaining useful life of 15 years, had been revalued to £4.5m from £3.0m. The managing director does not understand the accounting treatment in both the 19X5 and 19X6 accounts.

REQUIREMENTS:

(i) Discuss the accounting treatment required by the ASB in this situation.

(ii) Show how the above transactions would appear in the company accounts for the years ended 31 December 19X5 and 19X6 as required by FRS 3. Depreciation was charged in full in both years. **5 Marks**

(b) In the group's annual report, the following appears as a note to the group's consolidated profit and loss account.

INCOME STATEMENT RECONCILIATION
FOR THE YEAR ENDED 31 DECEMBER 19X6

	£m
UK GAAP: net profit	130
US GAAP: adjustments net of tax	
Amortisation of capitalised interest	(8)
Deferred tax	(55)
Additional depreciation and amortisation	
of goodwill for acquisition accounting	(280)
Results eliminated arising pre-merger	(200)
US GAAP: estimated loss as adjusted	(453)

There is also a reconciliation between equity as reported under UK GAAP and US GAAP.

REQUIREMENTS:

(i)   Explain to your managing director why it is considered that greater harmonisation of accounting policies and disclosures on an international level would be beneficial. Note the barriers which exist to such harmonisation.

(ii) In relation to the above income statement reconciliation, explain why each adjustment has been made.

(iii) Will equity under US GAAP be greater or less than equity reported under UK GAAP if the adjustments made in the equity reconciliation relate to those given in the income statement reconciliation? Explain your answer.

(iv) Supposing that a final dividend was proposed, and that under US GAAP this had to be included in the year in which the dividend is to be *paid*, state the effect on equity. **15 Marks**

Total Marks = 20

1   CHARACTERISTICS

Characteristics of financial reports

The suggested characteristics are, in general, present in company accounts prepared in accordance with normally accepted accounting rules and practices. SSAP 2 *Disclosure of accounting policies*, identifies **consistency** and **prudence** as two of the four fundamental accounting concepts. We can therefore assume that these characteristics are always present in audited company accounts. Moreover, one purpose of the entire series of SSAPs and FRSs is to improve **comparability** between companies by narrowing the range of valuation and reporting procedures available to them. However, in many areas alternative procedures remain permissible and a great deal of variety persists.

The use of historical cost as the basis for preparing financial reports is justified on the ground that it makes these statements more **objective**. On the other hand, use of historical cost conflicts, to some extent, with the need to provide *relevant* data; for many business decisions current values are more relevant than historical cost.

The need for company accounts to be **realistic** (complete in form and substance) to some extent conflicts with the desire for **economy of presentation** and the need for the data to be **understandable** to user groups. The accounts contain a comprehensive range of financial data within the constraints imposed by the money measurement concept, which requires transactions to be accurately expressed in financial terms before they are reported. For this reason resources such as human assets and created goodwill are excluded from the accounts. The preparation of final accounts inevitably involves a great deal of summarisation; it is impossible to report everything as an excessive amount of detail makes it difficult to identify the more important developments.

It is the job of the auditors to check that the information published is **reliable** and fairly reflects progress during the year. The preparation of the final accounts is a relatively slow process. Often the accounts are not made available to the shareholders until three or four months after the year end and, except for quoted companies which must publish interim results, no further information is received for another year.

Uses of accounting information

The users of accounting information are **many and varied**. They include the following.

(a)   The equity investor group which includes existing and potential shareholders.

(b)   The loan creditor group, including existing and potential holders of debentures and loan stock, and providers of short-term secured and unsecured loans and finance.

(c)   The employee group, including existing, potential and past employees.

(d)   The analyst/advisor group including financial analysts and journalists, economists, statisticians, stockbrokers and other providers of advisory services.

(e)   The business contact group, ranging from customers, trade creditors and suppliers to business rivals.

(f)   The government including tax authorities, departments and agencies concerned with the supervision of commerce and industry, and local authorities.

(g)   The public including tax payers, rate payers, consumers and other community and special interest groups such as political parties, consumer and environmental protection societies.

Satisfying user needs

Obviously, a set of published accounts **cannot satisfy all the needs** of this diverse range of user groups. The accounts are principally designed for the shareholders and one must assume that their requirements are met more effectively than those of any other group. A number of the groups can of course insist on the supply of extra data. For example, a bank manager may insist on the preparation of detailed management accounts and forecasts as a pre-condition for granting a loan. Similarly, the government can oblige companies to fill in substantial forms for a variety of purposes.

Specialist accounts

Some companies prepare specialist accounts, which often make use of pictorial presentations in the form of graphs and bar charts, for employees. Probably the main weaknesses of final accounts are that they contain out of date historical costs rather than up to date values, and that they omit valuable assets that cannot be expressed accurately in financial terms. They are also the victim of 'window dressing' in order to conceal the full extent of a company's liabilities.

BPP PUBLISHING

2 STATEMENT OF PRINCIPLES

The merits of the ASB's *Statement of Principles* should, ideally, be summarised in its objective, which is given in the *Foreword to Accounting Standards*:

> 'to provide a framework for the consistent and logical formulation of individual accounting standards (and to provide) a basis on which others can exercise judgement in resolving accounting issues.'

The following points may be made in favour of the *Statement of Principles*.

(a) The principles have in fact been used in the formulation of standards, for example its definitions of assets and liabilities have been used in FRS 5 *Reporting the substance of transactions*.

(b) The *Statement* helps reduce scope for individual judgement and the potential subjectivity that this implies.

(c) Financial statements should be more comparable because, although alternative treatments will still be available, there will be a consistent and coherent framework on which to base one's choice of a particular alternative.

(d) The *Statement* puts forward a consistent terminology and consistent objectives, for example in the definitions and the qualitative characteristics.

It could be argued that the *Statement of Principles* is too theoretical. It is certainly general rather than particular. However, as has been seen with FRS 5 and FRS 15, the general principles can be applied to very specific issues in accounting standards. Moreover, in areas not at present covered by accounting standards, the statement can give general guidance. Nevertheless, in the short term, the principles in the *Statement* may conflict with some accounting standards which had already been issued before it was written.

3 RYMACHINES

Notes for meeting with Arthur Isation, chief accountant of Rymachines plc on treatment of fixed assets.

(a) *Revaluation of plant*

Depreciation charge in the P&L account for the period should be based on the carrying amount in the balance sheet. The entire amount being charged through P&L account for the year.

Rymachines have revalued mid year, hence the appropriate depreciation charge for the year will be (assuming depreciation calculated on a monthly basis).

		£
1st 6 months $\dfrac{£80,000}{10} \times \dfrac{6}{12} =$		4,000
2nd 6 months $\dfrac{£97,500}{7.5} \times \dfrac{6}{12} =$		6,500
Charge for the year		10,500

Note that this is £2,500 higher than if no revaluation had taken place and this should be disclosed if material.

The revaluation as at 1 July 19X7 will amount to (£97,500 − (£80,000 × 7½/10)) = £37,500, and should be credited to a revaluation reserve.

It is possible to transfer an amount equivalent to the depreciation on the revalued amount from revaluation reserve to P&L account as the revaluation reserve in effect becomes realised.

(b) *Supplementary depreciation*

It is not possible to charge depreciation in excess of that based on the carrying amount of the assets, in the P&L account. This does not, however, preclude the appropriation of retained profits to, for example, a reserve specially designated for replacement of fixed assets.

The additional £25,000 should not be accounted for as conventional depreciation. The depreciation charge must be based on the balance sheet carrying amount and the additional £25,000 should merely be an intra-reserves transfer, ie from P&L account reserve to a plant replacement service.

Additionally if appropriate the asset could be revalued and this would automatically lead to higher depreciation.

(c)   *Revision of useful lives*

When, as a result of experience or of changed circumstances, it is considered that the original estimate of the useful economic life of an asset requires revision, the effect of the change in estimate on the results and financial position needs to be considered. Usually, when asset lives are reviewed regularly, there will be no material distortion of future results or financial position if the net book amount is written off over the revised remaining useful economic life. Where, however, future results would be materially distorted, the adjustment to accumulated depreciation should be recognised in the P&L account as an exceptional charge.

Such an adjustment will be dealt with in arriving at the profit on ordinary activities.

(i)   This is a standard revision in estimated useful life, and there is no reason to believe that future results will be materially distorted by the change. It would appear that the estimate of future useful life is being made at the balance sheet date, which would involve a normal £20,000 charge in respect of the year just finished (year ended 31 December 19X7), and a charge for the remaining two years of estimated useful life of:

$$\frac{£140,000 - £60,000}{2} = £40,000$$

If, however, one takes the view that the revision is to apply in respect of 19X7, then the depreciation charge for 19X7 (and 19X8 and 19X9) will be:

$$\frac{£140,000 - £40,000}{3} = £33,333$$

(ii)   Two points to bear in mind here are:

(i)   materiality, dealing with much larger figures; and
(2)   the change in useful life itself has arisen from an 'unusual' event.

It is likely that the costs of closure of the factory are to be accounted for in total as an exceptional item as provision should be made for the consequences of all decisions taken up to the balance sheet date. This specifically includes losses arising from the disposal of assets.

With this in mind, an immediate write-down is necessary in the 19X7 accounts, the write-down forming part of the exceptional item relating to terminated activities. if writing down to £10,000, the charge will be (£400,000 − £10,000) × 6/10 = £234,000.

(d)   *Impairment in value of warehouse*

If at any time there is an impairment in the value of an asset and the net book amount is considered not to be recoverable in full (perhaps as a result of obsolescence or a fall in demand for a product) the net book amount should be written down immediately to the estimated recoverable amount, which should then be written off over the remaining useful economic life of the asset. If at any time the reasons for making such a provision cease to apply, the provision should be written back to the extent that it is no longer necessary.

The write down required will be £80,000 + (£80,000 × 48/50) − £115,000 = £41,800, which should be charged against the 19X7 profits. The remaining buildings element should then be depreciated over the ensuing 48 years:

$$\frac{£115,000 - £80,000}{48} = £729 \text{ pa}$$

4   FRS 11

(a)   If there were an indication that a fixed asset in income-generating unit B was impaired, the value in use of B would be compared with £200m, not £150m.

(b)   An impairment loss of £20m is recognised in respect of income-generating unit Z, reducing its carrying amount to £120m and the total carrying amount to £370m. A further impairment loss of £10m is then recognised in respect of the goodwill.

5   **MILLER**

(a)   SUMMARISED PROFIT AND LOSS ACCOUNTS
YEAR ENDED 31 DECEMBER 19X2

	Units	*Direct cost* £	*SSAP 9* £
Opening stock (@ £9/£15)	6,000	54,000	90,000
Production (W1)	54,000	490,500	814,500
	60,000	544,500	904,500
Closing stock	5,000	49,500	79,500
Cost of sales	55,000	495,000	825,000
Sales	55,000	1,375,000	1,375,000
Gross profit		880,000	550,000
Production overheads		(324,000)	-
Other overheads		(210,000)	(210,000)
Debenture interest		(7,200)	+ (7,200)
Retained profit for the year		338,800	332,800
Retained profit brought forward:			
As reported		247,400	247,400
Prior year adjustment		-	36,000
		247,400	283,400
Retained profits carried forward		586,200	616,200

(b)   SUMMARISED BALANCE SHEET AS AT 31 DECEMBER 19X2

	Direct cost £	£	*SSAP 9* £	£
Fixed assets		600,000		600,000
Current assets				
Stock (W2)	49,500		79,500	
Debtors	252,000		252,000	
Cash at bank	44,100		44,100	
	345,600		375,600	
Creditors: amounts falling due within one year				
Trade creditors	119,400		119,400	
Net current assets		226,200		256,200
Total assets less current liabilities		826,200		856,200
Creditors: amounts falling due after more than one year				
12% Debentures		(60,000)		(60,000)
		766,200		796,200
Share capital and reserves				
Called up share capital		180,000		180,000
Profit and loss account		586,200		616,200
		766,200		796,200

(c)   REPORT

To:	Board of Directors
From:	Accountant
Subject: *Change in basis of stock valuation*	Date: XX/XX/XX

In the accounts for the year ended 31 December 19X2 stock will for the first time be valued, not at direct cost, but at direct cost plus production overheads. This is the valuation method prescribed by statement of standard accounting practice 9 *Stocks and long-term contracts.* Compliance with SSAP 9 will mean that we will avoid a qualified report from our auditors.

The effects of the change are set out below.

(i)   In the balance sheet, stock at 31 December 19X2 will be valued at £79,500 compared with a direct cost valuation of £49,500, ie stock will be £30,000 greater than if the previous valuation basis had been used.

(ii)   This will be matched by an increase of £30,000 in retained profits, arrived at as follows.

	£
Upward restatement of retained profits at 31.12.X1	36,000
Less reduction in profits reported for 19X2	6,000
Net increase in retained profits	30,000

(iii)   The upward restatement (£36,000) of last year's retained profits arises from valuing last year's stock at £90,000 (previously, £54,000).

(iv)   The reduction in 19X2 profits (£6,000) is the difference between profits on the old basis (£338,800) and profits on the SSAP 9 basis (£332,800).

Workings

1   *Production in 19X2*

		£
Direct costs:	$11/12 \times 54,000 \times £9$	445,500
	$1/12 \times 54,000 \times £10$	45,000
		490,500
Production overheads		324,000
		814,500

2   *Closing stock*

	Units	Direct cost £	SSAP 9 £
December production			
$(1/12 \times 54,000)$	4,500		
Direct cost (@ £10)		45,000	45,000
Production overhead (@ £6)			27,000
	4,500	45,000	72,000
November production (balance)	500		
Direct cost (@ £9)		4,500	4,500
Production overhead (@ £6)			3,000
	5,000	49,500	79,500

6   SOAP

> *Tutorial note.* The key to avoiding getting muddled in part (b) of this question is to set out the proformas (including those for workings) and present your workings logically.

(a)   The definition of a long term contract in SSAP 9 *Stocks and long term contracts* generally applies to contracts which last for more than one year, but does not exclude contracts of less than one year which fall into different accounting periods. The relevant wording of the definition is as follows.

> '(A long term contract is) one where the time taken substantially to complete the contract is such that the contract activity falls into different accounting periods. A contract that is required to be accounted for as long term . . . will usually extend for a period exceeding one year . . . Some contracts with a shorter duration than one year should be accounted for as long term contracts if they are sufficiently material . . . that not to record turnover and attributable profit would lead to distortion'.

The accounting treatment adopted by Soap plc for the shorter contracts would appear to be consistent with this SSAP 9 definition. It is also consistent with the treatment of the other contracts. It is important, however, that the same accounting treatment is used every year, even if the results are not as favourable, unless there are good reasons for changing it.

(b)   SOAP PLC
PROFIT AND LOSS ACCOUNT
FOR THE YEAR ENDED 31 DECEMBER 19X7 (EXTRACT)

	£'000
Turnover	5,680
Cost of sales	(5,165)
Gross profit on long term contracts	515

SOAP PLC
BALANCE SHEET AS AT 31 DECEMBER 19X7

	£'000
Current assets	
Stock	
Long term contract balances	137.5
Debtors	
Amounts recoverable on contracts	1,050
Current liabilities	
Payments on account	(350)

Workings

1   *Archers plc*

	£
Costs incurred to date	47,500
Machine write-off $(20,000 - (^6/_{12} \times 10,000))$	15,000
	62,500
Less cost of sales (W4)	(40,000)
Long term contract balance	22,500
Excess of payments on account over turnover $(40 - 30)$	(10,000)
	12,500

2   *Neighbours Ltd*

	£'000
Costs incurred to date	1,800
Cost of sales (W4)	(1,250)
Long term contract balance	550
Less excess of payments on account over turnover $(2,500 - 1,600)$	(900)
Current liability	(350)

3   *Emmerdale plc*

	£'000
Costs incurred to date	4,000
Cost of sales (W4)	(3,875)
Long term contract balance	125
Turnover (W4)	4,050
Payments on account	3,000
Amounts recoverable on contracts	1,050

4   *Profit and loss account*

	Emmerdale £'000		Archers £'000		Neighbours £'000	Total £'000
Turnover						
	$(45\% \times 9)$	4,050	$(20\% \times 150)$	30	$(25\% \times 6.4)$ 1,600	5,680
Cost of sales						
	$(45\% \times 7.5)$	3,375	$(20\% \times 120 - 20^*)$	20	$(25\% \times 5)$ 1,250	4,645
Additional costs						
	$(8 - 7.5)$	500		20		520
		(3,875)		(40)	(1,250)	(5,165)
Profit (loss) on						
long term contracts		175		(10)	350	515

* *Note.* Because the machine is being written off in one year, its total cost, rather than a percentage, is allocated to that year.

5   *Balance sheet*

	Emmerdale £'000	*Archers* £'000	*Neighbours* £'000	*Total* £'000
Current assets				
Stocks				
Long term contract balances	125 (W3)	12.5 (W1)		137.5
Debtors				
Amounts recoverable on contracts	1,050 (W3)			1,050
Current liabilities				
Payments on account			(350) (W2)	(350)

7   **QUOTED COMPANY**

(a)   The main argument for the maintenance of a deferred tax account stems from the accruals concept, ie that costs and revenue should be matched and dealt with in the profit and loss account of the period to which they relate. Where, for example, a company receives accelerated capital allowances which exceed the depreciation charge on the same assets in the period in which the allowances are received, the benefit of the allowances should be carried forward and matched against the depreciation charge over the asset's useful life. Similarly, where a profit is recognised by revaluing property assets in the accounts, the potential future tax liability on that profit should also be recognised and matched against the profit.

One argument that may be used against deferred tax accounting is that taxation is not an expense but a distribution of profits and as such is not subject to the accruals concept. This point of view is not, however, widely held.

On the other hand, there is considerable support for the view that whilst the principles of deferred tax accounting are generally acceptable, it should not be necessary to make a provision when it can be demonstrated that no liability is likely to arise in the foreseeable future. This argument would seem to have particular merit in cases such as property revaluations where there is no intention of disposing of the properties concerned. There is, however, less justification for ignoring timing differences on depreciable assets. There is, after all, no doubt that such timing differences originating from accelerated capital allowances will reverse over the life of the asset. The supporters of full deferred tax accounting would then argue that it is irrelevant that such reversals might be more than covered by future originating timing differences. To ignore the net position, however, is to risk having a situation under which a company's deferred tax balance will increase year by year without any possibility of a reduction in the foreseeable future. Deferred tax accounting would then have become a theoretical exercise of no real value, but with the considerable practical drawback that reserves would be understated.

(b)   The fundamental statement of principle in SSAP 15 is that deferred tax should be accounted for on timing differences which are expected to result in the crystallisation of a tax asset or liability.

The standard, therefore, reaffirms support for the concept of providing for deferred taxation, but takes the view expressed in part (a) of this answer, that no provision should be made where the reduction in liability is likely to continue for the foreseeable future. In the figures given in the question it may be seen that:

(i)   full provision is made on 'other timing differences' which are most likely to be short-term timing differences resulting from the use of the receipts and payment basis for tax purposes and the accruals basis in the accounts;

(ii)   with the exception of £450,000 full provision has been made in respect of accelerated capital allowances perhaps because management believe that the amount provided will become payable or, more likely, because, in view of the uncertainties of the economic climate and business forecasting they feel the provision is required by the concept of prudence;

(iii)   no provision has been made for tax on the revaluation surpluses on freehold land and buildings presumably because the management of the company do not consider that the properties will be sold in the foreseeable future.

The standard requires the full potential liability for each category of timing difference to be disclosed as well as provision made.

649

The standard provides that debit balances on deferred tax account should be carried forward only if there is reasonable certainty of their recovery in future periods. It is acceptable, however, to offset debits arising from one category of timing difference against credit balances arising from another. This has been done in the example given.

The other requirements of SSAP 15 are largely concerned with the details of disclosure and the application of those already discussed. The standard prescribes that deferred tax provisions should be computed on the liability method.

A discussion draft on deferred taxation produced by the ASB advocates the full provision method, perhaps combined with the use of discounting.

8   PENSION COSTS

(a)   (i)

Year	Funding £m	Profit & loss charge £m	∴ Balance sheet provision £m
1	-	0.6	0.6
2	-	0.6	1.2
3	-	0.6	1.8
4	-	0.6	2.4
5	1	0.6	2.0
6	1	0.6	1.6
7	1	0.6	1.2
8	1	0.6	0.8
9	1	0.6	0.4
10	1	0.6	-
	6	6.0	

Funding = cash paid into the scheme.
The profit and loss charge is the £6 million spread evenly over 10 years.
The balance sheet accruals is the balancing figure.

In other words, the profit and loss charge is as follows.

	£m
Normal contribution	1.0
Less the experience variation spread over the life of the employees	0.4
	0.6

(ii)

Year	Funding £m	Profit & loss charge £m	∴ Balance sheet prepayment £m
1	5	1.4	3.6
2	1	1.4	3.2
3	1	1.4	2.8
4	1	1.4	2.4
5	1	1.4	2.0
6	1	1.4	1.6
7	1	1.4	1.2
8	1	1.4	0.8
9	1	1.4	0.4
10	1	1.4	-
	14	14.0	

Profit and loss charge is £14 million spread over 10 years.

OR

	£m
Normal contribution	1.0
Plus variation $\dfrac{£4m}{10}$	0.4
	1.4

(b) In (i) above, at the end of year 1 the company still has an over-funded pension scheme but the balance sheet is showing a £0.6m provision.

Unsophisticated readers of the financial statements might think the contributions are in arrears. A suggestion is that it is reclassified out of provisions and into deferred income.

The ASB has been urged to review this aspect of the SSAP.

If we look at an example of an under-funded scheme (as in (ii) above), the same principle emerges. In this example a company which has an under-funded scheme ends up with a balance sheet asset. This could be reclassified as a deferred cost.

9   FRS 5 SCENARIO

Note. This scenario is based on an illustration in FRS 5 and it demonstrates the thought processes required to determine how an item should be treated.

The commercial effect of this arrangement is that, although the debts have been legally transferred to Farant Factors plc, Shaky plc continues to bear significant benefits and risks relating to them. Shaky plc continues to bear slow payment risk as the interest charged by Farant Factors plc varies with the speed of collections of the debts. Hence, the gross amount of the debts should continue to be shown on its balance sheet until the earlier of collection and transfer of all risks to Farant Factors plc (ie 90 days).

However, Shaky plc's maximum downside loss is limited since any debts not recovered after 90 days are in effect paid for by Farant Factors plc, which then assumes all slow payment and credit risks beyond this time. Thus, even for debts that prove to be bad, Shaky plc receives some proceeds. (For a debt of 100 that subsequently proves to be bad, the proceeds received would be 100, less the credit protection fee of 1, less an interest charge calculated for 90 days at base rate plus 2.5%.)

Hence, assuming the conditions given in FRS 5 for linked presentation for certain non-recourse finance arrangements are met, a linked presentation should be adopted. The amount deducted on the face of the balance sheet should be the lower of the proceeds received and the gross amount of the debts less all charges to the factor in respect of them. In the above example, for a debt of 100 this latter amount would be calculated at 100 less the credit protection fee of 1 and the maximum finance charge (calculated for 90 days at base rate plus 2.5%). Assuming the proceeds received of 80 are lower than this, and accrued interest charges at the year end are 2, the arrangement would be shown as follows.

	£	£
Current assets		
Stock		x
Debts factored without recourse		
Gross debts (after providing for credit protection fee and accrued interest)	97	
Less non-returnable proceeds	(80)	
		17
Other debtors		x

In addition, the non-returnable proceeds of 80 would be included within cash and the profit and loss account would include both the credit protection expense of 1 and the accrued interest charges of 2.

10   FRS 4 CALCULATION

At inception

DEBIT	Cash	£157,763
CREDIT	Liability	£157,763

Year	P & L a/c charge (a) £		Interest payable (b) £	Rolled up interest charged to P & L a/c (a) – (b) £	Liability in closing balance sheet £
19X1	14,988	(W1)	8,000	6,988	164,751
19X2	15,651	(W2)	8,000	7,651	172,402
19X3	16,378	(W3)	8,000	8,378	180,780
19X4	17,174	(W4)	8,000	9,174	189,954
19X5	18,046	(W5)	8,000	10,046	200,000
	82,237		40,000	42,237	

Workings

(1) $0.095 \times 157,763 = 14,988$
(2) $0.095 \times (157,763 + 6,988) = 15,651$
(3) $0.095 \times (164,751 + 7,651) = 16,378$
(4) $0.095 \times (172,402 + 8,378) = 17,174$
(5) $0.095 \times (180,780 + 9,174) = 18,046$

11   LEASES

Accounting for leases and hire purchase contracts is the subject of SSAP 21 issued by the ASC in 1984.

Definitions

General. A lease is a contract between a lessor and a lessee for the hire of a specific asset. The lessor retains ownership of the asset but transfers the right to use the asset to the lessee for an agreed period of time in return for the payment of specified rentals.

Finance lease. This is a lease that transfers substantially all the risks and rewards of ownership of the asset to the lessee. It is assumed that such a transfer occurs if, at the beginning of the lease, the present value of the payments to be made under the lease amounts to substantially all (normally 90% or more) of the value of the lease. A finance lease is usually issued by a bank or a finance house which is, in effect, simply financing an asset required by the customer.

Operating lease. This is defined as any lease other than a finance lease. This means that the risks and rewards of ownership remain with the lessor. The lease is usually for a relatively short period of time, and the expectation is that when the leasing period is complete, the asset may be rented by somebody else. The point is that the asset is leased for substantially less than its useful economic life.

Accounting treatment: lessees

Finance lease. The lease should be recorded in the balance sheet both as an asset and as a liability (obligation to pay future rentals). At the outset, the sum to be recorded should represent the present value of the minimum payments under the lease. This is arrived at by discounting the minimum payments at the interest rate implicit in the lease. In practice, the 'fair value' (the price at which an asset could be exchanged in an arm's length transaction) of the asset is often considered a reasonable approximation of present value for this purpose.

The asset should be depreciated over the shorter of the period of the lease and the useful life of the asset.

Rental payments should be apportioned between the finance charge for use of the asset (debited to the profit and loss account) and repayment of the loan (deducted from the outstanding obligation in the balance sheet).

Operating lease. There is no balance sheet entry and the amount of the rental payment is debited to the profit and loss account.

Accounting treatment: lessors

Finance leases. The amount due from the lessee should be recorded in the balance sheet as a debtor at the amount of the net investment in the lease. The rentals receivable should be allocated between repayment of the debt and profit so as to produce a constant return on the declining net investment.

Operating leases. The lease should be recorded as a fixed asset and depreciated over its useful life. Rental income should be credited to the profit and loss account on the straight line basis, over the period of the lease, even if the payments are made in an irregular fashion.

12   ANGUS

> *Tutorial note.* Aspects of FRS 3 could come up in all types of question - make sure you are familiar with all its statements and notes.

(a)   (i)   ANGUS PLC
PROFIT AND LOSS ACCOUNT FOR THE YEAR ENDED 28 FEBRUARY 19X7

	Continuing £'m	Discontinued £'m	Total £'m
Turnover	180.00	20.00	200.00
Operating profit (W1)	18.99	2.11	21.10
Loss on disposal of fixed asset (W2)	-	(1.50)	(1.50
Loss on disposal of discontinued operations		(0.35)	(0.35)
Cost of fundamental reorganisation	(1.25)	(0.35)	(1.25)
Profit on ordinary activities before taxation	17.74	0.26	18.00
Tax on profit on ordinary activities			(6.00)
Profit on ordinary activities after taxation			12.00
Dividends			(2.00)
Retained profits for the financial year			10.00

(ii)   STATEMENT OF TOTAL RECOGNISED GAINS AND LOSSES

	£m
Profit for the year	12.0
Surplus on revaluation of fixed assets (W3)	6.8
Total recognised gains and losses	18.8
Prior year adjustment	(1.5)
Total gains and losses recognised since last annual report	17.3

(iii)   RECONCILIATION OF MOVEMENTS IN SHAREHOLDERS' FUNDS

	£m
Profit for the financial year	12.0
Dividends	(2.0)
	10.0
Other recognised gains and losses	6.8
Net addition to shareholders funds	16.8
Opening shareholders' funds (originally £500m before deducting prior year adjustment of £1.5m)	498.5
Closing shareholders' funds	515.3

(iv)   NOTE OF HISTORICAL COST PROFITS AND LOSSES

	£m
Reported profit on ordinary activities before taxation	18.00
Difference between a historical cost depreciation charge and the actual depreciation charge for the year calculated on the revalued amount (400k − 280k)	0.12
Historical cost profit on ordinary activities before taxation	18.12
Historical cost profit for the year retained after taxation, minority interests, extraordinary items and dividends (18.12 − 6 − 2)	10.12

Workings

1   *Operating profit*

	£'m
Profit before tax	18.00
Add back losses	
Fixed assets	1.50
Termination	0.35
Reorganisation	1.25
	21.10

2 *Loss on sale of fixed assets*

	£'m
NBV	10.5
Proceeds	(9.0)
	(1.5)

3 *Surplus on revaluation*

	£'m
Revalued amounts	20
NBV at 28.2.X6 (16m − 2.8m)	(13.2)
Surplus	6.8

(b) (i) The purpose of the STRGL is to be an 'all inclusive' statement of gains and losses occurring in an enterprise during a period.

The P&L account excludes items deemed to be unrealised such as revaluations/forex differences that go directly to the reserves. These can, however, represent very material amounts. FRS 3 therefore requires companies to provide this extra statement to give increased prominence to these items.

(ii) As illustrated in parts (a) and (b) the two statements differ as dividends are not shown in the gains and losses statements as it represents a distribution of gains made not a loss.

By only including true gains and losses, not anything which changes net assets, the statement has a clearer purpose than the reserve statement.

Reserve notes are usually included at the end of the financial statements. The STRGL is a primary statement and must therefore be given due prominence within the financial statements.

One explanation might be that the statement of movement on reserves has not a regulatory or mandatory format so that it is clear that the movements contained in the statement are not presented in a uniform format and are not well understood by the user.

The efforts to improve the presentation of information in the accounts is designed to produce decision useful information. By advocating additional primary statements the ASB might be setting the scene for further primary statements that could be used to accommodate future developments, eg value statements with a reconciliation to the historical cost profit.

13   EXCLUSION

Exclusion of undertakings from group accounts

S 299 CA 1985 (as amended by the CA 1989) provides that a subsidiary *may* be omitted from the consolidated accounts of a group under certain circumstances. FRS 2 goes further and states that a subsidiary *must* be excluded from consolidation in the following circumstances.

(a) if severe long-term restrictions are substantially hindering the exercise of the parent's rights over the subsidiary's assets or management;

(b) if the group's interest in the subsidiary undertaking is held exclusively with a view to subsequent resale *and* the subsidiary has not been consolidated previously;

(c) the subsidiary undertaking's activities are so different from those of other undertakings to be included in the consolidation that its inclusion would be incompatible with the obligation to give a true and fair view.

The FRS requires the circumstances in which subsidiary undertakings are to be excluded from consolidation to be interpreted *strictly*.

Where a subsidiary is excluded from group accounts, FRS 2 lays down supplementary provisions on the disclosures and accounting treatment required.

Dissimilar activities

Where a subsidiary is excluded on grounds of dissimilar activities (which would be so exceptional as to be extremely unlikely), the group accounts should include separate financial statements for that subsidiary including:

(a) a note of the holding company's interest;

(b)   details of intra-group balances;

(c)   the nature of its transactions with the rest of the group;

(d)   a reconciliation of the subsidiary's results (as shown separately) with the value in the consolidated accounts for the 'group's investment in the subsidiary'.

In the consolidated accounts, the excluded subsidiary should be accounted for by the equity method of accounting (as though it were an associated company).

Long-term restrictions

Subsidiary undertakings excluded from consolidation because of severe long-term restrictions are to be treated as fixed asset investments. They are to be included at their carrying amount when the restrictions came into force, and no further accruals are to be made for profits or losses of those subsidiary undertakings, unless the parent undertaking still exercises significant influence. In the latter case they are to be treated as associated undertakings.

The following information should be disclosed in the group accounts:

(a)   its net assets;
(b)   its profit or loss for the period;
(c)   any amounts included in the consolidated profit and loss account in respect of:

    (i)   dividends received by the holding company from the subsidiary;
    (ii)   writing down the value of the investment.

Temporary control

If control is temporary (the investment is held purely for resale), the temporary investment should be included under current assets in the consolidated balance sheet at the lower of cost and net realisable value.

General disclosure

In all cases given above, FRS 2 states that the consolidated accounts should show:

(a)   the reasons for exclusion;
(b)   the names of subsidiaries excluded;
(c)   the premium or discount on acquisition not written off;
(d)   anything else required by the Companies Acts.

The Companies Act 1985 has only this to say on the treatment of excluded subsidiaries:

'The interest of the group in subsidiary undertakings excluded from consolidation under section 229 (4) (undertakings with activities different from those of undertakings included in the consolidation), and the amount of profit or loss attributable to such an interest shall be shown in the consolidated balance sheet or, as the case may be, in the consolidated profit and loss account by the equity method of accounting.'   (Sch 4A para 18 CA 1985)

On the treatment of subsidiaries excluded for other reasons, the Act is silent.

14   **ZED AND TEE**

Z PLC

CONSOLIDATED BALANCE SHEET AS AT 31 DECEMBER 19X5

	£'000	£'000
Fixed assets		
Premises (300 + 200)		500
Plant (250 + 140 − 10)		380
		880
Current assets		
Stock (160 + 90 − 3 (W1))	247	
Debtors (120 + 70 − 20)	170	
Bank (60 + 30)	90	
	507	
Current liabilities		
Creditors (90 + 35 − 20 + 3 (W2))	108	
Proposed dividend	20	
	128	
Net current assets		379
		1,259
Share capital		170
Profit and loss (W3)		995
Minority interests (20% × (480 − 10))		94
		1,259

Workings

1   *Unrealised profit on stock*

Profit on goods sold by Z plc to T Ltd
£(20,000 − 15,000) = £5,000

60% remain in stock ∴ unrealised profit on stock = £3,000

DEBIT	Group reserves
CREDIT	Group stock

2   *T Ltd dividend payable to minority*

£15,000 × 20% = £3,000

3   *Profit and loss*

	£'000
Post-acquisition reserves of T Ltd	
Reserves at 31.12.X0	400
Pre-acquisition	(350)
Additional depreciation	(10)
Add back proposed dividend	15
	55

4   *Group reserves at 31 December 19X5*

	£'000	£'000
Z (per question)		1,110
Add: dividend receivable from T (80% × £15)		12
Less: unrealised profit		(3)
		1,119
Tee (per question)	400	
Additional depreciation	(10)	
	390	
Less: pre-acq'n	(350)	
	40	
Group share (80%)		32
Less: goodwill fully amortised		(156)
		995

656

5   *Minority interest*

		£'000
Share capital		80
Reserves (400 – 10)		390
		470

470 × 20% = 94

6   *Goodwill arising on consolidation*

	£'000	£'000
Cost of investment in T Ltd		500
Net assets acquired		
80% × £80,000	64	
80% × £350,000	280	
		(344)
Goodwill		156

15   AXY

Stage 1. The dividend paid by Y Ltd has been accounted for in the books of Y Ltd and A Ltd, but A Ltd has treated it incorrectly. Of the £4,500 (75% × £6,000) received by A Ltd, £2,250 ($^6/_{12}$ × £4,500) comes from pre-acquisition profits. The following adjustment is necessary to A Ltd's draft balance sheet.

DEBIT	Revenue reserves	£2,250	
CREDIT	Investment in Y Ltd		£2,250

A Ltd now has a balance of £50,750 (£53,000 – £2,250) on revenue reserves, while its investment in Y Ltd is stated at cost less amounts written down £(48,000 – 2,250) = £45,750.

Stage 2. The current accounts differ by £3,000, being £2,000 cash in transit from Y Ltd to A Ltd, and £1,000 cash in transit from X Ltd to Y Ltd. £3,000 cash in transit will appear in the consolidated balance sheet as an asset.

Stage 3. The only cancelling items, apart from the current accounts, are A Ltd's investments in subsidiaries and the subsidiary companies' share capitals. These will be dealt with in the cost of control account.

Stage 4. We will make the prudent assumption that all of the unrealised profit in X Ltd's stock ($^{20}/_{120}$ × £6,000 = £1,000) is to be charged to consolidated reserves. No charge will be made against the minority.

Workings

1   *Minority interest*

	£	£
X Ltd		
Share capital (20% × £10,000)		2,000
Reserves (20% × £40,000)		8,000
		10,000
Y Ltd		
Share capital (25% × £20,000)	5,000	
Reserves (25% × £34,000)	8,500	
		13,500
		23,500

2   *Goodwill*

	£	£
Cost of investment in X Ltd		20,000
Share of net assets acquired as represented by		
Share capital	10,000	
Reserves	18,000	
	28,000	
Group share (80%)		22,400
Negative goodwill		2,400
Cost of investment in Y Ltd		48,000
Less pre-acquisition dividend		2,250
		45,750
Share of net assets acquired as represented by		
Share capital	20,000	
Reserves £26,000 + ($^6/_{12}$ × £8,000)	30,000	
	50,000	
Group share (75%)		37,500
Goodwill		8,250

3   *Reserves*

	£
A Ltd (£53,000 − £2,250)	50,750
Share of X Ltd's post acquisition reserves	
£(40,000 − 18,000) × 80%	17,600
Share of Y Ltd's post acquisition reserves	
£(34,000 − 30,000) × 75%	3,000
	71,350
Unrealised profit on stock	1,000
Goodwill amortisation (£8,250 × $^1/_5$)	1,650
	68,700

CONSOLIDATED BALANCE SHEET AS AT 30 JUNE 19X3

	£	£
Fixed assets		
Intangible assets		
Goodwill	6,600	
Negative goodwill	(2,400)	
		4,200
Tangible assets		65,000
		69,200
Current assets		
Stocks (less £1,000 unrealised profit)	42,000	
Debtors	32,000	
Bank (including £3,000 in transit)	11,000	
	85,000	
Current liabilities		
Bank overdraft	6,000	
Creditors	26,000	
	32,000	
Net current assets		53,000
		122,200
Capital and reserves		
Ordinary £1 shares		30,000
Revenue reserves		68,700
Shareholders' funds		98,700
Minority interests		23,500
		122,200

16   WATER

> *Tutorial note.* It is often useful, as a first looking, to lay out the group structure. You should then use it to check that you have the correct shareholding %. Look out for shares < £1 nominal value etc.

Workings

1   *Group structure*

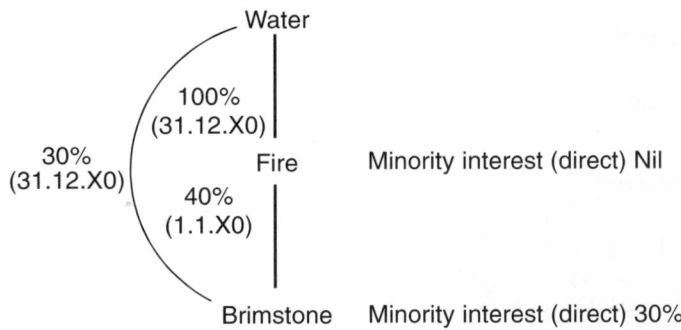

Water	
100% (31.12.X0)	
30% (31.12.X0)	
Fire	Minority interest (direct) Nil
40% (1.1.X0)	
Brimstone	Minority interest (direct) 30%

2   *Minority interests*

	£
Brimstone	
Share capital	100,000
Capital reserve	24,000
P&L account reserve	6,000
Profit for the year (12,000 − 4,800)	7,200
	137,200
× 30%	41,160

3   *Goodwill*

	£	£
Fire Ltd		
Cost of investment		280,000
Share of consolidated net assets acquired as represented by:		
Share capital	200,000	
Capital reserve	35,000	
Consolidated reserves (see below)	26,380	
		261,380
		18,620

Consolidated reserves of Fire Ltd as at 31.12.X0

	£	£
Fire (4,900 + 31,200 − 9,600)		26,500
Brimstone (12,000 − 4,800) × 40%		2,880
Goodwill on Brimstone		
Cost of investment	55,000	
Net assets acquired		
Share capital	100,000	
Capital reserve	24,000	
P&L account reserve	6,000	
	130,000	
× 40%	52,000	
		(3,000)
		26,380

Brimstone	£	£
Cost of investment		48,000
Share of net assets acquired		
Share capital	100,000	
Capital reserve	24,000	
P&L account (6,000 + 12,000 − 4,800)	13,200	
	137,200	
	× 30%	41,160
		6,840
Total goodwill		
Fire		18,620
Brimstone		6,840
		25,460

4   *Capital reserve*

Water Ltd	£80,000

5   *Profit and loss account*

	£
Water £(18,000 + 77,219 − 24,300)	70,919
Stocks: unrealised profit 20% (£42,820 × 25%)	(2,141)
Dividend	(10,000)
	58,778

WATER LIMITED
CONSOLIDATED BALANCE SHEET A AT 31 DECEMBER 19X0

	£	£
Fixed assets		
Intangible assets - goodwill (W3)		25,460
Tangible assets		
Freehold land and buildings		452,000
Plant and machinery at cost	228,186	
Less depreciation	(120,244)	
		107,942
		585,402
Current assets		
Stocks £(137,855 − 2,141)	135,714	
Debtors	108,643	
Cash and cash in transit £(10,827 + 2,419 + 220)	13,466	
	257,823	
Creditors: amounts falling due within one year		
Bank overdraft	1,613	
Creditors	112,974	
Current taxation	38,700	
Proposed dividend	10,000	
	163,287	
		94,536
		679,938
Capital and reserves		
Ordinary shares of £1 each, fully paid		500,000
Capital reserves		80,000
Profit and loss account		58,778
Shareholders' funds		638,778
Minority interest		41,160
		679,938

17   PROJECTION

FORECAST CONSOLIDATED PROFIT AND LOSS ACCOUNT
FOR ABC AND SUBSIDIARY FOR YEAR TO 31 DECEMBER 19X1

	£m
Turnover (W1)	917.5
Cost of sales (W2)	534.0
Gross profit	383.5
Distribution costs (W3)	96.0
Administrative expenses (W4)	63.0
Interest	12.0
Net profit before tax	212.5
Taxation (W5)	74.9
Net profit after tax	137.6
Minority interest (W6)	7.5
Net profit attributable to members of ABC	130.1
Dividends payable (W7)	36.5
Retained profit for the year	93.6

Workings

1   *Turnover*

	£m
ABC 800 × 105%	840.0
DEF 200 × 105%	210.0
Less intra-group sales (see below)	(132.5)
	917.5

Intra-group sales	£m
ABC's cost of sales	525.0
ABC's stock increase (5% of opening stock): 5% × 20% × 500	5.0
ABC's purchases in total	530.0
25% is purchased from DEF	132.5

2   *Cost of sales*

	£m
ABC : 500 × 105%	525.0
DEF : 120 × 105%	126.0
	651.0
Less intra-group purchases etc (see below)	117.0
	534.0

	£m
Intra-group sales as above	132.5
Profit on stock	
ABC closing stock = 525 × 20% = 105	
Of which 25% from DEF = 26.25	
Of which DEF profit = 40%	(10.5)
Increase in value of DEF opening stock for	
consolidation purposes only	(5.0)
	117.0

3   *Distribution costs*

	£m
Additional depreciation on sales vehicles	
15 × 20% per annum	3.0

4   *Administrative expenses*

	£m
Consideration	100.0
Net assets bought (80% × 75)	60.0
Goodwill	40.0
Amortisation @ 20% per annum	8.0

5   *Taxation*

	ABC	DEF
	£m	£m
Turnover	840.0	210
Cost of sales	(525.0)	(126)
Distribution costs	(90.0)	(3)
Administrative expenses	(50.0)	(5)
Dividend from DEF (W7)	10.6	-
Interest	(12.0)	-
Pre-tax profit	173.6	76
Tax @ 30%	52.1	22.8

6   *Minority interest*

	£m
DEF profit after tax (W5)	53.2
Intra-group profit on stock (W2)	(10.5)
Opening stock adjustment (W2)	(5.0)
Adjusted DEF profit	37.7
Of which 20% is minority interest	7.5

7   *Dividends*

	£m
ABC (173.6 − 52.1) × 30% (30/100)	36.5
DEF (76.0 − 22.8) × 25% (10/40)	13.3
Of which 80% is ABC's:	10.6

18   BOLD

> *Tutorial note.* The calculations in this question are quite straightforward as long as you are confident in the techniques of equity accounting. If you keep up to date with current topics you should be able to discuss the problems associated with equity accounting.

(a) (i) BOLD GROUP
CONSOLIDATED PROFIT AND LOSS ACCOUNT
FOR THE YEAR ENDED 31 AUGUST 19X1

	£m	£m
Group turnover		175.00
Group operating profit (90 − 5.8)		84.20
Share of operating profit in associate		20.00
		104.20
Profit on sales of property		15.00
Interest payable		
Group	2	
Associate	5	
		(7.00)
		112.20
Taxation		
Group	27.25	
Associate	5.00	
		(32.25)
		79.95
Dividends		(61.00)
Retained profit for the year		18.95

BOLD GROUP
CONSOLIDATED BALANCE SHEET
AS AT 31 AUGUST 19X1

	Notes	£m	£m
Fixed assets			
Tangible assets			135.00
Interest in associated company	2, 5		54.95
			189.95
Current assets			
Stock		72	
Debtors		105	
		177	
Current liabilities			
Creditors		95	
Bank overdraft		14	
		109	
Net current assets			68.00
			257.95
Capital and reserves			
Ordinary shares £1 each			135.00
Reserves	4		122.95
			257.95

(ii) NOTES TO THE ACCOUNTS

1 *Retained profit*

	£m
Retained by Bold and its subsidiaries	14.75
Retained by Face plc	10.00
	24.75

2 *Interest in associated company*

	£m
Group's share of net assets (25% × (340 − 200))	35.00
Less unrealised profit (25% × 13)	(3.25)
Unamortised goodwill (29 − 5.8)	23.20
	54.95

BPP
PUBLISHING

Additional disclosures for associates

The group has one associate, Face plc, in which the group's share exceeds 25 per cent with respect to the group.

	£m	£m
Share of turnover of associate		50
Share of assets		
Share of fixed assets (W)		45
Share of current assets		65
		110
Share of liabilities		
Liabilities due within one year or less	(30)	
Liabilities due after more than one year	(48.25)	
		(78.25)
		31.75

Workings

1 *Premium on acquisition*

	£m
Share capital	50
Reserves at date of acquisition (90 – 40)	50
	100
Group share (25%)	25
Cost	54
Premium on acquisition	29
Amortisation (29,000 ÷ 5)	5.8

2 *Reserves*

	£m
Bold reserves per question	122.00
Less: amortisation	(5.80)
Group share of post acquisition reserves of Face	
(40 × 25%)	10.00
	126.20
	(3.25)
	122.95

3 *Working: exceptional profit*

	£m
Profit per Bold's profit and loss account	20
Less unrealised profit	
(25% × 20)	(5)
	15

4 *Group tax charge*

	£m
Bold per question	29.00
Less tax on unrealised element of exceptional profit	
(7 × 25%)	(1.75)
	27.25

5 *Share of Face's fixed assets*

		£m
Face fixed assets per question		200
Unrealised profit		(20)
		180
	× 25%	45

6 *Share of Face's liabilities after one year*

	£m
Face liabilities per question	200
Tax element of unrealised profit	(7)
	193
× 25%	48.25

(b) Two of the main problems with equity accounting are discussed here.

(i) *Availability of earnings*

Face plc has not declared a dividend for the year to 31 August 19X1, and it can be seen from Face's balance sheet that the reason for this is severe liquidity problems. There is a large bank overdraft and the quick ratio is as low as 0.4:1 (although the current ratio is very favourable at 2.2:1.

This means that Bold is accruing income from an associated company under equity accounting, when in fact no funds are being received.

(ii) *Gearing*

In equity accounting, only the holding company's equity share in the associate is shown. This disguises the gearing of the associate and the effect it might have on the group. In this case, Face plc's operating assets are financed by debt to the extent of nearly 60%, but the net equity investment shown in the consolidated accounts gives no indication of this.

One of the effects of this is that return on capital employed is improved.

$$\text{ROCE} = \frac{104,200,000}{257,950,000} \times 100\% = 40\%$$

The rate should be adjusted to take the long term loan interest, which has been deducted from the associate's profit.

$$\text{ROCE} = \frac{£104,200,000}{£257,950,000 + (25\% \times £200,000,000)} = 33.8\%$$

Under FRS 9 the equity method is still used for associates but for material assets much greater disclosure is required of the group's share of individual assets and liabilities. This enables the level of borrowing in the associate to be more easily identified.

The profit and loss account now also distinguishes the group's share of operating results from group's share of interest payable allowing more meaningful ratios to be calculated.

Some critics, however, might argue that disclosure by way of note draws insufficient attention to the level of borrowing in the associate and inclusion of the investor's share of borrowings on the face of the balance sheet would be better (as in proportional consolidation).

(c) (i) Should this issue go ahead it would dilute Bold's holding in Face plc as follows.

	Current	With new issue
	£m	£m
Face plc total share capital	50	80
Bold's share	12.5	12
%	25%	15.625%

Under FRS 9 Bold would have to consider whether it was still in a position to exercise significant influence. If this is not the case, this would usually mean that the investment in Face plc would be treated as a fixed asset investment on consolidation, rather than an associated undertaking. Income would be recognised when dividends are received from Face plc.

In terms of the 19X1 accounts, it would seem necessary to disclose the transaction as a non-adjusting post balance sheet event, because the materiality is such that it affects the ability of the user to understand the financial statements properly. The materiality can be seen in terms of dividend cover.

Before issue

$$\text{Dividend cover} = \frac{76}{61} = 1.25$$

After issue

$$\text{Dividend cover} = \frac{(76 - 10)}{61} = 1.08$$

The holding company dividend is now only just covered by profits, because the associate company has not distributed a dividend, although it has made a profit.

(ii) In the 19X2 accounts, the carrying value of the investment should be the amount of its equity value at the time when influence was lost. (*Note.* Treatment as a deemed disposal is suggested by FRS 2).

The revised carrying value would be calculated as follows.

Carrying value of associate

		£
Before the issue	25% × £140,000	35,000
After the issue	15.625% × £(140,000 + 120,000)	40,625
Gain		5,625

19 ANGEL AND SHANE

(a) BALANCE SHEET

	£'000
Fixed assets	200
Net current assets (580 + 320 − tax on gain 66)	834
	1,034
Share capital	500
Profit and loss account (W)	534
	1,034

Working: reserves

	£'000
Angel	400
Add profit on disposal (320 − 120) × 67%	134
	534

PROFIT AND LOSS ACCOUNT

	£'000	£'000
Operating profit 110 + (30 × 9/12)		132.50
Profit on disposal of shares in subsidiary (W3)		147.15
Tax 40 + (12 × 9/12) + 66		(115.00)
		164.65
Minority interest (30% × 18 × 9/12)		(4.05)
Net profit		160.60
Profit b/f (W2)		373.40
Profit c/f		534.00

Workings

1   *Goodwill*

	£'000	£'000
Cost		120
Share of net assets acquired		
Share capital	100	
P & L a/c	10	
	110	
Group share (70%)		(77)
		43

2   *Reserve b/f*

		£'000	£'000
Angel			330.0
Shane:	Balance sheet date	72	
	Acquisition	10	
		62	
Group share (70%)			43.4
			373.4

3   *Exceptional item*

   (i)   *Holding company profit*

	£'000
Sale proceeds	320
Cost	(120)
Profit	200
Tax @ 33%	(66)
	134

   (ii) *Group profit*

	£'000	£'000
Gross H Co profit		200.00
Less post-acquisition profits now sold		
Brought forward	43.40	
Plus (9/12 × 18 × 70%)	9.45	
		(52.85)
		147.15
Less tax		(66.00)
		81.15

   Alternatively:

	£'000
Sales proceeds	320.00
Less net assets disposals of (190 − (3/12 × 18)) × 70%	(129.85)
Less goodwill	(43.00)
	147.15
Less tax	(66.00)
	81.15

(b) BALANCE SHEET

	£'000
Intangible fixed asset - goodwill	21.5
Fixed assets	200.0
Investment in Shane (190 × 35%)	66.5
Net current assets (580 + 160 − 33 tax)	707.0
	995.0
Share capital	500.0
Profit and loss account (W1)	495.0
	995.0

PROFIT AND LOSS ACCOUNT

	£'000	£'000
Operating profit 110 + (6/12 × 30)		125.00
Income from associate (30 × 35% × 6/12)		5.25
		130.25
Profit on disposal of shares in subsidiary (W2)		75.15
		205.40
Tax: 40 + (12 × 6/12) + 33	79.00	
Associated share (12 × 6/12 × 35%)	2.10	
		(81.10)
		124.30
Minority interest (18 × 6/12 × 30%)		(2.70)
		121.60
Profit b/f (per (a))		373.40
Profit c/f		495.00

Workings

1   *Reserves*

	£'000	£'000
Angel		400.0
Add: profit on disposal		
(160 − (120 × 1/2)) × 67%		67.0
		467.0
Shane		
Balance sheet	90	
On acquisition	(10)	
	80	
Group share (35%)		28.0
		495.0

2   *Exceptional item*

(i)   *Holding company profit*

	£'000
Sale proceeds	160
Cost (120 × ½)	(60)
	100
Tax @ 33%	33
	67

(ii)   *Group profit*

	£'000	£'000
H Co profit: gross		100.00
Less post-acquisition profits now sold on		
At disposal date 72 + (18 × 6/12)	81	
At acquisition	(10)	
	71	
Group share (35%)		(24.85)
		75.15
Less tax		(33.00)
		42.15

Alternatively:

	£'000
Sales proceeds	160.00
Less: net assets disposed of	
(190 − (6/12 × 18)) × 35%	(63.35)
Less goodwill (43 × 1/2)	(21.50)
	75.15
Less tax	(33.00)
	42.15

20   DYNASTY

Notes

1   The combination of Dynasty and Carrington satisfies the CA 1985 criteria for a merger. In particular, the cash element of the purchase consideration is less than 10% of the nominal.

	£'000
Cash paid	12
Nominal value of shares issued	130
	142

12/130 = 9.2%

2   An adjustment is required in respect of the £1,000 interim dividend received by Dynasty from Carrington. Dynasty has credited the amount to its cost of investment. This is not normally necessary under merger accounting principles and the following adjustment should be made to the draft balance sheet of Dynasty.

DEBIT	Investment in Carrington	£1,000	
CREDIT	Profit and loss account		£1,000

3   A second adjustment is needed to take account of the proposed dividend receivable from Carrington.

DEBIT	Current assets	£9,000	
CREDIT	Profit and loss account		£9,000

The revised balance on Dynasty's profit and loss account is £(344,000 + 1,000 + 9,000) = £354,000.

CONSOLIDATED BALANCE SHEET AS AT 31 DECEMBER 19X5

	£'000	£'000
Fixed assets		
Tangible assets		970
Current assets (W1)	988	
Creditors: amounts falling due within one year (W2)	470	
Net current assets		518
Total assets less current liabilities		1,488
Creditors: amounts falling due after more than one year		
10% debentures		140
		1,348
Capital and reserves		
Share capital (£1 ordinary shares)		730
Capital reserve (W3)		38
Profit and loss account (W4)		539
Shareholders' funds		1,307
Minority interests (10% × 410)		41
		1,348

Workings

1   *Current assets*

	£'000
Dynasty plc	598
Carrington plc	394
	992
Less unrealised profit in stock (25/125 × £20,000)	4
	988

2   *Creditors: amounts falling due within one year*

	£'000
Dynasty plc	299
Carrington plc	180
	479
Less dividend payable by Carrington to Dynasty (90% × £10,000)	(9)
	470

3 *Capital reserve*

	£'000	£'000
Nominal value of shares acquired (20 + 160)		180
Nominal value of consideration paid		
Cash	12	
Shares	130	
		142
		38

4 *Profit and loss account*

	£'000
Dynasty plc (see tutorial notes)	354
Carrington plc (90% × £210,000)	189
	543
Less unrealised profit on stock	4
	539

21 T GROUP

REPORT

To: The Managing Director
From: Group accountant
Subject: *Foreign currency translation*   Date: XX/XX/XX

With reference to our recent acquisition of a foreign subsidiary, this memorandum outlines how its financial statements will be translated into pounds sterling. This area of accounting practice is covered by SSAP 20 *Foreign currency translation*.

(a) *Foreign currency translation methods*

There are two permitted methods for translating the accounts of foreign subsidiaries for the purpose of consolidating their results with those of the rest of the group. These are the temporal method (whereby each item is translated at the rate applicable when the underlying transaction occurred) and the closing rate method (by which each item is translated at the rate at the balance sheet date).

SSAP 20 requires the temporal method to be used in respect of foreign operations which are essentially an extension of the activities of the UK parent (eg acting as a selling agent for products produced in the UK). The closing rate method is used where the overseas operation is autonomous. The operations of our new subsidiary fall into the latter category. The chosen method must be applied consistently.

(b) *Treatment of foreign currency exchange differences*

Foreign currency exchange differences are of two types, transaction differences and translation differences. Transaction differences occur when the sterling revenue or costs are recorded initially at the rate at the time the transaction occurs but this rate has changed by the time cash has been received or paid. Transaction differences are regarded as part of the normal business of the company or the finalisation of otherwise provisionally recorded transactions and are, therefore, charged or credited directly to profit and loss account. When the foreign operations are regarded as merely an extension of the UK operations (and therefore the temporal method is used) all foreign exchange gains and losses are regarded as transaction differences and are taken directly to profit and loss.

Translation gains and losses, on the other hand, are those that arise from the conversion of the accounts of an autonomous overseas operation into sterling for consolidation purposes. The investing company does not regard itself as having undertaken each of the foreign currency denominated transactions. It has made a net investment in the foreign operation in the expectation of receiving foreign currency returns by way of dividends and interest on loans. Where the foreign operation has taken on foreign currency debt this is considered to be matched against a corresponding amount of the foreign currency assets. Thus gains in the sterling value of the assets due to an appreciation in the foreign currency will be matched by losses on the increased sterling equivalent of the loans. Thus, the exposure of the UK holding company is limited to its net investment in the overseas subsidiary.

While transaction differences are considered to have been realised when the transactions to which they relate have been completed, translation differences are not considered to be realised until the net investment or part of it is disposed of. Consequently, translation gains and losses are retained in the reserves section of the balance sheet and only released to income when the associated net assets are sold or written off. This is an example of reserve accounting.

Where the acquisition of an overseas subsidiary is financed by foreign currency borrowings, there is a matching of foreign currency exposure although if there is more than one currency involved, this is not a complete match. Where the subsidiary is autonomous, and therefore the closing rate method is used, the translation difference on the borrowings may be offset in reserves against that on the investment in subsidiary. However, any excess gain or loss on the borrowings over that in the subsidiary must be taken to the profit and loss account. This concession can be applied both in T plc's accounts and in the T Group accounts.

(c) *Disclosure*

Disclosure must be made of the method used for translating foreign currencies and, if different methods are used for different subsidiaries, this fact must be disclosed. If, as allowed by SSAP 20, the profit and loss accounts of foreign subsidiaries are translated at the average rate for the period instead of the rate at the end of the period this should be disclosed.

Exchange gains on net foreign currency borrowings or holdings should be disclosed together with an analysis between the amount taken to profit and loss account and the amount taken to reserves.

The net movement on reserves due to exchange differences must be shown in the analysis of reserves contained in the notes to the accounts.

22 ROWEN

(a) ROWEN GROUP
CONSOLIDATED PROFIT AND LOSS ACCOUNT (DRAFT)
FOR THE YEAR ENDED 31 DECEMBER 19X8

	Rowen	Overseas	Group
	£m	£m	£m
Turnover	2,784	676.5	3,460.5
Cost of sales	1,822	449.2	2,271.2
Gross profit	962	227.3	1,189.3
Distribution costs	392	53.0	445.0
Administrative expenses	370	17.7	387.7
Depreciation	35	12.0	47.0
Dividends received			
Overseas	(12)		
Europe SA	(11)		(11.0)
Exchange difference		6.5	6.5
Profit before tax	188	138.1	314.1
Taxation	93	53.0	146.0
Profit after tax	95	85.1	168.1
Minority interest	60%		51.0
			117.1
Dividends			37.0
Retained profit			80.1

BPP PUBLISHING

ROWEN GROUP
CONSOLIDATED BALANCE SHEET (DRAFT)
AS AT 31 DECEMBER 19X8

	Rowen £m	Overseas £m	Group £m
Fixed assets			
Tangible assets	669	229.0	898.0
Investment in Europe	10		10.0
			908.0
Current assets			
Stock	675	27.5	702.5
Cash	46	75.3	121.3
Current liabilities			
Trade creditors	490	20.7	510.7
Long-term liabilities			
Loans	370	68.7	438.7
			782.4
Capital and reserves			=
Share capital			185.0
Profit and loss account			452.0
Shareholders' funds			637.0
Minority interest (60% × 242.4)			145.4
			782.4

GROUP RESERVES STATEMENT
AS AT 31 DECEMBER 19X8

	£m
Profit and loss account as at 1 Jan 19X8 (W8)	371.9
Retained profit for the year	80.1
Profit and loss account as at 31 Dec 19X8	452.0

Workings

1   *Translation of Overseas' P&L account at 31 December 19X8*

	US$m	Rate	£m
Turnover	1,150	1.7	676.5
Cost of sales			
Opening stock	57	2.0	28.5
Purchases	762	1.7	448.2
Closing stock	44	1.6	27.5
	775		449.2
Gross profit	375		227.3
Distribution costs	90	1.7	53.0
Administrative expenses	30	1.7	17.7
Depreciation	24	2.0	12.0
Exchange differences (W5)			6.5
Profit before tax	231		138.1
Taxation	90	1.7	53.0
Profit after tax	141		85.1
Dividends paid 31.7.X8	51	1.7	30.0
Retained profit	90		55.1
P&L a/c b/f (W7)	346		164.8
P&L a/c c/f (W2)	436		219.9

2   *Translation of Overseas' balance sheet as at 31 December 19X8*

	US$m	Rate	£m
Fixed assets			
Tangible assets	458	2.0	229.0
Current assets			
Stock	44	1.6	27.5
Cash	113	1.5	75.3
Current liabilities			
Creditors	31	1.5	20.7
Long-term liabilities			
Loan	103	1.5	68.7
	481		242.4
Capital and reserves			
Share capital	20	2.0	10.0
Profit and loss account			
Pre-acquisition	25	2.0	12.5
Post-acquisition	436	Balance	219.9
	481		242.4

3   *Group reserves as at 31 December 19X8*

	£m
Rowen plc	367.0
Overseas Inc (40% × 219.9)	88.0
	455.0
Less goodwill (W4)	3.0
	452.0

4   *Goodwill written off investment in Overseas*

	US$m	£m
Cost of investment		12
Share of net assets acquired		
Share capital	20	
P&L account	25	
	45	
Group share (40% @ $2.0)		9
Goodwill		3

5   *Exchange differences: P&L account*

	US$m	£m	£m
Opening net monetary liabilities of $148m (W6)			
At 31 December 19X8 translate @ $1.5		(98.7)	
At 31 December 19X7 translate @ $1.8		82.2	
	US$m		(16.5)
Profit and loss account at average rate			
Retained	90.0		
Depreciation	24.0		
Change in stock (57 − 44)	13.0		
	127.0		
At 31 Dec 19X8 @ $1.5		84.7	
At average rate of $1.7		(74.7)	
			10.0
Exchange loss			(6.5)

BPP PUBLISHING

6   *Opening net monetary assets/liabilities at 31 December 19X7*

	UIS$m
Share capital	20
Pre-acquisition profit	25
Post-acquisition profit (436 – 90)	346
	391
Deduct	
Fixed assets (458 + 24)	(482)
Stock	(57)
Net monetary liabilities	(148)

7   *Opening post-acquisition P&L account balance*

	US$m	Rate	£m
Fixed assets	482	2.0	241.0
Stock	57	2.0	28.5
Net monetary liabilities	(148)	1.8	(82.2)
Total net assets (481 – 90)	391		187.3
Deduct			
Share capital	20	2.0	(10.0)
Pre-acquisition profit	25	2.0	(12.5)
Post-acquisition profit (436 – 90)	346		164.8

8   *Group reserves as at 31 December 19X7*

	£'000
Rowen plc (367 – 58)	309.0
Overseas Inc (40% × 164.8 (W7))	65.9
	374.9
Less goodwill (W4)	3.0
	371.9

(b) (i)   If Europe SA is treated as an associated undertaking, then the profit and loss account for the year will be translated at the closing rate, as follows.

	Europe SA FFm	Rate	Consolidation figures £m
Profit before tax	2,122	8.0	265.3
Taxation	831	8.0	103.9
Profit after tax	1,291	8.0	161.4

Consolidated profit and loss account

	£'000	£'000
Profit before tax (as in (a))		314.1
Less dividends received from Europe		11.0
		303.1
Add share of associate's profit (25% × 265.3)		66.3
		369.4
Tax per consolidated accounts	146.0	
Share of associate's tax (25% × 103.9)	26.0	
		172.0
Profit after tax		197.4

	£'000
Retained profit in associate	
= 66.3 – 26.0 – 11.0	29.3

(ii)   Carrying value of investment in Europe SA as an associate:

	£'000
25% × FF4,431m @ FF8	138.5

23 SHIPCO

(a)

REALISATION ACCOUNT

	£		£
Yards account: NBV	80,000	Shipco (19X5) plc	155,000
Equipment: NBV	60,000		
Stocks	15,000		
	155,000		155,000

DEVELOPMENT EXPENDITURE

	£		£
Balance b/f	50,000	Sundry members-write-off	50,000

PATENT RIGHTS

	£		£
Balance b/f	15,000	Sundry members-write-off	15,000

YARDS

	£		£
Balance b/f (NBV)	160,000	Realisation a/c	80,000
		Bank	21,000
		Sundry members-write-off	59,000
	160,000		160,000

STOCKS

	£		£
Balance b/f	20,000	Realisation a/c	15,000
		Sundry members-loss	5,000
	20,000		20,000

DEBTORS

	£		£
Balance b/f	10,000	Sundry members loss	10,000

TRADE CREDITORS

	£		£
Bank	1,000	Balance b/f	5,000
Sundry members	4,000		
	5,000		5,000

PREFERENCE DIVIDENDS

	£		£
Sundry members	10,000	Balance b/f	10,000

BANK

	£		£
Yards account	21,000	Balance b/f	45,000
Shipco (19X5) plc	25,000	Trade creditors	1,000
	46,000		46,000

6% SECURED DEBENTURE

	£		£
Shipco (19X5) plc	65,000	Balance b/f	65,000

SUNDRY MEMBERS

	£		£
Profit & loss account	40,000	Ordinary shares	200,000
Development expenditure	50,000	Preference shares	30,000
Patent rights	15,000	Creditors	4,000
Yards: loss on disposal	59,000	Preference dividends	10,000
Stocks	5,000		
Debtors	10,000		
Shipco plc			
Ordinary shares	50,000		
10% preference shares	15,000		
	244,000		244,000

SHIPCO (19X5) PLC

	£		£
Realisation account	155,000	Bank	25,000
		6% debenture	65,000
		Sundry members	
		ord. shareholders	50,000
		pref. shareholders	15,000
	155,000		155,000

(b) SHIPCO (19X5) PLC: OPENING JOURNAL ENTRIES

		Debit	Credit
		£	£
(i)	Yards	80,000	
	Equipment	60,000	
	Stocks	15,000	
	Bank		25,000
	6% debenture		65,000
	Ordinary share capital		50,000
	Preference shareholders		15,000
	Being net assets acquired from Shipco plc		
(ii)	Bank	25,000	
	5% secured debenture		25,000
	Being discharge of bank overdraft taken over		
	from Shipco plc		
(iii)	Bank	50,000	
	Ordinary share capital		50,000
	Being payment of £1 per share outstanding		
	on 50,000 ordinary shares		
(iv)	6% debenture	65,000	
	Bank		65,000
	Being discharge of debenture taken over from Shipco plc		
	over from Shipco plc		

(c)   SHIPCO (19X5) PLC
      BALANCE SHEET AS AT 1 JANUARY 19X5

	£	£
Fixed assets		
Yards		80,000
Equipment		60,000
		140,000
Current assets		
Stocks	15,000	
Creditors: amounts falling due within on year		
Bank overdraft	15,000	
Net current assets		-
Total assets less current liabilities		140,000
Creditors: amounts falling due after more than one year		
5% debenture (secured)		(25,000)
		115,000
Called up share capital		
50,000 ordinary shares of £2 each		100,000
15,000 10% cumulative preference shares of £1 each		15,000
		115,000

24   CAPITAL MAINTENANCE AND PROFIT REPORTING

(a)   *Capital maintenance*

The capital of a business may be measured by attributing values to its net assets. There are many ways of calculating the relevant values but whichever basis a business chooses it will wish to ensure that its capital at the end of an accounting period is not less than it was at the beginning. This is the concept of capital maintenance. If capital at the end of the period is greater than capital at the beginning of the period (and assuming no new injections of capital have been made during the period) the business can be said to have made a profit. Indeed, profit may be defined as the amount which could be distributed to the owners of a business without reducing capital to below its original level. (This is very similar to the economist's definition of income as 'the maximum value which an individual can consume during a week and still expect to be as well off at the end of the week as he was at the beginning'.)

Historical/current cost accounts

Accounts prepared under the two accounting conventions commonly in use at present (historical cost and current cost) use a mixture of values to arrive at a company's capital:

(i)   historical cost (net of depreciation or amounts written off where appropriate);
(ii)   market values (for example, land and buildings, investments);
(iii) replacement costs;
(iv)   net realisable value.

The valuation problem is complicated by the existence of inflation. Because of inflation, the monetary units in which values are measured are not stable; the purchasing power of each unit (£1) declines over time.

Two capital maintenance concepts which attempt, in their different ways, to overcome the problems posed by inflation have been attempted in the UK. They are the concepts which underlie:

(i)   current purchasing power accounting (CPP); and
(ii)   current cost accounting (CCA).

CPP

CPP was introduced experimentally by PSSAP 7 *Accounting for changes in the purchasing power of money*. In CPP accounting the values attributed to net assets are measured in terms of a constant monetary unit, which may be called £ of current purchasing power or £CPP. Profit is measured after allowing for *general* price changes. Capital should be maintained in terms of the same monetary purchasing power, so that:

$$P_{CPP} = D_{CPP} + (E_{t(CPP)} - E_{(t-1)CPP})$$

where

P~CPP~ is the CPP accounting profit

P_{CPP} is the CPP accounting profit

D_{CPP} is distributions to shareholders, re-stated in CPP terms

$E_{t(CPP)}$ is the total value of assets attributable to the owners of the business at the end of the accounting period, re-stated in CPP terms

$E_{(t-1)CPP}$ is the total value of the owners' equity at the beginning of the year, re-stated in terms of current purchasing power at the end of the year

CCA

CCA reflects an approach to capital maintenance based on maintaining the 'operating capability' of a business. The conceptual basis of CCA is that assets in the balance sheet should be stated at their 'value to the business'. This is because value to the business is the amount of extra funds which would be required to maintain the operating capability of the business entity if it suddenly lost the use of an asset. This amount may increase over time in the case of like assets because of inflation specific to those assets, which may be quite different from the general level of inflation. CCA aims at preserving the operating capability of the company, but does not necessarily preserve it against the declining value of the purchasing power of money (ie, against general inflation).

(b)   In the long term, profits equate to cash flows. The management of a business might be content to carry on the day-to-day conduct of its activities, observing the inflows of cash and looking for no other indicator of success. Many small businesses, whose owners are not interested in accounting information and have no duty to account to anyone but themselves, are run on precisely these lines. In other cases, for example in large limited companies, the owners of a business may be remote from its day-to-day conduct. They will wish to ensure that the persons to whom they have delegated responsibility are exercising their stewardship function efficiently. This leads to the need for periodic accounts to be drawn up. Values need to be attributed to assets and liabilities before they have been realised or defrayed in cash. Some measurement must be made of the extent to which the business has been successful and is likely to maintain its success.

Profit is an important measure in accounting statements because:

(i)   it measures the efficiency with which the business has been managed;

(ii)   it is a starting point for the owners' decision on how much cash they can withdraw from the business;

(iii)   it helps creditors and investors to decide whether they can safely lend money to the business;

(iv)   past profit may act as a guide to predictions of future profits;

(v)   the government may use profit as a means of imposing direct taxation on the business;

(vi)   it may help management to make decisions about pricing, expansion, closures, etc.

25   COCOA

(a)   (i)   Historical cost accounts are stated at a particular amount in £s. However, the value of these £s change over time. Historical cost accounts do not reflect this change. For example an asset is recorded in £s at the date of purchase. A similar asset bought subsequently will be recorded at a different value in £s because of movements in the relative value of the £s. If the accounts were restated in order to eliminate these movements, similar assets would be stated at the same amount in these 'constant' £s. The method of restating the historical cost accounts would normally involve use of the Retail Price Index.

With regard to capital maintenance, again in historical cost accounts capital is shown in nominal money terms which takes no account of the 'real' value of money. If profits are distributed without taking account of any erosion in the capital value of the business due to the fall in the value of these £s, it will in effect result in a distribution of *capital* in real terms, to the detriment of the business.

The information needs of the directors of the company will determine the choice of capital maintenance concept. An operating capital maintenance concept might be more appropriate than a financial capital maintenance concept, for example where the business is required to operate at a constant level.

(ii) *System 1*

The use of constant purchasing power as the unit of measurement means that profit is only recognised after the purchasing power of the equity interest has been maintained in real terms as measured by the RPI. It is feasible to use this accounting system, but it is time-consuming to carry out and the resulting financial statements may present difficulties in comprehension for users.

System 2

Under this method assets are measured at current cost and the effects of changing prices are measured to ascertain whether a company's financial capital has been maintained.

(b)

	£
Profit after tax for year ended 30.6.X3	42,000
Add back dividends (200,000 × 15p)	30,000
	72,000
Add unrealised holding gains	
Plant £(62,000 – 55,000)	7,000
Stock £(44,000 – 39,000)	5,000
	84,000
Less inflation adjustment $(£100,000 + £75,000) \times \left(\dfrac{128}{116} - 1 \right)$	(18,103)
	65,897

26 CARVER

CARVER PLC
CONSOLIDATED CASH FLOW STATEMENT
FOR THE YEAR ENDED 30 SEPTEMBER 19X4

	Note	£'000	£'000
Cash flows from operating activities	1		372
Dividends from associates (W2)	2		250
Returns on investments and servicing of finance	2		7
Taxation (W9)			(250)
Capital expenditure and financial investment	2		(585)
Acquisitions and disposals	2		98
Equity dividends paid (200 + 400 – 300)			(300)
Cash outflow before financing			(408)
Financing	2		
Issue of shares		2,453	
Increase in debt		650	
			3,103
Increase in cash in the period			2,695
Reconciliation of net cash flow to movement in net funds	3		
Increase in cash in the period			2,695
Cash inflow from increase in debt and lease financing			(650)
Change in net debt resulting from cash flows			2,045
New finance leases			(850)
Other change			(40)
Movement in net debt in period			1,155
Net funds at 1 October 19X3			950
Net funds at 30 September 19X4			2,105

BPP PUBLISHING

NOTES TO THE CASH FLOW STATEMENT

1 *Reconciliation of operating profit to operating cash flows*

	£'000	£'000
Operating profit		1,485
Depreciation charges (W1)		325
Profit on sale of machinery		(100)
Increase in stocks (1,975 – 1,000 – 32)		(943)
Increase in debtors (1,850 – 1,275 – 28)		(547)
Increase in creditors (500 – 280 – 68)		152
Net cash inflow from operating activities		372

2 *Analysis of cash flows for headings netted in the cash flow statement*

	£'000	£'000
Returns on investments and servicing of finance		
Interest paid (W3)*	(100)	
Dividends from fixed asset investment	155	
Dividends paid to minority interest (W4)	(48)	
		7
Capital expenditure and financial investment		
Purchase of tangible fixed assets (W5)	(1,085)	
Sale of tangible fixed assets	500	
		(585)
Acquisitions and disposals		
Purchase of subsidiary undertaking	(14)	
Cash balances acquired with subsidiary	112	
		98
Financing		
Issue of ordinary share capital (W6)		2,453
Debt due beyond a year (W7)	920	
Capital element of finance lease rental payments (W8)	(270)	
		650
		3,103

* There is not sufficient information in the question to identify separately interest on finance leases.

3 *Analysis of changes in net debt*

	At 1 Oct 19X3 £'000	Cash flow £'000	Other changes £'000	At 30 Sept 19X4 £'000
Cash at bank	1,820	2,695	-	4,515
Debt due > 1yr	(500)	(920)	(40)	(1,460)
Finance leases	(370)	270	(850)	(950)
		(650)		
	950	2,045	(890)	2,105

Workings

1 *Depreciation charges*

	£'000	£'000
Freehold buildings (2,200 – 2,075)		125
Plant		
Closing balance	1,200	
Opening balance	1,100	
	100	
Depreciation on disposal	100	
		200
		325

2   *Dividends from associates*

	£'000	£'000
Opening balance		1,000
Share of profit	495	
Taxation	(145)	
		350
		1,350
Closing balance		1,100
		250

3   *Interest*

	£'000
Accrued interest b/f	30
P & L account	150
Discount	(40)
Less accrued interest c/f	(40)
	100

4   *Minority interests*

	£'000
Opening balance	-
Profit for year	100
On acquisition	63
	163
Closing balance	(115)
Cash outflow	48

5   *Purchase of tangible fixed assets: machinery*

	£'000	£'000
Cost at 30 September 19X4		3,000
Cost at 1 October 19X3		1,400
		1,600
Disposal		500
		2,100
On acquisition	165	
Leased	850	
		(1,015)
Cash outflow		1,085

6   *Issue of ordinary share capital*

	£'000	£'000
Closing balance		
Shares	3,940	
Premium	2,883	
		6,823
Non-cash consideration		
Shares	220	
Premium	55	
		(275)
Opening balance		
Shares	2,000	
Premium	2,095	
		(4,095)
Cash inflow		2,453

7   *Issue of loan stock*

	£'000
Closing balance	1,460
Opening balance	500
	960
Finance cost	40
Cash inflow	920

8 *Capital payments under leases*

	£'000	£'000
Opening balances		
Current		200
Long-term		170
		370
New lease commitment		850
Closing balances		
Current	240	
Long-term	710	
		(950)
Cash outflow		270

9 *Taxation*

	£'000	£'000
Opening balance		
Corporation tax	213	
Deferred tax	13	
		230
Profit and loss account transfer (391 + 104)		495
Closing balances		
Corporation tax	402	
Deferred tax	30	
		(492)
		233
On acquisition		17
Cash outflow		250

27 WRIGHT SHOES

Theoretical ex-rights price per share

	£
Value of 3 shares before rights issue (× £1.42)	4.26
Price of 1 rights issue share	1.10
Value of 4 shares after rights issue	5.36

The theoretical ex-rights price per share is $\dfrac{£5.36}{4} = £1.34$

To calculate the weighted average number of shares in the year, the shares in issue before the rights issue must be multiplied by a factor:

$$\frac{£1.42}{£1.34} = 1.0597$$

Weighted average number of shares

Period of year	Days	Number of shares	Adjustment factor	Hash total (millions)
1 Jan - 28 Feb	59	5,500,000	1.0597	343.873
1 Mar - 31 Jul	153	6,000,000	1.0597	972.805
1 Aug - 31 Oct	92	8,000,000	-	736.000
1 Nov - 31 Dec	61	8,200,000	-	500.200
	365			2,552.878

The weighted average number of shares is $\dfrac{2,552.878}{365} \times 1 \text{ million} = 6.994 \text{ million}$

Earnings

	£'000
Profit after taxation attributable to shareholders	1,550
Dividend of preference shareholders	42
Earnings available for equity	1,508

$$EPS = \frac{£1,508,000}{6,994,000} = 21.56p$$

Comparability with previous year: the EPS calculated for the previous year must be adjusted by the factor:

$$\frac{\text{Theoretical ex} - \text{rights price}}{\text{Market price per share before rights issue}}$$

in order to achieve a proper comparability. Comparable EPS =

$$21.2p \times \frac{£1.34}{£1.42} = 20.01p$$

28 CONWAY

(a) REPORT

To: Finance Director
From: Chief Accountant
Re: *Analysis of Uplift Ltd's results*   Date: XX/XX/XX

The ratio analysis prepared by my assistant is attached in an appendix to this report. I will cover the major areas which indicate the condition of Uplift Ltd.

1 *Profitability and sales growth*

Sales rose rapidly in 19X3 and 19X4, but the rate of growth has slowed substantially in 19X5, although it is still slightly higher than average. This may be a one-off for 19X5 and forecasts for the following years would be helpful. Alternatively, the company may have encountered difficult trading conditions due to competition, recession and so on.

Gross profit percentage is lower than industry average, but not by a great amount, and the percentage has fluctuated over the three years. The implication is that the costing structure is close to the industry average. The operating profit however, is significantly higher than the industry average (12% in 19X5 compared to 4%). this may indicate lower interest costs, higher additional income or lower administration or distribution costs than other industry competitors.

In addition, the profit after tax: total assets ratio is very high compared to the industry average, although once again there have been significant fluctuations over the three years. This might be explained by on-off receipts of other income, for example on the sale of property or investments; more information is needed here.

2 *Interest cover*

The company's interest cover greatly exceeds the industry average, so the company obviously has little difficulty servicing existing debts. This may mean that there is capacity to take on more debt should a change in the capital and financing structure become desirable.

3 *Gearing*

Although the company's long-term debt: total asset ratio, at 30% in 19X5, is significantly higher than the industry average of 10%, the interest cover is also a lot higher, as mentioned above. It may be that the company has been able to negotiate a lower than average interest rate, and it would be useful to see the extent to which this accounts for the high interest cover, rather than greater profits.

Uplift's reliance on current liabilities is lower than average and so the total liabilities: total assets ratio 'evens out' at around the industry average. So, while having roughly the normal proportion of liabilities, the company prefers longer term debt.

The debt/equity ratio can be calculated from the information given as it consists of:

$$\frac{\text{Long - term debt}}{\text{Total assets}} \div \frac{\text{Equity}}{\text{Total assets}}$$

	19X3	19X4	19X5	Industry average
Debt/equity ratio (%)	167	48	88	67

The company has no difficulty servicing the debt, in spite of the fact that the 19X5 debt/equity ratio is higher than the industry average.

4   *Liquidity*

The current ratio and quick ratio for Uplift Ltd are generally good, although lower than industry average. Lower stock and higher debtors and cash in 19X4 and 19X5 have kept the quick ratio higher and this indicates good working capital management. The company has ample supplies of cash, which is not necessarily a good sign from a takeover point of view.

5   *Asset utilisation*

The overall asset utilisation figure is low compared to the industry average. Although this could indicate low sales compared to available resources, it is necessary to look at individual asset and liability turnovers to discover where any problem might lie.

6   *Fixed asset turnover*

There is a huge discrepancy between the £2.90 sales per £1 of assets generated by Uplift, and the industry average of £17. Further information would be required to decide whether inefficient assts are being used or whether recent substantial asset purchases have been made to anticipate sales growth and expansion in production.

7   *Stock turnover*

A much higher stock turnover rate than the industry average could be due to higher sales, but the stock: total assets ratio shows that the real reasons is low levels of stock holding, as mentioned in relation to the quick ratio above. Stock holding in the rest of the industry in general is much higher. This is obviously a company policy as the stock: total asset ratio has remained constant for many years.

Low stock obviously means low stockholding costs, but there may be disadvantages in terms of stock-outs and hence customer dissatisfaction and lost sales. This seems quite unlikely, however, and stock control is probably very good.

8   *Debtors turnover*

The debtors turnover is *very* high compared to the industry average; however, the debtors: total assets ratio is very low. These differences are large enough to imply that Uplift Ltd is factoring its debtors, thus leaving very few days' sales in debtors. Factoring may be common throughout the industry.

9   *Cash*

The high cash: total assets ratio supports the argument that Uplift is factoring its debtors.

10   *Creditors turnover*

The company is taking a long time to pay its creditors, but the company is also not particularly exposed to short-term creditors, relying instead on longer term finance.

11   *Asset/working capital management*

It can be seen from the points made in (5) to (10) above that Uplift Ltd is managing its assets, both fixed and current, in a different way to the majority of the rest of the industry. Further investigation will be required to decide whether this demonstrates forward-thinking and innovative management, or whether the policies being used are inappropriate to Uplift's business. It may be possible to obtain average ratios which are more specific to Uplift's sector of the market, or which take account of the size of the company etc. This might produce more meaningful comparisons.

Summary

Substantial growth in 19X3 and 19X4 in turnover has not been maintained in 19X5 and forecasts are required to give some indication of the likely trend of sales and profits for Uplift.

Although gross profit has remained constant, variations in the profit before tax figure require investigation.

The company is probably not very vulnerable to takeover, as it appears to be cash-rich. However, the financial structure of the company might show capacity for improvement. Loan financing could be increased which could lead to an increase in share price and better equity return.

The main question is: what is likely to happen in the near future? Will the substantial growth of 19X3 and 19X4 be repeated or is the company stagnating? These questions will be crucial if we decide to approach Uplift with a view to takeover, particularly in terms of timing.

(b) A summary of limitations of this type of financial analysis are as follows.

    (i) *Information problems*

        (1) The base information is often out of date, so timeliness of information leads to problems of interpretation.

        (2) Historic cost information may not be the most appropriate information for the decision for which the analysis is being undertaken.

        (3) Information in published accounts is generally summarised information and detailed information may be needed.

        (4) Analysis of accounting information only identifies symptoms not causes and thus is of limited use.

    (ii) *Comparison problems: inter-temporal*

        (1) Effects of price changes make comparisons difficult unless adjustments are made.

        (2) Impacts of changes in technology on the price of assets, the likely return and the future markets.

        (3) Impacts of a changing environment on the results reflected in the accounting information.

        (4) Potential effects of changes in accounting policies on the reported results.

        (5) Problems associated with establishing a normal base year to compare other years with.

    (iii) *Comparison problems: inter-firm*

        (1) Selection of industry norms and the usefulness of norms based on averages.

        (2) Different firms having different financial and business risk profiles and the impact on analysis.

        (3) Different firms using different accounting policies.

        (4) Impacts of the size of the business and its comparators on risk, structure and returns.

        (5) Impacts of different environments on results, for example different countries or home-based versus multinational firms.

(c) The report in (a) above could be affected in the following ways.

    (i) *Profitability and sales growth*

        The substantial sales growth shown should be adjusted to take account of inflation, particularly in 19X3 and 19X4 where no industry average is given. The adjustments will reveal the rise in sales in *volume* terms, not just price terms, giving a truer picture of operational growth.

        The gross profit percentage could be affected by the composition of cost of sales, or by the choice of accounting policy, for example for depreciation on plant and machinery.

    (ii) *Gearing*

        Gearing could be affected by a variety of factors, including the decision whether to revalue fixed assets, particularly freehold property. A revaluation would improve the equity component of the debt/equity ratio.

        A decision as to whether to rely on short or long term credit will affect the gearing ratio and the quick ratio. The choice of policy may be forced on a company which is in danger of breaching loan covenants. Also, the use of different kinds of leases could help to manipulate such ratios.

    (iii)   *Liquidity*

Liquidity ratios may be manipulated around the year end (as they only reflect the position at that date) to produce a more favourable impression. For example, window dressing transactions may be undertaken. Such transactions would be unacceptable, but other acceptable procedures might be undertaken, such as paying creditors early. Also, window dressing transactions are hard to spot, particularly if two or more group companies are involved.

    (iv)   *Asset utilisation*

Again, revaluation of fixed assets will affect the ratios here. Also, the age of fixed assets, whether they have been fully depreciated, whether assets are leased (finance/operating?) or owned and so on. Such questions need to be answered, both for Uplift and the rest of the industry, before fixed asset utilisation can be analysed properly.

Working capital utilisation will be affected by any seasonal sales trends, particularly around the year end, as well as whether debtors are factored, whether the company runs a just-in-time stock system and so on.

Window dressing can also be a problem in this area.

Summary

The industry averages are a useful starting point in examining Uplift's results, but further investigations need to be carried out to determine the underlying reasons for the quite substantial differences highlighted.

29   TERMS FOR A MERGER

(a) *Current market prices*

Value of S plc shares (1,064,000 × £1.03)	£1,095,920
Value per T plc share	£2.40

Number of new T plc shares to be issued:

$$\frac{1,095,920}{2.4} = 456,633.33$$

This would mean issuing a one new share in T plc in exchange for every 2.33 shares in S plc. Three shares in T plc for seven shares in S plc might be a suitable rounded exchange ratio. With a three for seven share exchange, 456,000 new shares in T plc would be issued.

Combined earnings of the two companies	£404,000
Total shares in issue after the merger	
(800,000 + 456,000)	1,256,000
EPS	32.17p
	£
Earnings attributable to:	
old T plc shareholders (63.69%)	257,308
old S plc shareholders (36.31%)	146,692
	404,000

The market value of the merged firm would be difficult to predict. If, however, its market value were the sum of the market values of the two separate firms before the merger, the market value after the merger would be:

	£
Old T plc value (800,000 × £2.4)	1,920,000
Old S plc value	1,095,920
Combined	3,015,920

The effects of the merger would be:

(i)   to improve the EPS of old T plc shareholders at the expense of a worse EPS for the old S plc shareholders. This is because S plc has been 'bought' on a lower P/E ratio (6.6 compared with 8.0);

(ii)   on the assumption that market values remain constant, to share out the market value of the merged business between old T plc and old S plc shareholders in the ratio of the pre-merger market values of their respective companies.

Using a P/E ratio of 8

Value of S plc shares (£165,000 × 8)	£1,320,000
Value per T plc share	£2.40
Number of new T plc shares issued	550,000
Combined earnings of the two companies	£404,000
Number of shares in issue after the merger	1,350,000
EPS	29.9p

Earnings attributable to:	£
old T plc shareholders (59.26%)	239,410
old S plc shareholders (40.74%)	164,590
	404,000

Again, assuming that the market value of the company after the merger is the same as the combined values of the two pre-merger companies, £3,015,920, the market value of shares attributable to old T plc and old S plc shareholders would be as follows.

	£
Old T plc shareholders (59.26%)	1,787,234
Old S plc shareholders (40.74%)	1,228,686
	3,015,920

In this situation the effect of the merger would be to leave the earnings attributable to old plc shareholders and also to old S plc shareholders the same as before the merger, but old S plc shareholders would improve the market value of their shares at the expense of old T plc shareholders. This is because S plc would have been bought on a higher P/E ratio than its current P/E ratio.

(b) The factors influencing the choice of P/E ratio would include:

   (i)   how combined earnings after the merger would change, if at all;

   (ii) how the market value of T plc shares after the merger would change;

   (iii) the relative bargaining strength of the two companies, and the sort of deal that would be necessary to win shareholder approval in both companies.

30   SEGMENTAL REPORTING

(a) (See following page)

(b) (i)   *Non-trading items.* The profitability analysis provides information only at the operating profit level. It might be important to know the allocation (if it is feasible to provide it) of such non-operating items as share of income of associated companies, interest expense and taxation.

   (ii) Unallocated items. The proportion of unallocated expenses is very high in relation to the total and an analysis should be provided of this. The value of segmental information is very much reduced if unallocated items comprise too large a proportion of the total.

Exam answer bank

(a) SEGMENTAL REPORT FOR THE YEAR ENDED 31 DECEMBER 19X6

CLASSES OF BUSINESS

	Stationery 19X6 £'000	Stationery 19X5 £'000	Tissue 19X6 £'000	Tissue 19X5 £'000	Packaging 19X6 £'000	Packaging 19X5 £'000	Other 19X6 £'000	Other 19X5 £'000	Group 19X6 £'000	Group 19X5 £'000
Turnover										
Total sales	12,986	11,877	22,048	17,819	5,200	3,955	3,290	1,992	43,524	35,643
Inter-segment sales	1,227	1,398	3,658	3,211	-	-	-	-	4,885	4,609
Sales to third parties	11,759	10,479	18,390	14,608	5,200	3,995	3,290	1,992	38,639	31,034
Profit before taxation										
Segment profit	2,442	3,627	5,916	4,599	821	915	(201)	(321)	8,978	8,820
Common costs									5,004	4,833
Group operating profit									3,974	3,987
Net Assets										
Segment net assets	31,750	29,480	44,620	37,254	17,775	16,440			94,145	83,174
Unallocated assets									14,856	12,007
Total assets									109,001	95,181

GEOGRAPHICAL SEGMENTS

	United Kingdom 19X6 £'000	United Kingdom 19X5 £'000	United States 19X6 £'000	United States 19X5 £'000	Other areas 19X6 £'000	Other areas 19X5 £'000	Unallocated 19X6 £'000	Unallocated 19X5 £'000	Group 19X6 £'000	Group 19X5 £'000
Turnover										
Total sales	30,630	28,182	9,344	7,100	1,481	1,117	3,290	1,992	44,745	38,391
Inter-segment sales	2,430	1,270	2,117	1,180	-	-	-	-	4,547	2,450
Sales to third parties	28,200	26,912	7,227	5,920	1,481	1,117	3,290	1,992	40,198	35,941
Profit before taxation										
Segment profit	4,873	4,230	3,127	2,249	487	594	(440)	474	8,047	7,547
Common costs									4,073	3,560
Group operating profit									3,974	3,987
Net Assets										
Segment net assets	41,820	39,042	30,600	21,788	21,660	21,792			94,080	82,622
Unallocated assets									14,921	12,559
Total assets									109,001	95,181

(iii) *Definition of business segments.* The exact definition of market segments and the activities they cover are not self-evident to users of the accounts. Consequently, a short description of the activities concerned and clear definitions should be provided.

(iv) *Geographical segments.* It is not clear whether the geographical segments reflect the source of the activity or its ultimate location. For example, the level of inter-segment transfers in the USA might suggest that the profit may have been earned primarily in a business segment located outside the USA.

31 WORLD PROBLEMS

(a) (i) The accounting treatment required by the ASB is based on the recognition of assets, liabilities, gains and losses in the accounts. According to the *Statement of Principles:*

'At any stage in the recognition process, where a change in total assets is not offset by an equal change in total liabilities or a transaction with owners, a gain or a loss will arise. Gains and losses should be recognised in one of the two performance statements, ie the profit and loss account and the statement of total recognised gains and losses.'

It is necessary to consider all gains and losses recognised in a period when assessing financial performance and so FRS 3 requires a statement of recognised gains and losses in addition to the profit and loss account.

The statement of recognised gains and losses shows the profit or loss for the period along with all other movements on reserves which reflect recognised gains and losses attributable to shareholders. It does not deal with the *realisation* of gains in previous periods, nor with transfers between reserves. This means that the excess of the revalued amount over historical cost will never be recognised in the profit and loss account; profit or loss on disposal will be calculated as the difference between the net proceeds and the net carrying amount. This is a very important FRS 3 rule; previously, on disposal of a revalued asset, companies could transfer the surplus in the revaluation reserve which related to the asset to the profit and loss account.

The difference between historical cost depreciation and depreciation on a revaluation will appear in the note of historical cost profits and losses.

The basic principle here is that the same gains should not be *recognised* twice, for example, a holding gain *recognised* when a fixed asset is revalued should not be *recognised* again when the asset is sold. This approach reflects the effect of allowing figures not related to current values to distort the measurement of performance in the income statement (P&L a/c) because profit measured by return on assets is distorted.

(ii) *Year ended 31 December 19X5*

(1) *Profit and loss account*

Depreciation charge = £300,000

(2) *Statement of recognised gains and losses*

Gain = £1,500,000

(3) *Note of historical cost profits and losses*

Difference between the historical cost depreciation charge and the actual depreciation charge based on the revalued amount = £100,000.

(4) *Balance sheet*

	£
Fixed asset at revalued amount	4,500,000
Accumulated depreciation	(300,000)
	4,200,000
Revaluation reserve	
Revaluation during year	1,500,000
Transfer to realised reserves	100,000
	1,400,000

Year ended 31 December 19X6

(1) *Profit and loss account*

Depreciation charge = £300,000

Gain on disposal = £(5,500,000 − (4,500,000 − 600,000)) = £1,600,000

(2) *Note of historical cost profits and losses*

Realisation of property gains = £1,300,000 (W).

Difference between the historical cost depreciation charge and the actual depreciation charge based on the revalued amount = £100,000.

(3) *Balance sheet*

Revaluation reserve: transfer £1,400,000 to realised profits (£1,300,000 shown above plus £100,000 excess depreciation, also shown above).

Working: profit on disposal vs historical NBV

	£	£
Proceeds		5,500,000
NBV at historical cost		
Cost	3,000,000	
Accumulated depreciation	400,000	
		2,600,000
(£1,600,000 + £1,300,000)		2,900,000

(b) (i) The *advantages of harmonisation* will be based on the benefits to users and preparers of accounts, as follows.

Investors, both individual and corporate, would like to be able to compare the financial results of different companies internationally as well as nationally in making investment decisions. Differences in accounting practice and reporting can prove to be a barrier to such cross-border analysis. There is a growing amount of investment across borders and there are few financial analysts able to follow shares in international markets. For example, it is not easy for an analyst familiar with UK accounting principles to analyse the financial statements of a Dutch or German company. Harmonisation would therefore be of benefit to such analysts.

Multinational companies would benefit from harmonisation for many reasons including the following.

(1) Better access would be gained to foreign investor funds.

(2) Management control would be improved, because harmonisation would aid internal communication of financial information.

(3) Appraisal of foreign enterprises for take-overs and mergers would be more straightforward.

(4) It would be easier to comply with the reporting requirements of overseas stock exchanges.

(5) Consolidation of foreign subsidiaries and associated companies would be easier.

(6) A reduction in audit costs might be achieved.

(7) Transfer of accounting staff across national borders would be easier.

Governments of developing countries would save time and money if they could adopt international standards and, if these were used internally, governments of developing countries could attempt to control the activities of foreign multinational companies in their own country. These companies could not 'hide' behind foreign accounting practices which are difficult to understand.

For *tax authorities* it will be easier to calculate the tax liability of investors, including multinationals who receive income from overseas sources.

Regional economic groups usually promote trade within a specific geographical region. This would be aided by common accounting practices within the region.

Large international accounting firms would benefit as accounting and auditing would be much easier if similar accounting practices existed throughout the world.

The main *barriers to international harmonisation* are as follows.

(1) *Different purposes of financial reporting.* In some countries the purpose is solely for tax assessment, while in others it is for investor decision-making.

(2) *Different legal systems.* These prevent the development of certain accounting practices and restrict the options available.

(3) *Different user groups.* Countries have different ideas about who the relevant user groups are and their respective importance. In the USA investor and creditor groups are given prominence, while in Europe employees enjoy a higher profile.

(4) *Needs of developing countries.* Developing countries are obviously behind in the standard setting process and they need to develop the basic standards and principles already in place in most developed countries.

(5) *Nationalism* is demonstrated in an unwillingness to accept another country's standard.

(6) *Cultural differences* result in objectives for accounting systems differing from country to country.

(7) *Unique circumstances.* Some countries may be experiencing unusual circumstances which affect all aspects of everyday life and impinge on the ability of companies to produce proper reports, for example hyperinflation, civil war, currency restriction and so on.

(8) *The lack of strong accountancy bodies.* Many countries do not have strong independent accountancy or business bodies which would press for better standards and greater harmonisation.

(ii) The adjustments have been made to the income statement reconciliation between UK and US GAAP for the following reasons.

Amortisation of interest costs
Under UK GAAP companies have the choice of expensing or capitalising interest as there is no accounting standard governing this area. Under US GAAP the group has capitalised the interest (whereas in the UK it appears to have been written off) and the amortisation charge relating to this interest is £8m.

Deferred tax
The principal difference between UK GAAP and US GAAP in respect of deferred taxation is that under UK GAAP, deferred taxation is only accounted for to the extent that it is probable that taxation liabilities or benefits will crystallise; US GAAP requires that full provision is made for all deferred taxation liabilities and this has increased the deferred tax charge by £55m under US GAAP. (In addition, UK GAAP requires that deferred taxation is provided using the liability method, whereas under US GAAP, the deferred method is used and the £55m may incorporate adjustments for this fact.)

Merger accounting adjustments
It appears that a merger has taken place during the year which satisfies UK criteria for the use of merger accounting (per FRS 6). This is not allowed under US GAAP so adjustments have been made to adopt acquisition accounting, including the removal of £200m of pre-acquisition profits and the additional depreciation and amortisation of £280m.

(iii) The effect of the above items on the UK/US GAAP equity reconciliation is as follows.

Amortisation of interest costs
Any unamortised balance outstanding will increase equity under US GAAP (ie this balance will not be part of UK GAAP equity).

Deferred tax
The increase in the charge will have the cumulative effect of decreasing equity.

Merger accounting adjustment
The adjustments required to switch UK GAAP merger accounting to US GAAP acquisition accounting will *probably* cause an increase in equity because of the uplift to net assets given by a fair value exercise (a fall is possible, but unlikely).

(iv) If such a dividend was proposed, the effect on equity would be to increase it because under UK GAAP the dividend must be accounted for in the fiscal year to which it relates. Under US GAAP the reduction in equity caused by the dividend is delayed until 19X7.

Lecturers' question bank

1 BRICKSTOCK

Brickstock Ltd has decided to diversify its activities by purchasing plant to be hired out on a daily basis to the construction industry.

The company proposes to purchase two types of multi-purpose machines: type A at a cost of £30,000 each, and type B at a cost of £40,000 each. Both types of machine are estimated to have an effective life of 5 years or 1,200 working days, after which they will have a residual value, as scrap, of 5% of original cost.

After taking into account the warranties given by the manufacturers of the machines, the expected repair costs are as follows.

	Type A	Type B
	£	£
1st year	350	1,200
2nd year	750	1,600
3rd year	850	2,000
4th year	1,500	2,400
5th year	2,100	2,800

It is estimated that type A machines will achieve 230 working days per annum and type B, 267.

REQUIREMENTS:

(a) State the matters which should be taken into consideration in deciding the method of depreciation for the machine.

(b) Prepare schedules showing the application of two methods available.

(c) Draft a brief report to the directors of the company stating the method you recommend, giving your reasons.

2 LONG-TERM CONTRACTS

The following details refer to two contracts undertaken by AA Ltd.

	Contract X	Contract Y
	£	£
Expected final contract price	400,000	750,000
Expenditure during the year to 30 September 19X8		
Wages	37,670	41,560
Materials	59,430	54,260
Special plant	45,000	96,000
Progress payments received from customers		
30 June 19X8	40,000	40,000
30 September 19X8	60,000	80,000
Value of work certified, 30 September 19X8	200,000	250,000
Stocks of raw materials on site at 30 September 19X8	6,780	5,520
Expected costs to completion (excluding special plant)	140,000	295,000

The contracts started together on 1 January 19X8. Contract X is expected to be completed on 31 March 19X9 and Contract Y on 31 December 19X9. In addition to the special plant which will have no scrap value on completion of the contracts, specialised technical equipment was purchased for £60,000 at the start of both contracts. It will be used for these and other later contracts. The contract manager estimates the life of this technical equipment at thirty months. The equipment has been used on Contract X for three months and on Contract Y for six months, but it will not be needed again on these contracts. Head Office intends to charge £20,000 for the period up to 30 September 19X8. This should be allocated according to the proportion that the final price of each contract bears to its value certified at 30 September 19X8.

REQUIREMENTS:

(a) Prepare, in columnar form, the contract accounts showing clearly the net profits that can reasonably be taken against each contract for the year to 30 September 19X8. The basis of your calculations of profits should be shown by way of note.

(b) Indicate how the values of the contracts would be shown in the balance sheet of AA Ltd on 30 September 19X8.

(c) Explain why only part of the contract profits to 30 September 19X8 is taken to the profit and loss account quoting any relevant recognised accounting assumptions, concepts or practices in support of your explanation.

3 ARLENE AND AMANDA

Arlene plc acquired 135,000 shares in Amanda Ltd in 19X3. The reserves of Amanda Ltd at the date of acquisition comprised: revenue reserve £20,000; capital reserve £10,000. The draft balance sheets of both companies are given below as at 31 December 19X5.

	Arlene plc		Amanda Limited	
	£	£	£	£
Fixed assets				
Tangible assets		350,000		210,000
Investments				
Shares in Amanda Ltd at cost		190,000		
		540,000		
Current assets				
Stocks	83,000		42,000	
Debtors	102,000		48,000	
Current account with Amanda Ltd	5,000		-	
Bank and cash	40,000		12,000	
	230,000		102,000	
Current liabilities				
Trade creditors	90,000		37,000	
Current account with Arlene Ltd	-		1,000	
Proposed dividend	30,000		10,000	
	120,000		48,000	
Net current assets		110,000		54,000
Total assets less current liabilities		650,000		264,000
Capital and reserves				
Ordinary shares of £1 each		400,000		150,000
Revenue reserve		190,000		99,000
Capital reserve		60,000		15,000
		650,000		264,000

Arlene plc has not yet accounted for its share of the dividend proposed by Amanda Ltd.

On 29 December 19X5 Amanda Ltd sent a cheque for £4,000 to Arlene Ltd, which was not received until 3 January 19X6.

REQUIREMENT:

Prepare the consolidated balance sheet of Arlene plc as at 31 December 19X5. (Goodwill arising on consolidation is deemed to have an indefinite life and is to remain on the balance sheet.)

4 NELSON

From the information given below you are required to prepare the consolidated profit and loss account of Nelson Ltd for the year ended 31 December 19X3. Detailed workings including a consolidation schedule should be shown.

Nelson Ltd acquired 80% of the ordinary shares in Flagship Ltd when the company was formed five years ago. Nelson Ltd acquired 40% of the ordinary shares in Emma Ltd as from 1 January 19X3.

The abridged profit and loss accounts of Nelson Ltd, Flagship Ltd and Emma Ltd for the year ended 31 December 19X3 were as follows.

	Nelson Ltd £	Flagship Ltd £	Emma Ltd £
Turnover	3,000,000	1,000,000	800,000
Balance brought forward at 1 January 19X3	45,000	30,000	25,000
Profit on trading	240,000	120,000	70,000
	285,000	150,000	95,000
Directors' emoluments	25,000	8,000	4,000
Auditors' fees	2,000	1,000	800
Depreciation	40,000	22,000	15,000
Share issue costs, balance written off	3,000	-	-
Transfer to general reserve	30,000	-	-
Debenture interest	20,000	5,000	-
Tax charge on trading profits	70,000	40,000	20,000
Proposed dividends	40,000	25,000	10,000
Balance carried forward at 31 December 19X3	55,000	49,000	45,200
	285,000	150,000	95,000

The directors of Nelson Ltd are not directors of Flagship Ltd or Emma Ltd.

5 AX

The following balances were extracted from the books of AX plc, BY plc and CZ plc at 30 September 19X4.

	AX £'000	BY £'000	CZ £'000
Credit balances			
Ordinary share capital (£1 shares)	2,400	1,000	1,200
Reserves	1,352	520	640
	3,752	1,520	1,840
10% debentures	-	260	-
Proposed dividend	100	-	200
Current liabilities	1,046	640	936
Accumulated depreciation at 1 October 19X3	745	750	924
Depreciation charge for year to 30 September 19X4	290	150	100
	5,933	3,320	4,000
Debit balances			
Fixed assets at cost	2,443	1,500	2,600
Investment at cost			
BY (750,000 shares)	1,300	-	-
CZ (480,000 shares)	750	-	-
Current assets	1,440	1,820	1,400
	5,933	3,320	4,000

The following additional information is provided.

(a) AX purchased its investment in BY on 1 October 19X3 when the latter company's reserves stood at £300,000. At acquisition date the fixed assets of BY were considered to possess a fair value of £910,000. It was further estimated that, at that date, the fixed assets possessed a five year life and a nil residual value at the end of that time.

(b) AX purchased its investment in CZ some years ago, when the latter company's reserves stood at £120,000. Following this acquisition directors were appointed to the board of CZ to take an active part in that company's financial and operating decisions. There were no differences between the fair values and book values of CZ's assets at the acquisition date.

(c) Credit has not been taken in the books of AX for its share of the dividend receivable from CZ.

(d) Interest has been provided on the debentures to 30 September 19X4.

REQUIREMENT:

Prepare a consolidated balance sheet of the group at 30 September 19X4. Goodwill arising on consolidation is assumed to have an indefinite life and is to remain in the balance sheet.

6 CRERAND *63 mins*

During the year ended 31 December 19X7 Crerand plc, a UK registered company operating in several overseas locations, carried out the following transactions denominated in foreign currencies.

(a) Transactions with a French supplier of raw materials were as follows.

		FFr
1 January 19X7	Balancing outstanding	50,000
1 May 19X7	Purchases	280,000
1 August 19X7	Payment	(300,000)
1 November 19X7	Purchases	320,000
31 December 19X7	Balance outstanding	350,000

(b) In 19X6 Crerand plc purchased an 8% equity investment in a Belgian customer for 3,600,000 Belgian francs. The rate of exchange ruling at the date of purchase was £1 = BFr64. As a hedge against future exchange rate fluctuations, Crerand plc financed this investment with the proceeds of a German DM-denominated loan of DM 180,000 raised on the same date, when the rate of exchange was £1 = DM3.15. In 19X7 a dividend of BFr38,000 was payable to Crerand plc. This amount had not been remitted at 31 December 19X7. Sales to this customer are billed in sterling amounts.

(c) The company is the owner of a hotel situated in an Italian resort. This hotel is treated as an independent branch operation. The local management is responsible for all income and expenditure in local currency (Lira) with surplus cash being remitted to the UK from time to time.

The following financial statements, received from the hotel management, summarise the operations during 19X7.

BALANCE SHEETS

	31 December 19X7	19X6
	Lira (000)	Lira (000)
Property and fittings	520,000	520,000
Net current assets	106,000	84,000
	626,000	604,000
Loan from Italian bank	400,000	400,000
Head office capital account	100,000	100,000
Surplus retained	126,000	104,000
	626,000	604,000

PROFIT AND LOSS ACCOUNT
FOR THE YEAR ENDED 31 DECEMBER 19X7

	Lira (000)
Income from hire of rooms and sundry services	746,000
Less operating expenses	483,000
	263,000
Less local taxes	91,000
	172,000
Less remittances to Crerand plc	150,000
Surplus retained	22,000

The company received £69,450 from the branch during the year. No cash was in transit at the year ends.

Crerand plc accounts for its foreign currency transactions in accordance with the provisions of SSAP 20, with profit and loss accounts being translated at the average rate for the year. The company considers that its accounting for foreign currency transactions reflects their economic substance as far as possible within the provisions of SSAP 20.

Exchange rates prevailing during 19X7 were as follows.

Value of pound sterling (£) against:	French franc (FFr)	Belgian franc (BFr)	German mark (DM)	Italian lira (Lira)
At 1 January 19X7	62.50	9.60	3.12	2,050
1 May 19X7	9.45	-	-	-
1 August 19X7	9.50	-	-	-
1 November 19X7	9.50	-	-	-
31 December 19X7	9.65	60.10	3.05	2,130
Average for period	-	-	-	2,080

REQUIREMENTS:

(a)   Prepare the journal entries necessary to reflect the foreign exchange aspects of the above transactions in the books of Crerand plc for the year ended 31 December 19X7.   **20 Marks**

(b)   State the amounts which would appear in the balance sheet of Crerand plc at 31 December 19X7 in respect of the above items, including comparatives where possible.   **10 Marks**

(c)   Explain how the specific exchange differences arising during the year would be dealt with in Crerand plc's financial statements.   **5 Marks**

Total Marks = 35

---

7   **A AND B**   *54 mins*

Two privately owned retail companies, A Ltd which commenced business on 1 July 19X0 and B Ltd which commenced business on 1 July 19W8 agreed to form a new holding company AB Ltd to acquire the whole of the share capital of both companies at 1 July 19X2.

It was agreed that the accounts of A Ltd for the two years ended 30 June 19X2, should be adjusted, where necessary, to conform to the accounting policies followed by B Ltd.

In satisfaction of the purchase consideration AB Ltd would then issue loan stock and shares to the shareholders in A Ltd and B Ltd on the following basis:

(a)   £1 of the 12% unsecured loan stock 19Y6 for every £1 of net assets owned by each company as shown by the adjusted accounts at 30 June 19X2;

(b)   Ordinary shares of £0.25 each based on a two year purchase of the adjusted pre-tax profits. These profits are to be the average of the two years ended 30 June 19X1 and 19X2 with 19X2 being weighted on a 3:2 basis.

The following information is given.

(1)   BALANCE SHEETS AS AT 30 JUNE

	A Limited		B Limited	
	19X1 £	19X2 £	19X1 £	19X2 £
Tangible fixed assets				
Furniture and fixtures at cost	18,700	18,700	30,000	30,000
Less depreciation	1,870	3,740	8,000	12,500
	16,830	14,960	22,000	17,500
Quoted investments				
At market value	-	-	-	31,500
At cost (market value £18,000)	11,440	11,440	-	-
Current assets				
Stocks	51,500	77,600	91,200	94,000
Debtors	62,000	88,800	94,000	112,000
Cash	900	1,000	800	600
	142,670	193,800	208,000	255,600
Current liabilities				
Creditors	39,470	54,300	61,000	64,000
Bank overdraft	-	-	28,000	23,600
Taxation	21,000	27,700	23,000	30,000
	82,200	111,800	96,000	138,000

	A Limited		B Limited	
	19X1	*19X2*	*19X1*	*19X2*
	£	£	£	£
Share capital				
Ordinary shares of £1 fully paid	60,000	60,000	50,000	50,000
Reserves				
Unrealised appreciation on investment				7,000
Retained profits	22,200	51,800	46,000	81,000
	82,200	111,800	96,000	138,000

(2) SUMMARISED PROFIT AND LOSS ACCOUNTS
FOR THE TWO YEARS ENDED 30 JUNE

	A Limited		B Limited	
	19X1	*19X2*	*19X1*	*19X2*
	£	£	£	£
Trading profit	42,000	56,000	47,000	62,000
Investment income	1,200	1,300	2,400	3,000
	43,200	57,300	49,400	65,000
Taxation	21,000	27,700	23,000	30,000
	22,200	29,600	26,400	35,000

(3) A Ltd calculated the cost price of stock on the 'first in first out' basis whereas B Ltd use the 'first in last out' basis. Adjusting A Ltd's stock value to conform to the basis used by B Ltd would reduce the value at 30 June 19X1 by £1,200 and at 30 June 19X2 by £4,700.

(4) Depreciation of furniture and fittings in both companies is provided on the straight-line basis, A Ltd at 10% per annum and B Ltd at 15% per annum. There were no additions or sales in the two years ended 30 June 19X2.

(5) Debtors at the year-end were made up as follows.

	A Limited		B Limited	
	19X1	*19X2*	*19X1*	*19X2*
	£	£	£	£
Trade	52,920	82,320	93,400	110,600
Pre-paid expenses	1,080	2,480	600	1,400
Deferred advertising expenditure	8,000	4,000	-	-
	62,000	88,800	94,000	112,000

Both companies launched similar advertising campaigns in the year ended 30 June 19X1, but B Ltd wrote off its expenditure in that year.

(6) Trade debtors in A Ltd are shown after a provision of 2% to cover doubtful debts.

(7) It was agreed that directors' remuneration of £5,000 paid to non-executive directors in A Ltd in each year was really a share of the profits in lieu of a dividend.

Using the information given above, you are required:

(a) to calculate the value of the consideration to be received by the shareholders of A Ltd and of B Ltd, showing the amount of loan stock and the number and value of ordinary shares;

(b) to prepare the balance sheet of AB Ltd after the transactions have been completed (a consolidated balance sheet is not required).

No adjustments are to be made to the corporation tax liabilities. Calculations are to be made to the nearest £1.

30 Marks

8 **ROBERT** *63 mins*

Robert Ltd was incorporated with an authorised share capital of £250,000 divided into 600,000 ordinary shares of 25p each and 100,000 £1 10% cumulative preference shares to take over the existing businesses including cash of Alpha Ltd and Beta Ltd at 31 December 19X2.

The draft balance sheets of Alpha Ltd and Beta Ltd at 31 December 19X2 showed the following.

	Alpha	Beta		Alpha	Beta
	£	£		£	£
Capital: ordinary			Freehold property		
shares of £1 each	30,000	20,000	at cost	28,000	12,000
Reserves	18,000	6,500	Plant at cost	32,000	25,000
Trade creditors	13,000	26,000	Less depreciation	(10,000)	(8,000)
Bank	14,000	-	Development		
			expenditure	-	10,000
			Stock	15,000	7,500
			Debtors	10,000	2,000
			Bank	-	4,000
	75,000	52,500		75,000	52,500

You are given the following information.

(a) The purchase consideration for the business acquired is to be the amount which Robert Ltd would have to invest at 15% per annum to yield the weighted average profit of the past three years. The weights are to be 1, 2, 3 respectively.

Profits, which have been adjusted to take account of the adjustments required in note (d) following, were as follows.

	Alpha Ltd	Beta Ltd
	£	£
19X0	8,000	17,000
19X1	14,000	13,000
19X2	16,500	6,500

(b) The fixed assets have a fair value at 31 December 19X2 as follows.

	Alpha Ltd	Beta Ltd
	£	£
Freehold property	35,000	18,000
Plant	17,500	22,000

(c) The development expenditure of £10,000 has been reviewed. The project it relates to is technically viable but unless the new company is formed to acquire Beta Ltd and provide additional funds, there is doubt as to whether Beta Ltd is a going concern. However, subject to the amalgamation, it is felt that the carrying value should remain at £10,000.

(d) Provision is to be made as follows.

		Alpha Ltd	Beta Ltd
(i)	Obsolete stock	5% of balance sheet value	-
(ii)	Doubtful debts	3% of debtors	2½% of debtors
(iii)	Warranty claims	£6,000	-

(e) The purchase consideration is to be satisfied as follows.

(i) Preference shares are to be issued to the value of the freehold property.

(ii) 75% of the remaining purchase consideration is to be satisfied by the issue of ordinary shares in Robert Ltd at a premium of 5p per share.

(iii) The remainder of the purchase consideration is to be satisfied by cash.

(f) Robert Ltd is to issue sufficient ordinary shares at a premium of 5p per share to establish a liquidity ratio of 1:1.

(g) The shares received by Alpha and Beta are to be divided to the nearest whole number. If not exactly divisible the balance is to be sold for cash and the cash proceeds distributed.

REQUIREMENT:

(a) Prepare journal entries to close the books of Beta Ltd. **10 Marks**

(b) Calculate for a shareholder with 100 £1 shares in Alpha Ltd what consideration he would receive from Robert Ltd showing clearly the breakdown between shares and cash. **7 Marks**

(c) Prepare the balance sheet of Robert Ltd immediately after the amalgamation. **18 Marks**

Note. Ignore taxation. **Total Marks = 35**

701

9   METEOR   *45 mins*

GHI plc is a retailer of women's clothes. It was founded in London and still operates one shop there and more shops being opened in other cities. GHI plc has operated for five years and has gained a reputation for fast growth. Summaries of GHI plc's profit and loss accounts and balance sheets for the previous three years are given below.

SUMMARISED PROFIT AND LOSS ACCOUNTS
FOR YEAR ENDED 31 DECEMBER

	19X7	19X8	19X9
	£m	£m	£m
Turnover	3.70	7.10	18.72
Cost of sales	2.50	5.03	14.85
Gross profit	1.20	2.07	3.87
Distribution costs	0.42	0.92	1.61
Administration expenses	0.25	0.31	0.38
Profit on ordinary activities before taxation	0.53	0.84	1.88
Taxation	0.23	0.31	0.62
Profit on ordinary activities after taxation	0.30	0.53	1.26
Dividends	-	-	0.50
	0.30	0.53	0.76

SUMMARISED BALANCE SHEETS AT 31 DECEMBER

	19X7	19X8	19X9
	£m	£m	£m
Fixed assets			
Property (note)	1.21	3.62	9.59
Fixtures and fittings	0.74	1.32	2.04
Vehicles	0.18	0.24	0.32
Current assets			
Stock	0.57	1.82	4.16
Debtors	0.08	0.84	3.28
Bank	0.26	-	-
	3.04	7.84	19.39
Creditors: amounts falling due within one year			
Bank overdraft		1.65	3.04
Trade creditors	1.48	2.02	3.18
Taxation	0.20	0.28	0.52
Creditors: amounts falling due after more than one year			
Debenture loans	-	2.00	10.00
Shareholders' interest			
Ordinary share capital	0.50	0.50	0.50
Retained profits	0.86	1.39	2.15
	3.04	7.84	19.39

Note. GHI plc owns the freehold of all its shops. It does not depreciate its property.

You are an accountant with JKL plc, a competitor of GHI plc.

Required

(a)   Prepare a report to the board of JKL plc on the performance of GHI plc concluding with a clear identification of areas requiring further investigation.   **20 Marks**

(b)   Provide an indication of any information on these areas which would be available in the full annual report of GHI plc.   **5 Marks**

                                                                              Total Marks = 25

10   IAS 1   *45 mins*

The International Accounting Standard No 1 (IAS 1) *Presentation of financial statements* states that presentation of three considerations should govern the selection of and application by management of the appropriate accounting policies and the preparation of financial statements:

(a) Prudence

Uncertainties inevitably surround many transactions. This should be recognised by exercising prudence in preparing financial statements. Prudence does not, however, justify the creation of secret or hidden reserves.

(b) *Substance over form*

Transactions and other events should be accounted for and presented in accordance with their substance and financial reality and not merely with their legal forms.

(c) *Materiality*

Financial statements should disclose all items which are material enough to affect evaluations or decisions.

Required:

(a) Explain how these provisions differ from SSAP 2 *Disclosure of accounting policies* which was adopted in the United Kingdom in 1972. **6 Marks**

(b) Discuss the extent to which you think that SSAP 2 requires revision as a result of the different provisions of IAS 1 or as a result of accounting practices permitted under later United Kingdom SSAPs and FRSs. **12 Marks**

(c) Discuss the benefits of making international standards directly applicable in all countries in which financial statements are published. **7 Marks**

Total Marks = 25

11   PORTSLADE

Jones plc has acquired, as part of a recent business combination, 1,000 shares in Portslade Joinery Ltd and the financial director has requested a brief report advising whether to retain or sell the shares.

A trainee accountant was instructed to analyse the company's accounts and to draft a report. The accounts of Portslade Joinery Ltd have been obtained for the years 19X0 to 19X3 and are summarised below.

SUMMARISED ACCOUNTS OF PORTSLADE JOINERY LIMITED
FOR THE YEARS 19X0 TO 19X3

PROFIT AND LOSS ACCOUNTS

	19X0	*19X1*	*19X2*	*19X3*
	£'000	£'000	£'000	£'000
Sales	506,000	566,720	623,390	673,260
Profit before tax*	58,800	68,400	68,470	78,370
Tax	28,860	33,090	32,450	29,740
Profit after tax	29,940	35,310	36,020	48,630
*After charging depreciation	41,330	34,800	29,620	25,360
*After crediting gross dividends (grossed at 30%)	5,200	10,900	14,500	20,800

The trainee accountant prepared the following analysis and comments.

		19X0	*19X1*	*19X1*	*19X3*
1	*Sales* These are showing a steady growth	506,000	566,720	623,390	673,260
2	*Capital employed* This is showing a slight growth	372,910	374,220	376,240	382,870
3	*Profit after tax* This is showing uneven but substantial growth	29,940	35,310	36,020	48,630
	% growth		18%	2%	35%
4	*Return on capital employed* Profit after tax to capital employed is showing a steady increase	8%	9.4%	9.6%	12.7%
5	*Dividends per share* These are growing in line with profit after tax	14p	17p	17p	21p

Lecturers' question bank

'The analysis shows a company which is well managed and achieving steady growth in sales, capital employed, profit percentage, the rate of return and dividends paid to shareholders. The company would be advised to retain shares and should possibly consider increasing the number of shares owned in Portslade Joinery Ltd.'

REQUIREMENT:

Comment on the analysis and conclusions of the trainee accountant.

BALANCE SHEET

	19X0		19X1		19X2		19X3	
	£'000	£'000	£'000	£'000	£'000	£'000	£'000	£'000
Fixed assets								
Goodwill		18,000		18,000		18,000		18,000
Leasehold premises	60,000		60,000		60,000		60,000	
Depreciation	30,000		36,000		42,000		48,000	
		30,000		24,000		18,000		12,000
Plant and machinery	250,000		250,000		250,000		250,000	
Depreciation	90,000		118,800		142,420		161,780	
		160,000		131,200		107,580		88,220
Investments		52,000		100,000		140,000		176,740
Total fixed assets		260,000		273,200		283,580		294,960
Current assets								
Stock	109,910		127,780		149,000		166,440	
Debtors	83,600		102,540		121,160		142,970	
Cash	42,680		26,040		6,500		6,000	
	236,190		256,360		276,660		315,410	
Current liabilities								
Creditors	65,780		87,070		118,000		155,800	
Tax	29,900		34,270		32,000		29,700	
Dividend	27,600		34,000		34,000		42,000	
	123,280		155,340		184,000		227,500	
Net current assets		112,910		101,020		92,660		87,910
		372,910		374,220		376,240		382,870

	19X0		19X1		19X2		19X3	
	£'000	£'000	£'000	£'000	£'000	£'000	£'000	£'000
Capital and reserves								
Share capital £1 shares)		200,000		200,000		200,000		200,000
Reserves		172,910		174,220		176,240		182,870
		372,910		374,220		376,240		382,870
No. employees		17,500		18,750		20,000		21,000
Employees' remuneration		79,000		89,000		98,000		106,000

Mathematical tables

PRESENT VALUE TABLE

Present value of $1 = (1+r)^{-n}$ where r = discount rate, n = number of periods until payment.

This table shows the present value of £1 per annum, receivable or payable at the end of *n* years.

Periods					Discount rates (r)					
(n)	1%	2%	3%	4%	5%	6%	7%	8%	9%	10%
1	0.990	0.980	0.971	0.962	0.952	0.943	0.935	0.926	0.917	0.909
2	0.980	0.961	0.943	0.925	0.907	0.890	0.873	0.857	0.842	0.826
3	0.971	0.942	0.915	0.889	0.864	0.840	0.816	0.794	0.772	0.751
4	0.961	0.924	0.888	0.855	0.823	0.792	0.763	0.735	0.708	0.683
5	0.951	0.906	0.863	0.822	0.784	0.747	0.713	0.681	0.650	0.621
6	0.942	0.888	0.837	0.790	0.746	0.705	0.666	0.630	0.596	0.564
7	0.933	0.871	0.813	0.760	0.711	0.665	0.623	0.583	0.547	0.513
8	0.923	0.853	0.789	0.731	0.677	0.627	0.582	0.540	0.502	0.467
9	0.914	0.837	0.766	0.703	0.645	0.592	0.544	0.500	0.460	0.424
10	0.905	0.820	0.744	0.676	0.614	0.558	0.508	0.463	0.422	0.386
11	0.896	0.804	0.722	0.650	0.585	0.527	0.475	0.429	0.388	0.350
12	0.887	0.788	0.701	0.625	0.557	0.497	0.444	0.397	0.356	0.319
13	0.879	0.773	0.681	0.601	0.530	0.469	0.415	0.368	0.326	0.290
14	0.870	0.758	0.661	0.577	0.505	0.442	0.388	0.340	0.299	0.263
15	0.861	0.743	0.642	0.555	0.481	0.417	0.362	0.315	0.275	0.239
16	0.853	0.728	0.623	0.534	0.458	0.394	0.339	0.292	0.252	0.218
17	0.844	0.714	0.605	0.513	0.436	0.371	0.317	0.270	0.231	0.198
18	0.836	0.700	0.587	0.494	0.416	0.350	0.296	0.250	0.212	0.180
19	0.828	0.686	0.570	0.475	0.396	0.331	0.277	0.232	0.194	0.164
20	0.820	0.673	0.554	0.456	0.377	0.312	0.258	0.215	0.178	0.149

Periods					Discount rates (r)					
(n)	11%	12%	13%	14%	15%	16%	17%	18%	19%	20%
1	0.901	0.893	0.885	0.877	0.870	0.862	0.855	0.847	0.840	0.833
2	0.812	0.797	0.783	0.769	0.756	0.743	0.731	0.718	0.706	0.694
3	0.731	0.712	0.693	0.675	0.658	0.641	0.624	0.609	0.593	0.579
4	0.659	0.636	0.613	0.592	0.572	0.552	0.534	0.516	0.499	0.482
5	0.593	0.567	0.543	0.519	0.497	0.476	0.456	0.437	0.419	0.402
6	0.535	0.507	0.480	0.456	0.432	0.410	0.390	0.370	0.352	0.335
7	0.482	0.452	0.425	0.400	0.376	0.354	0.333	0.314	0.296	0.279
8	0.434	0.404	0.376	0.351	0.327	0.305	0.285	0.266	0.249	0.233
9	0.391	0.361	0.333	0.308	0.284	0.263	0.243	0.225	0.209	0.194
10	0.352	0.322	0.295	0.270	0.247	0.227	0.208	0.191	0.176	0.162
11	0.317	0.287	0.261	0.237	0.215	0.195	0.178	0.162	0.148	0.135
12	0.286	0.257	0.231	0.208	0.187	0.168	0.152	0.137	0.124	0.112
13	0.258	0.229	0.204	0.182	0.163	0.145	0.130	0.116	0.104	0.093
14	0.232	0.205	0.181	0.160	0.141	0.125	0.111	0.099	0.088	0.078
15	0.209	0.183	0.160	0.140	0.123	0.108	0.095	0.084	0.074	0.065
16	0.188	0.163	0.141	0.123	0.107	0.093	0.081	0.071	0.062	0.054
17	0.170	0.146	0.125	0.108	0.093	0.080	0.069	0.060	0.052	0.045
18	0.153	0.130	0.111	0.095	0.081	0.069	0.059	0.051	0.044	0.038
19	0.138	0.116	0.098	0.083	0.070	0.060	0.051	0.043	0.037	0.031
20	0.124	0.104	0.087	0.073	0.061	0.051	0.043	0.037	0.031	0.026

CUMULATIVE PRESENT VALUE TABLE

This table shows the present value of £1 per annum, receivable or payable at the end of each year for *n* years.

Periods — **Discount rates (r)**

(n)	1%	2%	3%	4%	5%	6%	7%	8%	9%	10%
1	0.990	0.980	0.971	0.962	0.952	0.943	0.935	0.926	0.917	0.909
2	1.970	1.942	1.913	1.886	1.859	1.833	1.808	1.783	1.759	1.736
3	2.941	2.884	2.829	2.775	2.723	2.673	2.624	2.577	2.531	2.487
4	3.902	3.808	3.717	3.630	3.546	3.465	3.387	3.312	3.240	3.170
5	4.853	4.713	4.580	4.452	4.329	4.212	4.100	3.993	3.890	3.791
6	5.795	5.601	5.417	5.242	5.076	4.917	4.767	4.623	4.486	4.355
7	6.728	6.472	6.230	6.002	5.786	5.582	5.389	5.206	5.033	4.868
8	7.652	7.325	7.020	6.733	6.463	6.210	5.971	5.747	5.535	5.335
9	8.566	8.162	7.786	7.435	7.108	6.802	6.515	6.247	5.995	5.759
10	9.471	8.983	8.530	8.111	7.722	7.360	7.024	6.710	6.418	6.145
11	10.37	9.787	9.253	8.760	8.306	7.887	7.499	7.139	6.805	6.495
12	11.26	10.58	9.954	9.385	8.863	8.384	7.943	7.536	7.161	6.814
13	12.13	11.35	10.63	9.986	9.394	8.853	8.358	7.904	7.487	7.103
14	13.00	12.11	11.30	10.56	9.899	9.295	8.745	8.244	7.786	7.367
15	13.87	12.85	11.94	11.12	10.38	9.712	9.108	8.559	8.061	7.606
16	14.718	13.578	12.561	11.652	10.838	10.106	9.447	8.851	8.313	7.824
17	15.562	14.292	13.166	12.166	11.274	10.477	9.763	9.122	8.544	8.022
18	16.398	14.992	13.754	12.659	11.690	10.828	10.059	9.372	8.756	8.201
19	17.226	15.678	14.324	13.134	12.085	11.158	10.336	9.604	8.950	8.365
20	18.046	16.351	14.877	13.590	12.462	11.470	10.594	9.818	9.129	8.514

Periods — **Discount rates (r)**

(n)	11%	12%	13%	14%	15%	16%	17%	18%	19%	20%
1	0.901	0.893	0.885	0.877	0.870	0.862	0.855	0.847	0.840	0.833
2	1.713	1.690	1.668	1.647	1.626	1.605	1.585	1.566	1.547	1.528
3	2.444	2.402	2.361	2.322	2.283	2.246	2.210	2.174	2.140	2.106
4	3.102	3.037	2.974	2.914	2.855	2.798	2.743	2.690	2.639	2.589
5	3.696	3.605	3.517	3.433	3.352	3.274	3.199	3.127	3.058	2.991
6	4.231	4.111	3.998	3.889	3.784	3.685	3.589	3.498	3.410	3.326
7	4.712	4.564	4.423	4.288	4.160	4.039	3.922	3.812	3.706	3.605
8	5.146	4.968	4.799	4.639	4.487	4.344	4.207	4.078	3.954	3.837
9	5.537	5.328	5.132	4.946	4.772	4.607	4.451	4.303	4.163	4.031
10	5.889	5.650	5.426	5.216	5.019	4.833	4.659	4.494	4.339	4.192
11	6.207	5.938	5.687	5.453	5.234	5.029	4.836	4.656	4.486	4.327
12	6.492	6.194	5.918	5.660	5.421	5.197	4.988	4.793	4.611	4.439
13	6.750	6.424	6.122	5.842	5.583	5.342	5.118	4.910	4.715	4.533
14	6.982	6.628	6.302	6.002	5.724	5.468	5.229	5.008	4.802	4.611
15	7.191	6.811	6.462	6.142	5.847	5.575	5.324	5.092	4.876	4.675
16	7.379	6.974	6.604	6.265	5.954	5.668	5.405	5.162	4.938	4.730
17	7.549	7.120	6.729	6.373	6.047	5.749	5.475	5.222	4.990	4.775
18	7.702	7.250	6.840	6.467	6.128	5.818	5.534	5.273	5.033	4.812
19	7.839	7.366	6.938	6.550	6.198	5.877	5.584	5.316	5.070	4.843
20	7.963	7.469	7.025	6.623	6.259	5.929	5.628	5.353	5.101	4.870

List of key terms
and index

BPP PUBLISHING

BPP
PUBLISHING

BPP PUBLISHING

REVIEW FORM & FREE PRIZE DRAW

All original review forms from the entire BPP range, completed with genuine comments, will be entered into one of two draws on 31 January 2000 and 31 July 2000. The names on the first four forms picked out on each occasion will be sent a cheque for £50.

Name: _____   Address: _____

_____

_____

How have you used this Text?
(Tick one box only)

☐ Home study (book only)

☐ On a course: college _____

☐ With 'correspondence' package

☐ Other _____

Why did you decide to purchase this Text?
(Tick one box only)

☐ Have used complementary Kit

☐ Have used BPP Texts in the past

☐ Recommendation by friend/colleague

☐ Recommendation by a lecturer at college

☐ Saw advertising

☐ Other _____

During the past six months do you recall seeing/receiving any of the following?
(Tick as many boxes as are relevant)

☐ Our advertisement in *CIMA Student*

☐ Our advertisement in *Management Accounting*

☐ Our advertisement in *Pass*

☐ Our brochure with a letter through the post

Which (if any) aspects of our advertising do you find useful?
(Tick as many boxes as are relevant)

☐ Prices and publication dates of new editions

☐ Information on Text content

☐ Facility to order books off-the-page

☐ None of the above

Have you used the companion Practice & Revision Kit for this subject?   ☐ Yes   ☐ No

Your ratings, comments and suggestions would be appreciated on the following areas

	Very useful	*Useful*	*Not useful*
Introductory section (How to use this text, study checklist, etc)	☐	☐	☐
Introduction to chapters	☐	☐	☐
Syllabus coverage	☐	☐	☐
Exercises and examples	☐	☐	☐
Exam focus points	☐	☐	☐
Chapter roundups	☐	☐	☐
Test your knowledge quizzes	☐	☐	☐
Illustrative questions	☐	☐	☐
Content of suggested solutions	☐	☐	☐
Glossary and index	☐	☐	☐
Structure and presentation	☐	☐	☐

	Excellent	*Good*	*Adequate*	*Poor*
Overall opinion of this Text	☐	☐	☐	☐

Do you intend to continue using BPP Study Texts/Kits?   ☐ Yes   ☐ No

Please note any further comments and suggestions/errors on the reverse of this page.

Please return to: Alison McHugh, BPP Publishing Ltd, FREEPOST, London, W12 8BR

REVIEW FORM & FREE PRIZE DRAW (continued)

Please note any further comments and suggestions/errors below

FREE PRIZE DRAW RULES

1   Closing date for 31 January 2000 draw is 31 December 1999. Closing date for 31 July 2000 draw is 30 June 2000.

2   Restricted to entries with UK and Eire addresses only. BPP employees, their families and business associates are excluded.

3   No purchase necessary. Entry forms are available upon request from BPP Publishing. No more than one entry per title, per person. Draw restricted to persons aged 16 and over.

4   Winners will be notified by post and receive their cheques not later than 6 weeks after the relevant draw date. Lists of winners will be published in BPP's *focus* newsletter following the relevant draw.

5   The decision of the promoter in all matters is final and binding. No correspondence will be entered into.

See overleaf for information on other
BPP products and how to order

CIMA Order

To BPP Publishing Ltd, Aldine Place, London W12 8AA

Tel: 020 8740 2211. Fax: 020 8740 1184

Mr/Mrs/Ms (Full name) _____

Daytime delivery address _____

Postcode _____

Daytime Tel _____

Date of exam (month/year) _____

	7/99 Texts	1/99 Kits	1/99 Psscrds	1/99 Tapes	1/99 Videos	1999 CDs
STAGE 1						
1 Financial Accounting Fundamentals	£18.95 ☐	£8.95 ☐	£4.95 ☐	£12.95 ☐	£25.00 ☐	
2 Cost Accounting and Quantitative Methods	£18.95 ☐	£8.95 ☐	£4.95 ☐	£12.95 ☐	£25.00 ☐	
3 Economic Environment	£18.95 ☐	£8.95 ☐	£4.95 ☐	£12.95 ☐	£25.00 ☐	
4 Business Environment & Information Technology	£18.95 ☐	£8.95 ☐	£4.95 ☐	£12.95 ☐	£25.00 ☐	
STAGE 2						
5 Financial Accounting	£18.95 ☐	£9.95 ☐	£5.95 ☐	£12.95 ☐	£25.00 ☐	
6 Operational Cost Accounting	£18.95 ☐	£9.95 ☐	£5.95 ☐	£12.95 ☐	£25.00 ☐	£39.95 ☐
7 Management Science Applications	£18.95 ☐	£9.95 ☐	£5.95 ☐	£12.95 ☐	£25.00 ☐	£39.95 ☐
8 Business and Company Law	£18.95 ☐	£9.95 ☐	£5.95 ☐	£12.95 ☐	£25.00 ☐	
STAGE 3						
9 Financial Reporting	£19.95 ☐	£9.95 ☐	£5.95 ☐	£12.95 ☐	£25.00 ☐	£39.95 ☐
10 Management Accounting Applications	£19.95 ☐	£9.95 ☐	£5.95 ☐	£12.95 ☐	£25.00 ☐	
11 Organisational Management & Development	£19.95 ☐	£9.95 ☐	£5.95 ☐	£12.95 ☐	£25.00 ☐	
12 Business Taxation (FA 99)	£19.95 ☐	£9.95 ☐	£5.95 ☐	£12.95 ☐	£25.00 ☐	£39.95 ☐ (FA 98)
STAGE 4						
13 Strategic Financial Management	£20.95 ☐	£10.95 ☐	£5.95 ☐	£12.95 ☐	£25.00 ☐	
14 Strategic Management Accountancy & Mktg	£20.95 ☐	£10.95 ☐	£5.95 ☐	£12.95 ☐	£25.00 ☐	
15 Information Management	£20.95 ☐	£10.95 ☐	£5.95 ☐	£12.95 ☐	£25.00 ☐	
16 Management Accounting Control Systems	£20.95 ☐	£10.95 ☐	£5.95 ☐	£12.95 ☐	£25.00 ☐	

£ _____

POSTAGE & PACKING

Study Texts

	First	Each extra	
UK	£3.00	£2.00	£ ☐
Europe*	£5.00	£4.00	£ ☐
Rest of world	£20.00	£10.00	£ ☐

Kits/Passcards/Success Tapes

	First	Each extra	
UK	£2.00	£1.00	£ ☐
Europe*	£2.50	£1.00	£ ☐
Rest of world	£15.00	£8.00	£ ☐

Master CDs/Breakthrough Videos

	First	Each extra	
UK	£2.00	£2.00	£ ☐
Europe*	£2.00	£2.00	£ ☐
Rest of world	£20.00	£10.00	£ ☐

Grand Total (Cheques to *BPP Publishing*) I enclose

a cheque for (incl. Postage) £ ☐

Or charge to Access/Visa/Switch

Card Number ☐☐☐☐☐☐☐☐☐☐☐☐☐☐☐☐

Expiry date _____ Start Date _____

Issue Number (Switch Only) _____

Signature _____

We aim to deliver to all UK addresses inside 5 working days. Orders to all EU addresses should be delivered within 6 working days. All other orders to overseas addresses should be delivered within 8 working days.

* Europe includes the Republic of Ireland and the Channel Islands.